MAINTAINING PERSPECTIVE:

A Decade of Collegiate Legal Challenges

by Dennis R. Black

Magna Publications, Inc.
Madison, WI

© 1997 Magna Publications, Inc.
2718 Dryden Drive
Madison, WI 53704

All rights reserved.

Printed in the United States of America

03 01 00 99 98 97   8 7 6 5 4 3 2 1

Cover design by Tamara L. Cook

This publication is designed to provide accurate and authoritative information in regard to the subject matter covered. It is sold with the understanding that the publisher is not engaged in rendering legal, accounting or other professional service. If legal advice or other expert assistance is required, the services of a competent professional should be sought.

Library of Congress Cataloging-in-Publication Data

Black, Dennis, 1956-

Maintaining Perspective: a decade of collegiate legal challenges
/by Dennis Black.
    p. cm.
Contains excerpts from author's articles appearing in Perspective: the campus legal monthly newsletter.
Includes bibliographical references and index.
ISBN 0-912150-39-4
  1. Universities and colleges--Law and legislation--United States.
2. College students--Legal status, laws, etc.--United States.
I. Title.
KF4225.b547 1996
344.73'074--dc20
[347.30474
                                        96-32404
                                          CIP

FOREWORD

When speaking with higher education professional organizations, at conferences, or during campus visits, I am frequently asked, "Where do you get materials for *PERSPECTIVE: The Campus Legal Monthly* newsletter?" The response is easy — "From you!"

For a decade, I have been fortunate to meet, speak, and correspond with many people interested in the law and higher education. Students, faculty members, administrators, legal counsel, governing board members, researchers, and the press have all shared with me campus stories, newspaper clippings, legal judgments, settlement agreements, journal articles, and research studies, along with seemingly endless, and always appreciated, personal or professional observations or opinions on every conceivable topic.

Through these contacts, from on and off campuses around the country, *PERSPECTIVE* has had a unique opportunity to observe and comment on colleges, universities, and the law.

The following materials are an accumulation of this shared knowledge, taken from the pages of *PERSPECTIVE*.

Please be reminded as you consider the compiled materials that no single approach or answer can work for every higher education institution or situation. The law is alive and changing at all times, so always consult with competent counsel in your jurisdiction on specific interpretations and needs.

From the beginning, our goal has been simple — each month, through the printed word, to promote an awareness and understanding of the myriad of legal issues facing higher education. It is our hope that, through these efforts and this collection of articles from *PERSPECTIVE*, we can help you in "maintaining perspective" in these and future challenging times.

Dennis R. Black

Acknowledgments

I am indebted to many individuals, but can name only a few, for their efforts as the text of *Maintaining Perspective* was developed. Helping to make a difficult task always easier for me have been Robert Magnan and William Haight of Magna Publications, Inc. and, for the first decade of *Perspective*, editorial assistant Linda Rayter Komdat, as well as several assistant editors over the years — James Rhem, Matt Gilson, Charles Bryan, Peter Vogt, Pat R. Dyjak, and Robert Magnan. Their cumulative efforts are greatly appreciated.

Table of Contents

Chapter 1
Academic Decisions *1*

    Introduction 1
    Advise with Care 1
    Advising Needs Advice (Legal, That Is) 3
    The Power to Evaluate 4
    Student Grades:
    What Courts Will (and Won't) Do 6
    Grades: Part II 7
    Grade Challenges: Best Left to Schools,
    Not Courts 9
    Case Law Defines Educational Malpractice 10
    Campuses Face Charges
    of Educational Malpractice 11
    Balancing Individual Rights
    and Commitment to Diversity 13
    Affirmative Action: Hopwood and Beyond 15
    International Students:
    What Are the Legal Issues? 16
    Student Evaluations Gain Legal Weight 17
    Evaluating Evaluations 19

Chapter 2
Academic Employment and Freedoms *21*

    Introduction 21
    False Credentials
    Can Quickly End Employment 21
    Not Whether You Win or Lose, But How You
    Break the Contract 23
    Termination Planning Key 24
    Managing Faculty Means Litigation 25
    Faculty Incompetence and Dismissals 26
    Supreme Court Opens Peer Review Files 26
    Freedom to Work on the Side 29
    Diverting Faculty Time: Problems
    with Moonlighting 30
    Court Contrasts
    "Official" and "Personal" Capacities 31
    Understanding the Charge of Defamation 33

    Defamation — or Free Speech? 35
    Word Wars Continue 36
    Employee Expression: How "Free" Is Free? 37
    Jeffries Suit Weighs Free Speech,
    College's Interests 39
    Academic Freedom and Campus Concerns 40
    Schools Test Language Proficiency
    ... and Laws 42
    Language Proficiency Laws
    Put Campuses at Risk 43
    Employee Tests May Flunk
    Legal Examination 44
    Job Interviews: Legalities and Realities 45
    Your Campus Can Prevent
    the "Zoe Baird Problem" 46
    Courts and Laws Support Whistleblowers 47
    Sex Discrimination: Laws and Litigation 48

Chapter 3
First Amendment *51*

    Introduction 51
    First Amendment on Campus:
    Four Exceptions 51
    Policies Confront First Amendment 53
    Anti-Harassment Policies
    Face Legal Challenges 55
    Speech Codes: Noble End, Ignoble Means 57
    Speech Code
    Takes on Constitution ... Again 59
    Can Hate Speech Codes
    withstand Legal Challenge? 60
    "Hate Speech" Codes Rejuvenated? 62
    The Effectiveness of Speech Codes 62
    Creed Promotes Different Way
    to Handle Hate Speech 64
    The Star-Spangled Banner
    and the Land of the Free 65
    Residence Halls:
    What's Private? What's Public? 66

Campus Art: The Limits
of the First Amendment..................................... 68
Is Art Protected by the First Amendment?......... 69
Separating the Church from the State 70
Top Court to Consider Higher Case................. 72
Courts Examine Church-State Relationships..... 73
Regulating the Press:
How Far Can Campuses Go? 75
Free Speech vs. Censorship 76
Theft as Censorship:
A Nationwide Campus Problem 78
Planning for Controversial Speakers 80
Who Can Read Your Email?.............................. 81
Electronic Communications............................... 82

Chapter 4
Governance and Regulation..........................85

Introduction 85
Decision Raises Questions About Residency 85
Deciding Who's a Resident and Who's Not 86
Residence Issues in the News............................ 88
Campuses Look Gift Horses in the Mouth........ 89
Relying on Estates and Pledges 90
No Such Thing as a Free Gift 92
When Is a Campus Exempt
from Property Taxes? 93
Avoiding the Tax Bite... 95
Campus Housing: A Taxing Problem 96
UBIT Takes Bite Out of Campus Income 97
Who Pays Taxes for This Event? 99
Communities Tighten Controls on Students ... 100
There's Battle Lines Being Drawn.................... 101
Gay, Lesbian Students
Challenge the Military...................................... 103
Federal Funds Have Strings Attached 104
Focus on Sexual Orientation 106
Campuses React to Sexual Harassment............ 108
Title IX:
It Affects More Than Athletics........................ 109
Lessons on Studying Abroad 111
Overlap Group: Final Battle 112
Schools May Lose Control Over Transcripts .. 114
Race-Based Financial Aid:
Confusion Thickens 115
Race-Based Financial Aid 117

Chapter 5
Health and Disability Concerns..................119

Introduction 119
New Law Renews
Access Issue for Campuses 119
ADA: Don't Let It Disable Your Campus 120
Expert Advice Needed
on Reasonable Accommodation 122
Learning Disabilities
and Test Accommodations............................... 123
Minimize the Risks
of Student Health Insurance 127
Mandated Health Insurance
Draws Challenges.. 128
"A-Word" on Campus 130
Abortion: Another Long, Hot Summer?.......... 131
AIDS and Discrimination:
What Precedent Suggests 133
AIDS and Confidentiality:
Privacy vs. Right to Know 134
AIDS and Campus Liability:
What Are the Risks? 136
Where There's Smoke, There's Fiery Talk 137
More Reasons to Become
a Smokeless Campus... 138
Schools Crack Down
on Drugs and Alcohol....................................... 140
Student Alcohol Abuse..................................... 142
Mandatory Withdrawal:
Policies and Problems 144
Withdrawal Policies Carry Risks 145
Coping with Environmental Risks 146

Chapter 6
Risk Management 149

Introduction 149
Alcohol Still #1... 149
How to Control Alcohol Use 150
Alcohol Marketing
on Campus Meets Resistance........................... 152
Campus Injuries:
What You Don't Know Can Hurt a Lot 153
Sports Injuries:
How Should Campuses Respond? 154
Campuses Less Immune to Litigation Virus..... 155
When Visitors Come 157
A Tale of Two Universities 158
Settling Doesn't Mean No High Costs 159
Risky Business: Campus Insurance 160
Campus Legal Counsel 162
Expecting the Worst:
Preparing for Calamities 164
Before the Controversial Speaker Arrives 165
Liability Waivers: Will They Protect You? 167
Waiver Failure: The Four Principal Areas 168
How to Develop a Policy for Student Deaths.. 170
Student Deaths:
When the Campus Must Notify 171
ACE Model Policy on Sexual Harassment....... 173

Table of Contents

Preventative Policy for Sexual Harassment...... 174

Chapter 7
Freedom of Information: Records and Meetings 177

Introduction 177
Freedom of Information Act Opens Federal Government 177
Determining What's Open, What's Closed Isn't Easy 179
Students' Rights Under the Buckley Amendment 181
Complying with Freedom of Information Laws 182
School Paper Beats Buckley: Now What? 183
Campus Security and Records: Whose Jurisdiction? 185
Social Security Numbers: Must They Be Protected? 185
Students Win War of Numbers 186
Schools and Media Fight Over Records 186
Courts Define "Student" 188
Student Disciplinary Records 190
Student Medical Files: A Danger if Not Maintained 191
Information: Uses and Abuses 193
Student Athletes Successfully Combat Drug Testing 194
Drug Testing Invades Student Privacy 194
Foundations Battle for Confidentiality 195

Chapter 8
Copyright, Trademarks, and Patents 197

Introduction 197
Copyrights, Copy Wrongs 197
No Appeal in Copyright Decision 199
Copy Decision Not Duplicated 199
Making the Permission Process More Efficient 201
Who Owns Course Lectures? 201
Texts, Laws, and Videotapes 202
"Fair Use" Guidelines Cover Television Programs, Too 204
Pirates on Campus: The Dangers of Sharing Software 205
Battle of Dictionaries Holds Lessons for Campuses 207
High Stakes Draw Campuses into Patent Wars 209

Chapter 9
Safety and security 211

Introduction 211
Time for a Crime Prevention Audit 211
Making Campuses "Smart" Havens for Safety 213
Securing the Campus 214
The Campus Security Act 215
Resources Help Reduce the Risk of Sexual Assault 217
Campus, Federal Forces Attacking Sexual Assault 219
The People Behind Sexual Assault Numbers 220
Fearful Students Turning to Court Protection Orders 222
How Far Must Campuses Go to Protect Students? 223
Searches Highlight Constitutional Questions 225
Warrantless Searches in Some Circumstances 227
At Risk Day and Night: Residence Hall Students 228
High Cost of Keeping Books 230
Big Brother Comes to Computerized Campus 232
Cover Your Assets 233

Chapter 10
Student Conduct 235

Introduction 235
Dealing with Dishonesty 235
Everyone Has a Story for Sale 237
Taking Ideas Without Credit 238
Courts Let Campus Arms Reach Out and Touch 239
Campus Hearing Option for Assult Victims 241
Alcohol Sanctions: Suggestions for Change 242
Due Process for Greeks 243
Be Sure It's the Real Thing 244
Fake Diplomas a Big Business 245
Campuses Try Mediation 247
Mediating Conflicts 248

Chapter 11
Student Life: Activities, Organizations, and Athletics 251

Introduction 251
Liability Risks for Greeks 251
Greeks and Alcohol Don't Mix Well 253

The Hazards of Hazing 254
Greeks: Initiation Rites New Wrong................ 256
State Hazing Laws Force Accountability 258
Student Organizations Fight to Survive........... 259
Who Controls the Right of Association? 260
Gay, Lesbian, and Bisexual Students
Fight for Rights... 262
Activity Fees Are Not for Political Usage 263
Mandatory Student Activity Fees 264
Student Control
of Student Fees Questioned 266
Campus Funding
of Student Groups — Again............................ 267
Sports in the Courts 269
Court Ruling Gives Title IX
Renewed Strength 270
Absent Supervisor Liable
for Cheerleader Injuries.................................. 273
Three Cheers for Safety.................................. 274
Guide to Advising Groups 276
'Tis Better to Have Won and Lost (Not!)........ 277
Unworthy Student Fund-Raisers:
Evaluating Charitable Causes.......................... 278
Concert Crush Teaches Lessons...................... 279
Student Stampede Raises Issues of Safety 281
Preventing Violence
at Student Social Events................................. 282

Final Thoughts 285

Index 287

Chapter 1
ACADEMIC DECISIONS

Introduction

> When judges are asked to review the substance of a genuinely academic decision, ... they should show great respect for the faculty's professional judgment. Plainly, they may not override it unless it is such a substantial departure from accepted academic norms as to demonstrate that the person or committee responsible did not actually exercise professional judgment.
>
> *Regents of the University of Michigan v. Ewing*, 474 U.S. 214 (1985)

Two principles apply to most cases involving higher education academic decision-making: judicial deference and contract theory. Courts have long stayed out of academic decisions, unless there is a showing of arbitrariness, unfairness, or capriciousness. Judges have said they cannot and should not substitute their judgment for that of the faculty. But will that trend continue?

In addition to fairness, courts also look to see if established campus rules and standards are applied. Where there are rules, says the court, the campus must follow them.

On issues related to grades, credits, evaluations, and degrees, courts generally uphold campus decisions if they find the decisions to be fair and determined by the rules.

Advise with Care

July 1991

"What do you mean my transfer credits are no good?" That's what some students wondered after spending several years at Southern Technical College (AL) and finding that they couldn't transfer. Two students went to court to get some answers. They got their answers — and $720,000 in damages!

A state court jury ruled that the private technical school and an admissions employee had defrauded the students when the employee advised them that STC credits could be transferred to four-year state colleges. When they tried to transfer to an area university, they found out the credits were worthless.

The jury awarded $20,000 in compensatory damages and $700,000 in punitive damages. As a result, the successful plaintiffs may have to spend more time in school than they'd planned, but they won't have any trouble paying their tuition!

The message to campus officials: remember that campus advisement is not free of liability risks. Understand the legal theories under which students can sue for damages, and then take steps to avoid litigation. Make sure your faculty and staff advise well — and wisely.

Contract Law

Most student suits over advisement are based on *contract law*. They contend that the school entered into an agreement and then breached that agreement. Written campus publications are often cited as being contractual: catalogs, applications, brochures, and handbooks set out terms under which students accept admission, select courses, and pursue degrees. A series of court cases have clearly established that representations made in these official documents can be contractual and, thus, enforceable.

In *Wilson v. Illinois Benedictine College*, 445 N.E. 2d 901 (1983), a state court ruled that the school catalog set out terms of the campus-student agreement concisely and completely, establishing a contract. The catalog said that only courses in which a grade of C was received would count toward majors, and that D courses might have to be repeated. The court found those terms complete and specific enough to form a contract.

A New York case, *Nieswand v. Cornell University*, 692 F.Supp. 1464 (1988), found that the various admissions materials sent to prospective students created an implied contract that must be performed.

In addition to written materials, courts have found advisement contracts in oral representations by campus agents. What you say can and will be used against you in a court of law!

In *Zumbrun v. University of Southern California*, 25 Cal. App. 3d 1 (1972), a state court ruled that contracts between students and schools can be formed through both written and spoken words.

However, spoken words must be specific and believable to form a contract. A student told by a school official "not to worry" about an academic problem cannot rely on those words. In *Abrams v. Illinois College of Podiatric Medicine*, 395 N.E. 2d 1061 (1979), the court found the official's words too vague and indefinite to create a binding oral contract.

What if an advisor makes a statement not in accordance with campus policy? Can the student rely on that "promise"? Yes, if it can be shown that the student's reliance was justifiable. That was the issue in *Blank v. Board of Higher Education of the City of New York*, 273 N.Y.S. 2d 796 (1966), in which a student followed an advisor's advice, which turned out to be wrong.

A student was told by faculty members, a department head, and an advisor that he could finish his undergraduate program at Brooklyn College while in his first year of law school at Syracuse. He completed the independent studies, but the college denied him his degree because he wasn't "in attendance" at Brooklyn. College officials claimed that only the dean of the faculty could authorize the program option.

The court ruled against the school. It found that the student had relied on permission granted by campus faculty and staff and shouldn't be penalized as a result.

So courts will hold campuses to promises, written or verbal, even when the promise is outside campus policy. That places a responsibility on advisors, as they can create contracts and breach them during everyday duties.

Tort Law

Advisement situations can also lead to *tort law* claims, including fraud and negligence. Fraud can be found when school officials or representatives make statements they know to be false. Negligence arises from claims that the college had a duty to a student and breached that duty. Tort claims haven't been as successful in court as contract claims, but increased efforts to "market" campuses to prospective students could give rise to more tort claims in the future.

An advisement fraud case could come from statements or nondisclosures in admissions materials or meetings. To prove fraud, a student would have to show that school officials

- Falsely represented a fact
- Knew the truth
- Misrepresented to make the student act
- Caused damage to the student
- The student would have to show that he/she was justified in accepting the falsehood

As in the Southern Technical College case, a credit transfer problem led to fraud charges in *Till v. Delta School of Commerce*, 487 So. 2d 180 (1986). A two-year degree student claimed to have been told that she could transfer easily to a four-year school, which wasn't true. The Louisiana court ruled that she'd been the victim of fraud and misrepresentation.

Generally, written fraud is easier to prove than verbal, and contract cases have been more effective for students.

In negligence cases, courts look to see if a special relationship exists between the parties giving rise to a duty to provide or perform, which is subsequently breached. Students often claim negligence in advisement cases, but few claims of this type have been sustained.

Agency Law

In addition to contract law and torts, student claims against advisement can be made under *agency law*. This makes schools responsible for words and deeds of officials or representatives having either actual or apparent authority. When a campus agent has the power to act, or appears to a student to have the power to act, the campus can be held responsible. Therefore, an academic advisor talking to a student about grades, credits, or degrees can be seen as being an authority that a student could consider reliable.

In *Healy v. Larsson*, 318 N.E. 2d 608 (1974), agency law was applied to campus advisement. A transferring student met with academic advisors, a dean, and the department chair about his planned course of studies. The student followed their plan, based on the advice received, and took all the specified courses. The college denied him a degree, saying he'd failed to complete all requirements. He took the issue to court.

The court awarded the student his degree. The officials were agents of the school, said the court, and their agreement on the program of study was binding on the college. The student had fulfilled the terms set by the agents, making the school responsible for fulfilling its part of the agreement, the granting of a degree.

However, courts are very hesitant to order schools to grant degrees and do so only in extreme cases. They are also reluctant to change degree requirements.

Take the case of an advisor who tells a student she'll be able to finish a program. Is the student then free of any responsibilities, such as attending class and passing other exams? In *Cuddihy v. Wayne State University*, 413 N.W. 2d 692 (1987), a student claimed that she couldn't be expelled because an advisor told her she'd be able to finish the program. The court did not find that promise enforceable.

In another instance, an admissions advisor thought an undergraduate grade would not be included, although school policy required its inclusion, and so advised an applicant. When the grade was included, the surprised applicant sued. Since written materials on the application process were clear on the issue, the grade was ruled to be part of the application, in *Shields v. School of Law, Hofstra University*, 77 A.D. 2d 867 (1980).

Writ of Mandamus

In advisement cases, a court may also use a *writ of mandamus*. This is a court order to school officials to act appropriately to correct abuses of authority.

An example of this writ can be found in *Bartlett v. Pantzer*, 489 P.2d 375 (1971). An applicant to the University of Montana Law School was told that to be admitted he had to complete a course at another school with a "satisfactory" grade. He received a D, which officials then told him was unsatisfactory.

The court found this denial of admission to be an abuse of discretion. The distinction in terms was not clearly established or explained, the court held, and the penalty imposed on the student was excessive. The court used a writ of mandamus to order the school to admit the applicant, correct an abuse of authority.

Play It Safe and Reduce Advisement Risks

As shown, institutional liability in advisement can be based on several legal theories. Students can use contract, tort, agency, and mandamus if they feel campus officials have dealt with them unfairly.

What can campuses do to prevent litigation of this type? Consider some of the following preventive steps:

1. Understand apparent and actual authority and take steps to limit agency legal exposure and threats of mandamus.

Specifically:

- When training and supervising advisors, outline the limits of their authority.
- Notify students of those limits.
- Review materials and advisement procedures to ensure that there are no accidental contracts.

2. Review the campus potential for contractual and tort law claims, and adopt a preventative strategy. This process should include a regular review of all campus publications to make sure that:

- The language is clear
- Promises made are intended to be promises
- The publications are factually accurate

3. Provide training programs for advisors to:

- Promote full understanding of campus policies
- Limit waivers of requirements
- Increase awareness of the potential legal consequences of advisement errors

4. Include in all campus publications language that reserves the institution's right to make changes in programs and services, as well as disclaimers for unintended errors. To err may be human, and change may be the only constant — but such philosophical defenses won't help in court.

Advising Needs Advice (Legal, That Is)

May 1992

A university student filed a $40,000 suit against her school, claiming that poor advising will force her to spend an extra year getting an undergraduate degree. According to the suit, the university advisors were negligent.

She says she told her advisors that she intended to get a pharmacy degree, but that she was never informed that the school's credits could not lead to that degree. Her claim for damages is based on her estimate for another year of school ($10,000) and the loss of one year's working income ($30,000).

Like many students, she was well into her program or nearing graduation when she discovered something wasn't right. Having planned an academic program leading to a particular degree, students may find they are not eligible for the desired degree, or any degree at all! Faced with this, students sometimes review what has happened and conclude that the school put them on a "path to nowhere." This student then sued, claiming breach of promise and negligence.

Colleges and universities need to provide good advisement information to students, train and supervise advisors, and consider alternative solutions to degree requirement problems when related to advisement difficulties.

Three Principles Govern Law

Student challenges to advising are generally based on one of three legal principles:

- Contract law
- Agency law
- Negligence

In each, a student will argue that the school had a duty or responsibility that it failed to carry out or that it carried out improperly.

Under *contract law*, courts consider whether the school followed its own regulations and guidelines in advisement situations, whether the school fulfilled "promises" made to students by persons or publications, and what the nature of the contract was between student and school. If a contract is found to exist, written or verbal, explicit or implicit, a student may be awarded monetary damages or other academic relief, if a breach of contract occurred.

Other claims could be based on *agency law*, viewing the college or university as responsible for the acts or omissions of its staff. If an employee who has authority — or one who merely appears to have authority — acts, a student can legally rely on that act. So when a department representative or advisor says that a course isn't required, a student may take that to be official college policy. If the representative or advisor is wrong, that may become their problem, not the student's. When an agent with actual or apparent authority waives a policy, the student can go into court to force the school to maintain the waiver.

Finally, under *tort law*, some students attempt to prove that their academic program or requirement problems are caused by *negligent* advising. They maintain the school has a duty to provide appropriate counseling, that it breached that responsibility, and that injuries were caused by the breach. In establishing negligence claims, a student may contend that damages are owed due to problems created by poor advising.

Case Law Established Mixed Record

A college student claiming improper advising sued his school in 1983. He contended that his advisor did not tell him that his class grades did not meet graduation requirements. While the catalog explained the policy, the student said the advisors failed to explain it in meetings and did not meet with him as often as recommended.

But in *Wilson v. Illinois Benedictine College*, 445 N.Ed. 2d 901 (1983), the court sided with the school. The school had not acted in violation of published guidelines and had not altered them, said the court, and the rules were clearly stated and binding. Failure of advisors to "remind" was not held to be a breach of contract.

When the school promises to update a student on academic progress and fails to do so, the school risks responsibility for damages. In *Kanton v. Schmidt*, 423 N.Y.S. 2d 208 (1979), the state court ordered that a degree be awarded to a student, even though the school questioned whether she had completed requirements. The State University of New York at Stony Brook had agreed "to inform students periodically of their progress and remaining obligations" and had then failed to comply. The court ordered the degree, as the college had failed to satisfy the contract.

When an advisor "waived" a required business course that was later needed for graduation, a student at the University of Montana sued. He claimed that an agent of the school had acted with apparent authority and that the school should be bound by the agent's acts.

But in *Holloway v. University of Montana*, 582 P.2d 1265 (1978), the court ruled the advisor did not have or appear to have power to waive courses. The school policies on waivers were clearly written and indicated that advisors could not change graduation requirements.

And what happens when there is a dispute over transfer credits? In a 1973 case, a student and his new school disagreed over how many courses were needed for graduation. In *Healy v. Larsson*, 360 N.E. 2d 419 (1974), the student sued after completing only the classes he thought were required. The court found that the school had earlier agreed on a transfer of credits and was bound to that previous agreement.

Summary

The last thing any court wants to do is award unearned credits or degrees, but if the school has broken its contract with a student, if an agent has acted to the student's disadvantage, or other aspects of advisement are negligently provided, courts will act. To avoid problems, campuses and students should consider the following:

- Periodically review graduation requirements and published guidelines.

- Periodically review the role of campus advisors, their supervision, training, manuals, and references to advisement in catalogs and other publications

- Make sure that other faculty and staff understand their role in advisement, establishment of requirements, and waivers.

- Make early attempts to identify problems that could negatively influence possible graduation, in order to allow students and the college an adequate opportunity to respond.

- Include disclaimer language in policy statements limiting the authority of campus personnel and allowing any necessary changes.

Students rely on campus advising. Campuses must protect student and institutional interests by properly establishing and maintaining advisement services.

The Power to Evaluate

July 1994

Organized student evaluations of collegiate instructors have officially been part of American higher education since the 1920s. When they first appeared, few people would have predicted the legal entanglements student surveys would face in the future. They began as a measure of teaching methods, contents, and skills. Decades later, they have become a factor in faculty tenure and promotion reviews, and subsequent lawsuits.

Presence in Case Law

Early class evaluations were used to assist students in course selection and to help instructors obtain feedback on their teaching performance. Today, they still serve those purposes, but they also are often used by schools in personnel decisions on renewal, tenure, promotion, and merit pay. When a faculty member challenges a school's personnel decision in court, student course and instructor evaluations often become part of the case evidence. Case law involving student evaluations in the past has included issues of sex discrimination, terminations, and academic freedom.

Colleges and universities have generally established criteria for judging faculty performance: scholarship, teaching, research, and service. An instructor challenging an unfavorable school decision must produce evidence to support his or her claim. Student evaluations are often submitted as evidence of performance. Courts have generally accepted these evaluation results as evidence in these cases, bringing student evaluations into the legal process.

Validity

While student evaluations are often considered in campus personnel decision-making and are accepted as evidence in court, many wonder just how valid they really are. Are they accurate? Do they really measure good teaching?

Some student evaluation research suggests that ratings of teachers do not measure effectiveness of teaching, intellectual achievement, or understanding of basic content. Instead, classroom instructor survey instruments may only measure instructor popularity and speaking abilities. Student evaluations may best measure teacher likability — *not* the reliability of their classroom teaching or the effectiveness of their methods.

However, a properly constructed and administered student evaluation can assess the characteristics of an instructor and student satisfaction at the same time. This information is helpful in assisting students and instructors, and in supporting litigation.

Evaluations in Court

In several instances, student evaluations have been critical elements in legal cases involving faculty personnel decisions. Denied tenure by the University of Connecticut, an English instructor filed suit, claiming sex discrimination. In *Lieberman v. Gant*, 474 F.Supp. 848 (1979), UConn argued that the tenure decision was based on the instructor's inadequate teaching and scholarship, not any form of discrimination. Student evaluations of the instructor's courses were introduced as evidence in support of the school's decision.

The student evaluations showed the instructor ranked 12th out of 15 members in her department. It also showed that her ranking had been dropping. Student complaints about her course methods and content were consistently included in evaluations. Based in large part on this type of evidence, the court found support for UConn's decision and upheld the tenure denial.

A similar outcome was reached in *Dyson v. Lavery*, 417 F.Supp. 103 (1976). A female business law instructor sued Virginia Polytechnic Institute over non-renewal, claiming sex discrimination and salary inequities. The court ruled that she had been underpaid but that the school was justified in dismissing her. Students complained about her lack of preparation for classes and lectures. The court carefully considered student evaluations, which ranked her 46th of 48 instructors! The court accepted the school's judgment, giving great weight to the student rankings.

Elsewhere, a tenured faculty member was dismissed in *Jawa v. Fayetteville State University*, 426 F. Supp. 218 (1976). The school said he was a poor teacher and did not work well with students. The instructor challenged his dismissal, contending it was actually race-based.

The court accepted much evidence from student evaluations in reviewing this case. Students had consistently complained about the instructor's teaching, poor advisement, unavailability, and poor grading processes. The court accepted the student evaluations and upheld the school's decision, based in part on the evaluations.

Can student evaluations affect instructor academic freedom? That was the issue in *Lovelace v. Southeastern Massachusetts University*, 793 F.2d 419 (1986). An instructor there claimed he lost his job because he was a "hard" teacher and subsequently got low student evaluations. According to his suit, his academic freedom would have been violated if he had been forced to lower his academic standards to keep his "popularity," and his position.

The court failed to find any connection between academic freedom and evaluations. Issues such as course content, grading, and homework were relevant in campus decision-making, said the court, as were student criticisms.

Similar issues were considered in a case involving an art instructor in *Carley v. Arizona Board of Regents*, 737 P.3d 1099 (1987). The instructor's contract was not renewed due to poor teaching evaluations, even though his chair supported continuation. The instructor argued that students who complained about his teaching were violating his academic freedom. But the court said "academic freedom is not a doctrine to insulate a teacher from evaluation" by his school. The dismissal was upheld.

Proper Usage

As demonstrated, student evaluations have a role to play in personnel decisions, and this can lead to their involvement in related litigation. Colleges and universities with student evaluation programs should consider the following guidelines:

- Gather data on instructors, over time, through well-developed, written instruments — well before they are to be used in litigation.
- Student evaluations should be only one part of personnel decision-making. Their use should be clearly stated in employee guides and policies.

- Evaluations should be used and reviewed in a consistent manner. Treat everyone and every situation the same.

Make sure your evaluations work for students, faculty, and the institution. Evaluate them!

Student Grades: What Courts Will (and Won't) Do

January 1992

Students go to school to learn, not just to get good grades. Right? Well, grades do count, and students have often gone to court when they haven't "made the grade" on campus. Will courts hear student complaints about grades? And will they order grade changes?

In principle, unhappy students can sue instructors and institutions over class grades. But courts are generally not inclined to get involved. They traditionally look to academe to make academic decisions and will only get involved where there is some showing of unfairness in the process. Most case law on grades developed from challenges filed by students fighting for their academic lives. In most reported cases, the students sued out of necessity to get a grade changed to avoid academic dismissal.

Consider the case of the student who needed to pass a course to graduate, but failed twice. On the second attempt, she received a grade of 69.7% but needed 70% to pass. When the school said she was finished, she responded with legal action. In *McIntosh v. Borough of Manhattan Community College*, 449 N.Y.S. 2d 26 (1982), the New York Court of Appeals considered her request. What did she want? Just make the school "round up" her grade! The court said no, out of deference to the instructor's decision. The school's refusal to round up the score was not deemed to be arbitrary, and the court upheld the campus' judgment. No grade upgrade!

Repeats Can Be Factored In

How about courses that are repeated due to a failure on the first attempt? Does the "F" have to be factored into the student's grade point average? Can't the try be forgotten? That was the issue in *Essignmann v. Western New England College*, 419 N.E. 2d 1041 (1981), in which a law student needed to get the low marks off his record to graduate. He argued that only the grade he received the second time he took the class should count.

The court agreed with the school, not the borderline student. The student cannot be surprised, said the court, that the grade he got on a second try won't be equated with the grades others got on their first try. Campus policies that average in earlier scores with repeated grades are not arbitrary.

How about the grade of "I" for incomplete? Can a student who failed a course then demand an "I," with a chance to improve the grade later? A medical student dismissed from the University of South Dakota sued for an "I" in *Hines v. Rinker*, 667 F.2d 699 (1981). The school had the discretion to award an "I" if the course work was not complete due to a satisfactory reason.

The dismissed student appealed the decision on campus and within the state university system without success. He fared no better in the federal courts. They found no rational basis for his complaint. The decision to dismiss the student was based on academic performance and the school had no obligation to give the student an "I." Unless the decision to dismiss was based on bad faith or ill will, the court supported the campus decision. No "I" on demand!

Schools Have A Right to Change Grades

What if the school agrees, on appeal, that a grade should be upgraded, but the instructor still says "no"? That was the case in *Parate v. Isibor*, 868 F.2d 821 (1989), in which a Tennessee State University engineering instructor refused to change a "B" to an "A." After reviewing the issue, the department dean said the student deserved an "A." The instructor refused to change the grade initially, but finally changed the grade after he felt his job was threatened. When the instructor's contract was not renewed, he sued the school, claiming that the pressure to change the grade violated his academic freedom and constitutional rights.

The court agreed but offered schools an alternative means of changing grades. The pressure to change the grade, according to the court, did violate the instructor's expectations of academic freedom and the First Amendment. However, what the court found objectionable was not the fact that the grade was changed, but how it was changed. The school should have altered the grade itself, said the court, noting:

> The actions of the defendants, who failed to administratively change [the] grade themselves, unconstitutionally compelled [the instructor's] speech and precluded him from communicating his personal evaluation to [the student].

If the instructor won't change the grade, the court told the school, "just do it yourself!"

Students Must Exhaust Campus Remedies

At what point will the courts hear grade appeals? A two-year college student found out the hard way in *Pfaff v. Columbia-Greene Community College*, 472 N.Y.S. 2d 480 (1984). The courts aren't interested until all campus remedies are exhausted. The student claimed that she received a low grade because of negative comments she made in class.

Claiming First Amendment violations, she went to court seeking a better grade. But the court said her claim was made too early, as there remained alternative means of getting the grade changed on campus. Since she had not exhausted all on-campus solutions, the court was unwilling to get involved. In the rush to court, students must make sure that all campus options are exhausted or they will find the judicial doors closed!

Changes in Support Services Don't Affect Outcome

Finally, what about the impact of tutoring? If the school changes academic support services, can a student sue, claiming that his grades have been negatively affected? Certainly the student can sue, but he or she will need a very strong breach-of-contract case to win. In *Marquez v. University of Washington*, 648 P.2d 94 (1982), the student sued but didn't have a case. The school had made changes in its tutoring program, but services were still available. They were not used by the student. The student just missed a passing grade, but the court refused to round up a grade based on changes in the tutoring program.

So when it comes to class grades, case law suggests several key principles for instructors and institutions:

- As long as grading policies are based on academic performance, courts defer to the campus, leaving academic decisions to academicians.
- Policies and decisions on grades will be upheld when they are not based on ill will or bad faith.
- Instructor grading may involve academic freedom and free speech issues.
- Campus appeals must be concluded before the courts will rule on grade challenges.
- Grade change requests based on changes in services or programs must demonstrate significant breach of contract.

When students don't make the grade in class, courts will hear their complaints — but only if there is some strong showing of unfairness and all campus appeals have been exhausted. And even if the court hears the case, students must still overcome a strong judicial preference for non-interference in academic decision-making.

Grades: Part II

June 1992

Since the most frequently asked questions on campus often seem to be, "Will it be on the test?" and "What did you get?," it should come as no surprise that test scores and grades occasionally lead to litigation. Students, faculty, and campuses often find themselves arguing over grades. And sometimes these arguments spill over into the courts.

Recently, a professor sued his college over student grades. Campus officials changed one of his student's grades from a "D" to a "C" over his objections. The student had filed a complaint with the school after the instructor's recommended remedial work did not improve the grade. A departmental review resulted in a higher grade, but the instructor responded with legal action against Irvine Valley College (CA).

Under state education law, an instructor has absolute authority to grade student performance, unless the school finds incompetence, bad faith, fraud, or error. The school contended that the instructor's failure to improve the grade after the completion of recommended remedial work constituted "bad faith" and made correction necessary. But the writing instructor said the extra work did not justify a better grade, so he went to state court, asking for enforcement of the state law and for the court to return the student grade to the instructor's grade, a "D."

Judicial Restraint the Norm

As a general rule, courts are very hesitant to substitute their judgment for that of campus faculty. Unless there is a showing of arbitrariness or capriciousness in grading practices, the courts have shown a strong preference to let academic matters decided by academicians stand unaltered. One example of this is a New York case, *McIntosh v. Borough of Manhattan Community College*, 449 N.Y.S. 2d 26 (1982). A nursing student had twice failed a required course and could not graduate. On her second try, her final grade was less than one percentage point below passing. She went to court and successfully argued that the multiple choice testing and failing grade were "arbitrary." The school was ordered to give her a degree.

But on appeal, the state's highest court ruled against the student. The court upheld the school's judgment on both how to test and what scores to award. The use of multiple-choice testing and an unwillingness to "round up" grades were not found by the court to be arbitrary or capricious. Academic decisions, said the court, will be free from outside interference unless the academicians act unfairly or fail to follow established campus regulations.

Students, unhappy with campus grading practices, have asked the courts to overturn grades, provide due process on grading issues, and alter policies on cumulative grade point averages, appeals processes, and related issues. In another New York case, a student claimed she received an "F" in retaliation for classroom comments. After retaking the class and getting an "A," the school averaged the two grades together for a final "C." She sued, in *Pfaff v. Columbia-Greene Community College*, 472 N.Y.S. 2d 480 (1984), claiming First Amendment violations and failure of the school to hold a full hearing on her complaints, although other remedies were possible.

The court ruled that it wouldn't consider the case until all possible campus options were exhausted. Since the school could still have reviewed the grade administratively, the court sent the case back to school.

Academic issues were also returned to the campus in *Woodruff v. Georgia State University*, 304 S.E. 2d 697 (1983). There, the state's supreme court heard various claims from a music department graduate student who claimed the faculty gave her consistently low grades that weren't deserved. She contended that they had tried to keep her from graduating because she succeeded in having a plagiarism charge dropped by an administrative committee. When she applied to a doctoral program, they gave her poor recommendations. She sued, asking a state court to overturn the faculty's assessment of her work. According to her suit, her grades and recommendations amounted to slander, negligence, breach of contract, and unconstitutional violations.

The court saw things differently. It found a legitimate dispute between members of an academic community over academic issues. And these issues, it ruled, should be decided on campus, not in the courts. Among the reasons noted by the court were confidence in the fairness and competence of instructors, litigation costs, legal turmoil, and fear that students and parents would or could "rely upon the legal process rather than the learning process." The policy of judicial non-interference was upheld.

Students Who Fail in Class Fail in Court

Failing grades have often led to judicial review. A graduate student who failed his doctoral degree oral examinations went into a federal court complaining that the committee was prejudiced against him from the start, due to his involvement in a commercial venture. But in *Stevenson v. Board of Regents of the University of Texas*, 393 F.Supp. 812 (1975), the court found no evidence of ill will or bad faith by the faculty. Some proof, beyond a student's contentions, must be provided before the court takes the extraordinary step of assessing academic performance.

When failing grades are factored into cumulative grade point averages, advancement or degrees can be threatened. In two notable cases, students have sued to get schools to treat failures differently once the course is retaken and a better grade is awarded. But in each case, school policies were upheld. The rewriting of a failing moot court brief could not save the academic career of a student in *Shields v. School of Law, Hofstra University*, 431 N.Y.S. 2d 60 (1980). The school stayed within its policies by refusing to eliminate the failing grade from her GPA, said the court.

Grading processes were also supported in another law school case, *Essignmann v. Western New England College*, 419 N.E. 2d 1041 (1981). Failing grades were factored into GPA, but one course could not be retaken because it was no longer offered. The student sued, claiming the school's policy was unfair. But the court said that eliminating failing grades simply because better grades were received on second attempts was unfair. Said the court:

As a matter of common sense, a student who passes a course only after failing and repeating it, is not academically equal to the student who takes the course but once and passes.

When Is Judicial Interference Justified?

Judicial interference has been justified where school decisions are arbitrary or capricious or where the school fails to follow its own rules. That was the case in *Heisler v. New York Medical College*, 449 N.Y.S. 2d 834 (1982). The school had a policy that a failing grade in four courses would result in dismissal. A review committee heard the cases of four students who had failed too many courses, but only dismissed one. The others were allowed to continue due to family situations. The dismissed student went to court, claiming judicial involvement was required because of a lack of fairness. And the court agreed, overruling the school's decision and ordering the student to be readmitted. The school had violated its own rules to the disadvantage of only one student. The court felt the error should be corrected.

Nevertheless, inconsistent policies on grading within an institution can be justified if properly administered. A law school student was in jeopardy of not graduating because failing grades were included in law school GPA calculations. But other schools on the campus did not include failing grades. So in *Johnson v. Sullivan*, 571 P.2d 798 (1977), the failing law student challenged the University of Montana. The state supreme court upheld university policy, allowing the law school to have alternative grading policies. Differing policies within the university were not found to be arbitrary or capricious. It was held that the policy was justified due to a law that waived state university law graduates from state bar exam requirements. The faculty had the right and responsibility to establish and maintain standards for assessing student academic performance.

Summary

The deferential attitude of courts to faculty decision making is perhaps best summarized in *Connelly v. University of Vermont*, 244 F.Supp. 156 (1965):

This rule has been stated in a variety of ways by a number of courts. Courts do not interfere with a school's internal affairs unless "there has been a manifest abuse of discretion or where action has been arbitrary or unlawful" or unless school officials have acted "arbitrarily or capriciously" or unless they have abused their discretion or acted in "bad faith."

Citing a longstanding policy of judicial non-interference, state and federal courts attempt to stay out of academic decision-making.

Before deciding any grade-based case, the courts will generally ask the following questions:

- Have all campus remedies been exhausted?

- Have applicable campus and state policies and regulations been followed?
- Is the grading decision or policy arbitrary or capricious?
- Is there evidence of bad faith?

Unless one of these questions can be answered affirmatively, academic decisions by academicians will not be subjected to judicial review.

But if the courts find inherent unfairness, the issues may be decided in the court, not the classroom. So the faculty member at Irvine Valley College has raised at least one of the key issues that get judicial interest in grade disputes — the alleged failure of his institution to abide by established regulations. If the school has violated state law in changing his grade, the instructor hopes the court will return authority over grades to its source, the faculty.

Grade Challenges: Best Left to Schools, Not Courts

September 1994

Just who is Susan M.? And why do or should so many colleges and universities care about her?

Susan was a fourth-semester law student in 1990 who went into court claiming that a school decision to dismiss her for academic reasons was both "arbitrary and capricious." The court ruling in her case, after extensive litigation, reaffirmed long-standing judicial deference given to academic decision-making. In the face of increasing student legal challenges over grading and other core academic decisions, Susan M's case reminds higher education of its duties to students in evaluating classroom performance and of the difficulties students have in pursuing such cases.

The Susan M. Story

She was just finishing her second year at New York Law School. During the previous year, her grade point average fell below accepted school standards and, as a result, she was placed on probation. She then barely met the standards in her third semester and, by the end of the year, she had again fallen below expected academic standards. The school, under existing policies, advised her that she was then subject to dismissal. It then gave her an opportunity to appear before a review committee.

Susan presented her case to the committee, citing "irrational" grading in three of her four recently completed semesters as the reasons for her academic difficulties. Her allegations:

- "A completely incompetent" instructor in one course, in which she received a poor grade.
- Another instructor's failure to clearly advise students that the final examination was "open book." She didn't bring her text and received a C-.
- A grading error on an exam in a third course. She claims to have provided an answer based on two different states' laws for extra credit. She received no credit for the multiple answers and ended up with a "D" for the course.

The Committee Story

The law school's Academic Status Committee gave Susan an opportunity to present both oral and written arguments on her failure to meet grade requirements. After considering her allegations, the Committee voted unanimously to dismiss her. The Committee did not find support for her first two claims and accepted the involved instructor's explanation of grading on the third class examination.

In the instance of the dual answer for "extra credit," the instructor maintained that the student had given two full answers and only one was correct. Since more than one answer was provided, the instructor judged that the student did not know which one was the correct answer, and so gave her no credit.

After receiving the Committee's initial ruling, Susan asked for a reconsideration of her case. She then provided additional explanations of her relatively poor performance. The Committee accepted her new pleadings but ultimately refused to reconsider its decision.

The Litigation Story

Susan then sought re-admission to the law school through New York courts. The trial court (known in New York as the Supreme Court) dismissed her initial petition. It held that the school's decision was not made arbitrarily, capriciously, or in bad faith. But in *Susan M v. New York Law School*, 544 N.Y.S. 2d 829 (1989), an intermediate appellate court reversed and remanded her grade contentions for further review. The Appellate Division was troubled by the grade given in the course with the exam on which Susan had answered with two analyses.

The court reasoned that a better grade on that one exam would have given Susan a C+ instead of a D for the course. And that would have given Susan an acceptable overall grade point average, allowing her to stay in school.

Said the court:

> If petitioner's transcript is any guide to her total academic performance, it does not appear that a C+ was utterly beyond her capabilities.

A rehearing by the lower court was ordered, in an attempt to make sure that there was not "an irrational reading of the exam" that could have impaired the grading process. At issue for the court was the extent to which no credit for Susan's exam answer was a reasonable exercise of academic authority.

The appellate panel questioned whether the school's decision was arbitrary or capricious. The court did not directly suggest that another grade be given, but noted that "concrete allegations of flagrant misapprehension on the part of the grader entitle the student to a measure of relief."

The lower court hearing on Susan's grade was never held. A petition to the state's highest court, the Court of Appeals, ended her legal challenge. In *Susan M. v. New York Law School*, 556 N.E. 2d 1104 (1990), the court ruled that the issues involved in her challenge were "beyond the scope of judicial review." Any further review of her grade, said the court, would inappropriately involve the justices in academic and educational decision making. In dismissing Susan's claim, the court noted that for students to receive any judicial relief in academic cases, they must first show "demonstrated bad faith, capriciousness, irrationality or a constitutional or statutory violation." They did not see that in Susan's case. Among the other stated concerns of the court was a judicial fear of being overwhelmed by the number of potential grading challenges if the court agreed to hear just one of them.

The Story's Lesson

Traditions of academic freedom have long held that academic decisions should be left to academicians, not the courts. As was the case in *Susan M.*, if the college or university follows its procedures and adheres to its standards, that tradition will continue into the future.

Case Law Defines Educational Malpractice

July 1991

Did I get a good education? Did my school give me what was promised? Did higher education really educate me? These are questions often asked by students as they sometimes unknowingly probe into the possibility of educational malpractice.

Malpractice is generally defined as a failure of a professional to render services exercising the degree of skill and knowledge commonly applied by other members of that profession, resulting in damages. While we're all very familiar with medical malpractice, the concept has slowly spread to the other professions. And in recent decades, courts have begun to hear more and more about educational malpractice at the elementary, secondary, and higher education levels.

For colleges and universities, malpractice cases have been based on the failure to provide the experience promised or on the student's failure to derive expected benefits. In recent years, case law has been developed on both of these points.

The most significant period of malpractice cases involving higher education came as a result of campus protests over American involvement in the Vietnam War. In the early 1970s, many school officials resorted to closing their doors to end growing violence on campus from anti-war activities. But as a result of the school closings, many students claimed that they did not get the education promised, and they went to court.

Closings in the University of Wisconsin System were explored in *Asher v. Harrington*, 318 F.Supp. 82 (1970). Students sued for malpractice, claiming that school officials had failed to maintain order: if the officials had acted professionally, school could have stayed open. The students had paid full tuition and should have been able to "pursue education [with the] unencumbered use and enjoyment of the facilities." They also claimed that the campus environment of dissent denied them their own rights of "free speech, free thoughts, free inquiry, and free assembly."

A federal court dismissed the action. It found no constitutional infringement and no way to judge what "normal" campus operations might be. The campus may have been in turmoil, but the court left it to school officials to determine whether there was any danger to the academic process. One appellate judge dissented, noting that, while the courts were open to protecting every other kind of student protest and demonstration, it was wrong for the courts to:

> close their doors to a group of students who seek merely their civil and contractual rights to pursue peacefully their studies without the violent interference of a well-organized disruptive movement allegedly supported by the university.

Strong words, but no malpractice.

Elsewhere around the same time, New York University canceled classes with only 19 days left in the semester. Officials felt that campus disorder made it impossible to finish the year.

One unhappy student went to court looking for a tuition refund of $277.40 for class time lost. A city court judge ruled in favor of the student and ordered a refund, even though NYU pointed out that the educational program was "subject to change without notice." But the court found malpractice.

In *Paynter v. New York University*, 319 N.Y.S. 2d 893 (1971), a state appeals court overturned the tuition refund. The judges noted that colleges are generally self-regulated and free from judicial interference, except when basic rights are violated. That wasn't the case. The court saw that school officials had a right to take steps to maintain order, and that the court should not question the wisdom of administrators on the scene. Officials had not violated professional standards in canceling classes; they had exercised professional judgment! The court found no malpractice.

One Thumb Up, One Thumb Down

Two other New York cases exemplify the types of educational malpractice cases filed by students in the troubled early 1970s. Cancellation of classes at Adelphi University and altered class schedules and grading policies at City University of New York Queens College both led to related litigation.

Adelphi students went to court seeking an order to fully reopen the school after it shut down in the aftermath of the Kent State University deaths. Officials were considering reopening the campus with special schedules and limited services. But some students went to court seeking the full university experience for their full tuition.

In *Harte v. Adelphi University*, 311 N.Y.S. 2d 66 (1970), the court supported the private school's right to make decisions in the best campus interest. Again, the court found good professional judgment, noting:

> that under ... unique and trying circumstances ... the defendants acted in good faith ... , which was not only their right but their duty.

The students failed to show evidence of a disregard for professional standards, and the case was dismissed.

Some CUNY students went to court claiming that changes made at Queens College in light of the protests represented malpractice. A state court heard these claims in *DeVito v. McMurray*, 311 N.Y.S. 3d 617 (1970). The students claimed that they wanted to attend classes, but that campus officials canceled instruction and altered grading policies.

Meeting in special term because of the need for an immediate decision, the state court reviewed the climate on campus and disagreed with the decision to halt classes. It found that officials had, in fact, overstepped their authority. Law and trustee policy mandated that instruction continue, and a well-meaning campus official cannot interpret the law differently. Back to school, said the court, finding campus administrators guilty of poor professional judgment.

In *Asher*, *Paynter*, *Harte*, and *DeVito*, courts looked at student claims of educational malpractice, due to class cancellations. In each case, the court reviewed campus authority and showed judicial restraint, preferring to leave educational decisions in the hands of educators. But when shown poor judgment or a lack of authority, as in *DeVito*, courts can apply judicial remedies to educational malpractice.

To avoid malpractice claims due to sudden program changes, campuses should:

- Understand the limits of administrative authority
- Use language in publications and handbooks that allows for program modification
- Exercise professional judgment, using the skills and education others in the profession would apply in similar circumstances

Campuses Face Charges of Educational Malpractice

August 1991

Why can't a college student read? That was the question in a suit filed by a former Creighton University basketball player. He complained that after four years of college, he still couldn't read a grade school textbook. His legal claim: educational malpractice. He contended that the school had simply failed to educate him, and he went to court seeking damages.

Educational malpractice is becoming more of an issue as college costs rise and the demand for skills and credentials grows. Suits over failure to teach, failure to educate, or failure to provide expected education benefits are based on claims of a special school-student relationship. Students sometimes contend that colleges and universities have been negligent in providing an education or that they have breached an agreement to educate.

They then look to the courts for remedies, basing their claims on:

- Program content
- Courses not presented as advertised
- Failure to meet standards
- Failure to anticipate academic problems
- Basic failure to teach

In all cases, courts must first decide if judicial intervention is appropriate and only then consider the merits of the claim. Many state courts have dealt with malpractice questions.

Program Content and Changed Courses

Doctoral students in a graduate management program sued their school, in *Lowenthal v. Vanderbilt University*, Tennessee Chancery Court A-8525 (1974). They claimed that the school which had a strong reputation, had started their graduate program in a "vague and ill-defined" manner without needed resources. The school had breached its contract with them to provide a quality education.

The court agreed. It found that a contract existed between students and the school, and that the school had breached the agreement by failing to provide necessary faculty and financial resources. The judge noted:

> Once it has made the promise to do so, the University has a duty to provide a high quality of academic training leading to an academically respectable doctoral degree which may be earned

by the satisfaction of reasonable and consistent standards and procedures.

The court rejected requests for lost future earnings but awarded eight students damages from $10 to $11,000 for registration fees and tuition costs. Said the court, "Vanderbilt received something of value from these plaintiffs and gave little or nothing in return."

In another case, an education major sued her school for $2,500 in damages, claiming that an education course she took was worthless. Her case, *Ianiello v. University of Bridgeport*, Conn. Trial Ct. (1977), focused on her claim that the course as taught didn't conform with the printed course description and that she didn't learn anything. She said there were no tests, no grades, no discussions, and no valuable content. She based her damage claim on lost tuition, wasted travel and class time, lost wages, and attorney's fees.

Bridgeport argued protection under academic freedom and claimed the class offering was not "unreasonable." It noted that the published course description was general and that the school reserved the right to make changes to fit changing situations. The court, finding evidence that the school may have been unreasonable, allowed a full trial. But in the end, the court upheld the school's authority to select courses, materials, methods, and instructors, as the case was thrown out before an appellate hearing.

Instructors and Equipment

It was a question of standards and qualifications for students in a telecommunications program who sued for malpractice due to negligence. Their argument: the instructor wasn't qualified and classroom equipment didn't meet standards. But the court dismissed the action, in *Beaman v. Des Moines Area Community College*, Law No. CL 15-8532 (1978), citing public policy. It ruled that state law had not yet expanded the principles of negligence to higher education.

This decision points out the difficulty often faced in educational malpractice cases, a new legal concept that courts are slow to accept. While malpractice suits based on negligence are common in other professions, they've only recently gained acceptance in higher education. Malpractice claims based on breach of educational contract are becoming more common and successful.

Failure to Adequately Prepare

Another student went to college in hopes of a career teaching English. He ended up suing his school for failing to prepare him adequately. A county circuit court considered the case of *Wai-Chung Ng v. West Virginia Board of Regents*, CA 82-404 (1982).

To earn his degree, the international student needed a passing grade in student teaching. Supervisors told him that his grade would be a C, but he received a D and couldn't be certified. In his suit, he claimed that he was never advised that his performance was "inferior or unsatisfactory." He completed his courses and teaching but wasn't eligible for certification. This was the school's fault, not his, he argued.

The case was dismissed on a technical issue, so the court never got to decide the issue of failing to advise or properly prepare. If the case had gone ahead, it would have been decided on the terms of the agreement and possible breaches.

Failure to Warn and Failure to Teach

What if a school fails to warn a student about potential academic performance difficulties? A former Alaska school teacher sued her law school for malpractice.

The plaintiff had failed three times to maintain the required grade point average and had been dismissed from the law program at Gonzaga University (WA). She completed her studies at another school, then wanted those credits counted toward a Gonzaga degree. When officials refused, the student took the case to court, claiming that the school failed in its duty to warn her of possible failure, which led her to finish elsewhere.

In *Maas v. Corporation of Gonzaga University*, 27 Wash. App. 397 (1980), judicial reluctance to intervene in academic issues was apparent. The court rejected the plaintiff's claims, saying that issues of credits and degrees should be left to campuses. It found no duty to warn students of potential failure:

> A graduate student seeking admission to a university knows a certain level of performance is necessary to earn a degree. It is unreasonable to require the university to warn applicants of the obvious.

In an earlier case, a plaintiff claimed educational malpractice based on a school's failure "to teach wisdom." When the school sued a former student for unpaid tuition, he filed suit for $7,000 in damages. In *Trustees of Columbia University v. Jacobsen*, 53 N.J. Super. 574 (1959), he contended that Columbia had failed to teach him as promised.

He learned a lesson. Wisdom, reasoned the court, was an end product. All the college can do, it ruled, was "through its teachers, libraries, laboratories, and other facilities ... endeavor to teach the student known facts, acquaint him with the nature of those matters which are unknown, and thereby assist him in developing mentally, morally, and physically."

Ross v. Creighton University, 957 F.2d 410 (7th Cir. 1992) was based on arguments similar to those presented in *Maas* and *Columbia*. In seeking damages, the former basketball player said the school should have known when recruiting him that he wouldn't succeed, and that it then failed to teach him. By the time he should have graduated, he was a full year behind in his studies and could read at only the second-grade level.

The court dismissed his claims. The school, it said, had kept its part of the education deal: it had taught. It was up to the student to learn. If he failed to do so, it wasn't institutional malpractice.

The court found that school officials had made an exception in admitting the student but had done so to give him an opportunity to perform. Creighton had success with other students in similar circumstances. The judge held that the school's judgment in admitting the student and teaching him seemed reasonable.

Summary

In cases ranging from *Lowenthal* to *Ross*, college students have claimed educational malpractice. Cases involving *breach of contract* have been more frequent and more successful than those based on *negligence*.

But in an increasingly litigious society, students unhappy with their higher education will head to court in greater numbers to argue every possible legal claim of malpractice. And courts, though reluctant to intervene in academic decisions, will deal with institutional actions that may be viewed as unreasonable or arbitrary and capricious.

Balancing Individual Rights and Commitment to Diversity

November 1994

Twice rejected by the University of California-Davis medical school, Alan Bakke began a challenge that would become one of the guiding pieces of litigation for affirmative action efforts in higher education. An aerospace engineer and a Vietnam veteran, he applied to a dozen medical schools in the early 1970s. Most rejected him, judging him to be too old to start school again. But UC-Davis read his application more carefully. He came very close to acceptance but was rejected.

Bakke wanted to know more about why he was passed over. What he found out made him angry. Sixteen of the school's 100 seats in 1973 and 1974 were reserved for "disadvantaged" members of minority groups. These 16 class spots went to students less academically prepared than he, if judged by college grades and standardized test scores. The engineer who wanted to be a physician sued the university, claiming that its use of a racial quota in admissions violated his constitutional equal protection rights.

Almost 20 years after Bakke was initially rejected by UC-Davis, four white applicants with high test scores were rejected by the University of Texas Law School. They sued, claiming that unlawful preference was given to Mexican American applicants. According to their suit, the school placed applications as they were received in color-coded files to indicate whether applicants were African American, Mexican American, or "other." In addition, separate admissions committees were used to evaluate white and minority applicants, leading to varying cutoff grades and test scores. The rejected white applicants claimed that UT Law School had violated their constitutional rights of equal protection. A federal district court judge ruled on their case in late summer 1994 in *Hopwood v. Texas*.

Bakke then and *Hopwood* today challenged higher education affirmative action efforts. Opponents of these efforts say they only fight discrimination with more discrimination. Proponents argue that admissions processes must be "race-conscious" to eliminate vestiges of discrimination or to promote required or desired diversity. What have the federal courts done? How do they affect current and future admission processes?

1976 and 1978

When the California Supreme Court heard *Bakke v. Regents of the University of California,* 18 Cal. 3d 342, 553 P.2d 1152 (1976), it ordered the medical school to admit Bakke. The university appealed to the U.S. Supreme Court in *Regents of the University of California v. Bakke,* 438 U.S. 265 (1978), maintaining that such an order would reverse required affirmative action efforts.

UC-Davis maintained that state universities should be free to consider the race or ethnicity of applicants in order to increase the number of qualified members of those minority groups trained for the educated professions and participating in them, professions from which minorities were long excluded because of generations of pervasive racial discrimination. The school had opened six years earlier, when minorities made up less than 2% of medical students. UC-Davis was committed to increasing those numbers through its admissions processes.

Attorneys for Bakke argued that the school had adopted a racial quota depriving Bakke of a fair opportunity for admission to medical school. His rejected test scores were more than double those of some students in the special admissions group.

The U.S. Supreme Court was badly split over the case, ultimately issuing two separate 5-to-4 majority opinions. One decision held that the government had earlier barred quotas like this in programs receiving federal funds. UC-Davis was found to have violated that standard and was ordered to admit Bakke.

Said the court:

> We have never approved a classification that aids persons perceived as members of relatively victimized groups at the expense of other innocent individuals. ... Although a university must have wide discretion in making the sensitive judgments as to who should be admitted, constitutional limitations protecting individuals may not be disregarded.

But a second majority on the court felt that campuses should retain race and ethnicity as factors in admissions. They held that a "plus" could be given to minority applicants to allow schools to achieve a better student "mix."

In doing this, the court noted:

> An otherwise qualified medical student with a particular background, whether it be ethnic, geographic, culturally advantaged or disadvantaged, may bring to a professional school of medicine experiences, outlooks and ideas that enrich the training of the student body. ... Ethnic diversity, however, is only one element in a range of factors a university properly may consider.

Bakke established a principle for later Supreme Court decisions that judged quota systems, on and off campus, on strong showings of past discriminations requiring remedies.

Today

In *Hopwood,* the four white applicants to UT-Law School challenged *Bakke*-type quotas. School officials argued, however, that admissions policies are narrowly tailored to encourage minority applicants without discriminating against others. The campus was under an earlier agreement with the federal Office of Civil Rights to address vestiges of segregation.

The case began with one plaintiff, then grew as others read about the challenge in newspapers and decided to join the effort. They were among the over 4,000 annual applicants for the program who had been ranked by the law school according to their college grades and standardized test results.

UT officials say that system policies require minority populations to be adequately represented in admissions. A strictly numerical decision-making process could have reduced minority acceptances by up to 75%. Under the admission process then in place, UT Law School admitted approximately half a class based on combined grades and law school exam forms. For the rest, minorities were compared with other minorities and the other applications were compared separately. Race, gender, age, and economic factors were then used as admission factors.

Under the "Texas Index" admission system, applications were reviewed separately by race. Each race had a separate accept or reject cutoff figure; minority applicants were admitted with scores lower than rejected white applicants. Applications that were subjected to further review were considered by race as well by the separate committees.

The four rejected white applicants went to federal court to challenge the index process. But before the case went to trial, UT law school changed admission policies. It announced, beginning in 1995, that all applications would be judged together, without any separation by race. A single admissions committee will be established to screen applications, but that one group will consider race and ethnicity in individual cases.

The court, in *Hopwood,* focused on the 1992 admissions process. Did university policies discriminate unlawfully against the white plaintiffs? Would the plaintiffs have been accepted into the law school if they had been treated lawfully?

The federal district court judge found that the campus affirmative action policies in 1992 had unconstitutionally discriminated against the four white applicants. The court found that the separation of applications and review by separate committees violated equal protection principles in the law.

The judge did not overturn all collegiate admissions affirmative action in his ruling. He found that it was "legal and appropriate" for the school to use affirmative action "until society sufficiently overcomes the effects of its lengthy history of pervasive racism." Said the ruling, colleges and universities must "provide a procedure or method by which qualifications of each individual are evaluated and compared to those of all other individuals in the pool, whether minority or non-minority."

The court also rejected the plaintiffs' reverse discrimination claim. It said the plaintiffs had not proven they were rejected only due to unlawful discrimination. Since the school had already changed its admissions policies, and the school year was about to start, the court ordered their applications re-evaluated next year at no charge.

The *Hopwood* decision attempts to balance the schools commitment to diversity and individual rights:

> Commitment to affirmative action programs in education institutions as just and necessary, however, does not imply that the individual rights of non-minorities should fall by the wayside or be ignored.

The judge said colleges could use affirmative action programs, but would subject them to the most searching judicial examination "to ensure they are necessary, fair, and narrow." The plaintiffs may appeal portions of the decision.

In the wake of *Bakke* and *Hopwood,* schools continue to seek appropriate and legal means of meeting campus and community commitments to diversity. More challenges to these practices are expected as those rejected will continue to press for their individual rights. Courts will have to continue to balance those rights with the demands of society.

Affirmative Action: Hopwood and Beyond

June 1996

> With the best of intentions, in order to increase the enrollment of certain favored classes of minority students, the University of Texas School of Law discriminates in favor of those applicants by giving substantial racial preferences in its admissions program.
>
> The law school has presented no compelling justification, under the Fourteenth Amendment or Supreme Court precedent, that allows it to continue to elevate some races over others, even for the wholesome purpose of correcting perceived racial imbalance in the student body.
>
> *Hopwood et al. v. State of Texas et al.*, No. 94-50569, U.S. Court of Appeals, Fifth Circuit, 1996

These two sentences express the basic facts and judicial outcome of an affirmative action challenge, with significant campus implications As the consequences of *Hopwood* develop, an understanding of the case, legal responses to it, and national reaction is important. Not since the establishment of admissions practices, based on *Regents of the University of California v. Bakke*, 438 U.S. 265 (1978), has affirmative action been subjected to this degree of college and university scrutiny.

Best of Intentions

The plaintiffs sought admission to the University of Texas law school for various reasons, but they were denied admission for only one reason, they claimed — their race: all were white. Brought together by a lawyer, they challenged the affirmative action admissions process that they believed had worked against them.

Claiming Fourteenth Amendment equal protection violations, they sued. They maintained that UT treated African American and Mexican American applicants differently than other candidates. They argued that, despite higher grades and test scores, they were not admitted, while members of protected minority groups with lower scores were accepted. They sought admission, an injunction to halt the affirmative action process, and compensatory and punitive damages.

In fact, the UT law school did operate with lower admission standards for minority applicants in an effort to provide a class each year that was at least 10% Mexican American and 5% African American. The admissions office color-coded applications to the school by race, rated applications separately by race, admitted applicants by race, and maintained separate race-based waiting lists.

In August 1994, a federal district court found that the UT approach violated the plaintiffs' rights. The court did not order relief, however. UT had already agreed to stop asking separate committees to review applications. Therefore, the court said, the applicants could apply in the future at no cost. The court said UT had only a limited right to consider race in admissions and had agreed to follow new rules.

But earlier this year, the Fifth Circuit Court of Appeals expanded on the lower court decision. It said UT had to eliminate altogether any consideration of race as a factor in admission. Campuses, said the court, can make admissions decisions on the basis of individual characteristics but cannot assume "that a certain individual possesses characteristics by being a member of a certain racial group." Discrimination by race to overcome past discrimination was held to be unlawful. Said the court:

> A university may properly favor one applicant over another because of his ability to play the cello, make a downfield tackle, or understand chaos theory. An admissions process may also consider an applicant's home state, ... relationship to school alumni, ... extracurricular activities in college. Schools may even consider factors such as whether an applicant's parents attended college or the applicant's economic and social background.

For this reason, consideration of race often is said to be justified in the interests of promoting diversity, not on its own terms, but as a way to assess other characteristics that institutions of higher education value but that do not raise similar constitutional concerns. Unfortunately, this approach simply perpetuates the very harm that the Fourteenth Amendment was designed to eliminate. The three-judge federal panel unanimously ruled that UT had failed to justify its policy favoring some racial groups. Use of race as a factor, a basic practice since *Bakke*, was rejected by the court.

Legal Maneuvers

Within weeks of the decision, several appeals were in the works. UT and civil rights groups involved in the case asked for U.S. Supreme Court review and a stay to prevent implementation of the ruling.

On behalf of the UT system, the state attorney general requested a hearing before the Supreme Court. He called the case "a matter of profound public impact" and said an appeal was necessary because *Hopwood* presented "dramatic potential consequences."

In its request for review, Texas has asked the court to reject *Hopwood* in favor of *Bakke*. Diversity, it maintains, must remain as a legitimate factor in selecting classes for admission. The Supreme Court has also been asked to consider the state's long history of discrimination as one important justification for the approach used by the UT law school.

Others have proposed alternative ways of reversing the *Hopwood* decision. Since only a three-judge panel of the Circuit Court heard the case, civil rights group plaintiffs have asked the full Fifth Circuit to rehear the case. Two plaintiffs, the Thurgood Marshall Legal Society and the

Black Pre-Law Association, have filed papers to have the panel decision overturned by the full court.

To allow all of the plaintiffs to get their appeals in order, the full Fifth Circuit Court ordered a stay of the panel's *Hopwood* order. It blocked implementation of the order until an appeal was formally filed. If the Supreme Court agrees to hear the case, the stay remains in effect until a final decision is reached. If the high court turns down the appeal, the *Hopwood* ruling will go into effect. In ordering the stay, the court acknowledged the difficulties faced by colleges and universities in swift implementation of the order.

While all of this is going on, the UT law school faces yet another class-action suit. Based on the success of 1992 applicants in *Hopwood*, a group of rejected 1994 candidates have asked for a judicial order supporting their admission to the school. They claim that race was unlawfully used as a factor in denying them admission two years ago.

Editor's Note: In July 1996, the U.S. Supreme Court refused to consider an appeal of *Hopwood*. That left three states under the Fifth Circuit ruling and the rest of higher education to consider the future of affirmative action in admissions.

International Students: What Are the Legal Issues?

March 1993

Despite tight finances and budget cuts at most colleges and universities, the enrollment of foreign students on American campuses remains significant. More than 400,000 international students are currently studying in the United States. Most hold F-1 student visas.

Last year, the National Association of Student Personnel Administrators (NASPA) published a monograph entitled *Working With International Students and Scholars on American Campuses*. One chapter, written by P.S. Levitou of the University of Nebraska, highlights the legal issues faced by many international students and the campuses that host them.

Admissions Regulations Complex

Most laws regarding the treatment and status of international students, on and off campus, are federal. The laws include the 1952 Immigration and Nationality Act and the more recent (1990) regulations on Aliens and Nationality. These laws specifically govern the admission and conduct of foreign nationals entering the country for educational reasons.

For admissions purposes, campuses may be certified by the federal government to enroll foreign students in the F-1 student visa status. The regulations involved are complex, but in short, they allow F-1 students to enroll if they:

- Are academically acceptable
- Have English skills that will allow them to successfully study in a full-time program
- Have the financial support to pay all their expenses in school

While there are several visa statuses for current and prospective international students, *Working With ...* says that over 80% of the current campus international population is F-1.

To maintain his or her visa status, and to stay in the country, an international student must be in a full-time study program at an authorized school. International students can generally be in the country only for the length of time needed to complete their programs.

However, the government will allow international students an additional two months to make arrangements to leave or to apply for a different visa status. It also allows a grace period of up to one year in some cases, along with additional time for students who want to stay for compelling academic or health reasons.

A Close Look at Employment Rules

Employment rules for international students — particularly laws governing off-campus employment — are currently under review.

On-campus employment regulations, however, have not substantially changed in recent years. On campus, international students who have full visa status compliance may work for commercial enterprises that serve students (e.g., the food service, residence halls, libraries) or in settings required for their educational program (e.g., the counseling center for a student studying to be a counselor).

Employment related to the academic experience, however, can be on or off campus. It might include, for example, an engineering company setting for an engineering student.

Previous restrictions on off-campus employment were temporarily lifted in 1991. Late that year, a pilot study of off-campus employment for international students began.

Until at least 1994, students who have been F-1 for at least one year can work off campus if:

- They are in good academic standing
- The off-campus employer has tried to but cannot fill an open position with a domestic worker

International students are also allowed to work in practical training environments related to their studies or as recommended by school officials. Such employment can extend to a full year of work experience after graduation if it is educationally recommended by campus officials.

Student Records

Since the early 1970s, all campus-maintained student records have been protected under federal law. The Family Educational Rights and Privacy Act (FERPA) of 1974 applies to all students, domestic and international.

The law says that campuses generally may not release student record information to third parties without student authorization. Directory information about an individual can be provided to others upon request, if the process is defined by the school and if the student consents.

While FERPA applies to international students, regulations of the Immigration and Naturalization Service (INS) require prospective international students to authorize the blanket release of their records for governmental purposes. Under visa requirements, foreign students must agree to allow INS to inspect any records held by the school in connection with its governmental purposes (e.g., employment records kept for tax purposes, academic records kept for INS compliance purposes).

In addition, INS review requirements place additional recordkeeping and compliance burdens on the host campus. Since the campus is conducting the initial student eligibility review, it must maintain proper records to ensure that enrolled students are still entitled to their visa status.

Other Concerns

On the topics of counseling, health care, and death, *Working With ...* offers several other issues for campus consideration. These include:

- Making sure that campus counselors have access to INS regulations and/or trained individuals, to ensure that advisors talk to international students with legal ramifications in mind
- A split in legal circles over the legality of mandatory health insurance programs, particularly when they're only required for international students (although there is case law to support such programs)
- Concern over the religious and cultural aspects of an international student's death

The monograph also examines financial restraints on F-1 visa status students while they're in the country. Nonimmigrant international students, for instance, are not eligible for any form of federal financial aid. Grant, loan, and work study programs also have regulations against awards to international students, and INS regulations prohibit international students from accepting such awards.

And while international students are exempt from Social Security payments (as are their employers), they may owe income taxes to the federal and some state governments. Generally, working international students will be liable for federal taxes on money they make in the country. State tax regulations, however, vary greatly.

Working With ... concludes its chapter on legal considerations with a look at asylum and deportation. For students who don't want to return home for fear of persecution, asylum may offer an opportunity to extend a stay or make it permanent.

For students who dabble in criminal activities or violate their visa status, however, deportation could result.

Conclusion

The impact of the INS regulations on international students and their campuses can be enormous. Campus policies on admissions, employment, records, health, and finance are directly involved, along with the procedures of many other campus units.

It's very important for international students, their advisors, and the entire campus community to be aware of the law — and to be sensitive to the circumstances and conditions of international students studying in America.

Note: Working With International Students and Scholars on American Campuses is available from NASPA at 1875 Connecticut Ave. NW, Suite 418, Washington, DC 20009.

Student Evaluations Gain Legal Weight

February 1990

The law student received a grade of D for the course. But he thought he knew why — and he didn't think his classroom work or examinations had anything to do with it. The alleged reason for his poor grade: his evaluation of the instructor.

According to his claim, the professor had talked to the class about the evaluation process and threatened students if they rated him low. The student also charged that the professor violated confidentiality by holding onto the evaluations until after the final examination. In *Mucklow v. John Marshall Law School*, 531 N.E. 2d 941 (1988), an Illinois state court was asked to consider the student's claims.

In an era of increased interest in the importance of teaching and in students as consumers, student evaluation of faculty and courses has taken on new meaning. And in the law, student evaluations may have ramifications in personnel matters, questions of discrimination, termination decisions, and issues of academic freedom. A series of higher education legal cases have helped to define uses and abuses in the student evaluation process.

Background

Student evaluations of instructors have existed *informally* throughout the history of education. Students frequently have shared their impressions of teachers and courses amongst themselves, in hallways, residence halls, and libraries, passing the word about what classes to take and which instructors should be avoided.

In the 1920s, Harvard University students independently began to compile informal evaluations and published them as a "confidential guide" to courses. Designed to advise students on class and instructor selection, the guide served as an early form of *formal* student evaluation. Since then, the basic format and questioning of student evaluations haven't changed radically.

Today, student evaluations are used to measure a variety of factors, including course materials, examinations, assignments, instructor interest and competence, teaching style, response to questions, and office hours. Most litigation surrounding the use of this information has been in personnel decisions. Student evaluations have been used to support faculty terminations and to refute staff discrimination charges.

While educational critics have long argued about the validity of student evaluations, courts have been more willing to accept their findings. Given a judicial tendency to support academic decisions unless shown to be arbitrary or capricious, campuses have enjoyed great latitude in using the results of student evaluations in faculty personnel decisions.

Terminations and Non-Renewals

The use of student evaluations to support termination of a faculty member was tested in *Jawa v. Fayetteville State University*, 426 F.Supp. 218 (1976). A faculty member was dismissed on the grounds of poor teaching and poor relations with students. The instructor, a native of India, filed a *race discrimination* suit against Fayetteville State. The school used student evaluations of the instructor to justify the personnel decision. The federal district court established a non-discriminatory reason for the termination and dismissed the suit. The legal validity of student evaluations was upheld.

Can student evaluations also be used to justify firing a physical education instructor and coach? That was the question in *O'Conner v. Peru State College*, 781 F.2d 632 (1986). A federal appellate panel reviewed charges that the instructor had been dismissed unfairly. To counter these allegations, the school then produced evidence of poor teaching, inadequate instruction, and low team morale. The court gave weight to student evaluations of the coach's skills and commitment and found that they supported legal termination of the coach for non-discriminatory reasons.

In a Virginia Polytechnic Institute case, a female lawyer was appointed to a department as an instructor. The rest of the department was male. After two terms, her contract was not renewed. In *Dyson v. Lavery*, 417 F.Supp. 103 (1976), a federal district court was asked to consider if the reason for her termination involved *sex discrimination*.

In addition to questioning her academic qualifications, the school used student evaluations to support the termination. Student complaints about the instructor were shared with the court, along with the results of formal student evaluations. Of 48 instructors in the department, students graded the plaintiff 46th in terms of effectiveness. The court accepted the use of the student evaluations, deeming them valid in establishing a non-discriminatory basis for the termination.

The growing trend of hiring husband and wife together led to conflict at the University of Connecticut in *Lieberman v. Gant*, 474 F.Supp. 848 (1979). Hired as part of an effort to recruit her spouse, the plaintiff was denied tenure after six years in the English department. She responded with legal action, contending that illegal sex discrimination was a factor.

Among the issues raised by the school in justifying the termination was poor teaching. Using student evaluations, the college provided numerical data to the court on the instructor's teaching abilities. The school showed that students had rated the instructor in the bottom 25% of the staff. Additional student and staff complaints about her teaching qualities supported the college's contention that poor teaching — not sex discrimination — caused her termination.

A school's failure to promote a female assistant biochemistry professor also led to litigation over sex discrimination. Student evaluations, formal and informal, were used to show reasons for denying promotion. In this case, *Johnson v. University of Pittsburgh*, 435 F.Supp. 1328 (1977), the federal court expressed confidence in the informal process of student evaluations. While dismissing the formal student ratings as being unreliable and "too general," the court considered other informal student complaints and concerns as solid indications of just cause.

Faculty Fight for Academic Freedom

Student evaluations of faculty members haven't met with universal faculty acceptance. At least two professors have challenged the process legally, charging that evaluations violate academic freedom.

A professor who was dismissed for poor teaching contended that students disliked his teaching methods. While his department chair supported renewal of his contract, the decision was made on the basis of student evaluations. The instructor argued that he treated his students as if they were already in the commercial art world, stressing attendance, timeliness, and independence in the classroom. Because of his high expectations, he claimed, he wasn't popular, so his ratings suffered. But his standards, he argued, shouldn't be for students to judge, and they shouldn't be held against him in personnel decision-making. So he responded with legal action.

The court, in *Carley v. Arizona Board of Regents*, 737 P.2d 1099 (1987), rejected his claims. It ruled that "academic freedom is not a doctrine to insulate a teacher from evaluation" by his employer. A school must remain free to evaluate teaching methods used in its classrooms.

A similar argument was raised — with similar results — in *Lovelace v. Southeastern Massachusetts University*, 793 F.2d 419 (1986). There, an instructor contended that he was dismissed because he wasn't "an easy grader." He claimed that the school's use of negative evaluations violated his academic freedom. His ratings were low, he argued, not because he was a poor teacher, but because he refused to lower his standards and grade students easily.

A state court disagreed, finding that the teacher had been legally dismissed. The school, ruled the court, retained the right to control grading policies, course materials, and class workload. These matters have a great impact on student life, and school control must be maintained to ensure a quality educational environment. Student evaluations can be a part of a school's effort to maintain that environment.

Summary

Despite a variety of legal challenges, student evaluations remain a legally viable means of assessing teaching abilities. The use of evaluations has not been found to violate basic academic freedoms (*Lovelace* and *Carley*), and they can be used to support terminations (*Jawa* and *Peru*) and to refute claims of sex discrimination (*Dyson*, *Lieberman*, and *Johnson*). In addition, the court has dismissed student claims of retaliation for poor evaluations (*Mucklow*).

To help make student evaluations valuable and usable, consider the following:

- Advise faculty — in advance — on the use of evaluations.
- Provide an opportunity for faculty review of evaluation instruments.
- Maintain evaluation procedures that ensure confidentiality.
- Establish simple testing instruments to reduce possibility of student error.
- Maintain other forms of teaching evaluations to complement student evaluations.

Evaluating Evaluations

April 1996

The request at the University of Kansas was fairly straightforward. Students wanted a chance to review their own evaluations of their instructors. Up until now, KU administrators have considered those evaluations confidential, calling them part of faculty personnel files. These files are not subject to the state Open Records Law, according to the school. Others aren't so sure. And now the student senate has adopted a resolution calling for the records to be open for review.

Access to student evaluations is only one of several legal issues related to the common campus practice of collecting feedback from students on their instructors. Evaluations are most often challenged in cases involving faculty rights and employment.

To what degree have courts accepted student evaluations? What role may they play in campus employment decision-making? Let's evaluate student evaluations!

History

The "Confidential Guide to Courses," first published in the 1920s about Harvard's curriculum, appears to be one of the earliest organized student evaluation efforts. Today, evaluations are commonly used by students and campuses to evaluate teaching — for purposes of renewal, promotion, tenure, and merit pay. If appropriately and successfully used, they can:

- Involve students more in the learning process
- Represent consumer assessment of a product
- Provide a look into a classroom's methods and content and an instructor's skill and approach
- Be the source of comparative data on how instructors are doing
- Provide feedback to help instructors improve their teaching

Basic Legal Issues

Many higher education institutions have used student evaluations in personnel decisions. As a result, when those decisions are challenged in court, the evaluations become part of the case. When courts review such evaluations, they give the most credence to those with established criteria and those that adhere to established standards.

Most student evaluation challenges involve dismissals, discrimination claims, and academic freedom issues. Confidentiality concerns, like those raised at KU, are somewhat less prevalent.

One example of dismissal cases involved an Arkansas instructor removed as a "poor teacher." The school used student evaluations to support that contention, in addition to sustaining allegations of poor advisement, unfair grading, unavailability to students, and declining class enrollments. The court accepted the validity of the student evaluations.

In another action, a female law professor was not renewed and claimed sex discrimination. The Virginia

Polytechnic Institute said the termination was due to her qualifications and teaching, and it used student evaluations to support that position. The court accepted evidence that the instructor was ranked poorly by students — as low as 46th out of 48 faculty members — in deciding in favor of the school.

A similar outcome can be found in a University of Connecticut case. As part of a deal to recruit a professor to the UConn faculty, the professor's wife was given a position in the English Department. After teaching for six years, she was denied tenure. She claimed sex discrimination, but the university successfully showed other causes for not offering her a permanent post. Itsr personnel process evaluated teaching, scholarship, and service in all tenure cases. The court was shown evidence that student evaluations and peer faculty observations had rated her poorly, as 12th out of 15 faculty members. The court found in those rankings an adequate basis for the tenure denial.

While not "highly valued," student evaluations were also given a judicial review in a University of Pittsburgh case. An assistant professor there was denied tenure and sued, claiming sex discrimination. Pitt maintained that poor teaching, research, and writing led to her situation. While the court found the student evaluation process to be "too general" to be given much credence, it concluded that student input was important to the review process. The formal student evaluations did support Pitt's contentions, and the denial was upheld.

Violation of academic freedom was alleged in other student evaluation cases. An instructor at Southeastern Massachusetts University (now the University of Massachusetts-Dartmouth) claimed that he lost his position because he refused to inflate his grades or lower his teaching expectations. He maintained that he was pressured to change his teaching approach because of poor student evaluations. According to his court papers, student complaints about homework assignments and hard courses led to threats not to renew his contract, violating his academic freedom.

The court sustained the termination of the professor's contract. It found that the personnel action was based on his conduct, not the content of his speech. It ruled that SMU legitimately considered student evaluations and used the information appropriately on policy matters, such as grading policies, course content, and homework load.

Academic freedom violations were also alleged in an Arizona case. An instructor there was denied tenure, primarily due to complaints about his teaching. He said his academic free speech rights were violated by school challenges to his teaching methods. The poor evaluations, he argued, were due to his "strict" approach. As his "popularity" suffered, so did his evaluations.

The courts, however, said academic freedom could not protect the instructor from serious employment reviews. Over 61% of his evaluations were negative. The school, said the court, was entitled to consider them in making employment decisions.

Validity

When student evaluations of instructors become a legal matter, their *validity* is often attacked. Some surveys indicate that they can be inaccurate and not the best measure of good teaching. A review of student evaluation systems raises legitimate questions about the ratings.

One is that most processes do not measure the effectiveness of teaching, intellectual achievement, or student understanding of basic concepts. Instead, they appear to assess student satisfaction, student attitudes toward teachers and classes, and instructor personality traits, speaking qualities, and even popularity.

Alternative teaching evaluations are often suggested to supplement or replace current student-based systems. These include peer evaluations and classroom observations. Student opinions, research suggests, can be most accurate for what they understand of course content and for the instructor's work habits and coverage of materials. It's suggested that students can best assess the characteristics of a teacher and their general satisfaction with a course. So, when using evaluations in making personnel decisions, administrators must carefully construct the process to allow appropriate student assessment.

Recommendations

Student evaluations of instructors can play a role on campus, but they can also lead to court, if not properly designed and used. Experts suggest several campus steps to improve the processes and protect the results from legal challenge:

- Student evaluations should only be one part of an overall review of an instructors teaching skills and competency.

- Evaluations should be based on personal observations.

- The process should be based on campus policies and should be conducted under those policies.

- The results should be shared as an improvement device for instructors.

- The forms used should be easy to read and understand, with questions focused, not open-ended.

- Good instructions should be given to evaluators, with someone other than the instructor conducting the evaluation.

- Results should be consistently applied.

Students at the University of Kansas want the results of their evaluations opened for their review. Campuses need to make sure that the evaluations, when used, are designed to provide appropriate, fair, and usable input, regardless of whether they are available under records access laws.

Chapter 2
ACADEMIC EMPLOYMENT AND FREEDOMS

Introduction

> Our nation is deeply committed to safeguarding academic freedom, which is of transcendent value to all of us and not merely to the teachers concerned. That freedom is therefore a special concern of the First Amendment, which does not tolerate laws that cast a pall of orthodoxy over the classroom. ... The classroom is peculiarly the "marketplace of ideas." The nation's future depends upon leaders trained through wide exposure to that robust exchange of ideas which discovers truth "out of a multitude of tongues."
>
> *United States v. Associated Press*, 52 F.Supp. 362 (1943)

A key relationship on campus, and within the entire educational process, is that between teacher and institution. The selection and employment of faculty involves many issues and principles, with academic freedom being most critical. In today's legal environment, employment issues are constantly being raised and reviewed, involving discrimination, speech and association rights, grievance processes, sexual harassment, whistleblowing, contractual rights, termination issues, false credentials, conflicts of interest, and basic tenure rights.

False Credentials Can Quickly End Employment

May 1993

When conducting employment searches, campuses often examine the credentials of hundreds of candidates from around the country. But some résumés may simply be "too good to be true."

Résumé fraud has become an unfortunate fact of life in today's competitive job world. To secure desirable employment, some people submit credentials that don't represent their actual work or education history.

Campuses, as major employers, must thoroughly review employment credentials. Meanwhile, students and other job-seekers must take equal care in preparing credentials to ensure accuracy and avoid problems.

Whether you're an employer or an employee (or both), be aware that according to court rulings, employees hired on false credentials can lose their jobs without the normal disciplinary proceedings.

Simply put, you need to understand this issue from several perspectives:

- Know the steps a campus can take when confronted with suspicions of résumé fraud.
- Know what rights the courts have given to employers who discover résumé fraud.
- Know the importance of reviewing your credentials and submitting an accurate résumé during your next job search.

When Suspicion Arises ...

A careful review of candidates' credentials is an essential element of any campus employment search. Campus officials should give the search committee the time and resources necessary to *fully* confirm the background information supplied by the most interesting prospective employees.

According to legal experts, the search committee should:

- Require credentials and references to be verifiable and submitted in writing
- Follow up on all materials, solicited and unsolicited
- Be specific in correspondence with past employers and educational institutions

Does your campus suspect that a *current* employee has submitted inaccurate credentials? If so, say the experts, take the following steps before confronting the employee:

- Check with the former employer listed by the employee. Ask the former employer to verify your employee's résumé claims in writing.

- Re-evaluate the employee's credentials based on any new verifiable sources that are different from those submitted originally.

- Check the original vacancy announcement that was used to solicit applications for the job. What work or educational experiences were required?

- Meet with the employee to review the discrepancies in his or her credentials. Ask for an explanation or comments.

If the employee can't provide satisfactory explanations or documentation, your campus can fire him or her — because false credentials void the original employment agreement.

Ruling May Have Campus Implications

Last year, a federal appeals court heard a case involving résumé fraud that may have campus ramifications.

In *Johnson v. Honeywell Information Systems, Inc.*, No. 90-2139/2205 (Sixth Cir. 1992), an employee who was fired fought her former employer to keep her job.

Initially, the company said the employee's work was unsatisfactory and asked her to resign. She refused and claimed that discrimination on the job was the real problem.

While preparing for litigation, however, the company reviewed the plaintiff's résumé and found some errors. The university she "graduated" from, for example, said its records indicated that she had completed only four courses. Another school listed on her résumé had no record of her attendance.

The employee's previous work experiences were also allegedly exaggerated or non-existent.

After gathering evidence, the company asked the trial court to rule in their favor before any hearing. Its request for a summary judgment was based on two items:

- The employee's misrepresentations were cause for her dismissal, even if the cause was discovered after the fact

- The misrepresentations prevented the formation of an enforceable work contract

The court, however, sent the case to trial, noting that the new evidence came too late to be "just cause" for termination. It also said the résumé fraud issues should be tried.

But an appeals court ruled that the summary judgment should have been granted. It said that termination for falsified credentials was a matter of law.

The company's strongest argument in the trial court had been that fraudulent misrepresentation had prevented the formation of an enforceable contract. The appellate panel found that evidence to be compelling and said the company had relied on the employee's résumé when it had made its initial hiring decision.

If the supervisor had known that the candidate did not have a degree, the court ruled, she never would have been given an interview. Said the court, her:

> misrepresentations, by virtue of their nature and number, and when viewed in the context of (the company's) expressed requirement of a college degree and its warning to applicants that misrepresentations may constitute just cause, ... provide adequate and just cause for dismissal.

The employee may have had a civil rights discrimination case originally. But the school's discovery of résumé fraud made it impossible for her to recover. In other words, because she never legally had the job, she could not sue for unlawful termination.

If You're Looking ...

Are you about to start a job search? One good way to avoid résumé fraud questions or concerns is to personally confirm your résumé details *before* the job search begins.

Consider what happened to a 1981 graduate of Rollins College (FL), for example. She went through several years of frustration because she couldn't get a job. Then she discovered why.

According to the college, she had never graduated. Now she wonders how many times prospective employers or supervisors were told by the school that she didn't have a degree.

The school finally checked its records at her request and confirmed that she did, in fact, have her degree. The school offered an apology, but the woman wants $10,000 in damages. Her case is pending.

Although this type of problem may be rare, take time to check your résumé details and references — because prospective employers will probably do the same. Check with former employers and schools to make sure your records are in order. Get copies of your transcripts and employment files. Check with the people you've named as references. Give them copies of your résumé and let them know that they might be called by your prospective employer.

Be advised, however, that prospective employers often do more than simply verify your past employment or your education. Some companies, for instance, hire outside firms to do more extensive screenings. Others may even check your credit history.

Remember also that, as a general rule, a prospective employer doesn't have to tell you why you weren't hired. In these times of expensive lawsuits, most won't.

If you're knocked out of the race for a job because of a credit check, however, the employer must notify you. That way, you have the opportunity to review your credit files for errors.

Summary

The *Johnson* case points to the ultimate risk in résumé fraud — termination that can be swift and legal. So if you're an employer, make sure you conduct comprehensive record reviews. And if you're an employee, take the responsibility to be accurate — and don't forget to confirm the details of your résumé.

Not Whether You Win or Lose, But How You Break the Contract

October 1990

You've read the story before. The team wins the championship, the trophy goes into the display case, and the coach gets a better offer at another college or university.

Or the team suffers through a terrible season, the fans blame the coaching staff, and the school decides the program needs "new blood" and terminates the coach.

The sports pages of your local newspaper are not what they used to be. In years gone by, you found box scores, scouting reports, interviews, and feature articles on your team. Today, those items are still there, but they're surrounded more often than not by evidence of the impact of the legal world on the sporting world. Recruiting violations, grade scandals, graduation rate reporting, and coaching changes get as much coverage as the scores.

One obvious area of growing concern in collegiate athletics is employment contracts for coaches. At the end of every season, dozens of college coaches, under contract, are publicly known to be considering other opportunities, courted by other schools and professional teams. What about their contracts? Aren't coaches committed to their current employers?

Employment Status

Given the relatively high turnover of collegiate coaches, their legal status becomes important when the school wants to make a change or the coach starts to look elsewhere. Some campus personnel work on a *contract* basis. Others are employed *at will*.

An employment *contract*, for coaches and others, has the same basic elements as any other contract to be effective. To be valid, a contract must reflect:

- *An Offer* — the willingness of both parties to enter into a bargain at terms
- *Acceptance* — an agreement by both parties to enter into the arrangement as stated
- *Consideration* — the exchange of something of value (i.e., dollars or effort) under the terms

Employment contracts that contain these elements obligate both parties to terms and conditions. Coaches and schools need to understand contracts — and be committed to fulfilling them completely — before entering into them. The contract itself is the entire legal arrangement.

Often, parties will contend that there's more to the agreement than the contract — that they agreed to other items in addition to those written down on paper. Courts generally will not enforce those "extra" terms, unless recorded in the same manner as the contract. If the contract is written, additional related agreements must be written as well.

Non-written evidence of other agreements will not be admitted into a court challenge on the contract. This is known as the *parol evidence* rule. So if the contract or agreement is to be valid, make sure that it includes all the necessary elements, and that the written terms reflect *all* the terms.

Coaches and other employees who work without contracts are most often considered *at will* personnel. They serve at the pleasure of the institution, and their status may be altered at any time. *At will* employees generally aren't entitled to an explanation of employment termination or alteration or to due process proceedings.

High Cost of Breaking Contracts

At certain times, coaches and campuses want out of contractual agreements for any of a variety of reasons. The time to plan for this possible occurrence is before the contract is signed, not when either party is trying to end it.

For campuses trying to break or end coaching contracts, the options used to be relatively simple. They could:

- Pay the coach not to coach for the remaining years of the deal
- Try to buy out the contract for a settlement figure
- Invoke a "morals" clause
- Breach the contract and hope for the best in court

The last choice wasn't highly recommended.

Today, those choices can be far more expensive, for two reasons: high salaries and outside income. Buying out or settling contracts at today's salaries can be very costly. Paying for the old coach and the new one at the same time can be a real budget-breaker. In addition, outside income has become an important consideration for the coaching elite. The loss of an institutional coaching position can also mean the loss of lucrative media contracts, product endorsements, summer camps, sports clinics, and speaking fees. This can be serious money.

In one prominent legal battle, a fired collegiate coach sued his former school for the lost value of outside income. In terminating him early, the school paid him the school salary due for the years remaining on his contract. But he felt he deserved more, to compensate for the lost outside income. In a disturbing decision, the court sided with the coach.

This factor is important to remember when developing any campus contracts that can lead to significant outside income. The contracts should deal directly with the issue, indicating what, if any, responsibility for outside income the school is willing to accept as part of the deal.

But when the coach wants to leave early, what can officials do? Can the school get damages?

Again, there are options to consider. The school can let the coach buy out the contract or it can build damages into the clauses of the contract. But these options don't guarantee a successful outcome.

Although clauses that indicate what damages will be due in the event of a breach are valid, they can be difficult to enforce. The damages requested cannot simply be punitive: they must have some relationship to actual damages expected to be incurred due to the breach.

In addition to the difficulty of identifying proper damages, schools may also have a recruitment problem if they "punish" coaches who break contracts. Other coaches considering employment at the school may be concerned about their careers and future opportunities. Schools that stand in the way of coaches trying to "move up" can face problems in attracting new coaches. That may not be right, but it's a reality that must be considered.

There's also the flip side of the coin. Some coaches have demanded such expensive severance packages that they may have acquired a reputation as being uncooperative, not "team players." A coach who gets terminated might have a difficult time getting offers elsewhere; if that coach tries to squeeze the school, the damage can be substantially greater.

Summary

While a contract sets the terms of employment for most coaches, the art of breaking the deal can be important in today's legal environment. How the employment ends — and at what cost — should be a key factor in any coaching arrangement. Especially after you win the championship.

Termination Planning Key

October 1991

It's often said that there are two or more sides to every story. That's certainly true in the termination or layoff of faculty and staff. Both sides need to fully consider many issues *before* acting.

Colleges and universities need to plan for employee cutbacks, decide how to handle the situation, consider legal release statements, and think beyond the termination. Campus employees must consider how to react if they are terminated, what to do and say, what plans to make, and where to go next.

In these times of budgetary uncertainty and new directions on campus, the termination of employees can quickly become a necessity. And that necessity can have significant legal consequences. It's important for employers and employees to understand termination "do's and don'ts"!

Institutions

Colleges and universities need to have a plan for terminations. They must consider the interests of the school, federal and state discrimination laws, and campus policies and staff contracts. They should also be as sensitive as possible to the position of employees.

Among the legal discrimination standards that administrators must understand and apply:

- Age Discrimination in Employment Act
- Older Workers Benefit Protection Act
- Civil Rights Act of 1964, Title VII
- Employee Retirement Income Security Act
- Other state discrimination laws

When terminations are necessary, make sure the employees affected cannot make any claims of violations of federal or state law. Also, review and follow all campus policies, employee handbook guidelines, state policies, union contracts, and other relevant documents. Where there are rules, follow them!

One good tip: make sure that performance-based terminations are supported by appropriate appraisals and counseling efforts. That's an institutional responsibility. Institutions should also consider severance packages when appropriate, other benefits, and outplacement services for employees being terminated.

When dealing directly with employees at the time of termination, supervisors should follow these guidelines:

- Be firm when giving them the news. Avoid giving false hopes and sending mixed messages. Be sympathetic without being defensive.

- Have someone in authority deliver the news. Also, consider having another person present, to document what takes place.
- Try to explain to the employees why they're being terminated.
- Document the termination for protection later on, if necessary.

In handling terminations, it's also important to consider what others are thinking. If there's media interest, deal with it directly and factually, without making derogatory comments or judgments. Other employees will also want to know what's happening and why. Give them the facts in a reassuring manner, noting your school's commitment to policies and fair play.

Employees

In response to growing concerns in higher education, the National Association of Student Personnel Administrators recently published *Involuntary Termination — What If It Happens to You?* The 24-page booklet views termination from the employee's perspective.

Among the issues considered are initial responses to the news, negotiating the terms of departure, seeking legal advice, taking care of yourself personally and financially, and seeking employment.

The booklet advises higher education employees to plan ahead for termination from the start, *before* they take jobs. Recommendations:

- Know your employment rights and termination potential, process, and options.
- Consider dismissal possibilities in accepting a new position, and attempt to get a long-term agreement or favorable termination clause.
- Get appropriate job performance evaluations, to understand what's expected of you and how you'll be reviewed. Keep your own records of performance and evaluations.
- Pay attention to the work environment to protect yourself. Keep your eyes and ears open, respond as appropriate, and work to resolve problems.
- Keep your other options open, just in case! Be prepared to act if necessary.

If terminated, do your best to *react properly*, not emotionally. The NASPA publication suggests that you try to buy some time to think and plan. Then, move slowly and carefully: talk out the situation, exit gracefully — and don't burn your bridges.

When *handling the details* of any termination, employees should make sure that they've considered such specifics as severance pay and benefits, how the news will be given to the media, what letters of reference will be available, and the possibility of outplacement services.

When considering obtaining *legal counsel*, remember that if an employee brings an attorney to the bargaining table, the school will call its own counsel into the process. If you use legal counsel, seek an advisor familiar with higher education and labor law and let the advisor know what you want. Don't be intimidated. It's your case, not the lawyer's!

Most important, if terminated, *take care of yourself*. Stay involved in higher education and remain active in other arenas as well. Keep looking forward!

When seeking your next position, use your network of contacts and plan out a good *job search*. Consider what you want to do and where. Then get to work.

Summary

Terminations are a fact of life in any work setting, including colleges and universities. Institutions facing the need to let employees go must take care to ensure that federal, state, and campus laws and policies are followed, and that the termination process protects the school against legal claims. For employees, the best advice is to plan for separation before hiring, by understanding the terms of employment and considering options in case of termination.

Terminations are never a pleasant story. But with proper planning, employers and employees can make the best of the situation, take care of their interests, and write a "happy ending."

Note: For a copy of *Involuntary Termination — What If It Happens to You?* contact: NASPA, 1875 Connecticut Ave., NW, Suite 418, Washington, DC 20009.

Managing Faculty Means Litigation

June 1992

Higher education employment and discrimination cases continue to fill the courts. Failure to follow proper termination procedures, inadequate minority employment, reverse discrimination, breach of contract, equal pay and sex discrimination, and access to unemployment insurance are all being litigated.

An English instructor at the University of California-Santa Barbara has filed suit, claiming *unlawful termination* after six years of employment. She claims she was not given proper performance reviews while teaching. According to the suit, she was denied reviews. She is suing for back pay and reinstatement. The school says that since it had no openings, there was no purpose in providing reviews to the then instructor. Since she wasn't going to have a job, why judge her fitness for future employment?

Meanwhile, the Supreme Judicial Court of Massachusetts has heard the case filed by Harvard University law students involving *minority hirings*. The students had filed suit alleging that the school had violated its contract with them by failing to improve the number of minority staff. The court will rule on the question of whether the students can sue on an employment issue even though they are not employees. Attorneys for the school are not impressed. They contend that even if the case makes it to trial, the students' complaint is without merit.

At Spelmen College (GA), a white male English professor is suing for $1 million, claiming *reverse discrimination*. He contends that the historically black college denied him tenure because of his race. After tenure was denied to the six-year employee, he filed charges with the federal Equal Opportunity Employment Commission. Spelmen "categorically denies" the charges.

Claiming *breach of contract*, a University of New Mexico associate professor is challenging tenure denial. He contends the decision violates his employment agreement with the school and infringes on academic freedom. He claims the decision to deny him tenure was based on secondhand information, not the evidence called for under his contract. But the school says that, however evaluated, the instructor's teaching and service was inadequate. That's despite faculty and review committee's favorable recommendations.

A dispute at the University of Alabama involves equal pay for equal work. Three female employees have filed claims of *sex discrimination*. They contend that school policies kept them in jobs that pay them less than male counterparts. On behalf of 1,800 women employed at UA, they want a court to award them back pay and benefits as if they had been historically promoted and paid as men have been.

And finally, The University of Alabama also faces litigation over *unemployment compensation* from a temporary political science instructor. Because the employee was a non-permanent alien, the school did not report his wages to state unemployment officials for a year. They changed the reporting policy, but not before the instructor was denied state benefits due to the non-reporting of income. The former instructor challenged the ruling and won, but the university appealed. It argued that the employee was actually unauthorized to work at all in the state due to his visa status. Therefore, UA argued he could not be entitled to unemployment benefits. The case is now before the state Court of Civil Claims. While only $3,900 is at stake, both sides claim that the principles make the legal challenge important.

Faculty Incompetence and Dismissals

November 1990

Incompetence isn't a pleasant topic, but campus administrators need to deal with it. A paper read at the fall 1988 meeting of the Association for the Study of Higher Education provides some interesting data on court cases dealing with faculty incompetence.

Titled "Dismissals of Tenured Faculty for Incompetence: An Analysis of Litigation Patterns," the paper reports on a study of state and federal court records from 1960 to 1988. A summary of the results: more incompetence cases are being filed now than ever before, and most of the cases come from public university settings.

The study was conducted by L.B. Helms and J. Seal of the University of Iowa. They found no cases prior to 1970, but cases appeared with increasing frequency in the years that followed. The 31 cases were evenly split between state and federal jurisdictions. Over 90% involved public institutions, and more than half were from comprehensive universities and doctoral institutions.

It was also noted that three-quarters of the claims were over process and procedure, not substance. Of the cases dealing with substantive issues, about half involved allegations of insubordination. The courts upheld the terminations in four out of five cases.

Supreme Court Opens Peer Review Files

May 1990

> The costs associated with racial and sexual discrimination in institutions of higher learning are very substantial. Few would deny that ferreting out this kind of invidious discrimination is a great if not compelling governmental interest. Often ... disclosure of peer review materials will be necessary ... to ... determine whether discrimination has taken place. Indeed, if there is a 'smoking gun' to be found that demonstrates discrimination in tenure decisions, it is likely to be tucked away in peer review files.
>
> Justice Harry Blackmun, *University of Pennsylvania v. Equal Employment Opportunity Commission*, 493 U.S. 182 (1990)

After years of conflict and controversy, the issue of disclosure and confidentiality in peer review personnel decisions on campus has been decided. Different courts in different jurisdictions had previously looked at the issues of *confidentiality, free speech*, and *academic freedom* and had developed differing standards. What was protected communication in one region was open to review in another. One faculty member could shield materials from disclosure with impunity, while others withholding materials could be sent to jail.

The case of a University of Pennsylvania business instructor who was denied tenure reached the U.S. Supreme Court. Now, the confusion is over: campuses enjoy no special privilege to withhold evidence relevant to bias cases involving faculty members. That's the law, according to Justice Harry Blackmun, *University of*

Pennsylvania v. Equal Employment Opportunity Commission, 493 U.S. 182 (1990).

Background

Disclosure of peer reviews in personnel matters is an issue of significant conflicting claims, on and off campus. Society has long placed a value on the open exchange of evaluation and recommendation materials, finding it to be in the best interests of public policy. In education, the exchange of peer group evaluations as a model for academic personnel decision-making came ashore from Oxford and Cambridge.

To make the system work, some have long argued, evaluators must feel free to openly review the work of colleagues, free from the "chilling" effect of possible disclosure. Disclosure, they fear, would result in a less candid and more non-judgmental process. They argue for a process that keeps peer reviews confidential, to promote the best possible exchange of important information on colleagues.

On the other side of the issue is the claim that closed files and closed decision-making protect various forms of illegal discrimination. A faculty member denied tenure or promotion needs access to peer review materials to prove his or her case. Without these materials, there is no evidence to support or to refute claims of discrimination.

Generally in litigation, both parties have an open opportunity to pursue evidentiary materials necessary to their case or defense. Materials pertinent to the issue and not protected or privileged are subject to review and exchange. In academic settings, the definition of *protected* or *privileged* communications has been contested. Courts have established tests for privileged communications but have interpreted the standards in differing ways when applying them to peer review materials.

Some communications are protected as privileged by law, such as a lawyer-client or doctor-patient relationship. Other privileges have a constitutional basis, such as the right against self-incrimination. Still other privileges have been developed through a history of judicial decisions. In arguing for protection of peer review materials, colleges and universities rely on common law, in the absence of specific legislation or constitutional language to address the issue expressly.

In determining if a common law privilege exists, courts generally look to see if certain factors support the claim. They ask the following questions:

- Was there an initial understanding between parties that the communication was to remain confidential?
- Is confidentiality necessary to maintain an appropriate relationship between the parties?
- Is public policy best served by promoting the relationship?
- Is the benefit of promoting the relationship greater than the benefits obtained through disclosure?

In higher education, these questions were asked in some early decisions. And conflicting answers were given, leading to the recent ruling by the U.S. Supreme Court.

Earlier Litigation

Four earlier cases of significance clearly demonstrated the difficulties faced by schools and courts in balancing conflicting interests in the area of confidential peer reviews.

In the case of *In re Dinnan*, 661 F.2d 426 (1981), the conflict led to jail time. An instructor at the University of Georgia sued, claiming that she'd been the victim of illegal discrimination in the tenure review process. In preparing her case, she discovered that one peer reviewer refused to discuss his vote or opinions. The court ordered the professor to respond to the inquiries. When he refused, he was sentenced to jail for contempt of court. In appealing the decision, the sentenced faculty member argued academic freedom.

The Fifth Circuit Federal Court of Appeals placed more value on the need for disclosure than on the need for confidentiality. Peer review confidentiality, said the court, should be protected only if its "societal values are more important than the search for the truth." The court balanced the competing interests and felt that in this case, discovering illegal discrimination was more important than protecting peer evaluation.

The court felt that academic freedom should be limited to questions of education, not administration. Although "the court feels that the government should stay out of academic affairs," the decision stated, at issue were the constitutional and statutory rights of a private plaintiff.

Society, ruled the court, must find and eliminate illegal discrimination, even at the high cost of disclosure: "To rule otherwise would mean that the concept of academic freedom would give any institution of higher learning a *carte blanche* to practice discrimination of all types."

Similar issues were reviewed in *EEOC v. University of Notre Dame du Lac*, 715 F.2d 331 (1983). There, a black finance professor denied tenure responded with legal action. On his behalf, the commission reviewed his claims and requested access to campus personnel files.

The campus offered to comply in part, providing access to the professor's file and those of others up for promotion at the same time. In addition, the school asked to delete information from the peer review materials that would have indicated their source and requested that the EEOC sign a nondisclosure agreement, allowing for no further release of the materials. After the district court ordered the university to provide the EEOC with complete and unchanged records, the case found its way to the U.S. Court of Appeals, Seventh Circuit.

At issue in the appeal was the school's request to delete personally identifiable information from the files and that the EEOC not release any of the data. The appellate panel ruled that a judge does have limited discretion in balancing the needs to find the truth with the demands of public policy.

The court supported the campus claim for limited confidentiality and partial compliance, understanding the need for candor in the evaluation process. And, the court added, it would require "a substantial showing of particularized need" before entertaining similar requests: "the identities of scholars would be released only under the most limited circumstances."

In *EEOC v. Franklin and Marshall College*, 775 F.2d 110 (1985), the Third Circuit Court of Appeals heard the arguments of an instructor who claimed tenure was denied due to his national origin. As is the practice, EEOC pursued the claim on his behalf. The commission asked the campus to provide a wide variety of related materials, including peer evaluations and annual reviews. The campus resisted.

Using the *Notre Dame* response, compliance after deletion of personally identifiable materials, a lower court ordered limited disclosure. The school appealed the ruling but found no support for its position, as the appellate panel ordered compliance based on the lower court ruling. The panel dealt with the school's concerns by noting that "we have no choice but to trust that the honesty and integrity of the tenured reviewers in evaluation decisions will overcome feelings of discomfort and embarrassment and will outlast the demise of absolute confidentiality."

A black professor's tenure denial led to similar deliberations in *Gray v. Board of Higher Education of City of New York*, 692 F.2d 901 (1982). The lower court refused to order disclosure of how two peer reviewers voted, saying a "qualified privilege" on voting existed because "confidentiality is integrally related to safeguarding academic freedom."

But the appellate panel reversed the decision, disagreeing with this reasoning and that of *Franklin and Marshall* and *Notre Dame*. The voting record, according to the court, was "an indispensable element ... without which proof of an intent to discriminate would be impossible." It implied, however, that if the college had given the plaintiff a statement of reasons for denying him tenure, the court would have treated the record of individual votes as privileged information. The court established a system determining when it was necessary to report voting results, siding clearly with those advocating full disclosure. The court ruled that the original records be opened.

University of Pennsylvania: A New Decade

Dinnan, Notre Dame, Franklin and Marshall, and *Gray* were all decided in the first half of the 1980s. By the end of the decade, the confusion resulting from these different decisions was sufficient to merit U.S. Supreme Court review.

In a unanimous decision, the Supreme Court ruled in *University of Pennsylvania* that colleges and universities may be forced to disclose confidential tenure files to federal discrimination investigators. The court sided strongly with the arguments that peer reviews may be needed as evidence in examining claims of unlawful discrimination.

The case involved a review of complaints against the school for discrimination on the basis of sex and national origin. The complaints were filed with the EEOC by a business faculty member denied tenure. The commission had requested various materials from the school as part of its initial investigation.

UPenn supplied all relevant data — except peer review files on five faculty members, including the file of the complaining instructor. In response, the EEOC went to court seeking complete compliance. The school then sought permission to delete personally identifiable information before releasing the materials.

The trial court and appellate panel ruled that the documents must be turned over to the EEOC. As a result, it was the task of the Supreme Court to balance the competing interests.

UPenn and supportive associations contended that the court should protect the confidentiality of peer review, basing their arguments on academic freedom and First Amendment considerations. But the EEOC argued for disclosure of all "potentially relevant" materials to aid in the discharge of its mandated duties.

Writing for the unanimous court, Justice Blackmun sided with the need to pursue the truth, even at the expense of other interests. When balancing the public needs and interests related to non-discrimination and confidentiality, the court saw that a compelling governmental interest was best served through disclosure.

As for concerns over potential damage to the evaluation process through the loss of confidentiality, the court stated:

> Although it is possible that some evaluators may become less candid as the possibility of disclosure increases, others may simply ground their evaluations in specific examples and illustrations in order to deflect potential claims of bias or unfairness. Not all academics will hesitate to stand up and be counted when they evaluate their peers.

Summary

The significance of this decision will become more apparent as time passes and its standards are adopted. Concerns exist over the prospect of less than candid evaluations or greater emphasis on unwritten reviews. The need for "ferreting out ... invidious discrimination" is apparent, and the Supreme Court has provided a powerful tool for those who would review the cases of instructors claiming discrimination in personnel decisions. The confusion is ending, though the conflict between the competing interests remains.

Freedom to Work on the Side

April 1991

The doctors thought they had the best of two worlds: public university teaching positions and a private medical practice. That was until the school advised them that it had limits on outside income.

They argued that the private practice was of no concern to the school and was constitutionally protected. So when the school asked them to sign policy compliance statements, they refused. And when the school fired them, they went to court.

Public employees, in education and outside, held their collective breath. Could they be forced to give up outside income? Yes, said the court.

Most of the recent case law on this issue involves faculty from professional schools, such as medicine and law, trying to engage in extracurricular employment activities. In reviewing the cases, courts have been forced to balance the desires of individuals with the rights and responsibilities of public employers, like state universities.

In response to a clear trend in legal decisions on outside employment, some states and the federal government have responded with restrictive policies. Public institution employees, beware! Big Brother can keep a watch on your pocketbook!

Case Law

The faculty physicians fired for refusing to sign a statement limiting outside income argued that they were entitled to constitutional protections. In *Gross v. University of Tennessee*, 448 F.Supp. 245 (1978), a federal district court found that public employees had no right to outside income. The school had decided that full-time staff should be devoted to full-time teaching. Noting that courts are reluctant to make academic decisions, the judge stated that if the ban or limit on outside income was based on a significant education-related goal, the court would support the rule. The doctors stayed terminated.

A law school faculty member challenged the same type of rule in *Atkinson v. Board of Trustees of the University of Arkansas*, 559 S.W.2d 473 (1977). The university barred full-time faculty members from outside legal practice, regardless of compensation. A trial court found that the faculty could do limited work on pro bono basis, for no fees. But the faculty appealed, wanting greater rights to outside practice.

What they got in *Atkinson* was a legal lesson: the state could in fact ban or limit outside practice of the faculty if it desired. Such a decision would have to be based on an educational need to require full-time attention of instructors or the intent to avoid conflicts of interest. In addition, any ban or limitation would have to be enforced uniformly for all faculty in similar circumstances.

In 1980, the terminated medical faculty appealed the *Gross* decision. The Sixth U.S. Circuit Court of Appeals heard their claims to a right to outside income, in *Gross v. University of Tennessee*, 620 F.2d 109. The outcome was the same. As long as the school rule limiting or barring outside income had some rational basis, it could be enforced.

Federal Government

Based on the *Gross* and *Atkinson* reasoning, the U.S. government recently adopted a policy banning federal employees from accepting honoraria for writings or speeches, even if the topic is outside their governmental scope of responsibilities. The new restrictions, part of the Ethics Reform Act signed by the president in late 1989, took effect January 1, 1991. Violators can be penalized $10,000 or the amount of any payments received, whichever is higher.

Political appointees have long been prevented from accepting pay for outside work in their fields. This was based on a need to avoid potential conflicts of interest and the possibility of interference in employee or agency duties. The new ban applies to all executive branch employees, including military personnel. An exemption exists for books and works of fiction: it allows for payments of $2,000 maximum, which must be donated to charity — with no tax deduction.

State Regulation: One Example

New York State's ethics regulations provide a good example of how state government policy can impact on public university employees. The law prohibits certain state employees, including college and university personnel, from accepting work-related outside honoraria and travel reimbursement.

However faculty may accept honoraria for publishing books or articles, delivering speeches, or attending meetings in their disciplines. Employees can accept reimbursements and honoraria for services that aren't work-related if:

- Payment doesn't come from an organization doing business with the institution
- The services aren't part of their official duties
- Institutional resources weren't used to prepare or deliver the services
- The institution doesn't reimburse the employee for travel

- The services are performed outside of work time or while on leave

In addition, many state employees must file annual financial disclosure statements. The forms solicit information on income, outside organizational positions, all extracurricular employment, sources of gifts and reimbursements, retirement plans, holdings in real estate and securities, and financial data on spouses.

Campus Impact of Regulations

In response to public interest pressures, many states have begun to adopt or modify similar ethics acts to prevent potential conflicts of interest. Campus employees can feel the effects of these efforts.

Instead of barring all outside activities, many campuses have merely adopted limitations and regulations. In doing so, they recognize the value of some outside work: it can keep people current in their fields and help attract strong candidates for positions. Most policies establish workload limits, approval processes, disclosure standards, and rules against use of campus resources or requirements that use be reimbursed.

The University of Wisconsin is adopting stricter regulations for reporting outside income by employees. In the past year, many states and the federal government have taken steps to limit employee outside incomes or to prevent conflicts of interest.

The UW-Madison Faculty Senate recently endorsed a plan that would require all faculty and academic staff in the 26-campus system to file an annual disclosure report, whether or not they earned any outside income. Currently, only faculty members with outside earnings exceeding $5,000 are required to report. Also, faculty currently may choose not to disclose income sources if they consider it "inappropriate" to do so. Under the new plan, faculty will need permission from their deans to avoid disclosure when it would damage "legitimate competitive interests."

A state audit recently criticized the Madison campus for inconsistent and loose reporting procedures. Currently, fewer than 10% of the entire statewide faculty report outside income.

A Louisiana State University System policy bars system employees from working as paid consultants for or against state legislation that's under consideration. But now, a state lawmaker has introduced a proposal to overturn the ban.

Rep. Gary Forster says the LSU policy is "absurd." He says it may have developed because some professors have worked on legislative issues that system officials don't agree with.

But LSU officials say the idea behind the policy is to avoid the impression that paid consultants speak for the system. They say an employee/consultant's "credibility" would come in large part from his or her association with the university.

System officials say the policy is not an infringement on academic freedom because it deals only with outside compensation.

Employees can still work as unpaid consultants or expert witnesses. But they must seek approval for outside employment, business action, or consulting work that does not involve state legislation.

The policy is the latest development in the ongoing debate over faculty and staff conflict of interest laws. After a series of questionable incidents involving schools and their employees, many states have adopted laws forcing campus employees to identify and/or curb outside income.

Case law supports the principle that public colleges and universities can limit their employees' outside work activities if doing so is in the best interest of the institution. Campuses with income limits or bans generally base them on the need to avoid conflicts of interests or the need for employees to devote full-time energies to campus work. Following the examples of *Atkinson* and *Gross*, the federal government, some states, and a number of campuses have moved to restrict outside compensation. Public higher education employees should be aware of the restrictions that their employment may place on them. Interested in outside income? It pays to understand the law.

Diverting Faculty Time: Problems with Moonlighting

October 1993

The old adage "you can't be in two places at once" was recently put to the ultimate test by a university professor. It seems the professor had been wooed by the University of North Carolina-Charlotte to join its faculty, and that he decided to do so. But when he told administrators at his current school, the University of Minnesota, that he had another offer, they raised his salary 20% and reduced his teaching load. The UM counteroffer sounded good, so he accepted. And when the fall semester started, he began to teach: two days a week at UNC-Charlotte and the rest of the week at UM! He ended up with two full-time appointments and didn't tell either school about his dual roles.

The "double dipping" was later revealed when colleagues from the two schools met at a professional meeting. Officials in Charlotte had also become concerned over the new faculty member's failure to swiftly relocate his family to the area. After the initial discovery, the instructor offered to repay UM his fall salary and reimburse UNC-Charlotte funds he took for moving expenses. He hoped that would end the growing controversy.

He eventually resigned his UM post, but he later accused the school of violating the terms of his agreement and sued UM to return. A lower court ruled in his favor, finding the resignation non-binding because UM had violated "a substantial part of the agreement," a confidentiality clause. As a result of the court decision, the academic department has begun termination proceedings against him. During this time, he also was pressured to resign his UNC post. So after one semester with two jobs, he suddenly found himself with none!

Many colleges and universities have adopted a variety of policies to control outside work by instructors. Both the University of Minnesota and the University of North Carolina-Charlotte have policies for faculty members on disclosing outside work. In addition to this, UNC-Charlotte requires employees to seek school approval for additional work.

One of the key administrative concerns about outside work is the possibility that it may divert faculty time, effort, and energy — the primary responsibilities they owe to their students and affiliated campus — to others. Officials fear that a pursuit of personal supplemental income may override a faculty member's dedication to his/her school. An additional concern is the extent to which other institutional resources may be diverted into outside efforts.

Campuses attempting to protect their resources, both personnel and material, have developed some form of a "conflict of interest" policy. These policies generally prohibit an employee from engaging in outside work that represents a conflict of interest to the institution. But where many institutions run into difficulty is in not clearly defining exactly what they mean by a "conflict."

Another common regulation on outside work by instructors and others *limits the amount of time* that can be devoted to such efforts. While some policies simply indicate that outside work cannot interfere with the performance of primary duties, others set specific days — per-week or per-term limitations on the work.

Yet another common policy that controls outside faculty work prohibits or limits the use of *institutional facilities and other resources*. These policies generally bar the use of campus materials (such as library resources, equipment, labs, etc.), require advance permission, or mandate reimbursement for non-institutional uses of campus materials.

Many colleges and universities also require *prior approval of outside work*. These policies generally require prior authorization from a supervisor any time a faculty member wishes to engage in any outside professional work. Employees usually must provide details on the outside work to allow a supervisor to properly review the request. Commonly, an employee may be asked to provide the name of the potential employing agency, a description of the type of work to be performed, the dates of the work, anticipated income, and a listing of any institutional resources that may be used in the work. Typical factors then used by supervisors to evaluate these requests include the:

- Amount of time required for the activity
- Possible conflicts with campus responsibilities
- Potential campus benefits from the outside professional relationships

In addition to these typical regulations and limitations, a majority of colleges and universities now require faculty and staff members to complete and submit some form of "disclosure report." These generally provide information on outside professional involvements. Some schools require an immediate disclosure when an outside work arrangement is initiated. Others require disclosure on a regular, periodic basis.

The case of the dual professor, split between UM and UNC-Charlotte, is an obvious reminder of the possible extremes that can be reached by "double dippers." Campuses are advised to weigh the negative and positive implications of outside work by campus professionals, then to adopt and enforce appropriate policies to ensure that the campus fully benefits from campus resources — especially its faculty members.

Faculty tenure termination hearings have begun in the case of the University of Minnesota professor who briefly held two full-time jobs at different schools. When the University of North Carolina-Charlotte found out what was happening, it fired the professor, who then returned to stay at his UM post. But Minnesota didn't welcome the professor back warmly. Instead, proceedings were initiated to fire him there as well.

A recent campus audit of his expenses concluded that over $16,500 in grant and donor funds he was responsible for were misspent. The expenses included international and domestic travel, additional personal salary, benefits, and other items. The audit covered the four-year period prior to the dual employment situation.

Attorneys for the instructor claim that the school worked on the audit for eight months but only gave them two days to review it prior to a key tenure hearing.

When the audit came up in the Department of Classical and Near Eastern Studies faculty tenure review hearing, the accused instructor and his legal counsel left in protest. The meeting, however, continued and the faculty voted unanimously to terminate the instructor. While the campus hearing is one of the early phases in a termination process, attorneys for the instructor say they will file suit to halt the proceedings due to "unfairness."

Court Contrasts "Official" and "Personal" Capacities

August 1993

It was a campaign promise that came back to haunt her.

Unlike some candidates, this public official in Pennsylvania tried to keep a pledge to voters. Once she took office, she fired everyone involved in a previous financial scandal, saying that some state employees had "bought" their jobs.

But one former worker took exception to the firings and sued the new state officer as an *individual*, not as a representative of the government. The suit claimed that the new officer had deprived the ex-employees of their constitutionally protected rights, and it asked that the officer be held *personally* liable.

The officer, however, argued that she had acted in her *official capacity* when she fired the staff members. Therefore, she claimed, she was protected from personal responsibility because she had acted as an agent of the state. In other words, she said, the *state* was responsible for her actions.

It was an argument made often in past cases, and the officer expected the case to be dismissed in court. But it wasn't — and appeals all the way to the U.S. Supreme Court still left her *personally* responsible.

What does this mean for campus decision-makers? Can they, too, be found personally liable for their acts on campus?

Case law suggests no clear answers to these questions. But previous rulings do provide *some* guidance for troubled decision-makers on campus.

Early Cases

State university physicians argued in a Virginia case that they could not be sued for their actions while working on behalf of the state. They cited laws providing for "sovereign immunity," a government exemption from suit.

But in *James v. Jane*, 221 Va. 43, 267 S.E. 2d 108 (1980), the state's highest court did not exempt the physicians from personal responsibility.

The court noted that immunity had initially been established to allow government to act without the restraints of possible litigation. Certain state officers, including the governor, legislators, and judges, may be exempt from suit, noted the court.

But immunity does not apply to all state employees, the court said, particularly for: "an ... employee who acts wantonly, or in a culpable or grossly negligent manner ... " and "[an] employee who acts beyond the scope of his employment, who exceeds his authority and discretion, and who acts individually."

Individuals, even when acting on behalf of the state, were to be judged by these standards, the court ruled. If people violated these standards, said the court, they could be sued as individuals and be held personally responsible for their actions.

Other Concerns

While *James* is only one state's decision, it highlights how similar public institution cases might be handled elsewhere.

Decision-makers at private institutions, however, can't argue the sovereign immunity principle when trying to avoid personal liability. Instead, they must face legal action by saying they acted appropriately within the scope of their institutional duties.

Several federal cases involving students and constitutional issues raise other problems for officials concerned about individual versus institutional liability. In one public high school expulsion case, for example, the U.S. Supreme Court reviewed school board members' concerns about personal immunity from a lawsuit.

The members, who were sued as individuals by several students who had been expelled, asked the Court to protect them from personal responsibility. They said they were doing official jobs and, therefore, could only be sued as officials, not as individuals.

The Court, in *Wood v. Strickland*, 420 U.S. 308 (1975), agreed, noting that:

> immunity must be such that public school officials understand that actions taken in the good-faith fulfillment of their responsibilities and within the bounds of reason under all the circumstances will not be punished.

The Court said that officials must truly believe they are acting appropriately, and that they cannot justify violation of students' constitutional rights by "ignorance or disregard of settled, indisputable law."

The Court also said that an official

> is not immune from liability for damages ... if he knew or reasonably should have known that the action he took within his sphere of official responsibility would violate the constitutional rights of the student affected, or if he took the action with the malicious intention to cause a deprivation of constitutional rights or other injury to the student.

The "Should Have Known" Rule

A key consideration in many liability cases is the level of knowledge decision-makers should have about the law or the Constitution.

In *Wood*, the Supreme Court said decision-makers could be judged on what they knew or "reasonably should have known" when carrying out their duties. This "should have known" rule was later applied to a campus president in a student demonstration case.

In *Perez v. Rodriguez Bou*, 575 F.2d 21 (First Cir. 1978), a federal court heard the arguments of students who claimed they had been unlawfully suspended from the University of Puerto Rico. The chancellor suspended the students without a hearing because of their involvement in a protest march.

The court did not protect the school or the administrator from the students' claims. It ruled that the administrator "should have known his action was unconstitutional" and that he should have understood prior court cases on student rights.

A more famous protest case provides further instruction on the responsibilities of campus officials, particularly when dealing with constitutional issues.

Student deaths during a May 1970 protest at Kent State University (OH) led to a suit against the school. In *Scheuer v. Rhodes*, 416 U.S. 232 (1974), the families of three victims sought damages from the school and several of its officials.

The administrators claimed they were immune from lawsuit because they had acted as officials of the state. But the court found such immunity to be limited by the circumstances, leaving each claim to be judged on its own.

The court considered what happens when a state officer deprives someone of constitutional rights while acting on behalf of the state. Simply put, the court offered no protection to the officials, noting that:

> when a state officer acts under a state law in a manner violative of the federal Constitution, he comes into conflict with the superior authority of that Constitution, and he is in that case stripped of his official or representative character and is subjected in his person to the consequences of his individual conduct.

At a lower court rehearing of the case, the suit against Kent State's president was dismissed — but not because of any protection from a lawsuit. Rather, a review of the facts showed that he hadn't personally violated any student's rights, according to *Krause v. Rhodes*, 570 F.2d 563 (Sixth Cir. 1977).

The Pennsylvania Case

The progression of cases, from *James* to *Krause*, points out the fine line between institutional and individual liability.

Public officers, including those on college campuses, have limited protection from liability lawsuits if they are working on behalf of the school, if they have reasonable knowledge of the law, and if they believe they are doing the right thing. In addition, when responding to constitutional issues, courts have established higher standards, including a "should have known" rule about the rights of individuals.

A Pennsylvania case, *Hafer v. Melo*, 112 S.Ct. 358 (1991), adds another important consideration. It draws a distinction between actions taken in an official capacity and those taken in an individual capacity. That distinction could be important to public campus decision-makers.

Hafer, the defendant, argued that she could not be held personally liable for her actions as a state official. The plaintiffs, on the other hand, all of whom the defendant had fired, said they had been denied due process, a federal constitutional right, by a state official acting "under the color of state law."

The Court ruled the officer was not protected from suit. It cited the legal difference between official and personal acts as justification for the ruling, and said that the mass firings were unconstitutional because they were done in a personal, not official, capacity.

Conclusion

People acting in an *official capacity* are sued when acting on behalf of agency policies or programs. The government itself is the target of such suits.

A suit filed over the enforcement of an agency rule, for instance, would involve an official decision. Therefore, under the *Hafer* ruling, an officer enforcing such a rule cannot be held *personally* responsible for his or her decisions.

Suits based on *personal capacity* involve an official's own decisions while in office. When an officer acts not on agency policy or regulation but on his or her own judgment, that judgment can be questioned in court, and it could lead to personal liability.

Make sure you understand the difference between acting in official and personal capacities. On campus, the distinction may seem slight. But in court, the difference could prove to be very important — and very costly.

Understanding the Charge of Defamation

June 1994

Defamation! That was the charge against Pennsylvania State University, as some staff members filed suit based on a research vice president's comments. They claim his remarks falsely blamed them for mismanagement of a campus research lab. The senior officer allegedly said the lab was in fiscal crisis, losing $750,000 due to poor leadership.

The remarks were made during a faculty meeting held while two of three involved staff members were out of town. The lab leadership returned and sued. Arguing that the remarks were false and harmful to their reputations, they have asked for damages of $120,000.

Defamation! That was also the charge made by a candidate for an elected position on the University of Nebraska Board of Regents. She claims she was the victim of a flier containing falsehoods mailed to over 40,000 potential voters. She demanded a retraction and didn't get it, so she sued.

Defamation! What is it? How is it proven? Does it have to be intentional? Can campus officials sue or be sued? What defenses are there for defamation charges?

Tort Law

Defamation is generally defined as language that tends to adversely affect someone's reputation. When claims of alleged defamation reach the court, the facts are reviewed for five key criteria:

- If defamatory language by a defendant exists
- If it is concerning a plaintiff
- If it has been communicated to third persons
- If it is causing damage to the plaintiff
- If it demonstrates fault by the defendant

When these elements are found, courts may order damages to compensate the victims.

Defamatory language usually impeaches a person's integrity, honesty, mental health, or virtue. It is usually judged by statements made, but it also can be found in pictures, satire, or drama. Only living persons can be defamed, although an organization might file a claim based on adverse remarks about its purposes, finances, or honesty.

The second element of a claim requires that the language be "of or concerning" the plaintiff. The standard for judging whether the language is such is how it would be understood by a *reasonable reader, viewer, or listener*. It also may be legally possible on campus to defame a group or members of a group. Those who can identify themselves as members affected by a slur can recover some damages.

How must a statement be *communicated* to constitute defamation? Simply said, a statement is not actionable unless it has been communicated to a third person who understood it. The communication does not need to be *intentional* to become *actionable*.

In an effort to determine *damages* in a college campus defamation case, it is necessary to consider the difference between *slander* and *libel*, because the proofs of damage differ. Defamatory statements that are recorded in some permanent form are automatically *libel* and are assumed to cause damage. Permanent forms could include printed materials as well as recorded television, film, and radio broadcasts. *Slander* is considered spoken defamation. Since it is in a less permanent form, plaintiffs must show specific damages. A plaintiff must prove to the court that he or she has suffered financial loss. Loss of friends, embarrassment, wounded feelings, or loss of reputation alone are not actionable. The loss of a job, canceled business deals or educational opportunities, or the loss of customers would show damages required for slander judgments.

The final element of defamation involves a finding of the defendant's *fault* or level of responsibility.

Of importance to some college and university cases are U.S. Supreme Court rulings that limit defamation damage awards to "public" figures. Public figures, said the court, may claim damage awards only if the defamation was intentionally "made with malice."

Are campus officials "public figures" with a limited ability to sue for defamation damages? Courts have held that "public figures":

- May hold a position in government with apparent importance, giving the public an interest in the office-holders beyond the general interest in the qualifications and performance of all government employees, or

- Could have achieved "pervasive fame or notoriety," becoming public figures as celebrities, or

- Voluntarily inject themselves or are drawn into a particular public controversy, as is the case for political candidates

In dual decisions, *Curtis Publishing Co. v. Butts*, 388 U.S. 130 (1967), and *Associated Press v. Walker*, 388 U.S. 162 (1967), the court ruled on the status of a college football coach as a public figure. The University of Georgia coach sued the *Saturday Evening Post* over a story accusing him of "fixing" a football game. Butts was found to be employed by a private school foundation, not the school, and was permitted, therefore, to seek damages.

More recent decisions, however, have broadened the public figure limitation to include major, national, and recognized campus leaders. These have been based on the freedom of the press principles and the opportunity public figures have to make rebuttals.

Defense

There are some effective defenses to defamation claims that should be understood. These include consent, the truth, and certain other privileges. A finding of defamation can be overturned or limited by these defenses.

In tort law, *consent* is a complete defense. If a party consents to defamation, he or she cannot later claim damages. The other most effective defense is *truth*. No matter how damaging a statement or remark may be about another, the speaker has an absolute defense to a defamation claim if the statement is true. Other *privileges* in the law also provide protection to certain types of speech. Court room remarks are fully protected from suit, as are those of legislators made in the course of their duties. Statements by government executive officers are also privileged when reasonably related to matters within their scope of responsibilities. At other times, privileges are extended to reports on public proceedings — including defamatory remarks made — and to fair comment and criticism on matters of general public interest.

In the event that defamation is found and damages are awarded, the amount owed can be reduced by some *mitigating factors*. These include:

- No finding of malice — this would include a showing by a defendant that comments were based on a source that appeared to be believable
- A retraction — an effort to negate or limit possible damage by withdrawing the statement
- Anger — based on a showing that the defamation was, in part, provoked by the victim

Back at Pennsylvania State, the research lab managers still say the vice president defamed them. They contend that remarks about their leadership were false and should be retracted. They've also asked for an apology from PSU and the officer. To succeed, they will have to meet the five elements of defamation.

And in Nebraska, candidates for the board of regents found themselves in court in *Hoch v. Prokop*, 507 N.W. 2d 626 (1993). The defendant, who circulated the allegedly defamatory flier, had asked the court to dismiss the case, using the "public figure" rule from *Sullivan*. He contended that the other candidate was a voluntary "public figure" and therefore needed to prove malice in order to proceed. The court agreed, ruling that damages could be awarded only if the defamed candidate showed that the flier was printed with the knowledge it was false or with a disregard for the truth.

Defamation! It's a claim often made in the "heat" of a verbal or written battle on campus, but it's rarely litigated to its conclusion. Speak and sue carefully!

Defamation — or Free Speech?

April 1996

The newspaper said the college basketball team was loaded with talent, but the coach "usually finds a way to screw things up." At another college, another women's basketball coach called one of her players a "disgrace" at a team meeting. Both statements led to defamation claims.

Were these statements defamatory? How have courts dealt with such claims in higher education? And how will they resolve these two recent athletic claims?

Scouting Report

Defamatory language is language that tends to adversely affect someone's reputation, usually by impeaching his or her honesty, integrity, virtue, or sanity. A statement is not actionable until there has been a "publication," which is generally communication to a third party who understood it. The two basic tort liability defamation claims are *libel* and *slander*.

Libel is a defamatory statement recorded in writing, or some other permanent form. Damages are presumed in libel cases, so plaintiffs do not have to prove losses. *Slander* is spoken defamation. In slander cases, damages are not presumed and must be proven, unless the comment involves a criminal offense, "loathsome" disease, business conduct, or sexual misconduct. Claims of these types are referred to as "slander *per se*."

Sometimes it's difficult to distinguish between libel and slander, in part due to new technologies. Several factors are considered in judging slander vs. libel, including:

- The permanence of the form
- How broadly the language is disseminated
- How premeditated the defamation is

These factors, when found, tend to indicate libel.

In the Courts

Many college defamation cases are related to employment matters. Non-renewed faculty and staff often allege defamation in legal attempts to retain their jobs.

Consider *Baker v. Lafayette College*, 504 A.2d 247, 532 A.3d 399 (1987). There, an instructor was let go after two years and sued the college for breach of contract and defamation. Student evaluations of his teaching were published, most of them leaving a negative impression about his teaching skills. The court did not find the release defamatory. It was permitted under the faculty handbook and the results represented only the "opinions" of students. The evaluations were found to be protected fair comments.

In *Small v. McRae*, 651 P.2d 982 (1982), a department chair at Eastern Montana College was removed from his administrative post. The school said the decision was made because he "failed to bring a polarized department into a smoother functioning unit." The comment was shared with others under the terms of an employment contract. The professor sued.

The ex-chair maintained that the statement was libelous. The court said the statements were protected because they were "made in the proper discharge of an official duty." Publication was necessary due to a collective bargaining agreement that mandated certain campus notifications.

A similar outcome was reported in *Cripe v. Board of Regents*, 358 So.2d 244 (1978). A terminated University of Florida staff member sued, claiming his unsatisfactory job evaluation constituted defamation. The court ruled in favor of the school. It noted that to hold otherwise would create an environment in which "a supervisor would not be candid in his evaluations because of a fear of being sued for defamation."

A different aspect of campus defamation was explored more recently in *Dilworth v. Dudley*, No. 95-C-072-S, W.D. Wis 1995. In a book published by a DePauw University professor, *Mathematical Cranks*, the plaintiff was identified as a "crank." In addition to naming the author as a defendant, the suit also included the college president — because he "paid the defendant's salary as a university professor during this time."

To pursue the case, the court ruled, the plaintiff had to show "a false statement that is capable of a defamatory meaning." The district judge ruled that "crank" did not fit that definition.

"Crank," said the court, was "no more than a rhetorical hyperbole and cannot be construed as a representation or misrepresentation of fact." Even the most careless reader of *Mathematical Cranks*, said the decision, "must have perceived the word was ... a vigorous epithet used by those who considered the plaintiff's positions unreasonable." The defamation claim was dismissed.

On the Courts

At the University of Kansas and the University of Wisconsin-Madison, defamation law moved from the basketball courts into the judicial courts. In the former case, a coach accused a sports magazine of defamation. In the latter case, a coach was accused of defamation by one of her players. Together, they represent legal actions in which a campus staff member is the accuser and accused.

In *Washington v. Smith*, 893 F.Supp. 60 (1995), the women's basketball coach at KU filed suit against a magazine over its evaluation of her. It reported that, in spite of good players, she "usually finds a way to screw things up." In addition to various other legal claims, the coach contended that the remarks, as published, were libelous. The coach had a strong overall won-lost record, but her teams had not been successful in recent playoffs. The magazine objected to her claim, stating that its comments were protected under the Constitution's First Amendment free speech clause.

The court reviewed the magazine article in detail. It found that statements of opinion, like those published, are protected if they:

- Relate to a matter of public concern
- Clearly express a subjective view, an interpretation, a theory, conjecture, surmise, or hyperbole, rather than claiming to be in possession of objectively verifiable facts

The court held that the team was of "public concern" but found that the comments were a "subjective opinion." Therefore, it dismissed the defamatory claim of the coach. It did not find the "screw things up" statement to be actionable.

The circumstances were far different in *Bauer v. Murphy*, 530 N.W.2d 1 (1995). After concerns of a sexual relationship between a coach and a player arose, the suspected coach was suspended. At a meeting where the suspension was announced, the allegedly involved player was said to be a "disgrace" by the head coach. The player then left the team and filed suit. Defamation was among the legal claims made against the head coach.

The coach's remarks were reviewed under slander laws, as they were made orally. Damages must be shown in slander cases, unless the claim involves "slander *per se*." The player did not provide any evidence of damage from the remark. Instead, she maintained that the "disgrace" remark was related to the alleged sexual relationship, making her claim "slander *per se*."

However, the court did not find any direct relationship between the remark and the sexual relationship allegations. In a 2-1 decision, it did not find slander *per se*. But the dissenting judge wondered what else the remark would have been related to, if not the sexual allegations.

Recap

Defamation cases are not new to higher education, and they are often related to employment situations. When they occur, a plaintiff generally has to show that:

- A statement of fact is made that is false
- Publication is made to a third party
- The statement is not privileged or protected
- The statement, if made orally, causes provable harm

Defamatory statements tend to subject people to hatred, distrust, ridicule, contempt, or disgrace. If they do, they may be actionable. Consider the cases of the basketball coaches. What's said on or around the court can lead into the courts!

Word Wars Continue

April 1990

Employee free speech issues continue to pit colleges against faculty and staff in a war over words. In a series of recent cases, courts have considered the balance between the right of an employee to speak freely and the right of employers to control employees.

Both faculty and staff speech have been subject to challenge. For example, several states have adopted statutes to protect employees who report problems to higher authorities.

In Michigan, a campus public safety officer argued that he was fired for carrying out his duties and that his termination violated the state's Whistleblowers' Protection Act. But in *Dickson v. Oakland University*, 429 N.W.2d 640 (1988), the court found no violation of the Act or employee free speech or expression. The officer was terminated for job-related actions, not whistleblowing or protected speech.

Another significant case is *Harris v. Board of Trustees of State Colleges*, 542 N.E.2d 261 (1989). After a faculty member made various remarks about the skills of colleagues and students, the Massachusetts Board of Trustees took disciplinary actions, then terminated him. He sued, claiming the school had violated his free speech rights and procedural protections.

In evaluating employee free speech rights, the court reviewed several cases that established standards for employee free speech, including Connick v. Meyers, 461 U.S. 138 (1983). The extent of "public concern" in the speech is the key factor. Public employees are free to speak out on matters of *public concern*, as an extension of their constitutional rights. However, employee speech that doesn't regard a matter of public concern and is disruptive to the workplace is not protected. In *Connick*, a survey on office policies and morale was found not to be protected speech or expression. This standard is used in evaluating other speech.

The critical faculty member in *Harris* was found not to be speaking on matters of public concern when negatively questioning the work of instructors and students. Discipline for such speech was held to be permissible, as employer and employee rights were balanced.

In another case, a staff member was fired for constant complaints — on topics ranging from scheduling to harassment — and sued, in *Berg v. Hunter*, 854 F.2d 238 (1988). The courts again looked to the *Connick* standards, ruling that employee speech can be protected when:

- It deals with a matter of public concern
- Does not disrupt the work environment
- Does not interfere with work performance

With speech that isn't related to matters of public concern, employer rights prevail. But where public issues or concerns are involved, the courts must balance the interests and rights of both parties. In this case, the court agreed that the employee's record of steady and unwarranted complaints was not on matters of public concern, and it ruled that discipline was justified.

Cases such as *Dickson*, *Harris*, and *Berg* should serve to increase college and university awareness of the issue of employee free speech. These recent cases provide basic guidelines on rights and responsibilities — for employees and employers.

Employee Expression: How "Free" Is Free?

March 1993

Staff, volunteers, and even some listeners of a University of Washington radio station filed a freedom of expression lawsuit against the station's management.

The suit accuses KCMU and the school of violating the First Amendment (and related state laws) by maintaining a policy that prohibits on-air criticism of the station. Eleven plaintiffs say they were fired without written warning two months before the suit was filed for trying to improve the station through their commentaries.

The plaintiffs say KCMU "should know more clearly than anyone the importance of the protection of free speech." But station managers, they say, are dismissing the plaintiffs' claims and calling the matter a "conflict between discontented staffers."

Those fired made on-air comments, drafted complaint letters, circulated petitions, and spoke out about the station at public events. They also objected to the station's policy of permitting news broadcasts from the *Christian Science Monitor*'s news network, which they say is biased and anti-gay in its coverage and content.

This case is just one example that calls into question the freedom of campus employees to speak freely. Are employees allowed to say what they please? Or may they only say things that please their employers?

And does it make any difference whether or not their topic is campus-related?

Public and Private Action

To review employee free-expression issues, you first need to understand the differences between public and private actions.

Free speech is a principle established by the Bill of Rights. It prevents government from infringing on a person's ability to express his or her views. Therefore, public colleges and universities, which are supported by government, are bound to uphold this constitutional tenant.

This line of reasoning doesn't automatically apply to private schools, however. Take, for example, the case of a law professor at a Catholic institution who claimed the dean lowered school standards and altered course requirements improperly.

According to the professor's suit, the school retaliated for his complaints by lowering his faculty rank, pay, and seniority, and forcing his early retirement. He claimed he was entitled to free speech protection under the Constitution, noting that the school received some federal funding.

But in *Spark v. Catholic University of America*, 570 F.2d 1277 (1975), the court ruled that since the government did not control the campus decision-making process, there was no "state action," or measurable level of government involvement, requiring the court to examine the free speech question. The rules governing the federal programs on campus specifically noted that the school maintained full control of its own actions.

Responsibility to the Public

If a court rules that the "state action" doctrine applies, the principle controlling free expression rights of employees is best detailed in a 1983 U.S. Supreme Court case, *Connick v. Myers*, 103 S.Ct. 1684.

An assistant district attorney, unhappy because she was being transferred to another assignment, circulated a survey to co-workers that criticized management. It asked workers to rate their confidence in superiors and the trustworthiness of management, and it included questions about alleged pressure to work for particular political campaigns.

After the survey, the assistant DA was fired. Shortly thereafter she sued, claiming First Amendment protection for her actions.

The Court, however, ruled that the survey was not focused on issues of public concern. (If it had been, the Court would have upheld the assistant DA's constitutional protection as a pulic employee.)

The issue of alleged forced political campaigning may have been of interest and value to the public — but viewed as a whole document, the Court found that the survey was not protected by the Constitution.

But the Court also said this principle must be carefully balanced with government's obligation to operate effectively on the behalf of citizens. The public employer, the Court ruled, has a responsibility to promote "the efficiency of the public services it performs through its employees."

The Court's ruling in *Connick* seems to overrule an earlier survey case involving higher education. A University of Georgia instructor lost his contract after circulating a survey questioning the trust and faith found at various levels of the university administration.

In *Lindsey v. Board of Regents*, 607 F.2d 672 (1979), a federal appellate panel reviewed the professor's First Amendment claim for contract renewal. The court ruled that the professor's survey had pursued a wide range of issues that impacted on the effectiveness of the whole public unit. The court awarded the professor monetary damages.

Are "Whistleblowers" Protected?

"Whistleblowers," individuals who report wrongdoing to other officials, have also been given free speech protection when the expression deals with matters of public concern.

One case involved reports of financial irregularities to state administrative officials. An academic department at Troy State University (AL) was discontinued after reporting the problems. So the involved instructors sued for their jobs in *D'Andrea v. Adams*, 626 F.2d 469 (1980).

A federal appeals panel ruled that the professors' negative reports were protected free speech. Questions of funding problems, the court ruled, were appropriate matters for public concern.

A federal court also protected speech in a case involving the improper registration of a leased car for the campus president at Phillips County Community College (AR). The professor who reported the situation to state officials lost his contract with the school and turned to the courts for help.

In *Hickingbottom v. Easley*, 494 F.Supp. 980 (1980), the professor got the help he was looking for. The court found that the instructor had a right to speak on issues of public concern — even the president's car lease.

In the years since *D'Andrea* and *Hickingbottom*, many states have adopted legislation protecting "whistleblowers" from retaliation.

Clear and Not-So-Clear Calls

Some examples of employee free expression are easy to define as unprotected under the Constitution. A faculty member who swore at some students about administrators, for example, was fired in *Duke v. North Texas State University*, 469 F.2d 829 (1973). The professor's claim of free speech was rejected by the court.

The court noted that the instructor had "a minimal duty of loyalty and civility to refrain from extremely disrespectful and grossly offensive remarks aimed at the administrators of the university."

Sometimes, however, it's harder for courts to determine whether expressions are protected. When a University of Arizona faculty member went on television to call the state board of trustees "hypocrites," for example, he wound up losing his teaching position.

He asked to be reinstated under First Amendment protection. The court ruled in his favor, saying the instructor "spoke or wrote as a private citizen on a public issue" and that he "spoke as any citizen might speak." That, in other words, was protected free speech.

Conclusion

An individual's rights to speak in a public employment setting must be balanced with government's responsibility to serve the people. While employees can speak out on issues of public concern, government units — including public colleges and universities — have a right to limit speech that affects service and efficiency.

As more faculty and staff speak out, more case law will help determine the balance between the rights of employees and the responsibilities of employers. The line between the two, however, is still being drawn.

Jeffries Suit Weighs Free Speech, College's Interests

July 1993

He claimed there was a "conspiracy, planned and plotted and programmed out of Hollywood" by Jews and the Mafia to destroy black people.

In the weeks following his 1991 speech at the state capitol, political and religious leaders denounced him. Within months, his term as chair of the Black Studies department at City University of New York City College had been reduced from three years to one. And by spring 1992, campus officials had voted to replace him.

Shortly thereafter, Dr. Leonard Jeffries sued the school, demanding reinstatement to the position he'd held for almost 20 years. At issue were the free speech rights of a professor balanced against the interests of his college.

In recent years, courts have heard various claims of tenure, promotion, or employment being unlawfully impacted by the exercise of faculty free speech rights. During Jeffries' suit, the school said that Jeffries was removed for poor administrative performance. But Jeffries argued that he was removed unconstitutionally because of his speech.

What are the legal trends in cases like this one? And how do they impact on the Jeffries situation? Let's take a look.

Earlier Cases

In 1989, the Supreme Court of Massachusetts heard arguments involving remarks made by a Bridgewater State College faculty member.

College officials had started disciplinary hearings against the tenured instructor, charging him with making negative statements about the intelligence of the academic community, the faculty, and students.

In *Harris v. Board of Trustees of State Colleges*, 542 N.E. 2d 261, the state supreme court considered various legal claims, including contentions that the faculty member was terminated for speaking freely.

Citing the U.S. Supreme Court's decision in *Connick v. Meyers*, 461 U.S. 138, the Massachusetts Supreme Court considered whether the faculty member's remarks were related to public issues (and were thereby protected) or to school affairs (and were therefore not guaranteed protection).

(Under the *Connick* decision, a campus can take action against an instructor or administrator who disrupts campus operations by speaking on matters that are not of public concern.)

Harris, said the court, commented on school affairs, not public policy. In doing so, the court ruled, he did not have constitutional protection, and the college was free to take action against him if the action was justified.

Last year, a college health center employee on another campus sought court protection for her free speech. She said she was terminated for speaking out on sexual harassment concerns on campus, and the U.S. Fifth Circuit Court of Appeals considered her claim in *Wilson v. University of Texas Health Center*, 973 F.2d 1263 (Fifth Cir. 1992).

The university said the plaintiff was fired for intentionally misrepresenting the nature of the harassing circumstance to others. But the plaintiff claimed she had been repeatedly harassed by several co-workers, and that when she complained she was fired.

While the court said it needed more information to make a proper ruling, it agreed that public policy protects and promotes open speech. A public employer may control or limit speech if it is in the best interests of government, the court said, but it can't prevent employees from speaking out on matters of public concern.

So clearly, employee speech is not always free, according to *Wilson*.

Another 1992 case considered free speech in the tenure review process. In that case, *Colburn v. Trustees of Indiana University*, 973 F.2d 581, several faculty members complained that they had been unfairly denied tenure.

When the faculty members asked for an outside review, due to their concerns about departmental "politics," they were dismissed. They saw the request for review as protected free speech, however, and asked the court to protect their right to ask for help.

The *Colburn* court, like others before it, looked to *Connick* for guidance. It understood that public employees retain certain free speech rights, but only on issues of public concern.

In *Connick*, a survey on office concerns and management styles had been ruled unprotected speech because it had dealt with the employment environment and not a significant public policy matter. Similarly, the Indiana University employees spoke out to protect their jobs, not the public interest, ruled the *Colburn* court. Because that was their goal, the court ruled that their speech was unprotected and allowed the school to take action against them.

In making its decision, the court reviewed correspondence written by the faculty members. The notes focused on their careers, not on matters of public concern.

The court also noted that the employees had shared their concerns internally, without informing the public. These factors supported the notion that the speech was not protected. They had spoken as unhappy workers, not as interested citizens, the court said, and, as such, their speech was unprotected.

The Jeffries Decision

Cases such as *Connick, Harris, Wilson,* and *Colburn* provide a basic framework for reviewing faculty free speech cases. But these principles were tested last year in another City College case, a precursor to the Jeffries suit.

In the case, a federal appellate panel found that the school had illegally censored a professor. The school had encouraged students to drop the professor's classes because of comments he had made about the relative intelligence of various races.

The Second Circuit Court of Appeals ruled in *Levin v. Harleston* 770 F.Supp. 895, *affirmed*, 966 F.2d 85 (2d Cir. 1992) that the college had "chilled" the instructor's First Amendment rights by taking action against him based on his commentaries.

That decision set the stage for the recent *Jeffries* ruling. Again, City College was accused of taking action against a faculty member (Jeffries) because of his comments.

At trial, lawyers defending the school in the $25 million suit claimed that City College had long been dissatisfied with Jeffries' leadership and lack of scholarship, and that he was removed for those reasons. The timing of the decision to remove him, just months after the controversy over his speech, was termed a "coincidence" by the school's lawyers.

The professor's legal team, however, had a different interpretation of the events that led to demotion. They said the evidence suggested that City College officials heard Jeffries' speech, didn't like it, and took action against Jeffries because of it. Jeffries' lawyers also pointed out that Jeffries had been reappointed to his post seven times over two decades, and that he had received several positive written performance reviews.

The federal jury agreed that the professor had been demoted unlawfully. It found that the chancellor of City University and five other officials had deprived Jeffries of his free speech rights, and that the school had taken action against him solely because of his speech at the capitol.

That talk, given by Jeffries at a state black arts festival, was found to be protected free speech. Jeffries had been asked to speak about multiculturalism, and the court found his comments to be on matters of public concern.

The jury awarded Jeffries $400,000 in damages. Individual award responsibility for the defendants ranges from $30,000 to $80,000.

Under state law, however, the administrators won't be personally responsible for payments. Because they were acting in their official college capacities, the state will make the payments.

The state and college say they'll appeal the ruling. Still to be decided: a possible court order to reinstate Jeffries and pay his related legal fees and court costs.

Conclusion

The *Jeffries* decision demonstrates the difficulties of campus response to "objectionable" faculty or staff speech on public issues. Faculty and staff are free to express opinions on public matters, even if those opinions are offensive or embarrassing to the college, the courts have said.

To uphold related disciplinary action, a campus must show that a staff member's speech jeopardizes campus interests. If the speech disrupts campus operations, officials can impose disciplinary sanctions — but only after appropriate processes, such as hearings.

The *Jeffries* decision teaches a lesson on the Constitution, free speech, matters of public concern, and faculty rights. What campuses will learn from it remains to be seen.

Academic Freedom and Campus Concerns

January 1995

Were they the best of words or the worst of words? In a tale of two cities, faculty members spoke out and there were severe consequences.

In Durham, New Hampshire, a professor's classroom remarks led to disciplinary sanctions and court action based on allegations of sexual harassment. And in New York City, a college department chair's right to speak out on issues off-campus remains under legal consideration. Both cases demonstrate current academic freedom issues on college campuses. As a result, the right of instructors to speak without fear of recrimination is being hotly debated on campus and in the courts.

"Jell-O™ on a Plate"

The University of New Hampshire professor had given the same basic lecture for at least 14 years in his technical writing class. In 1992, things were different.

So that his students could better understand how to focus on subjects, he put it in terms of sex: "Focus is like sex. You seek a target. You zero in on your subject. You and the subject become one." Several days later, he used a description of a belly dancer as a simile, saying it was like "Jell-O™ on a plate with a vibrator under the plate."

These classroom comments led to seven formal student complaints of sexual harassment against the professor. UNH had policies against "verbal conduct of a sexual nature" that creates a "hostile or offensive academic environment." The seven students were so offended by the comments that they filed grievances with their academic advisor. Then came 14 months of proceedings.

A campus committee reviewed the case and deemed the professor's classroom behavior "intolerable." After an appeal of the campus ruling, the campus president decided to enforce disciplinary sanctions, which included suspending the professor without pay for at least one year and professional counseling at his own expense.

The instructor sued UNH, asking a federal court to reinstate him with full back pay and damages. In preliminary proceedings, he won his case very easily.

The court ordered UNH to immediately reinstate the instructor until a full trial on the case could be heard. It also noted, in a 103-page opinion, that it was very unlikely that the college had any case at all to argue.

College students in the instructor's classroom, said the court, were not children. They were all "adult college students, presumed to have the sophistication of adults." The comments, it ruled, "were made in a professionally appropriate manner." Even if some students viewed the comments as "outrageous," they were not subject to disciplinary proceedings and sanctions because "the application of the ... sexual harassment policy to (his) classroom statements violates the First Amendment."

UNH officials at first considered appealing the temporary order. The school felt the ruling restricted its ability to supervise faculty, and that it would leave students "no recourse to complain about a professor's speech or behavior in a classroom setting." However, officials decided not to appeal for a stay of the order and allowed the instructor to teach, pending a full trial.

But in late 1994, UNH trustees decided to settle out of court. They agreed to pay the instructor, who was already back in the classroom, $60,000 in damages and back pay and another $170,000 in legal fees. The university also agreed to delete any records on the charges and suspension from files. The trustees issued a statement saying they felt they could have ultimately won their case, but that they decided to settle in the face of severe media and legislative pressures.

In the wake of the federal court's temporary order and the subsequent out-of-court settlement, campus administrators elsewhere are now reviewing their own speech codes and sexual harassment policies. While remaining sensitive to sexual harassment issues, campus policies must provide appropriate protections for free speech and expression, in and out of the classroom.

"A Conspiracy, Planned and Plotted and Programmed Out of Hollywood"

It was comments made outside the classroom that brought the City University of New York and its black studies department chair into a hot debate over academic free speech. A speech on the steps of the state capitol provoked an immediate reaction. Several years later, after campus administrative sanctions and legal challenges, the U.S. Supreme Court got involved. It recently ordered reconsideration of a lower court decision that gave the instructor his job back as chair and awarded him punitive damages of up to $360,000.

At issue were comments made at an arts and cultural festival. The tenured professor noted differences between "sun people" from Africa and "ice people" from Europe. He also blamed negative public images of Africans on "a conspiracy, planned and plotted and programmed out of Hollywood," noting further that "Russian Jewry had a particular control over movies, and their financial partners, the Mafia, put together a system of distribution of black people."

The comments were little noted — until they were broadcast on a state-operated cable TV network. Public and political reactions were then swift and intense. Some demanded that the college take action against the instructor for his professed "bigotry." Others maintained that freedom of speech principles protected him from institutional sanctions.

One year later, CUNY decided to retain him as an instructor but removed him as the department chair. Campus officials at the time cited his poor administrative performance, not the capitol speech.

He sued, claiming freedom of speech. In 1993, a federal district court ordered his full reinstatement. A federal jury then heard his appeal for damages for unconstitutional infringement on his expression and awarded him $360,000. In early 1994, an appellate panel upheld the reinstatement but ordered a new trial on damages.

That's when the U.S. Supreme Court got the case. CUNY asked the Court to consider "whether the First Amendment compels a university to retain, in a position of leadership, a person who has engaged in hate speech." It wanted the court to overturn the order to reinstate the instructor as chair, saying that the order "challenges the authority of university administrators to decide who may speak for the university."

Attorneys for the professor urged the Supreme Court not to consider the case. They argued that CUNY had not shown any damages and, therefore, was not entitled to a rehearing. Instead, they said, what resulted from the controversial speech was "an increase in the level and intensity of related research and debate." The attorneys maintained that such an impact should have been "welcomed by an academic institution."

In late 1994, the U.S. Supreme Court determined that CUNY should have a second chance to show that the demotion did not violate the Constitution. In a brief order, without any supporting opinion, the Court vacated the earlier rulings. It asked the appeals panel to reconsider its order to reinstate the chair and its damage award. This time, said the Court, the campus case should be decided according to principles established by the Court in a hospital case earlier in the year.

Workplace Disruption

In that case, *Walters v. Churchill*, the Supreme Court gave public officials seemingly greater powers to dismiss employees whose comments damaged morale or disrupted the workplace. The case involved a nurse terminated by a public hospital for criticizing the hospital's training program and her supervisor.

Lower courts had ruled in her favor, finding that her comments had not disrupted the workplace, and ordered her reinstated. But the Supreme Court disagreed.

In an opinion by Justice Sandra Day O'Connor, the Court gave greater credence to the concerns of administrators and managers over employee speech. The nurse's termination, said the Court, was supported by "reasonable predictions" by supervisors of workplace disruption. Actual disorder was not required.

Walters suggested that, under the First Amendment, "the government cannot restrict the speech of the public at large, but it can restrict the speech of its own employees." It went on to say:

> When someone paid a salary so that she will contribute to an agency's effective operation says things that detract from the agency's effective operation, the government employer must have some power to restrain her.

It may not be easy for the appellate panel to apply *Walters* to the CUNY case. Some contend that the ruling allows campuses to weigh the impact of offensive speech and conduct of officials in personnel decision-making. Others argue that *Walters* gave supervisors too much power over employee speech. They maintain that public academic institutions must preserve academic freedom, and that faculty and others must be free to speak out on issues of concern.

Tale's End

In two cities, on two campuses, issues of free speech for faculty have been severely challenged. In deciding these cases, the courts and campuses must balance institutional needs and faculty rights. In both cities, it was left to the courts to decide whether we live, work, and study in an age of reason or an age of foolishness.

Note: In fall 1995, the U.S. Supreme Court refused to hear an appeal of a lower court ruling that upheld CUNY's demotion of Jeffries. The appeal had held that his speech had interfered with the "efficiency" of the department, which justified the personnel action. His faculty rank was not affected.

Schools Test Language Proficiency ... and Laws

January 1991

"My TA can't speak English!" It's a growing complaint at colleges and universities. Over the years enrollment of international students has increased in many graduate fields. As a result, for many graduate assistants and teaching assistants, English is a second language.

These assistants help their departments cover required courses and provide educational support to undergraduate students. But can they teach? Do their students understand? Faced with growing complaints and concerns, campuses and state governments have begun to act. But have they acted wisely? Have they acted legally? If linguistic concerns can't be addressed out of the courts, litigation is sure to follow.

About a dozen states now have laws that deal with the English speaking proficiency of college instructors. Hundreds of campuses have also responded to the concerns. But in adopting language requirements and testing standards for international teachers, states and schools may be creating other problems. In the systems created to test English language skills, there are no uniform standards: different populations are tested in different ways in different states. One thing is consistent — most state and school language testing programs apply only to particular populations.

Concern is increasing over the trend to test only international instructors for language deficiencies. Educators fear the possibility of discrimination.

Certainly legal action over language tests for international instructors could claim discrimination on the basis of race, national origin, or alienage. If campus policies or state laws are found to discriminate unlawfully, courts could order awards of damages.

International assistants may use the Civil Rights Act of 1964, *Title VII*, which prohibits employers from discriminating on the basis of national origin. They would have to show that there is direct discrimination or that the policy of testing impacts disproportionately on one population. However, since Title VII deals only with employment situations, international assistants would have to be seen as employees. In many cases, they are considered students.

It would be easier to sustain a claim based on *Title VI* of the Civil Rights Act, which provides for sanctions against programs that discriminate on the basis of race, color, or national origin if they receive federal financial support. A school could be threatened with a loss of all federal funds if courts find discrimination in language skills testing programs.

One other legal claim that an international teaching assistant could make when faced with required testing would be based on the *equal protection* clause of the

Constitution. Under this provision, no person shall be denied due process of law or equal protection. This could apply if international teaching assistants are treated differently, solely according to national origin.

There's an obvious solution to the potential of lawsuits over language testing — test every applicant, not just those from other countries. Test everyone to make sure that any possible problems are identified and corrected in an academically and legally sound manner. Concerns over the language skills of classroom instructors may be increasing, but they cannot be addressed through means that might be discriminatory.

Language Proficiency Laws Put Campuses at Risk

August 1991

A $10,000 fine for colleges and universities that fail to test faculty properly for English fluency? That's the law in Pennsylvania, and several more states are now considering similar legislation. Other states are discussing bills that would bar some "non-native speakers" of English from campus classrooms for a semester and require a test of proficiency in a classroom setting before letting instructors teach. But while students and lawmakers want higher standards and more testing, others are questioning related legal risks.

Is language testing discrimination on the basis of national origin? Campus officials are concerned over potential liability; recent state actions have done nothing to ease their minds.

Concerns in the Heartland

In Nebraska, legislators, campus officials, and students are debating the pros and cons of an English language fluency bill. Known as LB 214, it would require faculty members at all state universities, colleges, and technical schools to be fluent in spoken English. A state coordinating commission would develop and conduct annual testing of all professors (full, associate, and assistant), instructors, and graduate teaching assistants.

Sponsors say the law is justified by the state constitution, which declares that English is the official language. At a legislative hearing, many University of Nebraska students testified that they couldn't understand non-native instructors when they lectured or answered questions.

Similar complaints in Arkansas led to a higher education English fluency bill that would require state college and university instructors to have "certificates of fluency" before they could teach. The state's department of higher education would award the certificates based on a testing program or on personal interviews and "peer, alumni, and student observations."

The law's sponsor cites a need to ensure that knowledge is being conveyed to students effectively and efficiently. But opponents say the problem should be addressed through employee reviews. They also argue that the law would be wrongly applied to some nationalities that already speak English, such as natives of Canada and Pakistan.

Opponents also claim that the bill sends the wrong message to students. The U.S. is one of the few monolingual industrialized nations. Some lawmakers and educators feel that the law would be another step in the wrong direction. Says one opponent, "By this, we send a signal that it's not even necessary for students to make an effort to accommodate people who speak English differently than we do."

Missouri is considering a statute that would keep non-native speakers of English out of the classroom for at least one semester. Anyone who hasn't received both "primary and secondary education in a nation or territory in which English is the primary language" would require training and testing before receiving a teaching assignment at a state college or university. As with other state efforts, the bill is aimed at improving teaching by improving communication.

So Pennsylvania and Texas have fluency laws, and at least 10 other states — Nebraska, Arkansas, and Missouri among them — are considering similar legislation. The demand for better English language skills is increasing, the demand for more testing is growing, but some concerns remain about institutional liability. Are language requirements or fluency testing programs discriminatory?

Concerns Over Liability

The primary legal concerns are over different treatment of different groups of potential employees and claims of discrimination due to national origin. One source of fear is the Civil Rights Act of 1964, which prohibits discriminatory hiring practices. Schools that require only certain nationalities to be tested could be accused of civil rights violations. International instructors could file complaints based on policies that affect them directly as individuals or on policies that may seem neutral but disadvantage an entire class of people.

Schools can consider the language skills of applicants for teaching positions. But where only applicants from certain countries are required to prove fluency, there may be claims of discrimination — that language skills testing disadvantages members of certain groups. A school would have to show that the testing was related to job performance and didn't serve to unfairly discriminate against one class of people.

Programs receiving federal funding are required to comply with the Civil Rights Act, which prohibits discrimination on the basis of national origin, race, or color. If campus employees or rejected applicants claim national origin discrimination due to testing, it could jeopardize federal support and result in back pay and damage awards. And the Civil Rights Restoration Act of 1987 reaffirmed the position that if any campus department receives federal support, the entire campus must comply with the law.

Constitutional considerations could also become factors in liability claims related to language fluency requirements. Under the Fourteenth Amendment, all persons legally in the country are entitled to due process and equal protection under the laws. Under some circumstances, discriminatory language-testing programs could be found to violate these protections.

Cause for similar legal concerns may also be found in other federal codes, some state constitutions and statutes, state and local civil and human rights regulations, and institutional policies. As concerns over instructor language skills are turned into new laws and rules, campus officials must pay attention to legal standards and the principles on which they're based.

Where Do We Go from Here?

There can be little opposition to the notion that instructors should be proficient in the language of their students. But given the concerns of students, higher education needs to consider:

- Increased self-governing efforts to indicate that this is an issue that can and should be resolved within the academic community, free from judicial or legislative interference
- Greater attention to student concerns, including well-defined and well-distributed policies, standards, and procedures for complaint resolution
- More research on the impact of language fluency on teaching and learning
- Increased efforts to make students more sensitive to differences in spoken English
- Improved opportunities for English language development programs for instructors
- Greater awareness of the potential risks in language skills tests that could be perceived as discriminatory

If language skills are important for teaching and you want to avoid claims of discrimination, test all instructors, not just those born abroad. Treat everyone the same in an effort to treat everyone fairly!

Employee Tests May Flunk Legal Examination

March 1990

"I refuse to be tested!" "It's an invasion of my privacy!" "It's demeaning and insulting!"

In today's legal environment, college and university personnel officers expect to hear protests like these whenever the subject of employee testing arises.

When dealing with campus employees, testing can mean either *drug testing* or *polygraph examinations*. Employee reactions to either are the same — but the law treats them very differently. While courts and legislators have moved gingerly toward allowing employers more drug testing, tighter regulations severely limit use of the lie detectors.

The federal Employee Polygraph Protection Act prohibits the use of lie detectors as an employment screening tool in most settings and limits its use on current employees. Backers of the bill estimated it will reduce polygraph testing of future and current employees by as much as 85%. One legislator saw the Act as outlawing "the massive misuse of these inaccurate machines to bully workers."

However, in the higher education arena, it's important to note that the Act does not apply to federal and state employment. This limits the effect of the Act to *private institutions* and their employees.

The exemption for public employees, however, does allow for polygraph examinations in the screening of government contractors. This exemption could be extended to permit testing of employees doing contract research work for the government. This could include sponsored research for the Defense or Energy Departments or national security agencies.

For private schools, the Employee Polygraph Protection Act virtually prevents the use of lie detectors in screening employees. The law does not allow private employers to "directly or indirectly require, request, suggest, or cause prospective employees to take a lie detector test." In addition, private institutions also may not use the results of previous polygraphs in the hiring process.

Exceptions

One exception to the law sounds like it might apply to campuses — but in fact it does not. It provides for an exemption for job applicants involved in the protection of "facilities, materials, or operations that have a significant impact on health and safety." Although it may seem to apply to security forces on campus, the exception is much more limited: it applies only to employers whose *primary* business is security. Thus, while a private security agency providing protection on campus may screen applicants with polygraphs, a private campus cannot test its own security employees.

A second exception exists for persons involved in manufacturing, distributing or dispensing controlled substances. The implications of this exemption remain somewhat unclear. It's conceivable that it could be extended to include many *health care professionals* on campus. Future case law will help define the extent of the law's exceptions.

In looking at the exceptions, it's important to note that even when pre-screening polygraphs are allowed, the results can't be used as the *sole reasons* for a negative employment decision. They can be only one of many factors in the decision-making process.

The Act is not limited to pre-employment situations; it also deals with the possible testing of *current* employees in private institutions and industries. Lie detector tests can be given to continuing employees as part of investigations into specific incidents. Testing for this reason is allowed when:

- Given as part of an inquiry into a business loss or injury
- The employee "had access" to the property or situation being investigated
- There is a reasonable suspicion that the employee to be tested is involved in the situation
- The employer has prepared and distributed a statement that these conditions exist

Several terms are critical here. A "loss or injury" must involve some economic loss or damage to the employer's operations. Employee "access" to the situation or incident is not clearly defined in the Act, but legislative reports all dealt with property. A "reasonable suspicion" could arise from employee actions, from information discovered in the investigation, or from the circumstances.

Where testing is allowed, it must be conducted under specific circumstances:

- An employee must have advance notice of the time and place of the test, be allowed to consult with counsel, and fully understand the nature of the testing.
- Employees cannot be asked questions about political or religious beliefs, labor union issues, sexual behaviors, or other degrading or intrusive questions.
- Employees are entitled to review the questions in advance, see a record of the proceedings, and have an interview with an employer on the test and results prior to any attempts to act on the test results.
- The results of permitted private employer tests cannot be released to third parties without prior authorization.

Violations

The Department of Labor can pursue violations of the Employee Polygraph Protection Act through government action and civil legal suits. It can assess penalties against employers who violate the Act, including fines of up to $10,000, or pursue other legal actions on behalf of employees whose rights are violated by seeking employment, promotion, and lost wages and benefits. Employees of private institutions who feel that the Act has been violated can sue for "equitable relief" in state or federal courts. Prevailing parties in such cases can recover legal and court costs.

The 1988 federal law is not the only control over employee polygraph testing. Where there are state laws or union contracts that have other conditions for testing that are more restrictive than the federal statute, they must be followed.

As shown, the laws regarding polygraph testing by private institutions and employers have radically changed in the past year. Under the Employee Polygraph Protection Act of 1988, private school employees and applicants have many new rights when faced with lie detectors. Except under very limited circumstances, private employers are no longer free to use polygraph testing in employment decisions.

Job Interviews: Legalities and Realities

June 1996

Some students recently complained to a campus career planning office about encountering inappropriate or illegal questions while interviewing for outside employment. What can they be told about responding to such questions? Also, how can employers be reminded, on and off campus, to be more careful when doing job interviews?

Students want jobs and have to survive interviews to get them. Employers need workers and have to conduct interviews. Both can suffer from inappropriate or illegal questions, which can have a very negative impact on the interview — and lead to discrimination lawsuits if not handled properly.

What Questions Are Inappropriate?

Generally, questions are illegal if they directly or indirectly lead candidates to reveal information about their race, creed, color, national origin, sex, marital status, disability, or age. If a candidate who is not hired can show that such a question was asked for the purpose of discrimination or had a discriminatory effect, that candidate may take legal action — and win.

Students pursuing employment and campus personnel searching for employees need to understand what questions are inappropriate and illegal. Students then need to be prepared for improper questions. Employers, on and off campus, need to be trained to avoid questions that can lead to claims of discrimination.

Staff involved in conducting interviews should be properly trained to develop suitable interviewing skills. Most often, inappropriate or illegal questions are asked by those who don't hire often enough to know the law as well as they should. They simply make mistakes in conducting interviews. Others follow patterns set by others long ago, asking questions that are now off-limits.

Finally, inappropriate or illegal questions may arise during "informal conversation." As interviewer and applicant try to get to know each other before or after the formal interview, questioning can go off in unexpected *and* unconstitutional areas! Regardless of purpose or circumstances, questions about race, creed, color, national origin, sex, marital status, disability, or age are inappropriate and can be unlawful. Hiring organizations need to ensure that all interviewers are properly trained to understand and comply with today's employment legal standards — at all times.

What Can Applicants Do?

Students involved in job searches need to be prepared for this type of question. Placement organizations suggest several ways in which candidates can respond to inappropriate questions:

- Answer the question, if you think it's necessary to get the job.
- Answer the question, but tactfully mention that it may be inappropriate.
- Refuse to answer the question — in a nonconfrontational manner.
- Reply by addressing the concern raised by the question, without answering the question.

Then, regardless of the method of responding to the inappropriate question, file a complaint with campus career planning officials, to help them deal more effectively with future situations like this.

Specifically, most inappropriate *gender* questions deal with marriage or family plans. Suggested responses to questions like, "Do you plan to get married?" or, "Do you plan to have children?" should assure a prospective employer that, regardless of any plans, the student is committed to working toward a successful career.

Questions dealing with *age* can be dealt with in a similar fashion. Inquiries related to a candidate's age or birth date might be deflected by responses suggesting that evaluation should be based on skills, competence, and experience, not age. Candidates, particularly older ones, might also effectively yet tactfully deal with questions of age by emphasizing "broad-based experiences."

Questions of *national origin* pose other difficulties. It is not appropriate for those hiring to ask where candidates were born or about their citizenship status before offering employment. When faced with such questions, students should point out the pride they have in their heritage and how it can help them deal effectively with people from different backgrounds.

"Do you have a *disability*?" That question seems to be asked more frequently as more persons with disabilities join the work force. To deal with a direct question of this type, a candidate needs to be ready to respond positively, not negatively, about his or her ability to perform the job. One suggested response: "Any disability that I might have would not interfere with my ability to perform all aspects of this position." This type of answer provides assurance that the candidate is reliable and able to do the work. That's what an employer needs to hear!

Sometimes *religion* can become an issue in the interview process. It should not be a factor except for a limited number of positions (*e.g.*, a theology professor at a religious institution). When an interviewer improperly raises the question of religion, the candidate could remind him or her that religious preference has no relation to ability to work. Any accommodations for religion, a candidate could say, could be discussed after a hiring decision is made.

Finally, sometimes questions are illegally asked related to *race*, such as, "Are you of a particular race?" or, "Would your race be a problem in working with others?" Professional organizations suggest that candidates:

- State that no one should be judged on race
- Cite their experiences with people from a variety of races
- Add that race should not interfere in the work environment

Answering an inappropriate or even illegal question may seem like the easiest way out for a student searching for a job. But answering these kinds of questions can lead to personal disappointment and possible discrimination.

Colleges and universities need to work as employers to ensure interviewing is done properly. More important, they need to work with students to be sure they are prepared when the questions are inappropriate.

Your Campus Can Prevent the "Zoe Baird Problem"

April 1993

The media referred to it as the "Zoe Baird problem" — the failure of an employer (a U.S. attorney general nominee, in this case) to pay Social Security taxes for two people she hired to work in her home.

That mistake cost Baird an opportunity for a federal Cabinet appointment at the beginning of the Clinton administration. A similar mistake cost a second nominee, Kimba Wood, the same appointment.

What does this have to do with you and other campus administrators? Well, the "Zoe Baird problem" can have campus implications. As an employer, your college or university must correctly withhold and pay FICA (Social Security), FUTA (unemployment), and income taxes as required by law.

Shortly before the latest Washington woes, related higher education issues were reviewed in NACUBO

Business Officer, a publication of the National Association of College and University Business Officers, based in Washington (DC). An article in the August 1992 issue discusses concerns surrounding employment taxes and provides sound guidelines for campuses to consider.

The key to understanding what your campus must do, the article says, is grasping the differences between an *employee* and an *independent contractor*. The article stresses that it's important for your school to appropriately classify campus workers. To do so, you have to determine whether they:

- Work for the *school*, or
- Work for *themselves* for the benefit of the school

What happens if you classify workers incorrectly? The biggest worries are tax and audit problems you might face, for your school as well as your workers.

The good news is that these difficulties are preventable — if you take the time to master the ground rules.

The Basics

Within the campus environment, you generally classify workers as either *employees* or *independent contractors*.

Your campus must pay and withhold employment-related taxes for employees. But your campus doesn't bear those responsibilities when it comes to independent contractors. If an independent contractor works for the school, *he or she is responsible* for his or her own taxes and withholdings.

In general, employees work under the control of supervisors, who direct what will be done, how it will be done, and when it will be done. An employee's supervision can be limited — he or she may even enjoy a significant amount of discretion in his or her work — but it is ultimately the employer who controls the outcome of the effort.

The work of independent contractors, on the other hand, is not subject to control or supervision. While campus supervisors may control the *results* of the work, they cannot control the contractor's *methods*.

The "Test on Employment Status"

If your campus has work to be done or needs goods or services, it has a choice: it can hire either an employee or an independent contractor.

There are cost and tax advantages to using independent contractors. You don't have to pay the employer's share of taxes for them or provide them with benefits.

But there can also be serious liabilities for treating what the government calls an employee as an independent contractor. Failure to pay or withhold proper taxes could result in back taxes, fines, and back interest for your institution, as well as possible criminal prosecution.

So what can you do to stay within your legal bounds? The tax laws for the United States, which are often less than easy to understand, are assembled in an official tax code and a series of Internal Revenue Service rulings. You can use the rulings as guidelines for determining a worker's correct status (employee or independent contractor) for tax purposes.

IRS Revenue Ruling 87-41 provides a series of scenarios that will help you determine the status of workers on campus (and elsewhere). These scenarios make up the "Test on Employment Status."

You can use the test to help you decide whether a person you're hiring should be classified as an employee or an independent contractor. That, in turn, will help you follow the correct procedures for tax purposes — before you unknowingly make a mistake.

Extra Help

By knowing the law and studying the scenarios in the "Test on Employment Status," you and your campus should be able to avoid the "Zoe Baird problem." But you can also get more help, either from legal counsel or from the IRS.

When in doubt, file Form SS-8 with the IRS for a formal ruling on whether a worker is an employee or an independent contractor for employment and income tax withholding purposes.

In other words, play it safe.

Courts and Laws Support Whistleblowers

May 1993

For years, employees who exposed the wrongdoings of employers often lost their jobs, benefits, and promotions. But now, courts and governments are increasingly protecting "whistleblowers" who step forward for the public good.

Court and campus actions in Michigan and South Carolina illustrate the growing concern about whistleblower protection.

Michigan

Big dollars are the answer to a research overcharge dispute at the University of Michigan.

A former UM employee blew the whistle on a computer time overcharge system that inflated charges to the federal government. To resolve the dispute, the university recently agreed to a $3.35 million settlement with the U.S. departments of Justice and Health and Human

Services. From that total, the former employee gets $570,000.

The settlement ends a year-old lawsuit filed by the former employee, who worked as a budget manager for the campus unit that supervised the computer center. In that role, he found overcharges assessed on government research projects.

He says he told his supervisors about the problem in 1989 but that they didn't respond.

University officials say the former employee's perception of the billing problem and timetable varies "wildly" from theirs. They say the employee was fired for insubordination, and that shortly after his termination the school reviewed its computer charging system and reduced its rates by about 70%.

In an attempt to resolve the matter, the employee was reinstated to another non-billing position at the school. But shortly thereafter, he joined the federal agencies in the suit, which alleged $15 million in overcharges.

The former employee gets a portion of the settlement because he told the government about the problem.

South Carolina

Last fall, the South Carolina Supreme Court ruled on a "whistleblower" case involving hazardous waste at the University of South Carolina.

Like many other cases, a whistleblowing manager sued after being fired. The employee was hired in 1989 to handle the storage and disposal of chemical waste. After a few months on the job, she found violations of environmental regulations.

She reported the violations to the appropriate government agencies and to school officials. But just one day before she would have been granted full-time employment status, she was fired for "insubordination and gross negligence."

She filed a legal claim based on a state whistleblowing statute. Under the law, state government agencies cannot terminate, suspend, demote, discipline, decrease the pay of, punish, or threaten employees for:

- Reporting violations of state or federal laws and regulations
- Exposing government waste, criminality, corruption, fraud, gross negligence, or mismanagement

If a whistleblowing employee is fired or otherwise disciplined within a year, the employer must prove that it did not violate the whistleblower statute.

At trial, the jury awarded the former manager $350,000 in damages (*McGill v. University of South Carolina*, 423 S.E.2d 109, 1992). Both sides appealed the ruling after the court reduced the damages to $250,000.

USC said the employee was negligent and had never proven that the school had violated any regulation or law. The plaintiff, on the other hand, said her judgment should not have been lowered by $100,000.

The state Supreme Court ruled for the plaintiff and told the trial jury that it shouldn't have ruled out retaliation as the cause of the employee's termination.

The court also ruled that the plaintiff did not need to prove the school's alleged violation to be protected under the whistleblower law. The court said she only needed a "good faith" belief of a suspected violation. Otherwise, the court said, the public might be discouraged from reporting suspected government errors, waste, and corruption.

The court also found no relationship between the state tort damage maximum of $250,000 and the whistleblower law. It reinstated the original claim.

Summary

The law and the courts have generally supported whistleblowers in order to best serve the public interest. So if you're an employer or supervisor at a public college or university, encourage your employees to step forward when they suspect problems.

Create an environment that promotes compliance with laws and regulations. You'll be better off rewarding people who expose wrongdoing rather than retaliating against them.

Sex Discrimination: Laws and Litigation

March 1991

A major area of campus litigation is sex discrimination in employment. To use gender as the determining factor in personnel matters, including hiring, promotion, wage, or termination decisions, is discrimination — and it may be grounds for legal action.

A variety of federal statutes and regulations require fair employment practices on campus. States also have a number of laws that can impact on campus hiring, promotions, salary levels, job assignments, and terminations. Sex discrimination laws can be complicated.

Four factors in higher education further complicate sex discrimination cases: tenure, confidentiality of the review process, difficulties in comparing academic assignments, and a tradition of academic freedom. It's difficult to achieve tenure as a remedy because of its permanence, making courts very hesitant to impose it. A history of confidential peer reviews in academic decision-making makes it difficult to obtain records for evidence. In judging discrepant pay levels, it can be difficult to properly compare teaching and research responsibilities. Are people doing the same jobs for different pay? And the principles of academic freedom have long inhibited judicial interference in academic matters. The tendency has been to leave academic issues to the academic process.

But despite the complex network of state and federal employment-related sex discrimination laws and regulations, and despite factors in higher education that complicate questions of sex discrimination, cases are consistently filed, heard, and decided. In the past year, various interesting and significant sex discrimination cases involving colleges and universities have been reported. The following provide a sampling.

University of North Carolina

An employee in the purchasing department at the University of North Carolina has filed federal suit, alleging violations of the Equal Pay Act and claiming salary discrimination and retaliation.

The purchasing agent charges that two men hired at her rank received over $5,000 more to do exactly the same job as she was doing. And when she was promoted to her supervisor's job when he left the position, she was given a salary of $7,000 less than he had been receiving. In addition, the plaintiff claims that after filing her complaints, she was denied secretarial assistance in retaliation.

Campus hearings have ruled that she wasn't a victim of discrimination, but she has appealed that ruling to the state level. The campus panel did find problems of favoritism and mismanagement in the department, and the plaintiff included these findings in her federal lawsuit. The plaintiff has claimed back pay and dam-ages in excess of the $10,000 necessary for federal courts to have jurisdiction in sex discrimination cases.

University of Minnesota-Duluth

Did the state university bypass qualified women for administrative positions in favor of hiring men? That's what 22 women at the University of Minnesota-Duluth claimed in a petition filed against the school in U.S. District Court.

All of the petitioners have tenure and administrative experience. Some currently hold staff positions. They all claim that the university has consistently given preference to hiring men for senior campus administrative positions. The men hired by the school, they argue, have credentials similar to their own.

In filing their petition, the women claimed university violations of a 1980 out-of-court settlement from an earlier sex discrimination case. A former female chemistry professor sued the UM system in the 1970s. Minnesota agreed to settle that suit by establishing new hiring, promotion, and salary increases for women.

Lehigh University

Sex discrimination in the form of denied tenure and salary inequities was reviewed by a U.S. District Court in Pennsylvania. A former assistant German professor sued Lehigh University for $150,000 in back pay and damages, under the sex discrimination provisions of the Civil Rights Act of 1964.

After seven years at the school, the plaintiff learned that she would be rehired for only one more year and would not receive tenure. The decision was based on research and scholarship that campus and outside reviews found "insufficient in both quantity and quality."

In legal papers, the plaintiff accuses the school of denying her tenure because of her sex. She contends that she wasn't promoted because the department already has women in a majority of tenured positions. In addition, the suit alleges that the school paid her less than men for similar work, and that she was given less time to complete her research than some men.

Lehigh disputes the claim. A spokesperson stated that the school doesn't have a "tenure cap" and that all faculty are hired "with the expectation they will receive tenure."

University of Virginia

A former instructor sought compensatory damages in excess of $40,000, claiming sex discrimination in a suit. She alleges that since 1984, the University of Virginia has engaged in inequitable salary distribution.

According to her claim, the school paid her less than men in the sociology department for doing equal work — work that requires equal skill, effort, and responsibility under similar conditions. She filed her suit under the federal Equal Pay Act, which prohibits wage discrimination based on age, race, or sex.

School officials claim the suit "actually boils down to small salary differences." They say that sex had nothing to do with her level of pay, and that UVA salaries are based on rank within the department and on years of employment.

The instructor also claims that the department took actions against her in response to her legal claim. Despite a departmental recommendation that she receive tenure, she didn't get it. After a faculty senate committee reviewed her case and agreed with her contentions, she expected a salary adjustment. She didn't get it. The school maintained that she wasn't entitled to promotion or salary increases.

The former assistant research professor is pursuing damages, back wages, an injunction against retaliation, and attorney's fees and court costs. She left UVA after the suit became public and is now teaching at the University of Wyoming and directing a women's studies program.

University of California-Berkeley

A claim of sex discrimination at the Berkeley law school led to tenure for a female professor. Two women under consideration for tenure at the same time were both denied. One filed a complaint alleging sex discrimination.

After that claim, the school awarded tenure to the other instructor.

What makes the Berkeley case notable is that an outside panel was formed to review the charges. The claimant agreed not to sue the school in exchange for a full review of her tenure application by an independent academic committee. The instructor and the school submitted nominations for the panel, but the provost made the selections, so neither party knew the identity of committee members, which included three professors from other leading law schools and two Berkeley professors from outside the law school.

The panel members knew that charges had been filed but were instructed not to consider the matter. They were simply to compare the female instructor's tenure case with the full files of six male law instructors given tenure at Berkeley in the last decade. The committee reported to the campus chancellor that the female instructor's work was of the same quality as that of the men who received tenure. The committee recommended tenure — which was granted 18 months after the sex discrimination charge was filed.

Boston University

A federal appellate court upheld a significant lower court finding of sex discrimination at Boston University. As a result, a female instructor received tenure and $215,000 in damages.

The lawsuit, *Brown v. Trustees of Boston University*, 674 F.Supp. 393, was filed in 1981 and decided in 1987, with the appellate ruling coming in late 1989. The instructor claimed that the school had denied her tenure because of her sex. Her department and a faculty panel recommended tenure, but the provost and president denied the request. The plaintiff said her academic work was held to a higher standard than that of male peers.

Boston University said tenure was denied due to a "lack of academic excellence." It also contended that the courts shouldn't become involved in judging academic issues. Said a spokesperson: "We believe that it is wrong for courts to substitute their opinions or the opinions of the jury for the scholarly judgment of the university in determining who shall teach."

The court ruled that while tenure was an unusual remedy, it was appropriate under these circumstances.

Summary

Sex discrimination is illegal, but it can be difficult to prove. Even when an instance of sex discrimination on campus is established, a tradition of academic freedom and judicial non-interference makes it difficult to appropriately remedy.

But when presented with facts, courts act. They can grant tenure. They can award damages. It's simple: understand the law and practice fair employment!

Chapter 3
FIRST AMENDMENT

Introduction

> The ordinance applies only to "fighting words" that insult or provoke violence, "on the basis of race, color, creed, religion, or gender." Displays containing abusive invective, no matter how vicious or severe, are permissible unless they are addressed to one of the specified disfavored topics. Those who wish to use "fighting words" in connection with other ideas — to express hostility for example, on the basis of political affiliations, union membership, or homosexuality — are not covered. The First Amendment does not permit ... special prohibitions on those speakers who express views on disfavored subjects.
>
> *R.A.V. v. City of St. Paul,* 112 S.Ct. 2538 (1992)

Added to the U.S. Constitution as part of the Bill of Rights, the First Amendment notes, "Congress shall make no law respecting an establishment of religion, or prohibiting the free exercise thereof, or abridging the freedom of speech, or of the press."

It remains a primary source of legal conflict on college and university campuses two centuries later. Most recently, attention has been focused on speech codes, in an attempt to address campus expression aimed at individuals due to their race, sex, or creed. But the First Amendment and its campus implications extend far beyond speech. Challenges to the arts — in music, in film, on stage, in photographs, and in paintings — involve First Amendment principles. The display of flags, symbols, and posters with messages on campus has also generated litigation as well.

Two other major areas of constitutional concern for colleges and universities arise from the First Amendment — religion on campus and the student press. Debate continues over worship services and symbols on campus and over prayer at commencement exercises. Student newspapers continue to generate a flow of legal decisions on the extent to which a campus may or should control or influence the student press.

First Amendment on Campus: Four Exceptions

January 1991

On college campuses across the land, one of the most difficult questions of our time is how to balance First Amendment rights against growing harassment and offensive expression. Many schools have adopted restrictive conduct guidelines designed to halt harassment and offensive behavior.

But in doing so, campus officials must clearly understand constitutional law, including the rights of individuals to express themselves and the rights of individuals to be free from harassment. Officials must also assess the impact of speech rules on the campus academic climate, weighing academic freedoms against the campus interest in controlling offensive speech and conduct. This is a difficult balancing act.

Free speech isn't completely free. Over the years, exceptions have developed to the constitutional provision prohibiting government from making laws infringing upon free speech, including considerations of time, place, and manner. In constructing rational policies on free speech and expression, campus officials must think carefully about any exceptions to the First Amendment. Campus attempts to address intolerance through rules and regulations without a careful assessment of legal risk and impact on academic freedom are destined for failure.

Courts have recognized four basic categories of speech that the Constitution may not protect:

- Fighting words
- Obscenity
- Incitement to lawlessness
- Defamation

Campus rules and regulations concerned with limiting free speech must find legal basis in these categories.

"Fighting Words"

Words "which by their very utterance inflict injury" may be restricted, as in *Chaplinsky v. New Hampshire*, 315 U.S. 568 (1942). In that case, and in few cases since that time, the court allowed regulation of words likely to cause retaliation and thereby a breach of the peace. In *Chaplinsky* a member of a religious group was sanctioned for addressing a police officer as a "damned fascist" and a "damned racketeer." The court held that this language was threatening, profane, and likely to cause the victim to respond by fighting.

The "response by fighting" standard was tested in *Cohen v. California*, 403 U.S. 15 (1971), in which "fighting words" were defined as words that would likely cause an average person to reply with his fists. In *Cohen*, the Court overturned the conviction of a man wearing a coat that had "F___ the draft" printed on it. He argued that his jacket message wasn't fighting words, as it wasn't directed at anyone in particular. No one individual could take the message as a personal insult, as it was directed to everyone.

In *Gooding v. Wilson*, 405 U.S. 578 (1972), the court ruled that a black war protester who called an arresting police officer a "white SOB" and said he would kill him wasn't using fighting words. Favoring free speech, the Court found it difficult to say that such language in today's society should not be expected. And if it is to be somewhat expected, how can it cause the average listener to respond in anger and violence?

As society has become more permissive, it appears that standards of acceptable language have been eased as well. Courts have found that state laws designed to control speech such as the *Cohen* message or the *Gooding* remarks are unconstitutionally vague: they don't meet current "fighting words" standards.

One other major Supreme Court decision has dealt with "fighting words." But, like *Chaplinsky*, it hasn't been tested in decades. In *Cantwell v. Connecticut*, 310 U.S. 296 (1940), the Court ruled that the use of "epithets or personal abuse is not ... safeguarded by the Constitution." This standard for fighting words could have campus implications in today's environment. But since *Cantwell* hasn't been reviewed recently, its significance in the current legal climate is uncertain.

Obscenity

If it's obscene, it's not protected by law. That's the simple part. But just what is obscene?

The decision in *Miller v. California*, 413 U.S. 15 (1973), based on earlier decisions, established a three-part test for obscenity. The Constitution will not protect speech and expression that:

- Taken as a whole, would be found by an average person to appeal to the prurient interests, when "community standards" are applied

- Depict or describe in a patently offensive way sexual conduct specifically defined by state law

- Taken as a whole, lack serious literary, artistic, political, or scientific merit

For campuses and communities, having the *Miller* test is very different from being able to apply the test. The recent unsuccessful attempt in Florida to prosecute musicians for allegedly obscene lyrics and performances points out the difficulties in limiting speech and expression on the basis of "obscenity."

Even if the *Miller* test were easier to use, its application on campus would remain limited. Most campus speech of concern doesn't seem to be obscene by contemporary legal standards.

Incitement to Lawlessness

The First Amendment doesn't protect speech that provokes violence or illegal actions. The standards for this free speech limitation were established in *Brandenburg v. Ohio*, 395 U.S. 444 (1969). According to this decision, government can limit or control speech or expression that is "directed to inciting or producing imminent lawless action."

Speech that makes people upset or angry is different from speech that incites violent or criminal behavior. The speech or expression must create a "clear and present danger" of violence or lawlessness.

In *Terminiello v. Chicago*, 337 U.S. 1 (1949), the Court dealt specifically with speech intended to excite people and create disruption. But did the speech incite violence or unlawful activity? That was the question. The Court ruled that even though the speech caused dissension, it was entitled to First Amendment protection. Said the court:

> A function of free speech under our system of government is to invite dispute. It may indeed best serve its high purpose when it induces a condition of unrest, creates dissatisfaction with conditions as they are, or even stirs people to anger.

Speech that promotes unrest is protected. Speech that prompts anger is protected. Speech that incites dissatisfaction is protected. But speech that creates a clear and present danger of imminent violence or unlawfulness has no First Amendment protection.

In both *Brandenburg* and *Terminiello*, speakers at public gatherings had been convicted of urging crowds to attack minority groups. But the Court said that more than "urging" violence was necessary to invoke limits on speech. Words must create an imminent danger or be accompanied by acts of intimidation that make the words more than simply threatening.

Defamation

There is no First Amendment protection for false statements of fact. Words or expressions of falsehood that cause personal injury can be controlled or limited. The Constitution permits the award of damages to individuals harmed by false words or expression.

The rationale for the control of defamatory speech may best be explained by the ruling in *Hustler Magazine v. Falwell*, 108 S. Ct. 876 (1988). The court noted that "false statements of fact are particularly valueless, they interfere with the truth-seeking function of the marketplace of ideas, and they cause damage to an individual's reputation that cannot easily be repaired by counter speech."

Some states and communities have tried to control "hate speech" through defamation control laws. In *Colin v. Smith*, 578 F.2d 1197 (1970), the Sevevth Circuit Court of Appeals overturned a local ordinance that banned distribution of materials that would "promote hatred toward persons on the basis of their heritage." The court didn't find defamation and looked for other ways to halt the materials. But "fighting words" and "obscenity" didn't apply, and the distributed materials didn't meet the "imminent violence or lawlessness" test. As a result, the speech was protected by the First Amendment.

Campus Considerations

In developing policies, campus officials must evaluate the four categories of speech and expression that can be controlled. *"Fighting words"* may be prohibited in face-to-face confrontations in which the words would cause an average person to respond by fighting. But the legal standards for "fighting words" haven't been tested recently and that exception to the First Amendment may be less viable in our more permissive environment. *Obscenity* standards, based on community standards, are difficult to interpret and difficult to enforce — and most intolerant speech and expression isn't what is commonly considered obscenity.

Words that *incite violence or lawlessness* can be subjected to controls — but only where there's a clear and present danger of specific violence and lawlessness, or where words or expressions will directly cause damage, harm, or illegal activity. Words that only cause anger and disruption are still protected by the Constitution. Monetary awards for damages can be obtained where *defamation* is shown, but this has limited applications for addressing campus concern over harassment and offensive expression.

Free speech and expression have long been essential to our society, with few legal limitations. Campuses wishing to attack intolerance through rules and regulations must do so in a manner consistent with today's legal standards. If new policies are part of your campus response to intolerance and harassment, make sure they're legally sound.

Policies Confront First Amendment

February 1991

With the understanding that free speech may not be truly free, many campuses have begun to adopt and enforce rules to control "hate" speech and acts. While approaches differ greatly, the intent behind the rash of new or revised policies is universal: to protect the campus and members of the campus community from harassing speech and expression. Concerns over the problem, and over freedom of speech, are reflected in many of today's campus conduct codes.

University of Michigan

In response to a court challenge of the university's initial attempt to address discriminatory conduct through regulations, U of M adopted a new policy in 1989. That policy created three different areas in which control over speech on campus is exercised: open forums, educational environments, and residential setting. The university established different standards for discrimination in each area, using a common system of complaints and hearings for alleged policy violations. The policy is based, in part, on permissible limitations on speech. The exceptions are for "fighting words" or words that intentionally injure.

Areas intended to be fully open for the free exchange of ideas essential to a campus are deemed *public forums* in the policy. As such, they're subject to the least control. Only speech or expression that represents "malicious and intentional verbal threats of physical violence and destruction of public property" through discrimination is a violation in a public forum.

Speech and conduct in campus *educational centers* are limited to a greater degree. While the Michigan policy indicates that the campus requires "free and unfettered discussion of the widest possible nature," it declares that discrimination and discriminatory harassment "have no place" on campus. As a result, in the academic environment:

> physical acts or threats or verbal slurs, invectives, or epithets referring to an individual's race, ethnicity, religion, sex, sexual orientation, creed, national origin, ancestry, age, or handicap made with the purpose of injuring the person to whom the words or actions are directed, and that are not made as part of a discussion or exchange of an idea, ideology, or philosophy, are prohibited.

The rule was intended to control speech or actions based on discrimination, in an academic setting, unless the speech or acts are part of the academic experience. Under the policy, academic settings include libraries, research labs, and recreation centers on campus, in addition to classroom buildings.

Free speech and expression may be even more limited in the campus *residential community*. In campus-owned housing, students are bound contractually to policies on harassment and discrimination that are, in part, based on an expectation of "privacy" in a living setting. The policies in housing areas are the most restrictive on the campus.

In an effort to avoid First Amendment problems, campus legal counsel initially reviews complaints about policy violations from any of the three areas — public forums, academic settings, and residential communities. Resolution of complaints may include informal and formal means, from mediation to a hearing process. Sanctions that can be imposed for violations of the U of M policy range from reprimands to expulsion.

University of Connecticut

After a 1989 challenge to initial campus anti-harassment standards, the University of Connecticut revised its student conduct code to limit speech and expression on the basis of "fighting words." The use of "fighting words" in face-to-face settings is a violation of campus standards, when the words are used to harass. The UConn conduct code defines "fighting words" as:

> personally abusive epithets which, when directly addressed to any ordinary person, are, in the context used and as a matter of common knowledge, inherently likely to provoke an immediate and violent reaction, whether or not they actually do so.

These "fighting words" include derogatory references to "race, ethnicity, religion, sex, sexual orientation, disability, and other personal characteristics."

University of California

At the start of the Fall 1989 term, the president of the University of California system issued additions to the state student conduct policy dealing with "mutual respect and tolerance." In distributing the new policies, the system noted that "nothing in the policy is intended to limit the protection of free speech accorded students by law and University policy."

The California policy applies to campus activities, organizations, and students, and it is based on the "fighting words" principle. The policy prohibits the use of words "likely to promote a violent reaction." Words that could be considered "fighting words" include "terms widely recognized to be derogatory references" to "race, ethnicity, religion, sex, sexual orientation, disability or other characteristics."

The policy expands the definition of "fighting words" to incorporate "harassment." It also covers campus speech and expression that:

> create a hostile and intimidating environment which the student uttering them should reasonably know will interfere with the victim's ability to pursue effectively his or her education or otherwise to participate fully in the university programs and activities.

In an effort to ensure that new rules don't infringe on "the free exchange of ideas," any individual campus policy based on the California system rule must receive system approval.

University of Texas

The new racial harassment policies at the University of Texas were developed by a nine-member committee that had an even distribution of faculty, students, and staff. The committee reviewed policies of other campuses and newspaper accounts of incidents and held a series of public meetings in formulating recommendations.

The UT policy is based on the First Amendment principle of limiting speech due to "severe emotional distress." The policy makes it a violation to:

> engage in racial harassment of any student, whether the harassment takes place on or off campus. Racial harassment is defined as extreme or outrageous acts or communications that are intended to harass, intimidate, or humiliate a student or students on account of race, color, or national origin and that reasonably cause them to suffer severe emotional distress.

In addition, the university rules call for an examination of other rule violations to determine if they were committed due to the victim's race, color, or national origin. If discrimination is found to be the cause of the act, it "shall be treated as an aggravating factor" in determining sanctions. Penalties for conduct violations can range from an admonition to expulsion for at least a year.

Complaints of racial harassment and intolerance at Texas are initially directed to a race relations counselor. If mediation efforts are unsuccessful, an advisory panel appointed by the president reviews complaints and makes resolution recommendations.

Stanford University

In May 1990, the Stanford Student Conduct Legislative Council proposed changes in campus academic and non-academic student rules and regulations as they relate to intolerance. The school conducted a required public comment process as it moved to adopt a new interpretation of an existing conduct standard.

Stanford policy makes "discriminatory harassment" a conduct violation because it "contributes to a hostile environment that makes access to education for those subjected to it less than equal." Prohibited harassment includes intolerant intimidation by threats of violence and personal vilification of students due to their "sex, race, color, handicap, religion, sexual orientation, or national or ethnic origin."

The Stanford definition of "harassment by personal vilification" indicates that the policy is rooted in a constitutional "fighting words" foundation. Under the policy, speech or expression constitutes harassment by vilification when it:

- Is intended to insult or stigmatize individuals on the basis of their sex, race, color, handicap, religion, sexual orientation, or national or ethnic origin
- Is addressed directly to the individual or individuals whom it insults or stigmatizes
- Makes use of insulting or "fighting words" or non-verbal symbols

University of Massachusetts

UMass addresses intolerant speech and expression through harassment standards. The campus definition of harassment includes "verbal and/or written invasion or violation of any individual's rights through graffiti, obscene telephone calls, or other means." Failing to provide others with equal treatment due to their "race, sex, sexual preference, religion, age, handicap, national origin, or ancestry" is also prohibited.

Emory University

Emory also uses "discriminatory harassment" to limit intolerant campus speech and expression. Prior to the Fall 1989 semester, the school issued a new policy statement dealing with the issue. The policy threatens employees, students, student organizations, and "persons privileged to work or study" at Emory with penalties up to expulsion for harassment violations. The policy restricts discriminatory conduct (oral, written, graphic, or physical) that:

> has the purpose or reasonably foreseeable effect of creating an offensive, demeaning, intimidating, or hostile environment.

The policy includes objectionable epithets, demeaning depictions or treatment, and threatened or actual abuse or harm.

University of Wisconsin

One of the most comprehensive racial and discrimination campus policies in the nation can be found in the University of Wisconsin System. The system's student non-academic disciplinary procedures deal with intolerant speech and expression in section 17.06 (2)(a). Under the code, printed in the August 1989 register of the state administrative code, a student can be disciplined for:

> racist or discriminatory comments, epithets, or other expressive behavior directed at an individual or on separate occasions at different individuals, or for physical conduct, if such

comments, epithets, other expressive behaviors or physical conduct intentionally:

- Demean the race, sex, religion, color, creed, disability, sexual orientation, national origin, ancestry, or age of the individual or individuals
- Create an intimidating, hostile, or demeaning environment for education, university-related work, or other university-authorized activity

To help students understand the conduct code, several examples are provided. It's a violation to utter racial slurs that make the education environment hostile. It's a violation to place visual or written materials demeaning the race or sex of an individual in that person's residence hall area when that act makes the environment hostile. However, it's not a violation of the code to express a racially derogatory remark in a class discussion.

Campus conduct violations are reviewed by an "investigating officer." The officer can use informal methods of adjudication or settlement, unless the potential sanctions are suspension or expulsion. In that case, a formal process is implemented.

Summary

Colleges and universities must find "state action" to extend the First Amendment to campuses. Intolerance policies at public universities must balance constitutional concerns with campus needs. In developing policies, most schools have turned to previously accepted free speech limitations including "fighting words," emotional distress, and harassment. A careful review of related policies at other schools can help campus officials make sure that their rules make sense — legal sense and campus sense.

Anti-Harassment Policies Face Legal Challenges

March 1991

Can campus policies designed to control discriminatory harassment and hate speech "chill" academic freedom? Can these policies be balanced against the principles of academic freedoms? Does the Constitution permit such policies? As more and more campuses turn to rules and regulations in response to intolerance, the courts can expect to hear more and more related cases.

How will the courts apply constitutional principles to new campus speech and expression policies? A significant ruling may provide colleges and universities with the beginning of an answer.

John Doe

In response to campus incidents, legislative concerns, and threats of litigation, the University of Michigan in spring 1988 adopted a policy on discriminatory harassment. The policy placed different levels of control on campus speech and expression, depending on the site of the conduct.

In academic or educational areas, physical or verbal behavior that "stigmatizes or victimizes an individual on the basis of race, ethnicity, religion, sex, sexual orientation, creed, national origin, ancestry, age, marital status, handicap, or Vietnam veteran status" could result in discipline. Policy violations could include threats to academic efforts, interference with an individual's academic efforts, or creation of "an intimidating, hostile, or demeaning environment" for academic efforts.

A U of M graduate student in psychology, using the pseudonym John Doe to protect himself, filed suit in U.S. Federal Court. He argued that the 1988 policy threatened him, as his classroom comments on race and sex might lead to discipline. He felt that his "right to openly and freely discuss ... theories might be sanctioned" under the anti-harassment rules.

Doe claimed the U of M policy was unconstitutional due to "vagueness and overbreadth." His case, *Doe v. University of Michigan,* 721 F.Supp. 852 (1989), provides colleges and universities with a recent judicial opinion on campus regulation of expression.

In reviewing the case, the court considered four primary issues of interest: Doe's *"standing"* or right to sue, *constitutional free speech and expression*, and regulatory *overbreadth* and *vagueness*. The final ruling was based on the court's finding for each of these issues.

Did Doe have *standing* to initiate legal action, since the policy hadn't been applied to him? U of M hadn't taken action against him, and it insisted that classroom speech was still protected. After consideration, the court ruled Doe could sue, as the policy had been "broadly and indiscriminately" enforced. Three other students had been subject to discipline for classroom remarks prior to Doe's suit.

Doe's suit could go forward, said the court, if he could "demonstrate a realistic and credible threat of enforcement" against him. The court found that Doe held certain views that he wished to express in class as a teaching assistant. Those views, dealing directly with differences in the races and sexes of individuals, could be viewed by some as "sexist" or "harassing." Based on the examples in a policy guide — which U of M subsequently withdrew from circulation — the court found that Doe had a significant stake in the case, which ensured that he would provide a strong presentation of the issues for court deliberation.

After determining that Doe could sue, the court then looked at the scope of permissible regulation of constitutional *free speech and expression*, reviewing federal and state case law. The court reiterated the general principles in law that have been established over time, including no protection for:

- Fighting words, which by their use inflict injury or incite immediate violence (*Chaplinsky v. New Hampshire*, 315 U.S. 568, 1942)
- Credible threats of violence or property damage due to the victim's background (state statutes)
- Speech that incites imminent lawlessness (*Brandenburg v. Ohio*, 395 U.S. 444, 1969)
- Obscene speech, as judged by community standards (*Miller v. California*, 413 U.S. 15, 1973)

The federal district court found that the university could attempt to enforce policies based on these principles. But campus regulations could not be based on the prohibition of certain speech due to content or message. The court used a 1969 case, *Street v. New York*, 394 U.S. 572, to best convey this, saying:

> It is firmly settled that under our Constitution the public expression of ideas may not be prohibited merely because the ideas are themselves offensive to some of their hearers.

Thus, courts may allow limited campus policies based on the well-established exceptions to the First Amendment, but policies that judge content won't withstand judicial review.

Was the new U of M policy *overbroad*? Did it go too far in controlling campus speech and expression? It well established in constitutional law that regulations of First Amendment rights must be narrowly constructed, to limit infringement to the least necessary level. Any rule that limits more speech than absolutely necessary is unconstitutionally overbroad.

The court found that U of M's policy was, in fact, overbroad. It subjected to disciplinary proceedings several students whose speech should have been protected, said the court. "Serious comments" made by students in the classroom, as part of academic pursuits, had resulted in complaints and sanctions. The court found the policy overly broad, as it made protected speech punishable.

Rules must also be understandable; they're unconstitutional if their meaning is unclear. Therefore, the court also considered *vagueness*. It held policy terms such as "stigmatize" and "victimize" to be generalizations that "elude precise definition." The court found it unclear just what words or acts were grounds for action. U of M had withdrawn its guidelines on the policy, saying they were "inaccurate." This suggested to the court that even school officials were unsure of the meaning of the policy.

In reviewing "vagueness," the court held that students reading the policy were forced to guess about its meaning. This is unconstitutional vagueness. Any effort to enforce the policy would violate due process standards.

Based on constitutional limits to free speech, overbreadth, and vagueness, the federal district court ruled against the U of M policy. While the court expressed an understanding for the school's desire to protect students, that protection "must not be at the expense of free speech." The policy, as it dealt with expression in the academic environment, was unconstitutional.

The university, noting that the original policy was never intended to be permanent, decided not to appeal that decision. Instead, campus counsel went back to the drafting room and developed another policy, more closely modeled along permissible restraints on free speech, such as "fighting words."

Rule 17.06(2)(a)

Commonly known as the University of Wisconsin anti-harassment rule, this policy too is under legal challenge from within the system. At last count, seven UW-Milwaukee students, two UW-Madison students, a UW student newspaper, and a UW-Green Bay instructor have all joined a federal lawsuit against the Board of Regents' policy.

Under the rule, UW can discipline students for discriminatory comments, epithets, or other expressive behaviors directed at an individual that demean the race, sex, religion, color, creed, disability, sexual orientation, national origin, ancestry, or age of the individual. Acts or speech that create an intimidating, hostile, or demeaning environment are also punishable.

While the policy is not as broad as the initial U of M policy challenged by *Doe*, the UW policy is under attack for similar reasons. The plaintiffs argue that the rule is overly broad and unconstitutionally vague. They say it affects protected free speech and doesn't clearly define its limitations on student expression.

Despite the ACLU-backed suit, this fall the regents, after reviewing policy impact to date on system campuses, voted to stay with the rule as written. During the previous school year, 21 complaints were filed under Rule 17.06(2)(a). As a result, one student was suspended and three others were placed on probation.

Advice on Making Campus Policy

In light of the U of M and UW experiences, it's appropriate to ask how campuses should approach anti-harassment policies. In *The Lurking Evil: Racial and Ethnic Conflict on the College Campus*, (Robert Hively, ed., American Association of State Colleges and Universities, 1990), attorney D.S. Tatel offers some advice to anxious campus officials. He suggests that they ask the following questions:

- *Are policies necessary?* Do existing laws allow campuses to address the problem?
- *Do we understand the Constitution?* Are we aware of the basic principles of the First Amendment? Do we understand the limited exceptions to it?
- *Do we know what we want to prohibit?* What words, acts, or expressions?
- *Can we develop a consensus* for the policies involving all impacted constituencies? Is a process in place that's inclusive? Open? Broad?
- *Are rules only one part of a comprehensive approach* to the problem? Are we also using counseling, mediation, communications, education, and affirmative action as responses?

These are good questions that campuses should answer fully in approaching intolerance through policies.

Summary

While the *Doe* decision is only a federal district court judgment, it well illustrates the great difficulties public institutions face when they address discriminatory harassment through regulation of free speech. Policy-makers must consider some constitutional standards, most of which haven't been scrutinized in recent years.

In the end, if campus officials decide to use regulations against intolerant expression, those policies must be based on permissible constitutional restraints they must be narrowly drawn to impact on only non-protected speech and specific enough to allow those affected to know the difference between right and wrong.

Speech Codes: Noble End, Ignoble Means

April 1992

Hate speech continues to hurt college students, poison the collegiate atmosphere, and vex campus leadership. Attempts to curb racist, sexist, and negative ethnic or religious conduct through campus conduct regulations have run afoul of the law. College hate-speech policies may send the right message to students about institutional standards, but they may be sending that message in a legally insupportable manner.

A series of legal battles demonstrate these pressures as does a municipal case recently heard by the U.S. Supreme Court.

Campus Cases Illustrate Dilemma

Three cases involving hate speech at colleges and universities in the past year help frame the ongoing debate. They involve campus conduct codes designed to curb personally hostile slurs and the conduct of student organizations.

Last fall, a federal district court struck down a University of Wisconsin system rule that barred speech intended to create a hostile learning environment through comments that demeaned a person's race, sex, religion, color, creed, disability, sexual orientation, or ancestry.

Violations of the rule could result in sanctions ranging from public service to suspension.

In *The UWM Post, Inc. v. Board of Regents of the University of Wisconsin System*, 774 F.Supp. 1163 (E.D.Wis. 1991), the court overturned the hate speech ban, noting that "content-based prohibitions such as the UW rule, however well intended, simply cannot serve as the screening which our Constitution demands." A school newspaper, several sanctioned students, and the ACLU had asked the court to act, asserting that First Amendment rights were being violated.

Adopted shortly after the University of Michigan's speech policy was overturned, the UW code was based on the "fighting words" standard, established almost 50 years ago. The Supreme Court ruled then that words intended to provoke imminent lawlessness was not protected under the First Amendment. The school argued that today's hate speech is directed at individuals with the intent of causing harm. UW said this met the "fighting words" test because it applies to instances in which someone intends to create a hostile learning environment, infringing on the rights of others.

But the federal court ruled that even if the "fighting words" standard was still valid law, it did not apply. Said the court:

> The problems of bigotry and discrimination sought to be addressed here are real and truly corrosive of the educational environment. But freedom of speech is almost absolute in our land, and the only restriction the fighting words doctrine can abide is that based on the fear of violent reaction.

UW officials noted that the rule was only "one tool in an array of tools to fight racism" and will continue other programs while appealing the decision and drafting new "fighting words" regulations. As this issue of PERSPCTIVE went to press, UW officials had sent a new regulation to prohibit *one-on-one confrontations* based on "fighting words" to the regents for system-wide approval.

A similar ruling was issued in a fraternity skit case involving students at George Mason University (VA). The school does not have an explicit hate speech code, but administrators acted against a fraternity chapter that sponsored an "ugly women" contest featuring one white student in black face makeup. The group was banned from campus activities for two years but challenged the campus sanction in court.

While the court and their own attorney found the skit "inappropriate and offensive," it was held to be constitutionally protected free expression. The judge ruled that the school could not discipline a group on the "perceived offensive content of the activity." Said the court:

> One of the fundamental rights secured by the First Amendment is that of free, uncensored expression, even on matters some may think are trivial, vulgar, or profane. ... A state university may not hinder the First Amendment rights simply because it feels that exposure to a given group's ideas may be somewhat harmful to certain students.

Campus officials, disappointed in the decision, said the court did not help "enhance the diverse educational environment" the university tries to provide.

A third judicial opinion on the issue was avoided by an out-of-court settlement involving the University of New Mexico. UNM had taken disciplinary action against a fraternity presentation found by some to be vulgar and ethnically offensive. The chapter went to federal court for relief from school sanctions.

The fraternity successfully argued, on the basis of free speech and association, for a temporary restraining order to forestall discipline. Faced with the prospects of a difficult trial, UNM dropped its sanctions and the fraternity dropped the lawsuit. The school, however, ultimately had to pay the fraternity's legal fees, which totalled more than $35,000.

The UW, George Mason, and UNM experiences demonstrate the serious constitutional problems faced by public institutions trying to discipline offensive student speech and expression.

Upcoming Decision

Why are campus legal observers interested in the outcome of a case involving a front-yard cross burning in St. Paul, Minnesota? Because the fate of a city ordinance being challenged could have a direct impact on campus speech codes.

The U.S. Supreme Court has heard arguments this term questioning the constitutionality of a city law that prohibits hate speech and expression. Under the law, it was a misdemeanor to place any symbol, object, or writing "which one knows or has reasonable grounds to know, arouses anger, alarm, or resentment in others on the basis of race, color, creed, religion, or gender" on public or private property.

In 1990, a man charged with burning a cross in the fenced yard of a black family was convicted under the law. But a state appeals court reversed the ruling, finding the statute violated the First Amendment. The Minnesota Supreme Court, however, found no fault with the law. Noting the violence and hatred a cross-burning symbolizes, the court said the city had "the responsibility, even the obligation ... to confront such notions in whatever form they appear."

At issue in the case are "fighting words" and flag-burning precedents. Many of the current campus hate speech codes, like the St. Paul law and the Wisconsin rule, are based on the fighting words standard which has not been seriously challenged in over 40 years. The principle is based on the notion that government can control words (and actions) directed at another person that would provoke a violent retaliation.

While the standard has not been reversed by the U.S. Supreme Court, over time it appears to have been limited by changes in society and related litigation. With more and more hate words found in common usage, it may be much harder today to find words that, when uttered, have such impact as to provoke swift and violent response. Words unspoken generations ago are now commonly found on bumper stickers and T-shirts and in the movies and daily life.

In addition, the Supreme Court has acted in recent years to invalidate a Texas flag-burning law, based largely on the fighting words standard. The state law was intended to sanction those who burned the American flag, as such an act would or could cause a violent response. But the court found flag-burning, even if politically repugnant, to be protected First Amendment expression.

While the Supreme Court could avoid a decision in the cross-burning case, observers feel the issue will be addressed. Unless the court overturns the city law due to its "vagueness," it will have to deal with the free speech principles and the fighting words standard.

Where to Go Next?

For public institutions, conduct codes that regulate student speech run the risk of violating the Constitution. The rules can be viewed as too vague to be enforced or too restrictive of student First Amendment rights. Speech-restrictive conduct codes can negatively affect the academic environment and cause manifold opportunities for expensive and time-consuming litigation.

For private institutions, the constitutional implications are less direct, but other right-based concerns can come from speech regulations. A private school could be subject to constitutional restraints due to governmental involvement on campus or through adoption of student and campus rights in handbooks and other campus policies.

In either setting, providing support for the fight against hate speech through conduct regulations may not be legally supportable. As an alternative, or in addition to a very carefully drafted and administered conduct rule, consider the educational response suggested by many. Use education to get to the root of the problem.

Speech Code Takes on Constitution ... Again

June 1992

The University of Wisconsin has a new "hate speech" code. It's out of the courts for now. But a question lingers: how long will the new code remain litigation-free?

The original Wisconsin anti-harassment rule was adopted by the System's Board of Regents in 1989. The speech code was established in response to a series of racial incidents on the UW-Madison campus, including a fraternity's mock "slave auction." The original rule allowed the school to take action against students who made racist or discriminating comments.

The rule, known by its state statutory designation as Section 17.06(2)(a), allowed student discipline for the following behaviors:

> racist or discriminatory comments, epithets, or other expressive behavior directed at an individual or on separate occasions at different individuals, or for physical conduct, if such comments, epithets, other expressive behaviors or physical conduct intentionally demeans the race, sex, religion, color, creed, disability, sexual orientation, national origin, ancestry, or age of the individual or individuals, and creates an intimidating, hostile, or demeaning environment for education, university-related work, or other university-authorized activity.

An investigating officer was to review conduct violations and impose settlements or sanctions. If suspension or expulsion was recommended, a formal hearing process was established.

That regulation was quickly challenged in federal district court and found to be unconstitutional. The court ruled that the code "goes beyond the present scope of the fighting words doctrine [and] is ... likely to apply to many situations where a breach of the peace is unlikely to occur." The U.S. Supreme Court ruled almost 50 years ago that "fighting words" could be sanctioned, but that doctrine has not been seriously tested in recent times. UW decided not to appeal the decision, deciding instead to develop a new code and battle hate speech with other tools.

The new code, based more closely on the "fighting words" doctrine, was drafted by a UW-Madison law faculty member. It differs from the former judicially voided version in several ways:

- It applies only to an "epithet," defined as a word, phrase, or symbol that reasonable people would recognize as abusive or as an insult or threat based on race, gender, religion, or sexual orientation. The old rule applied to "comments" and "other expressive behaviors."

- An "insult" is not actionable unless it would provoke "an immediate violent response" when addressed to a person of "average sensibilities." These phrases invoke a "fighting words" standard not found in the original version.

- Sanctions are strictly limited, requiring system approval for any campus disciplinary action under the rule. This is to prevent unequal application of the rule on various system campuses.

The approval process for new rules in the Wisconsin System involves extensive review steps. After campus endorsement, including faculty senate consideration, the hate speech code must be approved by the UW Board of Regents, and it is then referred to the state legislature. Public hearings and committee reviews are part of the overall process.

In the Madison campus faculty senate review of the proposed rule, code drafters noted that statements to general audiences would not be punishable. Only epithets shared in one-on-one confrontations could lead to sanctions. According to proponents, the code would not impede the free exchange of ideas on campus. Instead, it would allow action to be taken in response only to insults, abusive language, and harassment aimed at students based on race, creed, or sex. But opponents argued that the new rule, like the old, would "have an unconstitutional chilling effect on free expression." The senate endorsed the proposal, narrowly defeating a motion to reject the code.

The Board of Regents heard arguments on the new code after a subcommittee held public hearings. After debate, the regents approved the policy, voting 9 to 6 in favor. The regents who opposed the rule called the entire effort "an exercise in futility," citing the likelihood of renewed litigation. But supporters responded that the rule was narrowly written enough to pass judicial scrutiny.

The policy is now subject to legislative committee review and a final vote by state lawmakers. After final legislative approval, the regents must give the new code a final review before implementation. UW officials hope to have the new rules in place for the start of the next school year. They expect approval. But many others expect litigation.

Can Hate Speech Codes Withstand Legal Challenge?

September 1992

Over the years, campuses have enacted student conduct codes in an attempt to curb bias-related speech and behavior. The codes have been drafted to control expression deemed to inflict injury or incite violence.

But campuses haven't been alone in the effort to fight hate speech and actions through codes. Most states, and many municipalities, have adopted their own such regulations.

The U.S. Supreme Court recently heard arguments concerning the hate speech code in St. Paul, Minnesota. At issue: the authority of public institutions to regulate particular forms of speech or conduct.

In *R.A.V. v. City of St. Paul* (112 S.Ct. 2538, 1992), the high court was asked to consider the balance between an individual's free speech and a community's responsibility to protect and defend its members. The court's decision may have significant impact on hate speech and expression codes at public and private colleges and universities.

Campus Strategies

Many campus codes are based on a 1942 Supreme Court decision that established a "fighting words" principle. In *Chaplinsky v. New Hampshire*, 315 U.S. 568, the court held that language and words that "by their very utterance inflict injury" may be regulated. In other words, speech that provokes retaliation and violence can be limited, according to the ruling.

The fighting words principle has become the standard for many campus hate speech codes. But until recently, the principle hasn't been significantly challenged in court.

Campuses have used various language to try to gain control of hate speech and expression. The University of Michigan, for instance, prohibits "malicious and intentional verbal threats of physical violence and destruction." At the University of Connecticut, students may not use "personally abusive epithets ... likely to provoke an immediate and violent reaction." And the University of California System's rule prohibits "terms widely recognized to be derogatory references" to "race, ethnicity, religion, sex, sexual orientation, disability or other characteristics."

The policies have been challenged in some cases. The University of Michigan's code, for example, and the University of Wisconsin System's policy were both initially rejected as constitutionally overbroad and in violation of the First Amendment.

The St. Paul Case

In 1989, the city of St. Paul revised an ordinance that made it a crime to engage in speech or behavior likely to arouse "anger or alarm" on the basis of "race, color, creed, or religion." First adopted as an anti-hate crime law in 1982, the law was amended to make specific mention of swastikas and cross-burnings. It was revised again in 1990 to add "sexual bias" as an illegal motivation for actions.

St. Paul was among the dozens of cities, 46 states, and over 100 campuses to adopt or revise hate speech regulations to combat racially, sexually, or religiously motivated behaviors.

The first test of the St. Paul statute came in 1990, when a group of teenagers used broken chair legs to fashion a crude cross, then burned it in the enclosed back yard of a black family that had recently moved into the neighborhood. The teenagers were arrested and charged under the city's Bias-Motivated Crime Ordinance, which said:

> Whoever places on public or private property a symbol, object, appellation, characterization, or graffiti, including, but not limited to, a burning cross or Nazi swastika, which one knows ... to arouse anger, alarm, or resentment in others on the basis of race, color,

creed, religion, or gender, commits disorderly conduct and shall be guilty of a misdemeanor.

One of the arrested teens claimed the law violated his First Amendment rights. He asked state courts to dismiss the charges, saying the law was overbroad and unlawfully based on the content of the speech.

A trial court agreed, but the state's highest court allowed the charges to stand. It called cross burning "an unmistakable symbol of violence and hatred" that could be controlled.

So the teen appealed the case to the U.S. Supreme Court.

Can't Control Content

In a widely reported decision this summer, the Supreme Court ruled that control of speech or expressions cannot be based on content. The entire court agreed that the St. Paul law was unconstitutional — but for different reasons.

Five justices rejected the law because they said it contained "content-based discrimination" and "selected" for control only words that communicate messages of race, sex, or religious intolerance. Said the court:

> Selectivity of this sort creates the possibility that the city is seeking to handicap the expression of particular ideas. The point of the First Amendment is that majority preferences must be expressed in some fashion other than silencing speech on the basis of its content.

In short, the five justices said the St. Paul law was unconstitutional because it made some insults illegal, but left others alone. The court's decision noted that hate speech based on political beliefs, union membership, or sexual preference would have been legal under the law. According to the justices, "The First Amendment does not permit ... special prohibitions on those speakers who express views on disfavored subjects."

The other four justices, however, had different reasons for overturning the St. Paul effort. They found the law "overbroad" and said the statute created a risk that speech deserving constitutional protection might be deterred. Words that cause "hurt feelings, offense, or resentment" are protected by the First Amendment, the four reasoned, but would have been illegal in St. Paul.

Besides overturning laws and regulations controlling hate speech, the court may also have eliminated the practice of punishing hate crimes and expressions more severely than other crimes and expressions. Some campus codes, for example, contain provisions that create special sanctions for bias-related acts. By the Supreme Court's reasoning, such practices would now be seen as "content-based" discrimination and, therefore, unconstitutional.

Legal experts say the R.A.V. decision invalidates the St. Paul law and many other similar efforts by states, municipalities, and public institutions. Hate speech codes on public campuses, they say, will now be subjected to the court's "content-based discrimination" test — and will probably be ruled unconstitutional as currently written.

Campuses Respond to the Decision

Campuses with hate speech regulations may now be forced to go back to the drawing board. And campus reactions to the ruling seem to point in that direction.

At the University of North Carolina-Chapel Hill, the ruling casts doubt on the school's anti-harassment regulations. The regulations prohibit intimidation and harassment based on race, gender, religion, creed, sexual orientation, national origin, or disability. Verbal or physical conduct that creates a "demeaning environment" is also prohibited by the student conduct code.

The university is considering rewriting the regulations. New policies may be similar to an existing racial harassment policy, which calls for a balance between the First Amendment and the need to protect the educational process for all.

Administrators at University of California-Santa Barbara, who point out that no student has been charged with violating the UC code, say they may keep the rule until it is challenged. That, they say, could take years. But they also say they'll re-evaluate their response to hate speech and expression incidents on campus in light of R.A.V.

At the University of Wisconsin-Madison, the Supreme Court decision adds fuel to an already burning debate over speech codes.

A new regulation based on "fighting words" was recently drafted to replace the original, which federal courts overturned. The new code prohibits "epithets," defined as words, phrases, or symbols "that reasonable persons recognize to grievously insult or threaten persons" due to race, sex, religion, color, creed, disability, sexual orientation, national origin, ancestry, or age.

Legal counsel for UW says the new rule would be upheld if challenged, partly because it covers only one-on-one incidents. Others, however, disagree. Opponents call the new regulation an "abridgement of free speech," illegally based on content.

The rule's authors believe the minority opinion of the court may protect the rule. Four justices supported the notion that a city could place hateful speech in a special category for action, if it was based on the city's judgment of harm. Said one justice, in language that gives the UW rule some support, "conduct that creates special risks or harms may be prohibited by special rules."

University of Michigan officials, who have already had one code overturned by the courts, are also considering the impact of R.A.V. The current UM rules are content-based. Officials there are now considering a new rule that would generally prohibit violence and intimidation, no matter what the acts or expressions are based upon.

What's Next?

Campuses have been wrestling with bias-related speech and acts for years. Hate speech codes have been one leading solution. Even if they're not used regularly, the codes have allowed campuses to clearly outline their policies and standards.

R.A.V. may change that. But given the multiple decisions issued by the courts, it might still be possible to draft a limited hate speech policy. It may take another case to clarify the position of the Supreme Court.

In the meantime, colleges and universities — public campuses, in particular — should re-evaluate their student conduct codes. Does your campus code focus on content-based discrimination? Does it call for additional sanctions for violations based on the content of speech or acts? Is it overbroad? If you answered yes to any of these questions, your campus should probably consider revising its policy.

Private institutions may also want to review existing codes under the principles highlighted in *R.A.V.* Private campuses, of course, have greater latitude when dealing with Constitutional issues. But the Supreme Court decision may convince Congress to revive action requiring private institutions to provide constitutional free speech.

The *R.A.V.* ruling does not mean colleges and universities can't respond to acts of hate and violence on campus. But rather than focusing on the *cause* of the behaviors, campus conduct codes can prohibit *specific behaviors themselves* — as long as the prohibition isn't based on content.

"Hate Speech" Codes Rejuvenated?

August 1993

Last year's U.S. Supreme Court decision on a Minnesota hate expression law (*R.A.V. v. City of St. Paul*, 112 U.S. 2538) left many questions unanswered for colleges and universities — including the issue of taking stronger disciplinary action against students whose violation of campus conduct rules is bias-related.

But in June, the Supreme Court ruled in another case that people who commit "hate crimes" motivated by bias may be given longer prison terms, and that such punishments don't violate the First Amendment.

In the case, *Wisconsin v. Mitchell*, a black man, after discussing a movie scene in which a white man beats a black youth, asked his companions if they were "hyped up to move on some white people." When a white youth walked by, he shouted, "There goes a white boy. Go get him." The man's companions did just that.

Under Wisconsin's hate crimes statute, the two-year maximum sentence the man would have received for aggravated assault was extended to four years. The defendant, however, said he had been punished for exercising his free speech.

But the Supreme Court upheld the Wisconsin law. Writing for the Court, Chief Justice Rehnquist noted that:

> Traditionally, sentencing judges have considered a wide variety of factors in addition to the evidence bearing on quality in determining what sentence to impose. ... The defendant's motive for committing the offense is one important factor.

At least 27 states have laws providing for longer sentences for crimes motivated by bias. While this case involved a criminal action, its principles may be applied to campus situations.

The Effectiveness of Speech Codes

January 1994

Some free speech on college campuses can be distasteful, hurtful, and even repugnant to many. But it is protected free speech, and public college and university steps to limit expression continue to be overturned by the courts.

This trend continued in *Iota XI Chapter of Sigma Chi Fraternity v. George Mason University*, 993 F.2d 386 (1993). Attempts by the university to discipline a fraternity for its sponsorship of an "ugly women" contest were blocked by the federal courts.

In a series of legal cases, campus codes attempting to address speech concerns have not been legally supported. In two prominent cases, involving the University of Michigan and the University of Wisconsin-Madison, courts upheld student expression, not campus control. Both institutions had tried to draft conduct regulations to halt discriminatory harassment through expression. But the courts swiftly and strongly pointed to the First Amendment. In the "marketplace of ideas," not all expression will be appreciated and understood, but regardless of its basis, it remains protected

During the last two years, the U.S. Supreme Court has added to the free expression debate by considering hate expression law and hate expression sanction cases. Both dealt with governmental limitations on speech. Therefore, both can have public college and university implications.

In *R.A.V. v. City of St. Paul*, 112 U.S. 2538 (1992), the court overturned a municipal hate expression law. It ruled that a specific law that made speech illegal because of its discriminatory nature was a violation of the First Amendment. The law was found to be an unlawful attempt to control the content of speech and expression. Because many college and university speech codes were based on the same principles used to draft the municipal expression law, these campus codes became subject to additional legal challenges.

Illegal Acts, Not Speech

Campuses found more support for their efforts in *Mitchell v. Wisconsin*. In that case, the challenged law provided increased sanctions if an illegal act was bias-related. The Supreme Court upheld that statute. It noted that a variety of factors, including motivation, had always been considered in sentencing decisions. Campus codes that held additional or increased sanctions for bias-related incidents and violations were legally supportable.

While these cases worked their way through the legal system, George Mason University attempted to do what it thought was necessary to preserve its campus climate. Its attempt, however, led it into court with all of the other free speech and expression cases.

In spring 1991, the campus student union food service area was the site of an "ugly women" contest, a fundraiser for charity sponsored by one fraternity. Students were asked to select "winners" from a parade of fraternity members dressed as stereotypical women. While many judged the entire event to be distasteful, the most offensive entrant was dressed as a caricature of an African American woman.

George Mason began an investigation into the program after receiving many complaints about the racial and sexist nature of the program. The fraternity apologized, but sanctions were imposed against the organization. The school suspended its activities for a time, placed the group on a two-year probation, and limited activities to sanctioned pledging and charitable and educational efforts. Even these limited activities were restricted to programs related to sex and race discrimination.

The fraternity challenged the school's ruling in federal court. It argued that the skit and contest were protected by the First Amendment. The court ruled immediately in favor of the group, finding that the college had violated its constitutional rights. The decision was based on a presentation of case facts that were not in dispute. The university appealed.

Hostile Environment

George Mason wanted the court to understand the negative impact such events, if allowed, could have on the campus and on diversity efforts. It argued that the event created a hostile environment for women and blacks and would make future recruiting of a diversified population more difficult. But the appellate panel focused its attention on the First Amendment and its importance, not the event implications.

The court found the program distasteful and offensive, but noted that that was not the key issue. Of more importance legally was the right of the group to freely express itself. However, the conduct led the court to comment:

> The answer to the question of whether the First Amendment protects the fraternity's crude attempt at entertainment, however, is all the more difficult because of its obvious sophomoric nature.

The court found an answer to the First Amendment concerns based on case law. Generally, live entertainment, except that judged to be obscene, has been protected by courts. Several relevant examples were provided by the judge's decision, including offensive street performances (*Schact v. United States*, 398 U.S. 58 (1970)) and nude dancing (*Barnes v. Glen Theater, Inc.* 111 S.Ct. 2456 (1991)). Regardless of the entertainment value of the student event, the court found the performance protected by the Constitution.

George Mason failed in its attempt to convince the court that the entertainment was protected only if it portrayed a valuable message that was communicated to an audience. The court found that the skit had a message, but not one the school appreciated. Punishing the group for the message was not supportable. Said the ruling:

> The mischief was the university's punishment of those who scoffed at its goals of racial integration and gender neutrality, while permitting, even encouraging, conduct that would further the viewpoint expressed in the university's goals and probably embraced by a majority of society as well. The First Amendment generally prevents government from proscribing ... expressive conduct because of disapproval of the ideas expressed.

The institution was ordered to withdraw its sanctions against the organization. The expression, even though the campus and court found it racially and sexually offensive and crude, was held to be protected by the Constitution.

Of Significance ...

Two additional elements in the case are important for campus consideration. First, the case deals only with public institutions, leaving private colleges and universities more leeway in responding to speech and expression concerns. Finally, in a separate opinion, one justice did express other concerns over the campus attempts to sanction the group. These concerns were based on university approval of campus space for the event and the fact that this was not the first time the organization sponsored the event on campus.

All campus officials should keep in mind that when balancing the interests of a campus community with the

First Amendment rights of organizations and individuals, the courts have consistently sided with free speech and expression.

Creed Promotes Different Way to Handle Hate Speech

August 1992

You've probably read press coverage of the recent U.S. Supreme Court decision on free speech, which has focused on the difficulty of using regulations to control campus speech. Over 200 colleges and universities have attempted to attack the problems of hate speech and ethnoviolence through revised student conduct rules and policies. But many of these will be re-evaluated in the months ahead due to the high court's rejection of a municipal hate expression law. Some schools, particularly public institutions with codes based extensively on race or other key factors, will have to go back to the drawing board if they want to use regulations to control student speech.

One school that won't be redrafting regulations is the University of South Carolina. USC took a different approach to the national problems of attacks and insults based on race, sex, sexual orientation, or religious status. Instead of restrictive rules and regulations, USC went back to an old tried-and-true concept: an honor code. Using a traditional academic honor code as a base, what was developed was a social honor code. The end result, the "Carolinian Creed," promotes "civilized behavior" through an understanding of the obligations USC Community members have adopted. Of interest to other colleges and universities is the Creed, an explanation of it, and the steps that led to its development.

The Creed

The Carolinian Creed obligates members of the academic community to dedicate themselves to personal and academic excellence through allegiance to five institutional ideals. These require each member to pledge that they will observe the following precepts:

- Practice personal and academic integrity
- Respect the dignity of all persons
- Respect the rights and property of others
- Discourage bigotry while striving to learn from differences in people, ideas, and opinions
- Demonstrate concern for others, their feelings, and their need for conditions that support their work and development

As part of the Creed pledge, each member of the faculty, staff, or student body is required to "refrain from, and discourage, behaviors which threaten the freedom and respect every individual deserves."

Creed Comes with Explanation

To assist members of the academic community in implementing the Creed, USC developed a companion document to fully explain the Creed's intentions. In promoting the *integrity* ideal, the Creed requires a commitment not to cheat, lie, or practice "infidelity or disloyalty" in personal relationships. To respect *dignity*, the Creed asks that members refrain from activities that compromise or demean others, including hazing, intimidation, insults, harassment, and discrimination.

Respecting the *rights and property* of others involves avoiding theft, vandalism, and damage to property and behaviors that intrude on others' rights to enjoy privacy, move about, or express themselves freely.

To discourage *bigotry*, the Creed asks students and others to support affirmative action for all protected classes of persons.

To demonstrate *concern* for others, the explanatory statement from USC urges students and others to be "compassionate and considerate and to avoid behaviors that are insensitive or incited." Members of the community are also required not to act in a manner that would impact on the safety or feeling of welcome all deserve.

Implementation of the Creed requires all community members to avoid disrespectful or other acts of uncivilized behavior. It also demands that such inappropriate acts by others be "confronted and challenged" or reported to authorities.

Development of the Creed: A Consensus Approach

Several years ago, officials at USC shared the same concerns as others over hate speech and other offensive forms of expression. They looked at the efforts by other schools to deal with the problems through regulations. They found that many adopted regulations were limited in their effectiveness due to concerns over campus impact, political pressures, and First Amendment concerns and related litigation.

To develop an alternative campus response, a task force of leading and diverse faculty, staff, and students was formed. They were asked to explore how students are governed, why they don't observe or enforce the rules, and how campus standards could be promoted with new regulations. Because the group was large and represented a wide variety of interests, the task force started slowly, but still broadened its mission to include faculty and staff behaviors and other academic and policy matters.

The group studied what students bring with them to campus in terms of values and behaviors, how they learn while on campus, what they learn from each other, and how they can be influenced. The task force did a cultural audit of various subcultures on campus to understand what happens on campus and what influences each subculture.

After developing a set of values to be promoted, the task force needed a format for the values to be articulated. The group studied values and ethical statements from groups and organizations outside of higher education to get new ideas. After a review of many models, they decided to print a list of key values for wide distribution and a more explanatory version, including information on inconsistent behaviors.

The group's work was not done with the completion of the two texts. Task force members next established a plan for wide distribution of the Creed, with an emphasis on its use in orientation and first year experience programming. In addition, the group proposed that the Creed be introduced slowly and developed over time to build support.

Summary

The Carolinian Creed represents a significant and important departure from the traditional approach to campus hate expression. It takes the approach of firmly establishing standards for the community and clearly explaining them for all to understand.

Instead of focusing exclusively on negatives, the Creed adopts a positive vision of promoting values and respect and concern for others.

The Star-Spangled Banner and the Land of the Free

May 1991

Oh, say, can you see ... an end to the latest flap concerning flags on campus? Disputes have surfaced over the display of flags from residence hall windows, the burning of flags in protest, and the use of Confederate flags taken as a message of racial intolerance. If the flag serves as a political symbol, campus regulations must remain sensitive to First Amendment protections.

Campus Conflicts

Public displays of support for the troops serving in the Persian Gulf conflict involved yellow ribbons and the American flag. On some campuses, the displays included attempts to hang the flag from residence hall windows. In many cases, this practice violated campus policies based on safety and aesthetic factors. Most of the rules had been established to keep students from hanging unsafely out of residence hall windows or to keep campus buildings free of the unsightly clutter of banners, flags, signs, ribbons, towels, and underwear!

When campuses tried to enforce "no banners from the windows" rules, they ran into stiff opposition. Students, politicians, and columnists cried foul. They didn't understand how campuses could permit the flag to be burned, but not displayed. In response to public pressures, many campuses, such as the University of South Carolina and Cornell University (NY), relaxed their regulations and permitted expression through window flags. But now that the schools have altered their policies based on *content*, they'll have to redraw their regulations to limit speech and expression by only *time, place,* and *manner*.

How about protection for students who fly the Confederate flag, over the objections of some who claim it's a symbol of racism? At Harvard University, the display of the flag of the Old South from a house window sparked marches and protests. The campus president has indicated that he disapproves of the display, but that he understands that these students have First Amendment rights. Angry students have written the campus newspaper and demonstrated at the house flying the flag. In responding to student concerns, the president asked all students to be more aware of "the feelings and sensibilities of others."

The display of flags can send a message and evoke a response. But as we have seen, it's the issue of flag burning that can engulf a presidential election or disrupt a campus. Recent cases in Wisconsin, at Princeton University, and at the University of New Mexico involve disputes over flag abuse.

On the University of Wisconsin-River Falls campus, a political science professor trying to spark classroom debates over free expression burned a small desktop flag, sparking protests by students and parents. Accepting academic freedoms, the campus president has not condemned that act, but has called the display "extraordinarily bad judgment." Some 250 students reacted by gathering outside the professor's classroom with flags and singing the national anthem. The political science class was studying flag burning cases. Next class topic: abortion.

Two small flags were burned at Princeton University by a group known as Students for Social Responsibility. Students from another group grabbed a flag destined for desecration, and veterans' groups and conservative student organizations subsequently held counterdemonstrations. No charges were filed.

Attacks on flag burners this year at the University of New Mexico could result in legal action against UNM or the assailants. Two students burning a flag on campus were accosted by other students. The protesters complained that campus police had been notified in advance but didn't intervene to protect them. The two are considering a negligence suit against the force for breech of "duty and responsibility."

To fully appreciate these cases, it's necessary to understand the law of flag burning.

Flag Desecration

Can the flag be legally burned for a political purpose? While the laws have consistently said "no," in recent times the courts have moved toward "yes." Since the street protests and violence of the 1960s, the U.S. Supreme Court has protected those who use the flag to send a message. In the past two decades, the Supreme Court has decided several flag burning cases that led the way for the recent precedent-setting case, *Texas v. Johnson*, 109 S.Ct. 2533 (1989).

In 1969, the Court heard a case involving the burning of a flag on a Manhattan street corner. The burner was arrested for mutilating the flag and casting verbal contempt on it. Citing a lack of a record to show whether the arrest was for his "acts" or his "words," the Court overturned the conviction in *Street v. New York*, 394 U.S. 576 (1969). But in doing so, it gave little guidance to others on the status of the law.

Several years later, the Court faced the case of the student who used a small flag to patch the backside of his blue jeans! Was this "contemptuous treatment" of the flag?

Convicted and sentenced to six months in prison, the man appealed, in *Smith v. Goguen*, 415 U.S. 566 (1974), claiming First Amendment protection. Again, the Court overturned a flag abuse conviction, this time on the grounds that the statute was too vague to be enforced.

That same year, the Court considered a college student's protest over the Kent State University killings. The student taped a peace symbol on a flag, then hung it from a window upside down. When the police confronted him, he agreed to remove the flag but was arrested for "improper use." In *Spence v. Washington*, 418 U.S. 405 (1974), the Court reversed the criminal conviction.

In overturning the related state law, the Court raised three issues for consideration:

- Is the use of the flag a "communication" deserving judicial protection?
- How does the "setting" affect protection levels?
- What is the importance of the interests of the state being protected?

In *Spence*, the Court found that the student's use of the flag as a sign of protest was a legitimate expression, tied to a traumatic event and therefore protected.

Finally, in 1989, the Court again was asked to deal with flag abuse, as it reviewed the conviction of a demonstrator at a political convention. In *Texas v. Johnson*, 109 S.Ct. 2533 (1989), the Court devised a three-part test, asking the following questions:

- Is the flag act "expressive conduct"?
- Does the violated law serve a state interest?
- Is there a "compelling" need for the state to have the content-based law?

In overturning another flag burning conviction, the Court felt that the burning of a flag at a political convention sent a political message. As such, the act was protected. Said the Court:

If there is a bedrock principle underlying the First Amendment, it is that government may not prohibit the expression of an ideal simply because society finds the idea itself offensive or disagreeable. We have not recognized an exception to this principle even where our flag has been involved.

Summary

While the U.S. flag flies higher than all others by protocol, it is not protected from use or abuse to send political or social messages. The First Amendment protects free expression, even when the flag is involved. On campuses, students can use flags to send messages that are positive or negative, under protection of law. Campus policies and enforcement efforts need to be sensitive to these principles.

Residence Halls: What's Private? What's Public?

May 1991

It seemed simple: go door to door in the residence halls collecting signatures on a petition concerning environmental issues. The group's goal was to get students to write their legislators. Campus police gave their permission, but the students were stopped at the doors. It was campus policy: no canvassing in the residence halls.

That's the rule at the University of North Carolina-Chapel Hill and many other campuses. But some UNC students, like the environmental coalition, want the regulation changed to permit open access to students. Can they challenge the policy on legal grounds?

Protected Speech

Courts have held that there's a significant difference in constitutional protections between *commercial speech*, that is, for profit — and *non-commercial speech* — for social or political interests. Public institutions are allowed more freedom to place restraints on commercial speech than on non-commercial speech. Most canvassing in residence halls can be classified as non-commercial speech — generally student attempts to get other students involved in campus, local, and national political activities or social issues.

Restraints against campus commercial speech in residential areas have been legally tested in recent years, in the series of pots and pans sales cases from Pennsylvania and New York, including *Fox v. Board of Trustees of the State University of New York*, 841 F.2d 1207 (1988).

Three Principles Behind the Policies

Bans against residence hall canvassing are generally based on three principles:

- Student rights to privacy
- Security concerns
- The need to protect the educationaláenvironment

Campuses have argued that students in residence halls deserve *privacy* in their living areas. Bedrooms should not be considered public areas, open to all for solicitation or canvassing. Some campuses say students should be able to live in an environment free from unrequested contacts.

Open access by outsiders can also compromise *security* efforts. Restricting residence hall floors to residents and invited guests makes it easier to maintain security, a growing concern on campus.

Also of primary importance is the preservation of the residential *living and learning environment*. Residence halls do not provide lodging alone: they provide a system of education and student development. It's important to control that environment, which could be threatened by access by solicitors and canvassers.

Justifiably concerned with student privacy, security, and the learning environment, campuses have adopted rules and regulations that ban or restrict door-to-door canvassing in residence halls.

Campus Case Law

Students at Northern Illinois University were unhappy with a total ban on canvassing in residence halls. When they asked for changes, the university proposed loosening the rules if supported by a student referendum and a vote by individual floors. Some students took NIU to court to challenge the process, claiming that use of a referendum violated constitutional freedoms of expression and association. In *James v. Nelson*, 349 F.Supp. 1061 (1972), a federal district court ruled that use of a referendum was indeed an infringement on student rights and that the campus could not totally ban canvassing in the residence halls.

Restraints on voter registration were challenged in *National Movement for the Student Vote v. Regents of the University of California*, 123 Cal. Rptr. 1œ1 (1975). In conflict were local laws permitting registration at residences and UCLA rules limiting residence hall canvassing. Students complained about being approached in the halls by outsiders about voter registration. The campus decided to limit the registration process to open public residence hall areas, like the building lobbies. The voter registration drive went to court, seeking permission to go door to door.

The state court found no constitutional right to canvass in the residence halls. In order to serve a legitimate school purpose, UCLA could set reasonable time, place, and manner restraints. The court recognized the school's interests in providing students with privacy and security.

Access to the residence halls for non-commercial speech was also tested in *Brush v. Pennsylvania State University*, 414 A.2d 48 (1980). The state Supreme Court was asked to judge the constitutionality of a canvassing ban imposed by a student vote. Campus rules permitted floors to be closed to canvassing if the residents voted to adopt that policy. Canvassing was then limited to the building lobbies or by invitation to student rooms, but canvassers were free to seek invitations by phone.

Some students living in a restricted area challenged the policy. They argued that the floor hallways should be considered public areas like the lobbies, claiming they were like public highways, open for travel. They based their case on the Constitution, specifically on the freedoms of speech and assembly.

Viewing the case as a First Amendment issue, the court based its decision on a balancing of institutional and individual rights. The court noted that in some cases, reasonable limitations can be placed on speech. But limitations cannot be based on *content*; they can address only *time*, *place*, and *manner*. Above all else, the limitations must further a significant institutional interest. The least restrictive method of achieving the necessary results will receive the greatest judicial support. So campus rules must be crafted to limit speech and conduct only at the minimum necessary level.

In *Brush*, the court held that Penn State had met these conditions. The university enforced the ban on door-to-door canvassing uniformly, dealing with the time, place, and manner of the canvassing and not the content. And finally, the rule served a legitimate campus purpose, as it protected student privacy, security, and the educational environment. Since the university ensured other means for canvassers to contact students, including the lobbies, the telephone, group meetings, and the mail, the court held the restrictions on individual speech rights to be permissible. It should be noted that these same rules, when applied to the sale of pots and pans, led to the commercial speech cases, such as *Fox*.

Canvassing for political votes and voter registration were the issues before a state appellate court in *Harrell v. Southern Illinois University*, 457 N.E. 2d 971 (1983). The university had two policies: one that allowed election canvassing during the period just prior to elections, and a second that limited registration efforts to lobby areas. SIU also limited non-political canvassers and solicitors to lobby areas. The county clerk went door to door to get students to vote and was thrown out by school officials. So he went to court, claiming that SIU was unlawfully using two different standards on canvassing.

The court looked at the school's reasons for the rules, found valid interests in need of protection, and upheld campus rules designed to protect the living and learning environment in the least restrictive manner. But the court extended the time period for door-to-door solicitation from 30 to 60 days to allow for voter registration.

Summary

As shown by cases such as *Nelson*, *National Movement*, *Brush*, and *Harrell*, free speech isn't necessarily free. While the pots and pans cases dealt with commercial speech, challenges to campus canvassing laws have helped to define non-commercial institutional and individual rights. Campuses must adopt the least restrictive means in limiting residence hall speech to protect governmental interests of student privacy, security, and educational atmosphere. In drafting canvass restrictions, campuses should:

- Determine the important governmental need to be advanced by the restriction
- Establish regulations that are the "least restrictive,"
- Make sure that the rules and their purpose can be justified

Environmentally concerned students at the University of North Carolina-Chapel Hill can challenge the campus ban on canvassing. They will have to show that the rule isn't related to significant campus interests and that it is overly restrictive. Others before them, with similar arguments against restrictions on non-commercial speech, haven't been too successful.

Campus Art: The Limits of the First Amendment

February 1992

Consider this brief smattering of cases — only a sampling of a growing campus concern:

- An artist is suing her alma mater over the removal of art work from a community college campus. In a suit against Mohawk Valley Community College (NY), the artist contends that the school illegally removed a photographic display from a gallery, violating the First Amendment. College officials contend that the exhibit was not appropriate for a campus cultural center because it included nude subjects. They pulled photographs they found inappropriate because the gallery was visible from a child care center. In her suit against Mohawk Valley, the artist seeks damages to compensate for the time and money spent developing the display.

- Strong negative reaction to campus-imposed rules for an exhibit led to the cancellation of the entire show at the University of Wisconsin-Madison. A campus education center planned to sponsor a student show but prohibited the display of art with sexually explicit themes, religious or political messages, or works judged to be inappropriate for youth or the general public. Student artists objected to the restrictions, and instead of changing the rules cancelled the show.

- "Scents and Shivers," an art display at Valencia Community College (FL), caused community and political uproar. The contemporary art exhibit featured images of nudity and religious symbolism. Local ministers came to campus to complain and ultimately got their national religious organizations involved. Some members came in, took unauthorized photographs of the displays, and sent them — devoid of their contexts — to members of the state legislature. As a result, several lawmakers joined the protest, and vowed that such an exhibit would never be permitted in the future. The art exhibit was also used by the religious organization and a tele-evangelist for fund-raising purposes.

- Rosary beads and nude subjects in a student art display at LaGuardia Community College (NY) led to a conflict on campus. The work of two photography majors was covered with black paper by an instructor who was responding to campus complaints about "offensive" art. But in the end, the paper came down and the photographs stayed up.

- A photograph on display in an Arizona State University classroom has at least one student complaining of sexual harassment. On the classroom wall in the photography department are works by previous students, including some with nude subjects. An upset student complained to campus officials without success. Citing the First Amendment and academic freedom, officials kept the display up.

- Student art work involving sexual displays and religious objects has been challenged by community residents surrounding the University of North Carolina. While community and religious leaders call the display "blasphemous," campus officials support free expression.

- A student play, containing sex and violence, had serious problems at the University of Alabama, where the show didn't go on! Federal courts upheld the school's decision that the campus playhouse was not an open forum for unlimited free speech and expression.

- Few public schools, it seems, could avoid the temptation of challenging the film *The Last Temptation of Christ*. Legal actions and demonstrations at Oklahoma State and New Mexico State were examples of this. In most places, the film finally made it to the screen, and at NMU, the school ended up paying for the legal costs that got it there!

- Finally, response to a play about AIDS, *The Normal Heart*, almost overwhelmed Southwest Missouri State University. The president's insistence that "the show must go on" earned the wrath of several influential state legislators.

From Mohawk Valley to Southwest Missouri State, and at schools in between and beyond, the potential for controversy over campus arts is a very real and growing concern. In the aftermath of challenges to the public art gallery displays of the late Robert Mapplethorpe's photography exhibition, it is important for campuses to understand the law and how it can be applied to them.

A federal Circuit Court of Appeals heard a case of this exact nature over two decades ago. The art display on campus went up, then came down, after persons who were offended complained. In *Close v. Lederle*, 424 F.2d 988, an art instructor from the University of Massachusetts sued the state, complaining that the school violated his freedom of expression. UMass had earlier invited him to display his works in a public corridor. But after the work went up, school officials removed it after concerns were raised over offending persons who walked through the area.

In deciding the case, the court balanced the interests of both sides. It recognized that art is protected as free expression, but it also recognized that the public has rights as well. The court decided that the art works deserved less protection under the law than other forums of social or political thought and upheld the school's action. Said the panel, art of this type is "not entitled to the same degree of First Amendment protection as students' rights to hear unpopular speakers."

The *Close* decision is of interest to those concerned about these issues today, but is not necessarily controlling. Campus programs and policies should consider the following issues when dealing with the display of art and the potential for controversy and litigation:

- The First Amendment and the principles of academic freedom and free expression will apply to some extent to any such policies.
- Campus facilities are not public forums open to all, but use of facilities should not be governed solely by the content of programs, particularly at public institutions.
- Campus policies on art and artistic expression should be developed in advance of exhibitions, displays, or performances. The policies can be established after full consideration of the law and consultation with faculty, students, staff, and the community, if desirable.

Are you prepared for the next "questionable" campus art exhibit, film, or play? If not that one, the one that follows? Consider now the delicate balance between free expression and institutional rights and responsibilities and plan accordingly.

Is Art Protected by the First Amendment?

July 1994

Colleges and universities have watched with interest the disturbances at San Francisco State University involving a mural of Malcolm X. The painting, located on a student union wall, depicted the slain civil rights activist surrounded by Stars of David, a skull and cross bones, and dollar signs. After the 100-square-foot mural was splashed with red paint, campus officials ordered its removal. Jewish students had complained to officials that the painting was anti-semitic. Black students complained that its removal was "insensitive" to them and their interests.

Artistic expression on campus has always been a subject for much discussion and debate. In recent months, campus art has provoked contentious responses beyond San Francisco State, to higher education institutions in Alabama, Nebraska, and Texas. In each case, campus officials weighed carefully the balance between freedom of expression and offense to the audience. How might the law respond? The principles established in higher education free expression cases involving art and film may help guide future decisions.

Campus Concerns

The San Francisco State University mural is only the most recent and most widely publicized "art on campus" debate. It is not an isolated incident. The University of Alabama-Birmingham has taken some criticism for a purchase of artwork made last year. A photograph, purchased with private funds, that displays Michelangelo's *Pieta* in a tank of human waste and blood has created problems. Individuals and church groups have objected to the acquisition, claiming the work is "offensive." The state legislature has denounced the purchase as well.

Last fall, the state governor joined the protest movement, calling on UAB to take the artwork down from campus display. In a press release, the state leader called the piece "inappropriate and in poor taste." But UAB said the art *had never been* publicly displayed. To date, it has been used only for curriculum-related, educational purposes.

Campus officials defended the acquisition, arguing that the campus is a place for the exchange of ideas. Said a UAB spokesperson: "If we exchanged or explored only non-controversial ideas, we strongly believe that we would not fulfill our responsibilities as a university."

At North Lake College (TX), a painting depicting a Ku Klux Klan lynching was displayed; it got an immediate reaction. The artist involved said her painting was intended to send an anti-racist message. Local NAACP officials contended that the work was "insulting" and argued that students could not be "expected to learn" in a setting with that artwork. The painting had been hanging on a wall between the campus bookstore and a food service area. It has since been moved to a closed area, to be seen on request only.

In Nebraska, a painting of Nazi leader Heinrich Himmler, which hangs in the school library, has created a controversy. At Midland Lutheran College, a senior asked for removal of the artwork, which was done by a former faculty member. The painting of the man who headed the Nazi secret police in World War II is five feet wide and shows Himmler wearing a swastika arm band.

It has been hanging in the library for more than 10 years, without any comment or concern. According to the artist, the painting was intended to make viewers consider the "nature of evil." The student's request for removal has received a "cool reception."

Case Law

Artistic expression on campus has been tested in a variety of cases. Various principles of Constitutional rights have been explored in these legal challenges.

Consider the case of *Hail Mary*, a film that created a minor sensation in the mid-1980s. Attacked by some for blasphemy, the movie sparked debate and picketing nationwide and resulted in litigation on college campuses. At the University of Nebraska, the film was selected to be shown in spring 1986 by a staff member responsible for an art gallery theater. Two days after the schedule of the film series was first publicized, the complaints started coming in.

The most significant call came from a state senator opposed to the film. Based on reviews, she contended that the movie was offensive and could lead to unsafe protests and demonstrations. In conversation with the Center's director, she reminded him of past state debates over gallery funding and said she would personally introduce a resolution against the film in the legislature. Telephone calls to the campus president and system chancellor were threatened by the lawmaker. After a gallery attempt to defuse the situation, the director finally cancelled the film. He concluded that the movie was "offensive to a segment of society and did not merit the efforts it would take to defend it."

Unauthorized Use of Political Power

The director's decision was tested in *Brown v. Board of Regents of the University of Nebraska*, 669 F.Supp. 297 (1985). A federal district court considered the issue of a constitutional right of people to view artistic expressions. The Court did find a right in the law to receive information and ideas, using precedents set in public libraries. In cases involving books viewed by some as "Anti-American, Anti-Christian, Anti-Semitic, and just plain filthy," the courts ruled that First Amendment rights are "infringed by the removal of books from the library stacks." The courts supported the premise that:

> the right to receive ideas is fundamental to the recipient's meaningful exercise of his own rights of speech, press and political freedom.

In reviewing the Nebraska cancellation of a controversial film, the court found that the school cancelled the movie due to political controversy. It yielded to the threats of a legislator, who "threatened the peace and stability" of the gallery. According to the court, this was an unauthorized use of political power. It noted:

> What is at stake is the right to receive information and to be exposed to controversial ideas — a fundamental First Amendment right. If (the film) can be banned by those opposed to (the) ideological theme, then a precedent is set for the removal of any such work.

University students were denied the right to receive controversial ideas because a state legislator intervened, judging the content of the film to be offensive. *Hail Mary* was judicially returned to the campus film schedule.

Two decades earlier, a federal appellate panel considered the display of controversial artwork on college campuses. At the University of Massachusetts-Amherst, an art exhibit was quickly taken down by campus officials when complaints about its offensive nature were received. In *Close v. Lederle*, 424 F.2d 988, a faculty member in the arts sued his own school, claiming a constitutional violation of his rights of expression.

His exhibit was originally placed in a busy campus corridor for all to see. But after receiving complaints, the works were taken away. In hearing the case, the court attempted to balance the rights of expression with other rights. Artwork, said the court, was entitled to less protection than other forms of social and political thought. The panel supported the campus attempt to move the display away from passersby.

Cases such as *Brown* and *Close* can help campuses review art-related issues. But colleges and universities should carefully consider other issues as well in an effort to respect the law and balance competing interests.

Before the next controversy, develop campus policies on the showing of art and the demonstration of artistic expression. Share the policies in advance of all exhibitions, displays, or performances as part of any agreement with artists or program sponsors. The policies should be based on an appreciation of the First Amendment and academic freedom, and should not focus solely on the content of the expression.

Separating the Church from the State

June 1994

> Congress shall make no law respecting an establishment of religion, or prohibiting the free exercise thereof.
>
> — First Amendment, U.S. Constitution

As a nation originally founded by those fleeing religious persecution, an intentional separation of church and state was established by law. Over the past two years, several cases have brought colleges and universities to court on issues such as religion in the classroom, religious discrimination in employment, funding for religious student organizations, religious events on campus, and prayer at commencement exercises. These cases clearly demonstrate the "tightrope" higher education walks when dealing with religion.

Classrooms

Can a public university instructor speak of faith in the classroom? In *Bishop v. Aronov*, 926 F.2d 1066 (11th Cir. 1991), a federal appellate panel reviewed a University of Alabama order limiting the topics an education instructor could talk about in class. The school action came in response to student complaints. The instructor sued, asking for protection of "academic freedoms."

A district court ruled in his favor, ordering Alabama to stop interfering in classroom presentations as long as personal religious belief comments were made only occasionally. An appeal overturned that decision. In *Bishop*, the appellate court said a school can "establish the parameters of focus and general subject matter of the curriculum." A reasonable restriction by the campus could limit classroom materials to curriculum subject matter.

Employment

After working for the Catholic college for 20 years, finally serving as the vice president for student affairs for four years, he was fired. He sued, arguing that he was let go due to his religion. The college contended that it was exempt from laws against religious discrimination due to its church control.

In *Scheiber v. St. John's University*, 600 N.Y.SD. 2d 734 (1993), a New York court agreed that it was legal and appropriate for a church-related school to give a preference to members of the faith in high level administrative hiring under state law. The court also noted that the vice president served at will and was subject to termination without notice or cause at any time.

Student Organizations

Two cases considered use of campus or student activity funds for religious-based student organizations. At the University of Virginia and the University of Hawaii, funding was ultimately denied by the courts. At Virginia, campus Board of Visitors guidelines prohibiting student activity funding were challenged. A Christian organization that published a quarterly magazine said the denial violated constitutional free speech and free exercise of religious rights. The group filed suit in 1990 after a student council rejected the magazine's request for $6,000 in activity funds. The student council had funded Muslim and Jewish student groups but did so based on their "cultural activities." University officials said the funding policy was legal and noted that religious organizations have access to the students and campus, regardless of funding. A U.S. Court of Appeals (4th Cir.) ruled earlier this year that the UVa policy is constitutional. But *Rosenberger v. Rector and Visitors of the University of Virginia*, 18 F.3d 269 (1994), was appealed to the Supreme Court.

A similar suit against a University of Hawaii policy was filed by students in 1991. Four campus religious organizations had been granted funding by their student government in 1989. The money was for Bible studies and workshops on specific religious issues and perspectives. Saying the grants violated separation of church and state principles, the ACLU threatened to sue. In response, Hawaii developed a new evaluation process for student fee funds.

The process was based on a key U.S. Supreme Court case, *Lemon v. Kurtzman*, 403 U.S. 602 (1971). In judging public funding for student materials and services at non-public schools, the Court created a three part test for constitutionality:

- A law or regulation must have a secular purpose.
- It must not foster excessive entanglement with religion.
- Its primary effect must be one that neither advances nor inhibits religion.

Using the *Lemon* test, the University of Hawaii rejected funding for student religious organizations. The organizations responded with legal action, claiming that the denial violated their free speech and free association rights. After a federal district court upheld the Hawaii policy, the student organizations asked the U.S. Court of Appeals (9th Cir.) to review their claim. The court panel supported the university policy, noting that:

> Between the two extremes of denying student religious groups all financial support, on one hand, and subsidizing indisputably religious activities, on the other, the university has wide latitude in adopting a funding policy to allocate the limited resources available to promote student extracurricular activities.

Relying on a tradition of judicial deference to campus decision-making, the court respected the system of student activity fee funding evaluations developed by the university.

Events

Is the campus event a cultural program or a religious ceremony? Campus and university officials at Northern Illinois University dealt with this question when a Native American pow wow raised constitutional concerns. Administrators were informed that the program was a religious event, but student leaders contributed $9,000 in fees under the impression that it was a social or cultural activity. Student government policies prohibit the financing of religious programming.

To avoid problems with access to the campus and funding, program organizers quickly agreed that the event was strictly cultural.

Prayer

The public university debate over public prayer continued at the University of Nebraska, as prayer at commencement exercises was reconsidered. Prayer before football games at the University of Oklahoma was also ontested.

At Nebraska, prayer returned to commencement exercises after being replaced in the program by a moment of silence. After the U.S. Supreme Court indicated that prayer at public high school programs was unconstitutional, Nebraska dropped prayer. But students supported non-denominational prayer in referendum and negotiated its return with campus officials.

At Oklahoma, the prayer issue revolved around sporting events and Freedom of Information laws. A student who challenged prayer led by a faculty member before football games demanded and finally received copies of related university policies and legal opinions. The now graduated student had threatened to sue over prayer.

OU officials say the pre-game prayer is an "invocation," more like a speech than a prayer. It reminds "spectators and players of the importance of sportsmanship and fair play" without reference to a deity. The invocation, part of campus sporting events since 1957, passes the *Lemon* test, according to OU. The former student has consulted with counsel about possible litigation.

While separation of church and state is an accepted legal principle, it is consistently tested and re-interpreted in today's higher education environment And it is often determined by the courts, not the campuses.

Note: In summer 1995, the U.S. Supreme Court ruled in *Rosenberger* that the denial of student fee funding to a campus religious publication is unconstitutional. The University of Virginia shortly thereafter adopted a refund system for students objecting to the use of activity funds for all publications. (For more information, see "Campus Funding of Student groups — Again!," chapter 11.)

Top Court to Consider Higher Case

September 1991

It's hard to get the campus ceremony or special event off to a good start when the first activity is contentious. And that's the case with prayers at commencement ceremonies and other occasions.

Most of the disputes that have reached the courts have been at the elementary or high school level, but the debate won't stop there. Campuses need to understand the issues and consider responses before becoming a battleground over prayers.

Courts around the country have been divided over the issue.

In Virginia, a federal court allowed prayers to start a high school graduation ceremony where attendance was voluntary and students paid the expenses.

In two Pennsylvania cases, prayers were also upheld, because at commencement they were not part of the curriculum and not supervised by teachers. It was also noted that student attendance for the ceremonies was voluntary. In the classroom, attendance was compulsory, so no prayer was allowed. But at the voluntary graduation program, public prayer was found to be, at most, a "technical violation."

In a Michigan high school case, the Sixth U.S. Circuit Court of Appeals approved the delivery of a brief invocation and benediction at graduation ceremonies. Four factors were considered in the ruling:

- Ceremony attendance was voluntary.
- Parents and other adults were present, not just students.
- The prayers were short and took place only once a year.
- The prayers were not intended or used to promote any one religion.

However, prayer at other high school graduation ceremonies has not always been judicially approved. This spring, the California Supreme Court ruled against commencement prayers at public high schools and Texas courts have struck down prayers before public school sporting events.

Some courts have applied the U.S. Supreme Court's test for the separation of church and state to graduation and other education ceremony prayers. The test asks if:

- The government's prayer purpose is secular or religious.
- The effect of the government prayer promotes one religion or even religion in general.
- The prayer gets government too entangled into religion.

Courts applying the test have often concluded that ceremony prayers do, in fact, violate the Constitution's separation of church and state principles.

By next year, however, there may be a new test for education ceremony prayers. The Supreme Court has agreed to hear arguments over prayer rules in Providence, Rhode Island. At that time, the issues will be fully debated, and the decision may help settle what is becoming an increasingly hot issue.

Until then, consider the following:

- Remember that a split Supreme Court allowed the display of religious symbols on public grounds, as long as they are only part of a larger generic holiday display.

- Remember that the Supreme Court and Congress begin their sessions with prayers or references to God.

If prayers are offered at public education ceremonies, they should be on behalf of the general community, they should not promote any one religion or religion in general, and they should use words that can be applied to many faiths, not one in particular.

For the next year, pray at your own risk — and hope that the Supreme Court will establish clear guidelines for public ceremony prayer soon, before the issue splits higher education as it already has split high schools and communities.

Courts Examine Church-State Relationships

July 1990

Religious activities at public institutions always raise the same question: Whatever happened to the "separation" of church and state? A North Carolina State University student, going door-to-door in the residence halls to talk about his faith, ran into that question a few years ago. As is often the case in church-state disputes involving public facilities, the courts were called on to settle the matter. Whether it's door to door proselytizing or church services in campus facilities, religious use of public places raises legal considerations for close review.

An early test occurred in 1974. University of Delaware students went to court to seek permission to hold religious services on campus. One group, predominantly Roman Catholic, wanted to use a residence hall lounge, but the university refused.

It banned all religious use of facilities, citing the First Amendment's "establishment" clause — that "Congress shall make no law respecting an establishment of religion, or prohibiting the free exercise thereof." School rules prohibited campus involvement in what could be seen as the "establishment" of religion. But students and religious leaders read further into the language and argued that the ban infringed on their "free exercise" of religion. At trial, the court upheld the school ban, but the decision was appealed to the state supreme court in *Keegan v. University of Delaware,* 349 A.2d 14 (1975).

Three-Part Judicial Review

In reviewing the facts, the court first looked at legal tests for church-state involvements. A series of U.S. Supreme Court decisions has established a three-part judicial review for cases involving the "establishment" of religion. Courts can uphold government policies on religion if the policies:

- Have a secular legal purpose
- As a primary purpose neither advance nor inhibit religion
- Do not foster excessive government entanglement with religion

(See *Lemon v. Kurtzman,* 91 S.Ct. 2105, 1971; *Committee for Public Education v. Regan,* 100 S.Ct. 840, 1980; and *Roemer v. Maryland Public Works Board,* 96 S.Ct. 2337, 1976.)

In *Keegan,* the court found that student use of a residence hall lounge wouldn't violate the establishment clause. Students were free to use the rooms for various purposes, and religion could be one of those purposes — as long as the same rules that applied to other groups were applied to religious groups. The university could allow groups to use the room for services, but such permission didn't constitute support of religion: the school could still remain legally neutral as required by law.

The court went further to find that religious services on campus might even serve an educational purpose. It saw students coming together in a common area to share thoughts and ideas as an acceptable use of state facilities. Ruling that a ban on religious worship on campus prohibited students' free exercise of religion, the court overturned the school rule.

Use of campus facilities for religious services became a U.S. Supreme Court issue in *Widmar v. Vincent,* 102 S.Ct. 269 (1981). Students at the University of Missouri-Kansas City wanted to use campus space for religious meetings and worship. But the school's Board of Curators had earlier banned the use of facilities for religious worship or teaching, and the ban was applied to student organizations with religious affiliations. An evangelical student group filed suit against the school, claiming that the ban violated their free exercise of religion and free speech.

At trial, in *Chess v. Widmar,* 480 F.Supp. 907 (1979), the federal district court sided with the school, finding that the ban on religious worship and teaching was justifiable. But the Eighth Circuit Court of Appeals reversed the decision, ruling in favor of the students.

The court found the school ban to be unconstitutional. It violated free speech protection by placing restrictions based on content, allowing speech of some types but not speech on religion. While courts have upheld limited government rights to control the time, place and manner of speech, very few restrictions on the *content* of speech are permissible.

"An Open Forum"

The Supreme Court agreed with the appellate court. The Court also looked at the case from another free speech perspective. The campus was generally open to meetings and events by student groups. The Court saw this as creating a public forum. The school didn't have to open up as a forum; but once it did, it couldn't make decisions on use based on the content of speech.

The Court then applied the simple three-part test for violations of the establishment clause to conclude that the ban wasn't constitutional. The Court reasoned that a campus open forum, "including non-discrimination against religious speech," wouldn't necessarily advance religion unlawfully. Said the Court:

> We are not oblivious to the range of an open forum's likely effects. It is possible — perhaps even foreseeable — that religious groups will benefit from access to university facilities. But this Court has explained that a religious organization's enjoyment of merely "incidental" benefits does not violate the prohibition against the "primary advancement" of religion.

The Court went on to reason that religious use of a public forum can't be deemed state "establishment" of religion. Many other groups, some extremely objectionable to a majority of persons (the Court cited the Students for a Democratic Society and the Young Socialist Alliance as examples) were entitled to use campus public forums without necessarily implying state sponsorship or endorsement. Therefore, the "primary" focus of the campus open forum wouldn't be the advancement of religion, said the Court, since hundreds of varied groups were recognized to use facilities. Religious groups could or should represent only a minority of the public forum usage, making the forum lawful.

Summarizing its decision, the Court noted that:

> the state interest asserted here — in achieving greater separation of church and state than is already ensured under the establishment clause of the federal Constitution — is limited by the free exercise clause and in this case by the free speech clause as well. In this constitutional context, we are unable to recognize the state's interest as sufficiently "compelling" to justify content-based discrimination against respondents' (students') religious speech.

Widmar established important rights for students seeking to use public campus facilities for religious speech. However, the Court's ruling is not a blanket approval of all religious activity on campus. The decision allows equal access to campus services by all student groups; it doesn't open all doors to all visitors.

Campus regulations can appropriately limit access to open forums and limit access to non-members of the campus community. Campuses can still maintain and enforce controls over student groups, as long as the regulations promote a state interest and are not content-based. *Widmar* also included two possible exclusions for religious speech on campus in public forums:

- Where it is shown that the religious groups will dominate the forum, making it primarily for religious purposes

- Where the campus has limited facilities and must balance competing requests for space

The *Widmar* support of equal access in campus public forums has become the standard for judging religious services on public campuses. Courts review campus policies to ensure that they don't violate the three-part test for the establishment clause, and courts place great emphasis on students' claims of free speech and free exercise of religion.

Door-to-Door Religion

The North Carolina State University student attempted to go beyond the "public forum" when he went door to door in the residence halls to speak about religion. In *Chapman v. Thomas*, 743 F.2d 1056 (1984), the Fourth Circuit Court of Appeals was asked to rule on a campus ban of residence hall solicitations.

The campus allowed activities in residence hall commons rooms and lobbies, but not hallways. The student was disciplined for violating the rule but appealed to the courts. He claimed that the school unconstitutionally violated his rights to free speech and free exercise of religion by denying him access to the residence halls.

In court, the school cited various reasons for the ban on door-to-door activities, including safety, privacy, and quiet. Students running for student government office were the only exceptions to the ban.

The court upheld the door-to-door ban as reasonable. It found the residential areas of the residence halls to be non-public, so the *Widmar* principles didn't apply. The campus traditionally had kept residence hallways free from outside intrusion and had permitted public access to residents in common areas such as lounges and lobbies. The court supported the campus' right to establish time, place and manner regulations on speech in non-public forums on campus.

The court dealt with the claim of content discrimination in another manner. The student claimed he was disciplined solely for the content of his speech, since student politicians were free to go door to door. But the court found campus elections to be a critical part of student governance and understood why candidates were allowed into the residence halls.

Thus, in *Chapman*, free speech and free exercise of religion claims were argued, but to a different conclusion than in *Keegan* or *Widmar*. The key difference was the *location* of the religious speech. In a public forum, religious speech is entitled to equal access as any other speech. In non-public areas, speech and exercise of religion can be limited or eliminated, based on legitimate campus needs and concerns.

Campuses are not obligated to create campus public forums; once created, however, forums must be open equally to all. In open forums, discrimination against religious speech is unlawful and can be subjected to constitutional challenge, as shown by *Keegan* and *Widmar*. But reasonable campus controls over non-public areas will be supported, as in *Chapman*.

The First Amendment cautions public institutions to avoid either establishing religion or interfering in the exercise of religion. Cases such as *Keegan*, *Widmar*, and *Chapman* provide good guidance when dealing with the religious use of campus facilities.

Regulating the Press: How Far Can Campuses Go?

May 1993

The university's rule was simple: No one could hand-distribute publications on campus if those publications contained advertising. Such publications could only be dispensed at newsstands, tables, or booths, or through subscriptions.

Standing near building entrances or in parking lots to distribute commercial publications was also prohibited.

Southwest Texas State University officials said the school's rule was designed to control solicitation and help maintain an appropriate educational atmosphere on campus. But some challengers called the rule an infringement on free speech and freedom of the press.

The role of the press on campus continues to be debated, of course, despite case law that provides certain protections for published materials and their distribution on campus. In going to court recently, STSU became the latest of many public institutions that have attempted to limit the student press or distribution of publications on campus.

Past cases focused on:

- Suspensions of students whose publications printed "foul" language
- Rules against the hand-distribution of certain papers on campus
- Funding changes in response to controversial issues

If your campus wants to regulate the press or limit the distribution of certain publications, make sure you and other officials understand the impact of these court decisions.

Court Protects "Mere Dissemination"

In a 1973 case, a University of Missouri-Columbia student was expelled for her on-campus distribution of a newspaper judged to contain "indecent speech."

A conduct committee ruled that the student had violated "generally accepted standards of conduct." Her "offensive" action: distributing an underground newspaper that used explicit language and depicted the Statue of Liberty in sexual terms.

The student's challenge of her expulsion was reviewed by the U.S. Supreme Court in *Papish v. Board of Curators of the University of Missouri*, 410 U.S. 667 (1973). Lower federal courts had ruled in favor of the university, finding the student's publication "obscene" and, therefore, not entitled to constitutional protection.

An appellate panel had ruled that even if the publication had not been "obscene," it could still have been controlled by the school. Based on other campus interests, the court said, "The Constitution does not compel the University ... [to allow] such publications ... to be publicly sold or distributed on its open campus."

But the Supreme Court disagreed with that assessment. It noted that "mere dissemination of ideas — no matter how offensive to good taste — on a state university may not be shut off in the name alone of 'conventions of decency.'"

In other words, the Court said, the school had violated previous free speech rulings by punishing the student for the "content" of her newspaper rather than for the time, place, or manner of its distribution. The Court returned the student, and the newspaper, to campus.

Restricted Distribution

Efforts to control the distribution of newspapers on campus were challenged in *Texas Review Society v. Cunningham*, 659 F.Supp 1239 (1987).

In *Texas Review*, the student publishers of a conservative newspaper at the University of Texas at Austin went to federal court after the school kept them from handing the paper out at a popular campus location.

The UT system had a rule against campus solicitation. The rule reserved a system school's right to control the time, place, and manner of speech on campus.

Because the newspaper contained paid advertisements, school officials judged it to be a solicitation. So they prohibited students from handing it out on campus. Instead, they could only distribute the paper via vending machines or at approved sale locations.

To decide the case, the court reviewed the legal history of "public forums" — established areas in which speech and assembly may be restricted only slightly.

UT rules said the area in question was not a public forum. But the student newspaper publishers disagreed and pointed out that the area was the site of many unregulated student organization activities.

The court ruled that all newspapers in the area were being treated equally, and that the school could legally limit use of the area in question. The court said UT had a legitimate interest in maintaining "the special characteristics of the school environment," and that it could implement appropriate time, place, and manner controls.

The rule, said the court, was not based on the content of any paper. It simply served a campus need, without denying the conservative newspaper access to the campus population.

Funding Wars

What happens if campus officials don't like the student newspaper's "humor" issue? A federal court looked at that question in *Stanley v. Magrath*, 719 F.2d 279 (1983).

In *Stanley*, a University of Minnesota student newspaper lost its funding because the school's Board of Regents "deplored" the humor issue's content and called the publication "flagrantly offensive." While the paper was not found to be "obscene," it was generally perceived as offensive.

Six months after the issue was published, and following state legislative hearings, the university decided to alter the newspaper's funding. Previously, the paper had automatically received a portion of student fees. Under the new plan, it still would have received student fees — except from students who chose not to support the paper. They could get their money back.

The paper's editors went to court, claiming that the school's action was unconstitutional because it was based on the paper's content.

But a district court ruled in favor of the school. It said that "one of the motivations for establishment of the refundable fee system was to respond to the concerns of those students who objected to being coerced into giving financial support."

An appeals panel, however, saw the issue another way and ruled that the regents' motives were improper. "It is clear that the First Amendment prohibits the Regents from taking adverse action ... because the contents of the paper are occasionally blasphemous or vulgar," the court said.

The regents had responded to personal feelings and legislative pressure, all based on the paper's content, the court ruled. Before changing the funding system, the court noted, the regents had passed two resolutions disapproving of the paper.

The appellate panel also noted that the fee refund system was not instituted systemwide, but only on the Twin Cities campus. Said the court, "If the Regents had truly been motivated by the principle that a student ought not to be forced to support a newspaper that espouses views the student opposes," they would have taken similar action on the other system campuses.

The court said the rule was unconstitutional and damaging to the newspaper and ordered UM to reverse the refund policy.

The STSU Case

In its most recent campus free speech ruling, the U.S. Supreme Court raised more questions than answers by refusing to hear the appeal of the case involving STSU's limitation on newspaper distribution.

In *Supple v. Hays Guardian*, the Fifth Circuit Court of Appeals had ruled that STSU could not limit the distribution of publications solely because they contained advertising. The court had gone back to the "public forum" issue and had ruled that outdoor areas should be open to free speech.

STSU, of course, had objected to that ruling, arguing that it would open the campus to unrestricted solicitation and diminish the educational environment.

But the Supreme Court, like the appeals court, gave priority to free speech and declined to get involved.

The *Supple* decision runs contrary to earlier case law, which established time, place, and manner restrictions on newspapers (as long as the restrictions are not content-based). Cases like *Papish*, *Texas Review*, and *Magrath* determined what public campuses could and could not do when dealing with the campus press.

Will the earlier cases prevail? Or does *Supple* represent a new trend toward greater freedom of the press on campus?

Those are questions that are still open to debate — and, no doubt, future litigation.

Free Speech vs. Censorship

February 1995

It's become the campus version of the historic Boston Tea Party: in the 1990s, instead of tossing highly taxed tea into the harbor, today's college protesters toss campus publications beyond the reach of readers.

A series of well-publicized incidents in the last two years has focused attention on "censorship by theft" and appropriate campus responses. As colleges and universities consider what to do, at least one state has considered making a crime the taking of free newspapers as a protest. And a federal court has ruled on related issues in an off-campus civil rights case.

Campus Sanctions

According to the Washington-based Student Press Law Center, during one recent academic year, over 120,000 copies of 25 different campus publications were stolen on campuses nationwide. Beginning in 1992-93, the stealing of bundles — or the entire press run — of student publications spread from campus to campus. Incidents were reported at Penn State, Michigan, Dartmouth, Florida State, Northern Illinois, the University at Buffalo, Duke, the University of Massachusetts-Amherst, two University of Wisconsin campuses, Bucknell, and the University of Maryland. Campus responses to these incidents were varied.

Some argued that since student publications are generally free, students could take all of the copies, or as many as they wanted, without breaking any rules or laws. Other campuses charged those involved with theft, asking for restitution and other campus sanctions through disciplinary proceedings. In considering possible discipline, the issue in dispute seems to be freedom of speech. Does free speech prevent the theft of campus publications? Or does freedom of speech protect those who take publications in protest?

Those favoring discipline argue that perpetrators willfully acted to censor and stifle campus debate, a violation of basic campus "marketplace of ideas" principles. The student newspapers are also not really "free," they contend. They are financed through significant advertising revenues, student activity fees, paid subscriptions, and other forms of subsidies. Students who paid for their student newspapers through student fees, businesses and organizations that paid for advertising in the newspapers, and other donors and contributors may consider that newspapers destroyed or taken are stolen.

Some have also questioned whether the First Amendment even applies to campus student newspapers. Based on a significant series of common law decisions extending the Constitution to the student press, it clearly does.

Causes vs. Symptoms

Some campuses, faced with stolen papers, have steered away from student discipline as a response. They feel that campus responses should be directed at the root causes of the problems, not the ultimate student reaction. They fear disciplinary action against selected involved students acting in civil disobedience would only deepen campus tensions. One scholar argues that an appropriate college or university reaction would be to "address the root problem — the poisons of racism, anti-Semitism, sexism, homophobia — through the reasoned engagement of opposing forces or teaching embittered and impassioned students to respect the freedoms of the 'other' in a civil community." Respond with core principles — not police, speech codes, and lawyers — these campuses argue.

State Legislation

It wasn't the fall 1993 theft of 10,000 copies of the *Diamondback*, an independent newspaper at the University of Maryland-College Park, that drove state legislators to get involved. It wasn't the theft of over 6,000 copies of the *Retriever* (a student newspaper at the University of Maryland-Baltimore), allegedly due to racially insensitive contents, that got them to act. But the stolen *Diamondback*s and *Retriever*s were a factor in the lawmakers' decision to consider legislative approaches to "censorship by theft."

In an apparent protest against the College Park newspaper's content, half of its press run was taken in the late night hours. Left behind at the circulation sites were signs with the message: "Due to its racist nature, the *Diamondback* will not be available today — Read a book!" Three reasons were suspected for the thefts: only one photograph of an African American model in an extensive fashion supplement, misreferences to black leaders and publications, and continuing press coverage of the disciplinary suspension of a minority fraternity.

At UM-Baltimore, a "large quantity" of student newspapers were taken, allegedly by members of a minority student organization. According to the paper's staff, the papers were stolen in a dispute over published articles that dealt with civil unrest in California and that allegedly included some words or references some people found offensive. Campus police were called to investigate.

These 1993 incidents led to consideration of state legislation after the problem was compounded by a series of seizures of free publications from public libraries. All of the copies of a weekly gay newspaper were repeatedly taken without authorization from libraries in the Washington suburbs of Maryland. Apparently, they were taken by those claiming the publication was "anti-family" and, therefore, that it had no right to be in public libraries. In an effort to stop the seizures, the newspaper's staff watched distribution sites. They actually photographed a man taking the papers. But local prosecutors, when presented with the evidence, said it was not a crime to take something that is free.

In order to be a crime, said prosecutors, the legal elements of theft must be shown. These include property wrongfully taken from rightful possessors and some proven value. Since the papers were left on a library counter for anyone to take, the paper was said to have given up its "rightful possession." And, noted the state's attorney, a free paper has no "ordinary, objective, economic value," required under the law to prove a theft.

A Maryland state lawmaker said the taking of free papers in protest should be a crime. The lawmaker proposed legislation to make it a criminal offense. Under the new state law, it is now a criminal misdemeanor to take "one or more newspapers with the intent to destroy the newspapers or prevent other individuals from reading the newspapers." Conviction could result in fines of up to $500 and imprisonment for up to 60 days. Editorial pages in some leading city newspapers opposed the measure, suggesting that the seizure of free newspapers itself was an expression of free speech deserving equal constitutional protection.

Federal Court Action

While relatively few free campus newspaper cases have reached either the civil or criminal courts to date, the 1992 taking of a gay weekly in San Francisco did lead to a judicial decision on related issues that merits campus consideration.

The Bay Area *Bay Times* ran a story in May 1992 about the chief of police ordering thousands of demonstrators to be arrested after the first Rodney King trial. The front page of the newspaper contained a cartoon figure of the police official with a suggestively held nightstick, reacting to the Los Angeles riots. City police officers apparently seized nearly 2,000 of a press run of 40,000 papers from racks in the early morning hours before others could get them. Four days later, they were anonymously returned to the publishers. The new police chief, only two months on the job, denied that he or his department were involved. His boss, the police commissioner, investigated the incident anyway, and one week later the chief was fired.

The commissioner found that the papers had been taken by police officers in response to the chief's orders or suggestions. Three involved officers were suspended from duty without pay. Editors of the gay weekly sued the city; in federal court, they demanded damages, claiming that the officers' actions had violated their civil rights.

Last fall, a federal jury agreed with the paper after trial. The paper was awarded $5,600 for economic damage. The editors were awarded another $30,000 for emotional distress. The jury also ordered the city to pay all of the damages, in addition to both sides' legal fees. These alone could exceed $500,000.

At trial, the former police chief maintained that he hadn't directed the seizure of the papers. Instead, he contended that he had only told the officers they should get copies of the publication to read for themselves. City attorneys claimed that the officers did not violate protected expression rights of the gay paper by temporarily taking the publication. Since they were returned, no one was actually deprived of an opportunity to read the edition, according to the lawyers. But the jury believed the men had deliberately and unlawfully interfered with the paper's circulation. The court held the city liable for the officers' damages because they were found to be on duty, carrying out their responsibilities. City attorneys plan an appeal.

Summary

Are they thefts or pranks? Protests or criminal acts? Courts, legislatures, and campuses continue to debate the issue of taking free newspapers. As the primary sites of these incidents, colleges and universities must be prepared to respond in all manners — by protecting free speech and expression, upholding campus principles, and addressing the root causes of the actions.

Theft as Censorship: A Nationwide Campus Problem

January 1994

It used to be that if a newspaper printed something that made a person mad, that person would write an angry letter to the editor. Apparently, what used to be isn't the case anymore. Colleges and universities are dealing with a more modern approach to controversial publications: the theft or removal of papers. Some call it censorship, others say it's illegal. Still others think the publications are getting what they deserve.

Whatever it is, it's happening at an alarming rate on campuses across the country. The theft of free newspapers by students embarrassed, offended, or angered by publications is a growing concern. While controversy over the theft of University of Pennsylvania's *Daily Pennsylvania* grabbed most of the headlines, it was only one of over 20 reported cases in one year. And the trend continued, with reported thefts at the University of Maryland, West Virginia University, the University at Buffalo, Southeastern Louisiana University, Highland Community College (KS), and several other schools. At these and perhaps other schools, students, faculty, and staff are dealing with First Amendment, student conduct, and possible criminal implications.

A few years ago, nine students were charged with confiscating nearly 14,500 copies of the *Daily Pennsylvanian* as part of a larger campus protest. A UPenn Committee on Open Expression ruled the removal violated the University Open Expression policy, and the Committee's report was used in further investigations. A Special Judicial Inquiry Officer was appointed to investigate the complaint and make judgments concerning student behaviors.

Then, the campus decided to drop charges against all involved. This was based on the decision that mistakes "should be opportunities for education" rather than "occasions for punishment." Noting that the campus was in "need of healing," and that no charges were brought against a faculty member who had earlier removed papers, UPenn decided to halt its disciplinary action. However, the school said further thefts would be subject to the full range of judicial sanctions. Future UPenn students will be advised of campus policy on confiscation of publications in future editions of university handbooks.

However, the decision to drop the publication theft cases did not sit well with the UPenn trustees. The board's executive committee unanimously voted to criticize the campus administrator's decision not to pursue the cases. The trustees waited until the matter was completed to comment but said they had been uncomfortable with the campus process since early summer. According to the trustees, "the confiscation of any publication is wrong and will not be tolerated." However, the trustees gave support to the new campus administration's efforts to review campus policies and procedures, including those on free expression and judicial procedures.

In the Rest of the Nation ...

About 10,000 copies of the student-produced University of Maryland-College Park *Diamondback* disappeared.

Students looking for the morning newspaper found empty bins and a small computer-generated note. It read: "Due to its racist nature, the *Diamondback* will not be available today. ... Read a book." No one came forward to take responsibility for the theft of the free papers.

Campus officials condemned the act. They said "freedom of expression is a fundamental value in our society and university" and must be protected. Students suggest that some felt the paper had been insensitive to minorities, and this may have led to the theft.

At the University at Buffalo, an estimated 8,000 copies of a campus weekly magazine, the *Generation*, disappeared one week after a sexually explicit article angered some. University officials noted a First Amendment protection for the publication and ordered an investigation into the theft. No motives or suspects have been identified.

Official Censorship?

Did an unflattering article on housing benefits for the president at West Virginia University lead to the removal of campus newspapers? That's the question at WVU, after all copies of *The Athenaeum* disappeared in early October. The loss was initially reported by physical plant employees who noticed the empty bins.

On the campus of Southeastern Louisiana University, disciplinary proceedings against a student leader may lead to expulsion. The student body president has been accused of stealing over 2,000 copies of a campus publication that carried an unfavorable article about him.

And at Highland Community College (KS), over 1,000 campus newspapers disappeared. Who took them is not known, but the reason the newspapers were taken was told to student editors. The newspaper printed a photograph of an automobile in which a student had been killed in a wreck. Friends of the student were upset by the photograph and may have responded by removing the papers.

Repercussions

Most campuses have reacted to these cases with investigations, statements about campus policies and commitment to free expression, and campus charges where possible. Some have also looked into criminal charges, as did the University of Florida in 1988. Responding to the theft of campus newspapers, the state attorney's office filed criminal charges against the involved students. They eventually pleaded no contest to the charges and were sentenced to $100 fines, 25 hours of community service, and six months probation.

Two Penn State graduates have been charged with the theft of a campus newspaper, *The Lionhearted*. They objected to an editorial cartoon of a female columnist for the school's other student newspaper, *The Daily Collegian*, showing her wearing a bikini in bed with the slogan "Feminist at Work." Several hundred newspapers were reported to have been burned off-campus. Police have charged the former students with theft, receiving stolen property, and conspiracy.

Other Publications

Campus newspapers are not the only publications creating concerns this year on college campuses. Other schools are dealing with disputes involving free publications handed out at sporting events, materials for orientation programs, and pamphlets on sexual orientation.

At Ohio State University, officials dealt with a dispute between the athletic department and the campus. *The Lantern* had been publishing a weekend football edition and left it at locations around the stadium for fans. The papers kept disappearing before game time. What happened, student editors asked? This year, they found out: OSU athletic department officials ordered them removed. The department was placing them in trash dumpsters. Employees of the student newspaper saw this and photographed the perpetrators in the act.

The Lantern says the OSU actions violated student rights and cost the paper advertising lost due to the circulation problem. The paper asked the athletic department for $2,500 in restitution. Athletic department officials responded saying that the paper was distributed in an irresponsible manner, creating a maintenance problem.

But the athletic department swiftly changed its initial response to the complaint. Said one official: "We were wrong and we should not have done what we did." The department apologized in writing for removing the publication and agreed to reimburse *The Lantern* for lost ad revenues. The paper and the department agreed to work together in the future on publication distribution at major events.

The distribution of printed materials at orientation was disputed at the University of Minnesota. There, College Republicans were ordered to stop distribution of jokes about President Clinton during summer sessions for new students. Campus officials called the handouts offensive to gays and women and said the publication was "oppressive" and "not welcoming." Some, including local newspapers, questioned the campus' commitment to free speech. They contend that UM sends a terrible message to students and society when "universities start deciding what are acceptable forms or subjects of expression."

Similar concerns were expressed recently at Belmont University (TN). Campus officials removed pamphlets produced by the local gay community on a national "coming out" day. The pink pamphlets were taken down from bulletin boards. According to student services personnel, the pamphlets were removed because they had not been approved under campus posting policies. Materials must be approved in advance. Campus officials did not comment on possible sanctions against the individuals who put up the pamphlets.

The days of showing dissent by simply writing a responding letter to the editor for publication have turned into an era of missing publications. Regardless of the reason for the theft or removal, the loss of campus publications represents a loss to students and the campus community.

Planning for Controversial Speakers

August 1994

Controversial campus speakers, such as Nation of Islam leader Louis Farrakhan and his former spokesperson, K.A. Muhammad, focused wide community attention on higher education during the past year. Speakers presenting views from all across the political and social spectrum have used college campuses as platforms for their addresses. What can campus officials do to regulate such appearances?

In the 1960s and '70s, many campuses attempted to control speeches on campus through "speaker bans." They were intended to preserve campus "calm" by denying access to controversial speakers. During those years, most of the speaker denial attempts were directed at speakers opposed to the war or promoting communist-marxist doctrines. These regulations, however, did not pass judicial scrutiny. They were found to be in violation of the First Amendment: overly vague and without due process protection (*Dickson v. Sitterson*, 280 F.Supp. 486 (1968); *Brooks v. Auburn University*, 412 F.2d 1171 (5th Cir. 1969); and *Smith v. University of Tennessee*, 300 F.Supp. 777 (1969)).

In the 1990s, campuses have moved away from speaker bans. They are more directed by the principles reflected in the federal court ruling that allowed neo-Nazis to march in a largely Jewish community. Said the judge:

> When a choice must be made, it is better to allow those who preach radical hate to expend their venom in rhetoric rather than be panicked into embarking on the dangerous course of permitting the government to decide what its citizens must say and hear.

Campuses faced with the arrival of a controversial speaker should develop appropriate pre-event, during-the-program, and post-event strategies to protect people and property and to protect campus interests. Campuses can and may have to provide forums for controversial speakers, but they should do so in a manner designed to provide for the health and safety of the community. Certain forms of speech may be "free," but they can be subjected to reasonable regulations. Here, we consider constitutional advice.

Constitutional Perspective

An understanding of the First Amendment is critical to the development of an appropriate campus speaker policy. It is desirable to have all segments of the campus community contribute to the policy, and it should be regularly reviewed in an effort to keep it both legal and effective.

First Amendment considerations on a private college campus can be far different than those on a public campus. A private campus may not be legally bound by the Bill of Rights "free speech" principles. It may, however, be open to controversial speakers because of commitments to open debate, academic freedoms, and the exploration of ideas.

For public colleges and universities, *discretion* based on content is not an option, as campuses may not make judgments on the content of a speech. A speaker cannot be barred because his or her message is objectionable, offensive, distasteful, or even threatening. The mere apprehension that a speech could cause unrest or violence is not sufficient grounds for administrators to impinge on the First Amendment and withdraw an invitation.

Campuses can provide a forum for all types of speech, even controversial speech, without endorsing the expressed views. This can be done in the name of academic freedom and of promoting thought-provoking inquiry and discussion. Any campus policy must clearly state the colleges or university's reason for protecting free speech and the steps to be taken to balance that principle with other campus responsibilities.

Robert M. O'Neil, a former college president and the director of a constitutional law center, recently offered his views on the steps to consider when faced with controversial speakers. In a *Chronicle of Higher Education* article (Feb. 16, 1994), he suggested:

- Giving program sponsors a *full appreciation* of the negative campus impact of such events. While the college may not be able, or may not officially want, to cancel an event, program sponsors should be made fully aware of the divisive and intolerant reactions that can be fostered by controversial speakers and their impact on students and the community.

- Providing an opportunity for *full press coverage*. If the campus permits controversial events in an effort to promote a full exchange of ideas, press coverage should be permitted to allow the fullest exposure.

- Keeping campus *security*, not personnel working for the speaker, responsible for the event. The campus will be ultimately responsible for what happens within its facilities, and it needs to maintain a presence to ensure compliance with appropriate campus policies.

- Preparing the campus community to *respond* to hateful speech. While the forum for the address may be provided, the campus does not need to accept or agree with the views expressed. If the campus community strongly disagrees with a message, it should be free to express that opinion openly.

O'Neil recommends "careful planning and quick reactions to inflammatory speakers."

Who Can Read Your E-Mail?

August 1994

Electronic mail has become the voice of the people on and off campus. Controls over that voice may become the legal issue of the '90s.

A graduate student at the University of Texas-Dallas has charged campus officials with violating his First Amendment rights for barring him from the campus email and bulletin board system (*Steshenko v. Texas* (1994)). He has asked for a court order of $2 million in damages and a return to the network. Campus officials say he misused the network.

At the University of Nebraska-Omaha, officials have formed an internal committee to review allegations that private student email accounts were opened by campus administrators. A student claims to have witnessed staff members viewing messages. But the staff say they open student email only when there is a technical problem with an account.

As email networks grow in sophistication and popularity, campuses need to carefully weigh free speech and privacy rights of individuals with important campus interests, such as safety and security. *Steshenko* may provide much needed guidance to colleges and universities on balancing these principles.

Key Speech Rights

G. Steshenko was an electrical engineering graduate student at UT-Dallas with extremely controversial views on Russian and Ukrainian affairs. The views, which he widely and loudly expressed on a regular basis, cost him a private industry computer job in 1993 when a major corporation let him go after continued complaints from co-workers about his nonstop, disruptive comments on world issues. He then came to UT-Dallas, changing to an academic career but not changing his politics.

On campus during the last academic year, he regularly used the school's electronic bulletin board network to share his thoughts on issues involving the former Soviet states. His computer-shared comments provoked anger from other students and heated complaints from the off-campus community.

Campus officials told him the network was intended for educationally related uses and warned him to end the political messages. But he continued to send his views and was ultimately suspended from the campus email system.

The student maintains that he was punished solely because of his political views. A dissident deported from the USSR in the 1980s, he says he has been unconstitutionally sanctioned because of his beliefs. He contends that even though his viewpoint may be unpopular, he has a right to openly express it. UT-Dallas officials, he claims, reviewed his computer messages only in response to complaints from Ukrainian nationalists. He also contends that since he is denied access to the network, he is unable to complete his course work. Campus officials say that is simply not the case.

One issue the court will consider will be "selective enforcement." Did UT-Dallas take action because of the content of the student's message? Did the school apply the "educational use" policy fairly and evenly, or only to him?

UT-Dallas is certainly not the only school facing "free speech" network problems. Unfortunately, campus networks have been used to send threatening, harassing, and racist messages.

Hate messages sent from a University of Michigan account caused an international response, and a University of Illinois at Urbana-Champaign student has been arrested for email threats against President Clinton. At Dartmouth College, a student prank message on an email network announced the cancellation of a course exam. Half of the students read the message and skipped the class. Free speech? Campus responsibility?

Privacy Rights

At the University of Nebraska, officials say it's their policy not to view student email. However, they report they do make exceptions to serve campus interests. They open files when there are technical account problems or to trace sources if students report receiving threatening or obscene messages. This is a typical campus approach.

While Nebraska has adopted this policy and reports relatively few violations, a key question remains: just how private is email supposed to be? Everyone is aware of the federal privacy protection granted to the U.S. Mail. This same level of protection is *not* extended to email. Privacy cases, to date, have not been based on campus situations, but employment cases have already found their way into the courts. Campus cases won't be far behind.

The Corporate Experience

In *Alana Shoars v. Epson America Inc.* (1990), a company email coordinator was ordered by supervisors to read other employees' messages. The coordinator objected. She did not think it was right to be intruding on employee privacy.

In another corporate case, two companies are locked in a legal challenge over the privacy of email messages. In *Symantec Corp. v. Borland International Inc.* (1992), a company checked personal email files after a senior executive left to join a competitor. Finding "sensitive" materials, the company filed suit against the new employer for stealing corporate secrets. The executive who left claims his old employer violated state and federal privacy laws by reading his email.

Are there email privacy laws? If so, how do they work? The federal Electronic Communications Privacy Act (ECPA) of 1986 makes it unlawful for a party providing electronic communication systems to "knowingly disclose" the contents to others. The law only restricts communication firms, not employers or other institutions.

But proposed legislation under congressional review would provide further protection to communication system users and other employees. Under the proposed law, certain levels of email monitoring would be permitted after notice of the monitoring is provided to users. No notice would be required in investigatory situations. Monitoring could take place only during the first five years of employment, and an employee would have a right to review data obtained from the monitoring. Employers violating the Privacy for Consumers and Workers Act, if adopted, could be fined up to $10,000.

Resolving Problems

Clear campus policies and appropriate enforcement mechanisms must be in place to avoid email free speech and privacy abuses on campus. While system abusers represent only a very small percentage of network users, the campus must communicate policies and standards to all to protect the system for everyone. While serious offenders could face criminal proceedings, campus conduct boards should be prepared to handle less serious abuses. Some campuses have even created special disciplinary boards to hear electronic mail and computer network cases.

Campus privacy regulations need to be carefully thought out as well. They must consider student and staff privacy concerns, security and resource protection, employer rights, and potential abuse. Broad user input in policy development is always recommended.

The growth of electronic communication has been tremendous in recent years. E-mail has opened the door for almost unlimited campus communication. Some limits, however, may be necessary to balance student, staff, and institution rights and responsibilities. Campuses and courts will be developing those limits in the years ahead.

Electronic Communications

October 1995

Consider the following recent situations:

- An Ontario professor has filed a lawsuit against his campus supervisor for using a computer email system to send him a critical job performance review.

- Charges were recently dismissed against a former University of Michigan student accused of sending out sexual assault and death fantasies through a computer network.

- Washington State is debating legislation that could curtail Internet services on campuses throughout the state, by barring materials judged to be obscene from network services available to youth.

- At the national level, debate continues over the principles of the Exon Amendment proposed to Congress, which would also prohibit the distribution of obscene materials electronically.

Such situations, in and around higher education, have forced many college and university officials to carefully consider just what it means to be a stop on the information superhighway. As the Internet system continues to grow by as much as 20% each month, more and more thought must go into campus implications — and the many related legal issues.

Of particular concern to legal scholars and campus administrators are free speech and privacy considerations. How does current case and statutory law extend to the new frontier of communication?

Concerns about electronic communication are not new. Fearing the development of controls on electronic communication several years ago, before the current network explosion, a noted Harvard University law professor suggested the need to discuss a new amendment to the U.S. Constitution. L. Tribe proposed a 27th Amendment, which would have read:

> The Constitutional protections for the freedoms of speech, press, petition, and assembly, and its protection against unreasonable searches and seizures and the deprivation of life, liberty, or property without due process of law shall be construed as fully applicable, without regard to the technological method of medium through which information content is generated, stored, altered, transmitted, or controlled.

His proposal, not seriously acted upon, raises all of the key questions facing campuses today using email and the Internet. Is this type of communication protected by the Constitution? Is it personal and private? To what extent can or should messages be open to others, such as employers and law enforcement agencies?

Recent case law only begins to address these questions. A review of some key decisions may promote campus awareness of the issues and provide clues on how the judicial process is prepared to respond. Further legal developments can be expected in the years ahead.

Intervention and Privacy

Consider the responsibility of computer bulletin board network operators, a role served by many colleges and universities. Are they responsible for the content of messages posted on the system?

That was the issue in *Cubby, Inc. v. CompuServe, Inc.*, 776 F. Supp. 135 (1991). In this case, a libel action was brought against a commercial network provider. Everyone agreed that a message sent through the system was libelous. But was CompuServe, as a distributor of the message, strictly liable for resulting damages?

No, said the court. The company pointed out that it only had a contractual relationship with its clients to post their messages swiftly, without exercising any editorial control. In issuing a summary judgment without trial, the court accepted the principle that CompuServe was not a publisher, only a distributor, with far less responsibility and liability for message content. As such, the court said the service was responsible only if it knew or should have known of the defamatory comments. *Cubby* is an early case on the issue; no judicial trend has developed to date.

Many people use computer bulletin boards and discussion groups to say things they would not say face to face. Anonymity adds to the problem. But where email damages reputations or lowers professional esteem, inhibiting opportunities, defamation can and should be a concern.

How private are electronic mail messages? We all understand the protections provided to messages we send through the postal service. Are messages sent electronically any different? Various privacy rights are established in federal, state, and common law, but most were developed before email. How are these past privacy standards applied in our electronic environment?

Just how some related privacy issues may be considered can be found in a 1987 privacy case, *O'Connor v. Ortega*, 480 U.S. 709. There, the U.S. Supreme Court reviewed two competing legal interests — an employee's right to personal privacy and an employer's need to maintain, an appropriate workplace. It found the public employers interest to be paramount, extending only a limited personal privacy right and only to an employee's immediate desk area.

Outside the workplace, many personal email messages have also been accessed regularly now for legal proceedings. Parties in litigation increasingly seek electronic messages and backup files, as this form of communication has supplemented or replaced hard copy materials in some proceedings. In a recent legal battle between media and government, a year's worth of employee email was ordered released. The messages at issue in *Star Publishing Co. v. Pima County Attorney's Office*, Ariz. App. (1994), maintained on backup tapes, were held to be subject to a release order by a court.

Campus Policies

While there continues to be much confusion over protection of and access to email messages, one way to deal directly with the issue on campus is through well-developed and clearly communicated policies. These policies can help avoid misunderstandings, confusion, and, ultimately, litigation.

Campus policies can be effective in resolving problems if they reflect a good understanding of both the campus and the law. College and university computer network policies should include a statement on the rationale and principles behind them and indicate just who and what the policy covers. In addition, when dealing with computer bulletin board and email policies, consideration should be given to:

- Privacy — how protected should the communication be?

- Monitoring — how can or will the communication be monitored by authorities, such as supervisors or moderators?

- Access — to what extent, if any, is the system open to commercial, political, or religious messages and materials?

- Use — can the system be used for personal matters, rather than just educational matters?

- Enforcement — who is responsible for handling allegations of policy violations, and how?

To reduce problems and liability, institutions should make sure that all users — faculty, staff, students, and others — are fully aware of computer bulletin board and email institutional principles and policies. Avoid litigation by avoiding misunderstandings. If the system is subject to message retrieval and review, inform everyone in advance of use. If network use is limited to institutional, and not personal matters, make sure that's known before there's a problem.

New communication systems can speed up the exchange of information. But can also quickly lead to major problems. Avoid problems by developing good policies, providing appropriate training, and maintaining an effective compliance system.

Chapter 4
GOVERNANCE AND REGULATION

Introduction

> The students of each institution or campus subject to the responsibilities and powers of the board, the president, the chancellor, and the faculty, shall be active participants in the immediate governance of and policy development for such institutions.
>
> Wisconsin Statutes, Sec. 36.09(5)

Campuses are complex institutions with complex systems of authority and decision-making. Trustees, administrators, state officials, faculty, staff, and students are all involved in questions of authority, governance jurisdiction, institutional liability, and risk management.

Off campus, the complexity continues. No college or university is an "island," entirely free from external policies, pressures, and regulations. From outside the boundaries of higher education, colleges and universities are subject to a vast array of federal, state, and local laws and regulations. Among the constant concerns are zoning, taxation, business competition, and financial policies.

Decision Raises Questions About Residency

October 1991

Just who lives here, anyway? That's a question state institutions are asking with greater concern: Who is a "resident" and is entitled to pay in-state tuition?

A California state court decision — *Bradford v. The Regents of the University of California,* 276 Cal. Rptr. 197 (1990) — examined the issue when it considered the status of illegal aliens. Although they're not in the state legally, should they qualify for in-state rates?

The case was brought against the state university system by a former UCLA employee. He claimed that he was forced to resign in 1985 because he refused to register illegal aliens as in-state students for tuition purposes. By his estimate, the state spent between $1 million and $13 million subsidizing the tuition of illegal aliens over a five-year period. School officials disagreed with his figures and reasoning. In deciding the case, the state court ordered the school to consider undocumented aliens as out-of-state students.

That decision reverses an earlier ruling that separated immigration status (federal) and residency (state). Previously, courts have allowed state residency decisions for aliens undocumented by the federal government. Those rulings held that undocumented students living in the state were residents entitled to pay in-state tuition. (State university tuition averages $1,600 a year for residents and exceeds $7,400 annually for non-residents.)

The issue of in-state v. out-of-state tuition has always been sensitive, due to the personal and financial factors considered in any evaluation. State-supported educational institutions developed higher rates for out-of-state students so that state taxpayers wouldn't be burdened with educational costs for students who weren't contributing to the state tax revenues. And with the financial difficulties besetting states in recent times, the gap between in-state and out-of-state tuition has widened, making the issue of residency even more significant to campusess and college students' families.

Residency Tests

In 1973, the U.S. Supreme Court heard a challenge to residency requirements in *Vlandis v. Kline,* 93 S.Ct. 2230. The University of Connecticut required that applicants live in the state for a year to qualify as residents for lower tuition. A student's tuition status at initial registration remained unchanged for four years. There was no appeal process.

The federal courts struck down this policy. They noted that the state's failure to allow students an opportunity to challenge their status violated *due process*. If the state has a "reasonable means" of accurately assessing residency status, it must use it, out of fairness to students.

Courts have struck down strict residency rules in other states as well, where those rules did not allow students an opportunity to present their case for residency. The Supreme Court of North Carolina overturned rules that required students to keep their residency status as initially established, regardless of changed circumstances, in *Bauer v. Board of Regents of University of Nebraska*, 219 N.W. 2d 236 (1974). And in *Glusman v. Trustees of University of North Carolina*, 200 S.E. 2d 9 (1973), the court rejected rules requiring students paying out-of-state tuition to drop out for six months to establish residency.

What about *married students*? What's the status of a spouse? Two cases dealt with this question, one in Michigan and another in Pennsylvania. In *Blair v. Wayne State University*, 220 N.W. 2d 202 (1974), students challenged a policy that had different residency rules for single and married persons. The court found that the policy violated constitutional principles of *equal protection*. In *Samuel v. University of Pittsburgh*, 375 F.Supp. 1119 (1974), a federal court reviewed a rule declaring that a wife had the same residency status as her husband. It held that this type of automatic residency violated both *due process* and *equal protection* standards.

Residency rules based on the *age* of students have also been reviewed. In *Burke v. Raschle*, 428 F.Supp. 1030 (1977), the court overturned as arbitrary a North Dakota rule limiting to students over 21 years old the right to establish separate residency from their parents. A similar decision was reached in *Florida Board of Regents v. the Department of Education*, 338 So. 2d 215 (1976).

Aliens and Visas

In 1982, the Supreme Court was asked to rule on in-state tuition for non-immigrant aliens. The University of Maryland offered in-state rates to immigrant families residing in the state, but not to students in the state on special, non-permanent visas. These students had lived in the state for five years, paid taxes in the state, and registered cars in Maryland. They challenged the state policy in *Toll v. Moreno*, 102 S.Ct. 2977 (1982), in which the Supreme Court reviewed a series of district and appellate decisions.

The Court noted that the federal government, not the states, controlled the status of aliens in the U.S. State laws that placed other regulations or burdens on aliens could interfere with the federal process. In ruling against the school policy in *Toll*, the Court justified its decision on the Supremacy Clause, which makes federal law "supreme" over state legislation. Since Congress established the regulations for holders of various visas, the states were not free to alter or affect the status of immigrants. Separate tuition systems for different classifications of immigrants were not allowed.

Current Case: Bradford v. UC Regents

The California case was filed by a former employee angered by a policy that he claims cheats citizens and legal aliens of admission, housing, financial aid, and other benefits.

Many experts question the court's ruling, which denies in-state benefits to illegal aliens. Aliens who have been in the state for some time and intend to stay already receive other state benefits. As an example, previous legal battles elsewhere have established the rights of the children of undocumented aliens to attend public elementary and secondary schools in Texas and elsewhere.

An appeal may alter the judgment, as it may deny students the opportunity to present their case for residency. As established by case law, from *Vlandis* to *Toll*, residency policies must observe *equal protection* and *due process*.

Deciding Who's a Resident and Who's Not

October 1994

She lived in Michigan for less than a year but claimed to be a resident for tuition rate purposes because of her husband's new job. The University of Michigan applied a "one full year" residency requirement to her case and declared her to be an out-of-state student. This forced her to pay a substantially higher tuition, nearly $10,000 more a year. She sued.

He applied for in-state status after one year in the state. He said he planned to stay and figured he was a resident after being called for jury duty. The University of Michigan thought otherwise and billed him as an out-of-state student for his final three years. He figures that decision cost him at least $25,000, and he wants the money back, plus interest.

States may distinguish between residents and non-residents when determining tuition and fees at taxpayer-supported institutions. States may choose to charge out-of-state students substantially more, reserving the benefit of state financial support to those who live or intend to stay in the state.

But who is a resident of a state for tuition purposes? Someone who's been in the state for over a year? Three months? No absences from the state for more than 30 continuous days? Ownership of a home in the state? Marriage to a resident? These Michigan cases are just the latest legal challenges in a long-running battle over public higher education residency requirements.

Court Action

"Residency discrimination" received U.S. Supreme Court approval in *Vlandis v. Kline*, 412 U.S. 441 (1973). Said the court:

> A state has a legitimate interest in protecting and preserving the quality of its colleges and universities and the right of its own bona fide residents to attend such institutions on a preferential tuition basis.

In *Vlandis*, the court said a state could not judge residency solely on the basis of a "permanent irrebuttable presumption." Instead, it should apply standards of due process that allows an individual an opportunity "to present evidence that he is a bona fide resident entitled to the in-state rate." Overturned was a Connecticut policy that limited residency to those who had been in the state 12 months before applying to a state school. The rule maintained that determination for a student's entire academic career. The court suggested several other factors as proper criteria for evaluating residency, including year-round residence, voter registration, place of filing tax returns, property ownership, driver's license, car registration, marital status, and vacation employment.

Durational residency requirements have been tested regularly over the past several decades, for various reasons. Some interesting questions were raised in these cases. Does a higher tuition rate for non-residents put an unlawful "chilling effect" on the right of citizens to move freely between the states? That was the issue in *Starns v. Malkerson*, 326 F.Supp. 234, 401 U.S. 985 (1971). In this case, a Minnesota one-year residency requirement was found not to violate constitutionally protected interstate travel.

How about a requirement that students accept an in-state job to prove an intent to remain in the state for residency purposes? In *Kelm v. Carlson*, 473 F.2d 1267 (1973), such a rule was challenged. The court held that post-graduation employment in-state was not a valid, single criteria for residency. It could, however, be one of many other factors considered in making a decision.

What if the state accepts you as a voter? Doesn't that mean you're a resident of the state for tuition purposes? "Not necessarily," ruled a court in *Hayes v. Board of Regents of Kentucky State University*, 495 F.2d 1326 (1974). Proof of voter registration is not conclusive proof of residency, but it may be a factor in a decision.

Is marital status a key factor? In 1974, a campus presumption that a wife's residence was the same as her husband's was challenged. In *Samuel v. University of Pittsburgh*, 375 F.Supp. 1119, this policy was found to violate equal protection principles as unlawful gender discrimination.

An exhaustive review of general residency requirements for tuition purposes was conducted in *Frame v. Residency Appeals Committee*, 675 P.2d 1157 (1983). The plaintiffs in this case were husband and wife Utah State University students who were denied residency status by the school. The couple had moved to the state after leaving the military and attended the university as non-residents for two semesters. During that year, they rented an apartment, had a bank account, and registered to vote. They then left the state to conduct research in Africa, leaving behind some personal property back in Utah. They retained an in-state mailing address.

Six years later, they returned to Utah to enroll in school, but then spent several months out of the state, working, visiting, and traveling. Before starting classes, they returned to Utah and applied for the lower, in-state tuition rate. The university denied their request, on three grounds:

- They had not lived in the state continuously for a year before applying, and they had been absent for more than 30 continuous days during that year.
- They had come to the state strictly for educational purposes.
- They had failed to provide objective facts to support their residency claim.

In challenging the denial in federal court, the couple claimed violations of due process and equal protection principles. They also called the campus finding arbitrary and capricious. The court considered each claim separately.

No *due process* violations were found, as campus regulations had given the couple an opportunity to overcome the school's presumption of non-residency. The one-year presumption of non-residency was held to be valid, as was the exemption absence of less than 30 days rule, as long as the students had a chance to prove residency in another manner.

The court did not find *equal protection* violations. The couple complained that state standards for residency were "illogical," but the court said the rules had a rational relationship to legitimate state purposes. The tuition and residency system was found to be "reasonable."

Finally, the court found the campus decision to be supported by evidence. Therefore, it was not *arbitrary and capricious*. While the couple did establish some ties to the state, they did not register to vote, did not get state driver's licenses or car registrations, never filed Utah tax returns, and often used an office as their home address. The court said the school "could have ruled the other way," but that it's decision was not arbitrary or capricious. The campus residency decision was upheld.

Current Challenge

The two cases involving the University of Michigan demonstrate primary challenges to residency determinations: time requirements and the extent of evidence required to support a claim.

A federal appellate panel has ruled against the U of M "one year" residency rule. The court said it was "perfectly acceptable" to have differing tuition rates based on residency, but it found equal protection problems in the time requirement policy. In an earlier decision, the district court had sided with the school's rule.

But Michigan says the court misunderstood its policy and it wants a new trial to get the facts straight. The school says one year in the state is an important factor in its decisions, but individual exceptions have been made in the past.

In the other student's case for a $25,000 refund, a state court will hear the graduate's claim that he should have been given in-state tuition rates. The school was not convinced that he was a resident for tuition purposes. His claim to be a resident was based on a year in the state, jury duty, and an expressed intent to remain after graduation. Michigan thought otherwise and continued to bill him as an out-of-state student. To overturn the decision, he will have to show that the Michigan approach is unconstitutional and unlawful.

Public campuses across the country will be watching these cases carefully, as many use similar policies to determine who is entitled to preferential tuition. A legal defeat, however, won't open the door to everyone who wants to be considered in-state for low tuition. States have a right to limit benefits to residents, and state colleges and universities would develop new residency tests if needed. As was said in *Frame*, "The court has no such power. The prerogative and power to draw such lines belongs to bodies invested with the power."

Residence Issues in the News

April 1996

She was born and raised in the state. She went to elementary and secondary school in the state. When she applied to the state university, she still lived with her parents in the state. But they moved away, leaving her back in the state to finish her senior year of high school. The university accepted her application but designated her an out-of-state student for tuition rate purposes.

The case of the student with the "moved away" parents was recently reviewed by the Supreme Court of North Carolina. The justices were asked whether the University of North Carolina at Chapel Hill could charge out-of-state tuition to a student who had never moved out of the state!

Residency issues have become more complex in recent years as public colleges and universities have sought to maximize revenues and limit taxpayer-supported benefits to non-taxpaying families. The North Carolina case is only the latest challenge to campus student residency decisions.

Background

When the student plaintiff first applied for 1992 admission to the university, she used her home address to show she was a resident. However, she noted on the application that her father had taken a new job out of state and would be relocating soon to Vermont.

During her final year of high school, she remained in North Carolina, staying with family friends. Records show that during this period, she received family financial support from Vermont and was covered under her father's Vermont health insurance policy. Late in 1991, she amended her UNC application to show another North Carolina mailing address, possession of a car registered in the state, and a North Carolina driver's license. She also indicated that 95% of her personal property was in the state and that she worked two North Carolina summer jobs to help support herself.

In spring 1992, she was accepted into the fall UNC class, but as an out-of-state student. This designation resulted in significantly higher tuition and fees. She appealed the decision to a campus committee but was rejected. She then turned to the courts.

Court Action

The trial court quickly reversed the campus decision. While courts have a long record of sustaining campus residency decisions, in this case UNC was found to have unfairly denied the student lower tuition rates. In *Fain v. State Residency Committee of the University of North Carolina*, No. 9310-S.C. 911 (1995), the university challenged that reversal.

The state Court of Appeals carefully reviewed the campus residence committee's position. First, it considered the definition of "resident":

> To qualify as a resident for tuition purposes, a person must have established legal residence (domicile) in North Carolina and maintained that legal residence for at least twelve months immediately prior to his or her classification as a resident for tuition purposes.

Wasn't she a resident for a year before the school classification? No, said the committee, citing a common-law principle that presumes the domicile of a minor is that of the minor's parents. The UNC Committee used this reasoning to find the plaintiff to be a resident of Vermont at the start of her collegiate career.

However, the appeals court noted that the common law applies only if not "supplanted" by legislation. It found other state statutory language that dealt specifically with an applicant whose parent or guardian does not live in the state. That law provided:

> that the legal residence of an individual whose parents are domiciled outside this state shall not be prima facie evidence of the individual's legal residence if the individual has lived in the state

for five consecutive years prior to enrolling or re-registering at the institution of higher education.

The court ruled that the student had lived in the state for the required five full years. Therefore, she was entitled to consideration as a resident. The UNC residency committee, it ruled, relied on the common law, violating "the duty of the committee to determine the petitioner's status based on a correct understanding of the law." That decision, ordering in-state tuition for the longtime resident, was upheld by the North Carolina Supreme Court in January of this year.

Summary

This is a public college and university issue, as residency is generally not a tuition factor at private institutions. For over 100 years, some public schools have extended more favorable tuition to the children of taxpayers within their jurisdiction. Analysis of student residency is easy in most circumstances, but it can be made complex by the movement of students and their parents. Students, or their families in transition, have to deal with a variety of durational presumptions and tests to determine residence.

Given the growing difference between in- and out-of-state costs of tuition, more challenges are likely.

Campuses Look Gift Horses in the Mouth

October 1990

Campus fund-raisers and development officers are concerned about two legal decisions that could significantly affect the value of gifts to colleges and universities. At issue are management and disposition of funds donated through gifts, wills, and trusts.

In the past, schools generally had to worry only about how funds they received were to be spent. But today's legal environment makes it very important for higher education to know where dollars are coming from and how they are being managed en route.

Use of Funds

Traditionally, grants to schools through gifts, wills, and trusts are designated by a donor as being *restricted* or *unrestricted*. Restricted gifts can be used only in the manner established by the grantor, donor, testator, or settler of the estate or trust. Unrestricted gifts come to campus without conditions and generally can be used for any campus-related purpose.

Due to the lack of conditions on unrestricted gifts, most litigation in the past focused on restricted funds. In principle, schools must use these funds in accordance with the established guidelines. The only exception to this principle is when the funds, terms, or conditions are found to be illegal or impossible.

Courts May Allow Modifications

Discriminatory clauses in wills and trusts have caused the most problems for institutions of higher education, particularly those with governmental affiliations. When faced with illegal or impracticable clauses, the courts will entertain motions to modify the awards to serve similar, but more achievable, purposes, under the *cy pres doctrine*.

For example, Amherst College (MA) was unable to accept a gift that was restricted in a way that violated school policy. The gift stipulated that recipients be Protestant and Gentile. In *Howard Savings Institution v. Peep*, 170 A.2d 39 (1961), the court agreed to remove that restriction. The court justified the action under *cy pres*, noting that the doctrine is a judicial mechanism for the preservation of a charitable trust when accomplishment of the particular purpose of the trust becomes impossible, impracticable, or illegal.

The courts retain the right to modify such estates or trusts to meet the desires of the gift as nearly as possible. A similar decision was reached in *Wilbur v. University of Vermont*, 270 A.2d 889 (1970), in which a court, using *cy pres*, modified class size limitations contained in a trust document. The limits expressed by the donor were no longer practicable.

The involvement of public schools in the administration of discriminatory trusts has been reviewed in several cases. In *Shapiro v. Columbia Union National Bank and Trust Co.*, 576 S.W.2d 310 (1978), the Supreme Court of Missouri looked at the University of Missouri at Kansas City and its handling of funds designated for needy young men. A female law student challenged the school, claiming that state involvement in the trust was unconstitutional. The court disagreed, finding that the school could administer the private funds as long as they came from private sources and private parties made the actual award decisions.

In *Trustees of the University of Delaware v. Gebelein*, 420 A.2d 1191 (1980), a state court dealt with a challenge to a trust by a state school. The school wanted to eliminate references to gender in a trust fund. In this instance, the court found that state action in the trust was significant, making it susceptible to constitutional challenge. The state cannot lawfully be involved in discriminatory actions.

The decision noted, however, that, while the trust was discriminatory in that it allowed awards only to poor females, the intent of the trust was to remedy past discrimination. The court allowed the trust to continue because it promoted equal opportunity.

Cases like *Howard Savings*, *Wilbur*, *Shapiro*, and *Delaware* demonstrate clearly the legal maneuvering sometimes necessary to save gifts from failing or to make them usable. Given the legal challenges that may result from restrictions on gifts, campus development offices should give careful attention to such gifts.

Two Current Concerns

While past concerns primarily centered on school use of gift funds, recent legal decisions have raised concerns over the *value of trusts* intended for schools and the *reopening of estates* after disbursements have been made. Recent state court decisions on these issues have campus development offices paying close attention to legal counsel.

In Wyoming, the state's highest court recently ruled that the future beneficiaries of a trust don't have to be advised about trust transactions. At issue was the use of assets from *charitable remainder* trusts. These trusts are set up by donors to support a family member for life and then have the remaining assets transferred to a designated charitable organization, such as a college or university.

In the case before the court, a trustee sold assets for less than deemed appropriate by the charity that was to receive the assets in the future. But the court said the trust was not yet a legal interest of the charity. In the future it would control the funds, but until then it had no say in the use of the trust.

Colleges and universities that stand to benefit from charitable remainder trusts in the future are concerned that decisions like this one could damage their attempts to monitor trusts and preserve their value. The charity that expected to gain the Wyoming assets filed an appeal with the U.S. Supreme Court, but it was denied early this summer.

Another case that has raised campus concerns involves a battle over the estate of a country music legend, Hank Williams. Twenty-two years ago, state courts in Alabama awarded the full estate of the singer to his only son. Ten years after the estate was closed and all funds paid, a woman claiming to be an illegitimate child of Williams sued, claiming her share of the estate. The state supreme court sided with her and reopened the estate. The singer's son has petitioned the U.S. Supreme Court to overturn the decision and keep the estate closed.

College and university officials following the case fear what could happen if they received a testamentary bequest and spent it, then heard from the court that it wasn't theirs to spend. Would they risk spending the money? Or would they turn down the gifts and miss out on the benefits to students and the campus? All organizations that may benefit from estates will be watching the case closely.

Summary

In the past, campus legal difficulties with gifts, trusts, and wills have been generally limited to restrictions on use of funds. When faced with illegal or impracticable trust restrictions, courts allow modifications to meet the intended purposes in alternative ways. If the restrictions are discriminatory, schools can administer the trusts as long as involvement of state officials is limited.

But today, with a growing number of trusts and estates heading toward campus, legal decisions have clouded the picture. Campus officials are watching closely to see how legal decisions may alter their rights to know about trust transactions that might affect them in the future — and to see how the courts may establish precedents for reopening estates that colleges and universities receive in the future.

Relying on Estates and Pledges

November 1993

Colleges and universities often seek and receive support from benefactors through wills and estate plans or pledges of support to annual or capital fund campaigns. Based on established estate or pledge cards, campus programs are developed with the knowledge that they will be supported by benefactors.

But what happens if the will is suddenly changed, leaving the school without expected funds? Or what if a family decides not to honor a pledge? The school may have taken action in reliance on the estate plan or pledge, starting a building or awarding a financial aid grant. What can the college or university do, if anything, to reinstitute a favorable will or force the honoring of a donor pledge?

Contest of Wills

Western Kentucky University was looking forward to the $200,000 estate gift it expected from the will of a very prominent community member. Another local school, Lindsey Wilson College, was looking forward to $150,000 from the same estate. And the local school board was looking forward to even more — at least $300,000 from the estate when the will was probated.

The community member died in the summer of 1992. But now, instead of waiting for estate payments, the schools are waiting for litigation to begin.

A last-minute change in the will eliminated Western Kentucky and drastically reduced the bequests to the other schools. The institutions claimed in court that the new will was invalid, alleging that the testator was not mentally capable of making a second will and was under the influence of family members. Those same family members now stand to obtain the most significant portion of the estate, and they are named as defendants in the school's suit.

On what grounds can Western Kentucky and the other schools challenge the will? What conditions must the schools satisfy to get their case to court?

In most states, a challenger to a will must generally prove that the testator was not "of sound mind" or was under "undue influence" at the time the disputed will was signed. And to be heard in probate proceedings, a challenger must act at an appropriate time and have an interest in the outcome. These are the general conditions that must be met to get into court with a claim.

Time limits for a challenge depend on state statutes, varying from three to 21 years. A national probate model law suggests that challenges be filed within three years, with few exceptions. Nevertheless, a campus wishing to challenge an estate must act within the time frame established by state law.

A campus must also show an interest in the will. The law generally limits challenges to "persons who have some legal or equitable interest affected adversely by establishment of the will." If acceptance of the will negatively affects a person or an organization, that person or organization has a legal right to contest it.

Questions of "Testamentary Capacity"

Once the right to challenge is established by showing appropriate timing and interest, the legal grounds for contest must be considered. Most often, they focus on mentality and undue influence. A finding of either can lead to the judgment that the will-maker lacked "testamentary capacity." This could overturn the will.

State statutes rarely define specific standards for being of "sound mind." Courts have ruled that a will-maker can be found incapacitated mentally because of mental deficiency or because of mental derangement. These would be shown through psychiatric and medical evidence.

Probate courts also have found a will-maker mentally deficient for the purposes of making a will if he or she "lacks the ability to understand the general nature of his testamentary act, to know the nature and extent of his property, and the natural objects of his bounty, and to interrelate these factors."

A campus left out of a second will must prove more than that the will-maker was eccentric, old, ill, weak, deaf, dumb, or blind. These factors can be used to support a claim that the will-maker was not of sound mind, but proof of these facts alone will not invalidate a will.

A second claim made in many will challenges involves "undue influence." It is legally defined by most courts as "coercion" of the will-maker's mind. When a testator is subjected to undue influence, the intentions of a dominant party are found to have been substituted for the testator's own intentions. While undue influence need not consist of physical threats or harm, it has to consist of more than advice or even persuasion.

Undue influence is also found when, by his/her conduct, a person gains an unfair advantage by devices that reasonable people regard as improper. The nature of such influences is judged by the courts case by case.

Western Kentucky, named in the first will and left out of the second, has gone into court claiming both mental incapacity and undue influence. School attorneys note that the family had significant ties to the school and indicated that the deceased had planned to leave money to Western. To support its challenge, the school must prove the second will was invalid according to case law.

Honoring a Pledge

An active supporter of Hannibal-La Grange College (MO) served on various college committees and had been a member of the college board of trustees. So when the campus needed a new sports complex, no one was surprised that she pledged to donate $50,000 over five years. Her first payment was for $10,000.

Based on that pledge and others, the college was able to secure a bank loan for construction, hire an architect and contractor, and break ground on the complex. But before much of the complex was completed, the donor died. Her family decided not to honor the pledge, leaving the college $40,000 short of its goal and very surprised. To finish the project as planned, the college sued to enforce the pledge.

In *Estate of Buchanan*, 840 S.W. 2d 888 (1992), a Missouri appellate court heard arguments concerning the pledge, the college, and the law.

The court ruled that the college, not the donor's family, had erred. The pledge card noted that all donors had the right to change their pledges at any time. Therefore, since it could be changed at any time, the pledge never really promised anything. And since nothing was promised, there was nothing to be enforced.

The college argued that, since part of the pledge had been honored, it had a right to rely on the rest of the pledge. But the court, citing a precedent in *In re Estate of Bacheller*, 437 S.W. 2d 132 (1968), ruled that the pledge was enforceable only if it was irrevocable. While most promises become binding when they are relied on, in this case the court found no promise, so there was nothing to rely on.

The pledge was only a pledge, not a promise. The donor retained the right to change the pledge and her representatives exercised that right. The college was not successful in its efforts to force payment.

Summary

Unless it can be shown that a will-maker lacked "testamentary capacity" or was under undue influence, the courts generally support changed wills, not campuses that lose out on large gifts. And when a donor retains the right to change a gift pledge, the court will support the change, not the campus that loses a large pledge.

Colleges and universities counting on support from estates and annual and capital campaigns should be very clear in their understanding of the uncertain nature of such giving.

No Such Thing as a Free Gift

July 1995

For generations, parents have offered simple wisdom to youth, saying, "It's better to give than to receive." Today, for some colleges and universities, the acts of giving and receiving have grown quite complicated.

Campus development officers across the country are considering two recent higher education gifts gone "bad." In one case, officials decided to return a significant gift. In the other, officials decided to sue to get money promised but not received.

In both cases, the general principles of contract law may be applied. Was there appropriate mutual consent, a "meeting of the minds" when the deal was made? Did the school and donor agree to "the same bargain at the same time"?

Yale University

After more than four years of frustration and confusion, Yale officials apparently determined that they had a $20 million deal they just couldn't handle. And the donor, frustrated with the school's inability to do what he thought it had promised, demanded a full refund of his gift, with interest. Amid wide publicity and much second-guessing, a $20 million deal had gone bad.

The donor had offered the money to the school in 1992 to fund a program reintegrating Western civilization into the undergraduate curriculum. The gift came in response to a college dean's proposal and was solicited by the university president. The new program was to fund seven professors and four assistant professors.

Some members of the campus community did not judge the re-establishment of Western civilization on campus as "politically correct," and some opposition to the gift developed. Although Yale held onto the money, it did not develop the intended academic program.

Later — after three presidents, three provosts, three graduate deans, and three college deans had all served the school — Yale still had the money and still had not started the undergraduate program. Inside and outside the university, some wondered if the school was "dragging its feet" because of "a political agenda favoring a more multicultural value on history and social issues."

In late 1993, the donor asked about the promised program. A new campus president responded that status reports would be prepared and shared regularly. But the donor says he heard nothing from the school over the next 14 months.

When he finally learned about his gift to Yale, he was not pleased. Since his earlier contact on the money, the school had formed a task force to come up with alternative ways to spend his gift!

The donor, whose family had already given Yale over $85 million in the last decade, decided to act. Feeling that Yale had not stayed in contact with him and had not taken steps to implement the program as agreed upon, the donor asked for some input into the appointment of a senior faculty member to administer the new program.

This request, several years after the deal was made, ended up terminating the relationship. Citing principles of academic freedom, Yale said it could not permit a donor to intrude into academic matters, such as the appointment of faculty members. The donor — now without his money, his program, and an administrator he could work with — then asked for a return of his $20 million, with interest.

Yale acknowledged not "doing a very good job" with the donation and the donor. The contributor, in withdrawing his gift, noted the campus administrations that had come and gone in the four years, calling it "a very unusual period of time" at Yale. He complained of obvious administrators' "very poor handoff of the ball."

The donor felt that he had a contractual agreement with the school to start the new program. The school had failed to honor that agreement, he concluded, so he ended the deal. Yale also felt that it had a deal, but finally said it could not honor the agreement without violating academic freedoms. So the school too felt that it had to cancel the deal.

A basic legal tenet of any contract is that it should represent "a meeting of the minds," the mutual agreement of the parties. It was a lack of any meeting of the minds that ultimately ended Yale's $20 million deal.

University of California-Irvine

School officials solicited the gift; they agreed to name a new campus theater after a contributor who gave UC-Irvine what he called an "irrevocable pledge" of $1 million. The school borrowed additional funds to complete the project. When the theater opened, the main stage was named for the donor.

Two years later, he died. He had paid only $400,000 of his pledge. Since he left an estate in excess of $5 million, the school expected his widow to fulfill his pledge.

Wrong assumption. Citing a California recession, a depressed real estate market, and her lack of personal "loyalty" to the school, the man's widow decided not to pay the outstanding amount.

The school and the city tried to negotiate a settlement with her. UC-Irvine had borrowed city funds against the original pledge and needed the funds to pay off the debts. When negotiations with the family failed, UC-Irvine officials sued the widow for the funds.

Their case is based on contract law. According to the school, the parties entered into a binding agreement that both sides were obligated to uphold. UC-Irvine maintains that it performed as agreed by building the theater and naming it after the donor. The school and the city joined in a suit to force the donor's estate to perform as well by paying off the remaining pledge funds.

Attorneys for the estate argue that the pledge was only a gift, not "a business or trade debt" that would have legally obligated them to pay. The widow, they maintain, had objected to the pledge in the first place and never gave her consent. They have suggested that UC-Irvine reduce or forgive the pledge and simply remove the donor's name from the theater.

In this contract between donor and school, there was the essential "meeting of the minds" required for agreement and enforcement. However, before the contract was completely performed, one party was succeeded by another. That brought a different perspective to the agreement, which eventually forced the issue into court.

Gifts and Contracts

When parties agree to a contract and then perform as agreed upon, the contract language is usually clear on the terms and conditions. There is an obvious "meeting of the minds," and their performance reflects this.

But without a "meeting of the minds," or when there is a change of mind later, the resulting lack of performance can lead to embarrassment and litigation.

When Is a Campus Exempt From Property Taxes?

February 1993

The tax man "cometh." But one campus says, "Go away!"

That's the situation at Syracuse University (NY), where two community college tax issues went to court. Under review were school claims that a home for its former chancellor and a campus commercial food court are exempt from local property taxes.

A suburban town wants the school to pay taxes on the house. And local merchants say the school's tax-exempt status creates an unfair competitive advantage for its food court.

Tax-Exempt Status

Communities use property taxes to provide public services. The taxes are assessed under state laws, on a basis related to the value of the property and its improvements. The local municipality estimates the value of property and then taxes owners based on that evaluation.

There are, however, a number of common exceptions to most state property taxation laws. The property of public colleges and universities, for example, is generally exempt from taxation — as part of the state tax law or a "sovereign immunity" agreement.

State tax laws may exempt college properties as a matter of public policy to avoid taxation between different levels of government. Under the policy of sovereign immunity, a lower level of government can't tax a higher level. In other words, the sovereign (a state or its agencies) is immune from the laws of lower forms of government (cities).

Exemptions for private colleges and universities are also based on public policy, as are exemptions for most religious, educational, and charitable organizations. To remain exempt, however, such an organization must show that its activities are related to religious, educational, or charitable purposes.

Traditionally, municipalities have made little effort to tax schools because of state laws and the sovereign immunity principle. But the role of colleges and universities has expanded beyond classrooms and labs. Schools are becoming increasingly involved in revenue-producing ventures.

At the same time, the cost of community services continues to grow, while citizen support for increased taxes keeps falling. So now tax collectors are starting to challenge higher education institutions. They're beginning to tax schools for properties that aren't specifically related to educational missions.

Faced with cost problems of their own, schools are taking their complaints about possible property taxes to the courts.

What Constitutes "Educational Use"?

Just what is an "educational use" that is protected from local taxation? An answer first began to develop when the purpose of a campus president's house was reviewed in *Appeal of the University of Pittsburgh*, 180 A.2d 760 (1962).

The school wanted to avoid property taxes on the home it provided to its president. It argued that the president was an official representative of the school who hosted a variety of school-related programs in his home.

The court supported the university's position. It cited an earlier Massachusetts case, *Amherst College v. Assessors*, 79 N.E. 248, which noted that:

> The residence of the head of a university or college necessarily renders a real function, tangibly and intangibly, in the life of the institution. While its utility to the purposes and objectives of the institution is incapable of exact measurement and evaluation, it is nonetheless real and valuable.

The decision, however, did not establish a rule that was beyond challenge. In a second Pennsylvania case, for instance, a somewhat similar situation led to a different outcome.

A president emeritus, retained by the school on a "consultative basis," received campus-owned housing. His role for the school was to simply assist in development and public relations.

Did this justify a property tax exemption? No, ruled the court.

In *In re Albright College*, 249 A.2d 833, 835 (1968), the court reviewed the use of the home. It found that the home was not available for general use by the school, as were other "educational" facilities. Instead, the record supported the town's contention that the home was provided to the past president "to properly afford him an appropriate dwelling house commensurate with his past worthy service."

An even more detailed review of the issue was conducted in a 1976 case, *Cook County Collector v. National College of Examination*, 354 N.E.2d 507. In the case, the court examined the institutional uses of the college president's home, which was said to be "used as well for a number of educational, fund-raising, business, alumni, and social activities of the college."

The court, however, ruled against the school's tax exemption claim. It said the house was "primarily" a residence, and that others could gain access to the house only by invitation. That didn't cut it under state tax exemption laws.

All of these cases highlight issues a campus must face when trying to avoid taxation on residences for officials or official functions. While the required proofs may vary from state to state, it's clear that any exemption claim must be strongly supported by evidence of *educational* use.

Dining Services

What about commercial dining facilities on campus? Are they subject to property taxes because of private ownership or management? Or are they exempt from property taxes because they support educational institutions?

One early case established an exempt status. But it was long before the days of fast food franchises in the middle of campus.

In *Goodman v. University of Illinois Foundation*, 58 N.E.2d 33 (1944), a court found that the campus dining service was exempt from taxation, even though it was a revenue producer for the school because it was a support service of the institution.

In 1967, a court ruled that a private dining service that had a contractual relationship with a school was also exempt from taxation (*Blair Academy v. Blairstown*, 232 A.2d 178). The school used the private firm for food services and gave the firm rent-free access to the school's kitchens.

The local tax collector said the setup was commercial and taxed the kitchens as commercial facilities. But the court disagreed with that assessment. It ruled that the school's decision to "contract out" for necessary support services did not make the kitchen facilities taxable. Said the court:

> The use of a catering system to feed the students and faculty of this boarding school cannot be regarded as a commercial activity or business venture of the school. ... It has been found expedient by the management of the school to have such a private caterer, in lieu of providing its own personnel to furnish this necessary service.

Current Challenges

Exemption principles are being disputed again in the Syracuse case. The university, for obvious reasons, wants to exercise any rights it has to avoid taxation. The local municipalities, on the other hand, want to maximize tax revenues.

The property taxes on the residence SU purchased for the school's former chancellor would be about $5,500 annually. But the school has asked the city to exempt the two-bedroom ranch house, saying it fulfills "educational purposes."

The school's lawyers say the ex-chancellor serves educational purposes, including consulting and other professional activities. He also maintains an administrative relationship to SU, they say. And his home, they argue, is an extension of his educational and administrative roles.

But a suburban tax assessor rejects the school's claim. He says there is no legitimate educational purpose for the home, and that the town should not be asked to subsidize "retirement" benefits for a former SU officer.

The city has asked a court to order SU to pay property taxes as well as court costs.

Similar arguments have followed since a new food court appeared on campus. The enterprise — which includes commercial vendors such as Kentucky Fried Chicken, Taco Bell, Pizza Hut, and Burger King — claims to be tax-exempt because of the school's non-tax status.

But city officials, responding to the complaints of nearby businesses, are attempting to tax the operation. The businesses see the campus venture as unfair competition, since it doesn't pay taxes like everyone else does. And the city sees the operation as an opportunity for additional tax support.

The courts will have the final say in both SU cases. Unless SU can show evidence that the house and the food operation provide "educational support," the campus will probably have to open up its checkbook!

Avoiding the Tax Bite

December 1990

Taxes. It's not anyone's favorite word. And yet, as the saying goes, taxes are just one of two sure things in life.

Taxation is an important issue for colleges and universities, with campuses paying local taxes, property taxes, sales taxes, and admissions taxes to local governments. Legal battles over tax issues have created some confusion on campus.

And as if those taxes didn't cause enough problems, watch out for this one — a tuition tax! The city council of Evanston (IL) voted to tax students attending college in the city $15 each quarter. Northwestern University, the largest of the four institutions of higher education in Evanston, threatened to take the tax to court.

Taxes and Campuses

In almost all tax battles involving colleges and universities, two questions are raised:

- Does the government have the power to tax?
- Does the school have some type of exemption from the tax?

The taxing power of local governments is established by the states. Each state has empowered counties, cities, towns, and villages to levy taxes under certain conditions. A campus challenge to local taxation is often a challenge to the locality's interpretation or use of state taxing authority. Does the state statute allow the locality to tax? What can it tax? Whom can it tax? What penalties can it impose for failure to pay taxes? These are all tests of local taxing power.

Exemption from taxes is often an issue in higher education. Even when the locality has the power to tax, does the school have to pay? This question often has the same answer for public and private institutions — but for very different reasons.

Public colleges and universities often claim exemptions from local taxes for *constitutional* or *sovereign immunity* reasons. Since public schools are created by the state, they aren't subject to county or municipal levels of government, which are also created by the state. Public schools use these arguments to gain exemptions from local taxes.

Private colleges and universities also enjoy some protection from local taxes. They depend on exemptions granted to charitable, religious, and educational institutions in the state.

Tax Types

At the local level, three taxes are most common:

- Property Taxes — on campus properties, based on the value of land and buildings
- Sales Taxes — on sales or purchases involving the campus
- Use Taxes — on attendance at campus events or participation in other forms

For each of these taxes, colleges and universities challenge the authority of localities to tax them, and they seek exemptions from the taxes.

In most states, non-profit organizations and institutions are exempt from local property taxes, but only if the property is used for exempt purposes. Campus housing has often been tested, with colleges and communities arguing over "exempt purposes."

For instance, is a house for the campus president exempt from property taxes? In *Appeal of the University of Pittsburgh*, 407 Pa. 416, 180 A. 2d 760 (1962), the court sided with the school, which contended that the house served an educational purpose. Since the president's home was used to host events and serve as an institutional meeting place, the court supported the exemption claim. But in *Cook County Collector v. National College of Education*, 41 Ill. App. 633, N.E.2d 507 (1976), the court denied similar claims for exemption. The president's home, said the court, was only a home. No classes were held in it and access was by invitation only. If the purpose of the house wasn't educational, it couldn't be granted an educational exemption from local taxes.

Student housing has met similar challenges, generally known as the "primary use" test — Is the primary use of the facility or property for an exempt purpose? While student residence halls have generally been allowed educational exemptions from property taxes, housing for faculty, staff, married students, and fraternities has faced tougher challenges.

In *MacMurray College v. Wright*, 38 Ill. 2d 272, 230 N.E.2d 846 (1967), staff and faculty housing on campus was found to be taxable. The state court failed to see an educational purpose for the property, since its primary use was as housing:

> The record does not show that any of the faculty or staff members ... were required, because of their educational duties, to live in these residences or ... perform any of their professional duties there.

But for married-student housing, courts have tended to find an educational purpose. In *Southern Illinois University v. Booker*, 98 Ill. App. 3d 1062, 425 N.E.2d 465 (1981), a court ruled:

> We consider married student housing as necessary to the education of a married student as single-student housing is to a single student. Since the use of dormitory housing, serving essentially single students, is deemed primarily educational rather then residential, the use of family housing for married students should

likewise be deemed primarily educational, and such property should enjoy tax-exempt status.

Fraternity houses have also been put to the "primary use" test. When Greek houses are operated as part of a school's housing program, tax exemptions have sometimes been granted, as in *Alford v. Emory University*, 216 Ga. 391, 116 S.E.2d 596 (1960), and *Johnson v. Southern Greek Housing Corporation*, 307 S.E.2d 491 (1983). But in other cases, the social and recreational uses of Greek housing, whether owned by the school or the organization, have been seen as non-exempt. In *Cornell University v. Board of Assessors*, 24 A.D. 526, 260 N.Y.S.2d 197 (1965), the court ruled that, since the house wasn't used "exclusively" for educational purposes, it couldn't enjoy an educational exemption.

As shown, the key issue in exemption claims is the use of the facility or property. Where the court finds that use is exclusively or primarily for an exempt purpose, it will grant an exemption.

The ability of a community to impose *sales taxes* is based on state constitutional or statutory law. Such law may allow schools to be taxed when they make purchases or sales. In *New York University v. Taylor*, 251 A.D. 444, 296 N.Y.S.848 (1937), a city attempt to tax school purchases and sales was defeated due to an educational exception. The court found the school to be a "semipublic institution" and thus exempt.

Imposition of *use taxes*, including admission taxes, is also subject to questions of authority and exemptions. When a tax is imposed by one governmental entity on another, an exemption can be claimed. Thus, in *City of Boulder v. Regents of the University of Colorado*, 501 P.2d 123 (1972), the court overturned a city attempt to tax football tickets of the state university. The city didn't have the legal authority to tax. However, the court noted that if authority for taxation had been established, only events that were non-educational could be taxed.

Tuition Tax?

The Evanston city council has approved a tuition tax, which could raise over $500,000 from students studying in the city. Evanston claims the tax is fair, since the city provides the four schools with police and fire protection services without reimbursement.

Area schools object strongly to the new tax, and they've threatened court fights. Northwestern has mounted an extensive lobbying campaign against the tax and sent a special issue of the campus staff newsletter to every home in the city, detailing the school's many contributions to Evanston.

If the city persists in its attempt to be the first municipality in the country to tax tuition, the court will explore two basic questions: Does the city have the authority to tax? And do the school or its students have a right to a tax exemption?

Campus Housing: A Taxing Problem

February 1990

Can a community impose property taxes on campus housing? Many municipalities have tried, with mixed legal results, leaving this as a topic for serious consideration.

There are two key factors in considering exemptions from property taxes for institutions of higher education: the nature of the school (public or private) and the use of the property.

Generally, a public school's property is exempt from local taxation under state law. *Supremacy laws* limit the ability of governmental creations to regulate or tax their creators. So cities, which are creations of the state, are not in a position to tax state-operated schools. Since the municipalities' authority to tax comes from the state, the state can limit that authority, and it often does so to restrict taxation.

But what if the state-operated school doesn't hold title to the property in question? That was the issue in *Southern Illinois University v. Booker*, 98 Ill. App. 3d 1062, 425 N.E.2d 465 (1981). Married student housing was owned by the school's private foundation, and the community challenged the school's claim of exemption. The court sided with the school, noting that the school had control and benefits of the housing, even though it didn't have legal title. Since the foundation had been formed solely "to promote the interests and welfare" of the school, its property was found to be exempt.

Other exemptions may also be available. Most states have exemptions for *educational* organizations. Where property is used for educational purposes by *not-for-profit* organizations, including some colleges and universities, the property may be exempt from local taxation. When applying for this exemption, the definition of "educational" is often debated.

When a House Is Not a Home

Is the president's house used for educational purposes? How about faculty-staff housing? Case law isn't clear.

In *Appeal of the University of Pittsburgh*, 407 Pa. 416, 180 A.2d 760 (1962), a state court ruled that presidential housing could be exempt from property tax. The ruling was based on the needs of the "image" of a president as "official representative" and the business conducted in the home on behalf of the school. But in *Cook County Collector v. National College of Education*, 354 N.E. 2d 507 (1976), the court reviewed whether the president's house was "exclusively" or "primarily" used for educational purposes. While the home was sometimes used in support of the school, it was not used for classes, and its primary use was as a residence. Fundraising, business, social, and alumni activities were not held to be sufficiently "educational" to support an exemption from property taxes.

Similar uncertainty exists with regard to faculty-staff housing. Again, the test for exemptions can be "primary" or "exclusive" educational use of the property. In a key case, *MacMurray College v. Wright*, 230 N.E.2d 846 (1967), the court denied a tax exemption, applying a primary use test. Since faculty and staff weren't required to live in the housing for any educational purposes, the court found the housing to be primarily *residential*, not *educational*.

Greek housing is also subject to property tax challenges. If fraternity-sorority housing is owned by a school, an educational component must be established to support an exemption.

In *Cornell University v. Board of Assessors*, 260 N.Y.S.2d 197 (1967), the court applied the "exclusive use" test to university-owned fraternity houses. It denied them a property tax exemption, ruling that houses used for purposes other than "the essential functions of housing and feeding students" — houses "devoted, in substantial part, to the social and other personal objectives of a privately organized, self-perpetuating club" — weren't entitled to tax exemptions.

But houses that are operated as key components of the entire residential life program may be exempt, as in *Alford v. Emory University*, 116 S.E.2d 596 (1960), and *University of Rochester v. Wagner*, 408 N.Y.S.2d 157 (1978). In *Rochester*, "the social activity" of the housing use was held to be "essential to the personal, social, and moral development of the student," which established an educational use. The housing was exempt for the same reason as residence halls.

Questions to Consider

Just as campuses are very different, types of housing on campuses can differ widely. In assessing the possibility of tax exemptions for residential properties, consider the following questions:

- Is the institution that owns the residential property *private* or *public*?
- Is an exemption built into state taxing authority for state agencies like public universities?
- If the property is owned by an auxiliary organization, is the use of it for the "benefit of" and "controlled by" the school?
- Is the housing used "primarily" or "exclusively" for educational purposes by a not-for-profit organization?

While state and local laws and rulings control this area of the law, with inconclusive results, the answers to these questions can assist in assessing possible taxability of campus housing.

UBIT Takes Bite Out of Campus Income

September 1991

It seemed like an obvious money-maker, not the start of a significant legal battle between the federal government and higher education. Officials at Ohio State University thought they could raise over $1 million annually by selling advertising space on the football stadium scoreboard. And that's what they did — until the Internal Revenue Service came to play. And what they saw on the scoreboard was potential tax dollars!

Unrelated Business Income Tax (UBIT) regulations require nonprofit groups to pay taxes on income received from activities unrelated to the not-for-profit status. Ohio State University is in the education business, not the advertising business, said the IRS. Therefore, the income from the scoreboard advertising was taxable, since it was not directly related to research and education.

OSU initially settled with the IRS for $500,000 for scoreboard income from 1985 through 1989, but it is now appealing that payment. Why? Because of a 1990 appeals court ruling that questioned the regulations.

Figuring out taxes is not easy for individuals or institutions. IRS regulations and forms are often complex and difficult to apply to specific circumstances. While liability or contract cases are often decided on the basis of legal precedents, tax law does not provide similar guidance to parties trying to understand the law and responsibilities under it.

When the IRS rules on issues, it produces what is called a "private letter." That answers the questions of one taxpayer only. It may provide some guidance to others, but it cannot be cited as a precedent by others. So that leaves colleges and universities with the difficult task of applying IRS rulings and regulations without the benefit of case law.

Most colleges and universities find general exemption from taxation in Section 501 (c) (3) of the Internal Revenue Code. This section exempts educational and charitable organizations from taxes, based on a desire to advance knowledge and science and to lessen the need for greater government service or support.

Income generated by activities *related* to the nonprofit educational nature of a college or university is not subject to taxes. But income from *unrelated* activities may be if it is:

- Generated from a business or trade
- Regular activity

However, not all unrelated income is taxable. The IRS Code offers some exemptions for campus consideration, including income from:

- Services offered for the convenience of the campus community
- Activities in which the labor and goods are donated
- Research performed for government agencies
- Passive sources like royalties and rentals
- Student-generated income from educational programs

The OSU scoreboard advertising income is just one of many current concerns over the application of UBIT to campuses. Campus computer services, publications, athletic events, bookstores, gift shops, theater festivals, and medical services and products are all under IRS scrutiny. Are the goods and services related to an exempt purpose? Are they ongoing? Do they meet the requirements for an exemption?

Current Position on Advertising

Advertising on campus can be found in many forms: in campus newspapers and telephone directories, on radio and TV stations, in athletic program books, and on scoreboards. In each case, the IRS will look at the source of the income generated, what the advertising is for, and whether it's for the convenience of the campus community.

Ads sold in campus directories or schedules are tax-exempt, as they are related activities for the convenience of the students and staff. However, if the directories or schedules are run as businesses, taxes would be owed.

Advertising income in student newspapers was thought to be exempt if related to the academic purposes of the school. It was a standard campus practice to include campus announcements, academic articles, and other institutional or educational materials to maintain this status.

But an IRS audit of the University of Texas has ruled that all of the advertising revenues from the school newspaper may be subject to tax. The government ruled that the newspaper was not directly part of required student academic coursework and was not serving an important campus purpose related to its mission. UT is challenging that finding through an administrative appeals process.

Advertising in athletic programs has generally been taxed. When the NCAA used a professional marketing agent to sell space in the Final Four basketball program, the tax court ruled that tax was owed. But in a ruling that Ohio State is depending on, the U.S. Court of Appeals for the Tenth Circuit ruled that no tax was owed for the program because the activity was "not regularly carried on" by the schools or association. OSU would like to get the same ruling for its scoreboard advertising, since it is seasonal and ads are sold only for a brief period of time.

Radio and TV time sold to generate campus revenues will be judged for tax purposes by the nature of the station and its program. Stations operated commercially by campus for the purposes of generating income will be subject to tax.

Services, Activities, and Sales

The campus development of *computer services and software* has been seen as related to the academic functions of the institution. Revenues generated from the sale of these services have not been taxed unless done as a business enterprise.

Income from *university press operations* is generally exempt from tax if the publications are educational and published for educational uses. Factors to be considered would include the type of materials published and the method of distribution. The production and sale of publications that are academic and not distributed in a commercial manner will be exempt from UBIT.

What about income from *athletic programs and events*, such as admission tickets, souvenirs, and summer camps? Is it subject to tax? Generally, the IRS has agreed that athletic and recreation programs are part of higher education and not subject to taxes. Since the income is generated by an exempt activity and is used by the institution to support programs related to its mission, it is free from UBIT.

Many campuses generate significant income from *bookstores and gift shops*. These sales often cause resentment among local vendors, who complain that the campus is unfairly competing with them, using subsidy dollars from taxpayers.

Most campus bookstore sales have been held exempt from federal taxation under the "convenience" exception in the Code. Typical bookstore inventory items are exempt, with the exception of income from the sale of non-insignia clothing, plants, and furniture. These are subject to tax under a 1958 IRS ruling.

Sales from campus gift shops are subject to a different standard. Items sold in an educational setting that encourage further educational development are exempt if the setting and the educational experience are related. Thus, sales from a museum shop of items related to that museum's exhibits are exempt, while the sale of other educational items is not.

Much of the tax and business competition pressure on bookstore and gift shop sales has been from state and local officials. One example has been the application of the state Umstead Act on the University of North Carolina-Chapel Hill bookstore. The local prosecutor's office ruled that the campus stores could not sell non-insignia items readily available in the surrounding community, including gift cards, photo development, stuffed animals, and health care products.

State laws have also pressured campuses over campus *theater festivals* and some *medical products and services*.

After years of legal battles, Southern Oregon State University's participation in a local Shakespeare festival has been ruled as an exempt activity. To keep it that way, the school must keep an educational purpose behind its involvement. But several states, including Arizona, have ruled that the provision or sale of items such as hearing aids to clinic patients is not an exempt activity.

Summary

Tax exemptions due to educational status are limited to educational and related activities. Colleges and universities wanting to protect income from federal UBIT taxation need to generate income educationally, not commercially. Campus businesses run on an ongoing basis may produce income — but that income will be taxed.

At Ohio State University, officials estimate that $300,000 of every $1 million received from scoreboard advertising would go to the government if subject to UBIT. OSU hopes that the ads will be seen as substantially related to the institution's mission and not as an ongoing commercial endeavor.

For the time being, federal talk of rewriting UBIT to create greater campus taxation has slowed down. But obvious campus efforts to generate funds commercially without applying UBIT will incur the wrath of local vendors and place additional public and legislative attention on this sensitive and fiscally important topic.

Who Pays Taxes for This Event?

September 1993

Tax concerns are raised each time a commercial presence is found on a college campus. The federal government generally questions how the money is being made and who, if anyone, is paying taxes on it. The issue is federal Unrelated Business Income Tax (UBIT) regulations — and it remains a topic for debate.

Recent Examples

Scoreboard advertising revenues and major campus events ticket sales are only the latest examples of activities that have caught the attention of both local businesses and the Internal Revenue Service. In each case, questions are raised about the appropriateness of the activity to the schools' primary purpose. At Ohio State University and other schools, the issue recently has been taxes on revenues from advertising on stadium scoreboards. The OSU case is an example of differences of opinion between college campuses and the IRS over revenues.

The government ruled that advertising income is not related to the original and primary purposes of the school. The IRS ruled that OSU's $1 million in advertising revenues were subject to taxation, since the athletic stadium advertising revenues were not directly related to teaching, research, and education. The government demanded payment of taxes. Non-profit organizations are exempt from federal taxes from revenues generated for their primary activities, not unrelated business activities. Advertising was ruled "unrelated business income" in the OSU case. The school paid $500,000 in taxes over a five-year period before another court case gave it an opportunity to appeal.

In a case involving advertising in the NCAA Final Four game program, a federal appellate panel ruled income exempt from taxation because it didn't meet an IRS requirement that the activity be "regularly carried on." Based on that ruling, OSU argued that no taxes should be owed on stadium advertising, as it is only used on an occasional basis. Up to $300,000 a year from OSU depends on the definition of "substantially related ... to the primary not-for-profit enterprise and ... regularly carried on."

Also of concern is a 1992 IRS ruling on school-sponsored or school-hosted entertainment events. In a state university case involving an auditorium, the government ruled that "ticket sale" events in the building were taxable. Tickets were sold through commercial brokers, and the events were commercially produced. The events ranged from traveling theater productions to rock concerts. The IRS ruling (Ltr. Rul. 9147008) contends, "These events were not ... an integral part of the educational program."

The campus maintained that the facility was regularly used for educational events, such as class registration, athletics, and graduation ceremonies. During the audited year, it was used only 45 times for ticket sale events. The IRS found those events unrelated to the school's purpose.

The school argued against the tax vigorously. It claimed that promotion of the arts and exposure of students to the arts was substantially related to its purpose. A balanced program of out-of-the-classroom experiences supplemented the academic process. The IRS didn't agree. It said that, if money was made, it was unrelated business income and taxable.

Campus Response

Faced with difficulties related to disputes over advertising and ticket sales revenues, what can campuses do?

When considering advertising issues and possible "unrelated business income taxes," it's important to understand the factors that determine taxability. These include the intended audience, the type of advertising, competition with outside advertising, and convenience to the campus community.

Advertising in campus publications, like class schedules and directories, has been upheld as tax-exempt. They are judged to be a convenience for the campus. But if the publications operate like commercial enterprises, they will be taxed like commercial enterprises. Campus newspaper advertising is also exempt, if the publication serves legitimate campus interests through news, announcements, and other educational opportunities.

But sports-related advertising has not been so favorably judged, from the campus perspective. Most sports program advertising has been judged taxable. Some advertising may be exempt, due to its limited nature. This exemption cites the NCAA Final Four publication that was exempt because it was not a venture "regularly carried on." In exempting the income, the government looked at the period when the advertising was available, not the longer period during which it was sold.

To avoid problems related to the "ticket sales" events on campus, experts suggest a response based on the IRS letter ruling:

- The need to increase income should not be the motivating factor behind programming efforts; find a purpose closer to the campus purposes.

- Sell campus tickets for less than a commercially sponsored event would, to demonstrate an intent to "promote" the arts to the community.

- Use different contracts and terms than commercial enterprises would; don't limit commercial activities through the contract with clauses that prohibit other performances in the area.

- Provide significant student ticket discounts to assist in the educational purposes of the event.

- Involve academic personnel, such as fine arts faculty, in the event decision-making process.

Summary

For almost a decade, Congress has been considering ways to tighten UBIT regulations. Colleges and universities that continue to expand their revenue-producing programs and services should be aware that they are under the watchful eyes of local businesses and the federal government.

Communities Tighten Controls on Students

November 1991

You think you have some town-gown problems that need to be addressed? Wonder what the local community may think of next to control college students?

Consider the "Community Harmony Program," developed by the three towns surrounding Villanova University (PA). Through land zoning, housing and property maintenance codes, state and local ordinances, and alcohol beverage laws, the towns have set strict controls over student conduct.

The Township of Lower Merion has developed a series of regulations and an education program to "address those problems most generally experienced as a result of rental homes in residential communities." The "Harmony" program outlines community standards and enforcement efforts. It highlights the responsibilities of the town, its citizens, its judges, its police, and its college student residents.

Building regulations have been established to require property owners and occupants to maintain their premises. All rental properties must be inspected and registered annually in the town. Property owners and tenants are required to "protect the public health, safety, and welfare" by specific maintenance:

- Cutting grass and trimming overgrown hedges
- Maintaining the exterior and interior of the property
- Removing all trash and debris from the grounds
- Placing all trash in cans with lids
- Maintaining all steps, sidewalks, and curbs

Complaints of non-compliance are directed to town housing inspectors, who contact involved landlords and tenants directly. Violations can lead to fines of up to $1,000 each day.

Zoning regulations have also been established to limit occupancy of rental homes. The local code prohibits more than three unrelated individuals from residing in a single dwelling. In addition, the town has established a special zoning law for property considered "student homes." A *student home* is defined as:

> A living arrangement for a number of students unrelated by blood, marriage, or legal adoption attending or planning to attend either undergraduate colleges or universities, or attending or planning to attend graduate programs at colleges or universities; or who are on a semester break from studies at colleges and universities, or any combination of such persons. The residents of a student house share living expenses and may live and cook as a single housekeeping unit but may also only share access to cooking facilities.

Under the restrictive law, homes rented or used for student housing must meet specific standards:

- Limit of no more than three occupants
- Minimum yard area, setback, and lot size requirements
- Separation of student homes (limiting them to not being within 20 lots of each other)
- Minimum building size requirements
- Minimum of three off-street, on-site parking spaces
- Annual registration of the manager and home with local authorities

As part of "a determined enforcement/educational campaign," student residents are regularly cautioned about *state and local conduct laws* and local ordinances. The students are advised that disorderly conduct charges can result from these behaviors:

- Fighting or threatening, or violent or tumultuous behaviors
- Unreasonable noise
- Obscene language or obscene gestures
- Creation of hazardous or physically offensive conditions that serve no legitimate purpose

The campaign also stresses ordinances governing public drunkenness, alcohol purchase and possession, corruption of minors, and false police or fire alarms.

In delineating responsibilities, a *building regulation* department is charged with inspecting and licensing of rental properties and enforcing the maintenance and zoning codes. The *local police* work with the department and enforce state and local alcohol and conduct laws. The town has also established a "Special Incident File," based on complaints at specific addresses, to build case histories for use in possible litigation.

The education effort notes that the local *judges* are "sensitive to the concerns of residents" and committed to seriously hearing charges that disrupt town harmony. The town advises *students* to behave "in a lifestyle coinciding with those of the community" and urges *citizens* to report to authorities "conduct that affects the peace, tranquility or quality of life."

Other area municipalities have adopted similar measures to address the problems sometimes caused by college students in residential neighborhoods.

The Township of Radnor adopted a more restrictive zoning policy on non-family occupancy of residential properties. It limits occupancy of any unit to only one person not related to the others. While a family can occupy residential property without restriction, only two unrelated students can rent property.

Haverford has enacted student housing regulations similar to those in Lower Merion, including the minimum standards, distance apart, and parking requirements. And to make sure that landlords and student tenants obey the law, penalties for violations are fines of up to $1,000 per day per violation. Failure to pay can also result in 30-day jail sentences.

These small college communities have acted to control traditional student problems in what students consider to be a "Draconian" manner. The "Community Harmony Program" effectively eliminates most student housing in the area. Officials from colleges and universities, student leaders, and other municipalities will be watching closely to see what becomes of community harmony in these towns.

There's Battle Lines Being Drawn

December 1991

It's déjà vu all over again, as Yogi Berra might say. Students on campuses all across the country are battling military recruiters. But instead of opposition to war, which fueled protests of the '60s and '70s, today's battles are over recruitment policies. The U.S. Armed Forces won't allow gays and lesbians into the services and that has prompted student groups and some campuses to invoke anti-discrimination regulations.

Under some state, municipal, and campus guidelines, discrimination on the basis of sexual orientation is unlawful. Employers coming to these campuses must agree not to discriminate in order to use career planning and development services. For most, this is not a problem. For the military, however, it is a major issue. And across the country, military recruiting and the Reserve Officer Training Corps (ROTC) have become legal targets. But on whose side is the law? And what if state and federal laws are in conflict?

On-Campus Recruiting Causes Problems

The battle is over a long-standing policy of the Defense Department, prohibiting homosexuals from enlistment and retireing military personnel found to be gay or lesbian. Homosexuality, says the Armed Forces, is "incompatible with military service." A coalition of college and university presidents has asked the military to reconsider its policy, and other interest groups and institutions (including accreditation agencies) are trying to force a change. But so far, the policy remains intact.

The latest action comes from New York, where a state Human Rights Division office recently ruled that the State University at Buffalo Law School violated state policy by permitting military recruiters to use campus facilities. The Office of Gay and Lesbian Concerns ruled that the campus had unlawfully provided state benefits or services to agencies that discriminated on the basis of sexual orientation. The Office ordered the school to halt military recruiting and required proof of the school's compliance within 60 days.

The state order was not based on New York law, interestingly. State anti-discrimination laws do not specify protections based on sexual orientation. Instead, the state governor had issued executive orders to all state agencies requiring that state actions not discriminate against gays and lesbians. The agency used these orders to say that the state campus, as a state university agency, was bound to follow the governor's policy. By providing space to military recruiters, the Office said, the campus violated the executive order.

But even before the students, the campus, or the Armed Forces could react to the decision, the state governor himself said the ban on military recruiting was not enforceable. Since it was based solely on the executive order, the governor contended that the state did not have the power of law to enforce the decision. The Human Rights Division has no authority to sue other state agencies based on an executive order.

The SUNY system did not appeal the decision. The campus felt that the state law took precedent over the governor's executive order. The university also contended that the executive order, which bars discrimination on the basis of sexual orientation, applies to university decision-making — such as hiring — but not to the actions of others who may come in contact with the campus. Military recruiting will continue at Buffalo until the matter is resolved, although representatives will not be using career services.

Buffalo is only one of many sites in the growing national dispute. A policy of the American Association of Law Schools requires all members to bar recruiters who discriminate on the basis of sexual orientation. Many schools have adopted that policy, but not without a fight. When military recruiters were barred from the law school at Drake University (IA), the U.S. Marines Corps reacted strongly. The USMC reminded the school about a 1972 Vietnam War-era law linking military recruiting to defense-related research or financial aid. The law says that institutions that ban military recruiting may not receive federal defense-related funding. While Drake altered its policy and allowed military recruiting to continue, it noted that the law school itself did not receive any federal defense support. Drake made its decision, according to officials, to stay in compliance with the law.

The Marines faced a similar experience at the University of Kansas, where they were barred from campus career-counseling facilities. Campus officials reviewed the ban in light of the 1972 law and ongoing defense funds received from the federal government. While vowing to work with other schools to change military rules against homosexual persons, the school did eventually reopen its doors to Armed Services recruitment.

A ban on military recruiting at the University of Minnesota Law School has provoked a legal response. One student, complaining that the ban violated his constitutional rights, has asked a federal district court to overturn the school policy. He claims that the ban on armed service recruitment violates his rights to free speech, expression, and association.

ROTC: Back in the Limelight

The non-discrimination battle has also refocused state and federal attention on campus ROTC programs. After a decade of relative calm, the programs are again under attack.

Why? Because they bar homosexual persons from participation. As many campuses adopted or considered enacting regulations to ban ROTC programs, legislative attention was attracted. In two states, Ohio and Illinois, legislatures passed bills that would prevent public colleges and universities from removing ROTC programs. The Ohio bill was part of the state budget package and received little notice or debate.

Campus concerns over ROTC programs and sexual discrimination have also been raised at Kent State University (OH), Bowling Green State University (OH), Ohio State University, and the University of Cincinnati. Actions on these campuses included disclaimers on university publications, calls for program termination, establishment of study committees, and lobbying efforts designed to change Defense Department policy. Lawmakers acted to limit public college and university responses to the policy.

Illinois lawmakers' attempts to control campus decision-making on ROTC programs did not make it past the governor's desk. That law would have required public colleges and universities in the state to continue military recruiting and ROTC programming. But the governor vetoed the measure, calling it an intrusion into the authority of college and university governing bodies.

Meanwhile, at the University of Wisconsin-Madison, officials are planning to sue the federal government over its ROTC enrollment policies. It's been two years since the faculty asked that ROTC programming end unless the enrollment policies changed. The school had asked the American Council on Education to help finance the case, but ACE's board thought a statement condemning the ban on homosexual persons would be more appropriate.

The ROTC enrollment policy apparently violates campus and state regulations at UW-Madison. But the school estimates it would cost $500,000 to challenge the federal policy, and it wants financial help from organizations and schools. For UW-Madison to pursue the case, however, the state regents and attorney general's office would have to support the case. In the past, UW's regents have repeatedly stated their support for ROTC programs, so costs may not be the only factor delaying the challenge.

Congress Enters the Fray

Meanwhile, at the federal level, a congressman from New York introduced legislation that would deny federal funds to any school that denied access to the Defense Department. The bill was drafted in response to attempts by some secondary schools to bar military recruiting, but it could also be applied to college and university armed forces recruiting and ROTC programs if enacted.

The issue of sexual orientation and the military is in large part a conflict between state and local laws or policies and the federal government. Temple University (PA) learned that lesson when it found itself caught between the human rights laws of Philadelphia and federal policies. The school permitted military recruiters to use law school facilities, but objecting students claimed that the activity violated local human rights law. So when the school barred armed forces recruiters in compliance with the city ordinance, the federal government sued to get the military back on campus. In *United States v. City of Philadelphia* (798 F.2d 81, 1986), a federal appellate court considered these issues.

Citing a supremacy of laws principle, the court ruled that when laws are in conflict, federal law takes precedence over state law. The City of Philadelphia is only a creation of the state, thereby making federal law or policy supreme. Congress has authorized the military to establish its policies, and the military has done so legally, ruled the court. The city does not have the power to alter authorized national policies.

Summary

When conflicts exist among laws, the conflicts find their way into the courts. The status of state, municipal, and campus sexual orientation discrimination policies varies and is often at odds with the U.S. Defense Department policy barring homosexual persons from the Armed Forces. While the campuses are the battleground for today's scrimmages, the courts and legislatures will ultimately decide the issue. Until then, it's déjà vu on students vs. the military.

Gay, Lesbian Students Challenge the Military

November 1992

At schools across the country, the clash continues between gay rights and the federal military.

The military refuses to admit gays and lesbians into ROTC programs and won't recruit homosexuals for military careers or allow them to serve.

To many college students, these policies violate the protected rights of individuals, not to mention state laws and campus policies. The military, however, stands firm in its refusal of homosexuals.

Now the military's position is being tested in courtrooms, hearing rooms, meeting rooms, and classrooms across the country.

Background

Court challenges of the military's policy have not been very successful to date.

Most case law deals with homosexuals in active service, not those who are still in the recruitment process. The Department of Defense has had a public policy of discharging known gay and lesbian personnel since 1949. Discharge is required when personnel engage or attempt to engage in homosexual activity or openly state that they are gay or lesbian.

The military enforces the policy because it finds homosexuality "incompatible" with military service. Defense regulations note that:

> The presence of such members adversely affects the ability of the military services to maintain discipline, good order, and morale; to foster mutual trust and confidence among service members; to ensure the integrity of the system of rank and command; to facilitate assignment and world-wide deployment of service members who frequently must live and work under close conditions affording minimal privacy; to recruit and retain members of the Military Services; to maintain the public acceptability of military service; and to prevent breaches of security.

Federal courts have generally upheld Defense Department regulations. The courts have ruled that the policies do not violate rights of privacy (*Woodward v. United States*, 871 F.2d 1068, 1990), equal protection clauses (*Dronenburg v. Zeck*, 741 F.2d 1388, 1984), or free speech provisions (*Ben-Shalom v. Marsh*, 881 F.2d 454, 1989). Each case dealt with active military personnel.

In one reported ROTC case, *Matthews v. Marsh*, 755 F.2d 182 (1985), a student was tossed out of a program because she told a superior she was a lesbian. The student challenged the dismissal on First Amendment grounds and won an initial free speech judgment.

But her case was dismissed when she listed numerous homosexual activities on her re-application. The appellate court said the military could act on the student's known or admitted conduct, not just speech. So the student's dismissal from the ROTC program was upheld.

Based on cases such as *Woodward*, *Dronenburg*, *Ben-Shalom*, and *Matthews*, the military's ban on homosexual admission into ROTC programs or active service has been judicially protected.

Current Challenges

Across the country, campuses and systems are attempting to overturn the military's policy — using a variety of strategies.

At the University of Minnesota, for example, a federal court has ruled that the school may prohibit military recruiters who discriminate against homosexuals.

The campus has a policy of denying access to employers who discriminate by race, gender, religion, disability, or sexual orientation. Using a free speech basis, the court ruled that military recruitment is not a constitutionally protected right.

In *Nomi v. Regents for the University of Minnesota*, a federal district court judge ruled that recruiting speech is "commercial speech," which government can regulate to a reasonable degree for government purposes.

A law student had challenged the campus ban on military recruiting. The student, a former military officer, said the school had violated the military's "free speech" and used campus rules inconsistently.

The court, however, saw it differently. But it did allow the military to continue using UM's career planning facilities to promote general military service and issues.

At the University of Cincinnati, ROTC is at the center of a dispute. ROTC's ban on gay and lesbian students was challenged at a recent meeting of the school's board of trustees. The trustees say the policy violates the university's non-discrimination regulations.

A battle of campus regulations, state law, and military policy is also under way at Cornell University (NY). Campus policy prohibits discrimination based on sexual orientation. But state education law requires colleges and universities to give the military the same access to campus recruitment services that other employers have.

That law was adopted in the wake of the anti-war movement of the late '60s, when campuses were under pressure to bar the military and military suppliers from campus job placement services.

Cornell has joined a list of schools asking the Defense Department to reconsider its policy against homosexuals. In a letter to the Secretary of Defense, Cornell noted that it had dual, but in this case conflicting, traditions of support for the military and opposition to discrimination.

The military is claiming "breach of contract" at California State University-Chico, where the ROTC program has lost its accreditation.

The school ended ROTC's accreditation in response to its ban of gays and lesbians. Now the military is telling the school to honor its agreement or face court action.

The faculty senate has voted on a shutdown schedule for the program — unless the military changes its policy.

Recruiting is the controversy at the University of Alabama. The law school has a policy of non-discrimination but has continued to allow military recruiting.

After losing access to campus facilities for a time, military recruiters were allowed to return to campus last spring.

In Illinois, lawmakers are reconsidering legislation that protects ROTC programs on state campuses.

During the Persian Gulf War, the state adopted a law that prohibits state schools from terminating ROTC programs because of their ban on homosexuals. Now, several state representatives have proposed legislation to reverse that law and allow program termination.

In New York, the conflict between non-discrimination principles and government regulation has led to a state human rights complaint. A State University of New York at Buffalo law student challenged the school's policy on military recruitment, which was permitted despite extensive debate. The student filed a complaint with the state, claiming the military's practice violated a state non-discrimination order.

The student won a judgment against the school, but on appeal the ruling was overturned. The state's human rights division ruled that the complaint should have been denied. It said the school did not violate the state order because the military ban has been upheld by courts.

The human rights division also said that the state law on equal access for all recruiters was applicable in the case. Under the law, educational institutions must give the military the same recruitment facilities and services they give to other employers.

What's Next?

The pressure to change the military's ban on homosexuals has increased. But to date, there is little government movement on the policy. But students will no doubt continue to challenge ROTC and military recruitment programs — on campus and in the courts.

Federal Funds Have Strings Attached

October 1990

Linkage. It's not a word that colleges and universities want to hear when it comes to student financial aid packages. Linkage means the government has "linked" access to federal financial support with an unrelated interest or concern. For example, to compel states to adopt higher minimum drinking ages, the government "linked" drinking age to highway funds. States had to change their laws to get federal support.

The 1980s saw a linkage between financial aid and military service draft registration. And just as the legal battles over that issue faded away toward the end of the decade, financial aid packages became linked to substance abuse. College students and public interest groups have long fought linkages like this one, but, as legal challenges to the draft linkage indicate, government has traditionally enjoyed great latitude in controlling its resources.

Two Attacks Against Draft Linkage

In 1983, legal battles over draft registration hit the federal courts. Students who needed financial aid to attend school brought suit in Minnesota. They wanted to block enforcement of the government's linkage of financial aid to draft registration. In Doe v. Selective Service System, 557 F.Supp. 937 (1983), a federal district court heard arguments over the Department of Defense Authorization Act, section 1113. Under that law, those eligible for the draft who failed to register would be denied federally supported education aid. To get aid, students had to sign a compliance statement, which was then subject to governmental scrutiny.

The students claimed, in legal papers, that the process was unconstitutional. By denying aid in this manner, they argued, the government was punishing them without the benefit of any judicial process. This would be the equivalent of a bill of attainder, prohibited by the Constitution. They also complained that their legal protections against *self-incrimination* were being violated, since they had to refuse to sign the compliance statement if they didn't register. This could inform the government that they were in violation of the registration law. The students sought an injunction blocking enforcement of the law.

For a court to grant an injunction, there must be potential for "irreparable harm." The court saw that denial of aid would prevent some students from attending school. It considered this a legitimate harm. With regard to the Fifth Amendment issue, the court agreed that students couldn't apply for aid without risking self-incrimination. This, too, could be viewed as irreparable harm.

The district court sided with the students. It found that enforcement of the law could harm the students and that the students stood a good chance of success when their case came to full trial. The court granted the students an injunction.

In a similar test, a public interest group sought to fight the law before aid was denied to any student for failing to comply with the draft registration requirement. In *Minnesota Public Interest Research Group (MPIRG) v. Selective Service System*, 557 F.Supp. 925 (1983), a district court agreed that there was a legal issue to be tried but ruled that the public interest group lacked *standing* to pursue the case alone on behalf of individuals.

For a group to sue on behalf of an individual or a group of individuals, it would have to show that:

- Members of the group have a right to sue on their own.
- The interests of the suit are the interests of the group.
- Individuals are not needed in the suit to pursue the claim.

While the court saw the advantages of having a group pursue the claim, it found that the public interest group had no right to carry forward the student linkage case.

By 1984, the Minnesota issue of draft-aid linkage reached the U.S. Supreme Court. In *Selective Service System v. Minnesota Public Interest Research Group*, 104 S.Ct. 3348, 468 U.S. 841 (1984), the Court dealt with the district court injunction against enforcement of the rule. It explored the issues of bills of attainder and self-incrimination.

On the question of bills of attainder, the Court took a narrow view: it sided with the government and allowed the linkage to stand. The majority opinion cited the need for the government to properly handle its scarce resources and saw a rational connection between receiving government aid and living up to governmental responsibilities.

The Court also reviewed the issue of compelled self-incrimination; again it sustained the position of the government. The Court held that those who didn't register weren't compelled to seek federal financial aid; therefore, they weren't forced to incriminate themselves.

Two Other Arguments Fail

The two Minnesota cases were unsuccessful attempts to overturn the linkage with bill of attainder and Fifth Amendment claims. Meanwhile, students in other states were trying to overturn the aid-draft linkage using other arguments — that the government went beyond its legal authority in making the rules and that the law violated the First Amendment.

In *Dickinson v. Bell*, 580 F.Supp. 432 (1984), three female students challenged the law out of sympathy for male classmates. The women refused to sign the compliance forms mandated by the Department of Education. They claimed that the rules for the linkage as developed by the department exceeded the legislative mandate, and that their refusal to sign was protected First Amendment expression as a political statement.

While the court expressed displeasure with the whole system of linkages, it ultimately ruled in favor of the government. Congress had authorized the Department of Education to establish rules to carry out its mandate, and the court found the system created to be rational and defensible. As for the First Amendment claims, the court found the process to place only a "minimal" burden on free speech. By signing the form, students weren't being forced to say they agreed with government policy, only that they had complied with the law or were exempt. The court didn't hold this to be protected free speech. Claims of exceeding authority and free speech did not overturn the linkage.

Similar issues were raised the next year in a case that went to the First Circuit U.S. Court of Appeals. In *Alexander v. Trustees of Boston University*, 776 F.2d 630 (1985), the students claimed that the process violated their First Amendment freedom of religion protections and, as in *Dickinson*, they accused the Education Department of exceeding its authority.

The court examined the secretary's authority and found the department's policy to be legally sound. It also found the regulations and the collection of related data from students to be rational and within the limits of the law.

The court also found no substance in the students' freedom of religion claims. The Department of Defense Authorization Act, said the court, had no particular religious implications and had very limited impact on any student First Amendment rights. The court held that the needs of government, in ensuring military readiness, outweighed any limited burdens on constitutional protections.

Court Rules Draft-Tuition Linkage Legal

Ohio college students who do not register for Selective Service can be charged out-of-state tuition rates. That's the decision of the state's supreme court. It has overturned a lower court ruling that held that the practice violated the Ohio Constitution.

The high court ruled that the 1987 state Selective Service law was legal, as "Ohio has a legitimate interest, as does any state, in helping to promote the objectives of the federal government in providing for a common defense." The ACLU had argued unsuccessfully that there must be some relationship between the restriction and Selective Service. But the court ruled that the state could link its provision of state benefits to state residents who complied with the state law.

To identify non-compliance, OSU runs a computer student data check against Selective Service registration records. Females and males over the age of 26 do not have to register under the law. OSU officials say that almost all of the students discovered to be non-compliant register with Selective Service once they understand the implications of out-of-state tuition rates.

Through the mid-1980s, students and student groups fought the linkage between student financial aid and military service draft registration. However, claims of bills of attainder, self-incrimination, excessive governmental action, and First Amendment protections failed to overturn the linkage.

Linkage of Aid and Substance Abuse

Late in the decade, students faced a new challenge — linkage between Pell Grants and substance abuse. Under the 1988 Anti-Drug Abuse Act, students applying for federal financial assistance through the Pell Grant program must sign a statement indicating that they aren't involved in substance abuse.

The law, which went into effect in 1989, covers students and grantees or companies contracting with government. The students and vendors must, as a condition of receiving support or business, agree not to "engage in the unlawful manufacture, distribution, dispensation, possession, or use of a controlled substance" during the program. To date, the requirement hasn't been challenged in court.

For colleges and universities, the Pell Grant linkage is even more troublesome than the draft law linkage. For the latter, the campus simply had to collect compliance statements. But under the Anti-Drug Abuse Act, more is required. In addition to collecting compliance statements, higher education institutions are also required to act as reporting agents — to report student drug offense convictions and suspected fraudulent compliance claims to appropriate agencies, including law enforcement.

For many campuses, these regulations are burdensome, presenting work for all in an effort to identify and penalize a few. Another concern is the perception that through the grant-abuse linkage, campuses are keeping track of substance abuse by needy students but not by the affluent.

Summary

The federal government designs linkages as levers to achieve certain purposes. While students, student groups, and campuses may disagree with the principle and find linkages unnecessary and burdensome, courts have traditionally rejected legal challenges.

Cases such as *Doe*, *Minnesota*, *Dickinson*, and *Alexander* show the difficulties in resisting linkages. Whether it's the draft registration of yesterday, today's substance abuse concerns, or an as yet unidentified issue, the government will be given wide latitude in using its resources to achieve its purposes.

Note: With the advent of the U.S. military's "don't ask, don't tell" policy on sexual orientation in the ranks, the campus issue refocused on access to recruiters and possible federal financial support penalties for denying military access. The Department of Defense implemented in 1995 a rule against Department grants or contracts to any campus that has "a policy of denying, or that effectively prevents" the military from recruitment.

Focus on Sexual Orientation

January 1990

Responding to campus pressures and city regulations, Temple University Law School (PA) denied U.S. military recruiters an opportunity to appear on campus. The reason: the military's policy of not recruiting homosexuals. Campus and city officials found the practice discriminatory and responded with regulations and rulings designed to halt campus military recruitment altogether.

The resulting case, United States v. City of Philadelphia, 798 F.2d 81 (1986), involving career planning and placement services, is an example of the extent to which colleges and universities have struggled to establish appropriate relationships with homosexuals and homosexual groups on campus. In the classroom, in student newspapers, in recognition of student organizations, in the granting of degrees, and in employment, courts have helped define the appropriate campus status of homosexuals.

Military Recruitment

In deciding *City of Philadelphia*, the U.S. Court of Appeals, Third Circuit, was concerned with two issues: *discrimination* and *supremacy* laws.

State and federal laws have clearly established a variety of classes of individuals with special protections. The members of these classes, generally listed in campus anti-discrimination statements, cannot be treated any differently from others on campus because of their class status. Temple extended to its campus a Philadelphia statute prohibiting discrimination on the basis of sexual orientation.

The court found two reasons to overturn the ban. First, it noted that not all discrimination is illegal. For example, while it is generally illegal to discriminate in hiring on the basis of age, some professions have an exemption due to special circumstances. The early retirement age for airline pilots might be an example of legal age discrimination. The legality of some forms of discrimination may be established through litigation or legislation.

The court found that congressional language exempts the military from the legal need to open recruitment to homosexuals. Congress, in effect, created an exemption from the equal protection under the laws language found in the Constitution.

Second, faced with conflicting laws — a city regulation banning discrimination and a congressional exemption — the court sided with the federal government. Under a *supremacy of laws* principle, the federal government is a higher authority on such matters, and conflicts of law are decided in its favor.

The military's policy that homosexuality is incompatible with armed forces service has sparked debate and controversy beyond career planning offices. ROTC programs are again under attack on a number of campuses, including the University of Minnesota and the University of Wisconsin-Madison, and the return of ROTC to Harvard has also become embroiled in the recruitment debate.

In the Classroom and in the Press

A homosexual relationship between an undergraduate and a graduate teaching assistant was reviewed in *Naragon v. Wharton*, 572 F.Supp. 1117, 737 F.2d 1403 (1984). Fearing a *classroom* problem could develop, the Louisiana State University School of Music reassigned the graduate assistant to non-teaching duties. The grad assistant sued, claiming that the conduct of her personal life was of no consequence to the school, and that she was being discriminated against on the basis of her homosexuality. The school argued that it had changed her assignment only in response to her unprofessional conduct.

The Fifth Circuit Federal Court of Appeals agreed with the school, upholding the legality of the reassignment. The court didn't see this as a case of discrimination on the basis of sexual orientation. The school would have been justified in taking action, the court ruled, whether the instructor-student relationship was homosexual or heterosexual. This particular relationship was found to be detrimental to the interests of the institution, and appropriate response was justified.

College newspapers have had to review their policies and procedures as well, as a result of an incident at the State University of New York at Binghamton. A letter to the editor printed in the *Pipe Dream* stated that two students involved in a campus incident were homosexuals. The letter was reported to have been signed by the students, but the students later claimed they hadn't written or submitted the letter. The paper printed a retraction and an apology, but the students sued the newspaper and the state after being harassed and questioned about their sexuality, in *Mazart v. State*, 441 N.Y.S.2d 600 (1981).

Was it libel for the newspaper to designate the students as being gay? Could the press be held responsible for not taking steps to verify the authenticity of the letter to the editor? The state Court of Claims ruled yes on both questions. At the time of the publication, homosexual acts were a crime in the state. The paper, according to the decision, had a duty to ascertain the authenticity of letters to ensure protection of student rights.

Questions of Recognition, Degrees, and Employment

Recognition of gay student organizations continues to be an issue around the country. While Georgetown University (DC) has accepted the status of its gay student organization, compelled by District of Columbia laws, Congress continues to argue over the matter. Two other cases serve to remind colleges and universities of the rights of student organizations, including those representing or consisting of homosexual students.

In *Gay and Lesbian Student Association v. Gohn*, 850 F.2d 361 (1988), funding for a student organization was denied. The group charged discrimination, claiming that the decision was based on their beliefs and lifestyles, and it sued. Since the University of Arkansas had final approval over student budgets, the denial of funding represented *state action*, contended the plaintiffs, in violation of their constitutional rights of free speech and association. The court agreed, finding that the group met every criterion for funding but was denied support because of the *content* of its free speech. This was held to be unconstitutional.

A key case almost two decades ago established standards for campus recognition processes still in effect today. *Wood v. Davison*, 351 F.Supp. 543, 548 (N.D. Ga. 1972), involved a request for use of University of Georgia space for a gay dance. The school denied the request, but the courts said there had to be a better reason than simply stating it was not in the best interests of the institution. To deny the request or recognition, the school would have to show that:

- The group refused to obey reasonable campus rules and regulations, or
- The group represented a real danger of campus violence or disruption, or
- The activities would violate state or federal laws

Gohn and *Wood* established a legal foundation for the later Georgetown University case, upholding the rights of gay students and their organizations to be recognized on campus.

The *denial of an academic degree* based on the potential recipient's homosexuality was questioned in *Lexington Theological Seminary v. Vance*, 596 S.W.2d 11 (1979). There, a divinity student who disclosed his homosexual lifestyle while taking courses was advised that he might not be granted a degree. When he completed his studies, no degree was awarded. The school said he did not display Christian character as required for the ministry.

A trial court ordered that his degree be conferred, as it found the school's standards too vague and, therefore, unenforceable. The Court of Appeals of Kentucky saw the case differently. It ruled that the Christian language used in the seminary's catalog should have been very clear to any divinity student. The court was also not interested in asserting itself in what should remain an academic decision. So in these limited circumstances, the court ruled it legal to withhold a degree on the basis of sexual orientation.

Sexual preferences can also be a factor in *employment* settings. The homosexuality of an instructor at Oklahoma State University was at issue in *Corstvet v. Boger*, 757 F.2d 223 (1985). The professor was accused of soliciting sexual acts from a man in a restroom and was subsequently fired under a moral turpitude clause in his contract. While the Court of Appeals reviewed claims of due process failures in the case, it noted that the actions taken against the instructor were not based on his homosexuality. He was terminated, the court decided, for acts of solicitation, a state crime. This was found to be legally justified.

Summary

It's interesting to note how often key cases involving student services and activities or academic programs and employment have been based, in part, on matters related to homosexuality. The legal system is based on resolution of disputes, and the status and rights of homosexual students and staff have often been in dispute in the last two decades.

Campuses React to Sexual Harassment

June 1990

The key words are hostile and offensive, to characterize a campus work and study environment where there is sexual harassment. Complaints of harassment can come from faculty, students, or staff, against faculty, students, or staff. Concern over campus sexual harassment is on the rise, and with good cause. Experts claim that a large percentage of students and campus employees have been subjected to inappropriate sexual behaviors. The need for a strong campus response is apparent and supported by law.

Sexual harassment on campus is generally defined as unwanted sexual attention that interferes with a person's ability to work or study. As more and more people become aware of what harassment is, there are more and more reports of incidents. And campus officials need to react appropriately.

Title VII and the Supreme Court

An employer can be held responsible for the work environment, and employees can sue their employers for damages. More specifically, an environment of sexual harassment is a violation of Title VII of the Civil Rights Act of 1964; if that environment is hostile and offensive to women or men, their rights are being unlawfully violated.

In 1986, the U.S. Supreme Court found that a hostile and offensive workplace existed in a bank, and it upheld a civil rights action for damages against the employer (*Meritor Savings Bank v. Vinson*, 106 S.Ct. 2399, 1986). A campus is responsible, as an employer, for maintaining a workplace free of sexual harassment.

Title VII of the Civil Rights Act of 1964 was extended to campuses in 1972 as the basis of federal employment discrimination laws. It makes it unlawful for an employer to:

> fail or refuse to hire or discharge any individual, or otherwise to discriminate against any individual with respect to his compensation, terms, conditions, or privileges of employment, because of such individual's race, color, religion, sex, or national origin. (42 U.S.C. Sec. 2000)

Sexual harassment on campus can be a violation of the law, as demonstrated in *Meritor*. An environment of sexual harassment on campus places the school at risk.

EEOC Guidelines

Title VII is also the source for Equal Employment Opportunity Commission guidelines that can be applied to campuses as well. The guidelines make employers responsible for their own acts and the acts of their employees in the workplace. Under the EEOC guidelines, harassment on the basis of sex is defined as:

> unwelcome sexual advances, requests for sexual favors, and other verbal or physical conduct of a sexual nature ... when (1) submission to such conduct is made either explicitly or implicitly a term or condition of an individual's employment, (2) submission to or rejection of such conduct by an individual is used as the basis for employment decisions affecting such individual, or (3) such conduct has the purpose or effect of unreasonably interfering with an individual's work performance or creating an intimidating,

hostile, or offensive working environment. (29 C.F.R., Sec. 1604.11)

The guidelines apply a "knew or should have known" standard with regard to employee actions. The employer will be held responsible for sexual harassment of fellow workers when the employer *knew or should have known* the harassment was taking place.

As an employer, a campus is responsible for the harassing behaviors of its agents and supervisors, *regardless* of whether the specific acts complained of are authorized or even forbidden by the employer and *regardless* of whether the employer knows or should have known of their occurrence. Even if the campus has rules against harassment, officials still can be found responsible when a supervisor or an agent violates those rules.

The EEOC guidelines promote prevention, advising employers to:

- Take all steps necessary to prevent sexual harassment in the workplace
- Raise the subject affirmatively with employees to increase awareness
- Express strong disapproval
- Develop appropriate sanctions
- Inform employees of their rights and the procedures for making complaints
- Develop other methods to sensitize all involved.

Title IX

The Education Amendments of 1972 are also a basis for sexual harassment claims against campuses. Title IX of the law states: "No person ... shall, on the basis of sex, be excluded from participation in, be denied the benefits of, or be subjected to discrimination under any education program or activity receiving federal financial assistance." (20 U.S.C., Sec. 1681.) The law applies to both students and staff, and victims can use it to initiate legal action.

Campus Responses

Student, faculty, and staff concerns — as well as legal pressures — have motivated campuses to provide education about sexual harassment and take preventive steps. Many schools have established advisory committees and other working groups to address the problem. A variety of publications and presentations have been developed at the campus level to increase awareness. And definitions of sexual harassment and procedures for dealing with it have become important parts of faculty and student handbooks.

In adopting procedures to handle complaints, several considerations are important:

- It may be necessary to preserve the confidentiality of the complainant. Many victims are very reluctant to report incidents; they need to be assured of some level of protection.
- There should be a campus definition of sexual harassment that clearly conveys community standards.
- Reporting procedures should be as simple as possible, with appropriate follow-up contact with the complainant.
- Campus reporting procedures, including where and how to file complaints, should be well-publicized.

Conclusion

On campus, whether to work or to study, people have a right to be free of sexual harassment, a right supported by Title VII, *Meritor*, the EEOC guidelines, and Title IX. A campus definition of sexual harassment, a campus program of education and awareness on the issue, and clear campus policies and sanctions for incidents of sexual harassment are important steps toward an environment that is not hostile and offensive to members of the campus community.

Title IX: It Affects More Than Athletics

November 1992

A recent Supreme Court decision focused on Title IX and college athletics. Federal law, the Court ruled, prohibits sex discrimination in athletics at campuses receiving federal funding.

But the law covers much more than athletics. Employment benefits, promotions, admissions, sexual harassment, extracurricular activities, counseling, health care, advising, and placement are all covered under Title IX.

In other words, it's crucial that you understand Title IX and make plans to comply with it.

A Review of Title IX

Title IX of the Education Amendments of 1972 prohibits sex discrimination at institutions receiving federal dollars.

Enacted to end gender-based decision-making on campus, the law exempts single-sex schools, military academies, and religious institutions if compliance "would not be consistent with the religious tenets of such organizations."

But generally, the law says that sex cannot be the basis for providing differing opportunities, services, programs, or fees. Students of both sexes must have equal access to campus programs and support services.

According to Title IX:

- With only a few exceptions, admissions decisions and recruiting efforts cannot be based on gender.
- Sexual harassment of students and employees is prohibited.
- Financial assistance cannot be sex-related.
- Campus housing can provide separate housing based on gender — but the housing facilities, services, and fees must be equal for all.
- Restroom and locker facilities must be comparable.
- Campus health services and medical insurance programs cannot discriminate on the basis of sex.

Employees have separate protections against sex discrimination, under the Civil Rights Act of 1964 (Title VII). Title VII prohibits employment discrimination based on race, color, sex, religion, or national origin. Victims using Title VII have traditionally sued for back wages or job reinstatement.

Today's Concerns

In the past, campus victims of gender-based discrimination went to court without any promised outcome. The only apparent remedies were orders prohibiting campuses from similar actions in the future.

This clearly did not provide much motivation to students and employees who felt they had been treated unlawfully. The threat of losing federal dollars made some schools change policies and procedures — but it really wasn't a major deterrent.

However, a U.S. Supreme Court decision earlier this year may have changed the rules for everyone.

In *Franklin v. Gwinnett County Public Schools*, 112 S.Ct. 1028 (1992), a high school student said she left the school district because she was being sexually harassed by an instructor. The student went to court looking for damages, not injunctions, in a Title IX action.

Title VII back pay and re-employment were useless to her because she was a student. So was a Title IX court order prohibiting future unlawful action by the school.

The Court ruled that monetary damages could and should be awarded to victims of institutional sex discrimination. The Court clearly noted that sexual harassment by an employee is sex discrimination by an institution. That reasoning opened the door for other lawsuits.

Since *Franklin*, the potential for litigation has increased. Campuses that don't respond appropriately risk significant financial damage from suits filed by admissions applicants, students, and current and former employees.

Out of Bounds

There is no universally accepted definition of sex discrimination or sexual harassment. The law and language on these matters will continue to evolve as more conflicts are reviewed by the courts.

But it's clear from Title IX that, on the basis of sex, people at institutions receiving federal support cannot be "excluded from participation in, be denied the benefits of, or be subjected to discrimination."

Franklin established a clear link between harassment and discrimination, noting:

> When a supervisor sexually harasses a subordinate because of the subordinate's sex, that supervisor discriminates on the basis of sex. .... The same rule should apply when a teacher sexually harasses and abuses a student.

A victim doesn't have to prove discriminatory or harassing *behavior* to seek Title IX protection. If a campus creates a "hostile environment," an employee can seek a sex discrimination claim. In 1986, the Supreme Court found that gender-based, offensive behavior by co-workers and/or supervisors could create a "hostile environment."

Employees have successfully used Title VII when they've been victims of a "hostile environment." Students in similar circumstances may well use Title IX in the future.

Planning a Response

Campuses that don't comply with Title IX risk monetary damages or the loss of federal funds.

But money shouldn't be the only motivation to comply. The rights of students and employees are simply important to preserve. To do so, and to protect your campus:

- *Understand the law.* Do key campus administrators understand Title IX, *Franklin*, and their impact on higher education?
- *Create appropriate policies.* Are campus regulations concerning sex discrimination and sexual harassment strong and clear? Are they widely disseminated? A campus must have a policy prohibiting illegal discrimination and harassment. It must also ensure that the policy is widely publicized through handbooks, the media, posters, and notices to faculty, staff, and students.
- *Respond to complaints.* Are complaints or concerns handled by trained staff? Is the complaint process well-publicized? Is it followed? To avoid litigation, strong responses to complaints and concerns are vital. Devote resources to establishing, training, and publicizing a unit to deal with concerns. Follow your own rules — and if you generally don't follow them, change them.
- *Foster awareness.* Do campus groups and individuals know about your concern and commitment

with regard to sex discrimination? Do you have workshops and printed materials that promote your desire for compliance? An effort to motivate the campus will ensure that all members of the academic community are aware of concerns and committed to respecting the rights of others.

- *Review the program.* You may have already re-evaluated "gender equity" in intercollegiate athletics. But has your campus reviewed all programs and services to identify and correct potential sex discrimination, inequity, or harassment? Be aggressive. Ensure equity in academics, support services, and extracurricular activities. It will be an important part of your response to Title IX and the *Franklin* ruling.

The language of the law and related judicial decisions may change in the future, but the established principles are clear today. *Campuses are obligated* to prohibit sex discrimination and sexual harassment.

By developing a full understanding of the law, you and your institution can protect your own rights as well as those of individuals.

Note: In 1995, a federal district court ruled that Brown University (RI) does not provide female athletes with sufficient opportunities to compete in sports. Brown has filed an appeal, claiming that the court misapplied the law and that the test for Title IX compliance is flawed.

Lessons on Studying Abroad

May 1991

Students in overseas study programs have always needed to include personal safety in their curriculum. Part of the overall experience is learning how to take care of themselves in a foreign environment. Concern for safety grows in times of international crisis, so it's not surprising that students and campuses had to re-evaluate program plans as a result of the 1990 Persian Gulf conflict.

Indiana University halted a study program at Hebrew University in Jerusalem. Harvard University restricted student travel planned for Israel, Jordan, North Africa, and Greece. The University of Arkansas canceled a Rome program, but not other campus programs. University of Delaware programs went forward, although some students came home out of concern. And Yale University decided to curtail its London summer program.

Yet, with notable exceptions, most programs continued. According to some estimates, only 10 of over 500 study programs were canceled nationwide, affecting fewer than 4% of the participating students. But it was not — and should not have been — business as usual.

Administrators of overseas study programs need to be sensitive to safety and security concerns and adopt good risk management plans to protect students and their institutions. Good management programming has benefits in both routine administration and crisis response.

Here are some key elements to consider to ensure that your study program applies the principles of good risk management.

Travel

Travel to and from the program site, or while in the program, can present legal risks for students and sponsors. Students should be advised in advance about the program's level of responsibility for travel and be informed of their own assumption of risks. When the school or an agent of the school handles the group travel arrangements, it's important to use a reputable organization to avoid scheduling, financial, or other difficulties.

In time of uncertainty, information and advisories from the U.S. Department of State, Consulate General offices, and the Council on International Educational Exchange can help in assessing potential risks. In the event of an overseas emergency, such as war, the local embassy or the national specialists at the State Department would coordinate safety and evacuation planning. Staff and students should be advised to stay in contact with these offices. Each program should have a contingency plan to deal with emergencies.

During the recent crisis, the State Department and many schools advised program participants to avoid "looking American." Simple and logical advice, but it could make a crucial difference.

When in Rome ...

Students must be advised of the laws in host countries and of the consequences of violations. Program sponsors should emphasize laws that deal with issues likely to be of particular concern to college students, such as alcohol and drug standards and motor vehicle use. They need to understand local regulations and customs, help make students more aware, and encourage them to obey laws and respect customs.

A Sound Mind and a Sound Body

Sponsors should also consider health issues: the fitness of the applicant, health insurance, and access to health care overseas. Applications for programs should elicit appropriate information on applicant background, qualifications, and interest in overseas study. Administrators should seek and read letters of recommendation as important elements in ensuring student fitness.

Programs should require a comprehensive physical examination of candidates and a doctor's statement indicating that no medical, physical, or emotional conditions exist that could interfere substantially with overseas travel and studies. Conditions that may require treatment while overseas should also be indicated.

Participants should have adequate and appropriate health insurance. Coverage should include major medical benefits, reimbursement for care needed due to accident or illness, and benefits for medical evacuation or repatriation to a home country. Proof of alternative coverage should be required of students not participating in a program-sponsored insurance plan.

At the program site, students and supervisors should be aware of any *health care facilities* in the area for emergency and primary care. Supervisors should distribute to all participants written procedures on how to obtain care. They should establish emergency procedures in advance and periodically review them. In addition, they should secure as needed special authorization to provide care to students under the age of majority.

Supervision and Planning

Groups traveling or studying overseas under campus sponsorship must be adequately supervised. Personnel should be trained to provide direction and supervision. This role can also be played by officials of host institutions or others under appropriate arrangements. Supervision requires good training, oversight, and evaluation.

Programs should be designed to provide participants with an environment that ensures reasonable standards of care for staff and participants. Where there are potential hazards, program sponsors have a duty to provide *due warning* so that participants understand the risks inherent in an activity before they get involved. Program coordinators should carefully select, appropriately review, and properly supervise sites, facilities, equipment, and other program elements to provide a safe environment. This translates into providing a *minimum standard of care*.

Standards and Guidelines

Where there are third-party guidelines for campus programs or services, responsible professionals need to be aware of the standards and apply them as appropriate. The NAFSA: Association of International Educators has published *Study Abroad: Handbook for Advisors and Administrators* to provide guidelines. All program administrators should understand these guidelines and have a copy available.

Contracts and Liability Releases

Most litigation is based on miscommunication or misunderstanding. To prevent problems, full disclosure is the best policy for all. Sponsors should be explicit with potential participants about program services and responsibilities. What services will be provided? How? What will not be covered? What is the sponsor responsible for? The site? The student? Who is responsible for transportation to and from the site? Is the program responsible for the students' off-site activities?

After they completely understand terms and conditions, students may be asked to sign some form of an agreement or contract and a waiver of liability.

It should be noted that a waiver doesn't completely prevent students from suing schools or programs. But the less generic, the better. A specific and carefully crafted waiver can be used in litigation to show that the participant was fully aware of the program particulars and agreed to abide by those terms. Contracts and waivers can show assumption of risks and can be effective in limiting damages, as evidence that a participant completely understood the program and the rights and responsibilities of participation.

The Best-Laid Plans ... Often Go Astray

It may be necessary at times to alter program offerings due to changes in conditions, faculty, sites, or facilities, including circumstances such as warfare. To avoid legal complications, sponsors should include in all printed program materials disclaimers reserving their right to make changes as necessary. Program costs can be affected by international monetary policies and currency exchange rates. Therefore, students should be advised of the possibility of cost changes. Obviously, changes should be limited to the extent possible, and, in the event of any changes, program administrators should swiftly advise all affected students.

Conclusion

Study abroad programs offer many benefits to campuses and students. However, life is never risk-free: campuses must take adequate steps to ensure that opportunities for learning are carefully balanced against acceptable risks. Study abroad can be a rewarding experience. But programs should be safe, based on good planning and solid risk management.

Overlap Group: Final Battle

March 1994

In the end, the story contained two very familiar legal elements — a negotiated out-of-court settlement on the eve of trial and an ambiguous result.

For four years, the U.S. Justice Department pursued dozens of private colleges and universities, claiming that they shared information on students, financial aid, tuition, and salaries, which violated federal anti-trust laws. The case included records collection and review, consent agreements, litigation involving a trial, an appeal, and an order for a rehearing, and a final settlement.

In the last few months, the case has come to an end of sorts. The last holdout school, the Massachusetts Institute of Technology, has agreed with the government to halt litigation and abide by a complex agreement.

Background

For over 20 years, a score of private colleges, known as the Overlap Group, worked annually to develop common financial aid packages for students, to avoid competition. The group included Ivy League schools (Brown, Columbia, Cornell, Dartmouth, Harvard, Princeton, the University of Pennsylvania, and Yale) and about a dozen other campuses in the Northeast.

Their group efforts were intended to avoid a costly bidding war, using financial aid packages to "buy" students. By coordinating aid offers, the schools hoped to control excessive offers and let prospective students select schools without regard to financial considerations. The schools agreed on the level of aid to be offered to all jointly admitted applicants. A student accepted at more than one Overlap school received the same financial aid offer from all the schools. The schools found their collaboration successful over the years.

Then, in 1989, the federal government began asking questions and collecting records on the process. The Justice Department requested materials on financial aid systems from almost 60 private higher education institutions, including all of the Overlap Group schools.

The investigation was based on possible anti-trust law violations. The government wanted to determine if the annual meetings to fix tuition, faculty salaries, and financial aid offers to applicants accepted at more than one school created an unlawful educational monopoly. Federal officials were concerned that the annual process represented "collusion" that infringed on the rights of prospective students to negotiate for the best financial aid offers from competing schools.

The colleges and universities questioned whether the law applied to them. They did not see themselves as businesses engaged in interstate commerce. Instead, they argued, they should be seen more as charities, which would make them exempt from the law in their efforts to fix and limit financial aid. Because they were acting to make higher education more accessible to students with financial needs and to promote diversity, the colleges and universities contended, they should be judged as "charitable" organizations, free to work out cooperative relationships.

In response to the investigation, the Justice Department sued MIT and the Ivy League school group members. As a group, they agreed to end their spring meeting to compare finances; later in the year, all but MIT agreed to halt the practice to end the litigation.

MIT refused to sign the agreement, which set the stage for a 1992 federal trial. The court found that the Overlap Group, including MIT, had, in fact, violated anti-trust standards. But the Third U.S. Circuit Court of Appeals reviewed the decision and ordered a retrial. It held that the lower court had not adequately considered MIT's "social welfare" purposes behind its policy. While a policy on tuition and financial aid fixing could be an anti-trust violation, the court said further review of the issues was needed to see if the law applied in the MIT case.

To avoid extended litigation, the parties tried to settle out of court. But when talks broke down in late 1993, plans went forward for the court rehearing. The court gave the school and government a few more weeks to agree on the issues before it took over.

Settlement

Finally, based on a December 1993 settlement that allowed limited exchange of student information, the Justice Department agreed to drop the anti-trust action against MIT. As the dust settled after the four-year legal battle, both sides declared victory.

The Justice Department says the deal acknowledges that the past practice by the schools was unlawful, while MIT contends that it allows the school to continue with most of its information exchange on students.

Under the agreement, not-for-profit higher education institutions that admit students without regard to financial need can exchange limited information. Participating schools may agree on joint applications and financial aid review processes, and they can establish a central computer system for collecting and reviewing data.

Information from the system could be used to prevent students from providing different information to different schools in an effort to maximize aid offers. The collected and shared information would include student and family income, assets, and the number of siblings, including those in college.

In addition, campuses that agree to share information will send their materials through an independent third party to ensure that all participants follow the rules. However, campuses can no longer meet to discuss the financial aid packages they plan to offer to individual students.

Colleges can compare individual student records to prevent student fraud. But they cannot review cases in which aid awards are significantly different. And, to avoid further price-fixing charges, they cannot share information on tuition or faculty salaries.

The Bottom Line

While some call the settlement "workable and reasonable," others think the conditions are too complex and too costly. None of the schools in the Overlap Group have said they will participate in an information-sharing network under the negotiated terms. One spokesperson said complying with the agreement was "simply beyond the means" of most of the schools.

While the schools saw many benefits to the old Overlap Group process, they remain uncertain about the future. Some still want to share data, while others are concerned over the costs involved.

In the end, a process that private colleges have used to maximize access and diversity may have been lost to litigation and consent agreements. Prospective students face many choices and challenges. Financial aid considerations can overwhelm and confuse them. In light of the recent settlement, the same process may be overwhelming and more complex for private colleges and universities as well.

Schools May Lose Control Over Transcripts

February 1991

It's the campus version of the old "carrot and stick" routine: a student who pays his or her bill can get a copy of the academic transcript. But can the school legally withhold transcripts from students who have completed their courses? What about bankruptcy proceedings? Do they affect student or campus rights to records?

Until recently, colleges and universities felt that they were on solid ground when they refused to release records to students who still owed them money. But a recent ruling by a bankruptcy judge in California has many schools concerned: Is the court about to take from them their best weapon in the battle to collect bad debts? That's what's at stake in *Gustafson v. California State University-Fresno*, in which a federal district court judge was asked to rule on a rejected student request for transcripts.

Ruling

The university refused to release the records because the student had failed to repay student loans. Campus policies prohibited the school from providing a transcript until all debts were paid. But the student had filed for bankruptcy under federal law and was waiting for a discharge of his debts at the time. The court ordered the school to release the records.

According to the ruling, the school was obligated to provide the transcripts once the bankruptcy petition was filed, even when the requested discharge of debts might not cover student loans. The collection weapon was lost!

Despite objections from the school and several interested professional organizations, an appellate panel upheld the ruling providing the student with the records. Among the objections to the rulings were that the student could withdraw the bankruptcy petition after receiving the records and that the school would lose an effective debt collection tool.

But the court disagreed. The student, still owing money and with no bankruptcy ruling yet, got his transcript. This judgment was not consistent with earlier judicial decisions.

Relate Questions and Case Law

The first issue is the school's right to *withhold transcripts until all school debts are paid*. In 1980, a New York State court found the transcript to be part of a contract between student and school. The court ruled that if the student failed to keep his or her part of the deal by not paying his or her bills, the school could be justified in withholding some services, such as transcripts.

In *Spas v. Wharton*, 431 N.Y.S.2d 638 (1980), a former state university student sued to get his transcript released. But the school refused, citing the student's failure to pay his bills and a state statute in support of its position. State law said that no student should "receive credit or ... official recognition" for courses not paid for. The court, using the contract theory, ruled in favor of the school. Until a student satisfies his obligations to the school, the school isn't required to meet its obligations to the student, said the court.

Failure to pay parking tickets was the reason the University of Texas Law School gave when it refused to provide a student with records. And the court upheld this reason in *Haug v. Franklin*, 690 S.W.2d 646 (1985). Because the school had the authority to impose the fines, it could withhold academic records until the student paid in full.

A second issue: Can transcripts be used to *collect defaulted college loans*? That was the question in *Juras v. Aman Collection Service, Inc.*, 829 F.2d 739 (1987). A student took out several loans for school and subsequently failed to repay them. The bad loans were assigned to a collection agency, which threatened to have school transcripts withheld. In response, the student sued. He said that the collection effort, including the withholding of transcripts, violated state and federal collection practices laws. He argued that student loans are made without "security," and that withholding the transcript would constitute security.

The court disagreed. Since the school owns the record, denying access to it doesn't violate student unsecured loan regulations. The school could withhold the transcript to force payment of the bad loans.

Also, how do *bankruptcy* proceedings affect campus rights to withhold transcripts? Under old federal bankruptcy laws, schools could keep transcripts from students, even after the courts formally discharged school debts. That was the result of *Girardier v. Webster College*, 563 F.2d 1267, 1277 (1977). Two students who had failed to repay college loans had the courts discharge their debts, then asked for official transcripts. The school refused, since it hadn't been paid and now never would be paid.

Reviewing the case, the court found that the school hadn't violated any duty in withholding the records. Under the old bankruptcy law, the school couldn't take specific action or initiate any process to collect debts. But the court viewed transcripts as an additional benefit, a benefit that could be withheld since no payment had been made. It wasn't a collection tool, but a benefit that a non-paying student didn't deserve.

Law Changes Rules of the Game

In 1978, the federal Bankruptcy Reform Act changed the law. In addition to prohibiting formal collection efforts, the new law kept institutions from using informal or indirect methods to induce payment of debts. Debtors cannot be pressured in any way to prompt payment of debts discharged by the courts.

In *Handsome v. Rutgers University et al.*, 445 F.Supp. 1362 (1978), a student developed health problems and couldn't pay off her student loans. In bankruptcy proceedings, the courts discharged her debts to the school. After recovering from her illness, the student tried to get back into school, but the school denied her request for a transcript. She sued, asking the courts why the state school could withhold a transcript due to a debt when the federal government had discharged her obligation to pay that debt.

The court agreed with the student. The state must provide the former debtor with an opportunity for a "fresh start." Withholding transcripts for old debts doesn't serve this purpose, ruled the court; it further punishes a debtor. The court viewed it as continued pressure to collect on debts legally discharged. The Constitution's supremacy clause controls actions of the state, and in this case, federal bankruptcy laws took precedence over state attempts to withhold transcripts. If the school wanted its money, said the court, it should have taken advantage of the opportunity to participate in the bankruptcy proceedings. That was the time for school action — not long after the fact through withholding the transcript.

Finally, what happens if the student files for bankruptcy but the *college debts are not discharged*? Can schools then withhold transcripts? The Third Circuit Court of Appeals dealt with this question in *Johnson v. Edinboro State College*, 728 F.2d 163 (1984). Under a Chapter 7 filing, most of a student's debts were discharged, but not his student loans.

Since he hadn't repaid the loans, the school withheld his transcript. It argued that since the debt remained due, it retained the right to use the transcript as a collection tool. After the bankruptcy judge and a federal district decision both ordered release of the transcript, the college took the case to court.

The appeals court saw that repayment of the college debt wouldn't cause any hardship, since the amount owed was relatively low. Going back to the *Girardier* decision, a student owing money to the campus wasn't entitled to continued benefits from the campus.

Summary

Schools and professional organizations are disturbed by the latest in a long series of transcript decisions. In a reversal of the logic developed in cases such as *Girardier*, *Handsome*, and *Johnson*, the court has held in *Gustafson v. California State University-Fresno* that transcripts should be released even though no debt has been discharged.

Campuses have long used transcripts to encourage students to pay their debts. If the courts allow students to use loopholes to obtain records without paying their debts, transcripts may no longer be an important tool for collection. Schools will be watching further court action on this issue carefully.

Race-Based Financial Aid: Confusion Thickens

March 1992

What began as a compromise over Arizona's non-observance of the Martin Luther King, Jr., holiday continues today as a significant source of confusion and controversy. When sponsors of the 1991 Fiesta Bowl college football game wanted to appease those who felt the game should be moved out of a state that refused to honor the King holiday, they offered the two participating schools scholarship money for minority students.

But the U.S. Education Department ruled that the race-based scholarships were illegal, setting off a storm of conflict. The Department later modified the rule to say that it would allow public schools to offer minority scholarships with private money; the Department gave colleges and universities four years to comply. The new Education Secretary also asked for time to study the issue.

At issue is Title VI of the Civil Rights Act of 1964 and the Restoration Act of 1987. The law states:

> No person in the United States shall, on the ground of race, color, or national origin, be excluded from participation in, be denied the benefits of, or be subjected to discrimination under any program or activity receiving federal financial assistance.

The law extends to all college or university divisions that receive federal funds.

While colleges and universities scrambled to understand and comply with the rulings, some students went to court to settle the matter on their own. They wanted the federal courts to enforce the ban on race-based scholarships. Seven white students sued the Department in an effort to end what they perceived as "discriminatory" scholarships. They contended that federal law required public campus actions to be "race neutral," and that minority-only scholarships would violate the law.

But the judge dismissed their suit recently on several grounds. He said the students should be suing the schools — not the Department — if the schools were discriminating. And while the court appreciated the "important societal principle" of neutrality, it said that the Education Department should be allowed to complete its review of the issue without court interference. Said the court, give the Secretary of Education time to study.

Well, the Education Department used its time to develop a new policy on race-based scholarships that seems very similar to the original proposal last year, the one that set off the dispute in the first place. But many legal scholars advise colleges and universities not to get excited about the proposed Education rules. Since the issues in dispute are constitutional, they feel the Department guidelines will be challenged in the courts, and that the judiciary, and not the executive branch, will ultimately settle the issue.

The new guidelines proposed in the Federal Register for comments would prohibit most financial aid offered where race is a deciding factor. Exceptions to the policy would be for programs established by Congress, court-ordered programs or awards, or programs designed to overcome past discrimination. Minority-only scholarships awarded with privately donated funds would also be legal under the rules.

Under the plan, colleges and universities receiving federal funds could award minority student financial aid, including scholarships, fellowships, and loans, using certain rationales:

- *Need* — as awards to disadvantaged or low-income students without regard to race, even if more of the awards go to minority students
- *Diversity* — using race, as one factor out of many, in trying to vary the backgrounds, experiences, and cultures of the campus student population
- Discrimination — if needed to remedy past discrimination, based on legislative action or private donor wishes

The government proposed that, with these rationales, a tax-supported institution could still provide minority student financial aid without violating the law. But the Department cautioned that scholarships awarded solely on the basis of race would remain illegal. Many observers fear this regulation would threaten most current affirmative action efforts.

The proposed guidelines offer colleges and universities a few direct means of providing minority-based scholarships. It appears that these opportunities may be very limited. Examples of this may be programs to promote diversity or correct past discrimination or programs funded through private donations.

Back to Bakke

The exclusion to promote diversity is based on *Regents of the University of California v. Bakke*, 438 U.S. 265 (1978), in which the Supreme Court ruled that a medical school could not set aside specific slots for minority-only admissions. Race, however, could be used as a "plus" factor in selecting a diversified student body for education purposes. To "attract and maintain an educationally stimulating and diverse student body," a school may use race as a "plus" factor in making financial-aid decisions.

Scholarships under the new guidelines could also be race-based to correct past practices of discrimination, but only where there was a legislative or judicial finding of the past discrimination. Therefore, to be legal, the program would have to be based on a court order, administrative body order, case settlement, consent decree, or required compliance plan, or it would have to be authorized by federal, state, or local legislative bodies. To meet a constitutional challenge, this type of finding would have to be based on a true finding of past discrimination and not mere political decision-making.

Some schools had earlier stated that they would actively seek private funding to continue race-based financial aid, using this exception to get around the law. While a first reading of the proposed guidelines may encourage this, further review is necessary. There are restrictions on how the private money can be used and how it can be collected. These provisions are subject to serious questioning by legal observers. While the proposed guidelines allow tax-supported institutions to administer race-exclusive financial aid programs, the funds may be awarded based only on need or diversity.

Donor Wishes Not Affected

A donor can still give money to a school with the express desire that it be awarded based only on race. The school can accept the funds but must use the private dollars to replace institutional dollars that would have otherwise gone to a student, based only on need or diversity. The Department contends that this policy will allow schools to accept the donations and free up unrestricted funds for other students.

In addition to restricting the use of privately donated funds, Department officials are said to be considering another set of regulations that would not allow colleges and universities to solicit donors for race-exclusive gifts. But higher education lobbyists are quickly complaining that the Department doesn't understand how fundraising works, as often the school needs to approach a potential donor with a specific need in mind. Further consideration will be given to the gift solicitation issue.

Some school officials remain confused over the privately donated money exception. They contend that once the money is accepted by the campus, it becomes a campus asset and traditionally has been subject to all controls placed on the school. But the Department has proposed continuing private fund programs, reasoning that donors are not subject to the law, that such aid will be awarded to students previously found eligible for aid for reasons other than race, and that such programs will free up other institutional dollars for student support.

Final regulations on the issue of student aid and race will be promulgated later this year. And in an effort to prevent any current student receiving aid from being disadvantaged by the changing rules, the Department has proposed a four-year transition period to work toward college and university compliance.

The courts gave the Department time to complete its review of this important issue without judicial interference. Once the final regulations are established, it's expected that litigants won't wait long to ask for judicial review of conflicting principles — race neutrality versus affirmative action.

Race-Based Financial Aid

June 1995

He was a Hispanic student with a dream: successful undergraduate study followed by medical school. His father was a high-ranking federal official, so money shouldn't have been a major impediment.

Admitted to the University of Maryland-College Park in 1990, the outstanding student heard about an academic merit support program, the Benjamin Banneker Scholarship. The program awarded $800,000 each year to 80 or more gifted UM students. The funds were not based on need.

Daniel Podberesky applied for an award but was denied, although his academic credentials apparently surpassed those of all but two other applicants. The reason: the program was not open to all students, or even all minorities. Only African Americans were eligible.

Throughout the 1990s, the issue of race-based financial aid programs has been contested on campus, in the federal government, and in the courts. Where are these programs today? What are the underlying legal principles? What's next? *Podberesky v. Kirwan*, 38 F.3d 147 (1994), provides some insight.

Background

Relatively few campus financial aid programs in higher education use race as an absolute qualifier, with regulations that limit awards to members of particular races. Officials estimate that only about 5% of all undergraduate aid programs and up to 9% of professional and graduate school aid opportunities have race qualifiers for eligibility. But at least two-thirds of all schools have one or more of these programs.

Institutions developed these programs over the years for several reasons. These include:

- A recognized or mandated effort to reverse a legacy of past discrimination
- Attracting a significantly larger number of minority students
- Addressing negative institutional images and community relationships with minorities

However good the reasons for the programs may have been, they are now being scrutinized. At issue is the constitutionality of race-based programs under Title VI of the Civil Rights Act of 1964.

This sweeping federal civil rights act prohibits discrimination based on race, color, or national origin and extends to institutions receiving federal financial support. Within higher education, it provides legal protection to all who apply, are admitted to, or participate in campus programs and activities.

Early Case Law

Courts had reviewed affirmative action on college campuses to determine how race can be a campus decision-making factor. In 1978, attention was focused on a white male denied admission to a medical school. Was race the deciding factor in denying him admission? And in 1976, a case involving financial aid looked at how a campus tried to reserve funding for particular groups. Both decisions helped set the stage for the *Podberesky* race-based scholarship case.

In *Bakke v. Regents of the University of California*, 438 U.S. 265 (1978), the Supreme Court considered potential reverse discrimination in higher education. The plaintiff, academically well-qualified, was denied admission to the UC medical school due to a quota system. To ensure diversity, UC "reserved" specific slots for members of minority groups.

Bakke sued, claiming violation of the Fifth Amendment equal protection clause and the Civil Rights Act. A highly divided court ordered UC to admit him but left a confusing legal standard for others to follow.

The decision upheld college and university rights to consider affirmative action principles in admissions decisions. Campuses, said the court, have compelling interests to "make ... judgments as to ... the selection of the student body," and the court recognized the educational value of "wide exposure to the ideas and mores of students as diverse as this Nation of peoples." But the decision barred the use of fixed quotas.

In reviewing race-based financial aid programs since *Bakke*, some have questioned whether they, in fact, operate like quotas.

Financial aid allocations were directly challenged a few years earlier. In 1976, a law student charged that it was illegal for an institution to reserve up to 60% of available financial aid for the 11% minority student population. The court agreed, ruling in *Flanagan v. President and Directors of Georgetown College,* 417 F.Supp. 377:

> While an affirmative action program may be appropriate to insure that all persons are afforded the same opportunities or are considered for benefits on the same basis, it is not permissible

when it allocates scarce resources in favor of one race to the detriment of others.

The test of *Bakke* and *Flanagan* on minority scholarships did not begin to take shape until more than a decade later.

Department of Education

Since 1990, the federal Education Department has tried to deal with race-based scholarships in various ways, none with much success. The issue took off when the Department ruled that a corporate minority scholarship to a campus "would probably violate the law." Responding to immediate criticism and concern, the Department modified its position, noting that state and private funds for minority scholarships could be used.

Within a year, the Department scrapped all related rules pending review. Under later 1991 recommendations, race-based scholarships could have been offered:

- As part of specific federal programs, as created by Congress
- To remedy certified past discrimination
- To honor private donor gifts

With a change in federal administrations, a new study led to new guidelines, finally issued in 1994. They authorized race-based awards when:

- Given to "disadvantaged" students
- Part of a federal program
- Used to remedy past discrimination, even if not based on government certification
- "Narrowly tailored" to promote diversity
- Provided by private sources to remedy past bias or promote diversity
- Awarded by historically black colleges, when provided by third parties, if programs are open to all.

A two-year campus implementation process was established by the Department in an effort to protect current student aid that could be eliminated in the future under the guidelines.

University of Maryland

When his application for Banneker funds was rejected, Podberesky sued, saying the scholarship rules were unconstitutional and that they violated Title VI. In federal court, UM argued that the restrictions were needed because it had been subject to extensive investigation based on discrimination complaints.

In *Podberesky v. Kirwan*, 764 F.Supp. 364 (1991), the court upheld the need for such a program as demonstrated and allowed it to continue. On appeal, however, Podberesky was more successful.

In *Podberesky v. Kirwan*, 956 F.2d 52 (1992), the U.S. Circuit Federal Court of Appeals determined that the need was only assumed, not proven by evidence of past discrimination. To have a race-based program, the court ruled, UM would have to show effects of past practices needing remediation. The court ordered a new trial.

In 1993, the case went back to federal district court. The second trial produced the same outcome as the first — a lower court ruling in favor of race-based programs at UM. The court found the program limitations to be valid, based on the university's:

- Poor minority community relations
- Hostile campus climate for African Americans
- Enrollment underrepresentation of minorities
- Low retention and graduation rates

But again, there was an appeal. In October 1994, the Court of Appeals again reversed the lower court finding. In *Podberesky v. Kirwan*, 38 F.3d 147 (1994), a three-judge panel ruled that Maryland could not restrict scholarship eligibility by race. The court found that the need for race restrictions was not adequately demonstrated, and that the restriction was too broad to withstand constitutional scrutiny. Said the court:

> There is no doubt that racial tensions still exist. ... However, these tensions and attitudes are not sufficient grounds for employing a race-conscious remedy.

The court ordered Maryland to reconsider Podberesky's application without regard to his race.

Next?

The plaintiff, denied a scholarship before starting his undergraduate career, has graduated and now attends medical school. And his legal battle, which has taken more than five years, is far from over.

Maryland has asked for a final U.S. Supreme Court review of the issue. UM officials believe that they can show vestiges of past segregation, which would justify the use of restricted programs such as the Banneker scholarship. However, opponents of race-based financial aid programs call the latest *Podberesky* decision the ultimate victory, and they have asked the Education Department to withdraw its enabling regulation.

Note: Maryland and the student settled out of court in early 1996. The student received a check equal to the cost of the denied scholarship, and the school and state paid his legal fees.

Chapter 5
HEALTH AND DISABILITY CONCERNS

Introduction

> No otherwise qualified individual with a disability in the United States ... shall, solely by reason of his disability, be excluded from participation in, be denied the benefits of, or be subjected to discrimination under any program or activity receiving federal financial assistance.
>
> *Rehabilitation Act of 1973*, Section 504, as amended (29 U.S.C. 794)

The influence that health can have on an academic experience and an academic environment cannot be denied. Alcohol, drugs, AIDS, smoking, asbestos, and disability issues have all become a major part of campus discussions and decision-making.

Poor academic performance due to binge drinking, date rape, violence, vandalism, accidents, and hazing all have a relationship to *alcohol* on campus. Substance abuse in other forms led to the Drug-Free Schools and Communities Act — and to a series of challenges over employment and athletic *drug* testing. Liability and discrimination issues related to the advent and spread of *HIV* illnesses have had a significant impact on colleges and universities — for faculty, students, staff, and visitors.

Campuses have become battlefields as well in societal debates and disputes over *smoking* and *abortion*, creating tension between people and institutions, and among individuals, as the rights of some are weighed against the rights of others.

Finally, the latest civil rights movement in our history resulted in passage of the Americans with Disabilities Act. That law, and the earlier Rehabilitation Act of 1973, provide greater access to full campus opportunities through appropriate and reasonable accommodations.

New Law Renews Access Issue for Campuses

February 1992

Curb cuts. Ramps. Lifts on buses. Automatic door openers. Modified restrooms. Expanded door frames. Since 1974, these words and phrases have become part of campus language across the country. They are campus responses to the first significant federal regulation concerning discrimination based on disability, Section 504 of the Rehabilitation Act of 1973. But while campuses are still struggling to understand and comply with that law, they must now prepare to respond to a new piece of legislation: the Americans with Disabilities Act (ADA), modeled after the 1973 law.

Now more than ever, campuses must take the time to focus on the laws and try to respond appropriately. And that's what the laws are really all about: understanding and response.

Federal law in this area began with the 1973 Rehabilitation Act. It outlawed campus discrimination based on handicapping conditions. Students who are otherwise qualified for admission must be admitted. Once in school, the college or university must make "reasonable accommodations." In addition to modifications to facilities, reasonable accommodations could include study aids, tapes of lectures, note-taking services, interpreters for the deaf, and extended examination times or altered formats. The Rehabilitation Act of 1973 dealt with those programs, services, and campuses that receive federal financial support.

If the laws don't prompt campus attention, disabled students themselves will. A quick read of selected campus newspapers provides several examples:

- Disabled students at the University of New Mexico have gathered to seek an injunction to block construction of a new campus residence hall.

The project has 500 rooms, but only five designed as wheelchair-accessible. Critics note that when the federal government builds new housing, 20% of the facilities must be accessible, but that the UNM project will be only 1% accessible.

- In a partial victory for a disabled student, the federal government ordered the University of Washington to modify access to two campus buildings. The student had filed a complaint against the school, contending that two failing class grades were caused by a lack of accessibility in class buildings. In addition to making physical changes, UW was ordered to allow the student to retake the courses for free and to remove a failing grade.

- It took over $2.5 million to settle a lawsuit filed over handicap accessibility at Washington University (MO). The school has agreed to spend the money on facility modifications.

Pressures to make campus buildings and programs accessible continue to mount from student, faculty, and staff challenges and from changes in the law. In order to meet the challenges and comply with the law, colleges and universities need to consider new federal regulations and the ADA.

Earlier this year, the federal government proposed regulations that would govern campus construction and renovations after January 1993. The regulations would apply to private organizations, including colleges and universities, and they are similar to the principles found in the Rehabilitation Act of 1973. Similar regulations for public organizations are expected shortly. Among the basic requirements are standards demanding that:

- Hallways and restrooms be fully accessible
- Ramps and elevators be used where necessary
- Library card catalogs and book stacks accommodate use by wheelchair-bound persons
- A minimum of 5% of library study carrels be designed for use by disabled persons
- A minimum of 5% of dining hall tables accommodate the disabled and food service lines be accessible
- A minimum of 5% of residence hall rooms be designed for use by disabled persons

Before these guidelines take effect, the ADA will also become campus policy. The Act goes well beyond requiring physical modifications. It prohibits campus discrimination on the basis of personal disabilities and applies off-campus to public and private employers. For campuses, the ADA will apply to both employment and admissions situations.

With regard to facility modifications, the new watchwords under ADA will quickly become "readily achievable." Campuses must take immediate steps to make those modifications that are readily achievable. If physical barriers cannot be removed expeditiously, campuses will still need to develop alternative means of making programs and facilities available to those limited by the physical environment.

The campus transportation system will also be affected by the ADA. Regardless of whether the service is run by the school or contracted out, systems must be reviewed for accessibility and new vehicles must be designed to accommodate those with disabilities.

Standardized testing on campus may also need to be modified to meet the demands of the new law. All testing, whether conducted by the school or on campus by or for third parties, must be offered in an accessible environment. Reasonable accommodations must be made for those taking standardized tests on campus.

Summary

The times demand a renewed campus concern about barriers on campus to faculty, students, staff, and visitors with disabilities. With the new law will come new guidelines and standards that must be reviewed, considered, and fully understood, then applied by higher education. Colleges and universities should make the effort and the commitment to do what the times and the law expect; to understand and respond to the needs of disabled persons.

The federal Americans with Disabilities Act (ADA) means different things to different colleges and universities, but for all it represents a clear opportunity to review programs, facilities, and services and to renew commitments to non-discrimination and access. While most schools are already complying with the federal standards due to previous legislation, the ADA will expand the protection of the law into "public places of accommodation," such as transportation, housing, employment, and communications.

For campuses, the major impact of the new law will be on those few private campuses that did not comply with earlier similar laws, private employers, and service providers. The new law, combined with earlier significant legislation on the issue, Section 504 of the Rehabilitation Act of 1973, will ensure that colleges and universities, public and private, will be open and available to those with disabilities. It may also open the door to more civil rights litigation involving campuses.

ADA's Foundation: Section 504

Campuses that receive or benefit from federal financial assistance for operations, programs, and activities were covered previously under Section 504. A person who has a disability and meets academic and technical standards cannot be discriminated against on the basis of the disability. Campuses must operate in a non-discriminatory manner recruitment, admissions, educational programs, residences, counseling, transportation, financial aid, and other services.

In the U.S. Department of Education's Office of Civil Rights publication, *The Rights of Individuals with Handicaps Under Federal Law,* post-secondary institutions are advised that they must provide disabled students with:

- An equal opportunity to participate in and benefit from programs and activities offered by the school or others affiliated with the school
- Policies that do not limit the number of students admitted with disabilities and that do not make pre-admission disability inquiries
- Admissions testing that adequately measures qualifications of disabled students, including special testing provisions when necessary
- Modified academic requirements, such as completion time, unless those time requirements are academically essential
- Auxiliary aids, such as taped texts, interpreters, readers, and modified classroom equipment
- Modified housing at the same cost others pay
- Equal access to financial aid opportunities
- Equal opportunities to assistance in obtaining outside employment
- Equal opportunity to participate in intercollegiate, club, recreation, and other athletic activities
- Counseling and other services on a non-discriminatory basis
- Rules and regulations that don't adversely affect students with disabilities
- Measures of student academic achievement that don't discriminate against disabled students

Over the last 15 years, colleges and universities covered by the law have worked to meet the standards set by the government.

Americans with Disabilities Act

In addition to Section 504, all schools are now covered by the new federal ADA standards, approved in 1990. While many ADA requirements were first adopted in Section 504, the ADA standards now specifically extend non-discrimination and open access rules to the private sector, including some private schools not previously covered under the law.

The ADA affects private sector employment, state and local government transportation services operated by government and the private sector, accommodations, and communication services. For the purpose of federal regulation, the ADA defines "disability" as:

- A physical or mental impairment that substantially limits a life activity, such as self-care, walking, seeing, or working
- A record of the impairment(s), such as diagnosed conditions like cerebral palsy, HIV, emotional illness, specific learning disabilities, and others
- Regarded as having an impairment, such as disfigurement from burns or accidents, that limits major activities, such as work

Among the major features of the ADA that have implications for the hiring and employment practices of colleges and universities:

- Schools can't discriminate against an otherwise qualified individual with a disability in the employment process, including applications, hiring, and terminations.
- Schools must make "reasonable accommodations" for disabled employees, unless the accommodation would impose "undue hardship."
- Schools can't ask job candidates about disabilities or require medical tests before job offers; schools can, however, require medical tests of all who are offered jobs.
- Schools can't inquire about current employee disabilities, unless the inquiries are job-related and deemed necessary.
- Schools must make facilities readily accessible and usable by individuals with disabilities, in new construction and existing facilities.
- Schools may have to apply the law to private programs or services operating on campus.
- Schools with government support can't discriminate against disabled individuals by excluding them from the benefits of services, programs, or activities.
- Schools are required to modify campus transportation systems to be accessible.

Key ADA Language

Several key provisions of the ADA come directly from earlier Section 504 language, so they may be very familiar to most colleges and universities.

The term "reasonable accommodation" is an example. Under federal law, reasonable accommodations for colleges and universities could include:

- Facility modifications
- Altered work schedules
- Modified office or classroom equipment, and/or
- Readers, interpreters, and/or other auxiliary aids

Reasonable accommodations must be made for those with disabilities, says the law, unless the accommodation would impose an "undue hardship" on a school.

Just what is an "undue hardship"? For colleges and universities, it means that they do not have to make accommodations that require significant difficulty and delay.

This may involve an assessment of the necessity of an accommodation and the financial resources of the school.

A Timetable for Compliance

The ADA became law in July 1990 and its various sections took effect over the following four years. The employment discrimination sections became law immediately, as did the reasonable accommodation provisions.

The public accommodation sections of the law, which mandate full opportunity for those with disabilities to enjoy private sector goods, services, and facilities in public settings, became effective in January 1992, as did the section on services provided by government, such as communications or transportation. Requirements for new construction accessibility not already covered by Section 504 required compliance by January 1994.

Summary

Colleges and universities will be less affected by ADA than other segments of society because many of the standards contained in the new law have already been applied to campuses. Some changes in facilities and programs may come from a renewed examination of the law by campuses. What the ADA may also do, however, is open the door for increased litigation on the issues of discrimination and access for those with disabilities. To respond to the ADA and the interests of the impacted populations, campuses need to:

- Understand Section 504 and the ADA
- Develop and maintain appropriate employment and admissions practices under the law
- Make reasonable accommodations that can be accomplished without significant difficulty or delay
- Reinvigorate longstanding campus commitments to make colleges and universities open to those with disabilities

In addition, the American Council on Education encourages colleges and universities to use this period of renewed interest in and attention to persons with disabilities to strengthen "town-gown" relationships, by offering the resources and experiences higher education has developed over the past decade and a half to the community.

Expert Advice Needed on Reasonable Accommodation

December 1993

Due to a visual impairment, one law school graduate wanted to take the normally two-day bar examination over a four-day period. The state board of bar examiners said no to the request but offered alternatives. She would be given what it called "reasonable accommodation" for her disability, but not four days of testing. The law examiners suggested a separate testing room, enhanced lighting, a large print copy of the examination, a reader/writer to assist her, and unlimited time during the traditional two-day testing period.

The student took her demand for four days to federal court. The decision, based on a preliminary injunction in *D'Amico v. New York State Board of Law Examiners*, 3 NDLR 291 (1993), allowed the candidate two extra days. The court based its ruling on case law and the Americans with Disabilities Act (ADA). Medical evidence from the student's health care provider was a key element in the decision.

The court said that "reasonable accommodations" must be decided on a case-by-case basis. The disabling conditions will vary and so must campus and agency responses. The court said the law examiner's approach to "reasonable accommodations" may have worked from a testing perspective, but not for the student involved in the dispute.

The court's decision was based primarily on an affidavit from the student's physician. It said that extra time during only two days would make her disability *worse*. The judge noted:

> I view this principally as a medical issue and that, therefore, the opinion of the applicant's treating physician must be given great weight. The Board has no expertise concerning the plaintiff's medical condition as to what is the appropriate accommodation for her visual disability.

The ruling supported the view that the medical personnel, not the law board, was in the best position to determine what accommodations would be reasonable.

D'Amico is one of the earliest ADA reasonable accommodation cases dealing with issues related to higher education. It follows a pattern established in earlier cases that help define the obligations and responsibilities colleges and universities have under the law.

Generally, a student who — due solely to a disabling condition — cannot complete a program of study can request "reasonable accommodation" for campus assistance. The campus can deny requests that eliminate requirements or adjust inappropriate requirements for study or accommodations that are far too costly to make them "reasonable." But the burden of evaluating these requests is on the campus, not the student.

That was the case in *United States v. Board of Trustees for the University of Alabama*, 908 F.2d 740 (1990). In a Rehabilitation Act of 1974, Section 504 case, the University of Alabama at Birmingham (UAB) was sued for failing to provide free interpreters for hearing-impaired students on campus. The state offered free services to those unable to afford such services. The college directed students to that program. If they were ineligible for the free program, UAB would provide services based on the student's financial need. The students felt this approach was unreasonable.

The court agreed with the students, not the school. Said the court, cost was a deterring factor for the school only if it was excessively unreasonable. UAB was told that it must provide auxiliary aids and assistance if it was affordable and did not significantly alter the academic program or requirements.

In *Wynne v. Tufts University School of Medicine*, 976 F.2d 791 (1992), the court considered the program modification requests of a dyslexic medical student at Tufts University (MA). The student claimed he had failed his courses due to difficulties with multiple-choice exams. His legal claim was based on Tufts' failure to offer him the "reasonable accommodation" of alternative testing.

The court ruled that the school had a duty to adequately explore the situation and consider possible options. It gave the school an opportunity to do so. Back in court at a later date, Tufts demonstrated that it had offered reasonable accommodations short of modified testing, and that further accommodations would be academically unsound. Said the court:

> If the institution submits facts demonstrating that the relevant officials within the institution considered alternative means, their feasibility, cost and effect on the academic program, and came to a rationally justifiable conclusion that alternatives would result either in lowering academic standards or requiring substantial program alterations, the court could rule as a matter of law that the institution had met its duty of seeking reasonable accommodation.

Another federal court heard the case of a disabled college student seeking an accommodation in *Fleming v. New York University*, 865 F.2d 478 (1989). An NYU student with a disability needed a single bedroom due to his condition. The campus placed him in a double room by himself but charged him for the second bed. The student refused to pay his bill in protest. As a result, NYU refused to issue his degree. The student filed suit under Section 504, claiming discrimination due to a disabling condition.

The court found, as campuses sometimes do as well, that there was a second side to the story. The student had never "asked" to be moved out of the more expensive room. Less expensive, handicapped-accessible spaces were available, but the student apparently decided to stay in the larger room and fight the "double rate." The court did not rule in his favor. In order to make a claim, said the court, a student needs to make a request for a reasonable accommodation. NYU never received a request; therefore, it was not judged to have denied the student any reasonable accommodation to which the law may have entitled him.

Colleges and universities have dealt with "reasonable accommodation" issues since the passage of the Rehabilitation Act of 1974 (Section 504). Cases such as *D'Amico*, *University of Alabama*, *Wynne*, and *Fleming* are examples of this. But under the ADA, a new standard has developed that will be tested and interpreted over time by schools, students, and the courts. The newer law requires the removal of "barriers" to services and education by campuses if the removal is "readily achievable." Just what is "readily achievable" may, in the end, be a financial cost and campus resource issue.

Learning Disabilities and Test Accommodations

March 1995

The student informed state testing officials that he had a learning disability. So they gave him extra time, a quiet room, and other considerations when he took a law school admissions test. He passed the test.

During his years of law school, he received similar special treatment at exam time, due to the disability. He graduated, but when he went to take the state bar exam, questions were raised about the special arrangements he requested. The state relented, temporarily, when he filed legal action. Officials allowed him to take the two-day test under special conditions, and he passed.

Before he was admitted to legal practice, however, his special accommodations case went to trial. Now, if he wants to practice law in New York, he'll have to take the bar exam again — under the same conditions as everyone else. Why?

Under Section 504 of the Rehabilitation Act of 1973, and the more recent Americans with Disabilities Act (ADA), colleges and universities receiving federal support may not discriminate on the basis of disabilities. Related government regulations mandate that appropriate adjustments be made in the academic environment to allow equal access to those with disabilities without altering institutional and academic standards.

For many, accommodations can easily be realized by access ramps and curb cuts. The law involves far more, however. The problem and appropriate responses are not as easily identified in cases of students with learning disabilities.

Campuses need to evaluate student requests on an individual basis for special accommodations under the law. In cases of learning disabilities, these accommodations may include taped lectures, tutorial assistance, note-takers, and various examination accommodations, such as extended time and quiet rooms.

But what about specific legal cases? What accommodations have courts allowed or ordered? And why?

Academic Freedom vs. Learning Disability

Consider the case of the instructor who didn't believe that one of his students had a learning disability that required special accommodation.

Based on a diagnosis of a learning disability, the student had asked the instructor for special testing accommodation. The instructor turned him down, claiming that no learning disability had been shown to him that required special treatment.

One by one, various campus units and officers asked the instructor to change his mind — to obey the law and accommodate the student's request. The faculty member refused. He also rejected requests for cooperation from the campus disabilities services office, various administrators, and the university's legal counsel.

The instructor contended that the principles of academic freedom protected his right to test students in whatever manner he felt appropriate. He refused to allow the student any extra time for testing.

Ultimately, the student sued. In *Dinsmore v. Pugh and the Regents of the University of California at Berkeley* (1989) he challenged the instructor for violating his rights and the university for failing to enforce established and required non-discrimination policies.

Before trial, the parties agreed to settle out of court. The agreement was obviously in favor of the plaintiff. The university agreed to the student's demand that it develop clear policies and procedures to make it easier for students to receive appropriate accommodations under the law. In addition, the instructor had to admit to personal liability and pay damages to the student.

Certification Examination

At issue in *Pandazides v. Virginia Board of Education*, 752 F.Supp 696 (1991), was a request for extensive alterations in a statewide certification exam. The plaintiff, after graduating from college, could not pass a specific portion of a required teaching certification exam. Based on a diagnosed learning disability, Attention Deficit Disorder, the student claimed she was legally entitled to exam method changes to accommodate her needs.

The court disagreed, based on an earlier U.S. Supreme Court decision that recognized that some academic program factors are necessary and legitimate and should not be subject to alteration. To change them would lower academic standards, which should be protected under the law. That was the case in *Southeastern Community College v. Davis*, 99 S. Ct. 2361 (1979), in which the Supreme Court upheld physical requirements for a nursing program.

Classroom Testing

Was the medical school student with dyslexia entitled to alternative testing? Should he be tested by a method other than written multiple-choice questions? That was the issue put before the courts in *Wynne v. Tufts University School of Medicine*, 932 F.2d 19 (1991).

The plaintiff was dismissed from Tufts Medical School, according to his suit, because of a disability that impaired his opportunity to succeed academically. The student's suit contended that the school failed to make a "reasonable accommodation" by refusing to develop an alternative means of testing his knowledge.

At first, school officials simply contended that changing the multiple-choice exam process would fundamentally alter the school's program, and they refused to make the change. The court said the school had to do more than claim academic freedom when faced with a request for special accommodations. The court held that denial of accommodations should be supported by:

> undisputed facts demonstrating ... the institution considered alternative means, their feasibility, cost, and effect on the academic program, and came to a rationally justifiable conclusion that the available alternative would result either in lowering academic standards or requiring substantial program alteration.

Tufts then returned to court with a full report. It showed that it had provided various accommodations, including allowing the student to take his first year twice, tutoring, taped lectures, makeup exams, and untimed exams. But the student still failed eight of 15 required courses. Then came the request for untimed, oral, multiple-choice exams, which Tufts rejected.

On appeal, the student's complaint was dismissed. The court ruled that Tufts had considered test alternatives and come to a rational and justifiable conclusion that changing test methods would lower academic standards or necessitate major program changes not required by law. Tufts, said the court, had conducted a diligent assessment and made "a professional, academic judgment."

Wynne shows that institutions must be ready to demonstrate why their academic requirements and methods are critical and how an assessment of the critical elements was conducted.

Back to the Bar

In the case of the would-be New York attorney, a state court has ordered retesting without special accommodations. As part of a temporary legal compromise, the student was originally allowed to take the two-day exam under special conditions. The state board let him take the test, with the understanding that the results would not be accepted unless he won his lawsuit.

He was given four days to take the test. He passed. At trial, in *Argen v. State Board of Bar Examiners* (1994), he was not as fortunate. While two doctors testified that they had diagnosed learning disabilities in the student, the court ruled that the "plaintiff has failed to meet his burden of proving that he is a qualified individual under the Americans with Disabilities Act."

The court held that the state was correct to question the student's condition. The decision did not question his sincerity, but noted that experts were unable to agree completely on his condition or related needs.

Tests for Testing

Dinsmore, Pandazides, Southeastern, Wynne, and *Argen* suggest that campus officials take the following actions:

- Develop an understanding of Section 504 and ADA and appropriate campus policies.
- Establish a campus awareness of learning disabilities.
- Assess the core materials and requirements for academic programs.
- Require appropriate documentation of claimed student disabilities.
- Conduct good-faith reviews of alternative testing methods and other accommodations, on request.

Understand the law and comply — but do so with an understanding that compliance does not necessitate sacrificing academic integrity.

Learning Disabilities and Reasonable Accommodations

How can campuses make decisions about reasonable accommodations for students with learning disabilities? How should requests for academic adjustments be weighed under the law?

Process

An approach to campus decision-making in these cases is suggested in a recent article by Sally S. Scott of the Virginia Department of Rehabilitative Services, in *The Journal of Learning Disabilities* (Vol. 27, No. 7, 1994). In "Determining Reasonable Academic Adjustments for College Students with Learning Disabilities," Scott recommends a campus process based on responses to four key questions:

- Does the student have a learning disability?
- Has the student provided adequate documentation of the disability?
- Is the student qualified for academic adjustments?
- Is the requested accommodation reasonable?

By asking and answering these questions and making related follow-up inquiries, a campus can be guided toward appropriate and legal decisions case by case. They can be part of a written procedure for handling requests for accommodations from students due to learning disabilities.

Learning Disability

The law requires that colleges and universities provide academic adjustments only to those students with documented disabilities. Generally, a person with a learning disability is defined as someone who:

- has a mental or physical impairment that substantially limits one or more major life activities (such as learning), or
- has a previous record of an impairment of this type, or
- is regarded by others as having this impairment.

Students not meeting at least one of these qualifications are not eligible for academic adjustments.

Past records of college students may be helpful in determining the existence or perception of a learning disability. Many students who received academic accommodations in high school will maintain those services in college. Others with no previous diagnosis but having overcome a disability on their own may need services as well. Under the law, any past record of disability may make them eligible for accommodations.

Older, non-traditional students, many of whom last attended school before the growing national awareness of learning disabilities, may have associated difficulties without any past record of diagnosis or treatment. Because they did not have an earlier opportunity to develop a record, they may be entitled to legal protection now based on past difficulties.

Documentation

Determining whether or not a student without a record or history of disabilities has a condition that would entitle him or her to academic adjustments may require appropriate documentation.

The burden of providing adequate documentation of a learning disability rests solely with the student. But a college or university is responsible for establishing its own standards for any required documentation.

Such standards can include specific testing, establish required credentials for professionals who provide documentation, and mandate that any documentation of the nature of any impairment include the basis for diagnosis and the dates of testing or diagnostic visits. Documentation standards can also require a professional opinion of specific accommodations appropriate for offsetting any diagnosed impairment.

Adequate documentation of learning disabilities, for campus purposes, generally includes assessment data measuring student aptitude, achievement, and information-processing. An assessment should be conducted by an appropriate professional and based on recent evaluation.

Generally, documentation should be provided by a learning disabilities specialist, a licensed psychologist, or perhaps an educational therapist. Any credentialed professional providing diagnosis and recommendations should demonstrate appropriate experiences, based on work with other college students.

To be considered current, diagnostic testing should be no more than three years old, according to most existing standards. If the student does not or cannot provide adequate documentation meeting reasonable campus standards, the campus does not have to make the requested academic accommodations.

Qualified

A student with a disability is qualified for adjustments when he or she can meet the essential requirements of a class or program if given reasonable accommodations. This judgment must be made on a continual basis, as circumstances, conditions, and academic situations constantly change.

In determining if a student is "qualified" under the law, a campus should consider two primary issues:

- Can the student meet course and program standards, both technical and academic?
- With accommodations, can the student perform essential required tasks?

Students with learning disabilities must be able to meet the standards for admission, majors, grades, and graduation. If they cannot with appropriate accommodations, they are not qualified.

Reasonable Accommodations

What is a "reasonable accommodation"? It would be administratively easier if there were just one answer to this question, but that's not the case. What's "reasonable" must be determined case by case. It requires individually documented reviews of student conditions, needs, and the academic environment.

However, in making a campus judgment, several issues must be examined to determine what is reasonable for an individual. Consider the following key points in testing for a reasonable accommodation:

- It should be based on documented individual needs.
- It should allow for the most integrated student experience possible.
- It should not compromise essential requirements of a class or program.
- It should not pose a threat to personal or public safety.
- It may not impose undue financial or administrative burden on the campus.
- It must not be of a primarily personal nature.

An accommodation is reasonable if it meets this test. Campuses must provide such accommodations.

What Is "Unreasonable"?

When considering possible accommodations, legitimate campus concerns relate to possible academic program compromise and financial burdens. An academic accommodation does not and should not compromise essential academic or experiential requirements of a program. A program does not have to be "watered down" to satisfy the law. Courses or requirements expected of others should be modified for learning-disabled students only if such changes would not substantially alter content deemed necessary for competence.

Modifications that would necessitate substantial program changes or significantly alter standards are not required. The intention of accommodations is to allow a student with a disability the same opportunity as others to succeed or fail, but not compromise a program. If campus officials refuse an accommodation, they should be ready to document what they deem essential in courses or experiences and why.

Financial or administrative burdens may cause a campus to consider an accommodation unreasonable. But extreme care should be exercised before a campus uses this defense. While some accommodations may be too expensive or burdensome, a careful study of campus resources would be conducted if these were the sole reasons given for not providing an accommodation.

Campuses are not, however, required to provide accommodations beyond those needed or necessary to provide equal opportunity to pass or fail. The campus may choose to provide only the most basic or minimum accommodation available to meet a documented need.

Summary

As reviewed in "Determining Reasonable Academic Adjustments for College Students With Learning Disabilities," campuses need to establish a process and standards to deal with these requests. Experts advise institutions to:

- Develop written policies
- Implement them fairly
- Require students to provide specific documentation, including recommendations
- Make judgments about accommodations case by case, not relying on stereotypical assumptions
- Make accommodations that do not substantially alter program or academic standards

Minimize the Risks of Student Health Insurance

June 1990

One-quarter of American college students have no health insurance. They face years of significant risk —

risk of illness, accidents, and high medical care costs. They may also face the ultimate risk for students — that financial or physical burdens from illness or accident might force them to end their academic careers.

Concerned about students and their risks and burdens, institutions are turning to mandatory student health insurance programs; over 40% of four-year institutions have some insurance requirement for enrollment. Such requirements may address student health needs, but they can present other problems unless campuses carefully consider legal and non-legal factors. Good plans adequately serve student and community needs, with proper respect for existing legal standards.

News stories of double- and even triple-digit premium rate increases have become almost commonplace. Average student insurance costs today are in the $250- to $350-a-year range. Medical inflation continues to outpace cost increases in all other areas, and these costs are passed along to student consumers. In addition, as more and more hospital cost containment programs are developed, outpatient services are in greater demand and at a higher price.

Two other factors are contributing to student insurance premium increases: new catastrophic illnesses and a changing population. Diseases such as AIDS and greater mental health care needs have placed a heavier financial burden — or fear of a heavier financial burden — on student health insurance carriers. More students can be expected each year to reach the maximum major medical level of benefits policies allow. The shift from the traditional 18- to 22-year-old student population has also affected premium levels. Insurance carriers have always seen the traditional-age population as relatively healthy. As campus populations become older, health care needs can be expected to increase. As needs increase, premiums rise.

Protect Your Interests

Given the growing need for insurance coverage and escalating premium levels, campuses should take the following measures to protect student and institutional interests:

- Deal only with reputable brokers and carriers. Check references carefully. How is the carrier rated by the national ranking system?

- Get all promises in writing. Obtain a copy of the master insurance policy — as well as a letter of understanding among the campus, the carrier, the broker, and any claims payment agency involved.

- Consider employing an insurance consultant or broker of record to fully understand your population's needs and to represent your interests to the marketplace.

- Understand the basic underwriting principles used by the carrier and require reports to verify the financial status of the account. What formula will be used to establish a renewal quote?

- Check with the state insurance department. Is the plan on file? Is the broker licensed to do business in the state?

- Understand up front how disputes (and there will be disputes!) are to be resolved. By whom? When? What input will the campus have?

- Make sure the insurance materials distributed to students indicate the extent of responsibility the school accepts for the plan. Ask yourself, "Is it clear that the plan doesn't make the school liable for any payments or claims?"

- Check the brochure explaining benefits. Is it written clearly, in plain language? Do students understand the plan, the need for a plan, and how to use the plan they're paying for? Ask them.

- Have a clearly established claims review and payment timetable. Ask what students will be told when there's a delay. To what extent will providers seek additional medical records to substantiate claims?

- Have a firm understanding of the premium billing and collection process.

- Establish a central contact or telephone number for students to get answers to questions or to pursue concerns and complaints.

Confusion and frustration are often major factors contributing to litigation. Insurance programs that reduce confusion and frustration for students and the health care provider lessen the risk of costly and troublesome litigation. Good programs yield good results, and good programs involve quality carriers, quality brokers — and a full understanding by all parties of all duties and responsibilities.

Statutory and Constitutional Issues

The insurance plans themselves can lead to legal scrutiny on a variety of statutory and constitutional issues. In choosing or maintaining a student insurance program, officials should take care to understand potential legal problems.

In at least one significant case, students have challenged the right of an institution to require insurance of certain students. International students at the University of Toledo (OH) objected to the school's requirement that they carry health insurance. They filed a class-action suit, claiming that the requirement violated equal protection and due process rights as well as the First Amendment. They argued that the school was unlawfully treating them differently due to their status, and that it had deprived them of notice and an opportunity to be heard. They also claimed the insurance requirement interfered with their religious freedom.

In *Ahmed v. University of Toledo*, 664 F.Supp. 282 (1986), a U.S. District Court found the insurance requirement to be legal. The test for the rule, said the court, is one of *a rational basis*. "Under that test, it is the plaintiffs' burden to demonstrate that the University's health insurance policy is wholly unrelated to a legitimate state end." In this case, the state end was "to protect students' ability to exist in the community, taking cognizance of the high costs of health care."

The court looked at the several claims and found no legal basis for overturning the school rule. There was legitimate need for the rule, it said, citing high medical costs and an automobile accident that injured several uninsured students. The university met due process requirements by distributing notice of the requirement in all admission and registration materials, as well as through follow-up contacts with students who failed to meet the requirement.

The court saw the religion issue as "an afterthought" by the students and dismissed it. If the court had found the claim to be in good faith, it would have considered the issue on the basis of the *least restrictive means*. In doing so, the court would have looked at the policy and the burden, if any, placed on the students' practice of their religion, to see if the state's ends could met in another, less restrictive, manner.

An appeal of the decision failed, since the plaintiffs had left the school and the class-action status of 1,500 international students in the case had never been legally established (*Ahmed v. University of Toledo*, 822 F.2d 26, 1987).

While *Ahmed* deals only with an insurance requirement for international exchange students, it does point out several key legal principles in the area of student health insurance. If students challenge an insurance requirement, they'll have to show that the plan or rule doesn't serve some legitimate state end. In addition, if schools properly disseminate information on policies through catalogs and other enrollment and admissions materials, they provide adequate due process.

Questions of Discrimination

In addition to opposing insurance requirements, students can challenge the insurance plans themselves. Currently, the greatest legal concern is discrimination: plans are subject to review and challenge over alleged discrimination based on sex, handicapping condition, and age.

An example of such legal scrutiny is the attention focused by the Education Department's Office of Civil Rights on maternity benefits. The Department has ruled that if a school is involved in a plan, the plan must treat maternity as it does any temporary illness.

To avoid discrimination problems, insurance administrators should consider the following:

- Check all plans to make sure that the program doesn't exclude persons with disabilities.
- Make sure the coverage doesn't exclude specific illnesses.
- Make sure that policy provisions for pre-existing conditions are realistic.
- Avoid health and disability questions on group enrollment forms.
- Make sure that mental health and substance abuse care provisions don't violate Section 504 with regard to discrimination due to handicapping conditions.
- Avoid blanket age restrictions in plan enrollment, to avoid claims of age discrimination.

Concerns over discriminatory clauses in student health insurance programs are justified and must be carefully reviewed. Administrators can minimize difficulties by working with a qualified insurance broker and a reputable carrier. In addition to industry representatives, professional organizations, including the American College Health Association, regularly address insurance needs and problems.

A lack of coverage, rising costs, legal challenges and discrimination concerns are all problems with student health insurance in the 1990s. To meet the needs of students and society, colleges and universities must be prepared to consider mandatory insurance and its implications.

Mandated Health Insurance Draws Challenges

December 1991

To insure or not to insure? That was the higher education question tackled by a Kentucky court. College students, required by a new state law to buy health insurance if they enroll in college, went to court in an effort to stop the program. In addition to maintaining that the insurance requirement was unconstitutional, students claimed that the program was too expensive and didn't provide adequate benefits. Two students, one from a community college and another from a university, brought suit to challenge Kentucky health care reform laws. And these two students have had quite an impact!

Source: Health Care Reform

At issue was a small section of a comprehensive state health care reform law that was unanimously passed by the legislature. Under the law, if you wanted to go to college in Kentucky you'd need health insurance. The law required that all Kentucky college students taking at least 75% of a full course load have health insurance that met minimum standards. The required coverage included up to 14 days of hospitalization, 50% of inpatient physician's fees, and emergency room costs if subsequently hospitalized.

Students without alternative insurance coverage through their families, employers, or personally purchased plans would pay an additional $52 for six months of minimum coverage under the state plan. More comprehensive insurance plans were also available to Kentucky students without other coverage. One of those plans provided outpatient benefits, including X-ray and lab work, and cost $191 for six months' coverage for students under 35 and $526 for older students.

The state appropriated $8.8 million to buy insurance for those who couldn't afford it. The new law was intended to take effect on Sept. 1, 1991 — that was, until the students got involved.

Uninsured Population Causes Concern

Surveys by the Kentucky State Higher Education Council indicate that most of the nearly 150,000 two- and four-year college students in the state have medical and accident insurance. About 17,000 students have no health insurance protection. But over 700,000 state residents are without insurance, and the college insurance law was a small attempt to reduce that uninsured population.

In supporting passage of the college student insurance law, the state General Assembly cited two primary reasons:

- *Costs to the state for uninsureds*, as public resources are used to provide necessary health care to residents, including students, who have no personal resources to pay for health care.

- *State investment in education*, because the state subsidizes higher education. It is important to make sure that students receiving the benefit of the subsidy are protected from significant health care financial losses that could force them to end their studies without a degree.

Thus, as a small part of an overall state health care reform law, sponsors included a college health insurance requirement to reduce the health care burden placed on the public by those without insurance and to protect the state's investment in higher education.

Kentucky Students Try Politics and Courts

Students angered by the law first attempted to change it through the political process. Student leaders recently met in the state capital with leaders. They requested a special session of the legislature before the start of the semester to repeal the law. The legislature isn't scheduled to meet again until January 1992. The students asked that the insurance issue be placed on the agenda as quickly as possible. While legislative leaders say it's doubtful they will meet early, at least one state representative has already pre-filed a repeal bill for January consideration. Students are now lobbying hard in favor of that resolution.

But two students — with student government support — went to court to challenge the law before the school year started. They claimed the law was unconstitutional because it placed an insurance burden on them but not on other state populations. A county circuit court listened to their claim and granted a temporary injunction. It restrained colleges from imposing the rule on the two students until a final ruling on the case could be made after full consideration of the issues.

The court granted the temporary injunction, citing the irreparable harm the students would endure if they were barred from school. In addition, the court found that the constitutional issues the students had raised were worthy of additional judicial review. In response, several schools decided not to implement the law until the case was ruled upon.

And what started with two students became thousands when the state Board of Student Body Presidents asked the court to make it a class-action case on behalf of all Kentucky college and university students.

The court granted that request, suspending implementation of the law until after a trial on the issues sometime in the next year. The student governments have three attorneys working as volunteers on the case and have spent over $1,500 in court costs this year pursuing the matter.

Notification to all persons in the affected class will be the next step in the legal process. The plaintiffs plan to place legal notices in campus newspapers across the state. During the fall, attorneys for both sides will present written arguments on the issues to the court. Then, a trial date will be set.

A Constitutional Problem ... But Whose?

Is it constitutional to require health insurance as a prerequisite for attending a public college or university? That's the question before the courts as they consider state and federal regulations. Attorneys for students contend that the law is unconstitutional because it unfairly singles out college students when many others in the state are also without health insurance. They argue that for the law to be upheld, the state must show some important state need and a connection between the law's purpose and the affected population. Since college students represent less than 2% of the state's uninsured population, the students' lawyers claim that there is little or no relationship between the law and its purpose. According to them, health insurance and college simply don't go together!

State officials disagree. They cite the huge public subsidies provided to higher education students. Insurance is needed to protect the state's investment in them. One illness could ruin a student financially for life, were the student not adequately protected from loss. Public interest in keeping health care costs under control and the importance of teaching students about insurance are also cited by supporters of the law who seek to justify the act.

Hearing that some students objected to being singled out for required coverage, one lawmaker remarked:

> It seems to me that the taxpayers have a pretty substantial investment in college students, and students don't mind being singled out for that. We appropriate millions of dollars for education and for financial aid ... and one little illness ... even a day's hospital stay ... can financially ruin any student who's not covered.

Other State Schemes Are Similar

New Jersey and Massachusetts have mandatory college insurance laws, as do many state systems and private colleges. Some require students to purchase the endorsed plan or a plan operated by the school or system. Others require everyone to have insurance and to show proof of alternative insurance before being waived out of the endorsed plan. Variations on these programs exist across the country.

The existing state laws in Kentucky, New Jersey, and Massachusetts are similar. They all establish minimum statewide insurance standards for college students. Students with alternative coverage that meets or exceeds the state minimums don't have to participate in state plans.

The Kentucky case could affect student health insurance laws and programs around the country. Can health insurance be a requirement for college enrollment? Is there a relationship between campuses and health care? Does the state have an important interest in protecting higher education subsidies? How does the Constitution affect the rights of students and the responsibilities of the state? A court in Kentucky will begin its review of these issues shortly.

"A-Word" on Campus

November 1991

Abortion. The mere mention of the word today is enough to spark debate, controversy, even violence. And as the nation attempts to come to grips with the issue, it should come as no surprise that one battlefield in the war is our campuses.

In classrooms, student government offices, administration buildings, and health centers, colleges and universities are being forced to confront what may be the premier social, moral, ethical, and legal issue of the 1990s — abortion.

Campus Considerations

Campus debate can be all-encompassing. Consider the debate at the University of Texas-Arlington. There, students organized a referendum on the establishment of what might have been the nation's first on-campus abortion clinic. The proposal divided students and faculty at the 24,000-student institution.

Leaders of the student government, which supported the proposal, encouraged student governments across the country to get involved in the debate. Other students contended that state institutions and state dollars should not be used to support abortion services. And despite the efforts of the referendum organizers, the vote was only informational: the campus president, adamantly opposed to the idea, had the final say.

Many colleges and universities have tried to stay out of the abortion debate, often citing ethical issues, state regulations, and financial considerations. But the UT-Arlington students held their referendum anyway. They claimed that the school should respond to student concerns over funding abortion services. The campus health center, which provides pregnancy testing and contraception, took no stand in the debate. However, it regularly refers students to off-campus services that provide abortion and adoption services.

And while students debated in Texas, officials in other states are concerned over abortions in campus medical centers or teaching hospitals. The University of Arkansas School for Medical Sciences is currently under legislative investigation for alleged violations of the state constitution. In 1988, the state adopted legislation prohibiting the use of public funds for abortions.

According to records, the campus medical center performed at least 60 procedures during the past two years. University officials have said they do not believe the abortions violated the law, as they were privately paid for through fees. But others aren't so sure. The state governor has asked the attorney general to join in the investigation. Anti-abortion groups have claimed that the hospital should not perform abortions at all, because the facility and staff are publicly funded. Even patient fees are considered part of the state budget, they argue, and are public dollars, subject to the law.

In the classroom, one school has taken a different approach to make sure that the abortion issue is presented and debated in a balanced fashion. At George Washington University (DC), two instructors with strongly differing views are co-teaching a seminar on the "Abortion Controversy." While each instructor felt confident of being able alone to cover the topic appropriately, working together has given them and their 70 students a better appreciation of the issue.

The class focuses on the moral, political, and medical issues related to abortion. Students in the seminar will read articles and court cases, then present their own views and an analysis of an alternative view when the class ends. The classroom debate is intended to promote understanding, an element missing in much of today's national debate.

Student Fees

When students and student organizations get into the debate, they often bring up the issue of *mandatory student activity fees*. Can student activity fee dollars be used to pay for abortions and abortion-related services? Students at many schools are required to pay a student activity fee as a condition of enrollment. The fee dollars are used to support programs and activities that supplement the school offerings.

While there is little case law directly on this point, other fee cases indicate that the First Amendment may be a determining factor, in that it protects the free exercise of religion.

While some students object to the funding of particular services with activity fee dollars, courts have supported a variety of services as constitutional. Student objections to the use of fees have often been based on religious and political considerations. On the issue of abortion, some students have claimed that the use of fee dollars in support of such services violates First Amendment freedom of religion.

The law is clear: government cannot make regulations that affect the religious beliefs of the people. So school rules that require particular religious actions may be constitutionally objectionable. The courts balance the interests of individuals and groups. But when a student is given the choice between paying a fee and not attending a school, there's no infringement on religious freedom.

That was the case in *Erzinger v. Regents of the University of California*, 187 Cal. Rptr. 164 (1982). A state court considered claims of students who alleged religious infringement. According to the plaintiffs, the campus infringed on their First Amendment rights to exercise freedom of religion by requiring student fees that funded abortion counseling, abortion referral, and abortions. Failure to pay the fees would result in a termination of student status. If you wanted to attend the university, you had to pay. And your fees supported what you might consider religiously objectionable. The students saw this as wrong.

A California appellate court upheld the university's fee system. It ruled that the students could not complain of unconstitutional infringement unless they could "prove the university coerced their religious beliefs or unreasonably interfered with their practice of religion." While the students strongly objected to the use of their fee dollars for abortions, the court said, the fee policy did not force students to change their beliefs or to act against their beliefs. Since campuses have been given the right to collect and expend funds for the benefit of the campus population, compulsory payment is constitutional, even if some students object to certain programs funded by their fees.

But even if the students in *Erzinger* had shown an impact on their practice of religion, the court would have considered another test before declaring the school fee policy unconstitutional. The court would have asked the school to show that there was a compelling need for the fee policy and that the policy fulfilled the need in the least burdensome manner. If the school policy were justified in this manner, the court could have upheld it — even if it affected the free exercise of religion by some students.

Traditionally, campuses have enjoyed great judicial latitude in establishing policies. For student fees, administrative interest in promoting mandatory participation has withstood legal challenges in the past. And campuses have been given the responsibility for determining the types of programs students may need, including health-related services.

Summary

In and out of the classroom, in state capitals, in campus health facilities, and in the courts, the national abortion debate has engulfed campuses and communities. While colleges and universities have a duty to respect the beliefs of individuals, they may have a higher duty to the needs of the entire campus population. Consideration of the abortion issue must be balanced and public campus policies must be religiously neutral. And where student activity fee dollars are involved, campuses must consider the Constitution's free exercise of religion clause, compelling state interests, and the least burdensome means of achieving state needs.

Abortion: Another Long, Hot Summer?

June 1992

To the surprise of no one, the national schism over legalized abortion impacts college campuses. Off campus, the issue has proven to be very divisive and has put communities to severe tests when "pro-life" and "pro-choice" groups clash with the law or each other. College communities face similar risks. A variety of campus policies, programs, and beliefs may make the college or university campus a battleground in the continuing abortion conflict.

The power of the conflict was visible to all a few years ago during "Operation Rescue" in Wichita, Kansas. The forces of choice, life, and government clashed daily in the streets of middle America and nightly on national news broadcasts. For colleges and universities, one clear message should be, "It can happen here." Campuses should be prepared.

The campus opportunity for becoming part of, or the site of, community debate could develop from any number of sources:

- Student organizations: pro-life and pro-choice
- Student government involvement in social issues or the political process
- Faculty or staff involvement or participation in related off-campus organizations
- Policies or principles of church-affiliated institutions, perhaps stemming from governing boards
- Campus research projects on related issues, such as the use of fetal tissues
- Campus hospitals, medical schools, or affiliations with others that perform abortions
- Coverage for abortions under student or employee medical insurance programs
- Campus discipline for on- and off-campus protests
- Women's health services and publications
- Campus meeting space or demonstration areas
- Staff union involvement
- Student newspaper editorials

As the national debate intensifies, the campus debate may lead to acrimonious conflicts. Pro-life and pro-choice student groups at the University of Wisconsin-Madison, the University of Virginia, and Ohio State University demonstrate the potential for divisive conflict.

At Wisconsin, a conflict involving abortion-rights advocates tested student government bylaws. According to student association rules, organizations receiving annual funding cannot hold closed meetings on campus. The rule was questioned when a pro-life supporter tried to attend a meeting of a progressive student network.

Members of the network asked the student not to attend a lecture they were sponsoring because of earlier incidents. Network members said they felt threatened by the presence of a pro-life advocate who previously had been involved in altercations with other pro-choice supporters. Turned away at the door, the student filed a complaint with campus student affairs staff. He also wants the student government to withhold future funding. But the progressive network's members claim that the recently adopted rule they allegedly violated is unfair and should be reviewed. It allows persons to be excluded from group counseling sessions but does not allow other "safety exemptions." Both sides expect the clash to continue.

At the University of Virginia, an anti-abortion group and five students were recently subjected to campus disciplinary proceedings. The group, First Right, and the individual students were found innocent of violating student conduct regulations. They had been charged with disorderly conduct for their participation in an off-campus abortion clinic protest. During the protest, designed to halt operations at a community abortion clinic, the students were arrested for trespassing. Campus rules make students responsible for their conduct "on university-owned or leased property or at a University-sponsored event." Students can also be tried for conduct that "directly (negatively affected) the University's pursuit of its proper educational purposes." The group and students were accused of violating those standards of conduct.

They pleaded innocent at a judiciary committee hearing. The group successfully argued that the off-campus protest was not a sanctioned university event. It had been discussed at a campus meeting, but First Right was never mentioned as a sponsor or official participant in the rescue operation.

Student prosecutors argued that the group was formed to be a "vehicle for gathering support for the activities" of anti-abortion groups and should be held accountable for related activities. But group members persuaded the hearing committee that they did not serve as event co-sponsors and participated only as individual students. The charges of negative impact on the education process were also dismissed. The judicial panel objected to involvement in what it felt was a matter of "free expression." The committee did not want to judge "incompatible beliefs" of students or the institution.

Some on campus questioned the panel's failure to find student organization involvement in the protest. The judicial panel found that participation in an event by members of a university-affiliated organization does not make the event "university sponsored." Observers question whether future attempts to sanction groups like fraternities for the acts of their members may be hampered by the decision. In addition, others question why judicial charges were filed in this case and not other protests on unrelated topics. Did the fact that abortion was involved make a difference?

Must Publications Display Balance?

At Ohio State University, publications and their lack of anti-abortion messages are in conflict. A "Students for Life" coalition has been pressuring campus officials to include pro-life service and agency information in a women's calendar, a resource handbook, and crisis referral listings. The OSU Office of Women Student Services rejected the group's request. It ruled that the inclusion of pro-life materials would be inconsistent with the mission of the office, which promotes women's rights. The students then went off-campus for help, to the governor and legislative branches of government. They hand-delivered information packets, with campus documents and printed materials they felt discriminated against their beliefs, to political leaders. At least one elected official commented that "a balance, dialogue, and debate should be represented from both sides" of the issue in campus publications.

Not waiting for further government response, Students for Life took its case against OSU to federal court. The case contends that the failure of OSU to include the group's position in campus publications violates free speech and equal protection principles. An attorney for the group contends that the school refuses to include the pro-life materials because they are "not politically correct."

The disputes at Wisconsin, Virginia, and Ohio State are only some of many abortion-related conflicts today on campuses. Colleges and universities need to be aware of the potential for disputes and sensitive to campus principles and standards. They must also understand personal emotions and deal fairly with all sides in the debate. As the nation searches for common ground on the issue, campuses will have an important role to play, if they remain committed to awareness, sensitivity, understanding, and fairness.

AIDS and Discrimination: What Precedent Suggests

August 1992

The teacher had a history of tuberculosis. When it recurred and required hospitalization, the school system suspended her. Ultimately, she was terminated due to her illness. She claimed that her disease was really a handicap and that she was entitled to protection under the disability law. The school system said she was fired to prevent the spread of the disease.

The issue in *School Board of Nassau County v. Arline*, 480 U.S. 273 (1987), was whether an infectious disease is a handicap under the Federal Rehabilitation Act of 1973 (Section 504). Why is this particular issue of importance to colleges and universities today? Because of a modern and deadly disease: AIDS.

Beginning with the first reported deaths in the early 1980s, Acquired Immune Deficiency Syndrome (AIDS) has now grown into a major public health catastrophe, and has become a major concern for all. In one decade, the virus that attacks the body's immune system has also become a leading health and legal concern for higher education. Among the legal considerations for colleges and universities are possible discrimination in admissions or employment due to disease or sexual preference, responsibility for a safe study or work environment, the potential for negligence, and the question of confidentiality.

Beginning with *Arline*, several key cases and principles have laid down rules campus officials should be aware of when developing or implementing HIV policies. Understanding these rules can assist the campus in responding to and balancing individual and institutional needs.

The Question of Discrimination

Victims of HIV-related illnesses may fear campus discrimination in many places: admissions, housing, and employment are campus arenas where discrimination commonly occurs. Students, faculty, and staff who feel that campus actions against them are illegally based on their illness may turn to the legal system. They will look at the U.S. Constitution and the federal Rehabilitation Act of 1973 for support.

Within the Constitution, the "equal protection" clause of the Fourteenth Amendment is a basis for protection from some forms of discrimination. Originally adopted to protect the rights of blacks after the Civil War, the amendment applies directly to public institutions and those private institutions found to be engaged in "state action." That means that public colleges and universities and selected privates cannot discriminate against groups protected by law. Who is entitled to protection — and what level of protection must be provided — has been determined through court cases and legislation.

For private institutions, the Fourteenth Amendment is applied when "state action" is found. To look for "state action," courts will consider five factors:

- Receipt of state funding
- The level of state regulation
- The extent to which institutional regulations and activities connote state approval
- Service of state interests
- Strength of claim to private status

Courts will evaluate these factors when attempting to determine if a private school is subject to the "equal protection" clause. If a private school is found to engage in "state action," it is subject to providing "equal protection."

Application of the Fourteenth Amendment depends on the group affected and the degree to which it is affected. "Suspect groups" those based on race, sex, age, and national origin are given the highest protection (*Korematsu v. United States*, 323 U.S. 214, 1944; *Graham v. Richardson*, 403 U.S. 365, 1971; *Oyama v. California*, 332 U.S. 633, 1948). To make rules or decisions based on members of these groups and the impact on these groups, a campus must show a "compelling state interest" and show that the regulation or action is the least restrictive means of achieving much of the state interest (*Dunn v. Blumstein*, 405 U.S. 330, 1972).

Victims of HIV-related conditions have not been seen as protected "suspect" groups based on age, race, sex, and national origin. Their claims will be judged by a different standard. In order for a school regulation that discriminates against HIV victims to withstand constitutional challenge, the school must show an important state objective, such as a threat to public safety, that justifies the regulation a slightly lower standard to meet than the "compelling state interest" rule.

Under the federal Rehabilitation Act of 1973, disabled individuals can't be denied access to campus federally funded programs or services "solely by reason of the handicap." If a student or employee is "otherwise qualified," he or she cannot be excluded.

Disabled individuals who can be qualified for admission or employment if the school makes "reasonable accommodations" are also protected by the law. The school has a duty to make accommodations for disabilities unless the accommodations would cause an undue hardship to the institution (such as having to change a program) or causes the school to incur excessive expense. HIV victims feeling excluded due to their illness must therefore show that they have a "handicap" under the law. If AIDS is a handicapping condition, the victim has federal protection from discrimination.

That was the challenge facing the school teacher fired due to her infectious disease. She went to court, claiming that a handicap, TB, prevented her from working. After a series of reviews, the U.S. Supreme Court agreed and ruled that she should be protected by the Rehabilitation Act.

The court found that the woman's illness impaired her life activities and, in that sense, was a handicapping condition. If she didn't have the illness or handicap, she could have continued to perform her teaching duties. She was therefore "otherwise qualified."

The court did consider the school district's concern over the possible spread of disease. To justify a suspension or termination on this basis, there must be significant health and safety risks to others. To examine this, courts generally ask four questions:

- How is the disease spread?
- How long is a person infectious?
- What harm can come to those infected?
- How probable is the transmission of the disease?

The court said that it would look to public health agencies to respond to these questions in the future.

Arline's Protection Extends to AIDS Victims

What colleges and universities found after *Arline* was a new infectious disease, AIDS and HIV. Could campuses discriminate against the victims of these illnesses, based on fears of the possible spread of the virus? Or are AIDS and HIV "handicaps" under the law, giving victims some degree of federal protection?

Using the *Arline* infectious-disease decision, limited federal protection has been extended to those with AIDS and HIV-related illnesses. This does not mean that government and "state agents" can't act against those with the diseases. But given the protection of the law, victims are entitled to a review of their circumstances to see if they are "otherwise qualified" for programs/services or if their needs can be met through reasonable accommodations. If these conditions are met, the 1973 law applies.

If a student or staff member with an AIDS-related illness poses no significant health risk to others and can perform required duties, he or she is protected under the law. A series of cases has eliminated many reasons cited by some to discriminate against those with infectious illnesses. Fear of "complications" that could affect productivity cannot be considered in decision-making (*Chrysler Outboard Corporation v. DILHR*, 14 FED 394 (1976)). Fear of greater health insurance costs may also not be a decision factor. The key remains the illness itself, the likelihood of further spread of the illness, and its possible impact on the victims and others.

Campus Discrimination Needs "Case-by-Case" Scrutiny

Generally, campuses are advised to follow established guidelines developed by the federal Centers for Disease Control and other professional health organizations. AIDS or HIV-related illnesses do not allow a campus simply to reject a candidate for admission or employment. The Fourteenth Amendment and the Rehabilitation Act require a case-by-case examination of circumstances. The presence of the virus and its manifestations may eliminate some opportunities for some infected individuals, but only after careful consideration. Campuses should understand current public health guidelines and the court's analysis of infectious diseases before revising policies or making related decisions.

AIDS victims have non-discrimination rights under the law, and campuses must respect those rights.

AIDS and Confidentiality: Privacy vs. Right to Know

September 1992

Victims of AIDS and related diseases face more than discrimination on campus — especially from a legal perspective. Colleges and universities, therefore, must be sensitive to other concerns, such as:

- The confidentiality of victims' records
- The consequences of negligently exposing those records
- The diagnosis of victims
- The treatment of victims

Campuses have a duty to understand the law regarding these issues. They have an obligation to comply with proper standards and provide appropriate work and study environments for victims of AIDS and related diseases.

But it's usually easier said than done.

Two Colliding Arguments

Two key legal principles generally conflict in confidentiality cases: the "right to know" and the "right to privacy." As a society, we place great emphasis on respecting the privacy of the relationship between doctor and patient. But we're just as concerned about controlling the spread of deadly viruses.

On campus, protecting medical reports and other student records is an important confidentiality concern. So is avoiding the possible disclosure of health information to the government or other parties.

Protecting individual *medical records* has long been a required and accepted practice for colleges and universities. Professional organizations as well as state and federal laws support the maintenance of confidential medical records. Information about a student's medical condition or history, for instance, may not be given to others without the express consent of the student.

So if you unlawfully share medical information on a student, your institution could be sued. The victim could claim damages stemming from invasion of privacy, breach of duty, or violation of state or federal laws.

It's easy to imagine the damage a student could suffer from public disclosure of an AIDS-related condition. The more predictable consequences include the loss of employment, educational opportunities, and social and recreational opportunities. But the student might also lose his or her housing as well as some health benefits. The personal and economic damages could be enormous.

So, in short, you must preserve the confidentiality of medical records on campus — unless release is warranted due to extraordinary circumstances.

Sometimes, You Must Disclose

Disclosing a student's medical condition may sometimes be required by statutory or judicial precedents. Some states mandate the reporting of certain infectious diseases, and case law indicates that disclosure may be required if the public health or the well-being of another person is at significant risk.

Some states have adopted statutory regulations mandating the disclosure of specific medical conditions when they're diagnosed. Some laws, for example, require physicians to notify pubic agencies when they treat or suspect child abuse or gunshot wounds. Others require doctors to report particular infectious diseases to public health agencies.

Most states have some form of AIDS-related disease reporting, ranging from providing data on the number and types of cases to requiring a full report on each case (which includes the patient's name). A few state statutes even require that certain third parties, like emergency medical personnel, be advised of a patient's condition.

What Does Case Law Say?

Case law has dealt with a doctor's responsibility to warn third parties of a patient's condition in limited instances. The case currently being evaluated for its applicability to AIDS involves another sexually transmitted disease — secondary syphilis.

In a 1920 decision, a Nebraska state court ruled that a physician was justified in advising others of his patient's infectious condition because the patient failed to take recommended steps to prevent the spread of the disease. The court, in *Simonsen v. Swenson,* 104 Neb. 224, 117 N.W. 831 (1920), ruled that two factors should be considered in disclosure cases:

- the risk of transferring the disease from one individual to another
- the impact of the disease on a new patient

The higher the risk of transmission and the more serious the consequences of the disease, the more justified the release of a patient's medical condition would be, according to *Simonsen.*

For AIDS and HIV patients, the risk of transfer is seen to be relatively low — except for sexual partners and others who might come in contact with infected body fluids. Most health officials say household populations aren't at risk if they take reasonable precautions. Therefore, disclosure in most environments would not be justified.

However, where there is greater risk of transfer, there is greater justification for limited disclosure. Sexual activity, for example, increases the risk and must be considered in the collegiate environment. Your campus should provide students with good information on AIDS and its spread and should discuss the implications of identifying or not identifying infected students.

Do you have a legal duty to warn those who could come in contact with the disease? Case law suggests that in *very* limited circumstances, an individual or institution may be required to warn those at risk.

In one California case, a mental health professional failed to warn a potential murder victim who was subsequently killed by the doctor's patient. The case established "duty to warn" standards, which may be applied to AIDS and HIV cases where:

- A health care provider has a "special relationship" with a patient.
- A patient is unable or unwilling to take required precautionary steps.
- The risk to a specific individual or to a limited, identifiable third party is significant and likely.
- Other steps, including counseling and requests for authorization to disclose, have not altered the risk.

There is little or no AIDS-related case law on duty issues. Most agencies and institutions are providing notice to those at risk without naming the source of the risk, leaving it up to individuals to make informed decisions for themselves.

How will the courts deal with these cases? That remains uncertain.

Preserving Records

Regardless of potential "duty to warn" circumstances, campuses must maintain and preserve campus and student records in a legally appropriate manner.

Campus records are subject to a variety of controls, including federal and state statutes and campus policies. Make sure you understand regulations in the various jurisdictions. Take steps to ensure that HIV-related records are not subject to unintended and unlawful release.

Under the Buckley Amendment, certain *student* records are protected from release without student authorization. Educational records, for instance, including health and counseling records, are protected from disclosure by federal law. Take care to keep only those records that are necessary and appropriate. "Educational record" materials can be used by campus officials for campus business. But specific student medical information must be handled on a "need to know" basis.

Summary

AIDS and HIV-related illnesses represent a tremendous threat and challenge to campuses and communities alike. Based on medical evidence, the risk of transferring such diseases is slight under most circumstances.

So where does that place the balance between a student's "right to privacy" and the public's "right to know"? In favor of keeping student medical history and treatment information confidential. Warn the community of the real risks — but do so without naming names.

AIDS and Campus Liability: What Are the Risks?

December 1992

Campuses facing the social, legal, and medical pressures that accompany AIDS and other HIV-related illnesses must carefully manage the risks to their institutions, students, and staff.

Just what are those risks? Well, in addition to possible charges of discrimination, colleges and universities must be prepared to face other HIV-related legal issues, such as:

- Warning people about the disease
- Providing a safe work environment for employees
- Avoiding student or staff exposure to hazardous materials
- Properly treating or testing people for AIDS

As the affected population grows, the risk for tort liability against colleges and universities also grows. So it's crucial for you to understand the potential problems and concerns regarding HIV, AIDS, and related illnesses — and to then address them.

Issues

When a school knows that a student or staff member is infected with the HIV virus, does it have a "duty to warn" others about that person?

Generally, a legal requirement to warn people who are likely to come in contact with a medical danger is limited by state confidentiality statutes. In most settings and circumstances, a campus must simply advise a patient of the consequences of his or her infection, and give appropriate instructions on how to deal with it.

To date, there has been little case law regarding this issue. A related example came in a suit filed against comedian Robin Williams by a woman who claimed he gave her herpes in a 1980s sexual encounter. But the case was settled out of court a week before it was scheduled to go to trial.

As employers, campuses are obligated to provide a "reasonably safe work environment" for employees. To meet this requirement, it's important for campus officials to understand HIV transmission, evaluate the situations in which a campus transmission may occur, and enact and enforce appropriate policies to control possible exposure.

Decision-makers should also keep abreast of medical information and changes in programs to ensure that the campus develops, adopts, communicates, and follows good policies.

A strong education and awareness program for faculty and staff is the most important element of a safe work environment. Make sure employees understand the risks and response procedures designed for their own protection. Develop policies with appropriate staff input. Once you develop policies, disseminate them widely — and evaluate and update them periodically.

What Should Guidelines Cover?

Your regulations should include, among other things, policies for the handling of glass and needles, the handling of blood and other body fluids, and the use of protective clothing and equipment.

Concerns about potential "exposure to hazardous materials" are valid across the campus, from people who clean the residence halls to students in teaching hospitals and research labs. Again, the strongest weapon available in the fight against exposure is good education.

Treat all spills, for example, as potentially infectious. Your campus policy should address how spills can be handled safely and how exposed materials can be properly removed and disposed of. Campus personnel, in other words, must know how and when to respond and must have the equipment and supplies that will help them respond safely.

For individuals involved in student health care or health-related professions, the risks are more immediate. Your campus should aggressively and properly advise staff and students of the risks that come with HIV and AIDS. It should have control policies that limit the opportunities for exposure. And it should require adequate training for people in contact with HIV-infected students and staff, based on Centers for Disease Control precautions.

If your campus has its own hospital or extensive medical services, it may also be at risk for exposing patients to the HIV virus through transfusions of infected blood products. Several high-profile personalities who have publicly identified themselves as HIV-positive were initially infected by blood transfusions.

Now, of course, policies and procedures that require blood products to be tested are already in place. Your campus hospital or medical service, however, must ensure that staff members are following those procedures.

Failure to properly "diagnose, test, or treat" HIV infections can also result in legal action against your campus. Your medical staffs, of course, have a duty to properly identify and treat the disease. But beware that misdiagnosis is also cause for legal action. If the campus hospital diagnoses someone as HIV-positive, for instance, then says the diagnosis was an error, the victim could sue for emotional distress, the possible loss of employment and income, and other damages.

As the infection spreads, and as campus education and awareness programming begin to get their messages across, the demand for on-campus HIV testing will grow. Those campuses that can provide testing should provide it, despite the potential risks.

However, if your campus is going to conduct HIV testing, be prepared to provide the appropriate counseling. Student-patients need to understand the implications of a positive test result and their roles in limiting the risk to others. If your campus fails to provide such counseling, it might face a liability claim.

Conclusion

An aware campus is a safer campus, especially when it comes to HIV and AIDS. You and other campus decision-makers should understand the medical threat of AIDS and appreciate the policies designed to limit the related risks.

Most important, you *must* be aware of the potential for legal challenges regarding discrimination, breach of confidentiality, negligence (in failing to warn, failing to provide a safe workplace, or exposing someone to AIDS-related hazards), and improper diagnosis, testing, and treatment of the disease.

So do your homework. For starters, consider: *Educators' Guide to AIDS*, by B.J. Harty-Golder, College Administration Publications, Asheville, NC.

A little knowledge now could save a lot of heartache later.

Where There's Smoke, There's Fiery Talk

December 1990

A breath of fresh air is more common on campus as the national push for tougher smoking policies gains momentum. In the past few months, several campuses have become smoke-free, and others are seriously considering the move. What's behind this shift in policy? Most feel that it's a combination of concern over health factors and a sense of educational mission.

Past efforts to ban smoking on campus ran into legislative and legal problems. The rights of smokers and non-smokers were debated at length, with hostility the most common outcome. Campuses that acted to limit or eliminate smoking in states that had yet to take a stand on the issue ran into enforcement problems. They also suffered from a lack of understanding and awareness. The argument was made, often successfully, that if smoking was legal in the state, it should remain legal on campus.

Then governments began to enter into the debate. Year after year, the U.S. Surgeon General's warning language on tobacco products grew more ominous. But the warnings always focused on the dangers of using the product: smokers became more aware of the hazards they faced, while non-smokers simply suffered in their smoke.

Secondhand Smoke

In 1986, the situation changed with a new surgeon general's "Report on the Health Consequences of Cigarette Smoking," which said that non-smokers could be at risk from smokers. Of particular concern was the damage done to children exposed to smoke, for whom the report showed greater lung development and respiratory problems than previously reported. On and off campus, response was swift!

State governments, health departments, and the airline industry all took action as the dangers of secondhand smoke became known. They established smoking and non-smoking areas to reduce the health risks for non-smokers.

Further studies on the dangers of secondhand smoke have helped fuel the fire for greater restrictions. A Yale School of Medicine report indicated that 25,000 of the nation's 150,000 annual lung cancer cases occur among non-smokers, 40% of whom have never been smokers. The federal Environmental Protection Agency also reported that thousands of Americans die every year from smoke in their environment. It estimated that 3,800 citizens die from lung cancer without ever smoking, and that thousands of other non-smokers are victims of heart attack, stroke, or other diseases. The EPA report recommended banning smoking in all closed spaces, as practicable. A final smoking gun was found recently in the highly respected *New England Journal of Medicine*, in a study of the health risks of non-smokers raised in smoking households. It reported that their risk of lung cancer was twice that of those brought up in non-smoking homes.

The mounting evidence of risk led to action. Many states began to restrict public smoking, with most policies allowing smoking only in designated areas. Airlines went further, under Federal Aviation Administration guidelines. After years of separating smoking and non-smoking passengers, airlines banned smoking, except on long flights. And campuses joined the bandwagon.

Campus Response

Campuses began to seriously consider the rights of non-smokers. Some adopted policies that mirrored state law; others developed their own standards. But campus standards that exceeded state restrictions sometimes ran into trouble.

One early example of this situation was at the University of Louisville (KY). Campus administrators proposed a tough policy on smoking in the workplace, only to run into significant political opposition in that tobacco-growing state. The campus policy called for conflicts between smokers and non-smokers to be resolved in the favor of non-smokers, and it would have barred smoking in any open area on campus. State legislators responded with threats of budget cuts. In a negotiated compromise, the university adopted a policy weaker than originally proposed: workplace smoking disputes are now settled by supervisors, and there are separate smoking and non-smoking areas on campus.

The Heat Is On!

More inclusive and effective campus policies followed elsewhere. Now, coast to coast, the pressure is on to ban all smoking on campus.

Five University of California campuses have completely eliminated smoking. Berkeley climbed on the bandwagon, adopting a no-smoking policy for all buildings — except campus residence halls. Tobacco products are no longer sold in campus bookstores and other auxiliary services. Free classes on breaking the smoking habit are available to faculty, students, and staff, with employees receiving release time to attend.

Temple University (PA) also became smoke-free this year, after several years of study. Smoking is no longer permitted in classrooms, labs, offices, or residence halls, nor at any events sponsored by Temple, on campus or off. Tobacco products cannot be sold on campus, and cigarette machines have been removed. Violations of the ban can lead to disciplinary sanctions.

After Berkeley and Temple, the University of Wisconsin-Madison adopted a similar tough policy. Officials measured campus reaction to a proposal to ban smoking in all UW-Madison facilities. In a letter to the campus community, the chancellor cited three reasons for the proposed ban:

- *Health Concerns* — based on the surgeon general's report and other studies on the hazards of secondhand smoke
- *Precedents* — based on smoking policies at other schools and an American College Health Association recommendation
- *Education* — based on a campus mission to promote a healthy lifestyle by making a clear statement to students on the hazards of smoking

All campus constituency groups were asked for input on the proposal. The ban was preceded by a lead-in time period to encourage cooperation and by a smoke cessation program for all members of the campus community.

Summary

The battle over health rights on campus continues to spread. More and more campuses are considering their smoking policies in the face of health concerns. From times of no restrictions, through a period of separate facilities, to total bans on smoking. Stay tuned!

More Reasons to Become a Smokeless Campus

January 1994

"The Surgeon General reports ...." With those four words leading the way, a revolution in smoking has been taking place in the United States for almost 30 years. In recent years, attention has shifted from the dangers to smokers to the risks from secondhand smoke to others.

In an effort to protect college students from dangers associated with tobacco use, the Center on Addiction and Substance Abuse (CASA) at Columbia University (NY) recently supported a commission report on "The Smoke-Free Campus." That study, recently shared with numerous college and university presidents and chancellors, reviews the data supporting a ban on campus smoking and makes recommendations for campus consideration. Also of concern should be proposed federal legislation and its impact on colleges and universities.

Smoking in public places and the workplace has become heavily regulated in recent years. Many campuses have joined the trend toward a smoke-free environment, and the CASA report will become a consideration for others in further efforts.

Faculty, students, staff, and visitors are smokers and non-smokers, and any proposed change of smoking regulations can quickly lead to confrontation. The CASA report can be a tool in any campus effort to review its environment for study, work, and living for the benefit of all.

Background

After years of concentrating on the health dangers to smokers, researchers have now begun to actively seek links between illnesses and secondhand smoke. In 1992, the federal Environmental Protection Agency issued a report on the "Respiratory Health Effects of Passive Smoking." Its report strongly indicated that secondhand smoke is harmful. The EPA estimated that approximately 3,000 cases of lung cancer each year are related to secondhand smoke. Far more cases of lesser risks were reported, including reduced lung function, coughing, and chest discomfort. For young children, the EPA found secondhand smoke to greatly increase the risks of pneumonia, bronchitis, and asthma.

Several years ago, the American College Health Association (ACHA) developed a policy statement on campus tobacco use. The ACHA, in its 1988 report, suggested:

- Establishing campus wide smoke-free environments
- Prohibiting smoking in public areas
- Forbidding the advertising, sale, or distribution of free tobacco products on campus
- Using education programs to highlight dangers and help smokers quit

Colleges and universities have reason to be concerned about smoking. They legitimately should be worried about student and employee health. Also, they need to consider potential future litigation related to smoking and possible claims against schools for failing to provide a safe environment. These concerns, and others, are motivating reconsideration of campus smoking policies.

Study Group Recommendations

The CASA Commission felt that a smoke-free campus environment was important for a number of reasons, including:

- The risk to others from secondhand smoke
- The lack of a significant decrease over the years in smoking among first-year students
- The vulnerability of college students away from parental supervision, and under social and academic pressures
- The awareness that most smoking begins in the teens and early twenties

This makes the college years critical in addressing this health, social, and potentially legal concern.

To create smoke-free colleges and universities, the Commission recommends:

- Banning smoking in all campus buildings and at all campus events. This would apply to residence halls and faculty offices in addition to other areas. Well-ventilated, designated smoking areas could be provided if appropriate.
- Providing smoking cessation programs and making sure that student and employee health plans provide support for participants. Programs must be readily available, particularly to those who relapse.
- Eliminating the sale of tobacco products on campus.
- Prohibiting all tobacco advertising.
- Eliminating the distribution of tobacco products on campus.
- Prohibiting the use of school's name and logo on smoking-related items, including lighters and ashtrays.
- Working to create an environment in which smoking is viewed as unacceptable and unhealthy.

The Commission acknowledges the difficulties campuses may face in adopting a smoke-free environment and offers suggestions to aid in making a change.

Implementation

Positive and negative campus interventions are recommended to ultimately achieve a smoke-free campus. To aid in the transition, campuses are encouraged to sponsor classes that educate people on smoking hazards. An assessment of the types of smoking cessation and treatment programs should be conducted and made readily available. A range of these programs should be offered on campus at convenient times to make it easy for students and employees to attend as needed.

Fair and effective enforcement of the policy is important to its success as well. Compliance can be promoted through campus security officers and other staff members as well as student staff, such as resident advisors. Sanctions for violations of the policy must make sense if the program is to be accepted on campus. Enforcement of the rules should be uniform but reasonable. This requires appropriate policies and training. Colleges and universities, as educational institutions, are encouraged by CASA to use sanctions against violators that stress education and treatment.

Federal Proposals

At the federal level, proposed legislation could have some campus impact. Under one bill, called the Tobacco Education and Child Protection Act, current health warnings on products would be revised. New language would say that cigarettes can:

- Kill
- Cause lung cancer, emphysema, and heart disease
- Harm babies in the womb
- Be harmful to child development
- Cause cancer in non-smokers

The law, if adopted, would ban distribution of free samples at sports stadiums and other locations attracting students. It would also ban distribution within 2,000 yards of schools. Tobacco sports sponsorships would be prohibited, unless the sponsor hands out health information about the effects of tobacco.

Summary

The CASE Commission report was forwarded to colleges and universities in an effort to encourage schools to review current smoking policies, become more aware of smoking risks, and consider creating a smoke-free environment. Given the growing concerns over secondhand smoke, increasingly restrictive state and local regulations, the proposed federal legislation, and successful smoke-free efforts at some schools, further campus review is in order.

Note: In spring 1996, the federal Centers for Disease Control issued a new report on smoking in the workplace. It found that almost 90% of non-smokers have detectable levels of nicotine in their bloodstreams and that twice as many reported being exposed to tobacco smoke at work than at home.

Schools Crack Down on Drugs and Alcohol

December 1990

When it comes to preventing substance abuse, the federal government is hoping that the pen is indeed mightier than the sword. That's one of the messages behind the Drug-Free Schools and Communities Act (Public Law 101-226).

As a basic requirement of the law, every college or university has to certify that it has adopted and implemented "standards of conduct that clearly prohibit, at a minimum, the unlawful possession, use, or distribution of illicit drugs and alcohol by students and employees on its property or as a part of any of its activities." What is it that the institutions have signed? What have they agreed to do? What does it mean?

From Strategy to Implementation

Legislation calling for campus policies was a significant part of the 1989 National Drug Control Strategy submitted to Congress. It was suggested, and ultimately legislated, that campuses be required to adopt and maintain a substance abuse program to be eligible for federal financial support. The resulting Drug-Free Schools and Communities Act was signed into law in December 1989 with implementation guidelines. Final regulations were adopted in August 1990.

The Act requires campus certification of prevention programs, dictates requirements for program content, spells out the consequences of violations, and details available appeal processes.

Most campuses developed initial compliance statements based on adaptations of existing programs. Full compliance requires additional efforts from most schools.

The Act requires any campus receiving or seeking federal support to do two things, at minimum: provide each student and employee with a written statement on drug prevention, and conduct a biennial review of the campus substance abuse program. Standards for complying with these minimum requirements are important parts of the law and must be clearly understood on campus.

Prevention Statement

Five components are required in the *annual prevention statement*. It must communicate to students and staff:

1. Standards of conduct that clearly prohibit unlawful possession, use, or distribution of illicit drugs and alcohol by students and employees on campus property or as part of campus activities.

At a minimum, campus rules must meet the legal standards in the community. The standards of conduct should indicate that all participants in campus-sponsored events understand and adhere to the law. Most standards of conduct are already developed and available as part of student rules and regulations, employment agreements, and legal standards.

The standards must apply to campus conduct and off-campus conduct at school-sponsored activities. The final regulations suggest that the conduct rules should also extend to "officially sanctioned field trips," social activities, and even professional meetings.

2. A description of applicable legal sanctions under local, state, or federal law for unlawful possession or distribution of illicit drugs and alcohol.

A summary of the legal sanctions that prohibit use, distribution, or possession of illegal substances will satisfy this requirement. An attempt to provide all applicable standards would require thousands of pages. Campus summaries should focus on local, state, and federal laws and the penalties for violations.

In response to requests for federal standards, the Act's final regulations provide a summary for campus use, almost two full pages of charts and text. The regulations state that these materials satisfy the requirements, but campuses "are not precluded from distributing additional or more detailed information." Campus legal counsel, area district attorneys, the state prosecutor's office, or the area U.S. Attorney can provide assistance in preparing such materials, as can regional offices set up under the Act. In addition, it might be most effective and efficient if area schools work together on summaries of legal sanctions.

3. A description of the health risks associated with the use of illicit drugs and the abuse of alcohol.

A summary of information can be used to satisfy this requirement. The materials provided in the final regulations list various controlled substances, their level of dependence, possible side effects, effects of overdose, and withdrawal symptom information. The same material is provided on alcohol. Some campuses have also included information on nicotine.

4. A description of any drug or alcohol counseling, treatment, or rehabilitation or re-entry programs available to employees or students.

This is a resource listing of on- and off-campus assessment, counseling, and treatment programs for students and staff. This section should highlight the campus office or individual responsible for prevention programs and list support groups and peer groups on campus, as well as employee assistance programs for faculty and staff. Information on how to contact the services should also be included.

Since many treatment facilities are in the community, a referral listing and service would be an appropriate part of the statement and prevention program. If no campus referral listing exists, contacts should be made with local health department officials. At minimum, this section should detail campus counseling and treatment opportunities. A description of off-campus programs can be helpful as well, but it is required only where there isn't any on-campus program.

5. A clear statement that the institution will impose disciplinary sanctions on students and employees for violations of the standards of conduct (consistent with local, state, and federal law), and a description of those sanctions, up to and including expulsion or termination of employment and referral for prosecution. A disciplinary sanction may include completion of an appropriate rehabilitation program.

This section of the statement is to make members of the academic community aware of the penalties for violations and to inform students and staff that the rules will be followed. It would be helpful, for informational purposes, if the statement details procedures for police searches, drug tests, warnings, parental notifications, and similar matters.

While many campuses have objected to the required annual distribution of this statement, the final regulations are clear: a copy must be distributed each year to each student and each staff member. The decision on method of distribution is up to the individual campus. It's acceptable to publish the statement in student and employee handbooks or include it in course selection materials or with paychecks or grade reports. It's not satisfactory to simply tell members of the campus community that the information is available: it must be given to them.

Biennial Program Review

The Drug Prevention Program Certification *biennial review* requirement has two components. Campuses must:

- Determine program effectiveness and implement any needed changes
- Ensure that disciplinary sanctions are consistently enforced

To satisfy these requirements, schools will have to demonstrate how well their programs work and how they intend to make necessary program changes. In addition, they'll need to show some evidence that sanctions are being uniformly enforced.

In measuring "effectiveness," the Act's final regulations suggest that schools "track" data related to drugs, alcohol, and the campus. Among these areas:

- Disciplinary sanctions
- Referrals for counseling and treatment
- Law enforcement contacts
- Instances of vandalism
- Self-help or support group participation
- Perception and attitudes of students and staff

The review process could consider data that measure drug- and alcohol-related activity and outcomes. It should assess the effectiveness of activities that promote prevention and intervention; this could include health fairs, workshops, seminars, and support/counseling efforts. Evaluation would include a measure of the value of campus prevention and intervention programs, level of participation in these programs, and a review of the program outcomes. A survey instrument may be used to help assess program impact.

In reviewing the "consistent enforcement" requirement, some campuses have expressed concerns. Does "consistency" mean that disciplinary processes no longer should have the discretion to make punishments suit the crimes? The final regulations deal with this concern. Although they note it's understandable that differing circumstances may lead to differing sanctions, schools must "treat similarly situated offenders in a similar manner."

To make the review process work, it's suggested that a committee conduct the evaluation. Constituencies that should be represented include student leaders, student services staff, public safety, personnel, faculty members, health and counseling services staff, health educators, and support groups.

Summary

The Drug-Free Schools and Communities Act was designed to promote campus substance abuse prevention and intervention programming. By requiring a detailed program statement, annual statement distribution, and a biennial review process, lawmakers hope to have significant impact on campus. And by tying the program to eligibility for federal funds, lawmakers hope to keep the attention of campus decision-makers. The challenge is to keep up the interest and momentum — and address the root problem.

Student Alcohol Abuse

November 1995

Sometimes, it's difficult to reconcile the newspaper headlines. That's the case in higher education recently, as media have focused both on a new report on binge drinking and on student efforts to get around alcohol rules and laws.

The study points to staggering levels of collegiate binge drinking, while the newspapers remind us of the consequences of alcohol abuse. The dangers are obvious, yet the headlines continue:

- "Fraternity DUI ruling may set precedent"
- "Students looking for a way around new drinking law"
- "Students say new alcohol policy played role in kidnapping"
- "Students file complaint against alcohol agent"

Awareness of the continuing problems and the latest survey results may help campuses work toward resolving an old problem — alcohol use and abuse.

Stories in the Headlines

The extent of the problem has been evident in the pages of campus newspapers in recent weeks. Several stories deal directly with the consequences of student alcohol abuse in Arizona, Louisiana, and North Carolina.

In Arizona, a state court of appeals recently ruled that a national fraternity can be held responsible for a car wreck. The 1988 accident involved college students who had been drinking at a fraternity house party. The crash left a University of Arizona student paralyzed, leading to his death two years later.

The student's car was hit by a car operated by a drunken, underage member driving home from a fraternity party. The court held that the national Greek organization cannot legally claim to be powerless to control the activities of its chapters. The decision will be appealed, according to newspaper reports.

At Louisiana State University, a new restrictive campus alcohol policy has sparked negative student response. The regulations prevent most student organizations from serving alcohol on campus. Alcohol can now be served by organizations only at events where 90% of the members and guests are over the legal drinking age of 21.

LSU planned an extensive awareness campaign, starting with meetings for student leaders, since organizations that violate the policy can lose campus registration. Student leaders say they have had many complaints, that are unhappy with the policy, and they want it changed. But LSU officials say they are responding as they must to a recent change in state law barring alcohol sales to those under 21.

In North Carolina, a Duke University student says campus restrictive alcohol policies led to the recent kidnapping of two students. She contends that a Duke ban on campus kegs and beer distribution forced students to party unsafely off campus.

Two students were assaulted and robbed leaving an off-campus apartment one weekend in September. One of their assailants has been arrested. A student says the crime is a result of the campus policy, while the director of university relations called it "more than a stretch to think the university policy forces criminals to assault people off of the university campus."

Finally, consider a recent report on student complaints at the University of North Carolina-Chapel Hill. Two students there who were stopped as part of an alcohol enforcement crackdown have filed complaints.

They allege that they were harassed and illegally searched by alcohol law enforcement officials — after buying a six-pack of soft drinks! Police say they are cracking down on illegal alcohol sales and pull over only those suspected of violating state laws. They say, however, they will fully investigate the complaint.

These stories, and many others like them, show the consequences of student alcohol abuse and student resistance to campus and community alcohol controls. This is the collegiate environment recently studied for binge drinking.

Study of Binge Drinking

The Harvard School of Public Health College Alcohol Study sought to explore three questions in its research:

- How extensive is binge drinking among college students?
- Who is affected by binge drinking?
- What can be done about the problem?

For the study, "binge drinking" was defined as having four drinks (for women) or five or more drinks (for men) in a row one or more times in a two-week period. The study indicated that this level of consumption was "indicative of a heavy drinking lifestyle" for students.

The study involved 140 four-year colleges and universities. A third of them are private. A third of them are in small towns or rural suburban settings. Over 25,000 students at these schools were asked to complete a 20-page survey on drinking behaviors; almost 70% replied.

The study results explored what drinkers do to themselves and others. Bingers reported excessive hangovers, regrets over actions while drinking, missing classes, forgetting where they were or what they did, falling behind in school, arguing with friends, and engaging in unplanned or unprotected sexual activity.

Among the key findings:

- 84% of students drink during the school year
- 44% of all students are binge drinkers
- 19% of all students are frequent bingers (three or more binges in a two-week period)

However, researchers say that the most troubling finding was on how binge drinkers impact others. They referred to this as a "secondhand binge" effect.

On campuses with a majority of binge drinkers, over 87% of all students report having experienced problems from those who binge. Even at schools with fewer bingers, over 60% of all students reported negative impacts due to bingeing. Among the secondhand binge effects the students reported:

- Insults and humiliation
- Unwanted sexual advances
- Serious arguments, pushing, and assaults
- Interruption of sleep or studying
- Having to watch over a drunk friend

"Who is a binge drinker on campus?" asked the survey. According to results, 50% of male students and 39% of female students reported binge drinking. The highest percentage of bingers was in the 21- to 23-year-old age group (48%), with those under the legal drinking age of 21 the next largest binge group (45%).

Where students live has a definite relationship to levels of binge drinking: 84% of those living in Greek-letter housing binge — significantly higher than in other residential settings, including coed dorms (52%), off-campus housing (40%), and single-sex dorms (38%).

Recommendations from the Research

After a careful review of the study results, the Harvard Public Health survey team suggested a universal approach to campus binge drinking problems.

It recommended beginning with a full *understanding of the problem*. We must overcome institutional denial, with campus officials becoming more aware of the problem and its impact on student life. The best approach to this denial is through active involvement of campus leaders.

A systematic campus effort, according to the research, begins with the commitment and *leadership of the president*. Getting the chief administrative officer actively involved in solutions, they note, may help create a positive environment for change.

The study notes that "colleges and universities offer our most formidable aggregations of specialists in human and organizational behavior." To successfully attack the problem, the study recommends that *all campus constituencies must play an important role*. It is suggested that the institution convene a working group on campus to address alcohol abuse, using the variety of resource people available.

Because most binge drinkers begin in high school, campuses are also urged to *change the expectations of incoming students* before they arrive on campus. All materials and presentations provided to them should be designed to convey the quality and standards of student life. Orientation programming and materials should also show how far the school is willing to go to protect student life.

Since the Harvard study shows that more than 80% of students in Greek-letter housing are binge drinkers, campuses have to *work closely with national fraternity and sorority organizations*, holding them and their members accountable for "serving underage students ... and providing an environment where binge drinking is the norm."

It is also crucial for the *campus and community to cooperate* in efforts to combat binge drinking. Campus and local officials need to work together to enforce underage drinking laws and to limit the supply of illegal alcohol to students.

Finally, the most important influences on student binge drinking come from other students, according to the research. The study urges campuses to empower students to take the lead in making student drunkenness unacceptable. Students bothered by the effects of binge drinking need assistance to help them speak up and act.

Summary

Alcohol abuse remains a significant problem in higher education. Newspaper headlines and the Harvard study reinforce the need for new approaches to an old and continuing problem.

Mandatory Withdrawal: Policies and Problems

November 1990

Perhaps the solution is a problem. After years of frustration and consideration, colleges and universities have begun to address the problem of dismissing from campus students with significant emotional difficulties. National meetings and media have focused on this issue, with over 40% of schools now reporting that they have some procedure for dealing with the problem.

Many of the current policies are based on the work of G. Pavela of the University of Maryland. His proposals establish a framework for institutional decision-making. But even as this model gains greater national administrative acceptance, some question the basic premise. Consider the debate.

Mandatory Withdrawal Policies

Campuses have developed two tracks for dealing with student behavioral difficulties: discipline and medical withdrawal. In most cases, traditional judicial codes and enforcement processes serve the needs of the campus well. In most cases, campus rules are drawn to properly control student conduct and to provide for appropriate responses to misconduct. Long gone are the days of broad disciplinary discretion. Today, campus codes and processes are carefully crafted to balance institutional needs with student rights, under contractual and constitutional restraints.

However, many campuses have found it necessary to resort to an alternative form of decision-making when dealing with the mandatory withdrawal of students with psychiatric difficulties. Two reasons are often cited for developing an alternative process:

- Students under these circumstances are unable to defend themselves or respond in a traditional disciplinary process.

- As a result of a student's condition, he or she may have been unable to judge between right and wrong at the time of an incident.

Given these factors, it's argued, traditional discipline approaches aren't appropriate. Now, under the terms of many campus policies, circumstances other than violations of existing conduct rules can lead to mandatory psychiatric withdrawals.

Under the policy standards outlined by Pavela, students could be:

> subject to involuntary administrative withdrawal from the university or from university housing if it is determined by clear and convincing evidence that the student is suffering from a mental disorder and as a result of the mental disorder (a) engages or threatens to engage in behavior which poses a danger of causing physical harm to self or others, or (b) engages or threatens to engage in behavior which would cause significant property damage or directly and substantially impede the lawful activities of others.
>
> (*The Dismissal of Students with Mental Disorders: Legal Issues, Policy Considerations, and Alternative Responses,* G. Pavela, 1985)

Many campus policies have been adopted from *Dismissal* to incorporate an informal hearing process to review withdrawal circumstances. Called by the dean of students or a designee, a student and his or her representative appear at the hearing, along with a faculty member and appropriate mental health professionals.

The faculty member and the representative can challenge the recommendation, and it's expected that the mental health professional will present evidence in support of any withdrawal recommendation. The result of the process is a decision whether or not to require a medical withdrawal from the institution.

Case Law and Section 504 Implications

Campus discipline standards have gone from vague to specific in the last three decades. Initially, schools disciplined or terminated students without any standards or processes. Over time, schools accepted the need for basic fairness: it became standard to give notice and an opportunity to defend. But only in the last 30 years have standards of conduct become specific and widely distributed.

As an example, campus rules that allowed only activities of a wholesome nature were overturned in *Shamloo v. Mississippi State Board of Trustees*, 620 F.2d 516 (1980). The standard was found to be unconstitutionally vague, as it didn't provide advance notice of right and wrong to possible offenders.

However, disruptive activity language, which could be applied to some psychiatric student incidents, has been allowed. In *Lowry v. Adams*, a 1972 Kentucky case, the court upheld the following campus conduct standard:

> any disruptive or disorderly conduct which interferes with the rights and opportunities of those who attend the university ... to utilize and enjoy facilities provided to obtain an education.

Students found in violation could be subjected to discipline. This suggests that campus policies can be structured to allow traditional judicial processes to deal with most disruptive behaviors.

Under Section 504 of the Rehabilitation Act of 1973, colleges and universities receiving federal funds have to certify that they don't discriminate against persons solely by reason of [their] handicap. The definition of handicapped included any person with record of, or regarded as having, an impairment that limits one or more of such person's major life activities. The law covers mental health impairments, including mental or psychological disorders.

There was initial concern that Section 504 would bar any campus actions involving disabled students, but a U.S. Attorney General's opinion has clarified this aspect. According to the Justice Department, the Act doesn't require unrealistic accommodations if a person's disability and its behavioral manifestations would be unduly disruptive to others. Department of Health, Education, and Welfare implementation guidelines support this contention. They note that schools need to be protective only of those disabled students whose attendance or behavior doesn't impede the performance of other students.

Thus, under Section 504, the campus retains the right to take appropriate action against an impaired student, regardless of the disability, if that student's behaviors hinder the education of others.

Challenges to the Current Model

While many have seen campus adoption of mandatory psychiatric withdrawal procedures as an appropriate means of addressing a difficult problem, not everyone is convinced. Certain mental health professionals and student advocates express two major concerns over the informal hearing process that can lead to mandatory withdrawal:

- It places mental health professionals in an adversarial role with students.
- It may create difficult standards for students with mental disorders, threatening them with expulsion or suspension for acts that wouldn't result in those sanctions for other students.

Mental health professionals, on and off campus, have a difficult time being seen as a help resource for students when officials are asking them to advocate mandatory student withdrawals. They argue that they cannot, and should not, wear both of these hats at the same time. It could affect the long-term usefulness of professionals on campus if students develop a sense that in seeking their help, they could be helped right out the door!

There's also some concern over the lack of conformity in sanctions for campus behaviors. Under case law and Section 504, a campus's right to act isn't unduly limited. It can respond appropriately to campus misconduct that is disruptive to others or the education process. It can use established procedures and impose established sanctions. But in a mandatory withdrawal model, there's concern over what constitutes a crime and whether the punishment fits the crime.

Under conduct rules, students with disabilities or impairments have an opportunity to understand the limits of their behaviors and likely outcomes of non-compliance. They can know the rules and know that a sanction for violations will be appropriate under the circumstances.

This may not be the case for the mandatory withdrawal model. Students could be subjected to withdrawal for actions that wouldn't have been treated as seriously under traditional judicial processes. In addition, conduct that hasn't been previously defined as objectionable can result in the mandatory withdrawal of students with mental or psychiatric difficulties. Finally, critics contend that the withdrawal model doesn't clearly enumerate standards, and that it fails to provide appropriate sanctions for minor, rather than major, difficulties.

Summary

There's no dispute that students with mental, emotional, or psychiatric difficulties can present serious problems for the campus community. Regardless of the cause, behaviors that disrupt, impede, or threaten to interfere with campus education and life can be referred to campus judicial bodies for review. Only under unusual circumstances should an alternative means be used.

When a psychiatric withdrawal model is used, schools should take care to ensure the following:

- The problem can't be properly handled by traditional campus disciplinary processes.
- Students understand the process and have adequate preparation and representation.
- Withdrawals aren't authorized inappropriately for incidents that would have resulted in lesser sanctions if handled judicially.
- Mental health professionals help all parties in the process but leave the ultimate decision to administrators.
- All campus treatment and intervention resources are used to avoid mandatory withdrawal.
- Mandatory withdrawal is accompanied by a clear referral for continuing treatment, and it provides a means for the student to return to school in the future, as appropriate.

Withdrawal Policies Carry Risks

February 1993

It's difficult for everyone when a student faces mandatory withdrawal from school for emotional or mental health reasons. You can learn more about the related campus risks — and find out about a model withdrawal process — by reading an article in *The Journal of College Student Psychotherapy* (No. 3, 1991).

In "Mandatory Psychiatric Withdrawal from Public Colleges and Universities: A Review of Potential Legal Violations and Appropriate Use," K.M. Coll of the University of Wyoming reviews applicable federal laws and constitutional considerations.

Of major concern, Coll writes, are the implications of Section 504 of the federal Rehabilitation Act of 1973. The legislation prohibits discrimination based on a person's disabling conditions when reasonable accommodations can be made for that person. Under this law, diagnosed emotional or mental health problems can be considered disabilities.

The law applies to students at public or private institutions receiving federal financial support. It's designed to protect students from discriminatory withdrawal policies.

Public institutions making mandatory withdrawal decisions must have some form of constitutional due process in place. A campus must notify a student of the concern, for example, and arrange a hearing where the student can present his or her case.

Mandatory withdrawal for psychiatric reasons, Coll writes, is most appropriate when a student:

- Suffers from a mental health disorder and does not recognize the problem or understand it
- Represents a threat to himself by displaying suicidal behaviors
- Has a serious eating disorder related to the campus environment

Coping with Environmental Risks

February 1994

Lead. Radon. CFCs. Bloodborne pathogens. Asbestos. Indoor air pollution. These are not the chapter headings in a science textbook. They are real health and safety risks on today's college and university campuses that demand attention.

Contaminants and hazards can be found in any building at anytime. Campus officials must be aware of the risks, familiar with related regulations, and prepared to respond appropriately to the hazards that surround student, faculty, and staff while they study, work, and live on campus.

Lead

Lead can leach into the drinking water on campus from a variety of on- and off-campus sources. It is a significant health hazard, particularly for children, and campuses should be testing for dangerous readings on campus in sinks, showers, kitchen and food service areas, and drinking fountains.

The federal Environmental Protection Agency (EPA) suggests vigilant maintenance of several areas when dealing with lead pollution in facility water supplies. These include:

- A check of plumbing for lead pipes or lead solder on pipe joints
- A review of water coolers and tanks used for storage for lead linings
- Checking on the softness or acidity of the water. More lead is generally found in soft water.
- Not letting water stand in pipes and equipment too long. Regular flushing of the plumbing system removes much of the hazardous lead.
- Replacement of lead pipes, outlets, and joint solder with other non-polluting materials
- Use of cold water in food service preparation. Lead apparently can leach more into hot water.

Given the high level of water use on campus, regular monitoring of lead contamination and quick response to problems should be a high priority for colleges and universities.

Radon

There is a growing concern about the level of radon gas in collegiate buildings in some regions of the country. Radon is a radioactive, gaseous element formed by the disintegration of radium. Concentrations of radon in soil gases can seep into buildings through foundations, creating a health hazard for occupants.

The presence of radon in a campus building is dependent on many factors, including the level of radon in soil gas, the permeability of the soil surrounding the facility, building design and structure, and the structure's air circulation and ventilation system. Tighter construction and better air circulation systems contribute to much lower and safer radon levels.

When radon is found, it can usually be dealt with by sealing floor cracks and improving building ventilation. In areas prone to radon problems, vapor retarder systems can be designed into new facilities to prevent exposure. Campuses should be aware of this possible health threat and monitor the situation.

CFCs

Many schools have refrigerants that depend on chlorofluorocarbons (CFCs). They can be found in building air conditioning systems, refrigeration processes and units, and campus vehicles. With the production of CFCs ending in 1995 due to ozone concerns, alternative refrigerants are now becoming available and more visible on campuses. But as colleges and universities switch over to new products, care must be taken to deal with existing campus CFCs in an appropriate manner. Federal regulations call for heavy fines for institutions and individuals that improperly handle or release CFCs.

Campuses should be aware that the government has established certification requirements for CFC recycling and recovery equipment and technicians. It also restricts the sale of refrigerants to certified personnel, requires persons servicing or disposing of refrigeration or air conditioning equipment to certify compliance with the

Clean Air Act, mandates repair of substantial leaks in existing equipment, and mandates safe disposal requirements to prevent CFC release into the waste system.

Campuses dealing with refrigeration and air conditioning issues should be aware of the concerns and regulations dealing with CFCs. The EPA has established fines of up to $25,000 a day for violations.

Bloodborne Pathogens

In daily campus life, members of the college community may be exposed to risks from bloodborne pathogens. These are infectious diseases, such as AIDS and the Hepatitis B virus, spread from person to person. But in addition to the risk of contracting the disease from another person, personnel exposed to blood and other body fluids as part of their job face additional risks. Protection of those workers most likely to come in contact with hazardous fluids or situations is mandated by the Occupational Safety and Health Administration.

Campus policies must effectively control exposures, work practices and equipment, in addition to promoting awareness and understanding. Members of the campus community must have access to pertinent safety information. In recent years, much attention has been focused on campus HIV-AIDS issues. However, the same attention needs to be given to the other bloodborne pathogens as they also put campus community members at risk.

A campus policy for infection control should include universal precautions, engineering controls, work practices, and provision of personal protective devices. The plan may deal with related issues, including exposure control and methods, vaccinations, post-exposure evaluation and follow-up, hazard communication, waste disposal, and training and education.

Asbestos

Asbestos, a potentially deadly fiber, can be found in many campus buildings across the country. Except for those facilities most recently constructed, asbestos has been commonly used in floor and ceiling tiles and as insulation wrapped around pipes or behind walls. The danger in asbestos is that the fibers can easily separate from building materials, become airborne, and then be inhaled. Asbestos fibers are carcinogens and have lead to significant litigation involving manufacturers and institutions, like colleges and universities.

According to medical evidence, asbestos fibers remain in human lungs, causing a fatal form of cancer. They also can cause a scarring of lungs that leads to respiratory problems.

Asbestos is a significant health concern for many campuses because it was an extremely prevalent building material from the mid-1940s until the '70s. This time period includes higher education's great expansion after World War II, thus increasing the possibility that some of your campus buildings contain asbestos. The use of asbestos was limited by the EPA in 1973 and finally banned in 1978.

While there is some debate over the extent of campus health risks related to the presence of asbestos materials, campus response options are limited — and sometimes very expensive. Governmental regulations insist that campuses:

- Remove asbestos
- Cover it with a spray type barrier
- Enclose it with non-penetrating materials

Removal is the most effective, and the most expensive, option for campuses. But improper removal can generate even greater health and legal risks by releasing asbestos into the environment. Covering or shielding the asbestos is easier and less costly, but only delays and doesn't prevent fibers from becoming airborne and causing health risks.

Indoor Air Pollution

It was recently estimated that Americans spend 90% of their lives indoors, and that indoor air is up to 70 times more polluted than outdoor air! Given these facts, the quality of campus indoor air is important. The quality of indoor air can be affected by building design, operational and maintenance practices, insulation, filters, and related intake and circulation systems.

Campuses concerned about the risks of indoor air pollution in campus facilities should consider three forms of action. These are:

- *Source Control* — identifying the source of an indoor air pollutant and removing it or isolating it from the area.
- *Ventilation* — bringing additional outdoor air into the building to dilute the level of existing pollution.
- *Engineering* — using technology to avoid possible contaminants in area construction.

The key to air control is air intake and good circulation. Monitoring air quality and responding promptly to problems can lead to a better and safer indoor campus environment.

Summary

A campus should be free of recognized hazards. However, college campuses potentially contain a variety of environmental risks. And where risks exist, campus officials must understand and control them for the protection of students, faculty, staff, and visitors — and to prevent potential litigation.

Chapter 6
RISK MANAGEMENT

Introduction

> If a man does a thing, he is bound to do it in such a manner that by his deed no injury or damage is inflicted upon others.
>
> *Anonymous, Kings Bench,* 1466, Y.B. Edw. IV, f.7, pl.18.

A tort is generally defined as a civil wrong that a court may remedy in an action for damages. Institutions and individuals in higher education may have a responsibility toward those with whom they come in contact to care for them in a responsible manner. Student organizations and leaders can be held to these same standards. What is a duty to care? How is it applied on campus and at campus events?

During the past decade, concerns over potential liability and risk management responses to it have become prominent on campus. Defamation and negligence (including duty of care and breach of duty) are the most common campus tort complaints.

On campus, concerns must remain for the safety of the campus community and visitors, liability waivers and releases, alcohol use, injuries, and accidents.

Alcohol Still #1

January 1990

Few issues on campus have caused more legal consternation than alcohol. While the legal drinking age has been raised to 21, the legal problems associated with alcohol and campus life persist, and legal fears have increased for schools and student organizations.

Campuses have long relied on a Pennsylvania case from the mid-1970s to allay their alcohol-related concerns. There, a student injured in a car accident following a class picnic sued. Beer had been available at the off-campus site, and the faculty advisor had participated in the planning and marketing of the event. A trial court found both the school and the advisor responsible for more than $1 million in damages.

Of course, that's not the decision that reassures nervous schools. But on appeal, in *Bradshaw v. Rawlings*, 612 F.2d 135 (1979), the judgment was reversed. The federal appellate panel ruled that the school had no legal duty to protect a student from riding with an intoxicated driver. Students are adults and can be expected to make adult decisions and live with them.

Enforcement of Rules and Supervision

While *Bradshaw* has generally held up for a decade in spite of serious challenges — including Whitlock v. University of Denver, 744 P.2d 54 (1987), trampoline case — other cases have examined more specific alcohol issues. Two more recent cases have reviewed campus *alcohol rules* and school *field trips*. In both instances, liability for alcohol-related injuries to students was not extended to the campuses.

In *Allen v. Rutgers State University*, 523 A.2d 262 (1987), a student sued his school for failure to enforce alcohol rules. Sports event rules prohibited alcohol at the stadium, yet some students brought in liquor and were injured jumping a concrete wall. They had sneaked a large container of alcohol into the stands and had been drinking throughout the game. One of the drinkers, severely injured, sued the school, claiming negligence. He argued that if the school had enforced its rules properly, no injury would have occurred.

The court didn't agree. It found that the school had no duty to protect intoxicated students from themselves. The court ruled that Rutgers, even with its "no alcohol" rule, had no "common law or statutory duty to protect patrons against the results of their voluntary intoxication."

What duty does a school owe to a drinking student on a field trip? That question was reviewed in *Beach v. University of Utah*, 726 P.2d 413 (1986). An injured student argued that her instructor had failed to protect her, through improper supervision, poor training, and failure to enforce "no alcohol" rules. The injured student had been drinking and had wandered off, leading to a serious fall.

The court ruled that the school had no duty to protect the student from herself. It found no "special relationship" between the student and the instructor. No extra attention or supervision was required to protect the student from her own negligence. As in *Bradshaw*, college students can be seen as adults, living with the consequences of their own decisions.

Greek Organizations

As may be expected, a number of the most recent campus alcohol cases involve fraternity activities. Among the issues: supplying alcohol, injuries after parties, and searches for alcohol.

In *Fassett v. Delta Kappa Epsilon*, 807 F.2d 1150 (1986), a fraternity was charged with purchasing alcohol for sale to and use by minors. Following the party, an accident led to the death of one participant and serious injuries to another. A trial court ruled that while there could be liability for furnishing alcohol to minors, it was limited to those who actually handled the alcohol.

Not so, ruled an appellate panel. Pennsylvania law, said the court, could be extended to find liable those who "in aiding, agreeing, or attempting to aid, a minor in consuming liquor, did so in substantial fashion." The court established a test for alcohol "social host" responsibility:

- How much help was given by the accused
- The proximity of the accused to the injury
- The state of mind and intent of the accused
- The predictability of possible harms

In *Fassett*, the court put campses and students on notice that there was *no tolerance* for the provision of alcohol to minors.

The search for alcohol in fraternity houses became an issue in *State v. Pi Kappa Alpha Fraternity*, 491 N.E. 2d 1129 (1986). Alcohol agents gained entry to a house by posing as fraternity members. While in the house, they saw a soft drink machine loaded with beer. They purchased a can, then came back with a search warrant. Following the search, the fraternity was charged with a variety of alcohol violations. But the fraternity argued that the search had been illegal, supported by "deception."

The court agreed that the search was illegal, a violation of the group's Fourth Amendment rights. While the battle lines have been drawn against illegal alcohol use and sales, the state is not justified in violating individual or organization rights to enforce this policy.

Liability for Sales

Two New York cases provide some additional insights into the liability associated with alcohol sales on campus. They suggest an answer to the important question: Is a campus pub responsible for the death of a patron?

Only under specific circumstances, ruled the court in *Allen v. County of Westchester*, 492 N.Y.S. 2d 772 (1985). The community college pub had no duty to prevent all patrons from all harms. Simply furnishing alcohol does not create liability.

But there are notable exceptions. Primarily, the server becomes responsible when he or she knows that control is needed and has an opportunity to provide that control. Service to minors and service to intoxicated patrons also create responsibilities. In *Allen*, the patron drank to excess and injured only himself. The court found no liability on the part of the campus.

A similar ruling came in *Wellcome v. Student Cooperative of Stony Brook*, 509 N.Y.S.2d 816 (1986). A patron who drank and was injured sued, without success. He argued that the pub was negligent in letting him drink. The court found no cause of action in "voluntary consumption." The decision distinguished this case as being different from others in that harm came only to the patron, not "innocent" third parties. If injuries had been suffered by others, the pub could have faced *dram shop* liability.

Summary

So what are some of the principles we've learned since *Bradshaw* and other earlier key cases?

- Failure to enforce rules fully will not create liability to an injured rule-breaker, barring a showing of bad faith.
- Field trip supervisors have no special duty to prevent participants from alcohol harm, unless the supervisors are aware of a problem.
- When considering service of alcohol to minors and intoxicated persons, liability can be extended beyond those handling alcohol to those "assisting" in the service.
- Searches for alcohol cannot exceed legal limits previously established.
- No pub responsibility extends to drinking patrons who injure only themselves, unless a need for controls is established and ignored.

Despite the higher drinking age, alcohol remains a vexing campus problem. But the legal concerns related to alcohol on and off campus can be addressed through responsible service and careful application of the law.

How to Control Alcohol Use

October 1994

Party if you must, but party safe and smart — that's the message being given to student leaders and organizations nationwide. As survey data indicates a growing concern over alcohol use, the "safe and smart" theme takes on greater importance at colleges and universities.

How can students party "safe and smart"? By considering *and* applying "common sense" risk management techniques at their activities and programs. Everyone in today's society should be aware of the dangers of programming involving alcohol, but that important message should be reinforced whenever and wherever possible. Organizations and individuals can be held responsible for injuries and losses associated with sponsored alcohol use.

What are those risk management strategies that groups should employ to protect themselves and others when alcohol is present? Consider these approaches:

- *Understand legal principles.* Social chairs and student event planners should understand liability issues associated with alcohol use, particularly social host responsibilities, which vary from state to state. Check with legal counsel on the duties group leadership may have to members, guests, and others.

- *Understand legal standards.* Make sure everyone involved is fully cognizant of the legal restrictions placed on the purchase and distribution of alcohol. Know the standards in your area for possession, consumption, false identification, service to those intoxicated or not of legal age, open containers, and legal level of intoxication for motor vehicle use.

- *Provide server training.* Ensure that those who distribute alcohol do so under the law. Make sure that proper attention is paid to the age and sobriety of consumers.

- *Provide non-alcoholic beverages and adequate food.* Don't make alcohol the focus or theme of group events. Non-alcoholic beverages should be available in appropriate quantities, prominently displayed, and easily accessible to all. A variety of food and snack items should be available as well.

- *Limit the advertising of alcohol.* Try not to promote an event through the presence of alcohol. Alcohol may, in some cases, be an element of a program, but it should not be the program itself.

- *Avoid "open" parties.* Limit attendance at events to appropriate invited and expected guests. A guest list allows an organization to select its visitors, limit attendance to a responsible number, keep out minors, and know just who is at its party.

- *Check proof of age.* The law is clear and it's simple to enforce: no proof of age, no service. In any setting where it is available, program sponsors must make sure that only those of legal age have access to alcoholic beverages.

- *Consider use of professional caterers or bartenders.* They are trained to check IDs and to assess consumption of alcohol. Let them do their job. Use of appropriate professionals can also shift liability away from an organization.

- *Have appropriate insurance coverage.* Make sure that groups and leaders are protected as best they can be from action through insurance. Check with a local agent or broker for more information on coverage benefits and costs for liability, alcohol liability, "errors and omissions," and other policies.

- *Develop other organization events.* Don't just rely on alcohol for the success of an event or an organization. Establishing other events and activities that are not based on alcohol — like sports, recreation, and cultural activities — can contribute to organization success.

- *Offer safe transportation options.* Avoid drinking and driving accidents. Take away keys. Make sure that guests who need assistance are given a ride home. Consider the use of designated driver programs or shuttle services.

- *Place limits on the amount of alcohol and the hours of service at events.* Be smart about the volume of alcohol available and the hours of service. The amount should be reasonable, based on the number of people, type of event, and duration of its service. And limit the service hours to a reasonable length, ending service before the event ends.

- *Control the party site.* Make sure that only invited guests are welcome, area capacity is not exceeded, and there are not difficulties in the area due to parking, noise, or crowds. Consider the use of a "bouncer" or doorman, but remember that the organization may be responsible for that person's actions.

- *Limit use to a controlled area.* Don't allow alcohol outside of sponsor control.

- *Adopt a statement on use or non-use of alcohol at functions.* Think through the organization's use of alcohol.

- *Make sure that proper municipal permits are secured.* Distribution of alcohol is controlled by state and campus regulations.

- *Adopt alcohol education efforts.* The group should promote and participate in programs and activities that help educate grouop members and others on the risks of alcohol use.

- *Post notices of restrictions.* Remind guests about the law and policies. Make them fully aware of their own responsibilities.

- *Eliminate open bars, "happy hours," discount prices, etc.* Limit access to alcohol to only trained servers, and don't take steps that encourage the consumption of alcohol.

Smart and safe — two key principles for student leaders and organizations that are even more important where and when alcohol is served.

Alcohol Marketing on Campus Meets Resistance

August 1990

These days, "When you say 'Bud' ... ," you've broken the law! That could be the case on campuses in at least two states, where laws prohibit sponsorship of campus activities by the alcohol beverage industry. In addition, other states have placed legal restrictions on alcohol marketing, which can have a campus impact. As shown by these actions and related campus debate across the country, the issue of alcohol advertising and marketing is a topic of growing concern.

In the area of alcohol education, campus substance abuse brochures and workshops are not in a fair fight. Their messages compete with alternative messages from the alcohol beverage industry. The education message is campus-oriented and limited in resources and impact. The industry message is national and supported with millions of dollars. The battle over the future lifestyle of young Americans is being won by the industry through creative use of television, radio, newspapers, magazines, T-shirts, Frisbees, parties, and giveaways — all to sell a product.

Campuses and states have become increasingly concerned with the media barrage that young people face. And slowly but surely, a response is developing.

Promotion Dollars Less Welcome

Over strong industry objections, states and campuses are eliminating or restricting alcohol advertising on campus. Several states have adopted statutes to limit alcohol advertising or ban advertising from college sponsorships. Campuses have followed the lead of the Inter-Association Task Force on Campus Alcohol Issues and adopted guidelines similar to that group's "Guidelines for Beverage Alcohol Marketing on College and University Campuses." Through these efforts, states and institutions are addressing health and safety issues — and limiting their liability.

Two states currently with general restrictions on alcohol advertising are Mississippi and California. In Mississippi, a state statute banning liquor advertising in in-state media has been upheld by the courts. The state tax commission has promulgated a similar rule, prohibiting publications produced in the state from running alcohol advertising. In California, a state Business and Professional Code outlaws advertising designed to encourage minors to drink alcohol.

Two other states, Washington and Minnesota, have statutes that directly address campus alcohol marketing. The law in Washington prohibits the alcohol beverage industry, including manufacturers, wholesalers, and retailers, from promoting alcohol products on campus or sponsoring activities to promote alcohol consumption by students. However, several limitations significantly weaken the impact of the law. Alcohol advertising is permitted in campus media, the alcohol industry can provide commercial support to campus-based radio and television broadcasting, and alcohol industry financial support for campus events can be accepted and acknowledged.

Minnesota's laws are more direct. They prohibit the alcohol beverage industry — alcohol manufacturers, wholesalers, and retailers — from sponsoring, conducting, or supporting campus activities.

Why Worry About Marketing?

The impact of alcohol marketing on college students is unknown, although we know that students and campuses suffer greatly from alcohol-related problems. Those in favor of restricting marketing often cite surveys of college newspaper advertising. Over half of all national ads in campus newspapers in a recent year were for alcohol. When combined with local advertising from bars, taverns, and liquor stores, almost 70% of all the ads seen by students in their own newspapers were alcohol-related.

The extent of the problems of advertising and related difficulties was thoroughly studied in the *Journal of the American College Health Association* (February 1979). The study, "The Problems of Alcohol Advertisements in College Newspapers," looked at a random sample of college papers. Although conducted prior to national adoption of the 21-year-old drinking age, the study dramatically demonstrated the strong relationship between alcohol marketing and campus media.

To assist campuses in developing a response to the problem, the Inter-Association Task Force on Campus Alcohol Issues — composed of concerned higher education professional and student organizations — developed a set of standards. The guidelines address promotion, provision, and informational efforts. Key recommendations:

- Promotion of alcohol beverages should not encourage any form of alcohol abuse, nor place emphasis on quantity and frequency of use.

- If permitted, advertising on campus or in institutional media, including that which promotes events as well as product advertising, should not portray drinking as a solution to personal or academic problems of students or as necessary to social, sexual, or academic success.

- Alcohol beverage marketers should support campus alcohol awareness programs that encourage informal and responsible decisions about the products represented.

- Alcohol beverage marketing programs specially targeted for students and/or held on campus should conform to the code of student conduct for the institution and should avoid demeaning sexual or discriminatory portrayal of individuals.

Other Task Force guidelines discourage the use of alcohol products as awards, restrict product sampling, and encourage industry members to consult with campus officials when developing and conducting promotional and educational efforts.

Some 25 years ago, when the dangers of tobacco became apparent, restrictions on the marketing of tobacco products began to develop. Today, the health risks associated with alcohol are well-known. States and campuses have begun to react, to restrict alcohol marketing and sponsorships for students.

Campus Injuries: What You Don't Know Can Hurt a Lot

June 1991

When the baseball player collapsed, did anyone in the area know CPR? That was the question at Dartmouth College (NH), where officials are reviewing campus health care practices in light of the sudden death of a team member after practice.

He suffered a heart attack and collapsed after a two-mile run that was part of an informal training session. By chance, a teammate and a man working out in the school gym knew CPR and kept him alive until a medical team arrived. But the player, the son of the governor of Maine, died nine days later in the hospital.

Dartmouth and the NCAA had no CPR requirements for coaches or fieldhouse staff. The school employed student gym monitors and paid them more if they voluntarily learned CPR. But now, the entire athletic department — from secretaries to coaches — has stepped forward to learn basic lifesaving techniques.

Be Prepared — or Be Sorry

First aid for sports injuries can be both a physical and legal lifesaver for colleges and universities. There is a duty to care for participants in athletic and recreational activities, which higher education cannot ignore.

The courts reviewed the duty of a campus to provide first aid in *Stineman v. Fontbonne*, 664 F.2d 1082 (1981). During a softball game, a player was hit hard in the head by a ball. The coach applied ice to her injury and sent her back to her residence hall. The injury caused her to eventually lose vision in one eye, and she sued her school. She claimed that the school had failed in its duty to provide medical assistance. A jury trial awarded the student over $800,000 in damages.

The school appealed. The U.S. Court of Appeals, Eighth Circuit, applied a test for determining campus duty to provide medical assistance.

First, the court looked to see if the school appreciated the *severity* of the injury. The accident was witnessed by coaches, the sound of the impact was heard far beyond the playing field, and the injured student was deaf, so she depended more on her eyesight. Accordingly, the school should have known that the injury could have been serious.

A second test involved the school's *skill to provide assistance*. The court felt that even if the coaches didn't have the training to treat the injury on site, they were capable of directing the student across the street to the health center. They had that duty.

In *Welch v. Dunismur Joint Union High School District*, 326 P.2d 633 (1958), a football coach had team members carry an injured student off the field. Even though a neck injury was suspected, the student could move his hands and feet, so they carried him off. When they arrived at the sidelines, he was paralyzed.

The court ruled that, given the potential gravity of the injury, the school personnel should have waited for the team doctor before moving the injured player or providing other assistance. Providing the wrong type of care can lead to liability.

In another case, *Mogabad v. Orleans Parish School Board*, 239 S.2d 456 (1970), a high school football player died from heatstroke after the coach treated him with a warm shower and blanket. The coach tried to treat the injured player himself for over two hours before calling for assistance. It was too late, and the coach was held liable for giving improper treatment and for failing to call for assistance when needed.

Medical assistance given by trained professionals can also be challenged in courts. Take the case of *Gillespie v. Southern Utah State College*, 669 P.2d 861 (1983). When a basketball player injured his ankle, a student trainer applied tape and ice. Several days later, the player was seen by a physician, who continued the treatments. The player spent several days and perhaps nights with his foot in ice water. He eventually lost most of his foot to amputation due to frostbite. He then sued the school and trainer, claiming negligence.

At trial, the jury found that the student had taken the treatment too far, causing his own injuries. While acknowledging that "reasonable persons could ... differ on the outcome," the appeals court didn't find grounds on which to overturn the decision. The college and student trainer were not held responsible.

Transportation of injured students can also be a concern. In *Clark v. State*, 99 N.E. 2d 300 (1951), the sponsor that couldn't provide full treatment on site was held to a duty to provide swift transportation to care facilities. The court said the injured bobsledder should have been moved "with reasonable expedition" and taken to the hospital "without unreasonable delay."

"I Don't Want to Get Involved"

While recognizing the need for first aid and care, many non-professionals hesitate to respond because of liability concerns. They're afraid of providing inadequate or wrong care that further injures students.

Many states have adopted *Good Samaritan* statutes to deal with this problem. As a rule, they exempt caregivers in emergencies from civil liabilities. However, many states place restrictions on these laws. Some extend protection only to physicians or trained health care experts. Others provide legal protection to anyone who attempts to aid or rescue in an emergency. Carefully check state statutes with local counsel.

Summary

When campuses sponsor sports programs, they have a duty to provide reasonable medical assistance to injured participants. Officials should:

- Assess the need for health care and emergency first aid on campus
- Develop procedures to provide medical assistance for injured students
- Develop appropriate training programs on first aid for coaches and staffs
- Have emergency procedures for the transportation of injured parties
- Establish a system to follow up on injuries and evaluate current and future first aid needs

Use the three-part test established in *Kersey v. Harbin*, 531 S.W. 2d 76 (1975), to help campus personnel respond to injuries, on and off the playing field:

- Does the campus know — or should it know — of an injury and the severity of it?
- Does the campus have — or should it have — the skill, means, or training to respond? and
- Would an appropriate campus response reduce or eliminate the harm to students?

Today, students are involved in sports all over the country. Help make sure that your campus can provide the medical care your students may need.

Sports Injuries: How Should Campuses Respond?

August 1993

Injuries in collegiate athletics may be limited — but they can't be avoided.

Given the size and scope of campus athletic programs, and the size of college athletes, injuries are bound to occur. When they do, they may require timely and proper medical treatment.

Is your campus prepared to respond?

That was the question considered by a federal appellate panel in a case involving Gettysburg College (PA), *Kleinknecht v. Gettysburg College*, 989 F.2d 1360 (1993). The parents of a deceased student athlete sued the school, claiming that it was unprepared to respond to emergencies. The plaintiffs' son died of a heart attack in 1988 while practicing with the school's lacrosse team.

After a trial judge ruled that the school had no duty to anticipate catastrophes like this one, family members appealed. They argued that the school had a unique responsibility to their son — and other scholarship athletes — since it had recruited them to attend the college and participate in its sports programs.

The appeals court agreed. While it sent the case back to a trial court for further review, it said that the college had a special duty to recruited athletes. The majority noted that there is a difference "between a student injured while participating as an intercollegiate athlete in a sport for which he was recruited and a student injured at a college while pursuing his private interests, scholastic or otherwise."

The panel ruled that Gettysburg had a duty to anticipate life-threatening injuries in sports, and it asked the lower court to decide if that duty had been breached.

Cases like this one, and similar actions in other states, highlight the risks campuses face when it comes to athletic injuries. While duties may vary from case to case and circumstance to circumstance, it's clear that courts expect schools to provide first aid, medical assistance, and transportation as needed. Failure to provide adequate, proper, and timely care, therefore, can create liability problems.

Notable Cases

Another example of this concept comes from Texas, where a state workers compensation commission ruled that a paralyzed college football player was entitled to compensation as an employee for his severe injuries.

Disabled on the playing field in 1974, the Texas Christian University student was found to be an "employee" at the time of the injury. His claim was for compensation of at least $500,000, along with related medical benefits.

Meanwhile, a women's basketball player has sued the University of California-Santa Barbara, claiming that the school failed to properly diagnose an injury that ultimately ended her sports career.

The plaintiff says that medical personnel misdiagnosed a stress fracture that led to related medical problems. In her suit, the ex-player seeks compensation for pain and suffering, along with damages based on negligence.

Campus Responsibilities

Given the recent federal court of appeals ruling, and the Texas and California claims, what duties to injured athletes should a college or university anticipate?

Generally, a campus faced with an injury claim will be judged on how responsible it was in providing medical assistance, rendering proper medical care, and transporting the victim to medical facilities. Campus plans for injuries, then, should consider all three of these potential duties.

Courts often rule that athletic program sponsors have some *duty to provide medical assistance*. In an early case involving a bobsled injury, for example, a New York State court ruled that a sponsor acted responsibly when it provided stretchers, blankets, a doctor, and prompt transportation to a hospital (*Clark v. State*, 99 N.E. 2d 300 (1951)).

Thirty years later, a federal court of appeals found that a Missouri college had violated its medical assistance duty in a softball case. During practice, a deaf softball player was struck in the eye by a thrown ball. A coach applied ice and sent her back to her residence hall.

Coaches did not suggest any medical treatment, nor did they recommend that the victim see a doctor, even though her eyes were particularly important to her.

When the victim failed to attend practice the next day, no one contacted her to check on the injury. The student finally contacted her parents after a day of pain and dizziness. At their urging, she sought professional care. Specialists diagnosed a serious injury that ultimately led to the loss of vision in her injured eye.

In *Stineman v. Fontbonne College*, 664 F.3d 1082 (1981), the injured player claimed that the college had failed to provide medical assistance. The college, however, argued that it had no duty to the student.

The court ruled for the student. It relied on a test developed in an earlier medical assistance case, *Kersey v. Harbin*, 531 S.W. 2d 76 (1975). In that case, the court found a duty to provide medical assistance when the defendant:

- Was aware of the severity of the injury
- Had the skill to provide assistance or treatment
- Would have prevented ultimate harm by acting properly

In *Stineman*, the court ruled that the coaches knew how hard the student's eye had been struck and that they only needed to guide the player to medical care. If they had done so, the court said, they would have prevented the ultimate loss of vision.

The court awarded the victim damages of at least $600,000.

A second campus concern involves a *duty to provide proper medical assistance*. High school football cases are often used to demonstrate this idea.

In *Welch v. Dunismur Joint Union High School District*, 326 P.2d 633 (1958), a coach moved a student with a neck injury off of the playing field, resulting in extensive paralysis to the victim. The court ruled that the coach should have known to wait for the team doctor and proper equipment before moving the injured player.

Improper treatment was also the charge in *Mogabad v. Orleans Parish School Board*, 239 S.2d 456 (1970). There, a football player suffering from heat exhaustion was given a warm shower and a blanket. The player later died, and medical experts agreed that the coach had rendered improper care.

A final concern for campuses involves *transportation to medical facilities*. When proper care cannot be provided on site, program sponsors need to get injured students to appropriate care facilities as soon as possible.

An early case involving a broken arm during a school activity points out how this issue can be obviously and easily resolved. In *Sayers v. Ranger*, 83 A.2d 775 (1951), a New Jersey court approved a school's straightforward approach — it involved first aid and transportation to a local treatment facility.

Conclusion

The Gettysburg case and others highlight the responsibilities campuses have to their athletes. If you're not sure how your campus would fare in a similar case, push for a review of your emergency response plans.

First, make sure medical assistance is available. Then, see that it's provided *properly*. Finally, make sure that you can easily transport injured athletes to appropriate medical facilities.

In *Gettysburg*, the court found an even higher campus duty to scholarship athletes. But campuses should be aware of the potential for harm to *any* athlete. That way they'll respond appropriately when injuries do occur.

Campuses Less Immune to Litigation Virus

September 1990

He went to the health center for a flu shot but got much more than that. As a side effect of the shot, the student is now a quadriplegic.

A student broke his leg in a bicycle accident and went to the health center. The bones were set but an infection spread. He suffered permanent damage.

With medical malpractice a leading cause in the proliferation of legal disputes, it's no wonder students are suing their campus health services for negligence. The flu shot and bike accident point out the potential for liability claims against campus health care units and providers for preventive care or clinical treatment. In their defense, schools often claim immunity.

Immunities

Public institutions have long claimed immunity from certain liability suits, stemming from the 11th Amendment to the Constitution, which provides that the states may not be sued. But over the years, the impact of this statement has been greatly diluted.

Years ago, a public campus health service sued by an injured student-patient would simply claim *sovereign immunity* and the case would be dismissed. According to this principle, based on English common law and the Constitution, government acting on behalf of the people was free from suits over liability. Government agencies and institutions couldn't be forced to pay damages.

Government employees had protection as well, through *official immunity*. Under this doctrine, a public official working within the scope of his or her duties and responsibilities couldn't be held personally liable for tort damages.

Thus, through sovereign and official immunity, acts of government and government employees were exempt from early liability claims. Private institutions didn't enjoy immunity and had to defend themselves against tort claims and damages. The most protection available to them was a limited concept of *"charitable" immunity*, for actions taken on behalf of the public.

Over time, the system of a blanket governmental immunity has broken down. The 11th Amendment has been held to prevent suits against states only in federal courts. A series of state court actions around the country also served to weaken the coverage of sovereign immunity.

Courts Make Crucial Distinction

Many courts have ruled that governments could be liable for damages caused through *proprietary* acts, as opposed to *governance* acts. Propriety acts involve the delivery of services, while governance acts are policy-making decisions.

And finally, as a matter of public policy, state governments have agreed to partially open up to citizen suits through legislation. State laws dictate how and why a state agency or official can be sued for liability. Most states have recognized the need for fairness in dealing with citizen claims and have established special courts and procedures for these cases.

The ability to sue a public college or university for negligence is thus controlled by state law. Two questions are critical in any such legal effort: Does the law provide for liability suits? Was the school engaged in state action when it caused injury or harm? If both questions can be answered affirmatively, damages can be pursued.

Campus officials as individuals can be found liable for damages caused in the course of employment. Individuals cannot claim sovereign or charitable immunities. They can be sued for negligence if they committed, directed, or participated in the activity or decision that caused harm.

So even at a public college or university, an individual employee isn't free from all forms of liability. Employees must carry out their duties in a reasonable manner, as would others with similar jobs and experiences.

Some individuals do have one protection they can claim, *official immunity*. This principle protects officials working within the scope of their duties from damages due to discretionary acts involving policy-making. Therefore, an official immunity defense to a negligence suit is usually available only to senior university administration.

With lower levels of protection from liability, campuses and their officials have had to face a growing number of legal challenges in the past several decades.

Case Law

Public campus medical services and providers often claim immunities — sovereign and official — to prevent liability suits. The courts then must decide if the service can be sued and, if so, for what type of damages.

That was the case in *James v. Jane*, 221 Va. 43, 267 S.E.2d 108 (1980), as physician-faculty members at a state university medical center claimed immunity when a patient charged them with negligence. At the trial level, they were given protection from suit in the state due to sovereign immunity.

The Virginia Supreme Court disagreed and allowed the suit. The court adopted a narrow definition of immunities, designed to protect policymakers but not those providing services to the public. Sovereign immunity, it ruled, should be reserved for:

> Certain state officials and state employees ... required by the Constitution and by general law to exercise broad discretionary powers, often involving both the determination and implementation of state policy.

The court suggested several tests for limiting sovereign immunity in cases in which a state employee is charged with simple negligence. Among the issues to be considered:

- Did the employee fail to use reasonable care in performing a duty?
- What is the function of the employee?
- What is the state's interest and involvement in the function?
- What is the extent of judgment and discretion necessary for the job?
- What is the degree of state control or supervision of the employee?

The higher the level of employee authority, the greater the likelihood of being granted sovereign immunity. In *James*, the court found that as employees the physicians were practicing medicine, not making public policy. Therefore, they weren't entitled to immunity protection. Their role was *proprietary*, not *governance*.

Sovereign immunity and official immunity were tested in the flu shot and broken leg cases. When students sued over the quality of campus health service care, institutions and individuals responded with claims of immunity.

In *Dunlop v. University of Kentucky Student Health Service Clinic*, 716 S.W.2d 219 (1986), the state's supreme court was asked to rule on sovereign immunity. A graduate student, left paralyzed after receiving a flu shot, claimed that the service had been negligent. He contended that the shot had been wrongly given and that he hadn't received adequate and appropriate warnings of possible side effects.

At trial and on appeal, state courts rejected the student's case. They agreed that the state was free from medical malpractice suits due to *sovereign immunities*. But the state supreme court disagreed. Kentucky, it noted, had established a medical malpractice insurance fund to protect against claims and judgments. In doing so, the state waived its sovereign immunity and could be held liable for health service negligence. The state statute opened the door for liability claims.

The case of the bike rider with the broken leg highlights the extent or limits of *official immunity*. In *Gleeson v. Beesinger*, 708 F.Supp. 157 (1989), an injured student filed malpractice charges against the director of the Texas A&M University health center. The student was first treated at a local hospital, then transferred to the campus facility.

There his condition took a turn for the worse: an infection spread, resulting in permanent damage. The student sued the director who'd been treating him. Among the claims were improper diagnosis, improper treatment, and improper referral. The school and the health service director asked the court to dismiss the case entirely, citing official immunity.

The court evaluated the difference between *ministerial* (proprietary) and *discretionary* (governance) acts by public officials. It held that official immunity under state law was available only to those making policy decisions.

For a medical director, *discretionary* powers could include deciding who can be treated and what facilities were to be provided. Negligence in these areas could be covered by immunity. But actual patient care and treatment is *ministerial*: a physician provides such care without the blanket of state protection. When making policy, immunities can apply. But actual care must conform to good standards and practices in the medical profession.

Summary

Just as the number of off-campus medical malpractice cases is soaring, student health services are becoming more and more entangled in litigation. While official and sovereign immunities still exist on a limited basis, they don't provide full protection to physicians. Immunities were designed to allow government employees to make decisions — not provide services — free from lawsuits. They do not ensure complete protection for all state actions.

When Visitors Come ...

February 1992

A large number of outside groups hold meetings and events on campuses. What duty does a school owe to these guests on campus? Is there a higher standard of care for them than for the people who are working or studying on campus every day? For members of the campus community? These questions were reviewed in *Doelker v. Ohio State University*, 573 N.E. 2d 809 (1990).

In that case, an employee of the school came back to campus as a spectator of a special event. While watching a Special Olympics program, he visited some participants in the residence halls. To enter the building, he traveled through a glass entranceway with glass panels on the sides. After entering once, he came back into the entranceway, but mistook the glass wall for a door and walked into it. The glass panel shattered and he was injured. In response, he sued the school, claiming negligence in the design of the entranceway.

The state Court of Claims considered two issues in making its decision: Was the school negligent? Did the plaintiff contribute to his own injuries?

State law controls the level of care that must be provided on campus. In Ohio and in many other states, the level of care differs, depending on who may be harmed. If injured parties were "invited" to campus and the campus benefits from their presence, a higher duty is owed. But visitors coming to campus on their own are entitled to less protection. Said the court, a visitor is protected from "wanton, willful, or intentional injuries" and the school has a duty to warn of known or hidden dangers.

Guest's Status All-Important

The court ruled that, while the plaintiff was an employee, his visit to campus to see the Special Olympics was solely for his personal benefit. Thus, the school had the lower duty of care under these circumstances.

Doelker and similar cases consider the common law elements of *negligence* and *premises liability*. To establish liability, the record would have to show that:

- The school *had a duty* to protect others from unreasonable risks
- The school *breached that duty* or failed to conform to required standards
- There was a *connection* between school conduct and the resulting injury
- There was a *harm*

As reviewed by the court, the extent of campus liability can be determined by the status of the injured party. While some states have abolished the distinctions and treat all persons equally, many still consider *why* a person is on campus when determining liability. There are generally three categories of persons on campus under these laws:

- *Trespassers* — persons who enter without permission. They assume all risks of entering and the property owner has no obligation to exercise care to prevent trespassers from harm. For example, persons who enter over fences or other barriers are considered trespassers.
- *Licensees* — persons who are on the premises for their own purposes rather than for the benefit of the property owner. The owner has no obligation to inspect or warn of conditions that should be known or obvious to licensees. Persons coming to campus for social visits or personal business are licensees.
- *Invitees* — persons who are on the property for the benefit of the property owner or holder.

In most cases some financial relationship between the invitee and the landowner will exist. The latter has a duty to exercise *reasonable care* to:

- Not ignore hazards through negligence
- Warn of hidden hazards
- Inspect premises to discover dangers
- Take precautions to protect people from dangers that are foreseeable
- Provide first aid or care for known injuries or ones that should be known

Therefore, it is easy to see why, in some states, the visitor's purpose on campus is a key factor in assessing liability. The highest level of care is owed to invitees — persons such as students, faculty, and staff who are on campus for the benefit of themselves but also the campus. Needless to say, campuses should never turn a blind eye to any guest's safety, no matter what the purpose.

A Tale of Two Universities

August 1992

It is the best of times; it is the worst of times. This is the tale of two universities and the legal activity they face. Perhaps these schools represent two ends of the spectrum, with most colleges and universities finding themselves somewhere in between. All campuses should have an interest in their levels of litigation — both the number of cases and the costs of trials, judgments, and settlements.

Data collected from two schools, Brigham Young University (UT) and the University of California-Santa Barbara, during the late '80s and early '90s demonstrates the range of impacts that legal actions can have on a campus.

At Brigham Young University, officials studied cases filed against the school from 1986-1991. They found that the school remained "relatively immune" from the plague of litigation that otherwise swept the nation. An attorney for BYU noted that other schools in the area receive about 10 times as many lawsuits as the Latter-Day Saints-sponsored institutions. That LDS connection is thought to be a primary reason why BYU has remained relatively "suit-free." Officials feel that people try harder to settle matters without litigation within the church because the church and its institutions get funding from member donations. While this factor may limit the number of suits, BYU still faces some litigation.

According to examined court records, about half of the cases filed against BYU involve personal injury claims. These are filed by injured students, faculty, staff, and visitors who blame the school for their injuries. But medical malpractice cases from the university hospital account for most of the cash damages ultimately paid out, even though malpractice claims represent only one-quarter of all cases filed. Debt collection and other civil matters make up the remaining cases filed against the school during the five-year period studied.

What's the largest growth area in cases involving BYU? According to legal counsel, lawsuits involving former intercollegiate athletes. Some former athletes have recently sued the school for large amounts. BYU officials feel this is due to the high expectations players have of the tremendous amount of money currently available in professional sports. Intercollegiate athletes suing their schools seem to aim high when it comes to claiming damages.

In a society feeling heavily burdened by a litigation explosion, BYU represents the best of times. The school is subject to litigation, but only in limited numbers and amounts due to its predominantly religious population and religious institution sponsor.

On the Other Hand...

But from a legal activity perspective, it may be the worst of times for the University of California-Santa Barbara. In a three-year period ending in 1990, the school had paid out over $1.3 million to lawsuit-filing students and staff. The payments were made to settle cases out of court, to avoid the high costs of litigation and the possibilities of even higher damage awards. According to the school, it handles about 250 cases a year, and the settlements are "not unusual for a campus of this size."

Among the settlements agreed to between 1987 and 1990 were several involving personnel matters, including payments of $400,000 to a campus architect, $265,000 to a vice chancellor, $75,000 to the police chief, and $135,000 to faculty members involved in various disputes with the school. UCSB also settled a number of general negligence, liability, and contract disputes during the same period. These included a $200,000 payment to an employee injured in a work-related accident, $140,000 to a student rape victim, $37,500 to another college to settle a contractual matter, and $35,000 to settle several on-campus injury cases.

Campus officials cite a number of factors used in the decision to settle cases or prepare for trial on the merits. Their considerations include:

- Evaluation of the actual exposure or negligence
- Amount of the damage claim against the school
- A legal evaluation of the issues and the likelihood of campus success at trial
- The way the university or case is perceived in the community
- Cost of preparing for a full trial
- Cost of conducting a trial and possible appeals

The university contends that the amount and number of settlements is normal, but others worry that UCSB may become perceived as a "deep pocket," ripe for nuisance suits from faculty, staff, students, and others. It should also be noted that during the same three years in which these cases were settled, the school was also in court battling a former chancellor.

Campus attorneys were handling a case involving their former chancellor, who was convicted of two felonies. He was suspended without pay a year after the convictions for using $250,000 in UCSB funds to redecorate his home and for a related tax evasion case. He continued at the school for over a year while appealing the convictions, but was then suspended by the regents. The former chancellor has sued for full pay throughout the appeal process.

So between this case and the $1.3 million in other legal settlements, the UCSB legal staff stayed very busy. For campus administrators interested in protecting the campus, litigation to this extent may represent the worst of times.

Summary

Today, BYU and UCSB represent the best and worst of times for campus litigation. Some schools may limit the opportunity for suits due to tradition, history, and sponsorship, while others manage to avoid suits through good operating and risk management techniques. Others must deal more directly with the flood of litigation that has swept the nation over the last decade. What kind of campus are you affiliated with? Is it experiencing the best or worst of these legal times?

Settling Doesn't Mean No High Costs

August 1994

It's often said, "It's not the money, it's the principle." But sometimes, in the world of law and higher education, it *is* the money that gets our attention. It's not just a little money; it's the enormous figures that seem to have become commonplace. In Utah, California, Mississippi, and Washington, schools are dealing with the implications of millions of dollars in legal fees, judgments, and settlements due to campus actions. Understanding their circumstances may help others avoid or limit the damages associated with similar cases.

Utah

The University of Utah has a $1 million legal problem. That's what it cost, in just one year, to defend the campus hospital system during an extensive anti-trust investigation. The federal government has been reviewing allegations of price fixing, salary coordination, and a secret plan involving the campus hospital and a children's medical center to divide patient loads. The criminal investigation closed with no charges filed. U of U is trying to negotiate an end to the civil claims.

According to campus officials, at one point in the investigation U of U had 12 separate law firms working on the case at a cost of over $250,000 a month. Costs for campus defense in the federal investigation totaled over $4 million. Over two years, the state provided $1.75 million to help U of U with its costs. But now the state legislature has recommended that U of U use its operating dollars to pay for legal bills related to the ongoing anti-trust case. U of U has cut $2.3 million from its budget due to enrollment shortfalls. It says it can't absorb another $1 million cut to pay the legal bill.

Throughout the investigation, the university contended that it had done nothing wrong. In addition, U of U has argued with the state that anti-trust issues are not related to its educational mission, and that associated costs should not be taken from the educational system.

California

Campus officials at UCLA and USC have been forced to deal with the high costs of today's legal process. At UCLA, documents indicate that the school paid over $1 million in confidential settlements over the past four years to end the legal claims of four women in sexual assault, harassment, or discrimination cases.

UCLA says its settlements were intended to do the "right thing" for victims and to avoid more extended and costly litigation. In one case, $300,000 was given to a female student residence hall rape victim. In another settlement, $330,000 was paid to an employee who alleged sexual assaults and abuse involving a figure of "power and prestige" at the school. The involved faculty member was suspended without pay. The female employee suffered an emotional breakdown.

In a third settlement case, a UCLA supervisor was fired and the campus paid a sexual harassment victim more than $163,000. A campus investigation agreed with her complaints, finding that the supervisor's behavior was "filled with sexual language, gestures, racial jokes, stories of rape, and even an alleged suicide attempt." The abuse began on the employee's first day of work.

A fourth UCLA case, also settled out of court, involved harassment and discrimination related to a pregnancy. An employee contended that she was harassed because she took an extended leave due to maternity complications and was harassed when she returned to only a four-day work week.

At USC, a jury award of $2.1 million has been given to a former athletic director who charged that racial bias kept USC from giving him a long-promised promotion.

In 1991, a week after his negative comments on USC's treatment of black athletes appeared in a national magazine, he was transferred from athletics to a business office in the medical school. The article quoted him on the problems black athletes had in getting services they needed and had been promised, including counseling and tutoring. When the case went to trial, USC placed the plaintiff on unpaid leave.

The jury hearing the case awarded him $1.1 million in economic damages and $1 million in emotional damages. The jury viewed campus actions against him as unlawful retribution, but was undecided on his claims of bias.

His attorneys say they'll be back in court soon on that claim. USC counsel plan to appeal the economic damage award. They have also asked the court to set aside the emotional damage award as contrary to state law.

Mississippi

For 19 years, state taxpayers have paid the costs of litigation in a crucial collegiate desegregation case. While some say the importance of the issues in the federal case outweigh the costs, others aren't so sure. One cost to date: $2.2 million to the state's lead law firm over the last decade. Plaintiffs in the case estimate that the Justice Department has spent over $1 million on the case. These legal battles resulted in a 1992 Supreme Court ruling that Mississippi must end segregation in its university system, with a new trial to work out the process. The state has budgeted another $800,000 for expenses associated with the new trial. Among the costs are consultants for both sides on standardized tests, facilities, and other issues; legal expenses for staff and supplies;

travel expenses; and the expense of the staff involved from the state's education board and each of the system's campuses.

In addition to these costs, some individual campuses concerned about their future and separate identity have raised funds for their own independent counsel.

Washington

Settling employee grievances involving harassment, discrimination, and wrongful discharge has proven to be costly to the University of Washington. Since 1991, UW has paid out over $1 million to employees to settle these cases out of court. Not included in the settlement costs are the campuses own legal fees associated with the cases. Payments made by UW in 19 separate employee cases have ranged from $870 to $384,000. Officials say the campus settled the various cases primarily because of the cost of extended litigation.

Among the costly settlements paid out by the university in three years:

- A wrongful termination case resulted in a $384,000 payment. An unhappy employee filed an Equal Opportunity complaint and was then fired from her job. She lost the initial complaint, but won her suit to get reinstated under a wrongful discharge claim. Instead of taking a jury award and her old job, she agreed to drop the matter in exchange for a cash settlement.

- A claim of $162,500 was paid to the women's gymnastics coach to settle his sex discrimination claim. He argued that he'd been subjected to unfair criticism and greater scrutiny than previous, female coaches. He also contended he was more qualified than the coach hired to replace him after termination. He settled his case before trial.

- UW paid $34,800 to end a case of alleged harassment by an investigator for the campus human rights office. That's the office that usually investigates these claims! A report found that the investigator had "intentionally abused her position" and acted as a vigilante.

Regardless of whether it's the principle or the money, what is obvious to all is the enormous levels of resources being diverted from today's higher education for legal fees, judgments, and settlements. Be aware of the legal realities of our times and take effective steps wherever possible — or be prepared to pay.

Risky Business: Campus Insurance

July 1990

The insurance crisis of the 1980s left its impact on campuses in the form of reduced programming, greater concentration on risks, and increased liability awareness. Students, faculty, staff, and visitors all were seen as part of the problem, and today in some fashion they're paying for the solutions. Just half a decade ago, campus insurance discussions centered on whether coverage was available, not what it would cost. As the insurance industry has stabilized in recent years, questions remain with regard to campus risks.

From an insurance perspective, the campus is a small or large city, with a little bit of everything. A campus has research using dangerous chemicals, sporting events, rare books and art, food and alcohol service, a medical service, buildings, sidewalks, parking lots, and a child care center. The campus is indeed a microcosm of society, with tremendous risks. Insurance protection is essential.

Student Life

Student conduct is one primary area of risk. To some extent, student "rowdiness" is somewhat routine. A certain level of damage is expected and understood within the insurance industry. However, as always, a few spectacular incidents can upset carrier actuaries with national impacts, like the recent burning of the artificial turf at one Midwestern college. That claim, for more than $500,000, will be remembered by rate calculators and claims payment departments for some time to come.

Other significant areas of student conduct raise insurance issues. Campuses have to be concerned with allegations of sexual harassment and hazing — and generally without insurance coverage, since many standard policies have exclusions for claims related to these behaviors. When faced with these claims, campuses often turn to student organizations that purchase their own liability coverage and assume responsibility for the actions of members.

In addition to personal and institutional implications, date rape and sexual assault can also have insurance implications. Carriers can provide defense counsel and be responsible for limited damages. Claims generally involve charges that the campus was unsafe and failed to provide adequate security.

From an industry standpoint, efforts to educate students on potential risks are beneficial. Sharing knowledge of possible harm encourages students to make informed choices and lets them know the limits of the institution's ability to protect. Subsequent claims against the school would then be considered within this context. The insurance industry generally favors state laws, like Pennsylvania's, which require schools to disclose criminal activity information to students.

Athletics

Participation in athletic competition represents another area of campus exposure to risk. Athletic injuries are common, and they can be severe. With severe injuries can come catastrophic costs.

One national insurance program addresses this risk. The National Collegiate Athletic Association offers membership institutions a comprehensive catastrophic insurance plan for student athletes. Underwritten by an Indiana firm and administered by National Sports Underwriters of Kansas, the program provides unlimited lifetime benefits to injured athletes. Premiums vary by school, based on the division of competition, the type of program, and the number of participants. The program is comprehensive, providing protection against catastrophic loss, but it can also be expensive. Without such a plan, however, campus and student athlete exposure to loss is beyond measurement.

The insurance industry is also concerned with what happens in the stands at athletic events. In recent years, fan behavior has become more of a problem, leading to greater liability exposures. Consumption of alcohol, the throwing of objects, and victory celebrations all create the potential for injury. Campuses face pressure to limit or eliminate dangerous practices at athletic events. Collapsible goal posts are only a small step toward safety.

Medical Centers and Research

Medical malpractice cases are numerous and costly on campus and elsewhere. Medical centers or teaching hospitals can become a significant source of insurance claims. Campuses and insurance carriers are looking for tort reforms at the state level to place financial caps on runaway judgments.

As campus research develops more products and resources for commercial use, exposure to liability increases. A school wants to take enough credit to share in the wealth but limit its exposure from related product liability. Insurance executives see this as being "a narrow line" between taking profit but not taking responsibility. Campuses should secure appropriate protections to limit potential loss.

Sponsored research should be done on a contract basis, with the contract clearly limiting campus responsibility. For corporate research, the company should agree to pay all costs and cover all risks.

Faculty consulting services can also be worrisome. When a campus resource is used off-campus for a commercial purpose, the campus needs to ensure that it is adequately protected against potential claims.

Environmental Hazards

Hazardous wastes, pesticides, and asbestos expose campuses to considerable risk. Each area is highly regulated by government standards and campuses are generally subject to auditing. Insurance policies can have exclusion clauses for these risks and always should be carefully reviewed. Campuses with potential losses from environmental hazards need specialized coverage, available on a limited basis at a high premium.

Discrimination

Faculty and staff discrimination claims are a growing area of insurance concern. Tenure disputes lead the list, with payroll inequities not far behind. Cases involving age, sex, race, national origin, religion and handicapping conditions are filed on a regular basis. Even those without merit require a response.

Campus insurance policies and indemnification clauses are constantly being reviewed to determine coverage for these basic areas of employer-employee disputes. Increasing levels of employee protection have made the discrimination cases a more troublesome topic for campus and industry risk managers.

Field Work and Food Service

Two final areas of insurance concerns exist on campus — off-campus internships and practica and dining services. Each represents significant risk to campuses and carriers.

Field work assignments expose the school to risks of losses offcampus. Affiliation agreements and insurance contracts need to spell out campus, student, and site duties and levels of responsibility when students go off campus. Food service claims are frequent, due to the large volume on most campuses and the strict liability the law imposes on food service.

Conclusion

Insurance for campus risks is generally available today, but with more limited coverage and higher premiums than only five years ago. In response, campus risk managers are no longer just purchasing agents for insurance. Out of necessity, they've become educators, working to reduce or eliminate losses.

Loss control efforts involve:

- Monitoring local, state, and federal laws and regulations to ensure campus compliance

- Applying risk management principles in planning campus programs, activities, and facilities

- Educating students, faculty, and staff on safety procedures and common sense

- Developing and purchasing adequate insurance to meet a wide variety of needs

Campus efforts to control losses will help shape the insurance marketplace for colleges and universities in the years ahead.

Campus Legal Counsel

September 1995

What is the role of legal counsel on today's campuses? Just what do they do? To provide effective legal services on behalf of higher education communities, its important for everyone to understand the many roles and responsibilities legal counsel play on campus.

Responsibilities

Counsel provide legal services to a client. That's the basic role. For most colleges and universities, the client is the school itself, not individuals like the president or trustees. Legal counsel generally provides services to the school through its governing board and officers as the best representative of the school itself.

At a recent conference, campus legal counsels noted that they have what amounts to a "general practice" on campus, dealing regularly with a wide variety of matters. Among the most common areas of concern:

- *Procedures* — Counsel develops and reviews policies for operation of institutional affairs, particularly governance and rules and regulations, including guidebooks and handbooks.

- *Personnel* — Counsel develops and reviews policies and procedures for staffing, hiring, firing, compensation, searches, and related issues.

- *Contracts* — Counsel reviews agreements ranging from common purchases to estate agreements, including loans and leases, research, and service deals.

- *Real property* — Counsel reviews and conducts transactions involving property and facilities.

- *Education* — Counsel provides review of specific legal issues for campus consideration, promotes awareness, and provides opportunities for questions and answers and training programs for staff.

- *Off-campus relationships* — Counsel facilitates interaction with outside agencies and organizations, government entities, community board affiliations, and organizations.

- *Grievances and proceedings* — In on- and off-campus processes, counsel works on behalf of institutional interests. For internal proceedings, counsel reviews and monitors policies and procedures designed to review claims and settle grievances. When facing litigation, counsel works to prepare cases and represent the institution.

These areas represent only the basic areas of legal services needed today on campus. Given the wide variety of colleges and universities and the programs and services they offer, almost every area of the law can become an issue today. Colleges and universities need to be prepared for everything.

Roles

In a *Journal of College and University Law* article (Vol. 2, No. 3), R.K. Danne describes the roles of university counsel in a different manner. He identifies six roles commonly played by counsel on campus:

- *Advisor-counselor* — helping the institution and others avoid legal problems or deal with them early and effectively, through advice and consultation

- *Educator-mediator* — working between parties on issues, explaining options and alternative approaches, and teaching the campus community about legal issues and concerns for effective problem prevention

- *Manager-administrator* — managing legal affairs through appropriate staffing and allocation of resources and outside counsel, as needed

- *Draftsman* — drafting and reviewing documents used by the institution

- *Litigator* — representing the institution and its interests, in and out of the courtroom

- *Spokesperson* — representing the "client" school before agencies and in the media

An examination of these roles and responsibilities indicates the extent to which the law and legal counsel are present within higher education today. The need is apparent. But where does such counsel come from?

Source of Counsel

Over the past decades, the times have dictated a change in how campuses have needed legal counsel. In earlier and "easier" times, a trusted member of the Bar, serving on the school governing body, would offer legal advice and services as they were needed. But as legal needs grew, so did alternatives for obtaining campus legal services.

For many public institutions, legal services are now provided through a designated state agency, like the attorney general or a system counsel's office. Other large institutions, and many smaller ones, have developed in-house legal officers to meet campus needs. Some campuses have retained private outside legal counsel to provide services on a retainer or for an hourly fee. Each approach has its positive and negative features.

Representation through another state agency can be difficult for public institutions, unless the work is concentrated in some way to allow counsel to develop an understanding of campus needs and operations.

For schools with in-house counsel, needed institutional familiarity is developed, but expertise and resources can become issues. In-house counsel may not have all of the necessary specialization or time to deal with all required matters. Therefore, outside private counsel may be needed at times to supplement those efforts.

When outside legal counsel serves as an institution's primary source of legal services, expertise and time may not be a factor, but other concerns arise. Will outside counsel be available, early on, to help avoid or resolve small legal matters on campus before they can become major issues? Does one retained attorney develop enough working knowledge of the school and its mission to be effective?

Campus administrators must carefully assess legal needs and then develop the best model for the interests of the institution, considering in the process agency, in-house, and outside legal options.

Practice

Two decades ago, R. Bickel noted in *The Journal of Law and Education* (Vol. 3, No. 77):

> Although attorneys play a vital role in the defense or presentation of litigation where formal adversary proceedings are necessary to the resolution of university matters, the primary thrust of the attorney's responsibility to the university and the primary definition of his or her role within the institution is the provision of preventative advice which will save the institution from formal litigation or other challenges to its management decisions.

That preventative approach is critical. Campus counsel's role should not be reactive; counsel must actively work to prevent legal problems by educating the campus community, reviewing processes, and recommending approaches and procedures to avoid problems. In an effort to establish a campus "preventative law" system, William A. Kaplin suggests in *The Law of Higher Education* (3rd ed., 1995, pp. 65-67) preventive considerations, including:

- Assessment of the current organization of campus legal services for preventative effectiveness

- Establishment of a "teamwork" approach among counsel and campus officers, involving all in a continuing awareness of each other's responsibilities and concerns

- Conducting routine "legal audits" of campus operations to examine how well the campus deals with legal needs and to consider alternatives

- Developing a communication system to identify problems in their earliest stages, allowing for the maximum opportunity to resolve them

- Maintaining a campus "legal plan," based on the audits and problem identification system, to effectively manage the institution's legal needs

- Providing adequate means of internal grievance resolution, such as consultation, mediation, and arbitration, in an effort to resolve problems within the campus community, if at all possible

This preventative legal approach is important. But regardless of how an institution handles its legal needs, in the end final decisionmaking belongs to campus decision-makers. Legal counsel can only counsel; campus leaders must lead.

Expecting the Worst: Preparing for Calamities

May 1994

What can be done to protect the campus and community at major sporting events? Crowd safety has always been a concern. But after the rampage that followed a University of Wisconsin-Madison football victory late last year, campus officials have focused even greater attention on the liability risks associated with athletic facilities, major events, and large crowds.

Crisis Management Plan

Despite prevention planning efforts, things can go wrong. When a crisis occurs, it must be managed by the campus to limit loss and harm, which is what happened at UW-Madison.

Experts suggest that any plan designed to deal with risks from major events be based on four basic planning and implementation steps:

- Establish priorities
- Conduct brainstorming sessions
- Develop a written plan
- Practice

First, the campus should consider its *priorities* for large spectator events. Obviously, the safety and security of attendees is critical. Secondary priorities should be considered as well, including limiting financial losses, reducing operating problems, and maintaining good community relations and the campus reputation.

Next, what else can go wrong? Use *brainstorming* to think about this at your next planning or staff meeting. Imagine everything that could possibly go wrong and write down those possibilities. Equipment failures, power outages, fires, weather problems, overcrowding, inadequate staff presence, demonstrations, and illness should be on the list — as should much more.

Now, address the concerns raised during the brainstorming sessions in writing. What will you do if this happens? A *written response plan* should be developed in this manner. How will the campus respond? What is needed to enable the campus to respond? The response plan needs to be well thought out and then properly disseminated.

Finally, no crisis management plan can be effective without *practice*. Involved personnel should understand the plan and become familiar with its elements before they need to put it into action. A process of regular review and practice can help the campus maximize its ability to respond to a crisis involving athletic events and large crowds.

Self-Assessment

In tandem with an emergency plan, campuses are encouraged to assess campus athletic facility and spectator liability risks on a regular and organized basis. To assist in that process, an insurance group has created a review process for campus use — "Athletic Liability: Self-Assessment Audit," developed by United Educators Insurance Risk Retention Group.

The audit approaches athletic program and event liability issues by asking administrators to consider questions based on ideal or model "practices." It also encourages identification of persons responsible for follow-up or further review on key issues. The self-assessment audit program is a good prevention planning effort for campus administrative use.

Prevention planning for events and facilities should include an effort to identify risks through *careful inspections*. The audit asks:

- Are safety inspection programs conducted on a regular basis for all facilities?
- Are inspection reports kept on file? Who is responsible for this?
- Is staff appropriately trained to conduct inspections?
- Are corrective actions recommended, prioritized, and documented?
- Are the inspection reports reviewed to identify trends or problems?

This inspection process helps a campus identify problems in advance, providing an opportunity to prevent, not just respond to, an emergency.

Risks at *athletic facilities* must also be properly identified and addressed to avoid excessive liability. When considering these risks, a campus should ask itself about the need for:

- A formal annual review of facilities to correct unsafe conditions
- Designating a staff member (or several) to be responsible for observing safety elements at facilities and events and promoting changes based on observations
- Adequate staffing plans to provide for safe spectator experiences
- Establishing crowd control policies at all events and activities
- Providing adequate and appropriate safety and liability warnings to spectators

Other elements of suggested loss prevention efforts for athletic events and facilities are *insurance* and *legal issues review*.

Good administrative understanding of insurance coverages and exclusions in policies is important, with liability, property, student accident and medical, and volunteer issues of particular importance. Institutions that are self-insured need to understand that process and the claim procedures as well.

Effective legal counsel can also be helpful in limiting litigation in athletic facilities and major spectator events. Counsel should be involved early on in "activities, accidents, and injuries" that could become legal issues. In addition, consideration should be given to obtaining immediate legal counsel in the event of a major accident or significant loss.

Safety considerations to avoid losses should be an important element in *staff training and policies*. The audit suggests that campuses consider campus safety responsibility in position descriptions for athletic administrators. Safety duties also should be included in the descriptions of support personnel and security officers working in athletic facilities and at major events. Risk reduction strategies should also include appropriate training to ensure that the staff is adequately prepared to respond as needed. Staff training should cover emergency procedures, hazard recognition, use of emergency equipment and accident and injury reporting, and investigation, crowd control supervision, and "catastrophic incident management."

Another important prevention element for campus athletic event consideration involves review of previous situations that led to accident and injuries. Campuses are encouraged to *report and investigate incidents* to limit liability and avoid similar future occurrences. The United Educators Insurance Risk Retention Group's audit process suggests that campuses have incident reporting systems, designate persons responsible for investigations, have an incident review process, and use the system to develop corrective steps. Follow-up contact with injured persons and periodic review of policies and procedures are also recommended to athletic facility, event, and program administrators.

Finally, as the UW-Madison incident highlighted, effective *emergency procedures* are an important part of any risk reduction strategy. Among the response elements:

- Access to communication equipment and contact telephone numbers
- Presence of emergency medical personnel
- An emergency transportation plan
- A directory of available emergency care in nearby health care facilities
- Appropriate identification for key emergency personnel
- Regular emergency drills
- Review of the credentials of emergency health care providers
- Communication plans to contact relatives of injured parties
- Adequate training for staff and support personnel
- The presence of appropriate safety equipment and supplies

A commitment to protecting the campus and community at major athletic events with spectators is critical in today's legal times. Campuses should give special attention to careful inspections, athletic facilities, insurance and legal issues, staff training and policies, the reporting and investigation of previous incidents and emergency procedures in developing a campus risk reduction program.

Before the Controversial Speaker Arrives ...

September 1994

President's Perspective

Trenton State University (NJ) served as a site for a lecture by K.A. Mohammed from the Nation of Islam on a controversial tour a few years ago. Because of widespread press coverage of earlier presentations, Trenton State knew the presence of Mohammed on campus would be controversial.

The campus president, reporting on the event in *The Chronicle of Higher Education* (June 22, 1994), noted that school officials dealt with the event with "remarkable calm," in large part due to their careful planning and good communications. He cited several reasons for their results:

- Not underestimating the "volatility" of the event. This prompted development of an appropriate planning and communication process
- Full communication, on and off campus, on the history of the event and the campus rationale for permitting it, including contacts with trustees and legislators
- Close coordination of key campus personnel on operational details
- Contact with legal counsel on First Amendment rights and restrictions and on campus responsibilities for safety and security
- Careful control of media involvements, through sharing information and scheduling interviews in an orderly and timely manner
- Acknowledgement that the event was part of an overall campus academic environment and was part of a larger consideration of issues that may

included a variety of speakers and forums. These strategies demonstrate planning and communication, activities that protect both the First Amendment and campus interests.

Organizational Perspective

The Council for the Advancement and Support of Education (CASE) recently distributed an issues paper on "Coping with Controversial Speakers." The document (May 1994, No. 17) suggests a series of actions and considerations for the three major time periods on campus: before the event, during the event, and after the event. The CASE paper was developed from the perspective of campus public affairs and advancement personnel. As with the Trenton State experience, careful planning and good communication are key elements of the CASE recommendations.

Before the event, the paper suggests development of an appropriate campus policy, based on the First Amendment and the institutional mission. Coordination with the sponsoring organization is also critical. In addition, the campus should prepare an official position statement on the event and establish a spokesperson. Keeping key constituency groups and leaders well-informed is another important pre-event activity.

Clear guidelines, developed in advance, can greatly assist in the planning and coordination of controversial events. A planning team, under the direction of a top school administrator, could be asked to consider and recommend campus policies on advance notice for events, budgeting and scheduling, security, and media relations. Policies for dealing with disruption can also be established in advance of events.

Campus communication with the sponsoring organization and key campus constituencies is also important. A sponsoring organization needs to clearly understand its responsibilities and clearly demonstrate an ability to conduct an event in an appropriate manner. Campus officials working with the group can help the group identify issues and suggest ways of addressing concerns before they become serious problems.

Campus leaders must be advised of tentative plans to allow for appropriate input and to avoid unnecessary institutional conflict that can occur without consultation. Trustees, foundation boards, alumni leadership, and others should be advised of impending controversies and given an opportunity to understand and, hopefully, support any institutional stance. Contact with affected community groups is also recommended by the CASE paper. Event planning should consider ticket distribution, security, and media access. The campus should be prepared to deal with media pressure and demonstrators.

It should come as no surprise that controversial speakers attract significant media coverage. Generally, it is the media coverage that creates an aura of controversy surrounding certain speakers. The CASE paper extensively reviews media considerations for a campus serving as a forum for a controversial speaker. Some of the things to be done:

- Direct campus communication with important audiences if the media's message seems distorted
- Protect open media coverage to ensure wide communication and consideration of a speaker's message
- Establish a media access policy in advance, perhaps placing a priority on access by student reporters, those who cover the campus regularly, and then others, as space permits
- Give advance notice, if possible, to the media of any expected restrictions or limitations

When the presence of protestors and demonstrators is predictable or possible, the campus should be prepared to respond. How does the campus normally handle such problems? Are there existing rules or policies? Has an appropriate policy been developed in consultation with campus leaders, legal counsel, and law enforcement personnel? Advance consideration of these issues can help make the event run better — for the program sponsors and for the campus.

Following the event, CASE suggests continued communication through educational forums, official publications, follow-up statements, and a thorough program evaluation.

After an event, the campus should carefully consider a further review of issues raised by the speaker. Campus officials may want to take this opportunity to reiterate the school's policy on access to the campus or to distance the school from any troublesome expressed views. This can be done through a follow-up statement or news release or through prepared coverage in campus media outlets.

The campus community can also be encouraged to further consider an issue or a speaker's perspective through campus-sponsored educational forums. Faculty, staff, and student interest and involvement can help make this type of program beneficial and successful.

Finally, careful post-event evaluation can be of great assistance to those who will be responsible for the next controversial speaker, on your campus or elsewhere. Did the plans work? Was the event successful? Was there a real exchange of ideas? What could have been done differently to protect campus values and interests?

Summary

College campuses have long been the "marketplace of ideas" — some popular, some offensive. To preserve this "marketplace" and to protect the institution, colleges and universities are urged to deal with upcoming controversial speakers through careful planning and communication, as developed from a variety of perspectives.

… *Risk Management*

Liability Waivers: Will They Protect You?

December 1992

One result of the litigation explosion of the '80s was a dramatic increase in the use of language and releases that shift liability.

These days, it seems that everywhere you turn you're asked to sign a waiver of liability to participate. The forms just keep circulating, yet an important question remains: Do liability waivers have any legal value?

Background

A typical liability release asks a participant to waive the right to claim damages from injuries, accidents, or deaths caused by or emerging from a sponsored program.

The release is an agreement between participant and sponsor, intended to relieve the sponsor of responsibility for losses or damages. It typically indicates that the participant has agreed to "assume" the risks and responsibilities of the activity and "hold harmless and release" the sponsor from responsibility for property damage or personal injury.

The form generally describes the activity the sponsor is conducting and contains a line where the participant can indicate agreement with the release's terms by his or her signature.

"Assumption of risk" language is generally included to show that the participant is aware of the risks inherent in the activity and that he or she voluntarily chooses to participate with full knowledge of those risks. In other words, if something goes wrong, the participant was already aware — ahead of time — of the likelihood that something *could* go wrong.

Legal Concerns

Colleges and universities use liability releases all the time. But that doesn't mean the courts always accept or respect such releases.

Liability releases may be ineffective if courts find that they are:

- Against public policy;
- Designed to absolve a sponsor from its own negligence
- Poorly drafted, leaving their intent unclear
- Executed by a minor (under the age of majority)

A dental school case, *Emory University v. Porubiansky*, 282 S.E.2d 903 (1981), best illustrates the "against public policy" provision. The case involved students in a clinical setting, where patients signed liability waivers before their dental procedures.

The Supreme Court of Georgia was asked to rule on the case of a patient whose jaw had been accidently broken by a dental student. The school said the patient had signed a liability waiver and, therefore, had no case against Emory.

But the court disagreed, saying the form was against public policy. The judges ruled that health care professionals must exercise "care and skill" when treating patients. If they don't, the court ruled, they should be subject to suit.

The public is best served, the court said, when it denies waiver protection to highly trained and regulated health care professionals. In other words, the court said, health care providers are bound by *professional standards* — waiver or no waiver.

A similar judgment came from *Tunkl v. Regents of University of California*, 383 P.2d 441 (1963). The Berkeley campus hospital routinely asked patients to release the facility — before they were admitted — from responsibility and negligence.

But the state's highest court said the action was against public policy because it did not encourage the hospital to provide the highest level of care, as required.

Waivers also face legal challenge when they're designed to protect a sponsor from its "own negligence." A college or university is responsible for what it does or fails to do. A waiver that attempts to relieve a campus from its *own responsibilities* — whether it covers intentional acts or gross negligence by staff or in facilities — would probably be challenged.

To be effective, a sponsor must clearly outline, *in the agreement*, any attempt to release itself from its own "express negligence." An example explains it best. The classic illustration comes not from a campus, but a case involving a popular tourist attraction — Disney World.

A participant on a horse ride was thrown and injured. He sued for damages.

Disney contended that it was not liable because the rider had signed a release form. The language protected Disney from "any and all claims resulting" from the rider's participation.

But in *O'Connell v. Walt Disney World Company*, 413 So. 2d 444 (1982), a court allowed the rider to seek damages because the waiver he had signed failed to say that Disney would not be responsible for its *own negligence*. Without that explicit language, Disney was clearly responsible for its own conduct and activities.

As shown in *Disney*, waiver language must be *clear* and *fully understood* to be effective. A campus case involving a cheerleading injury drives this point home.

A Marquette University (WI) student had signed a release as a member of the cheerleading squad. He was injured during a stunt at a sporting event and lost the use of his limbs.

In suing the school, he argued that the waiver he signed was not clear. He claimed that the language was too broad and vague, leaving him without an understanding of the risks or the implications of the waiver itself.

But a court ruled in favor of the university. The cheerleader was experienced, the court ruled, and the waiver indicated that he had "full knowledge of the risks" and that he was "sufficiently informed to participate." According to the court, that language was clear, concise, and understandable — and therefore enforceable.

The execution of waivers by minors could be a concern on some campuses — particularly those with early entry programs, secondary education summer programs, and youth camps.

Courts have consistently ruled that minors are "not legally competent" to sign waivers. Minors are generally seen as lacking the capacity to sign away rights or assume responsibilities.

Parents, however, cannot simply *waive* children's rights to make liability claims unless authorized to do so by state law.

To get around this problem, some campuses use "indemnification" agreements. The campus asks the parents to agree to "indemnify" the school for any damages it incurs due to suit from the child. If the child sues and wins, the parents reimburse the school for its losses!

Such agreements may be effective because they're between the school and the parents, not the school and the minor. At the very least, they can severely impact the risk of suit by minors.

Know the Laws, and the Risks

The effectiveness of liability waivers is a state issue. So it's important that you fully appreciate state legislation and judicial rulings before drafting waivers for your campus.

You should also evaluate the risks of activities, so that any waivers you write are based on a full understanding of all the issues.

It's also important for program sponsors to determine the purpose of waivers. Is a waiver simply designed to be a release from general responsibility? Is it designed to absolve the sponsor from responsibility for its own negligence? Is it seeking indemnification from others?

The goals must be clear *before* you draft the waiver language — because the final language has to be very clear to withstand legal challenge.

In *Am I Liable?*, published by the National Association of College and University Attorneys, the following elements are suggested for waivers:

- An assumption of risk by the participant
- A clause that says the participant understands the dangers
- A description of the specific dangers
- An agreement to indemnify and hold harmless, even if sponsor is negligent
- Language that waives an individual's right to make a claim and — in event of that individual's death — the right of his or her family to pursue a claim on his or her behalf
- The state law(s) to be applied to the agreement
- An acknowledgement that the participant is of age to sign the waiver and does so voluntarily

Why Bother?

After considering the concerns a waiver must address and the circumstances in which a waiver is not valid, it's fair to ask whether waivers are worth the effort. The answer is usually yes, because a well-drafted waiver can:

- Protect an institution from liability
- Advise students and other participants of risks, and help them make good decisions about their involvement
- Help your campus properly assess the risks of activities and promote steps to ensure greater event or program safety
- Remind an injured party that he or she agreed to accept responsibility for outcomes (which may discourage interest in legal action)
- Become an important element in your campus' defense in liability litigation

A well-drafted release may not end your campus' liability on its own, but it can be effective. So go ahead and use liability waivers — but use them wisely.

Waiver Failure: The Four Principal Areas

February 1994

A West Virginia University sophomore, a member of the rugby club, suffered a blood clot at the base of his skull during a rugby game on campus. The 1990 injury affected his speech, memory, emotional control, walk, and grip. Medical expenses to date exceed $200,000. He sued for damages, contending that WVU was responsible and so compensation was required.

The claim was dismissed by the state court without even considering its merit. Why? Because the student had signed a release absolving the university of responsibility before he joined the team. The circuit court held the form to be an absolute bar to litigation. But is that how liability waivers really work? Are they that effective? All the time?

It is a common campus practice to require program participants to agree to assume all activity-related risks and to release a sponsoring institution or agency from responsibility. This is done in advance and in writing. These "voluntary" actions foregoing claims or damage actions are often referred to as releases, liability waivers, consent forms, or permission slips. And they have "hold harmless clauses" or "indemnification provisions."

Liability releases attempt to exempt a party from responsibility or require one party to pay for outcomes caused by another. Although commonly used, releases are not commonly accepted. Courts have carefully reviewed waivers and releases and have often deemed them unenforceable. As a general rule, courts strictly construe liability release efforts (*Doyle v. Bowdoin College*, 403 A.2d 1206, 1979; *Gross v. Sweet*, 400 N.E.2d 306, 1979).

Releases That Don't Work

For activities and programs that are not inherently dangerous, liability releases can be effective in certain circumstances. There are, however, four key conditions or principles that can void releases:

1. Releases are found to be against the interests of the public.

2. Obvious negligence is present; unless this is expressed in the agreement, responsibility cannot be waived.

3. Language ambiguities in the agreement make it difficult to determine the extent of the rights waived.

4. Parents or minors sign the release.

Public policy principle. Releases are found to be unenforceable when they adversely impact public interests. For example, courts have held that public agencies providing services cannot "contract away" their responsibilities (*Gore v. TriCounty Raceway, Inc.*, 407 F.Supp. 489, 1974). A case involving treatment at a campus hospital demonstrates how waivers can be found to be against the public interest. The patient, in *Tunkl v. Regents of University of California*, 383 P.2d 444 (1963), had signed a waiver of liability before receiving treatment. When he later sued, the court rejected the waiver, saying it did not encourage the hospital to provide the best possible care. The court ruled that, as a result of the transaction, the patient was placed under the control of the hospital, subject to the risk of carelessness by that party, which is against public policy.

In *Emory University v. Porubiansky*, 282 S.E.2d 903 (1981), the Georgia Supreme Court used the same rationale to void a dental school release. The school put language in patients' consent forms that waived all claims against the school. The court voided the waiver when challenged, noting that it sought to relieve professionals from their duties.

Waivers are overturned for public interest reasons when the activity is important to the public and the waiver is not the result of equal bargaining. Risk transferring does not work in these circumstances.

Negligence principle. In addition to the public policy principle, courts have also voided waivers that cover willful, wanton, or reckless behavior, gross negligence, or intentional acts. This is referred to as the express negligence principle (*Boucher v. Riner*, 514 A.3d 485, 1986). It voids releases that try to waive responsibility for the initiator's own negligence while not stating that information clearly to the signee in the release.

Consider the case of the summer camp that "forgot" to give a young camper his required medication. His family had signed a waiver releasing the camp from any responsibility for him while at camp. The waiver was voided in *Goyings v. Jack and Ruth Echerd Foundation*, 403 So.2d 1144 (1981), because it did not clearly indicate that the camp would not be liable for its own negligence.

Ambiguous language principle. Waivers can also be voided if they contain ambiguous language. Courts demand that waivers clearly indicate possible liabilities and name the parties seeking to avoid and transfer responsibility. In *Rosen v. LTV Recreational Development, Inc.*, 569 F.2 1117 (1978), a snow skier was injured when he hit a pole set in concrete. His season ticket had a notice warning him that "skiing was a hazardous sport." The court, in considering his claim for damages, found the notice ambiguous. At best, it warned skiers of the dangers from other participants, but it did not relieve the resort of liability for its own negligence.

Courts, in assessing ambiguous language, look to see if the affected party fully understood the agreement and agreed to give up claims for damages.

Minor/parent principle. A final reason some courts have invalidated waivers is when they are *signed by minors or executed by their parents*. Courts have consistently ruled that a minor lacks the legal capacity to make an agreement releasing someone from a responsibility to her/him or an agreement accepting responsibility for herself/himself (*DelSanto, Jr. v. Bristol County Stadium, Inc.* 273 F.2d 605, 1960). A parent's ability to waive liability is limited as well. It has been generally accepted by the courts that a parent can waive only his or her own future claim, but cannot surrender the independent claim of a minor child (*Kaufman v. American Youth Hostels*, 174 N.Y.S.580, 1957).

Where Waivers May Work

While releases can be invalidated for the reasons listed above, there are settings in which they have been enforced. One primary area is inherently dangerous activities on and off campus. Where a person is well advised of all related dangers, waivers can limit liability in risky endeavors. These have included mountain climbing, sky diving, and scuba diving (*Blide v. Rainier Mountaineering*

Inc., 636 P.2d 492, 1981; *Poskozim v. Monnacept*, 475 N.E.2d 1042, 1985; and *Hewitt v. Miller*, 521 P.2d 244, 1974).

On Campus

Liability releases are most often used by colleges and universities for student field trips and provision of medical services. Court-developed waiver exceptions can be applied to these common campus circumstances. Medical treatment waivers or consent forms, from student health services or campus hospitals, are subject to the against public policy principle. And field trips using releases to try to transfer liability are reviewed under the *ambiguous language (expressed liability)* rules.

While many waivers are found to be unforceable, signed releases may serve other important purposes. If the form is well written and provides specific information on risks and hazards, it can be used to show that an injured party *assumed risks* knowledgeably. This could be a defense to any liability claim. The signed release legitimately increases participant awareness of program risks, rigors, and hazards. A release may also have a value in discouraging an injured party from filing a claim.

Summary

While waivers are often used, they are often not as effective as most drafters would hope. In the case of the injured West Virginia University rugby player, the court initially upheld the release. But on appeal, a higher court will reconsider the waiver based on the various exemption principles. Was the waiver against public policy? Did it expressly indicate that the school would not be responsible for its own negligence? Was the waiver language unambiguous? Was the signer an adult? Was the activity inherently dangerous?

These are the questions the court will consider. Administrators should consider the same issues whenever contemplating waivers of liability.

How to Develop a Policy for Student Deaths

December 1991

How campuses react to tragedies can often influence subsequent litigation. If a college or university handles student accidents or deaths poorly, the potential for lawsuits increases, as survivor families react out of frustration, confusion, or misunderstandings. When a student dies at school, the campus must be prepared to make notifications, involve campus security and other key units, consider other student needs, and deal with the media. Advance planning regarding student deaths can benefit families and institutions and minimize legal risks for the latter.

In old movies, death notifications are often portrayed by a car slowly pulling up to stop in front of the home, then a long walk up the sidewalk by a police officer and a minister. Today's process for colleges and universities may not be all that different. A campus needs to plan for a coordinated response to student deaths. The response must be sensitive to the needs of the student's family and sensitive to the institution. It must do what needs to be done for all and restrict the potential for litigation.

In creating a campus policy on student deaths, it is important to *involve campus units* in a wide discussion of the purpose of the policy. Generally, such policies are designed to establish and clarify campus regulations, procedures, and policies in responding to student deaths. To develop the policies, it is important for decision makers to understand fully the existing regulations, the needs of various departments and populations, and other campus needs.

One key to any effective policy is the answer to a basic question: Who is in charge here? A campus death policy should clearly designate who is responsible for implementing the plan and managing the campus response. It is also important to establish who will handle the *media contacts* that inevitably follow a campus incident. Campus officials and public relations officials must also contact campus safety officers to determine what information can be released and in what manner. Therefore, the policy should open with a statement of purpose and a clear definition of overall responsibility for coordinating campus response and involving other units.

In the event of a student *death on campus*, public safety officers generally respond first. They should be responsible for making necessary campus notifications, including senior administrators and ministry officials. Student affairs staff should then make arrangements for on-campus responses that involve students, including counseling. Public safety officers must conduct their investigation in cooperation with local law enforcement departments and medical services. Campus *notification* of next of kin must also be considered if the family has not been contacted by medical or police officials.

When a *student dies off campus*, local hospitals and law enforcement agencies should be encouraged to contact the campus as quickly as possible. This allows campus officials to begin necessary work on campus and with campus populations without delay. If outside agencies make initial contact with the family of a deceased student, it's important to have that agency refer the family back to campus officials for important follow-up and support.

In responding to a student death, a college or university must understand the needs and responsibilities of various people and units. A good plan should consider:

- *Family* — One staff person needs to be designated to assist and advise the family of the deceased and coordinate a campus visit if desired.

- *Residence halls* — Reactions within the residential community must be anticipated and dealt with swiftly. Counseling for roommates and staff should be arranged, and a vehicle for good information must be established to avoid rumors and other complications. If appropriate, the campus should make plans to control local media access within the residence halls.

- *Legal counsel* — With any death, litigation is a possibility. Therefore, legal representatives of the college or university should be advised of any death and relevant details to assist the campus in developing an appropriate response — with attention paid to possible legal actions.

- *Media* — Any death is news, and campuses need to understand and prepare for the media attention likely to be focused on the school and its students. Campus and student needs and the needs of the media should be reviewed in advance to develop a policy on information releases and media access that is sensitive to all needs.

- *Counseling* — Efforts must be made to work with students, faculty, and staff. In addition to contacts in the residence halls, counseling should also be offered to classmates, off-campus housemates, student volunteer medical corps, parents, and the larger community. It is also important to arrange for follow-up to counseling contacts made after a student death or contacts made where immediate counseling was refused.

- *Campus ministries* — Where available, representatives of religious organizations can provide support to the deceased student's family and network of campus contacts. They can also play a key role with students in planning a campus memorial service.

- *Contacts with campus units* — Establishing contacts with many units on campus after the death of a student is important to the family and the institution. The student's *academic department and advisor* need to be made aware of the death. Consideration may be given to a posthumous degree, honor, or award if the deceased was near the end of an academic program or would have achieved other honors.

Departments such as *food service* and *student accounts* should be contacted under any response plan to arrange for a simplified return of any tuition, housing, or other fees. The campus *development* or fund-raising unit should also be advised to avoid unwanted contacts with family.

The campus response plan should also build in consultations with the campus *health insurance program* to expedite the payment of any related medical expense claims or possible death benefits.

In summary, it is important for colleges and universities to make appropriate plans *in advance* for responding to student deaths, on or off campus. Policies must be established to serve the needs of students and the school, especially to prevent litigation. To accomplish this, campus response plans must:

- Understand the needs of the family, students, and the campus
- Provide for appropriate notifications, consultations, support, counseling, and follow-up services
- Involve all necessary campus units in the planning and response effort
- Deal with important law enforcement and media considerations
- Keep one person in charge of each situation
- Conduct post-incident reviews to develop better approaches for future situations

Student Deaths: When the Campus Must Notify

January 1992

A college or university must be prepared to respond under difficult circumstances to address a variety of immediate concerns. In notifying the family of a suddenly deceased student, the school must do what needs to be done effectively, but in a sensitive manner.

Litigation often arises out of anger, frustration, or confusion. So when dealing with the family of a deceased student, the school should exercise care. To accomplish this, the college or university must be ready to make death notifications and handle family and campus responses appropriately.

Before making any death notification, it is important to get all of the facts. Campuses should be sure to answer the following questions:

- What has happened?
- To whom?
- When?
- Where?
- Were there other participants or victims?
- Has a positive identification been made? How?
- Who is the next of kin (name, address, and telephone)?

Who will make the contact with the family, and when? The circumstances often dictate the answer. If death occurs at a medical facility or enroute, the facility will generally notify the next of kin. However, when outside agencies make the notification, contact with the campus should be established to facilitate appropriate follow-up support. If requested, the hospital could provide the school's name and telephone number to the family or suggest that the school will be calling shortly.

If the campus has to make the initial contact, who should make the notification? Most schools suggest that a senior administrator with public safety or campus ministries be responsible. Contact needs to occur as soon as a positive identification has been made. Some policies limit notifications to day and evening, never before 7 a.m. However, in today's milieu of instant communications, immediate notification is required to avoid unseemly notification from other sources.

Most experts strongly suggest that death notifications be made in person. This can be done by campus staff when the next of kin is local or within a reasonable distance. If the family is out of town, personal notification can be arranged through law enforcement agencies, other schools, or ministries in the out-of-town area. After notification is made, the family can then be urged to call the campus directly for support and assistance.

Under some circumstances, it may be necessary to make death notifications to the family of a deceased student by telephone. When this is the case, extra care must be taken to ensure that all of the key elements of the notification process are observed.

Some important considerations for contacts:

- *Identification of the notifier* — Who is making the contact? Name and relationship to the school are most important to share with the family.
- *Identification of family member* — What is the member's relationship to the deceased? Is this the proper person to be given the news?
- *Identification of staff person* — He or she will serve as the school's assistance coordinator for the family.

When notification occurs, the person making the notification should take into account some common-sense suggestions:

- *Give slow, but direct, notice of death* — Try not to draw out the notice or withhold news of death until the end of a recitation of known facts.
- *Provide an opportunity for silence or other reaction.*
- Be prepared to *repeat facts*, often on family request.
- Be prepared for *identification of the deceased* to be challenged or disbelieved.
- *Ensure that there is someone else available* — a family member nearby or a neighbor — who can be called upon for support.

Finally, post-notification procedures should consider the following family needs:

- A *campus visit* — While not absolutely necessary, this can often prove helpful to the understanding and healing process
- A *liaison with the local mortuary* — To handle contacts with medical examiner or health care facility
- An *offer of assistance* — On behalf of the school, such as help with travel plans or counseling
- An *immediate follow-up system* — For the contacts to follow

Beyond the need to notify the family, many other responsibilities must be appropriately handled by the campus in these difficult circumstances. A variety of campus units must contribute to the process.

Campus security must get the facts on what has happened and all available information on the student involved. It must make necessary notification of the death and work with local law enforcement officers, when appropriate, on related investigations. It helps if the department can identify one individual to serve as the primary contact person within the department.

Of immediate concern for *campus counseling* should be roommates, friends, family, and participants in, or witnesses to, the incident. Counselors need to establish contacts, offer support, and arrange for follow-up assistance. Other considerations could include residence hall meetings, individual or group counseling, contacts with instructors or classmates, letters to campus media on support services available, and follow-up upon the death or notification process.

If the family desires a campus visit after a death, it is important to understand their needs in advance. This will help the campus satisfy them and simplify the visit. Assign one staff person to work with them and have that person prepared to get immediate responses to their questions and requests.

Within the *residence halls*, care for roommates and floor residents must be the first priority. They must be contacted and given necessary support and understanding. The property of the deceased student, if a resident, must be left undisturbed for the family and for investigative purposes if required. If the family comes to campus, materials should be available to assist them in packing and transporting personal belongings. It is also important to consider the needs of residence hall staff under these difficult circumstances and provide them with support as needed.

At the time of a student death, the involvement of *campus ministries* can be most appreciated by the campus and affected family. A system of contacting chaplains must be in place for emergency circumstances. Access to any student record of faith can be helpful. Campus ministries' role in campus counseling efforts, contacts with families, and memorial services should be considered in advance of any incidents to ensure appropriate responses. And in planning for campus memorial services, it is important to understand and respect the wishes of the family.

Summary

The need for a campus policy on responding to student death is based on concern for the campus and the family. Consideration must be given to the needs of the deceased student's roommates, classmates, friends, and family. But while caring for the living, the institution must be sensitive to the potential for litigation and do what it can to avoid family anger, frustration, and confusion.

ACE Model Policy on Sexual Harassment

August 1993

The American Council on Education (ACE) recently issued a revised statement on sexual harassment entitled *Sexual Harassment on Campus: A Policy and Program of Deterrence*. Its stated goals include reducing the incidence of sexual harassment on campus and limiting related campus liability.

The policy statement stresses the importance of campus responses, highlights key program elements, provides definitions of sexual harassment, considers grievance procedures, and establishes guidelines for developing effective campus programs. A review of the statement can greatly assist campuses that are revising or reviving sexual harassment policies.

The ACE model suggests that campus plans be developed to:

- Discourage acts of sexual harassment
- Encourage members of the campus community to report incidents as soon as possible
- Inform community members that sanctions will be imposed for violations of policy
- Provide protection for individuals and the institution

Definition Is Crucial

Campuses should establish a *definition* of sexual harassment to help community members understand what constitutes harassment and avoid improper contacts or circumstances.

The ACE policy provides a general definition. It describes sexual harassment as unwelcome sexual advances, requests to engage in sexual contact, and other physical and expressive behavior of a sexual nature, where:

- Submission to such conduct is explicitly or implicitly made into a condition of a person's employment or education
- Submission to or rejection of such conduct is used in academic or employment decisions affecting the individual
- Such conduct has the purpose or effect of substantially interfering with an individual's academic or professional performance, or creating an intimidating, hostile, or demeaning environment for employment or education

To assist the campus community in understanding the definition, the policy should also include written examples of sexually harassing conduct.

Guidelines for Programs

The ACE policy statement includes suggestions for campuses that are either creating new programs or modifying existing ones. ACE recommends:

- A strong sexual harassment policy that prohibits unwelcome conduct or contacts, protects those who report sexual harassment, explains harassment and the importance of the policy, and includes guidance on discouraging romantic relationships between faculty and students.

- A formal grievance and investigation process that encourages people to report incidents, allows for informal resolution when possible, and establishes a formal process for situations that can't be resolved informally. The investigation should include interviews, written statements, and the collection of other evidence. Confidentiality should be respected, but it may "give way to the institution's obligation to investigate and take appropriate action."

- A system of providing policy information and education to the campus community. The dissemination plan should include publication of the policy in student and employee handbooks and other commonly read materials (tuition bills, payroll checks, etc.). The plan should also include publication of complaint resolutions to encourage future reporting.

- A campuswide education and training program to promote awareness, understanding, and prevention of sexual harassment. The program should include brochures, posters, orientation for new faculty, staff, and students, and training for supervisory personnel and other campus leaders.

- The appointment of a campus coordinator for complaint reporting and resolution. This staff member would be responsible for publicizing and enforcing the policy, investigating and resolving problems, maintaining records, and pursuing campus action.

Summary

The ACE model suggests a comprehensive plan for campuses that want to effectively respond to growing concern about sexual harassment. Consider applying this model on your campus.

For a copy of Sexual Harassment on Campus: A Policy and Program of Deterrence, *contact: American Council on Education, Office of Women, 1 Dupont Circle, NW, Suite 800, Washington, DC 20036; Ph: 202/939-9390.*

Preventative Policy for Sexual Harassment

September 1994

What have the courts really said, and just what can campuses do, to limit the potentially damaging development of hostile, and now unlawful, work environments? Court decisions will have a significant impact on how a campus work environment is judged when claims of sexual harassment and gender-based discrimination are made by college and university employees.

Judicial Guidance

She was the manager of an equipment rental company for over two years. While on the job, the company president made a series of comments about the manager's ability to work. The remarks were based on the fact that the manager was a women. That, in his mind and words, made her unfit to perform certain duties. She was also subjected to various forms of sexual innuendo from the president.

The fed up female manager filed suit, naming the company as a defendant, under Title VII. She contended that the company president's actions created a "hostile work environment," which changed her working conditions. Under Title VII of the Civil Rights Act of 1964, an employer cannot "discriminate against an individual with respect to his competition, terms, conditions, or privileges" because of a person's gender. Federal courts have held that sexual harassment may be seen as sexual discrimination under the law. That was clearly demonstrated in *Meritor Savings Bank v. Vinson*, 477 U.S. 57 (1986), in which the U.S. Supreme Court found gender-based discrimination in violation of Title VII.

In *Meritor*, the court accepted a definition of unlawful sexual harassment in the workplace that included unwelcome sexual advances or requests for sexual favors and other verbal or physical conduct of a sexual nature, when:

- Submission to such conduct is made either explicitly or implicitly a term or condition of employment
- Submission or rejection of the conduct is used in employment decisions
- The effect of the conduct substantially interferes with work performance by creating an "intimidating, hostile, or offensive" working environment

This type of conduct in the workplace can lead to Title VII damages. Before 1991, these damages were limited to back pay and court orders preventing further harassment. But today, a sliding scale of damages exists, with sanctions ranging from $50,000 to $300,000 for intentional sexual harassment under the Civil Rights Act of 1991.

While the courts have consistently ruled that sexual harassment can be seen as unlawful sexual discrimination, different jurisdictions have required different showings of proof. Some courts have ruled against conducts "reasonable" persons found to be offensive, while others have required evidence of serious psychological harm to award damages. In the equipment rental service case, the U.S. Supreme Court considered Title VII issues of hostile work environments and levels of proof. As major employers, colleges and universities need to be fully aware of changing rules in the workplace.

In *Harris v. Forklift Systems, Inc.*, 126 L.Ed. 2d 295 (1993), the court ruled unanimously that a plaintiff does not have to show physical or psychological harm to demonstrate an unlawful hostile work environment. The conduct, not the impact, was what the court measured in deciding complaints of discrimination due to sexual harassment.

Writing for the full court, Justice Sandra Day O'Conner noted:

> Title VII comes into play before the harassing conduct leads to a nervous breakdown. A discriminatorily abusive work environment, even one that does not seriously affect employees' psychological well-being, can and often will detract from employees' job performance, discourage employees from remaining on the job, or keep them from advancing in their careers. ...
>
> The very fact that the discriminatory conduct was so severe or pervasive that it created a work environment abusive to employees because of their race, gender, religion, or national origin offends Title VII's broad rule of workplace equity.

Under *Harris*, an employee does not have to show physical, psychological, or economic harm to claim Title VII protection from a gender-based, discriminatorily hostile work environment.

Preventative Actions

In examining employee claims of on the job sexual harassment, courts generally consider four key factors before making determinations:

- Frequency of the alleged harassing conduct

- Severity of the conduct
- Whether the conduct was humiliating or physically threatening
- Whether the conduct unreasonably interfered with employee work performance

By understanding these factors, campus employers can better avoid the creation of illegal hostile work environments, protecting employees and the institution.

When examining the *frequency* of allegedly harassing conduct, courts review when the conduct began and how often it occurred. They will also consider the length of the period of time during which the conduct took place. Whether it has stopped or continues is also an issue.

Several issues are given judicial consideration when assessing the *severity* of allegedly harassing conduct by employers. Of concern to courts is whether the conduct was verbal or involved physical contacts. In addition, the severity of the claim may also be judged by any escalation of the harassment over time.

Just how *humiliating* or *physically threatening* was the conduct? That's another question asked by courts assessing sexual harassment work site claims. Reviewing courts will consider whether the conduct took place in front of others, involved more than one person, and whether it went beyond "offensive" utterances.

A final issue before courts in these cases involves the extent to which the harassing conduct *unreasonably interferes with an employee's work performance*. When conducting this portion of its review, the court considers whether the employee:

- Complained about the conduct
- Participated in similar conduct
- Was discouraged from remaining on the job or was discharged from seeking advancement

Courts hold employers liable under Title VII when the employers knew or should have known that sexual harassment was occurring in the workplace and failed to promptly respond. A college or university, as an employer, is responsible for the actions or inactions of supervisors, co-employees, and other agents of the institution or persons having a relationship to the school. The school is responsible for their violations.

The most effective tool in preventing or limiting sexual harassment claims on the job site is the development and implementation of a campus sexual harassment policy. Among the important policy elements:

- A statement that the campus doesn't tolerate any form of sexual harassment
- Encouragement for employees to report incidents
- Descriptions of unlawful behaviors
- A review of the campus claim review process
- Identifying a central location for claim reporting
- Careful review of formal and informal complaints
- Good record-keeping of complaints, investigations, and resolutions
- A statement ensuring confidentiality of complaints
- An explanation of disciplinary sanctions imposed in sexual harassment claims

The complete policy should be included in faculty/staff handbooks and prominently posted at campus work sites. These campus policies can be supported through training sessions and other educational settings.

Summary

In light of the sexual harassment definition in *Meritor* and the level of proof established by *Harris*, colleges and universities should carefully review how courts assess Title VII sexual harassment claims in the workplace. With that awareness, they should develop and implement appropriate preventative policies.

Chapter 7
FREEDOM OF INFORMATION: RECORDS AND MEETINGS

Introduction

> It is vital in a democratic society that public business be performed in an open and public manner so that the electors shall be advised of the performance of public officials and of the decisions that are reached in public activity and in making public policy.
>
> Arkansas Code Annotated, Sec. 25-19-102

Access to records of government and its agencies, including public colleges and universities, is subject to various federal and state public information laws. Generally, the laws deal with records and meetings, providing an opportunity for the public to inspect government documents and to observe government meetings. Within higher education, the laws apply to most campus records and governance meetings. But do they apply to auxiliary enterprises or foundations? Are those bodies governmental units or are they private in nature? Right-to-know laws promote openness and accountability in public higher education.

Of particular interest in higher education for the past two decades has been the Family Education Rights and Privacy Act and its implications on the access and use of student educational records.

Freedom of Information Act Opens Federal Government

September 1990

We generally read about "freedom of information" acts when they don't work. Parties seeking information from government make news when they don't get what they want and respond with legal actions.

But these cases are exceptions to an otherwise relatively simple process. Every day, government agencies at the local, state, and federal levels receive and honor requests for information. Understanding the process can help campuses, student organizations, researchers, and media use it wisely.

The federal Freedom of Information Act (5 U.S.C. 552) applies only to documents held by the administrative units of the executive departments and offices (such as at the cabinet level), military departments, government corporations, federally controlled corporations, and regulatory agencies. All executive branch records are available on request, unless the materials fall within one of nine categories of exemptions.

Among the items that can be obtained are: agency final opinions and orders, policy statements and interpretations (including materials not published in the Federal Register), administrative staff manuals, and other records. However, presidential papers are not considered "government records" and therefore are not covered by the Act.

Where Are the Records?

The Freedom of Information Act (FOIA) isn't designed for initial research. You have to have some idea of where to start looking.

One good guide is the *United States Government Manual*, which lists all federal agencies, describes their functions, and provides a listing of local and regional offices and telephone numbers. The federal *Congressional Directory* can also be helpful, as it gives information on agencies and administrators. Both resources can be found in most libraries or purchased from the U.S. Government Printing Office (Washington, DC 20402).

In most cases, the title of an agency or the description of the agency's work should indicate the probable source of the desired records. However, if you're unsure of the location of the records, contact the agency most likely to have them. In most cases, if that agency doesn't have the records, staff will forward your request or direct you to the appropriate agency.

Local and regional field offices of federal agencies have access to a tremendous volume of records. It may be helpful to phone them in advance of a request. The agency office may be able to identify specific records or direct you to a more appropriate source. Most local telephone directories provide a listing of area federal offices. The government also publishes regional federal telephone books, which list offices and agencies operating in specific areas and provides the names and titles of policy-level employees. These directories are available from the Government Printing Office.

Requesting Information

After locating the records in question, you make a written request. Direct it to the agency head or the agency FOIA officer. If you can identify an individual responsible for the information, send your request to that person. In any case, it's a good idea to mark the envelope "Freedom of Information Request" to make sure it's handled properly.

You should identify the desired records as specifically as possible. While the law doesn't require you to provide the name or title of the materials, you must "reasonably describe" the information. "Reasonably describe" is defined as a description that "would be sufficient if it enabled a professional employee of the agency who was familiar with the subject area of the request to locate the record with a reasonable amount of effort." The more specific the request, the more likely a prompt and appropriate response.

Your request doesn't have to indicate your intended use of the information. But in some cases, this may be helpful. Agency officials have discretionary powers to release information beyond that required by law. If they understand the intended use, they may be more inclined to provide more than the minimum information.

Costs for Searches and Copies

"Freedom of Information" doesn't mean that the information itself is free. Each agency has a schedule of fees to cover the actual cost of searches and copying. Search fees cannot be charged for time spent by the agency to determine whether the records should be released. When setting fees, Congress warned the agencies that "fees should not be used for the purpose of discouraging requests for information or as obstacles to disclosure of requested information." Fee schedules are available on request.

Agencies have the power to waive or reduce fees if "furnishing the information can be considered as primarily benefiting the general public." For this reason, it may be helpful to state the intended use of the data requested. Fees can also be limited or waived due to financial hardship. Requests for modification of the standard fees should be part of the written request for information where appropriate.

One other cost-saving tip: ask to view the materials at the agency itself. That way, you can make sure it's what you need *before* paying to copy it!

Responses to Requests

Agencies have to respond to requests for materials within 10 working days of receipt of written requests. You can use certified mail with a return receipt to verify the 10-day turnaround period. After allowing time for return mail, follow up via letter or telephone if you don't receive a timely response.

Sometimes, a backlog of requests will slow down the process. Under "unusual circumstances," the government can get a 10-day extension for requests and will notify you that extra time will be needed. You can use the courts to force a timely response, but it's generally not worth the cost and time.

As indicated earlier, agencies can refuse to release information if it falls into one of nine specific exempt categories. If an agency denies a request, it must provide you with a reason and the name and address of the person responsible for the decision.

When establishing exemptions, Congress didn't call for the automatic denial of all related requests. Legislative history indicates that agencies should use the exemptions to withhold certain information under certain circumstances. Understanding the exemptions may help you tailor requests for best results. The Act authorizes the following exemptions:

- Classified documents concerning national defense and foreign policy. Executive orders may be used to keep secrets "in the interest of national defense or foreign policy."

- Information "related solely to the internal personnel rules and practices of an agency."

- Information exempt under other laws. Certain federal statutes provide for the protection of specific records, files, or types of information.

- Confidential business information. The law exempts "trade secrets and commercial or financial information obtained from a person."

- Internal communications. Letters and memos within or between agencies, dealing with matters in litigation, are not available.

- Protection of privacy. Under the Freedom of Information Act, personnel medical files and similar files, "the disclosure of which would constitute a clearly unwarranted invasion of personal privacy," are exempt.

- Investigatory files. Files collected for law enforcement purposes are exempt under certain circumstances: if disclosure could impact upon enforcement proceedings or a fair trial, invade privacy, identify a confidential source, reveal investigation techniques, or endanger the "life or physical safety" of law enforcement personnel.

- Information concerning financial institutions. Data collected from banks as part of federal regulatory efforts is exempt.
- "Maps of wells and geological and geophysical information."

Request Denied

If your request for materials is denied, you can file a written appeal. A normal agency denial letter should indicate the appeal process and where requests should be directed. Include a copy of your original request and a written argument on behalf of your request. Legal citations in support of your request may be helpful, so some consultation with legal counsel may be appropriate at this stage. An explanation of the intended use of the materials, if not provided in the request, may also help in an appeal.

Regulations generally call for appeals to be filed within 30 days of denial and allow the agencies 20 days to respond to appeals. Agencies can take an additional 10 days if they didn't seek any extension on the initial reply. If the agency rejects an appeal, the matter is then left for the courts to decide.

Time and money will be necessary to pursue a Freedom of Information case through the federal courts. But the rules favor those seeking information.

Before the Justice Department will defend a federal agency in a FOIA case, the agency must convince the department that they will win the case. If Justice is not convinced, the agency will have to release the data.

Even if the case goes to court, the plaintiff still has some strong advantages. You go to court with a *legal presumption* that you are right: the government has to convince the court to withhold the data. In addition, if there is doubt as to which side is correct, the courts are instructed to rule in favor of disclosure.

Federal courts have been advised as a matter of public policy to expedite FOIA cases and, where possible, move them ahead of other cases. Attorney's fees can be awarded to plaintiffs in cases where it's clear to the court that the records should have been released.

Summary

The government has a wealth of information, but it's not always readily available to students, researchers, and campus media. The Freedom of Information Act requires federal agencies to disclose materials, with certain exceptions. Those seeking information improve their chances by doing advance research, identifying the proper agency, making specific requests, and indicating an appropriate use for the information.

Determining What's Open, What's Closed Isn't Easy

June 1993

The campus meeting is either open to the public or closed. Campus records are either available to the public or unavailable.

These are the simple choices facing campuses as part of a complex system of laws developed over the last two decades. Under state open meeting laws, open record laws, and other versions of "sunshine" laws, the public has access to public processes. In other words, public matters are open to public involvement — that's the law.

But figuring out what's public, and therefore open, can be very difficult on an individual campus. Across the country, colleges and universities are involved in disputes over search committee records, expenditure files, various meetings, and foundation fundraising information. In each of these cases, "open" or "closed" is at issue.

Search Committee Records

In Michigan, public access to the names of candidates for college presidencies is being questioned on campus and in the courts.

In a case involving the University of Michigan, for example, a state appeals court recently ruled that UM violated the law by discussing candidates privately during a 1988 presidential search. The state's highest court is now reviewing that ruling.

Meanwhile, Michigan State University's attempt to conduct the early phases of a presidential search in secret was also stopped — not by the courts, but by leaks.

The search committee planned to review in private, but not take action on, some applications that had already been submitted. Committee members said the "private" meetings were legal since a trustee quorum was not present and the group was only advisory. They also said an exemption in the law allowed them to privately review applications that were submitted in confidence.

But the plan went awry when the student newspaper obtained and printed a complete list of the 136 candidates for the job. The paper said the list came from "someone close to the search" who might have objected to the policy of secrecy.

Expenditure Records

Citing the public's right to know how public money is being spent, a Montgomery (AL) newspaper filed a disclosure lawsuit against Alabama State University.

The newspaper wants to find out how much the school spent on private photographers who were hired last year to record a student protest. The newspaper also wants the court to determine what the school intended to use the pictures for.

According to the suit, ASU hired a local photographer and an advertising agency to photograph and videotape 20 students who staged a sit-in last fall. The students were protesting campus parking fees and their lack of a voting seat on the board of trustees.

Campus Meetings

Access to meetings of campus officers, trustees, and committees has been debated at the University of Alabama, the University of Nebraska-Lincoln, and Oakland University (MI).

At Alabama, officials recently excluded media and the public from some campus meetings. They cited an exemption in the state's open meeting law that says that a meeting can be closed "when the character or good name of a woman or man is involved."

While some people said that character issues were discussed at the meetings, others objected to the exclusions. They felt the law was improperly used by the school to "shield a discussion of policy" that should be open to the public and the media.

Elsewhere, the Nebraska attorney general is looking into open meeting law issues involving UNL, the state's largest university.

A lobbying group and the local media have complained that UNL violated the sunshine law by closing regent and budget reduction meetings. According to the complaints, the school closed meetings as it began budget planning for the next year.

The school says the committee meetings can legally be closed to the public because they are only advisory. It also argues that the regent meetings being questioned were not full meetings — again allowing them to be closed.

But the outside groups disagree. They say the school violated the intent of the law, if not the law itself, and they want the school to reopen its meeting doors.

At Oakland University, trustees have decided to end a longstanding tradition of holding closed committee meetings. For several years, the student press has continually objected to the practice.

The new open-door policy contains a loophole, however. The chair remains empowered to close meetings when "an open meeting would not be in the best interests of the institution."

Foundation Records

Information from multimillion dollar fundraising organizations affiliated with public campuses in Florida and Ohio is also being sought under public record laws.

In a case involving Palm Beach Community College (FL), for example, a state court ruled that foundation records were not exempt from state public record laws. The foundation had been sued by a local newspaper, which argued that the records should be open.

Prior to the decision, the foundation made public only an annual report and an outside audit. Now, all records, except the names of anonymous donors, will be made available to the public.

While Florida community college foundation records start to open, Florida State University officials want the whole state disclosure law changed.

Under state pressure to open foundation records, FSU boosters claim the release would actually be illegal. They cite a state law indicating that only foundation audits, management letters, and materials sought by the regents are available to the public.

Releasing anything else, the boosters say, would break the law. So they want the law changed before they open any files to public inspection.

In Ohio, a state court decision dealing with the University of Toledo's foundation may have broad impact.

The court ruled that the foundation is a public entity whose records should be open. A local newspaper had asked the court to order the release of donor names and amounts.

In recent years, the foundation has tried to distance itself from the school. But the court found a history of school involvement that extended to the foundation, making it subject to the law.

Other foundation executives in Ohio are now worried about the impact of the decision on major donors.

In other areas, public college and university foundations have had mixed results in trying to keep records closed.

Records have been protected recently in Michigan and West Virginia. But donor confidentiality is threatened in Indiana. The Indiana University Foundation is going to court in an attempt to protect donor records from disclosure. That case is scheduled to go to trial later this year.

Summary

Across the country, courts are trying to balance public needs with campus needs in this ongoing debate. The public's right to know about meetings, expenditures, and records is the law — but how that law will be applied by various campuses and courts still remains to be seen.

Students' Rights Under the Buckley Amendment

September 1992

May students read the comments that college admissions officers made on the students' applications? The U.S. Department of Education answered that question recently — and the answer may not be what some campuses want to hear.

Early in 1991, an undergraduate student at Harvard University (MA) contacted the admissions office and requested access to the "summary sheets" used by the school in selecting students. He said he wanted his sheet for a research project.

But campus officials rejected his request, saying the records were confidential and that Harvard had "no legal obligation" to make them available. The student then complained to the DOE that Harvard was violating the Family Education Rights and Privacy Act (FERPA), commonly known as the Buckley Amendment.

Buckley's Provisions

Adopted in 1974, the amendment applies to public and private colleges and universities that receive federal support. The law establishes students' rights to access and challenge the content of educational records. It also controls the distribution of record information to outside parties. Under the law, institutions must:

- Provide students with access to educational records
- Give students the opportunity to challenge records that are "inaccurate, misleading, or otherwise in violation of privacy or other rights"
- Get written consent before disclosing personally identifiable information about students
- Keep records of third parties who request or obtain student records
- Provide students with information about their rights under the law.

The law also says that third parties receiving information about students must agree not to further distribute the information without written consent.

FERPA applies to all current and former students and gives them rights to records that are *directly* related to them. Some records, however, like health care files and directory information, are exempt under the law.

The federal government operates a Family Policy Compliance Office to receive, investigate, and rule on complaints. Institutions that don't comply with Buckley risk losing federal funding.

Harvard's Response

The DOE eventually opened an investigation of the Harvard student's request.

Harvard contended that admissions summary sheets should remain confidential because they include excerpts from teacher recommendations that applicants waive the right to see. The school also said that since the summary sheets are kept in separate files, they are not part of the student records subject to review. And, the school claimed, the sheets aren't used to make decisions that "affect the life of a student," so they should not get FERPA protection.

"Not so," said the DOE. It ruled that students *should* have access to admissions files. According to the DOE, the summary sheets and related files are subject to FERPA as educational records. Students, the DOE ruled, have a right to "inspect and review" the files — but only after the confidential information they've waived the right to see is removed.

A Final Twist to the Story

After the DOE ruling, the student who filed the complaint and several dozen other students asked to review their summary sheets.

During the investigation, Harvard had said that it keeps the summary sheets for possible use in outside agency reviews. But when the students filed their requests last spring, they got a different answer. According to admissions officials, the school routinely *destroys* files after three years, due to file space limitations.

Under FERPA, institutions are not required to maintain any files. If campuses maintain records, they are subject to the law, but that doesn't mean schools have to keep specific files.

Harvard, for instance, can destroy files after a certain period of time, as many other schools do. The DOE will pursue an investigation only if someone can prove that the school destroyed records *after* a student asked to review them.

The latest FERPA ruling does not affect the records of rejected applicants. Since the Buckley Amendment applies only to current and former students, unsuccessful candidates do not have the legal opportunity to review admissions files. FERPA regulations say that applicants must be admitted and in attendance before they get review rights.

What about undergraduates seeking admission to their school's professional or graduate school programs? What are their record access rights? The original FERPA guidelines were unclear on this issue, but later Congressional amendments clarified the matter.

According to the amendments, a person applying for admission to a "component" unit of an institution is not considered a "student" of that component. Therefore, an unsuccessful applicant has no right to review graduate or professional admissions files — even if that person is an undergraduate student at the same institution.

Complying with Freedom of Information Laws

December 1993

Open government is good government. That's the concept that fostered the development of state and federal open meeting and records laws. For public colleges and universities, Freedom of Information (FOI) laws give the public an opportunity to see campus decision-making at work, not just learn about decisions after they're made. Students, faculty, staff, bargaining units, the public, and the media all have rights under various laws to view campus decision-making.

Information and Record Laws

An understanding of the law by campus officials can help colleges and universities use and comply with Freedom of Information statutes. These include state open records laws, the federal Freedom of Information Act and open meeting laws, and similar state open meeting laws.

In addition, campus records may be made available to the community through other legislation. Primarily, these include the federal Crime Awareness and Security Act, various state crime statistic laws, and the federal Campus Sexual Assault Victim's and Student Right-to-Know Act. Taken as a group, these sunshine laws open public campus meetings and records and require various forms of data reporting on colleges and universities.

Under the federal Freedom of Information Act, all federal records not specifically exempted are open for public review. For example, documents generated by campuses and filed with the government can be obtained through this act. To obtain records, a student request should be made to the federal agency that maintains the documents. If the request is turned down, appeals can be filed for administrative review, and ultimately the case could be heard in the federal courts.

Meetings of most federal agencies and commissions are open as a result of the "Federal Government in the Sunshine Act." In addition to opening meetings, the law also requires advance notice of meetings, including their topic, location, and time. It should be noted that there are 10 exemptions to the Act.

State government meetings, including related agencies such as public colleges and universities, campus security bodies, and campus related organizations are covered by most "state open meeting" statutes. The laws open the meetings where official business is conducted. Advance notice of meetings is generally required, and an agenda, in advance of the meeting, is mandated. Minutes of meetings are usually required.

While regulations vary from state to state, all states allow for closed sessions on particular matters. Commonly accepted reasons to close public campus meetings include real estate purchases, collective bargaining issues, personnel, litigation, and negotiation matters. In some states, officials violating the law can be subject to fines. Actions taken at meetings that violate the federal statutes may be voided in other states.

At the state level, "open record" laws are somewhat less formal than federal regulations. Some states honor oral requests for records, while others require a written request. Records requests should detail materials required and identify the agency holding the records. Generally, state records, including campus documents, are accessible under the FOI laws. Penalties for non-compliance vary across the country.

Reporting Laws

In addition to materials available from open meetings and records, college communities can obtain a variety of other information through mandated reporting laws. These laws require public and private schools receiving federal support to make annual reports to the campus or public on issues related to crime, personal safety, graduation rates, and other matters.

Under the federal Crime Awareness and Campus Security Act, all campuses with federal funding must distribute annual security reports. They include:

- Security policies and procedures
- Information on the status of campus security personnel and their relationship to local law enforcement agencies
- Campus crime prevention and substance abuse programming data
- Efforts to encourage the reporting of crimes
- Policies on drug and alcohol law enforcement
- Campus crime data on murder, rape, robbery, aggravated assault, burglary, and motor vehicle thefts

Liquor law, drug abuse, and weapon possession arrests also must be included in the report. Campus crime information must provide "timely reports" to the campus community on threats of crime against staff and students. Failure to comply with any elements of the law can put continued campus federal funding at risk.

Campus crime information can also be obtained through some state reporting statutes and police crime logs. Many states require campuses to publish more crime data than needed to satisfy the federal requirements.

Some states require campus law enforcement agencies to provide open public access to daily incident police records and logs. While most of these same records can be obtained through open record laws, some states have adopted specific laws on crime records to ensure their accessibility.

Information on the status of some campus disciplinary proceedings also can be obtained. Under the Campus Sexual Assault Victim's Bill of Rights, the federal government requires campuses receiving federal support to advise both student parties — accused and accuser — of the status of disciplinary proceedings. Outcomes of campus judicial proceedings must be reported to them when the case involves sexual assault.

Information on campus graduation rates is available through the federal Student Right-to-Know Act. Under the law, campuses must compute and produce data on graduation rates for prospective students. Generally, colleges and universities receiving federal financial support must report the percentage of students who graduate within 150% of the established time for an educational program (i.e., within six years for traditional four-year undergraduate programs). The act requires additional reporting on financial aid and athletic scholarships. Failure to comply with the Student Right-to-Know Act, adopted in conjunction with the Campus Security Act, places federal aid in jeopardy.

The Law at Work on Campus

In many cases, student leaders and journalists attempt to use freedom of information laws to attend campus meetings or obtain specific information from a college or university. A national interest group, the Student Press Law Center, advises students to "just show up" for meetings on campus and assume they are open. If the meeting is closed, student journalists are told to ask why and explain the law to the meeting chair. If the students are still not admitted, the Center advises them to have objections be recorded in the minutes and to call for a lawyer.

To obtain records, student leaders and newspaper reporters are urged to make formal written requests to the person or unit maintaining the records or to an established records access officer. The letter should cite legal authority for the request and reasonably describe the documents sought. A public college or university needs this information to make an effort to locate the materials on a timely basis. Under general freedom of information laws, a records request denial should be accompanied by an explanation and information on how to file an appeal. Students are urged by the Student Press Law Center to appeal denials to higher authorities or to the courts.

Summary

Public access to information exists on college campuses, both public and private. Federal and state open meeting and record laws provide members of the public campus and community members with an opportunity to attend business meetings and obtain various documents. Information on other issues, including graduation rates and crime data, can be obtained through reporting statutes from public and private institutions with federal funding. Campus failure to comply with the regulations can lead to fines, reversal of actions taken, and threatened loss of federal funding.

School Paper Beats Buckley: Now What?

June 1991

Does the 1974 Buckley Amendment protect campus crime records from release? In the past few months, that law — more formally known as the Family Education Rights and Privacy Act (FERPA) — has been subjected to Education Department interpretation, a federal court challenge, and widespread press coverage. So where does all of this attention and action leave colleges and universities? That all depends on whom you ask!

The latest confusion began with a simple request from a campus student newspaper editor. Her paper, the Southwest Missouri State University *Standard*, wanted access to campus crime reports. A woman alleged that she'd been sexually assaulted on campus by a basketball player, and the paper wanted to write a story on the attack.

Campus officials denied the request. The school considered campus law enforcement records to be educational records, and as such those records were protected by the Buckley Amendment. If the records were released without authorization from the accused student, officials argued, it would jeopardize all federal aid to Southwest Missouri State.

The student editor took the case to a federal district court in Missouri. At issue was students' right to know about crime on campus. The editor felt that the campus policy unconstitutionally infringed upon freedom of the press, and that state "government in the sunshine" laws allowed for records release.

Focus on Campus Crime

National attention to crime on campus has increased dramatically over the years, with the death of a Lehigh University (PA) student, the Gainesville, Florida, murders, and other incidents prompting legislative actions. Several states have adopted campus crime reporting statutes, finally leading to adoption of the federal Campus Security Act.

Recent studies indicate that campus crime is indeed a serious issue for many people and schools. A recent report by the Towson State (MD) Center for the Study and Prevention of Campus Violence indicates that 37% of all undergraduates will become victims of crime before they graduate. Another study indicated that fewer than 27% of the nation's colleges and universities release campus crime reports to campus media.

Education Department Warns Campuses

The results of a survey of selected campus policies were presented as evidence in the Southwest Missouri State case. Upon learning that some schools regularly release crime reports to students, the U.S. Department of Education responded swiftly.

The Department wrote to tell each surveyed school that it was in violation of the Buckley Amendment and that further violation of the privacy law could result in loss of Department funding. Half of the contacted schools suspended release of names and crime reports, while others reviewed the law with their own counsel.

The Department's position was that campuses could not release crime reports containing student names without student permission. Some campuses had kept crime reports separate from other campus records in the hope of distinguishing them from educational records. But the Department ruled that where or how the records were kept was not the issue. If any record contains data that is "personally identifiable," it's subject to control under the law, according to the Department.

Reactions to the Department ruling varied. Many campuses felt justified in their practice of withholding crime data. Others had a difficult time reconciling the growing public demand for disclosure with the Department's restrictive interpretation. Lobbying groups, including one founded by the family of the deceased Lehigh student, demanded congressional action to remove the Buckley shield of protection for campus crime records.

District Court Rules for Release of Reports

They didn't need to wait long for action — but the response was judicial, not legislative. In the Southwest Missouri State case, affecting the Western District of Missouri, a federal judge ruled that the Buckley Amendment did not bar the release of data on campus crime.

The student newspaper editor, in filing her suit in January 1990, called for the release of crime reports under state open records laws. Southwest Missouri State had argued the position of the Education Department. Without authorization, they said, no student records with names should be released.

The federal judge went to the Buckley Amendment's thin legislative history. He ruled that the Act wasn't intended to treat law enforcement records as educational records, and that the Act was meant to protect students from harmful information in school files, not to limit access. The Act, over its 17-year life, has become much more encompassing than originally intended. Students, said the judge, are not a protected class of criminals; their crime records and names should be available.

In his 49-page ruling, the judge said that the crime records of campuses should be available for review under the First and Fifth Amendments. He wrote:

Criminal investigation and incident reports are not the same type of records which FERPA expressly protects. ... The fact that the statute specifically exempts records maintained for law enforcement purposes demonstrates that Congress did not intend to treat criminal investigation and incident reports as educational records.

Mixed Reactions

As a result, Southwest Missouri State started to provide crime records to the campus paper. The school trustees voted not to appeal the decision and paid the ordered $1 damage award.

The Department of Education is unsure about the meaning of the decision. A spokesperson has advised schools to "comply with the law as written" — which was the Department's advice before the suit. Consultations with the Justice Department have led to a government appeal.

The decision and the Department's intervention have caused many colleges and universities to review their records policies.

In the past, the University of Alabama released crime reports, with the names of students deleted, and the campus newspaper published a weekly summary of crime reports, to promote student awareness. That policy will be reviewed in light of the Southwest Missouri State decision.

The University of Kansas is taking a different approach. Officials intend to follow the Education Department guidelines, pending government revision.

Ohio State University has turned the matter over to the state attorney general. The campus currently follows state records laws, which require open access. Officials withhold from the public only the names of rape victims and suspects not yet charged. They will do what their attorney general tells them to do.

And at West Virginia University, the conflict continues. Student newspaper editors want campus officials to release more crime reports. But WVU administrators intend to follow the Buckley Amendment, as defined by the Education Department. They provide the paper, on a daily basis, with only summary reports.

Summary

After a flurry of activity over campus privacy rights, the Buckley Amendment, and crime reporting, it's back to a "wait and see" posture for most campuses. The Southwest Missouri State case is law only in the Western District of Missouri and is subject to appeal. But the Education Department hasn't formally filed an appeal yet. Meanwhile a Missouri state judge has already used the federal decision to order another school to open its files.

The Education Department's interpretation of the Buckley Amendment goes against the national trend toward disclosure of campus crime. Some lawmakers are beginning to talk about revising Buckley or amending the next higher education authorization act to clarify the matter.

Lots of questions, lots of concerns. And the conflict will continue as the privacy rights of students are balanced with the right to know and the First Amendment.

Campus Security and Records: Whose Jurisdiction?

February 1992

Another challenge to campus records policies has been filed, this time involving police files at Jacksonville State University (AL). Campus security there have refused to release the names of two students arrested on rape and attempted rape charges.

The student newspaper claims that the campus refusal to "name names" goes too far in protecting student privacy. The paper wants to print the names of the accused to help other students protect themselves. The school says it cannot release the names without violating the Buckley Amendment.

The U.S. Department of Education contends that the disclosure of names without student consent violates federal law. By Department standards, discipline records are part of protected student files. Earlier in the year, 15 schools were warned about the possible loss of federal funds if the Act was violated through such a release. But the department's warning seems to conflict with a federal judge's ruling in Missouri that campuses cannot use Buckley to shield crime reports from public scrutiny.

The campus and the student newspaper are waiting for a decision they hope will clarify the situation. A Washington-based interest group, the Student Press Law Center, has filed suit against the Department of Education. It wants the courts to allow schools to treat student arrest records as crime records, not protected student files.

Jacksonville State had been releasing names until the warnings started arriving on campuses.

Social Security Numbers: Must They Be Protected?

October 1992

It seems that students are always being asked for their Social Security numbers — to register, to get grades, even for a part-time job. But is it legal? Does everyone have a right to know and use Social Security numbers?

A small group of Rutgers University (NJ) students had a similar concern. They said the continued "forced disclosure" of individual Social Security numbers violated the 1974 Family Education Rights and Privacy Act (FERPA), commonly known as the Buckley Amendment.

The students expected some sort of fight from the school over the issue, but not the one they got. Instead of arguing about the law, Rutgers questioned whether it even applied to the campus. The school, which calls itself "the state university of New Jersey," said it was not a state agency.

That left the courts to deal with two questions concerning the law: its scope and its intentions.

Students Go to Court

A student lobbying group took the issue to federal court, naming the university and its president as defendants, in *Krebs v. Rutgers, The State University of New Jersey*, 797 F.Supp. 1246 (D.N.J. 1992). Seven current or former Rutgers students — who, for the most part, represented themselves — challenged the school's policy on the collection and use of Social Security numbers. They wanted the court to force Rutgers to advise students about the voluntary nature of disclosing their Social Security numbers. The plaintiffs also wanted the court to limit the school's distribution of individual numbers.

The students said the school routinely circulated classroom rosters — which included names and Social Security numbers — for students to sign. In addition, the students said, Social Security numbers were printed on identification sheets and posted with examination scores.

The students said such uses promoted "uncontrolled distribution" of names and numbers, creating a potential for false identification and credit card fraud.

According to Buckley, protected "personally identifiable" information includes "a personal identifier, such as the student's Social Security or student number."

So the plaintiffs asked for:

- An injunction to halt Rutgers' "improper use" of Social Security numbers
- An order to force the school to advise students of related rights
- An order to force Rutgers to delete *all* Social Security numbers from student files

The university countered by offering to include some information about students' rights on fall semester tuition bills. But that wasn't enough to satisfy the students' demands.

Rutgers Fights Back

Attorneys for Rutgers argued that the federal privacy law cited by the students "does not apply to the university." They said Rutgers was not subject to "extensive day-to-day supervision" by the state, was not audited by the state, and conducted its business outside of standard state controls.

In addition, the school's lawyers argued that even if the privacy law were applied, Rutgers used Social Security numbers only for "internal purposes."

The students challenged both contentions. In examining the relationship to the state, they noted that New Jersey provided $250 million annually to the institution. They pointed out that the state's governor appointed a majority of Rutgers' trustees, and that the school referred to itself as "the state university of New Jersey."

The campus president, they added, drove a state car. And campus security vehicles, they said, had state government license plates.

After hearing the arguments, the court urged an out-of-court settlement. But that failed — so the court decided the case based on presentations and legal briefs submitted in support of each side.

A Win for Both Sides?

In mid-summer, the court issued rulings that both Rutgers and the students claimed as victories. The court said Rutgers had the right to ask students for their Social Security numbers without telling them disclosure is voluntary. But it also ruled that the school had to curb its internal distribution of the numbers.

The court agreed that Rutgers did not qualify as a "state agency" under the law. "Although there are many aspects of Rutgers' operations which touch and/or intersect with the state," the court said, "the overall effect is an independent institution, divorced from direct, let alone day-to-day, control."

The court did ask Rutgers to correct its policies and procedures to better control the "disclosure of ... confidential ... highly personal information." The court found no "meaningful response" from the school to the charges of widespread, uncontrolled distribution of the protected information. Said the court:

> Although the court determines herein that the university has the right to request and utilize the Social Security numbers of its students, there is evidence that the confidentiality promised and required has been and will continue to be breached. Such future breaches must be enjoined.

In addition, the court said, Rutgers' initial response to the students' concerns about confidentiality was "antagonistic and dismissive." Students, said the court, had "every right to feel violated."

To comply with the decision, Rutgers will now prohibit the distribution of student rosters that include students' names and Social Security numbers. The students' request for the deletion of all Social Security numbers was rejected by the court — along with their inclusion of the president as a defendant in the case and their motion to make the case a class action.

In a statement, Rutgers noted that it was "sensitive to the need and requirement to protect the privacy of educational records of its students." The court has now given Rutgers, and other campuses, some guidance on the importance of maintaining that sensitivity.

Students Win War of Numbers

February 1993

Rutgers University (NJ) has agreed to stop displaying students' names and Social Security numbers on materials commonly circulated to students.

The decision is part of an out-of-court settlement ending a privacy lawsuit against the school.

Rutgers has agreed to:

- Quit using names and Social Security numbers to post students' grades
- Remove Social Security numbers from mailing labels and students' meal cards
- Conduct open forums on privacy rights twice a year
- Allow students to use a number other than their Social Security number for campus identification purposes

In their lawsuit, students said the school's widespread use of Social Security numbers violated federal privacy laws. They argued that other people could potentially use stolen Social Security numbers to gain access to personal or academic records or create false birth certificates, credit cards, and the like.

Schools and Media Fight Over Records

August 1990

The question of "open records" is a major concern on college and university campuses. Around the country, journalists are turning to their attorneys to gain access to campus records. Through an understanding of how the issue is developing elsewhere, campus administrators can better appreciate the ramifications of their own records decisions.

Nowhere is the issue more debated than in Wisconsin, where the press, the state university system, the state attorney general, and the courts are all parties in disputes. At least four separate recent incidents in a year have focused attention on the University of Wisconsin's open records policies and principles:

- The UW-Madison campus refused to release the names of applicants for two positions in the athletic department.
- The UW-Platteville campus refused to release records pertaining to charges of nepotism against a dean.
- The UW-Madison campus refused to release a listing of employees in a specific campus unit.
- The UW System board refused for three days to release its decisions on administrative pay raises.

Campus officials contend that they are "committed firmly to the letter and spirit" of the state open records law. But others, including the media and attorney general, are not convinced. State courts have been asked to make the final determinations.

Media Put Pressure on University System

A state newspaper sued UW-Madison to get access to the names of candidates for the positions of football coach and athletic director. A county circuit court judge ruled earlier in the year that the school's refusal violated the law, but an appeal is pending. No names will be released until the appeal is heard.

UW-Platteville is in the same situation with regard to records on nepotism charges against a dean. The school refused press access to the files, but a newspaper sued and won. The release of these records is on hold, awaiting an appellate ruling.

And finally, another court has ruled against UW-Madison's attempt to withhold the names of employees whose unit supervisor resigned after a student filed a claim of sexual harassment against him. The school had argued that release of the names of the employees, combined with previous press reports on the incident, could lead to public identification of the student, to whom UW had guaranteed confidentiality.

The judge dismissed that contention, noting that acceptance of the school's position would open the door to "multi-faceted excuses" based on "kaleidoscope speculations." Said the judge, "Such a result would be disastrous to the letter, spirit, and purpose" of the state open records law. In addition to seeing employment records, the newspaper now wants to recover more than $4,000 in attorney fees and receive punitive damages. State law allows for such damages when the refusal to release open records is arbitrary and capricious.

During the spring meeting of the Wisconsin Associated Press, newspaper editors unanimously adopted a resolution expressing "dismay that the state's highest educational institution continues to indulge in such blatant disregard of the state's openness statutes." They've called for the state and university to reverse their "unopen" open records policies. Several state newspapers are keeping pressure on three system campuses currently searching for two chancellors and a vice chancellor.

Moreover, the state attorney general has stated that he's considering a suit against UW for what he sees as repeated violations of the records law. State law allows him to take legal action over such violations.

In spite of all of the legal battles, trials, and appeals, UW has basic concerns that it feels must be appropriately addressed. The school fears that releasing the names of job candidates will greatly limit future searches, as most potential candidates would prefer that their interest in other employment not be made public. In the case of the nepotism charge, the school argued that it was keeping the accused dean's file closed to protect his rights. And in not releasing the names of office employees, UW-Madison contended that it was trying to protect the confidentiality of the victim. The courts have ruled that the law doesn't allow for these exemptions or that the school has failed to support the need for exceptions. But it's not over until the four appeals are decided.

"Confidence and Trust" vs. "Right to Know"

In another records battle, a federal court ruled that the University of Utah must release documents related to a sexual harassment suit filed by the former interim director of the campus women's resource center. The school had been trying to keep certain employment and administrative documents classified, including records of the search for a new center director. But, upon a motion by the plaintiff's attorneys and local media representatives, the court ordered disclosure.

As in the case of the UW-Madison search records, the University of Utah maintained that the "integrity of the university's hiring and recruitment process depends on its ability to maintain the confidence and trust of potential employees and applicants for positions." The university's motion stressed that "a public employee does not lose all rights to dignity or privacy merely by virtue of his or her employment."

But the magistrate maintained that the law gives the media, and the public, a "right to know" with only limited exceptions, and he signed a court order mandating release of the records.

FERPA and Crime Information

Campus journalists often fight the same battle to open records as members of the community media. Recently, they've begun to complain that campuses are wrongfully using the Family Education Rights and Privacy Act, commonly referred to as the "Buckley Amendment," to withhold crime data. The law was designed to open records to students, but it allows many exceptions.

Campus police information is generally seen as data that can be withheld, according to many limitations incorporated in FERPA. Out of concern over privacy, campuses regularly withhold the names and addresses of campus victims, those accused of crimes, and accident victims.

Campuses generally respond to student press inquiries by noting that they want to provide information that's relevant to the community, but can do so only by the letter and spirit of the law. The recent push at the state and federal level for better disclosure of campus crime statistics can in part be traced to this Buckley Amendment dilemma.

Open record issues can be complicated and emotional, with critical implications for all parties involved. Institutions and journalists need to know the law, know their rights and responsibilities, and act accordingly. If the law doesn't meet or satisfy the legitimate needs of higher education, administrators should try to change the law — but through *legislation*, not *litigation*. There can be legitimate exceptions to open records, but these should be determined by *lawmakers*, not *record-keepers*.

Courts Define "Student"

January 1991

When is a student a "student"? Only when enrolled in a degree program? How about people who audit courses? Are they students?

These questions were central to the first case to reach the U.S. Supreme Court under the 1974 Family Educational Rights and privacy Act (FERPA). Known generally as the Buckley Amendment, the law has remained largely unchallenged. Among the issues at stake before the Court were the definition of the term "student," institutional rights to withhold admission files from denied candidates, access to letters of recommendation, and the constitutionality of the Act.

A student applied for admission to a university graduate program and had three letters of recommendation sent in support of his application. When he wasn't accepted, he wanted to know why. The school turned down his attempts to review the admissions file and the letters of recommendation, so he sued.

But how could he sue, wondered many school officials. Didn't FERPA apply only to students admitted to the school? As the law was understood, a school had to share records only with its own students. And this applicant had been turned down!

But he sued for the records anyway, claiming that since he was auditing graduate and undergraduate courses at the school, he should be considered a student and allowed access to the records. The school disagreed. So the issue went to court in *Tarka v. Franklin*, 891 F.2d 102 (1989).

Background

FERPA is relatively easy to explain. It applies to most educational institutions that have students and establishes student and parent rights regarding school records. The law places several conditions on post-secondary school record-keeping:

- Students must have access to their own records.
- Students must be given an opportunity to challenge data in records that may be "inaccurate" or "misleading."
- Records cannot be disclosed to third parties, with few exclusions.
- Schools must keep records of third-party inquiries.
- Third parties given records must agree not to share them with others.
- Schools must inform students of their rights under the law.

Given the wide scope and impact of the law, it's interesting to note that it attracted little attention when it was proposed and passed. It was attached to a routine higher education funding bill and adopted by the House and Senate without being referred to committees or subjected to public hearings.

Complaints about FERPA and its approval process led to modifications less than six months after its passage. But the new amendments weren't studied by the committee or presented at hearings. In fact, they were attached to a bill that dealt primarily with a conference on library science! Given this history, it's surprising that FERPA hasn't created more problems or been challenged more often.

FERPA applies to all public and private schools that receive any federal financial funds or support. Students with complaints about school interpretation of the Act have access to a review process, which includes campus and Education Department investigations and consideration of complaints.

All students enrolled or formerly enrolled, regardless of age, have rights to records that are "directly related" to them as students and maintained by the school. Some records held by the school aren't subject to FERPA, including:

- Directory information, without consent of the student
- Private records, held by the person who created them and not available to anyone else
- Law enforcement records kept separate from student records
- Employment records of students in attendance, unless employed as a result of being a student
- Health care records
- Records created about an individual after his or her years of attendance, such as alumni files

Given all of this, including the definition of student and rights to access, how can an applicant for admission use FERPA to sue for access to records?

Admissions Records

Access to admissions files was one of the major problems corrected in the amendments to FERPA. Originally, candidates apparently could inspect admissions materials, including support documentation such as letters of recommendation. Congress acted quickly to close this open door, establishing complex guidelines to control admissions records.

Under the amendments, applicants for admission have no rights. FERPA applies to "student," defined by the then-HEW Department Final Regulations as:

> a student who has attained eighteen years of age or is attending an institution of postsecondary education.

The Department modified this definition in 1988 to include former students — "any individual who is or has been in attendance at an educational agency or institution." But these definitions still deal only with students, not with candidates for admission. If you're not "in attendance," you're not a student.

What if someone is attending one part of an institution and applies for admission to another? Does that person have access to those files as a "student"? Not according to the Department guidelines. Persons applying for admission to "component units" of an institution while attending another unit of the same institution don't have FERPA rights to admissions files. Therefore, an undergraduate who has applied to his own school's law program can't review his law school admission files.

Looking at the university as separate parts isn't how FERPA generally works. For violations of the Act, the school is seen as a whole: violations by one component could threaten federal support for the whole campus. The FERPA definition of an "education agency or institution" supports the broad reach of the Act. But records are covered by different definitions under the law, which allows for separating rights to records by student class distinctions.

Letters of Recommendation

The original law seemed to provide students with the right to review all recommendation letters in the school files. But this opportunity existed only between the original effective date of FERPA (Nov. 19, 1974) and the date of the modifying amendments (Dec. 31, 1974) — only 50 days. Congress and the departmental guidelines then provided a system for preserving the privacy of letters of recommendation.

Letters put into student files before January 1975 could remain closed if they were intended to be confidential and are being used only for intended purposes. For letters written after January 1975 — for employment, admission, or honorary recognition — students can waive inspection rights. The student must exercise the waiver on his or her own, not through a parent, and waivers can't be tied to admission or any other service or benefit. Students must be free to sign or not sign without the threat of loss of service or benefits from the institution.

Previous Challenges

Except for the 50 anxious days in 1974, there have been relatively few challenges to the law. For the most part, FERPA requests and interpretations have been adequately handled at the campus level, with few cases being forwarded to the Department of Education for review judgment. One factor has been the availability of advisory opinions from the Department: schools in doubt can ask for guidance.

Another factor has been court uncertainty over the rights of individuals to sue under FERPA. Students injured by FERPA violations may not have a "private cause of action" for suit. The law requires institutions to comply, but it doesn't specifically say that students injured under the law can use it to sue for damages. In *Girardier v. Webster College*, 563 F.2d 1267 (1977), a U.S. Circuit Court of Appeals refused to hear such a claim under FERPA.

More recently, the "private right of action" issue was reviewed in *Smith v. Duquesne University*, 612 F.Supp. 72 (1985). There, a federal district court judge heard arguments from a dismissed student that he had been denied access to records in violation of FERPA. The school contended that the federal government, not a student, has the right to interpret and enforce the Act. It also claimed that since it didn't receive federal financial support, it wasn't even covered by FERPA.

The federal court agreed. Under the law, said the court, there is no right to a private remedy. Designed to control school use of records, the law should be enforced through the schools. The school has a process for judging violations and imposing sanctions; judgments are limited to this process. A student can't sue the school to force it to comply with the federal law. The government must act to enforce its own laws.

Of the few FERPA cases heard by courts in the past 15 years, most have focused on *student directory information*. Off-campus agencies have tried to get information on students for private purposes, claiming it should be available to them as directory information.

In *Kestenbaum v. Michigan State University*, 327 N.W. 2d 783 (1982), the state supreme court ruled against such a request. The university had turned down a request for directory information that was to be used for political purposes, maintaining that the release of such student data would violate the Buckley Amendment. A divided court allowed the school to withhold the student listings, citing FERPA and a state freedom of information act as support.

In *Krauss v. Nassau Community College*, 469 N.Y.S. 2d 553 (1983), a New York State court ruled against a request for a listing of all student names and addresses. The school claimed that it hadn't designated names and addresses as open directory data. Again, the court relied on the Buckley Amendment in its decision.

Since Kestenbaum and *Krauss*, the Department of Education has clarified the definition of directory information: it can now include a student's name, address, telephone number, date and place of birth, major, campus activities, sports participation, dates of attendance and degrees, awards, and most recent other school attended. The school has discretion in releasing all or part of this information, and can do so only with student consent.

Current Challenge

In the latest legal test, *Tarka v. Franklin,* the federal courts were asked to look at the definition of "student." While it's understood that FERPA doesn't cover applicants for admission, is a person auditing courses a "student" at the school?

A federal district court ruled in favor of the school, noting that FERPA wasn't intended to give any rejected applicants a right to see their files and letters of recommendation. According to the court's review of the legislative record, FERPA as amended wasn't intended to affect admissions decisions or procedures in any way. The court ruled that a person must be admitted to the school to have any rights to school files. The district court considered those who audit classes to be visitors, without full campus rights and privileges.

An appeal review upheld the district decision. In support of school rights to control admissions files and letters of recommendation, the U.S. Supreme Court rejected the *Tarka* case, leaving the earlier decisions unchanged. A student, under FERPA, is a "student" only if regularly enrolled in classes.

Student Disciplinary Records

May 1995

It was a case of allegations of hazing. The involved student group had faced a hearing before a campus organization court. The student newspaper wanted to report the details to the campus.

The University of Georgia, considering federal and state privacy principles, conducted related disciplinary hearings behind closed doors. When university officials refused to open the hearing or provide records of charges and sanctions, the student newspaper went to court. It sued the campus president, school regents, and others, seeking access to the records of the organization court proceedings.

In *The Red and Black Publishing Company, Inc. v. Board of Regents,* 427 S.E. 2d 257 (1993), the courts considered the confidentiality of college student disciplinary proceedings. A final decision in the case was ultimately made by the Supreme Court of Georgia.

The question would appear to be relatively simple: Are disciplinary records open or closed? But the ultimate answer remains elusive, due to a series of legislative and regulatory adjustments to the Family Educational Rights and Privacy Act (FERPA) and court cases testing state open meetings and records laws.

FERPA and the Past Five Years

Without the benefit of legislative hearings, Congress enacted the Family Education Rights and Privacy Act in 1974. Since that time, the law has been modified several times, providing a confused history on access to student disciplinary records.

The Act originally protected records and files "maintained by an educational institution" that contained information "directly related to a student." This covered most campus files, including disciplinary records. But changes since 1990 have caused some confusion.

Out of concern for victims of campus violence, the 1990 Student Right to Know and Campus Security Act altered FERPA. The change allowed campuses to notify victims of campus crime of the outcome of related disciplinary proceedings.

The Higher Education Amendments of 1992 extended this provision to allow disclosure of proceedings and sanctions to the victims of sexual assault. Under governmental regulations for implementation, the guidelines provide that:

- Accuser and accused should have an equal opportunity to be present at campus proceedings.
- Both accuser and accused should be informed of the outcome of disciplinary proceedings.

These provisions deal exclusively with sexual assault campus disciplinary proceedings and records.

But what about campus law enforcement agency records? They may contain significant information pertaining to students and allegations of wrongdoing. Are they as protected as campus disciplinary records?

Not according to the Higher Education Amendments of 1992. They contain new language that creates a FERPA exception for:

> records maintained by a law enforcement unit of the educational agency or institution that were created by that law enforcement unit for the purpose of law enforcement.

This allows campus media and other interested parties access to public safety records, including incident reports, that are originally generated for law enforcement reasons.

Last summer, the Department of Education proposed draft regulation language to implement the new amendments. It contained a definition of "disciplinary proceedings" that remained protected against disclosure. It included the investigation, adjudication, or imposition of sanctions by an educational agency related to internal rules and policies. Those records remain closed.

Because of the large number of campus responses to the proposals, the Department issued revised final guidelines earlier this year. The Department has maintained protection of disciplinary records but has allowed for the release of campus security records. These records could contain similar information. The Secretary has asked Congress for guidance on the issue, to further clarify the distinction between disciplinary records and security records and to define legislative interest in their accessibility.

Red and Black

The University of Georgia withheld student organization disciplinary records from the campus media, based on FERPA. But the student newspaper argued that it was entitled to the records under a state open government law.

The state supreme court held that state law applied. The student organization court was held to be acting on behalf of the state and, therefore, subject to state law.

The court considered the FERPA implications of the case for Georgia. It noted that FERPA does not explicitly prohibit the release of disciplinary records. An institution can release the records, but at the risk of losing federal funding. In addition, the court held that the particular records sought by the student press should not be protected under the law as "educational records," which should be related to a student's scholastic performance or financial records, not other matters.

The court also concluded that the university was protected from FERPA when complying with court orders. Since the courts ordered the release, University of Georgia should comply without federal sanctions, the court reasoned. *Red and Black* has resulted in the opening of disciplinary proceedings in the entire state university system.

Other Decisions

Two cases last year dealt with similar issues and reached different conclusions.

In *Society of Professional Journalists and Millhollen v. Louisiana State University* (1994), the campus student newspaper, with the assistance of a professional organization, sued LSU for access to student disciplinary records from campus proceedings related to the alleged theft of funds by student leaders. The paper sought release under state open records laws, while the university maintained FERPA protection.

Finding that the LSU proceedings were not "criminal-type," the court applied FERPA. It denied media access to records related to the alleged theft. The court considered the state open records statute and found release of campus records not to be related to the law's purpose. It found "no compelling interest" for the public in releasing records related to internal campus policies and issues.

In Selkirk v. University of Oklahoma (1994), a student requested access to campus disciplinary records for the names of students disciplined for campus vandalism. The court denied that request. Citing FERPA, the court declared campus disciplinary records exempt from disclosure as educational records. Since the acts did not include acts of violence or sexual assault, there was no legal requirement to notify victims of any outcomes.

What Next?

With federal implementation regulations protecting disciplinary records on campus, at issue remains access to law enforcement records and the applicability of state open records laws. The law does not *require* release of law enforcement records, but only *allows* for it, at institutional discretion. In the months ahead, we can expect further clarification on just what constitutes "accessible" law enforcement records.

Student Medical Files: A Danger if Not Maintained

January 1993

All student records are sensitive — but none are more sensitive than student medical files.

Student health records, of course, serve a variety of purposes. But they can also be dangerous if they're not properly collected and maintained.

Guidelines for doing so have been developed by the American College Health Association (ACHA). The "Recommended Standards for a College Health Program" outline principles schools can use to develop their own policies for student medical files.

Member campuses and other institutions are not bound to follow the guidelines in their entirety. But the guidelines represent the "best thinking" of a professional organization dedicated to promoting students' physical and mental health, along with related issues.

The guidelines suggest ways to maintain records while serving students and protecting your institution from liability concerns (mistreatment, improper release of records, etc.). Let's take a look at some of the basics.

Standards for Health Records

Generally, the campus health service is responsible for the "collection, processing, maintenance, storage, retrieval, distribution, and safeguarding" of student medical records.

Your campus should have a clear records policy in place to protect students and limit campus liability. The policy should outline the types of records covered and should be based on a full understanding of medical and legal ethics. The policy should also address confidentiality issues and related legal matters, such as informed consent of patients.

The records, of course, must be available to campus healthcare providers to ensure that students receive appropriate treatments. But they can't be accessed by unauthorized persons or used for unauthorized purposes.

The ACHA guidelines are very specific about protecting students' medical records:

> Patient information is not revealed to any other college or institutional personnel without the informed consent of the patient, except in cases of extreme urgency where there is an obvious "need to know."

Records that include clinical, social, financial, or other personal data should always be treated as confidential. To prevent their disclosure, your campus must protect them from "loss, tampering, alteration, destruction, and unauthorized or inadvertent disclosure." Again, those preventive steps should be in your policy.

You should also appoint an individual as the "custodian of health records." That person should be responsible for protecting the records — with regard to confidentiality, security, and physical safety. An annual evaluation of the records process would also be a good idea.

The records custodian should make sure that the policy includes specific guidelines for:

- The retention of current records
- The storage and disposal of inactive records, as required by state laws or other applicable regulations
- The timely entry of information on all records to ensure accuracy
- The release of records, as authorized by patients or required by law
- The maintenance of separate records, as appropriate and necessary, for "counseling, substance abuse, mental health, HIV, or family planning" matters

The Importance of Accuracy

To protect your students and your institution, you must make sure that students' medical records are accurate. The ACHA offers several guidelines.

First, include a "problem list," a summary of significant personal health issues or problems, with each student's records. It's useful because it can help focus staff attention on immediate medical concerns and issues — particularly if a student's health record is lengthy.

(Care providers, of course, should review the student's entire record. The summary can simply point out "trouble" spots — quickly.)

To make the summary most effective (for promoting care and limiting liability), you should record:

- Important surgical procedures
- Important medical diagnoses — specifically those involving continuing conditions and continuing treatment
- Conditions that could affect care, including drug and other allergies and medications the student uses regularly

The format of medical records is also critical. The ACHA says that records should be easy to read, with information consistently reported in the same place on each record.

Uniformity helps healthcare providers find what they need effectively and efficiently, and reducing the chances for errors or omissions.

We often make fun of the handwriting of some healthcare professionals. But keep in mind that another key to effective medical recordkeeping is legibility.

People must be able to understand the recorded information. Good medical treatment limits the potential for campus liability, but only if information is properly — and legibly — recorded in the students' health files.

What else should you keep track of? Dates and times of visits, purposes of visits, findings, studies or tests ordered, treatments, referrals and recommendations, informed consents or refusals of treatment, and the health provider's name. Do so for every on-site visit.

And remember to record information provided to student-clients over the telephone.

What about sharing students' records with other providers? Well, with written consent, you can transfer health records to other providers, as long as you've developed some way to ensure maximum confidentiality.

Once the student receives care somewhere else, get copies of those records and include the data on the student's campus record. It will help you ensure that subsequent campus care is appropriate.

Summary

By maintaining good student health records, you'll be able to do a better job of managing care for students and reducing the significant liability risks involved in today's medical and legal environments.

The ACHA's guidelines can help you meet those needs. Review and apply the recommendations as appropriate. Your students and your institution will benefit.

Information: Uses and Abuses

March 1996

It is said that "information is power." On campus, information is powerful. But used improperly, it can become a major problem.

Consider the implications of an unauthorized job reference, a leaked criminal pre-sentencing report, a published computer image of a woman's breast, a term paper, and a faculty member's announcement of a student AIDS case. In each scenario, information released in the campus community resulted in angry legal action.

Job References

She had been involved in college fund-raising for almost a decade, but was now hunting for a higher-paying position. After a series of interviews, it appeared that only a meeting with board members separated her from a new, very desirable, post.

But the new organization called her current supervisor for a reference. And after that conversation, the board interview was canceled and no job offer was made. A month later, the woman's own campus asked her to leave that job as well.

Apparently, when called for a reference, the supervisor reported that the employee was difficult to work with and performed poorly. According to campus policies, all personnel records were confidential, subject only to limited release with employee permission. The employee handbook said that no other information would be revealed, without authorization, and never by telephone.

The former Northwestern University (IL) fund-raiser sued the institution. She claimed defamation, citing economic damages from the loss of the new job. A lower court dismissed her claim, but an appeals decision will allow her case against the school to go forward.

At trial, the plaintiff will have to prove economic loss and defamation. The appeals court found that it was legitimate to consider the loss of the job offer as a potential monetary loss. On the issue of defamation, the court considered the negative nature of the comments and the context in which they were given. Subject to judicial review were the truthfulness of the statements and the violations of the campus policy. The plaintiff's claim, said the court, could be successful if it is shown that the supervisor knew or should have known that the statements over the telephone were unauthorized.

Pre-Sentencing Investigation Report

A University of Nebraska football player has filed a $500,000 claim against the state over the leak of a pre-sentencing report to the media. He contends that the report, prepared for judicial review after he was convicted of sexual assault, was unlawfully provided to national medical representatives. The report was compiled to help the court determine an appropriate sentence.

State policy is to restrict access to the reports, which contain confidential medical information and correspondence and statements on an offender. The player's report was leaked after sentencing and detailed additional incidents in which the football player was accused of crimes.

According to his suit against state officials, the disclosure caused the student to suffer "significant and substantial" damage to his reputation, in addition to "humiliation and embarrassment." His invasion of privacy case contends that the unauthorized release will have a negative impact on his ability to earn a living through a professional sports career.

State officials admit that the material about the student should not have been made public.

Computer Image

Her case included 12 tort claims, including medical malpractice, invasion of privacy, breach of contract, and intentional infliction of emotional distress. She sought $2 million from various defendants, including the University of Minnesota and a local newspaper. The basis of her claim: an MRI image of her breast published as part of a newspaper story on implant dangers — with her name visible on the photo.

She had earlier been treated by a campus medical practice group, which newspaper reporters then asked to provide background materials for a story. The group gave the paper an MRI slide on which the patient's name was too small to be seen — at least before it was enlarged for publication! The practice group, seeing the potential for liability, has sued the newspaper, saying it violated an agreement to preserve patient confidentiality.

In an effort to resolve the matter prior to trial, the parties entered into a mediation process. As a result, they settled out of court but released no information on the monetary value of the settlement.

Term Paper

The students wrote the term paper in 1993 for a class, but it was also circulated around the local jail. The 11-page paper by University of Washington management students, "The Impact of Affirmative Action — King County Jail," detailed employment tension at the jail. The report section on "The White Perspective" noted that white officers complained that less-qualified minority employees received promotions and that African Americans faced race-based hostility on the job.

One African American jail official, saying the class paper defamed him, has filed suit against the school and its four former students. He maintains that "racist" comments in the paper were directed at him, resulting in damage to his career. He's suing, the jail supervisor says, because the students shared a copy of their project with the jail, not just with their teacher.

The plaintiff'sHis attorneys claim that the paper was part of an organized effort "to destroy ... and irreparably damage" their client's career. The ex-students, now far away from the campus, are stunned by the litigation against them.

AIDS

Fellow music students at the University of Minnesota started to call on him, expressing sympathy. They knew he had AIDS and wanted to wish him well. But how did they know? According to a civil case, an instructor announced the student's condition to classmates after the student left school. The ex-student is now seeking more than $50,000 from the instructor and the institution.

According to the plaintiff, he enrolled in the UM music school in fall 1994. But when diagnosed with AIDS, he told his instructors he was taking a medical leave of absence to deal with the illness.

Court papers indicate that one teacher informed a class about the student's condition, without permission, after the student took his leave. The plaintiff, not expected to live another year, has said he will share any monetary damages with charities.

Summary

Information may be powerful, but its misuse can have powerful consequences, causing harm, both personal and financial, and exposure to liability. To avoid problems:

- Understand campus policies on the use and release of campus records.
- Obtain advance permission before disclosing records.
- Make sure that released information is accurate.

Use your information power well.

Student Athletes Successfully Combat Drug Testing

September 1993

Two intercollegiate student athletic drug testing cases were recently reviewed in the *Journal of College and University Law*. In an article by W. L. Schaller, the legal relationship between student-athletes and schools and the parties' legal rights are explored. The article, entitled "Drug Testing and the Evolution of Federal and State Regulation of Intercollegiate Athletics: A Chill Wind Blows," suggests that testing be limited to circumstances in which there is a "reasonable suspicion" of wrongdoing.

While courts have not generally found college athletes to be employees with due process rights, they may have contractual rights that must be considered in any testing environment. Courts faced with student challenges to random drug testing balance individual rights of students with the responsibilities of their institutions. Two significant rulings now favor the athletes.

In *Hill v. National Collegiate Athletic Association*, 273 Cal. Rptr. 402 (Cal. Ct. App. 1990), the California Court of Appeals ruled that any "intrusive" testing, such as urine sampling, violated protected privacy rights. The court said that random testing could be justified only if taken in response to known widespread drug abuse. Since the NCAA did not prove to the court that the problem was widespread, the court disallowed the testing system.

A trial court that heard *Derdeyn v. University of Colorado*, 832 P.2d 1031 (Colo. Ct. App. 1991), ruled similarly. There, the school program used a "rapid-eye test" as a predictor of drug impairment. A student athlete claimed that testing was an unreasonable search of his person, and the court agreed. It ruled that schools could not test unless there was some founded suspicion of wrongful activity.

These two cases, Hill and *Derdeyn*, suggest that, absent a finding of widespread student-athlete drug use, a college or university should consider drug testing based on reasonable suspicions, not random sampling.

Drug Testing Invades Student Privacy

June 1994

Drug testing of college athletes has met with U.S. Supreme Court opposition. The Court upheld, without comment, a Colorado Supreme Court decision invalidating a University of Colorado-Boulder intercollegiate sports testing program.

In the mid-1980s, many colleges and universities adopted drug testing programs in an attempt to keep intercollegiate sports substance-free. Many programs were initiated after the death of a University of Maryland-College Park basketball star.

Colorado began testing student-athletes for drugs on a random basis in 1984. By 1986, testing had expanded beyond athletes to include students, team trainers and managers, and cheerleaders. Under the school policy, students in the sports program found to be using illegal substances were suspended for a year. Repeat violators were subject to expulsion.

But shortly after the program of mandatory urinalysis began, a cross country runner filed suit against the university. He argued that random drug tests of this type constituted an "unreasonable search" under the Fourth Amendment. State courts agreed, finding the program an unlawful invasion of privacy. A U.S. Supreme Court ruling upheld that position.

Foundations Battle for Confidentiality

February 1995

After decades of relative privacy, college and university foundations have come under increasing legal scrutiny. All across the country, pressure has been brought on these non-profit fund-raising organizations to open their donor and expenditure records for public review. In addition to a key legal battle involving the University of Toledo's (OH) foundation records, recent spending and record disputes have been reported at Michigan State, the University of South Carolina, the University of Minnesota, the University of Nevada-Reno, Eastern Michigan University, the University of South Alabama, Oklahoma State University,

Indiana University

The IU battle demonstrates the various legal issues and on- and off-campus perspectives involved in today's foundations. Should the records of the Indiana University Foundation be subject to an official state audit that would open its donor rolls to public review? Foundation officials say no. As a result, they have spent the last four years in and out of court, trying to maintain the privacy of their records.

The IU Foundation has more than $300 million in assets, solicited and invested on behalf of university programs and services. Foundation officials maintain that opening foundation records would damage efforts on behalf of the university and education. They fear that a state audit would open donor files to public review under the state's sunshine laws. They also are concerned that it would open up the foundation's correspondence files. These files contain "sensitive" materials about donors, their finances, prospects for giving and planned giving, and other personal matters.

The legal battle over records access and donor privacy began with a 1989 state attorney general ruling. The state's highest legal officer, the attorney general, ruled that IU Foundation records were subject to a full and public audit by the state Board of Accounts. The state official ruled that the foundation received direct support from a state agency — the university — and, therefore, was subject to state audit. According to the attorney general, the foundation received approximately $2.3 million in direct annual support in public funding. Under state law, organizations and agencies that are "maintained or supported" by public funds are subject to public audit.

A leading state newspaper reviewed the attorney general's ruling and decided to put it to a test. The paper requested copies of IU Foundation donor records. It argued that the listing should be made available under state freedom of information laws. It reasoned that if the state audit laws applied to the foundation because of its public support, then the state freedom of information or sunshine statutes should as well.

IU's foundation refused to provide any of its records to the paper. It argued that the state funds it received did not make the foundation a public agency. Instead, the foundation said it was paid only a "contract fee" for fund-raising by the school. Its position was that it did a job for the university — development work — and was paid for that service, as any other vendor would be paid for work completed.

In an effort to resolve the records access matter, the IU Foundation filed suit against the state. It sought a judicial ruling that it was exempt from state audit and sunshine law release of donor records. After three years of legal maneuvers, in October 1993 a state court finally agreed with the foundation's position. It ruled that Indiana authorities had no legal right to audit the foundation records or force their release. The decision was based on a judicial finding that the foundation "is not maintained in whole or in part by appropriations or public funds or by taxation."

Continued Litigation

The foundation's "victory party" was relatively brief. The attorney general filed for an appeal quickly, and the case may now find its way to the state's supreme court.

So four years after the initial ruling, the attorney general is back in court on behalf of the state. The appeal is an effort to defend the state law and to ensure that it is properly applied to agencies and organizations. The state maintains that the very close ties between the foundation and the university make the fund-raising unit subject to state regulation and oversight. According to the state appeal, the foundation purchases property and materials for IU, rents space back to the school for its use, and directly manages a $40 million IU endowment, in addition to other IU related funds. The state argues that the close relationship demonstrates state "support" for the foundation, opening it to public scrutiny.

Public Disclosure of Private Donors

The issue of donor privacy vs. public disclosure has created dissension on the IU governing board as well. One current member, a former state legislator himself, has argued that the school should side with the state, not the foundation, in the dispute. He maintains that state review of foundation records and public disclosure of donors and expenditures would give greater accountability to contributors and taxpayers alike. The board member feels that the court ruled only on the funding issue, finding that the $2.3 million given to the foundation was, in fact, payment, not an appropriation of state money. This was a technical issue, not a substantive one, he maintains, so board members would like IU to pressure the foundation to authorize complete financial disclosure.

Higher education foundation officials remain concerned about increasing state involvement in their management and record-keeping. Their primary concern is the reactions of donors if their names and specific contributions are widely published. In the past, givers have understood the confidentiality of the foundation's records. Today, donors may be more uncertain that information about them will be kept confidential. Officials fear that this could make donors less forthcoming and, ultimately, less willing to give.

National attention about the privacy of donor records was heightened by a 1993 Ohio Supreme Court decision involving the University of Toledo. It ruled that the Toledo Foundation had to open its contributor files to public review. In 1990, a South Carolina court issued a similar order. But recent court cases on campus foundation records in Michigan and West Virginia came to a different conclusion — these states protected donor records. Judicial indecision on the matter has contributed to campus, foundation, and donor concern and confusion.

Concern over the potential release of planned gifts information is a major issue for foundation officials. Donors make arrangements for gifts at their death, in confidence. Foundations fear that forced public disclosure of these plans could lead to pressure on donors by others to make alternative arrangements. They are concerned that family members, and other charitable organizations, may target known donors in an effort to significantly alter their gift plans, costing the foundation support and involving it in litigation and "family feuds."

Competing Interests

College and university foundations find themselves in the middle of a legal minefield as they attempt to promote campus interests in public settings. To be effective in today's environment, separate campus fund-raising organizations must consider the balance between donor privacy and the public's right to know. Achieving this balance and foundation success may be more challenging in these changing legal times.

Chapter 8
COPYRIGHT, TRADEMARKS, AND PATENTS

Introduction

> To promote the progress of science and useful arts, by securing for limited times to authors and inventors the exclusive right to their respective writings and discoveries.
>
> U.S. Constitution, Article I, Section 8, Clause 8

Federal *copyright* laws control how protected materials may be reproduced and used on campus for teaching, research, and other forms of scholarship. The laws also extend to other forms and developing technologies, including videotapes, computer software, and one of the oldest forms of the arts, music. Often debated are "fair use" educational exemptions and ownership and rights to campus lecture notes.

Trademarks are symbols or marks of an institution or product that serve to identify the institution or product to others. The law gives the user of the symbol a property right in it that can be used to challenge unauthorized use. Names, symbols, and mascots of colleges and universities may be covered by trademark law.

The products of campus research can be protected by *patent* laws, a growing area of concern in this era of growing profit potential. It deals specifically with what discoveries can be owned and by whom.

Copyrights, Copy Wrongs

October 1991

The courts have fired a "shot across the bow" at higher education to protect copyright law against a growing textbook trend: "professor publishing."

For years, Kinko's Graphics Corporation has been preparing in its stores customized anthologies for classroom use. Instructors could excerpt material from books, texts, magazines, newspapers, and other printed sources and the company would photocopy and bind the materials for sale to students.

It was a good deal. Instructors could prepare texts as they wanted them, students could pay less for class readings, and the company made a good business from this arrangement, which it promoted as "less wasteful" and "more economical."

But these arguments didn't convince everyone. "What about copyright laws?" asked the major book publishers. "Aren't the works reprinted in the anthologies protected under the law? Don't instructors have to get permission to use the materials? Doesn't someone have to pay royalties?"

Eight publishers were concerned enough about the answers to these questions that they took the copy company to federal court in 1989, in *Basic Books v. Kinko's Graphics Corporation*, 758 F.Supp 1522 (S.D.N.Y. 1991). They claimed that "substantial portions" of the customized texts were copied without authorization, and they demanded over $1 million in damages.

Background

In 1982, New York University, nine instructors, and an off-campus copy center were sued by copyright holders for printing anthologies and student course packets without permission. That case was settled out of court when NYU agreed to develop and enforce strict policies on copying and using protected materials for classroom and other campus purposes.

That case was an initial attempt to clarify the 1976 Federal Copyright Act. The law allows "fair use" of protected materials, without permission, for limited teaching, scholarship, and research. But it has never been fully determined just what "fair use" means and how the law should be applied.

An early report on the law by the U.S. House of Representatives suggested some guidelines, but these did not carry the force of law. The report noted that "fair use" could include single photocopies for research and teacher preparation and multiple copies for classroom use — if a copyright notice is attached, only one copy is made for each student, the excerpts copied are not significant, and students are only charged copying costs.

The report also tried to establish guidelines for usage based on word counts. Poetry of up to 250 words could be copied. For major texts, 1,000 words or 10% of the text, whichever was less, could also be copied legally without permission. However, the House report conceded that the "fair use" doctrine might allow more copying than this.

After the NYU case, the American Library Association developed a model policy for photocopying to address growing national concerns. Based on a University of Wisconsin policy, the model prescribed a system for campuses to use for copying. The model suggested that:

- Single copies of protected materials could be made for academic purposes

- More extensive text could be copied if the materials were not readily available elsewhere, the materials were to be used once and discarded, and the amount copied was in "reasonable proportion" to the entire work

The ALA guidelines viewed most single copy uses as permissible under the law. But it created different standards for other uses of protected materials. If copies were to be made and *used annually* in instruction, permission should be obtained. The copying of workbooks, tests, and exercises also needed permission, as they were *consumable works* for one-time use. And the ALA guidelines suggested that permission would be needed to create "anthologies."

Like the House report, these guidelines were not created by legislation. However, they were based on interpretations of the law, and they have become the basis for copying policies on many campuses and at other institutions.

Around the same time as the eight publishers were filing suit against Kinko's, the Association of American Publishers and the National Association of College Stores produced their own guidelines for campus copying. Somewhat similar to the ALA model, the industry standards made the following proposals:

- Unauthorized copying should not replace or substitute for anthologies or collective works, whether bound together or available separately.

- Unauthorized copying should not be a substitute for purchase of a book; the unauthorized copying of an entire work or a substantial portion of a work for personal use is illegal.

- The same item cannot legally be copied repeatedly, year after year.

- Campus authorities may not direct or order unauthorized copying.

These industry guidelines were intended to restrict campus interpretations of the "fair use" provisions and to protect the interests of copyright holders.

Case Law and Recent Legislation

Can public colleges and universities be sued for copyright violations? Are they exempt from damages?

In recent years, the U.S. Supreme Court has steered away from the issue. In 1989, it twice refused to hear cases involving claims against campuses. In both cases, one involving UCLA and the other Radford University (VA), courts said the schools were free from liability due to *governmental immunity*.

Copyright holders had sued the schools, claiming damages for unauthorized copying. But U.S. Court of Appeals had rejected their claims. The Eleventh Amendment to the Constitution protects state government and agencies of the state from federal suit. Since copyright laws are federal, are public schools free from the law? Can they copy at will? The Supreme Court didn't provide a clear answer, but Congress recently has.

In 1989, the Copyright Remedy Clarification Act was filed in the House and Senate. It authorized copyright holders to claim damages from schools previously protected by governmental immunity. While higher education was not accused of ignoring copyright law, the Clarification Act would give copyright holders a right of action against possible violators.

Schools and associations objected to the new act as unnecessary, since courts could stop unauthorized use without obtaining damages through injunctions. But copyright holders argued that the threat of damages would be a strong deterrent to state-sponsored unauthorized copying.

In fall 1990, the act passed and was signed into law. Colleges and universities are not subject to suit for damages for copyright violations — at least until they challenge the constitutionality of the new law.

Current Case: Basic Books v. Kinko's

In *Basic Books*, the publishers took on the photocopy company alone and did not name colleges or instructors as defendants. At trial, the copy firm defended its actions, noting that its 440 stores request copyright permission over 13,000 times a month and paid close to $1 million in royalties last year. It argued that the anthologies it copied were for classroom use only and were legal under the "fair use" doctrine.

The instructors whose materials were caught up in the suit say they were surprised to learn that the company hadn't secured copyright permission. According to a "professor publishing" brochure, the company provides "free assistance in obtaining permission to reproduce documents protected by copyright." Most instructors thought that meant the firm would secure needed permissions on their behalf.

But this spring, a federal court disagreed with the company's practices and ruled against its "professor publishing." The judge ordered damages to the plaintiff publishers totaling $510,000, plus court costs. The company was also prohibited from future infringement. The court termed copying of selected protected materials without permission complete frustration of the copyright law, which has been the protection of intellectual property and, more importantly, the encouragement of creative expression.

Summary

The battle continues over fair use of copyrighted materials, but recent legislation and legal decisions clearly point out that campuses must exercise great care in using protected materials. Schools can be held responsible for damages for unauthorized copying — and the law does not protect custom anthologies.

Perhaps the best advice comes from a Kinko's brochure:

> If you are wondering if you need permission on a particular work, chances are you do. Unless you are sure that the "fair use" doctrine applies, it is best to obtain permission.

Reports from various campuses indicate that Kinko's is now more actively showing concern for the copyright law. Instructors and students are complaining about greater inconvenience and higher cost, after years of enjoying a sense of immunity. Copyright permission: it's not just a good idea, it's the law — and higher education isn't above that law.

No Appeal in Copyright Decision

January 1992

There will be no appeal of the Kinko's copyright suit. A federal district court recently ruled that the photocopy company had been reproducing materials at instructor request for classroom use in violation of copyright law. The court said the company failed to seek permission from publishers to use protected materials.

The company claimed that the "fair use" provisions of the 1976 Copyright Act allowed it to make "customized" texts, but the court ruled that the company's interests were commercial, not educational. Kinko's had considered appealing the ruling but instead has agreed to settle the case without further legal proceedings.

The company has agreed to seek publisher authorization in the future for permission to copy protected materials and it will pay a publishing association over $1.8 million in damages and legal fees.

Note: While the Kinko's case was settled in favor of the publishers and copyright protections, in spring 1996 a federal appeals court ruled against those interests in a case involving course pack anthologies. The court ruled that the copying of limited articles for class use was a protected "fair use." An appeal is expected.

Copy Decision Not Duplicated

March 1996

He owned five small photocopy shops in Michigan, in and around Ann Arbor. His business serviced clients from the University of Michigan, Eastern Michigan University, and other schools.

Elsewhere, things had changed since 1991. That's when publishers won a big national legal victory over a major copy service for violating copyright laws. Copy shops everywhere had been preparing course anthologies without authorization, reproducing excerpts from books and entire articles without getting permission or paying any royalties. After a 1991 U.S. District Court decision that found the practice illegal and ordered it halted, many copy shops stopped producing course packets. But the Michigan shop owner kept copying, despite the ruling.

To the surprise of no one, several publishers swiftly sued him. To the surprise of others, he beat them, in *Princeton University Press, MacMillan, Inc. and St. Martin Press, Inc. v. Michigan Document Services, Inc. and Smith*, No. 94-1778 U.S. Court of Appeals, 6th Cir. (1996).

How did this happen? What's next?

Background

In the early 1980s, publishers made their first significant attempt to control the growing practice of photocopying copyrighted materials for educational purposes without permission or royalty payments. In December 1982, nine book publishers sued New York University and several of its faculty members, claiming copyright infringement. The publishers believed that NYU was copying protected materials without authorization and asked the court to stop the practice and order damages.

Campuses around the nation watched the case with great interest, as many were doing similar copying. But before the courts could decide the matter, the publishers and NYU agreed to settle. Under the agreement:

- NYU and the faculty members said they were "troubled that they may have infringed the copyrights of one or more publishers."

- NYU said it would adopt and implement specific rules and procedures to tightly govern photocopying of protected materials by faculty members.

- Faculty and staff at NYU agreed to abide by the new, tight rules.

- The publishers agreed to drop their legal action against them.

The publishers hoped the NYU agreement would help determine a national approach to the issue and "favorably influence the assumption of similar undertakings by other colleges and universities."

The 1990s started with another significant photocopy case. This time, the publishers went after a major company, Kinko's Graphics Corporation. They filed suit in spring 1989, accusing the company of "widespread unauthorized photocopying and sale of portions of the publishers' books, as part of college course anthologies."

After a federal district court ruled in favor of the publishers in March 1991, the parties agreed to settle to avoid further appeals. But unlike the NYU agreement, this settlement cost big money: Kinko's agreed to pay eight publishers $1.875 million in damages and attorney fees.

The federal court ruled that copying excerpts from copyrighted works without permission for sale in bound course anthologies was a clear copyright infringement. The judge delayed a final order to give the parties a chance to settle, which they did months later.

As part of the settlement, Kinko's agreed to abide by the court decision on infringement and acknowledged that it would copy only under established principles:

- Copyright-protected course anthologies can be reproduced and distributed only with permission.

- Use of a work for educational purposes does not justify copying without permission.

- Infringements and copying without prior permission are punishable by substantial damages.

Again, publishers and the Association of American Publishers, Inc., hoped this victory would settle the issue nationally. Copying protected works without authorization was illegal, or so they thought ... until Michigan.

Michigan

After the Kinko's settlement, many copy shops got out of the business altogether; others saw the demand for course books drop significantly. Kinko's gave up copying anthologies, and other national chains set up extensive processes to secure needed permissions before copying materials. Campus bookstores got into the business as well, but most in compliance with the developing law.

The Michigan shop owner stayed in business but made up his own rules. Instead of seeking advance permission to print protected materials and paying appropriate royalties, he copied on demand for faculty and sent a penny a page to the publishers as royalties.

The publishers were not amused. Fresh from the Kinko's victory, they filed suit in Michigan, claiming copyright violation and seeking $600,000 in damages. The publishers maintained that production of course books violated their exclusive rights to the materials. The shop owner claimed his course books were a protected "fair use" of copyright material for educational purposes.

In 1994, the defendant lost by a summary judgment. A federal court ordered him to pay $30,000 and legal fees and to stop copying protected material without prior permission. He quickly filed an appeal.

Early this year, the U.S. Court of Appeals for the Sixth Circuit ruled in favor of the copy shop! It accepted the defendant's argument of "fair use" for educational purposes. The court defined "course packs" as "compilations of various copyrighted and uncopyrighted materials, which may include journal articles, newspaper articles, course notes or syllabi, sample test questions, and excerpts from books."

Under federal law, the copyright holder's monopoly on the materials has an exception for fair use for purposes such as "criticism, comment, news reporting, scholarship, or research." The law establishes four factors for judging fair use:

- The purpose and character of the use, including whether such is of a commercial nature or is for nonprofit educational purposes

- The nature of the copyrighted materials

- The amount and substantiality of the portion issued in relation to the copyrighted work as a whole

- The effect of the use upon the potential market for or value of the copyrighted work

The appellate court applied these standards to the Michigan copy shop and determined its course packs to be protected "fair use."

First, the panel found the ultimate use of the materials to be educational and nonprofit, even though there was a charge for the service.

The court also found that there was "no evidence that the (copied) excerpts in the course packs are so substantial as to supersede the original works." Only a small percentage of each original work was copied, and the instructors said they would not have used the materials if students had to purchase the entire work for one section.

Finally, the court again considered the impact of the photocopying on the market values of the protected works and found no damage.

Said the court:

> Photo reproduction of limited excerpts, even if bound, are poor substitutes for a published work for any use beyond the precise scope of the course. ... It is unlikely that students who wish to build a personal library of books from their college years will retain loosely bound ... course packs. ... Moreover, the students who used the course packs were not a market for the purchase of the original works; the professors

would not otherwise have required students to purchase the original works.

The court, again issuing a summary judgment, ruled the copying a protected "fair use," opening the door for further challenges and an appeal in the Michigan case.

In a dissenting opinion, one judge noted that a generation ago "the notion that it could be 'fair use' for a commercial vendor, acting without authorization from the copyright holder, to copy and sell as much as 30 percent of a copyrighted work of scholarship is a notion that would once have seemed patently absurd." But given to-days technologies, the dissenting justice thought that the notion "at the very least might be the subject of a trial."

Said that judge:

> If the decision in this case stands, and if our sister circuits follow our lead, it seems likely that some academics will find it harder to get their books published. Perhaps these academics will not perish as a result but book publishing ... will clearly have taken a hit, an unfair hit, in any judgment.

The Future of Reproduction

The publishing industry is big business. The photocopy industry is big business as well. Further litigation will follow in the Michigan case and on other challenges to copyrights, as both industries strive to control the material — and the college marketplace.

Making the Permission Process More Efficient

December 1991

In response to concerns and confusion created by the recent Kinko's photocopy case, an interest group has begun an informational advertising campaign aimed at higher education. Produced by the Association of American Publishers, the advertisements encourage faculty members to request copyright permission to use protected materials in class.

To improve the permission request process, publishers note that larger and more computerized request departments have been established to handle more efficiently requests to use protected materials. To expedite the process, the publishers group suggests that instructors:

- *Request permission early,* ideally before other textbooks are ordered, but no later than when orders are placed. This allows publishers time to review requests and gives instructors time to obtain alternative materials if permission is withheld for some reason.
- *Direct requests to publishers,* not authors or others.
- *Include full information* on the source, the materials to be used, copies to be made, the school and course, and when and how the materials will be presented.
- *Specify* exact passages, pages, charts, and illustrations to be used.
- *Request authorization even for works out of print,* as they are still legally protected.
- *Provide the name and address of a contact person* for necessary follow-up. Responses will vary among publishers, but most will provide information on higher education classroom usage and fees on request.

Who Owns Course Lectures?

March 1994

The jury sat through testimony, but trial rules prevented members from taking notes. Some found the rules ironic, since the case dealt with notes from college and university course lectures.

The U.S. District Court jury was told by the University of Florida that a private, off-campus notetaking service violated school copyrights. The company countered that most lectures are recitations of previously known materials, containing little or no original information.

The company filed legal action against the school for damages, saying its opposition had hurt the business. At issue before the court were 23 claims by UF that the company had used protected materials without authorization.

The impact of this dispute is not limited to Florida. The legal and educational implications of commercial notetaking services are being debated at colleges and universities around the country, including Indiana University, Arizona State University, and the University of New Mexico.

What are the issues? How are colleges dealing with them? And what have the courts said in the early decisions?

Indiana University-Bloomington

At IU, a private, off-campus notetaking service began to seek copyright protection for the notes its employees were taking of faculty lectures. The company says the notes are taken by students and, therefore, belong to the students. What use they make of their own notes is up to the students, according to the company.

The firm says the notes serve as a "study aid," not a replacement for attending class. It currently offers lecture notes for more than 25 courses. Costs for lecture summaries range from $2.50 for a single class up to $26.50 for a full semester of notetaking services.

IU recently notified instructors that the notes from their lectures were being sold to students for a profit. Campus officials claim the notes are filled with the work of the instructors and belong to the instructors. But the company contends that the notes represent a student's "interpretation" of the lecture and, as such, belong to the student to use freely. Faculty argue that, if the notes reflected only the student's thoughts, they wouldn't have much retail value.

Unhappy with the commercial sale of class notes, several IU faculty members have offered to participate in a court challenge. They want a court order establishing their ownership of class notes and summaries based on their lectures. But the company sees things quite differently, arguing that there is academic value in their product. According to the company, its services allow students to concentrate on the lectures, not on writing thoughts down on paper.

Arizona State University

At ASU, the price and services are almost the same as at IU. On sale in a local drugstore are class notes from about 50 college classes. The private notetaking service concentrates on large, lower-level undergraduate courses that are often required. The notes even include a full review of what took place in class and any instructor announcements of interest. The service has been in place — and the subject of some controversy — since 1986.

ASU has responded aggressively to the service. The campus student code of conduct prohibits selling class notes. Notetakers who are not registered for a class can be removed from the class by campus security and charged with operating a business without a license.

Angry faculty have also taken on the note-taking service. Some instructors have started providing students with copies of their own notes to take business away from the company. Others have spotted errors on the commercial notes and have based exam questions on the faulty information, placing students who depend on company notes at risk. Campus legal counsel says some instructors are contemplating legal action to halt the practice.

University of Florida

At UF, officials decided to challenge a private notetaking company in court. The off-campus service offers lecture summaries for about 70 popular classes. The commercial notetakers are students enrolled in the courses, paid $50 a class each semester. The student notetakers also receive a percentage from each sale of their products.

After UF sued the service for copyright violations, the company, run by a UF graduate, filed a countersuit, claiming damage to the business.

UF filed suit to protect what it felt was the product and possession of its faculty members. The school has invested over $100,000 in legal costs to pursue the case.

In its suit, UF did not object to all note services, challenging only those operating without the permission of instructors. Faculty had complained that the service was profiting from faculty efforts and enabling students to skip classes without difficulty. Faculty had also expressed concern over the quality of the notes sold to students.

Were the commercial notes protected "property" of the lecturers? The federal jury didn't think so.

It found that lectures were not original materials entitled to copyright protection. Instead, the court held, they were simply recapitulations of publicly known and fixed knowledge, not subject to much interpretation. The court upheld the right of the private company to operate. UF lawyers immediately requested that the judge overturn the verdict and planned for an appeal if needed.

University of New Mexico

At UNM, a service suddenly shut down, leaving employees, landlords, and subscribing students bereft and bewildered. The employed students and those who purchased notes are considering legal action, but they may be afraid of academic retribution. Students fear the faculty's response if they learn students took notes for profit or paid for notes instead of taking their own.

The students may have solid grounds for such fears: one professor has said he'd have "a hard time" writing a positive letter of recommendation for a student who sold notes to others. And because the company operates from another state, the case would have to be filed in federal courts.

Summary

The issues are clear and remain in dispute. Who owns the rights to notes from faculty lectures?

The first court ruling on the issue took the side of the students and the notetakers. But there will be many more rulings to follow before this issue is finally settled. As this story develops ... take note.

Texts, Laws, and Videotapes

June 1990

> *FBI Warning:* Federal law provides severe civil and criminal penalties for the unauthorized reproduction, distribution, and exhibition of copyrighted motion pictures and videotapes.

What do hotel rooms, retirement homes, and campuses have in common? That's what everyone is trying to figure out as higher education continues to struggle with texts, laws, and videotapes. While the issues involving reproduction of printed materials, including texts, maps, graphs, and excerpts, still cause confusion, increased attention is focusing on campus use of videotapes, both commercially prepared and recorded from public broadcasts. Administrators need to review campus policies, in and out of the classroom, to ensure that they're legally appropriate and effective.

Campus Concerns

Videotape technology is rapidly growing on campus. There are few limits to the potential of video programming in education and entertainment — but there are some significant legal considerations.

Most video presentations, whether marketed or recorded from broadcast, are protected under federal copyright laws. The law gives the copyright owner the exclusive right to display, perform, distribute, or copy the work. When campuses and campus organizations want to use copyrighted video materials, that use is controlled by the owner and the law.

The right to "display" a copyrighted work is a most important campus consideration. Protected materials can be used for *private* purposes, not *public*. Use of a copied television movie or commercially prepared rental tape is allowed at home or in other settings limited to family and friends.

Can a classroom be considered comparable to "family and friends"? How about a student union lounge? A residence hall cafeteria? While court cases in this area are limited, the general sense of the law is that such showings would violate copyright laws. Fraternity houses make a separate argument that they are "family and friends," but this claim has not been recognized in law. Classroom use of videotaped materials may be entitled to limited educational exception from the law. Case law and experiences involving hotels and retirement homes can help explain the current state of the law and lead us to some thoughts for campus consideration.

Hotels

The use of videodisc technology was tested in the hospitality industry. A hotel rented videodiscs to guests to view on equipment installed in their rooms. A motion picture company sued, claiming that this presentation of their products violated copyright law. It wanted the practice stopped and asked for damages from the hotel. In *Columbia Pictures v. Professional Real Estate Investors, Inc.*, 866 F.2d 1394 (1988), the court reviewed two key issues: transmission and public presentation.

Under the law, to be a copyrighted transmission some form of a signal needs to be sent out or received. If the program had been "transmitted" in some manner, copyright protection could have been expected. But because the product was on a disc played on site, not broadcast, it wasn't "transmitted," according to copyright law.

But what about "public use"? Is a movie shown on a disc in a hotel room a public showing? The court said no, that such a viewing didn't require copyright action.

The court held that limited presentations to limited audiences in this setting are the equivalent of showing the video to a family.

The *Columbia* decision is often used as legal justification of non-hotel distribution of commercially copyrighted videotapes, such as when libraries and campus organizations collect tapes and loan them out to students and staff for home or residence hall room viewing. There should be regulations to prevent any unauthorized "transmission" of protected materials and to prevent any "public" showing of the materials.

Retirement Homes

In retirement homes, strict enforcement of "public display" standards is on the way out. Copyright holders trying to restrict the use of videotapes in retirement, nursing, skilled care, and similar clinical settings have met with stiff opposition and strong public backlash. Legislators and journalists have criticized industry efforts to block the use of videotapes in care and service facilities. Federal lawmakers have introduced legislation to exempt these facilities from "public display" standards, to allow them to use videotapes without copyright penalties.

Public outcry has provoked industry response as well. At least one major film production company has offered care facilities a license for legal public display of its protected works at a nominal fee, with fee revenues to be donated to charities. The industry wants to protect its markets, but it knows that successful compliance depends on government and public support and that pressure on retirement homes could threaten support from both areas.

Time-Shifting

Modern video technology has made it very easy for equipment owners to copy and save broadcast materials for later or repeated use. This "time-shifting" allows instructors and campus programmers to copy transmitted copyrighted programs for later use. However, because the broadcast materials are protected by copyright, campus use should be regulated.

Broadcasts licensed for distribution may be shown only under the conditions set by the license. Information on the "fair use" status of any production or broadcast can be obtained from the production company. In most educational settings, an exemption from copyright standards exists when the video is presented:

- Free of charge
- In a classroom or other site normally used for teaching
- By a not-for-profit entity
- For the purpose of face-to-face teaching

Educational and fair use of videotapes and videotaped products has been tested in the courts. In the most significant decision, *SONY Corporation of America v. Universal City Studios, Inc.*, 464 U.S. 417 (1984), the motion picture and television industry wanted the courts to prevent distribution of equipment that easily copied protected materials — or to require the equipment manufacturers to compensate them for lost revenues from copyrighted materials. But the court didn't hold the manufacturers responsible for the unauthorized use of their equipment, ruling that the users should be responsible for copyright infringement. The case should serve as a warning to equipment users that copyright laws will be enforced. Programs copied from transmission can be shown on campus only for limited educational and fair use.

What if the program copied is commercially available for purchase or rental through some form of licensing arrangement? A New York State school library recorded broadcast programming and loaned copies for classroom use. The same programs were being marketed for the same use by the production company.

In *Encyclopedia Britannica Educational Corporation v. C.N. Crooks*, 558 F.Supp. 1247 (1983), the state court ordered the library to stop copying and distributing copyrighted materials without permission. It ruled that there was an appropriate licensing arrangement, and that the copyright holder had experienced economic damages. Where materials are available, campus use must conform to the licensing conditions.

The FBI warning is placed on video products and presentations for a reason: to advise users of the consequences of copyright infringement. Sanctions can include injunctions, monetary damages, lost profits, attorney fees, court costs, and statutory damages. To avoid campus videotape copyright problems, consider the following:

- Understand the law. Work with local counsel to prepare a brief question-and-answer fact sheet for faculty, students, and staff.

- Educate the community. Let everyone on campus know what the law says and the implications of violations.

- Adopt campus policies. State your commitment to comply with the law. Make it a violation of campus rules and regulations to improperly present videotaped materials.

- Use the faculty/staff handbook to make employees aware of use restrictions.

- Provide training. Residence halls and student activities staff and student organization programmers should know the law and how to avoid problems.

- Make sure that library policies reflect the needs of copyright protection and that appropriate restrictions are marked on videotapes available for loan.

- Work with campus organizations and housing officials to ensure that they understand and comply with copyright laws.

- Post campus policies on campus equipment, including video recording and playback machines and large-screen monitors.

- Consider entering into licensing agreements for presentation of commercially available products.

- Request permission — in writing and in advance — to use copyrighted materials.

- Limit the use of campus funds or student activity fees to rent videotapes for unauthorized presentations.

"Fair Use" Guidelines Cover Television Programs, Too

June 1993

The world of television has changed dramatically in the last decade. Video cassette recorders have gone from curiosity items to everyday home appliances. Programming has expanded from a few broadcast network affiliates to a seemingly endless myriad of cable choices. College instructors can take advantage of broadcast or cable programming for classroom educational purposes — if they follow some simple rules.

Broadcast and cable programming is copyright protected material. The re-use of television programming is restricted under the same laws that regulate photocopying and distribution of protected printed materials.

Generally, protected materials cannot be reproduced without permission. But the law provides a limited exception for educational purposes, allowing instructors to make "fair use" of protected materials, like television programs or cable programs, in their individual classrooms.

In the late 1970s, after passage of the latest federal copyright law, a committee of legislators, educators, copyright holders, and others gathered to establish guidelines for the academic use of broadcast materials. The guidelines attempted to define permissible "fair use" of television programming and clarify areas of confusion.

The committee members believed it was important for educators to understand the restrictions on the recording, retention, and use of television programming. Today, the guidelines provide standards for those who own and those who use copyright-protected television materials.

Before recording, saving, or using a videotape of a television broadcast for educational purposes, consider the following:

- The guidelines governing "fair use" for educational purposes apply only to not-for-profit institutions. Others must seek advance authorization and may have to pay rebroadcast fees.

- Programs recorded for institutional use should be retained for no more than 45 days. The guidelines allow educators to use the programs they record in the classroom at a later time. But they do not permit the retention of videotaped programs for *unlimited* future use. They expect users to erase or record over copied programs at the end of the 45 days.

- Generally, recorded programs may be shown once by a teacher in a course. They can be repeated once for teaching reinforcement, but the second showing should occur within 10 days of the first one.

- Schools should record broadcasts only at the specific request of the instructor who intends to use the program for specific teaching purposes. Schools should not tape programs for general future use that is not specifically defined.

- Any individual program should be recorded only once for any individual teacher's use, regardless of how many times the same program is rebroadcast.

- The school may make a limited number of copies of the videotape for legitimate teaching purposes. The "fair use" guidelines, however, apply to all copies of the videotape.

- After the program is used for teaching and reinforcement, it may be used again only for teacher review and future application consideration. For example, a teacher could review a videotaped program after classroom use to consider adding it to the curriculum. However, future use would require authorization from the copyright holder.

- Instructors don't have to use recorded materials in their entirety. But the portions used may not be altered in any way.

- Recorded programs cannot be physically or electronically combined to make an "anthology" or compilation for class use.

- All copies of broadcast materials intended for classroom use must include the copyright notice broadcast on the original program.

- Educational institutions are expected to establish policies to protect television programming copyrights and to control educational "fair use."

Television today offers instructors a wealth of information, often presented in an exciting and entertaining manner that will grab students' attention. But you don't want to attract the wrong kind of attention from copyright holders. So make sure you know and follow the "fair use" guidelines.

Pirates on Campus: The Dangers of Sharing Software

July 1994

> To promote the progress of science and useful arts, by securing for limited times to authors and inventors the exclusive right to their respective writings and discoveries.
>
> U.S. Constitution, Article I, Section 8, Clause 8

Using two computer workstations at MIT, a college student allegedly established a computer bulletin board system that is now subject of a federal indictment. A grand jury has recommended action against the student on charges of wire fraud.

The computer network apparently allowed users to distribute and use copyright-protected software without a license. The network also made copies of the software and allowed them to be shared with others on the system, i.e., with people all over the world. The system included programs from games to word processing. According to the FBI, the copyright-protected materials available for general use were worth at least $1 million.

Software piracy is a growing legal concern, with some companies estimating they lose 30% to 50% of potential revenues to unauthorized copies — over $12 billion — each year. Every computer on campus has an ability to make and store perfect copies of protected programs. Industry attempts to safeguard against illegal use through locking systems made software difficult to use and were abandoned several years ago.

To protect a campus or student organization from piracy charges, college and university software users need to understand licenses and know what to do if accused of copyright violations. As is often the case, education is the best form of campus protection!

Software Licenses

Generally, consumers don't buy software for use, even though they think they do. They purchase a license allowing them to use the product. Software is provided to consumers and end users in this manner for a specific reason. By only licensing software, a vendor is permitted to establish restrictions on the product's future use and duplication, which would be more difficult or impossible if the software were actually owned by a user. The software distributors hold the copyright, an "exclusive" right to control its use and distribution, which they do through licensing.

Programs purchased for campus or personal use generally provide limited authorizations and restrictions on use. License agreements limit the number of copies that can be made, prohibit program derivatives or modifications, and prohibit use of the software on more than one computer. They also usually restrict the transfer of the license to others, except under strict control of the license. And the agreements remind users that they are purchasing only a "use" license, not actual ownership in the software. No proprietary rights are transferred to a purchaser. Users of the license are advised that the license is subject to immediate termination if they violate any terms of the license.

License arrangements may also deal with exclusive uses (i.e., personal or business use only) or computer networks with different fees and conditions for different levels of usage. The large, boldface type on the software box usually reads: "Please Carefully Read This Document Before Opening This Package!" This is the license and it should be read! When you break the seal, you have agreed to abide by all of the terms. No signature is required — just opening of the product and subsequent use. So when it says "Read," you should read it!

When Problems Arise

Software experts note that protected programs "have an uncanny way of multiplying" and getting onto hard drives. Unlicensed software is almost everywhere, and can get there intentionally and unintentionally. But intent doesn't matter — licensing does! Your campus or organization can be viewed as a software "pirate," either when protected programs are copied to save money or when an employee "shares" programs with another worker. Both acts are illegal and could result in a visit by the "software police."

National and international software developers have now joined forces to protect their copyrights and battle the pirates. They have formed professional organizations to elicit tips on illegal software usage and investigate the allegations. The two primary organizations, the Software Publishers Association and the Business Software Alliance, say they get dozens of calls a day reporting violations in business, industry, and service organizations. The tips may come from unhappy employees, part-time/temporary help, or visiting computer representatives and technicians.

How do these firms respond to complaints about campus software use? Generally, the "software police" will react with:

- *A cease-and-desist Letter* — This informs an organization that it must immediately stop using any and all unlicensed software. Receipt of this type of letter gives a school or organization an opportunity to get in compliance without further actions. Infringing copies, if any, should be removed from computer units.

- *An audit request* — The enforcement organizations may request an opportunity to do an on-site inspection of computers, software, and back-up documentation. They will want to inspect hardware and software and review license and purchasing documents to ensure that only authorized software is in use.

- *A lawsuit* — At any time, a computer software copyright holder can file suit against an alleged infringer. Particularly vulnerable are those that don't respond or cooperate with "cease and desist" letters or audit requests.

There is not much you can do if your organization or institution is caught with unlicensed software. Most experts suggest full cooperation in the audit process to get a complete inventory of software use, a careful examination of purchasing documents, and a review of existing licensing agreements.

Important defenses to unauthorized use allegations include copies of license agreements, registration cards, original disks, user manuals, and original sales receipts. Most audits in which unauthorized software use is found or in which there is subsequent litigation result in *settlement negotiations*. Generally, the enforcement units seek compensation of up to twice the retail value of the software discovered to be in illegal use on campus or in the organization. The actual settlement can vary, depending on the amount and type of unauthorized software discovered and its level of use.

Avoiding Problems

A visit from the "software police" can be unpleasant and costly for a campus or organization. To avoid these problems, colleges and universities are urged to do the following:

- *Adopt a strong anti-piracy policy.* Advise employees and students that illegal sharing of protected software will not be tolerated.

- *Educate the campus community.* Advise members about appropriate use of software and what uses are illegal. Education can promote awareness. Use letters, memos, newsletters, student and staff guidebooks, and other training methods to share the message that "sharing" is not allowed.

- *Enforce policies.* Ensure that action is taken when unauthorized software or its use is discovered.

- *Keep track of software.* Do this to accurately know what software is installed and is in use on site, and to make sure that it is properly documented and authorized.

- *Conduct audits and self-studies.* Do this to make sure that campus organization and license agreements are being followed.

Software is copyright-protected under the law, and collegiate users are permitted to use the programs only under the terms and conditions established by licensing agreements. Users who read the terms and comply should be applauded. Those who don't are placing their campuses and organizations at great risk!

Battle of Dictionaries Holds Lessons for Campuses

January 1992

Merriam-Webster, Inc., publishes *Webster's Ninth New Collegiate Dictionary*. Since 1973, it has had a red cover with the word "Webster's" printed in white on the spine. Then, Random House, Inc., began publishing *Webster's College Dictionary*. It has a red cover; printed in white on the book's spine is the word "Webster's."

Merriam-Webster sued Random House, claiming trademark violations. At issue was the similar name and appearance of the two products. Is the newer product named and packaged in a manner designed to confuse consumers and therefore profit unlawfully?

Names, slogans, and symbols can all receive protection under a federal law reserving their use to individuals or groups that register the marks. Colleges and universities, and their related organizations, can both use and abuse trademarks. Schools can register their symbols for use or licensing. And organizations on and off campus can infringe on trademarks when they use, without authorization, names or symbols that are protected. Campuses and campus organizations need to understand trademark law to protect their names and symbols and to avoid the risks of infringements.

Trademarks have long been recognized in English common law, which is the foundation for the American legal system. The establishment of a trademark created a property right that the holder can protect by court action.

In the United States, the power to regulate trademarks is implicit in the Commerce Clause of the Constitution (Article I, Section 8). It gives Congress the power "to regulate Commerce with foreign nations and among the several states." A federal system for establishing and controlling trademarks did not develop until 1870, and then only as part of a patent and copyright law revision. The laws establish an exclusive right to the person registering a mark to control that mark. Wrongful use by others can be addressed in civil actions.

Descriptive Names Not Protected

An early trademark case set several standards in the law over the use of names. A company that marketed a product called "Coco-Quinine" sued a manufacturer who later began selling the same product under the name "Quin-Coco." In *Warner v. Lilly*, 265 U.S. 526 (1924), the Supreme Court ruled:

> A name which is merely descriptive of the ingredients, qualities or characteristics of an article of trade cannot be appropriated as a trademark and the exclusive use of it afforded legal protection. The use of a similar name by another to truthfully describe his own product does not constitute a legal or moral wrong, even if its effect be to cause the public to mistake the origin or ownership of the product.

Therefore, a name that only describes the product cannot be protected from use by others.

The use of descriptive names was also explored in an early case, *Canal Co. v. Clark*, 80 U.S. 311 (1871). At issue was the use of the word combination "Lackawanna Coal" as a trademark. A company claimed ownership of the phrase for their products, but other companies in the region sued, claiming the phrase was merely descriptive and, as such, should be available to all.

The court ruled that the name should be free from trademark restrictions. It said that the company "has no right to appropriate a sign or a symbol, which, from the nature of the fact it is used to signify, others may employ with equal truth, and therefore have an equal right to employ for the same purpose."

Can confusion over names create unfair competition? That's been considered often, in cases involving music companies, food products, and restaurants. In *Cleveland Opera Co. v. Cleveland Civic Opera Association*, 22 Ohio App. 400 (1964), the court said that "a generic word or geographic designation cannot become an arbitrary trademark, [but] it may nevertheless be used deceptively by a newcomer to a field so as to amount to the unfair competition." This supports the principle that the use of words in public use, including names and places, can be unlawful if intentionally used to create confusion.

Who owns or controls the name of an organization like "Metropolitan Opera"? One group used the name without the permission of the association using that name and produced record albums of "inferior" quality. In *Metropolitan Opera Association, Inc. v. Wagner-Nichols Recording Corp.*, 107 N.Y.S. 2d 795 (1951), the association sued, claiming trademark violation. According to the suit, the corporation tried to "appropriate and trade on the name and reputation" of another and did so to mislead the public. Courts have long protected the right to exclusively own a name and reputation for commercial purposes. Thus, when one firm takes the name of another to mislead consumers, it violates trademark laws.

Most trademark cases are based on confusion. Usually, this comes about when:

- It is likely that consumers will believe that goods from one party are the products of another, and this is intentional
- Consumers cannot be sure who is the source for a product or service

Campuses need to make sure that they use names appropriately, not infringing on the trade names or marks of others.

Loss of Word to Public Use

In the current dictionary case, the two rival publishers did not argue over who had the right to use the name "Webster." Why not? Because of its common use in today's language, the name is no longer protected. It is said to be in the public domain and free to be used by everyone. At some point in the past, it may have been protected, but over time it became part of everyday, common language to define a dictionary and therefore lost its protected status.

The best examples of this in early trademark law are the words "aspirin," "cellophane," and "thermos." Each word was developed by a product manufacturer and used to market the product. In each case, the product name became synonymous with the actual product. The public lost track of the fact that they were only trade names.

For example, acetylsalicylic acid was a product. "Aspirin" was the name it was given by one manufacturer. But the consuming public's use of the name cost the firm its exclusive trade name, in *Bayer v. United Drug Co.*, 272 F.505 (1921). Aspirin became a generic term for all similar products, not just that of one manufacturer.

The trade names "cellophane" and "thermos" suffered similar fates in *DuPont Cellophane Co. v. Waxed Products Co.*, 85 F.2d 75 (1936) and *King Seeley Thermos Co. v. Aladdin Industries, Inc.*, 321 F.2d 577 (1963). In both cases, public understanding of the words replaced generic descriptions of the products. The name given to the product by one manufacturer eventually became the name for all similar products. Once it becomes a "household word," its protection under the law is lost.

Holders of trade names and trademarks must take steps to avoid losing their protected status to the public domain. They must continually educate the public on the fact that the name or symbol is protected, and that it is a trade name; holders must halt unauthorized use to prevent products from becoming household words.

This is not ancient law, pulled from dusty law books. Today, manufacturers who have skillfully marketed their products and popularized their names must take steps to protect them from becoming available for others as public domain. Examples: you don't make a "Xerox" of something, you make a photocopy of it. "Xerox" is the trade name of a major product manufacturer. And if you have a cold, you do not need a "Kleenex," you need a facial tissue. "Kleenex" is a trade name for a product, not the name of that product.

For colleges and universities, understanding of the law is needed to prevent problems. Campuses should avoid using trade names for product names and take steps to protect school names and symbols from becoming household words available in the public domain. The Webster family probably wishes it had taken steps long ago to preserve its family name and product under the law.

Books Can Be Judged by their Covers!

Can a product be packaged or designed in such a way as to violate the law? Certainly — as is often the case in infringements on products with college and university logos.

The law on cases of this type was considered several decades ago in *In re Swift and Company*, 223 F.2d 950 (1955). Two companies had similar products, and the newer manufacturer packaged its product in a manner similar to earlier products. The court held that "a definite and lasting impression [can] be created by the use of the design ... whereby the average consumer will regard it as an unmistakably certain, and primary means of indemnification pointing distinctly to the commercial origin of the product."

So where packaging is distinctly identifiable as the packaging of one manufacturer, it can be given a protected status.

Two Remedies Are Available

Under the law, there are two basic actions courts can take against infringers: *injunctions* and *cash awards*.

Injunctions are used by courts to halt infringement actions. A temporary injunction can be ordered before trial when the court sees the likelihood of irreparable harm and there is some merit to the plaintiff's contentions. A more permanent injunction can be ordered as the result of a trial or judicial decision on the issues. An injunction generally is an order to halt a practice, such as the use of a name or symbol that is protected. An injunction order can also require further steps to avoid confusion and deception, such as corrective advertising, changed product labels, or altered marketing strategies.

Money can be used by courts as a remedy for *damages* and *lost profits*. Damages can be awarded when the unauthorized use of a trade name or trademark causes financial loss. A plaintiff must prove that losses were suffered from the infringement, from factors such as loss of business or injury to reputation. Any profits from unauthorized use of a trademark or trade name belong to the owner of the name or mark. The court can order an accounting of the profits to make sure the holder gets his profits. Cash remedies are generally awarded only when the defendant's infringement is deemed to be willful or in bad faith; in other words, some responsibility to protect a trademark rests with the trademark's holder.

Since the word "Webster's" was already in the public domain, the publishers went to court arguing over the combination of several words and the packaging. The use of the word "College" with "Webster's" and "Dictionary" created concerns about two books printed with red and white covers.

Random House had previously published a *College Dictionary*, but it decided to add "Webster's" to the title to better compete with others who already had the name on their products. But Merriam-Webster cried foul. For almost 20 years, it had printed *Webster's Collegiate Dictionary*, and it argued that customer confusion was likely and intentional. Merriam-Webster asked the court to issue an injunction against Random House's *College Dictionary* and award damages.

And that's just what a federal district court jury recently did in New York. It ruled that Random House had violated Merriam-Webster's trade name and trademarks, and it awarded $2.3 million in compensatory and punitive damages.

Summary

Trademarks and names have long been recognized in law as having a protected status. Colleges and universities must:

- Understand the law.
- Register names and symbols.
- Protect existing trade names and marks from infringement.
- Avoid infringements on the names or marks of others.

High Stakes Draw Campuses Into Patent Wars

September 1990

Colleges and universities have entered into a new arena of competition: patents. It takes just a few statistics to tell the tale. The number of patents issued to colleges and universities has grown dramatically in recent years. It has become a multimillion dollar industry for colleges and universities.

But as campuses race to enter this technology and invention sweepstakes, those already in the game are experiencing the "joys" of patent law. In past years, several significant patent legal cases have been filed. For example:

- The University of Pennsylvania sued one of its leading research professors over rights to a profitable skin medication.
- Harvard University (MA) is suing a drug manufacturing firm in Sweden over rights to a biomedical product.
- Most recently, the University of California has sued a major American pharmaceutical firm over the rights to a new type of insulin.

In each case, the key question is the same: Who owns the rights to profit from inventions? While the courts consider this issue, campuses are left to contend with a larger, related question: What will be the impact of this new wave of capitalism on the academic-research community?

Two factors worked together in the 1980s to draw more and more campuses into the patent process: potential revenues and government deregulation of funded campus discoveries. During the past decade, as campus budgets continually tightened, new revenue sources became more critical. Initial successes in the marketing of campus discoveries — such as the University of Florida's "Gatorade" — led others to pursue discoveries with financial prospects.

This new interest in initiative developed around the same time the federal government adopted new guidelines concerning the ownership of discoveries. Prior to 1980, campus patent discoveries developed using federal funds were owned by the government. But that year, in an effort to improve our nation's standing in international commerce, Congress gave colleges and universities rights to their federally funded discoveries in the future.

The intent was to foster further and faster development for the public benefit. And that's occurring — with some profitable consequences and resulting legal entanglements.

Background

U.S. patent law is as old as the nation itself, with the first patent acts passed 200 years ago. The Constitution calls for the federal government to "promote the progress of science and useful arts," and the patent system is designed to serve that purpose.

Research, development, and innovation are rewarded through patents. The law works on behalf of the public and nation in several ways:

- It encourages invention and investment of private capital in research and development by offering rewards to inventors and supporters.
- It advances further development and marketing of products. The patent owner has the right, for a limited time, to exclude others from making, using, or selling the product or process.
- It promotes early disclosure of information that might otherwise be kept secret. Release of this information limits the waste of duplicate efforts and resources and allows others to work on advancing, not recreating, progress.
- It provides for a means of exchange of information within and out of the country with adequate protected interests.

Colleges and universities are now beginning to significantly benefit from these advantages of patent law. Campus research and development can advance the interests of both society and the academic community — and generate much-needed revenues.

Basics of Patent Law

In moving into the patent arena, it's important for campus officials and researchers to understand the basics of patent law. Relatively unchanged for 130 years, the patent system defines inventions, provides a process for recording them, establishes rights for patent holders, and sets penalties for infringers.

Patents can be issued for *inventions* and *processes*. An invention is a discovery, while a process is a method of manufacture, composition of matter, or material. The patent is issued to "whoever invents or discovers" an innovation, process, or product.

Campuses and campus research foundations generally have well-defined policies on the ownership of patents granted for campus-based or campus-supported work. A patent will be issued to a discoverer unless the invention or process was previously known in this country, previously patented, or described in a publication (American or foreign) prior to the claimed invention. The individual who invented the subject matter must submit the patent application.

A patent contains a short title of the invention and "a grant to the patentee, his heirs and assigns, for the term of seventeen years ... [of] the right to exclude others from making, using, or selling the invention." A copy of the product or process drawings and specifications is also attached to the patent.

Patent infringements are subject to civil court actions. Courts are advised to issue injunctions where necessary to protect the rights of patent holders. Those found to have unlawfully infringed on valid patents are liable for damages and, in exceptional cases, attorney's fees as well. Damages awarded, according to the Patent Act, should be "adequate to compensate for the infringement, but in no event less than a reasonable royalty for the use made ... by the infringer, together with interests and costs as fixed by the court."

Campus Issues

The campus impact of increased patent filings can be measured in two ways: through the advancement of knowledge and through enhanced revenues. In both areas, there are serious concerns and problems.

The "technology transfer" push, from campus to marketplace, has dramatically increased the number of patents issued to campuses. But it may be having a negative effect on the collegiality of the academic community. Concerns exist that the push to develop marketable products for their revenue value will be at the expense of other research with pure academic value. The failure of two University of Utah researchers to release data on a reported cold fusion breakthrough last year is a good example of the "profit first" mentality that many fear may be creeping onto campus.

To remind campuses of their roots, the National Science Foundation in 1989 issued an "important notice" to campus presidents. The NSF message was direct and to the point: there's a need for "open scientific communication" and researchers must continue to share ideas, research, and discoveries.

But secrecy is inherent in research designed to produce patents and marketable products. While the patent system was designed to transfer technology for society's benefit, potential profitability has been and will remain an important motive, on and off campus.

And with potential profit comes the likelihood of litigation. As more schools attempt to move into the million-dollar-a-year royalty category, legal disputes over patent ownership are likely to increase. The UPenn, Harvard, and University of California cases are good examples of the potential legal difficulties in this area.

Three sets of concerns are entangled in campus patent cases: the rights of schools, the rights of researchers, and the rights of private enterprise. As money divides former allies, they call on the courts to settle their disputes.

UPenn took one of its leading professors to court over the rights to a skin care product invented years ago. Neither the school nor the researcher expressed much interest in the patent rights of the product as a medication. But when it was discovered that the cream removed wrinkles and would be highly profitable, a new mentality took over. The school sued the professor over the product rights, which he'd sold to the Johnson & Johnson personal care products firm.

Harvard filed suit in federal court against Pharmacia, a Swedish pharmaceutical giant, for infringing on a school patent. At issue is the sale of kits used to determine the materials of genetic structures. Harvard claims to hold rights to the process, and it says the company's sale of products violated the school's patent.

University of California has taken one of America's largest pharmaceutical companies, Eli Lilly and Company, into court. The school has charged the company with violating patents the school holds on the manufacturing of a new genetically engineered insulin.

In all three cases, the schools are doing what all patent holders eventually have to do: defending themselves against infringers or alternative inventors. The decisions in these cases, and cases expected to follow, will inform higher education on the need to balance patent-related research with patent law.

Campuses need to examine current policies to ensure that all involved in the "discovery chain" understand and agree to their role, that all understandings are complete and recorded, and that resources are available to secure and defend campus patents. Patents can advance knowledge, with benefits to both society and the campus — if handled properly.

Chapter 9
SAFETY AND SECURITY

Introduction

> A university has a duty of reasonable care to protect a student against certain dangers, including criminal actions against a student by another student or a third party if the criminal act is reasonably foreseeable and within the university's control.
>
> *Nero v. Kansas State University*, 861 P.2d 768 (1993)

Crime is a reality in our society and, unfortunately, on college campuses. A series of significant cases has questioned the extent to which a college or university is responsible for crime on campus. Liability has been found in instances in which the crime was foreseeable.

In addition to significant case law, there has been a recent trend toward legislatively mandated crime reporting and awareness standards, both from the state and federal government.

Among today's campus concerns are assaults, threats, disruptive actions, access to residence halls, control of personal property, search and seizure, and surveillance.

Time for a Crime Prevention Audit

March 1990

Concern about campus crime can be found everywhere today. Newspaper headlines chronicle the latest assault or theft, orientation programs stress commonsense personal safety protections, and state legislators demand release and publication of campus crime data. It may be time for a crime prevention audit.

Several publications have focused on campus crime, suggesting steps for greater safety. These checklists can help responsible administrators examine today's campus to prevent tomorrow's crime.

Plan for Security Review

In *Hospital and College Security Liability* (Hanrow Press, 1987), authors Leonard Territo and Max L. Bromley recommend a three-point campus security review. They advise administrators to consider the following areas:

- *State government and professional organizations*, like the International Association of Campus Law Enforcement Administrators, *establish standards for campus law enforcement*. When developing security forces, campus officials need to understand governmental and professional standards as well as campus needs.

- *Criminal activity information.* Campuses should review crime data from the past two years, examining *prevalence* and *patterns*. Security measures should be adjusted based on the review results. Data should also inform educational efforts, to keep the campus population aware and alert.

- *Physical security and design.* Territo and Bromley recommend constant attention to the physical environment, with special monitoring for lighting, groundskeeping, residence hall security, emergency phone systems, and construction projects.

Lighting standards have been established by the Illuminating Engineering Society of North America. The Society has designed safety and health standards for classrooms, cafeterias, residence halls, building entrances, parking lots, and recreational facilities. Failure to follow established professional standards can raise liability concerns.

Failure to maintain a responsible *groundskeeping* program can also contribute to crime — and liability. Shrubs, hedges, and greenery, if improperly maintained or placed, detract from attractiveness and can create opportunities for crime. Periodic groundskeeping surveys are recommended, with careful records of survey results and corrective actions.

One major area of concern remains the *residence halls*, where student lifestyles have not promoted secure environments. The need for controlled access to residential areas is becoming more apparent.

While no security review or preventative audit can eliminate campus crime, steps can be taken to reduce its incidence and severity. One response has been the installation of *emergency telephone systems*. Business and pay phones are "of limited value" when speed is important, and there is a trend toward direct-response emergency phones at key campus locations.

To improve overall security and hold down costs, safety planning should be included in any campus *construction projects*. There should be a good-faith effort to make the campus facilities as safe, through design, as possible.

The specifics of some recommendations in *Hospital and College Security Liability* are covered in two other recent guides: *Sexual Assault on Campus: What Colleges Can Do* (Santa Monica Hospital Medical Center, 1988) and *Crime and Campus Police: A Handbook for Police Officers and Administrators* (College Administration Publications, 1989). Both provide good checklists for campus crime prevention audits.

Residence Halls

Sexual Assault on Campus suggests the need for a campus "task force responsible for reviewing crimes on campus and implementing ways to prevent dangerous situations." The guide also reprints, from a 1987 University of California report, a list of tips to reduce the likelihood of student victimization in the residence halls. Among the suggestions:

- 24-hour, card-entry control system for the main doors of each residence hall
- Self-locking doors on each residential room
- Front desk staffing in each residence hall lobby from midnight to 6 a.m.
- Periodic external and internal building patrols by security.
- Hiring of extra students to increase first floor entry control and floor monitoring, particularly on weekends
- Placement of "card readers" inside buildings at key access points

Security Personnel

Crime and Campus Police offers a valuable checklist of "campus policing concerns." Among the considerations identified by author M.C. Smith as being important for a competent campus police force:

Selection. Careful screening and testing of candidates is required today. Educational standards have increased, with many departments now requiring a college degree as a minimum standard.

Training. Training with state or municipal police agencies is recommended. Some form of continuing training should also be required for officers already in service.

Jurisdictional issues. Full understanding of the extent and boundaries of legal authority is necessary to prevent errors that could impede effectiveness.

Protocols. Written procedures for dealing with other law enforcement agencies are important.

Policies. Procedures are necessary to ensure safe and responsible law enforcement in matters involving arrests, firearms, searches, and pursuits. Policies should be widely distributed and updated regularly.

Supervision. Proper management is needed to ensure that security work is performed in a competent and professional manner.

Oversight and support. A senior campus official is recommended as the appropriate oversight individual. Among his or her duties should be improving cooperation between the unit and other campus operations.

Educational programs. Campus security departments should be committed to programs designed to educate the population and help modify behaviors. Joint programming with academic units is recommended.

Other Considerations

Evening hours and weekends — "low-traffic times" — present special concerns for campus safety and security. Campus workers need to be particularly alert if working during off-hours, and security personnel should take extra precautions on their behalf, such as checking to ensure that appropriate doors are secure.

Security should also be an issue in *scheduling classes*. Night classes should be centralized in high-traffic areas or patrol activity increased in response to the potential for crime. *Student patrols and escorts* can increase the presence and perception of security on campus, if aides are well-selected and trained to perform limited functions.

In addition, academic institutions should take advantage of their training and expertise to promote *crime prevention training* for students and staff. Classes, workshops, group presentations, newsletters, brochures, and films can help reduce the risks of and opportunities for crime.

Checklists, such as those found in *Hospital and College Security Liability*, *Sexual Assault on Campus*, and *Crime and Campus Police*, offer a framework for ensuring a safe environment for students, faculty, staff, and visitors and for reducing liability. Use of checklists can enhance the campus safety plan if consideration is given periodically to important areas of potential problems.

Security audit programs and checklists stress the need for basic *cooperation* and *communication*. A task force — composed of public safety, physical plant, space planning, academic and student affairs, and legal counsel — should be charged with performing an audit of campus safety and developing an action plan to reduce the potential for campus crime. More needs to be done to prevent crime, to properly respond to crime and its victims, and to promote campus cooperation and communication. Conducting a security review using checklists and forming a task force are two important first steps toward ensuring a safe and secure campus environment for all.

Making Campuses "Smart" Havens for Safety

July 1992

The truth hurts. Headlines and real life experiences of college students have painfully taught us that colleges and universities are not "safe havens" from crime. All too often, unfortunately, the lessons are learned by students, campuses, and communities the hard way: after they've become victims of crime.

While college campuses might never be safe havens, they can become "smart havens" with the right combination of commitment and concern. Recently, a New York state legislative task force studied issues related to the safety of women on campus. It researched the issues and held open forums in an effort to learn how to combat crime on campus. Its report noted that the task force's efforts were "not an end, but a beginning, to achieving greater safety for women attending or working at colleges."

The final report recommended that colleges and universities respond by re-examining three areas:

- Security and crime prevention measures
- Victim assistance and support systems
- Safety and security education efforts

In each area, the task force developed a series of recommendations that may be applied to campuses around the country. They provide a good framework for establishing a safety "smart haven" and for evaluating current campus crime prevention and awareness programs.

When considering *security and crime prevention* measures, campuses should consider a variety of actions:

- Expanding sexual assault training for security personnel and retraining them regularly
- Improving coordination with local police agencies when responding to assaults
- Assisting in the formation of student escort services
- Making sure that residence hall security systems are effective
- Increasing campuses' exterior lighting
- Supplementing security patrols in dark or less-traveled areas
- Installing or expanding emergency telephone systems
- Remaining aware of the needs of students with disabilities

These measures place emphasis on efforts to diminish opportunities for crime to occur. Some require significant capital or operating financial support, but others are more economical. The improvement of lighting, the development of "blue light" telephone systems, and the establishment and support of a student escort service, for example, may well assist a campus unable to fund increased security patrols or expanded staff training.

Women's Security Deserves Attention

Of particular concern are the security needs of women. In focusing on their safety and security, the training of security personnel is critical. They must be prepared to respond swiftly and appropriately to the needs of victims, the campus, and on- and off-campus prosecutors.

Campuses understand that even the most exhaustive commitment to crime prevention and personal safety awareness cannot prevent all crime. So campuses that are realistic will make sure they are more than adequately prepared to deal with the human consequences of crime. That's why *victims' assistance and support services* are vital.

The legislative task force recommended a series of steps for college and university consideration when responding to the victims of campus crime:

- Establishment of a campus intervention plan involving all appropriate units and an advocate for the victim
- Immediate medical and psychological treatment by trained professionals sensitive to victim needs
- Provision of, or referral to, long-term counseling care, as needed
- Access to appropriate legal advice and consultation, to facilitate reporting and prosecution on and off campus
- Training for members of the campus community likely to come in contact with sexual assault victims, to help prevent further trauma and maximize chances for recovery
- Wide distribution of a written policy on campus response to sexual assault cases, highlighting victim rights and investigation and disciplinary procedures

In sum, these measures are intended to protect the victims of campus crime to the fullest possible extent.

Campuses need to develop a victims' assistance program, make sure it's widely known to the campus community, and make sure it meets the needs of victims. Thorough preparation by the campus will lead to the most effective response. The victim needs support to promote recovery, while the campus needs to act to prevent further crime and to pursue appropriate punishment against offenders.

Education: A Crucial Component

It should come as no surprise that *education* is recommended as a key component in efforts to provide a safer environment for all, particularly women. The state task force worked with students, security personnel, student affairs staffs, and others in their review and recommended several steps campuses can take to combat crime through education:

- Messages to students that sexual assaults are felonies that will be fully prosecuted, on and off campus

- Mandatory orientation programs on sexual violence, campus policies, and victim support efforts

- A series of programs to educate students as part of the curriculum, with an emphasis on workshops and symposia

- Increased efforts to encourage victims to report campus crimes, and a review of reporting systems to reduce the reluctance to report crimes

- A focus on the extent to which alcohol and drugs contribute to sexual assaults and other crimes

- Promotion of peer education

- Development of campus women's centers and clearinghouses for information on campus violence

- Presidential recognition, through award programs and media acknowledgments, of organizations committed to making campuses safer

- Involvement of campus organizations and state systems or coalitions in the education of campus leaders on the issues

The focus on education helps the campus understand crime in all its tragic implications. A campus population with an understanding of crime will be a safer population.

Through safety and security measures, victim assistance and support systems, and greater education, campuses can combat crime and become "smart havens."

Securing the Campus

December 1993

The basketball players say they were arrested by campus police due to an avoidable misunderstanding involving a language problem with a foreign student. They feel they were falsely arrested. On another campus, the search of campus property by public safety concluded with the involved students claiming unlawful search and seizure. Elsewhere, a student claims that a campus security guard "roughed him up" during an arrest. He claims police brutality. And on yet another campus, a high-speed chase involving campus public safety and local law enforcement comes to an end on the campus. The students' concern: possible accidents involving bystanders.

In the performance of their duties, campus security personnel face a variety of challenges. They are often at risk of personal injury, and yet they are equally subject to charges of misconduct. The response, or lack of response, by public safety officers to incidents on college campuses can often place the school and employee in a liability concern situation. False arrests, illegal searches and seizures, use of unnecessary force, and high speed chases by campus security can all lead to legal action.

Students who feel they have been mistreated, or even injured, due to the conduct of campus law enforcement personnel may turn to the courts for support and damages. Generally, the courts will look to see if the campus had or assumed a duty or responsibility, violated that duty, and, as a result, caused harm. Where these conditions are found, an officer and an institution may be held responsible.

Arrests

Arrests on college campuses can be made only under specific circumstances. A campus law enforcement officer with the authority to make arrests may do so only when:

- A judge has issued a warrant based on "probable cause"

- The officer has "probable cause" that a serious crime has been committed

- A minor crime has been committed in front of the officer

Consideration must also be given to the various elements that constitute crime, as established in state or federal law. Many require a judgment that the offender acted with the knowledge that a law was being violated or that the act in question was deliberate.

"False arrest or imprisonment" (denying a freedom to leave) charges arise on campus when an arrest is claimed to be invalid and unlawful. Criminal charges can be brought against individual officers for false arrest, and civil damage suits may be filed against officers and institutions involved in false imprisonment.

Searches

Campus searches of students and residence halls, have always been a hot debate topic at colleges and universities. What are the rules? Are there exceptions? What happens if campus police go "too far"? The Bill of Rights severely limits the search rights of government — including public colleges and universities. The Fourth Amendment states:

> The right of the people to be secure in their persons, houses, papers, and effects, against unreasonable searches and seizure, shall not be violated.

Generally, campus law enforcement personnel should conduct searches based on a court warrant or only when an arrest is made, evidence is in "plain view" of the officer performing his or her duties, or the person or property owner consents. These searches are legal, and evidence obtained through them can be used in off-campus criminal proceedings. Evidence obtained through "illegal or unauthorized searches" may not be used in criminal courts. However, this evidence may be used in other civil or campus proceedings.

Search warrants are issued by courts based on probable cause "that a crime has been committed" and an understanding that the search will produce evidence. Campus and other law enforcement officials must support requests for searches with more than their personal opinions. They generally must provide some facts to support the request.

Warrants are not required for searches that take place "incident to a lawful arrest." An authorized campus security officer may search an individual and the area around the individual to find weapons, prevent escapes, and protect evidence. Other evidence found in these searches can be used in criminal cases.

Public safety officers also have a right to seize evidence they inadvertently come across in "plain view" while on duty. Materials officers come across during the performance of their duties may be seized without a warrant.

Searches can also be conducted with the "consent" of an individual or property owner. The consent must be freely given; it cannot be obtained through coercion or deception.

Physical Violence

Public safety officers and other law enforcement personnel may use "reasonable and necessary force" to make arrests. On campus or off, physical force must be limited to the type and level minimally needed to achieve its lawful purpose. The use of "excessive force" can lead to battery and brutality claims against the officer and subsequent institutional liability.

In one notable campus case, the issue of excessive force was reviewed after the shooting of a student by a security guard (*Jones v. Wittenburg University*, 534 F.2d 1203, 1976). A federal appeals panel questioned the use of force in apprehending a student escaping from custody. The student had been found on a ledge outside a women's residence hall. He was then apprehended. Without searching him, the student was placed in a patrol car and the security officers went to look for a supervisor. When the car stopped to question someone, the youth ran from the car. A security officer fired two shots. He later claimed that the shots were to serve as warnings, but the second shot killed the student. The campus was held responsible for the officer's excessive use of force and damages were awarded.

High-Speed Chases

While public safety emergency vehicle chases may be unusual on campus, they can happen, starting with routine vehicle and traffic violations on any campus street. They can start off campus with local law enforcement efforts and cut through a campus or end on campus property. Along the route, risks to bystanders can be significant.

At colleges and universities, emergency vehicles should be equipped with sirens and warning lights. Public safety officers should use safety equipment whenever pursuing another vehicle. When exceeding speed limits or not abiding by established traffic regulations, officers must do everything they can to protect others and themselves. Chases should terminate if they become too hazardous, even if the result is the loss of the suspect or vehicle.

Campus law enforcement departments need policies, based on sound police practices, to protect officers and institutions from liability in chase situations. Campuses should be aware that, nationally, juries have been very generous in awards to high-speed chase victims.

Summary

Campus security officers are at risk daily, and they place colleges and universities at risk when they fail to follow accepted policies, practices, and laws. Among the situations that can lead to liability concerns in campus security are false arrests, illegal searches, excessive force, and high speed chases.

Campuses can limit liability through good officer selection, training, and supervision and with well thought-out policies and adequate equipment. Campuses must understand and support the efforts of security officers for the benefit and protection of everyone. But they also must be aware of the inherent liability risks.

The Campus Security Act

November 1994

The rules are final. After several years of government advisories, interpretations, and rule-making, the Department of Education has issued final implementation regulations for the Campus Security Act. The law requires colleges and universities to provide information on security and prevention efforts and to publish related crime statistics. It also requires timely notice to the campus community of particular crimes.

The Student Right-to-Know and Campus Security Act of 1990 requires campuses to record and report information related to graduation rates and crime. Higher Education Amendments in 1992 revised requirements related to policies and reports on campus sexual assaults.

Initial compliance with the law was based on two advisory letters from the Department of Education and its drafts of proposed regulations circulated for public comment two years ago. Campuses used those materials as guidelines, waiting for final government resolution.

Final Regulations

The Department of Education published the final crime awareness regulations (*Federal Register*, Vol. 59, No. 82) based on previously published drafts and the Department's review of over 300 comments.

Under the implementation rules, colleges and universities must continue to provide an annual security report to members of the campus community by September 1 of each year. The report must provide policies and statistics related to crime prevention, reporting, and occurrences. At a minimum, the annual campus security report must include:

- Policies regarding procedures and facilities for reporting campus emergencies and crimes, including institutional response to reports. Specifically, the policy should note where and to whom students and staff should report criminal activities.

- Policies related to security and access to campus facilities, including security concerns in maintenance programming.

- Policies on campus law enforcement, including authority, relationship with off-campus agencies, powers of arrest, and efforts to encourage the reporting of crimes.

- Descriptions of programs advising the campus community about security programs and encouraging members to be responsible for their own safety and the security of the community. The descriptions must also include the types and frequency of awareness efforts and indicate how students and staff are informed about crime prevention.

- Statistics on certain crimes on campus.

- Policies on how off-campus student crime is monitored and recorded by off-campus law enforcement agencies.

- Statistics on arrests for campus violations of drug, alcohol, and weapon laws.

- Statements on campus policies on the possession, use, and sale of alcohol and other drugs. Statements on campus drug and alcohol abuse education programming are also required. They should be related to the school's Drug-Free Schools and Communities Act compliance efforts.

- A statement on institutional policy concerning programming to prevent sexual offenses, and on institutional response to such violations.

Changes were made in the requirements for reporting crimes. The annual campus security report must provide "a list of the titles of each person or organization" on campus to whom crime reports should be directed. The law requires any person or agency that is a "campus security authority" to report crimes. The governments definition of "campus security authority" has been narrowed by the final regulations but differs from general campus practice. The definition includes:

- Law enforcement agencies

- Individuals and organizations listed in the annual security report as having campus responsibility for receiving crime reports from the campus

- Institutional officials with "significant" responsibility for student and campus activities but without "significant" counseling responsibilities

The Department adopted this new definition of "campus security authority" in "an attempt to strike an appropriate balance between the need of individual crime victims for confidential counseling and the need of the broader campus community for prevention and a complete reporting of crime." Many concerns had been raised that forcing campus officials to report would discourage counseling and support opportunities. The annual security report must now identify the campus officials who are included or excluded from the definition.

As indicated, the annual security report must provide statistics on crimes reported to security authorities, including murder, forcible and non-forcible sex offenses, robbery, aggravated assault, burglary, and motor vehicle theft.

Prior to 1992, rape was the only reportable sex offense under the law. This reporting category was enlarged by the 1992 Higher Education Amendments to include all sex offenses. And a separate law, the Hate Crimes Statistics Act, also requires the campus to maintain records on crimes that involve prejudice based on race, religion, sexual orientation, or ethnicity.

Campuses have been reporting crime statistics under the law since September 1992. Each year's annual report must now include three years of data for the required crime categories. In addition, the report must also provide the arrest statistics for alcohol, drug, and weapons violations for the most recent year.

The offenses for which statistics must be collected and reported are defined by the law in accordance with the

FBI Uniform Crime Reporting (UCR) program. Data must be collected and reported in a manner consistent with that program, even if the college does not participate in the UCR system.

Campus plans under the new regulations should include a review of current year publications and an effort to improve compliance. For September 1995, a campus report on statistics should contain:

- Offense statistics for calendar years 1994, 1993, and 1992, with the 1992 report including rape statistics through August 1 and forcible and non-forcible sex offenses for the remainder of 1992

- Alcohol, drug, and weapons arrests for calendar year 1994

In addition to the annual security report, the law also requires campuses to report to the campus community on crimes considered to represent a threat to other students and employees. This notice is to be provided in a manner that is timely and that will aid in the prevention of similar crimes. The regulations don't specify reporting requirements, but they do suggest an appropriate procedure be in place to make prompt decisions on when and how these notices will be provided. Among the suggested means of providing timely reports: local and campus media, residence halls and food service areas, bulletin board posters, and letters to the campus community.

The 1992 law's revision added several elements to annual security reports related to sexual assault. In addition to mandating the reporting of sex offenses, the law requires campus education programs to promote awareness of rape, acquaintance rape, and other offenses. The published campus policy statement must now provide:

- Descriptions of education programming on sex offense awareness

- Procedures for students to follow when an offense occurs, including information on reporting to authorities and on using counseling and other services, available on and off campus

- Campus disciplinary procedures, including accuser and accused rights to equal presence at proceedings, possible sanctions for sex offenses, and notification of outcomes

- Notice that the campus will alter (as possible) victim academic and residential situations if requested

It should also be noted for reporting purposes that, while the statistics are limited to campus occurrences, the regulations' definition of a campus is somewhat broad. Crime reporting is required for all buildings and properties owned or controlled by the institution or student organizations recognized by the institution. Branch campuses and off-site programs may have separate crime reports, but organizational housing, like fraternity and sorority residences, are considered part of a campus, no matter where they are or how they're owned.

The new regulations also provide guidance on how to distribute the required information. The regulations note that the security report should be provided annually to current and prospective students and employees through appropriate publications and mailings. They suggest distribution through U.S. mail, campus mail, or computer networks and individually received publications. Prospective students and employees may be advised of the reports contents and availability and need only be given an opportunity to request a full copy.

Complying with the final regulations for the Campus Security Act requires an effort to understand the law and its implementation standards, as well as a commitment to its purpose — prevention of crime through awareness.

Resources Help Reduce the Risk of Sexual Assault

July 1991

Fear of sexual assault has greatly changed campus life. Several states have adopted legislation requiring campuses to advise students on the risks of assault and on campus policies, programs, and prevention methods. Campus officials and student organizations emphasize awareness and prevention programming, attempting to communicate the need to understand where assaults occur and what can be done to prevent them. Several recent publications dealing with campus security issues provide some good suggestions.

Prevention Programming

Hospital and College Security Liability, by Leonard Territo and Max L. Bromley (Hanrow Press, 1987), examines the issue in a variety of ways, looking at the problem of rape on campus, gang rape, and institutional responsibility. The text suggests many prevention strategies, beginning with a campus self-study to review the security force, high-risk areas, lighting problems, crime reporting, and victim support services. In addition, the authors offer suggestions for security patrols, the physical environment, education programs, and campus services. Among the suggestions:

- *Security staffing.* Use student patrols to supplement trained staff. Make more frequent patrols of high-risk areas. Establish residence hall guards. Increase foot patrols. Ensure that a female officer is on duty.

- *Physical environment.* Rekey locks. Leave classroom lights on in dark areas. Use ID card systems for building access. Eliminate pathways surrounded by shrubs and trees. Conduct a lighting survey. Provide warning signs. Maintain telephone systems.

- *Education programs.* Use campus publications to promote safety. Relay progress reports to the campus community. Provide presentations and training sessions. Distribute pamphlets, fact sheets, and booklets. Offer self-defense courses.
- *Other services.* These could include transportation and escort services and shelter house programs.

Crime Prevention on Campus, a booklet published by ELL Security Consultants, Inc. (1989), offers specific self-defense tips for students. Authors Edward L. Lee and William J. D'Urso stress that avoiding any crime situation is "far preferable to any type of confrontation." They suggest many ways to avoid violent crime on campus:

- Avoid dark and lonely areas. Stay in lighted areas and go with a friend.
- Lock your car, house, or room but have your keys ready when you get there. Don't waste time getting into a more secure environment.
- Be careful in risk areas: know where to go and when to go.
- Travel in groups. Remember that there's greater safety in numbers.
- Be aware, keep your eyes open, and know what's happening around you.
- Don't flaunt money or possessions. Don't attract unwanted attention.
- Carry a loud whistle — and be prepared to use it.
- Don't carry weapons: they can easily be turned against you, and they are often illegal on campus.
- Walk with confidence. Don't appear vulnerable or unsure of yourself or of where you're going.
- Avoid wearing headphones when out alone: they can disguise warning signs of danger.

Crime and Campus Police: A Handbook for Police Officers and Administrators, by Michael C. Smith (College Administration Publications, Inc., 1989), offers a checklist for preventing sexual assault. It suggests that campuses consider:

- Extra surveillance of problem areas, using patrols, lighting, and emergency phones
- Lighting standards, to provide adequate illumination
- Groundskeeping standards, to keep paths clear and visible and eliminate places where assailants might hide
- Scheduling night classes to avoid unnecessary student isolation
- Emergency telephones for walking routes, parking lots, and recreation areas
- Tighter residence hall security, particularly in coed facilities
- Coordination of after-hour and weekend work to avoid unnecessarily isolating employees and exposing them to risk
- Education and prevention programming

The National Crime Prevention Council several years ago produced a kit and a program guide to promote a campus community response to crime. The program, "Together for a Safe Campus," looks at a variety of awareness and prevention programs. It includes sample posters, fliers, and suggestions for events.

To combat the threat of sexual assault and rape, the kit offers the following recommendations to students:

- *Be alert and assertive.* Don't let substances cloud your judgment. Be aware of your surroundings.
- *Trust your instincts.* If you're in a setting or a situation that makes you uncomfortable or uneasy, get out!
- *Adopt safe habits.* Don't prop open security doors. Lock room doors and windows, and keep track of your keys. Watch out for unknown or unwanted visitors — and ask them to leave. Don't hitchhike. Keep your car in good working order to avoid getting stranded, and stay on the well-traveled routes!

A second text by Bromley and Territo offers additional tips on where assaults occur on campus and what to do if attacked. *College Crime Prevention and Personal Safety Awareness* (Charles C. Thomas, publisher, 1990) notes that assaults can occur anywhere, but that many happen in residence halls (rooms, restrooms, and showers), parking lots and garages, laundries, classrooms, stairwells, hallways, and walkways.

Although only the potential victim can judge how to respond to a threatened attack, the authors suggest several alternative tactics to consider:

- Make a diversionary noise to send a warning or attract attention. Shout or use a whistle.
- Run — especially if you're certain of a place you can reach quickly that will provide protection.
- Gain a psychological advantage. Think through in advance a reaction other than fear or panic. If attacked, try to defuse your assailant's anger by doing something unexpected, like going limp.
- Talk. Speak calmly and clearly. Try to be sincere in making the assailant view you not as a victim but as an individual.

Summary

Two brutal facts: sexual assault occurs on campus, and the victims may be anybody — faculty, students, staff, or visitors. Through better security staffing, physical plant improvements, educational programming, and other support services, campus officials can reduce the risk of sexual assault. Resources like these publications can help.

Hanrow Press, *Hospital and College Security Liability*, Box 2729, Columbia, MD 21045.

ELL Security Consultants, Inc., *Crime Prevention on Campus*, 1350 Beverly Road, Suite 115, McLean, VA 22101.

College Administration Publications, Inc., *Crime and Campus Police*, Dept. CP, P.O. Box 8492, Asheville, NC 28814.

National Crime Prevention Council, *Together for a Safe Campus*, 733 15th Street, NW, Room 540, Washington, DC 20005.

Charles C. Thomas, Publisher, *College Crime Prevention and Personal Safety Awareness*, 2600 S. First St., Springfield, IL 62794-9255.

Campus, Federal Forces Attacking Sexual Assault

February 1993

The risk of sexual assault and increasing efforts to hold campuses liable for attacks, are grabbing attention around the country.

You probably remember the University of Southern California's damage award of a $1.62 million lawsuit by a USC student assaulted in an off-campus residence hall. That judgment points out important considerations for other campuses.

The Council for the Advancement and Support of Education (CASE) has responded to the issue, as has the Association of Governing Boards of Universities and Colleges (AGBUC). A federal reauthorized Higher Education Act tackles the problem as well.

Sexual assault, it seems, is an issue that won't be brushed away.

USC: One Case and Response

A California state jury found USC negligent because it had concealed the dangers of living in the off-campus residence hall and hadn't warned students about a previous assault.

The student plaintiff in the case, who was attacked at the site, was awarded $1.62 million by the court. But she settled out of court for $1.5 million to avoid lengthy appeals.

The implications of the award and the settlement are staggering for higher education communities. Some say colleges and universities, if held responsible for crime against students, have only two equally unrealistic options — lock students in or provide no security whatsoever. That way, schools will know that everyone is safe or know that safety is only an individual's responsibility.

USC issued a report on dealing with campus rape in the future. Among the key recommendations:

- Swift notification of sexual assaults on or near the campus, to ensure that everyone is aware of dangers in their environment and able to protect themselves

- Mandatory sexual assault education and awareness prevention programming for all new students

- Improved communication and coordination among the campus and community law enforcement agencies investigating assaults

- Required response training for all security personnel

The problems USC hopes to address through these and other recommendations are national in scope, as reinforced by recent AGBUC and CASE actions and new federal legislation.

AGB Suggestions

In *AGB Reports* (March/April 1992), Antioch University (OH) Trustee K. Mulhauser tackles the issue in an article entitled "Taking a Stand Against Sexual Assault."

Included are suggestions for an effective campus sexual assault policy and related obligations of collegiate governing boards.

The suggested keys to a strong policy include specific campus definitions, education, processes, and support. "Taking a Stand" suggests:

- Creating a *policy statement* prohibiting sexual offenses. It should be clear and free of gender, culture, or sexual orientation language bias. It should also specifically define prohibited conduct.

- Defining *consent* to help the campus community understand and recognize "yes" and "no." Consider language that promotes "willingly and verbally agreeing to engage" in sexual activity — language that is obtained at each level of physical or sexual contact and that doesn't confuse consent with submission.

- Emphasizing *policy education* for faculty, students, and staff.

- Establishing programs designed to reduce the opportunities for sexual assault. Programs on healthy relationships, dating, gender roles, values clarification, self-defense, power and control, and sexism all help address the problem.

- Making *due process* available and fair for the accused and the accuser, including "notice" of a hearing and "opportunities to be heard." A campus policy should also include information on witnesses, confidentiality, and possible sanctions.

In addition, it should indicate the role and availability of the off-campus legal system as well as the on-campus system.

- Providing *support* to campus community members when sexual assault occurs. Offer counseling and other support services to victims in a sensitive environment. Give offenders an opportunity for some form of treatment and counseling as well.

"Taking a Stand" concludes with a challenge to trustees to inform *themselves* about sexual assault and the related laws.

CASE's Response

Another example of the impact this issue has had on campus comes from a recent "CASE Issues Paper for Advancement Professionals" (December 1992). The paper focuses on how campus advancement and development officers can best use their "skills and resources to deal with this important issue."

Entitled *Acquaintance Rape on Campus,* the document was developed due to one school's experiences with the issue. It's designed to be a forum on the issue sponsored by the organization.

The paper highlights efforts officials should make to ensure that the campus has appropriate policies and procedures in place and can react to all assaults with a sense of understanding and support.

Keys to making this approach work:

- Developing strong ties among campus units
- Educating the community
- Developing a sense of trust within the institution
- Promoting peer group programs

Prompt campus response to assaults should include support for all parties, and the release of appropriate information under the law.

Also, the paper says, open up communications with students (even those who don't support campus policy) and carefully respond to the interests of all constituency groups. In other words, CASE says, it's better to err on the side of "over-communication."

Of particular concern is the federal Campus Security Act requirement to *provide timely notice* of crimes that could be threats to the campus community. Give notice so that others can avoid similar occurrences. Appropriate notice should include the type and location of the crime and precautions that students, faculty, and staff can take to improve their safety.

Give advance consideration to the legal balancing act regarding crime and student records. Under a new law, crime reports not kept for educational purposes are subject to release.

But at the same time, it's also wise to take the steps you can to ensure privacy for victims.

Legislative Response

A final measure of the current concern over campus sexual assaults is the latest legislative response.

Along with the federal Crime Awareness and Campus Security Act and related state laws, additional federal legislation was adopted. Under the early 1990s Campus Sexual Assault Victim Bill of Rights, campuses will need to establish policies for sexual assault cases and spell out procedures they will follow when assaults occur.

The reauthorization of the Higher Education Act, adopted last year, requires campuses receiving federal financial support to "develop and distribute" a campus policy on sexual assault prevention. The policy should include:

- Procedures for handling assaults
- Provisions for education and awareness pro-grams
- Sanctions for sexual offenses on campus
- Procedures for student victims
- Disciplinary procedures

The law also says that campuses must build protections into their disciplinary procedures. These include:

- The right of those accused and accusers to have someone accompanying them at hearings
- The right of those accused and accusers to be notified of hearing outcomes

Under the new law, students must also be informed of their options regarding off-campus law enforcement, notified of existing counseling and support programs, and advised of campus options for victims (adjustments in academic programs, living arrangements, etc.).

Summary

Concern over campus sexual assault continues to rise. In higher education, the USC experience, the *AGB Reports* article, the CASE report, and the new federal legislation all point to a growing awareness of this critical issue.

Make sure your campus is also committed to making a difference.

The People Behind Sexual Assault Numbers

March 1993

With the publication of campus crime statistics, the stark numbers of reported sexual assaults on campus are available for all to see.

What the numbers don't reflect, however, is the human impact of sexual assault. To begin to appreciate its dimensions, it's good to take a look at the altogether too many schools, situations, and people behind the numbers.

Was Student Pressured to Leave?

At George Mason University (VA), a first-year student who left campus after one semester in 1991 sued the school, claiming that it impeded the investigation into her alleged rape and pressured her to leave.

The local prosecuting attorney's office did not find sufficient evidence to pursue criminal charges. The woman, however, is suing her three alleged attackers, as well as the campus president, trustees, board of visitors, and several campus police officers. She says the school didn't gather proper evidence at the time of the alleged rape and pushed her to leave school entirely.

A rape-related lawsuit against Central Michigan University was ultimately dismissed, but called into question the rights of victims.

A former student had sued CMU, claiming the school had failed to properly discipline a varsity athlete who had assaulted her. The school held a hearing, found the accused student responsible, and suspended him from classes.

The victim, however, thought the accused student should have been permanently barred from CMU, and she filed a federal lawsuit to that effect. But the court ruled that the victim had no standing to sue. Because she was not the person who was disciplined, the court ruled, she did not have any basis to sue the institution.

Charges stemming from a 1990 sexual attack at Indiana University have led to a civil case against a student, his fraternity, and its national office.

The defendant had previously pleaded guilty to criminal charges in the case. He spent a year under "house arrest" and was ordered to pay the victim's medical and counseling expenses.

According to the victim's civil suit, however, the assault took place after a homecoming party in the fraternity house. Alcohol was provided at the party. The victim says her assailant was clearly intoxicated but continued to receive drinks just before the attack.

Legal papers filed in the case say that the victim suffered physical and mental pain and suffering, shame, humiliation, depression, and other impairments that have affected her life since the incident.

A five-year jail sentence has been imposed on a former University of Southern Maine student who was convicted of attacking a female student at a fraternity party.

The assailant, who was not a member of the fraternity, followed his victim into an unlocked restroom and assaulted her there. Charged with rape, the defendant maintained that the sex was consensual.

But more than 15 other students who were at the party said they had seen no contact between the two before the rape. They also said the victim left the restroom in tears, with blood on her clothing.

A Long Wait

A judicial battle in Texas long delayed a day in court for a 1984 University of Houston rape victim.

The then student had a volleyball scholarship that required her to live on campus. According to her suit, she and other residence hall students had repeatedly complained to UH officials about a building fire door that was left open due to faulty locks.

Later that year, an armed man entered through the door and attacked the plaintiff. The assailant was captured and convicted, and the victim filed a civil suit. In it, she said UH had failed in its responsibility to provide safe housing.

In court, however, UH argued that state law protected the school from liability, because the victim was injured in an intentional act committed by a criminal.

It took six years for the case to reach the state's highest court. It then took another year and a half for the court to issue its ruling to allow the case to go to a full trial.

The off-campus assault of a West Virginia University student led to similar charges and countercharges.

The student filed a civil damage claim against her off-campus landlord, contending that failure to properly fix a window contributed to the assault. Her suit asked for $2 million in punitive damages and $3 million in compensatory damages.

The landlord, however, filed a countersuit. He said the victim was not an official tenant but an unauthorized visitor, since she was "unofficially subletting" the apartment.

His countersuit also named as defendants the owners of an adjacent property, the bank holding its mortgage, and the city itself. The landlord said the run-down house next door was unsafe and was used by the attacker to plan his assault.

The city had previously condemned the property next door, but had failed to tear it down as ordered.

A Different Approach

Another trend in campus rape emerged at Yale University (CT), where a group of women marked a fraternity as the home of a rapist.

The group's signs appeared after a student accused an unidentified member of the fraternity as her attacker. The group, "Women Breaking the Silence," demanded that the fraternity turn in the alleged attacker.

Fraternity members responded by saying that the group was too quick to accuse, and they threatened a slander suit because of the signs and banners the group hung.

Then, athletes were involved in sexual assault charges at the University of South Florida. There, documents reviewed by state officials showed that USF broke and manipulated university procedures for over a year to keep a basketball player on the team.

The files showed that, throughout the period, the player was repeatedly accused of harassing, battering, or raping female students. A faculty senate review found that many of the victims had withdrawn their complaints after being harassed by other athletes and their girlfriends.

The campus president has responded with promises to make extensive modifications of USF policy. The changes will include new reporting relationships for members of the athletic department and staffing to assist campus crime victims.

Syracuse University (NY) also dealt with allegations of leniency toward students found guilty of rape. Student victims have complained that SU refuses to release disciplinary transcripts, and that it has a system of disciplinary withdrawals that is "soft" on offenders.

Students charged with conduct violations at SU are given three options: they can plead guilty, plead innocent, or agree to withdraw from school. Students who decide to leave get only a "withdrawn" mark on their transcripts. If employers or other schools want to find out why a particular student withdrew, they have to request a full copy of the student's records.

But to do that, they must have the student's permission.

Conclusion

On campuses around the country, the issues and concerns remain essentially the same. Sexual assault is real; it involves real people and real pain.

By keeping abreast of reports from around the nation, campus decision-makers will reinforce campus awareness of this issue.

Fearful Students Turning to Court Protection Orders

July 1993

A tragedy involving the murder of a University of Massachusetts student highlights a growing concern for many campuses: students' fear of violence committed by other students or people they know.

The UMass student was killed by her former lover. Less than a month earlier, the victim had sought a court protection order to keep her ex-companion away from her. Unfortunately, it turned out that she had good reason to fear.

As violence related to student relationships increases, more potential victims are turning to the legal system for help. While the courts hear the victims' stories, people outside the courts feel equal impact.

Popular Precaution

In response to similar situations, an increasing number of Massachusetts college students are seeking court protection orders.

Campus police throughout the commonwealth have been asked to enforce the orders under a 1991 state law. The statute permits judges to issue restraining orders against people who have been involved in "significant dating relationships."

The law gives students a protection opportunity that was previously unavailable. Before the law, protection orders could only be issued when the parties involved were married or related or if they had lived together.

According to UMass officials, the protection order in place when the student was killed was not uncommon. At that time, at least 18 other students had notified UMass police about protection orders. Most of the orders were a result of previous dating relationships.

Officials at smaller schools in Massachusetts report similar cases involving their students. Court clerks say that over 1,000 orders a week are processed in the state, up 25% since the law went into effect. State officials say the increase is directly related to dating relationships gone sour — many involving students.

Lawmakers introduced the extended protection to increase the safety of women and men, particularly students, who may be victims of violence even though they're not married to or living with an abuser.

Initially, however, there was concern that some students might abuse the law. Some campus officials, for instance, feared that unhappy roommates might use protection orders to harass each other instead of resolving problems on campus. But now, it appears that most orders are based on real fear of harm.

Widespread Concern

The circumstances that cause students to live and go to school in fear exist on many campuses.

A week before the UMass student's death, another student was attacked at Northeastern University (MA). The victim's former partner, who was under a restraining order, eluded campus security and kidnapped his former girlfriend at knifepoint. The victim escaped unharmed about an hour later.

The *Boston Globe*, reporting on the increasing need to protect college students in abusive relationships, recently reviewed state court records. The paper found that at least four Boston College students had sought court protection in recent months.

Among the people barred from contact with BC students were a former boyfriend who threatened to kill a female student, a man who made repeated late-night phone calls to a female residence hall student, and a male who punched an international student and then used racial slurs against him.

Court records also showed that a campus-related protection order had been filed by a male Pine Manor College (MA) student. The student had sought protection from attacks by his former girlfriend.

According to papers filed in the case, the woman had intentionally damaged the student's car, pounded on his windows early in the morning, threatened him, and made harassing calls to the student's new girlfriend.

The Massachusetts Statute

Under the new state law, victims of relationship harassment involving threats to personal safety can seek protection by court order. The order generally establishes rules the harassing party must follow to avoid criminal prosecution.

Most orders prohibit contact between the parties. Many mandate a specific distance to be maintained between the accused harasser and the complainant, and many others prohibit specific behaviors by the accused harasser.

If the non-contact rule is broken, the violator is subject to immediate arrest and lengthy incarceration.

Some of the Massachusetts protection orders have dealt specifically with campus situations. The most recent case surrounds the off-campus death of the UMass senior. Her former boyfriend stabbed her to death, then burned her home in an effort to cover the evidence.

The couple had been involved in altercations before. They had placed court restraining orders on each other only a month earlier, and after one previous fight, the victim had been treated for injuries at the campus health service.

Conclusion

One way or another, a campus can often find itself involved in cases of relationship violence. College and university decision-makers need to understand the intense fear some students live with and support efforts to protect students from harm.

The Massachusetts system of court-enforced protection orders is an example of one state's effort to do what it can on behalf of those in need — particularly students. Court orders can't prevent all harm, of course, but they may be important tools in the effort to protect potential victims of relationship violence.

How Far Must Campuses Go to Protect Students?

January 1993

She walked across the street leaving campus and went into a popular bar. The nightspot catered to the college crowd, advertising on campus and displaying items that had the school logo. It even got its name from the school mascot.

The student used her school ID to get into the bar. She was 17 and the state drinking age was 21.

She had a drink and left with two men who eventually sexually assaulted her. The assailants had no relationship to the school or the bar.

The victim sued the school, claiming it had failed to protect her from harm while she was at the bar. She also said the school hadn't warned her about the bar's potential dangers or made her aware of several state and local laws — including laws on drinking.

In *Hartman v. Bethany College*, 778 F.Supp. 286 (1991), a federal court in West Virginia considered issues of concern to many campus administrators: rape, campus responsibility for student behavior, and a school's duty to warn or protect students.

Hartman isn't the first case to bring campuses and students into court over these issues. Several cases involving the assault or death of students have established legal principles for campuses to use in their efforts to limit crime against students — and reduce related litigation.

Most claims are based on *negligence* — a contention that a school had a duty to warn or protect but failed to act accordingly. A duty to warn or protect could arise from:

- "Assumption" of duty, through promises made by the school
- A campus' control over security efforts
- Landlord-tenant relationships in residence halls
- The foreseeability of future crimes against students, based on a school's knowledge of previous incidents

Attacks On and Off Campus

A 1983 case, *Mullins v. Pine Manor College*, 449 N.E.2d 331, explored the duty of a small, private college (located in the Boston suburb of Chestnut Hill) to protect a student from crime.

The student was sleeping in her residence hall room when she was abducted by a man. The man later sexually assaulted the victim in a food service area on campus.

The campus had no history of this type of crime. But it was ultimately held legally responsible for it.

The campus, located near a city subway station, has a system of locked doors and security patrols. But these security efforts, the court said, failed to protect the victim. The court ruled that the school had assumed responsibility for campus safety and had then breached that duty.

The student had relied on the campus to perform its safety functions — she didn't or couldn't take further steps of her own to protect herself, the court ruled. It also said that the school's system of fences, locks, and patrols was not adequately used or maintained, and that simple and inexpensive improvements in campus safety could have prevented the crime.

A court made a similar liability ruling against a campus in *Miller v. State of New York*, 467 N.E.2d 493 (1984), a case involving the landlord-tenant relationship in the residence halls.

A residence hall student at State University of New York at Stony Brook was forced out of an unlocked laundry room by a man and subsequently attacked. She filed a liability claim against the public university, saying she had complained earlier about people "hanging around" the residence halls. She said she had also complained about similar campus assaults and had expressed concern about the school's failure to lock exterior doors.

The court found the school responsible. It said the school had a duty to protect but had failed to take simple measures, like locking doors, that could or would have protected the student.

The courts reviewed another campus assault case in *Peterson v. San Francisco Community College District*, 685 P.2d 1193 (1984). At issue was the foreseeability of crime.

A female student was attacked while she was walking to a campus parking lot. There was a history of crime on the exterior stairway leading to the parking area, and the assailant had hidden in thick shrubbery to wait for the victim.

The victim accused the campus of failing to maintain the area in a safe manner. The campus, however, didn't provide extensive security arrangements and, therefore, did not "assume responsibility" for security beforehand. But it did fail to warn the student of the potential for crime, the court ruled.

More recently, a California superior court jury awarded $1.62 million to a University of Southern California student who was attacked near her off-campus — but university-controlled — residence.

The jury said the school was liable because it had concealed from students the dangers of living in downtown Los Angeles. The court said the school had also failed to warn students about previous incidents, including one that occurred two days before the one involving the plaintiff.

Schools Aren't Always Liable

Despite these rulings against schools, it's important to remember that campuses aren't always held responsible for on-campus crimes against students.

A Florida case provides a good example. In *Relyea v. State of Florida*, 385 So.2d 1378 (1980), two female Florida Atlantic University students sued after they were attacked in a campus parking lot.

But the school had no history of crime. And, like San Francisco Community College, the campus did not have an extensive security system.

The court eventually ruled that the school could not be held responsible for every incident on campus — including the crime against the plaintiffs.

What About Off-Campus Crimes?

We've already seen how cases like *Pine Manor*, *Miller*, and *Peterson* outline the extent of possible campus liability for *on-campus* crimes against students. But those cases don't necessarily pertain to *off-campus* crimes against students.

In 1987, for example, a recently paroled prisoner who was attending State University of New York College at Buffalo through a special support program attacked and killed two classmates in an apartment near campus.

Other students who survived the assault, along with the families of all the victims, filed a liability claim against the school, saying it had breached its duty to protect. They said the school had a responsibility to either avoid admitting students with dangerous pasts or keep them away from other students to promote safety.

But in *Eiseman v. State of New York*, 511 N.E.2d 1128 (1987), the State Court of Appeals ruled that such requirements were beyond the capabilities of a college or university and so were not required.

In another case, *Donnell v. California Western School of Law*, 246 Cal. Rptr. 199 (1988), a court ruled that the school was not responsible for an assault on a sidewalk adjacent to campus. While the school could be held responsible for what happened on campus, the court ruled, it could not be held liable for what happened across the street.

After much litigation, a similar result came from *Whitlock v. University of Denver*, 744 P.2d 54 (1987), a well-publicized case involving a trampoline, not an assault.

At issue was whether the campus was responsible for the safety of fraternity members using a trampoline at an off-campus, rented facility. The university knew that the students would be using the trampoline and that it could be dangerous.

Sure enough, a student using the trampoline fell. He sued the school, claiming that, since it had recognized the danger, it had had a duty to protect him.

The student received significant damage awards at the trial and appellate levels. But the Colorado Supreme Court refused to extend campus responsibility into the off-campus community, and it ruled in favor of the school.

The Hartman Case

In *Hartman*, a federal district court was asked to consider several issues — including the possible campus liability for an off-campus crime against a student.

The court acknowledged that schools may have certain duties to protect and warn students from foreseeable crimes *on campus*. But since the bar was *off campus* and not affiliated with the college, the court ruled that the school was not responsible for the victim's safety.

The court noted that:

- Students and parents hadn't expected the school to take responsibility for off-campus incidents.
- The campus hadn't done anything to indicate that it had assumed responsibility for off-campus crime.
- It was not "practical to require a college to supervise the activities of its students off campus" without significant staff regulations and other efforts.
- The college had no duty to warn students about threats or activities that were beyond the control of the school.

In other words, the court said, the student — not the college — was responsible for the consequences of her off-campus activities.

A campus, then, may have a duty to warn and protect students on its premises or in its programs. But that responsibility rarely extends into the outside community.

Searches Highlight Constitutional Questions

July 1992

Campus officials were very worried about fire safety and vandalism in the residence halls. A series of events had caused concern, including the use of firecrackers and the discovery of burned paper towels in the hallway. Utah State University housing officials had warned students that if the dangerous activities did not stop, rooms would be searched. The incidents continued. So staff, worried about safety and campus peace, searched several residence hall rooms.

In one student's room, they didn't find materials tied to the safety problems, but they did discover stolen property unrelated to the search's objectives. Among the items they seized were school signs and banners taken from university facilities. The student was charged with theft, a state misdemeanor. But at trial, the evidence against him was thrown out of court! The prosecution could not submit the university signs and banners because they were obtained in a *warrantless search*. The court ruled that the school had violated student constitutional rights in an illegal search and seizure.

At issue in this and similar cases is the Fourth Amendment to the U.S. Constitution, which says, in part:

> The right of the people to be secure in their persons, houses, papers, and effects, against unreasonable searches and seizures, shall not be violated.

Search and seizure is a sensitive topic of special concern to colleges and universities. The Fourth Amendment applies differently to public and private schools, and exceptions to the rule make generalizations difficult. Still, campus officials, particularly those involved in residence halls, need to understand the Fourth Amendment and judicial interpretations of it.

Private vs. Public: An Important Distinction

Generally, the Fourth Amendment exists to protect citizens from unreasonable government actions. As such, courts have held that it applies directly to public institutions and officials, because they are part of the government. They are seen to be "public" officers, and they must abide by the law. If they conduct an unauthorized search, the materials seized may not be used in court proceedings.

Officials at private institutions, however, may not be similarly restrained. Materials they obtain in warrantless searches may be used by the government for prosecution, as long as government does not play a role in the search decision or process.

Consider the case of *People v. Boettner*, 362 N.Y.S.2d 365 (1974). Using information provided by a parent, officials at the Rochester Institute of Technology (NY) targeted a residence hall room for a search. Security personnel at the private school entered the room, found drugs, and turned the drugs and the student over to local police. The student complained that his constitutional rights had been violated. But the court ruled that the Fourth Amendment did not restrict the activities of private citizens.

In this case, the campus was acting as a "private citizen," the court said. Local law enforcement agencies were not directly or indirectly involved or even aware of the drug allegations or search. The search was allowed.

While this is the accepted rule for private schools, such campuses should still be aware of some state privacy laws that may protect students from unreasonable searches. Check in your jurisdiction.

Exceptions to the Fourth Amendment

The Fourth Amendment restricts government only from "unreasonable" searches. That leaves a variety of "reasonable" conditions and circumstances under which a college or university can search student property without warrant:

- When items are in *plain view*
- When there are *emergencies*
- When students *consent*
- During *health and safety* inspections
- To maintain campus *discipline and order*

The law generally respects these exceptions, but advance notice to students of the conditions that permit campus searches makes for good policy. Clear policies avoid the possibility of misunderstandings and confusion, both prime causes of litigation. Campuses need to understand the exceptions and give students notice of them as well.

The law on searches does not apply to items found in *plain view*. If a campus official finds something illegal in the course of performing regular duties, it is held to be in plain view and subject to seizure. When a student needing identification took a security guard to his room, what the officer saw in the room was in plain view. In *Washington v. Chrisman*, 102 S.Ct. 812 (1982), the officer saw drugs on a desk. The arrest that followed was found by the courts to be legal.

Courts have also upheld a warrantless search during an *emergency*. A campus must remain free to respond to emergency situations, regardless of privacy expectations. Two noted examples of this involve a "noxious odor" and a lost purse. In responding to both, campuses found illegal materials without using a warrant, but the searches were justified under emergency circumstances.

In *People v. Cohen*, 292 N.Y.S.2d 706 (1968), campus officials smelled a problem. They went looking for the source of a particularly "noxious odor." They opened 20 rooms before they found the problem: marijuana that had been treated with a special preservative. The students were not in the room during the search but were arrested when they returned. In court, they claimed the warrantless search was illegal, but their position found no judicial support. The court held that campus officials had to respond to the odor with "prompt" inspection. What officials found during that inspection could be used in court.

The emergency exception has also been applied to a lost purse case. In *State v. Johnson*, 530 P.2d 910 (1975), an Arizona court held that campus police had a duty to open a lost purse to look for identification and to inventory the contents. They found illegal drugs, and the evidence was used in court. They had a duty, said the court, to respond to "emergency" circumstances in a responsible manner.

Rules for Consent: Voluntary, Specific, Without Reservation

A search can also be conducted by a campus with the *consent* of the student. In an Ohio case, *State v. Wingerd*, 318 N.E.2d 866 (1974), a student allowed a campus official searching for drugs to enter his room and then gave the official the drugs he had been searching for. When the case came to court, however, the student claimed that the official was engaged in an illegal search at the time. But the court held that the official was invited into the room knowingly and freely by the student. The student "consented" to the search, said the court.

Generally, courts have ruled that consent to searches without warrants must be specific, without reservation, and voluntary. In addition, one resident of a residence hall room cannot consent to the search of another's property.

Courts have also approved warrantless searches in some cases for routine *health and safety* inspections. While few college or university inspection cases have been tried, higher courts have ruled that this is a very limited exception. In municipal cases, courts have ruled that a city must review the need for each health and safety inspection in advance. This is not realistic on campus, so colleges and universities are advised to notify students in advance of non-emergency health and safety inspections.

The final exception to the search rule occurs in cases involving the maintenance of *discipline and order*. In very limited circumstances, courts have allowed warrantless searches by campuses that are attempting to uphold conduct and discipline standards. When a campus has reasonable cause to believe that a student area is being used for illegal or other activities that would undermine campus discipline, a search may be authorized. These searches, however, must have an institutional purpose; materials found cannot generally be used for criminal prosecution.

In *Keane v. Rodgers*, 316 F.Supp. 217 (1970), a cadet at a state-supported maritime academy was dismissed when a warrantless search of his vehicle revealed illegal drugs. Officials had been looking only for a lost flag. The student complained that the search was illegal, but the court allowed it, reasoning that it "was a reasonable exercise of ... supervisory authority to maintain order and discipline."

In a similar ruling, a warrantless search was upheld in *United States v. Coles*, 302 F.Supp. 99 (1969). Staff at a federal education center searched bags entering the facility for security reasons and discovered drugs. The student was disciplined and appealed, arguing violation of the Fourth Amendment. But the court noted no violation: "Quite plainly, the investigation was conducted solely for the purpose of ensuring proper moral and disciplinary conditions." The discipline was upheld.

Current Case:
Second Reversal Makes Sense

At Utah State, the trial court threw out the case against the student who had campus signs and banners in his room. It said the search was warrantless and, therefore, that the evidence could not be used against him. But a state court of appeals, after reviewing the law and earlier cases, including *Cohen*, *Keane*, and *Coles*, ruled that the room search had indeed been legal. The campus, said the court, had a duty to respond to the safety and discipline problem, and a warrantless search was, therefore, justified.

Most early law on campus searches dealt with illegal drugs. Today, the issues remain the same, even though officials may be in search of other contraband or property. Private schools have greater discretion to search and seize than do public institutions because the Constitution restricts governmental actions. In addition, courts have recognized that a variety of conditions may exist on a college campus that warrant a search without law enforcement approval or involvement.

Warrantless Searches in Some Circumstances

April 1993

> The right of the people to be secure in their persons, houses, papers, and effects, against unreasonable searches and seizures, shall not be violated, and no Warrants shall issue, but upon probable cause, supported by Oath or affirmation, and particularly describing the place to be searched, and the persons or things to be seized.
>
> Fourth Amendment to the U.S. Constitution

Students living in a University of New Mexico residence hall were angered by some actions of the campus housing staff.

The residents say their rooms were unlawfully entered and inspected by school employees conducting an equipment inventory. They vigorously complain that their rooms should not have been entered without their consent or prior knowledge. They want to use the "search and seizure" provision of the Fourth Amendment to the U.S. Constitution to prevent future "violations" of this type.

Whenever your campus is considering entry without consent into student residential areas, you need to consider several legal issues:

- The differences in legal status between public and private institutions
- Previous Fourth Amendment court applications
- Exceptions to constitutional protections against searches
- Contractual arrangements that may exist between residential students and the campus
- Individual privacy rights under common law

Administrators can protect their institutions, and students, in search and seizure cases by understanding the law — before they proceed.

Public vs. Private Institutions

Many elements of the Constitution's Bill of Rights, including the Fourth Amendment, were established to protect citizens from certain *acts of government*.

Private citizens and their agencies are not constrained by the law the way government is. Therefore, the principles of searches and seizures are applied differently to public and private college campuses.

A taxpayer-supported school, for example, is considered "government," so it must follow the restrictions of the Fourth Amendment. A private institution, on the other hand, which is not controlled or managed by the government or its agents, is generally not subject to the restrictions against unreasonable searches and seizures.

Fourth Amendment Applications

After the American Revolution, there was great interest in ensuring that the new government of the independent nation would not have power to act unacceptably. The British, in their ruling years, had angered the colonists by limitless searches and seizures and by warrants that were issued to the government at will by British courts.

That's why the Fourth Amendment exists. Because of the amendment, students at public institutions expect privacy protection, free from unjustified government intervention (see *Katz v. United States*, 389 U.S. 347, 1967).

The key to the amendment is that materials found in unlawful searches cannot be used in criminal prosecutions. This *exclusionary* rule was reiterated by the Supreme Court in *United States v. Payner*, 447 U.S. 727 (1980).

An unreasonable warrantless search by a public school official would violate the rule. But a private school's search under the same circumstances could produce criminal evidence, as in *Walter v. United States*, 447 U.S. 649 (1980).

In spite of these rulings, materials found in warrantless searches on campus may still be used in *campus* disciplinary proceedings in most cases (*Morale v. Grigel*, 422 F.Supp. 988, 1976).

In other words, under the Fourth Amendment, students have a right to expect privacy in residential rooms — although illegally seized evidence may be used in *campus* conduct hearings. (It would no doubt be challenged, however.)

Exceptions

Courts have outlined several "reasonable" exceptions that allow campuses to conduct warrantless searches in limited circumstances.

One exception deals with items found in *plain view* by public officers doing their jobs in places where they have a right to be (*Washington v. Chrisman*, 102 S.Ct. 812, 1982).

An official can also follow disturbing noises in a residence hall area (*People v. Volpe*, 452 N.Y.S.2d 609, 1982) or view items in a room if invited to the room for other legitimate purposes (*State v. King*, 298 N.W.2d 168, 1980).

The courts have ruled that campuses may also conduct warrantless searches:

- In emergencies, to protect the public and "abate [a] nuisance." For example, in *People v. Lanthier*, 97 Cal. Rptr. 297 (1971), a university official was trying to find the source of an offensive odor. He was allowed to search residence hall rooms as required.

- In situations in which someone might have a legal need to inventory. In one case, a police officer found a lost purse and went through it trying to identify the owner (*State v. Johnson*, 530 P.3d 910, 1975). Instead, he found illegal items inside.

- When officials have the specific consent of an individual, as in *Morale*. A "blanket" authorization, however, which is often part of a residence hall contract, may not be specific enough to withstand judicial challenge (see *Commonwealth v. McCloskey*, 272 A.2d 271, 1970). And keep in mind that, in the residence hall setting, one roommate cannot consent to the search of another roommate's property.

- For health and safety reasons. But while courts have authorized some warrantless searches to conduct health and safety reviews, the Supreme Court requires a warrant and a review of the specifics of each case (*Marshall v. Barlow's, Inc.*, 436 U.S. 307, 1978). Therefore, if you conduct these types of searches on your campus, you should limit their use and control them through notices in housing contracts and advance announcements.

- For security and disciplinary reasons. Searches conducted to maintain order on campus have been protected in the past, when they're not conducted for the purpose of criminal prosecution. But in *Piazzola v. Watkins*, 442 F.2d 284 (1971), the court suggested that such searches should be limited to cases involving serious disruption of a school's academic mission.

In addition to these exceptions, some *vehicle searches* and searches connected to *lawful arrests* may also be permitted. These exceptions may particularly apply to public safety officers on campus.

Housing Agreements

Under *contract law*, parties to an enforceable agreement must perform as agreed. The terms of a housing agreement, therefore, must be followed.

If agreements establish expectations of privacy or limitations on searches, the rules are enforceable. This is of particular concern to private campuses, where student rights are established through these contractual means, not via the Constitution.

The current complaint at the University of New Mexico involves the Fourth Amendment *and* the contractual agreement. Residents say the law *and* their contracts protect them from unauthorized inventory "searches."

According to the "Student Living Guide," officials can search a room only in the presence of a resident. In an emergency, however, another student can be called upon by staff to represent the resident during the search. This was not done in UNM's equipment inventory process.

Privacy Rights and Common Law

The Fourth Amendment may not be the only controlling principle on search and seizure issues. Some state and federal laws and court decisions (records access laws, limitations on use of Social Security numbers, etc.) have upheld privacy rights based on state and federal constitutions.

In one Supreme Court case involving search issues (*Rekas v. Illinois*, 439 U.S. 128, 1978), the court pointed out that plaintiffs could recover damages under the *Constitution* or under *state law* "for invasion of privacy."

Summary

Concerns about privacy and searches are as old as the nation. Through an understanding of the related laws and their applications, your campus will be able to adequately address search and seizure concerns.

In the end, your search for knowledge will protect everyone.

At Risk Day and Night: Residence Hall Students

September 1993

Residence halls are targets for crime both day and night. As the threat and fear of serious crime rises, how prepared are campuses to respond? A leading insurance carrier addressed the issue by developing questions for campus consideration. The answers to the following questions should lead administrators to a review of campus policies and procedures and, perhaps, a safer living environment.

CIGNA Education Insurance Services regularly considers issues that place their insureds at risk, providing information on risk assessment and avoidance. The group recently focused on residence hall security concerns, suggesting five elements for review:

- Campus housing policies
- External doors and access points
- Key control
- Personnel
- Reinforcement

The carrier suggests that campuses review these elements to develop ideas for positive and safe change.

Housing Policy

Campus housing policy is the "heart" of the campus housing security plan. The procedures used to operate the residence halls can make a huge safety difference. The insurance carrier suggests several areas of immediate concern. These include:

- *Monitoring* — Does the school use personnel or technology to log in and log out residents? Are areas of concern observed by security or residential staff, or by surveillance equipment?

- *Guest access* — Is there a policy on guest/visitor access? Is it known to the students? Is it enforced by the staff? Are violators of the policy sanctioned?

- *Communications* — Are phones available for use in all rooms in case of emergencies? Are alternative communication systems (such as alarms or speaker systems) available? Are staff trained and available to respond to emergency communications?

- *Assignments* — Are single-sex residence halls available on request? Can a student get a new room assignment swiftly if he or she feels that a current roommate is involved in illegal or unauthorized conduct?

- *Administration* — Do students know where to go if they have a problem or who to petition for change? Are residents adequately advised of how to resolve problems?

- *Student Involvement* — Is there an *active* residence hall safety committee with adequate student representation? Does it meet regularly to review concerns and share ideas?

- *Information* — Is the crime prevention effort visible in the residence halls through posted notices and other materials? Are the residents informed of problems or situations that may put them at risk?

- *Discipline* — Is the campus student conduct discipline program working? Are violators caught and sanctioned?

- *Review* — How often are the residence hall policies reviewed from a safety and security perspective?

External Doors and Access Points

We often read that a security system was in place but not working at the time of an incident. How often does your system fail? Or do residents intentionally bypass the system? Access to the facilities is an important security concern. A review of the entry systems can help limit or control unwanted outsiders. Some of the access and entry concerns:

- *Lighting* — Are the entranceways, corridors, steps, and walkways adequately lighted? Does the campus maintenance program regularly assess the condition and effectiveness of exterior residential lighting?

- *Entrances* — Do exterior doors lock? Are they electronically monitored? Is there a buzzer or intercom system for student communication? Are doors equipped with electronic alarms that go off if the doors are propped open?

- *Security personnel* — Are safety officers stationed at entrances? Are they visible elsewhere? Do they enter the residence halls and patrol the hallways?

- *Equipment* — Are doors solidly built and properly maintained? Are they self-closing and self-locking? Are the hinges inside? Are the locks adequate? Do interior doors have peepholes? Are sliding glass doors secured? Do they have warning labels to promote proper locking? Are lower floor windows adequately secured?

Key Control

Good key control helps control crime. It's a critical element of any residential safety and security plan. With the advent of electronic card access systems, the use of keys may be on the decline. But where used, keys presents a risk that must be controlled.

Insurance experts suggest that decision-makers and staff members consider the issue of key control regularly. When planning a new key control program, they should review:

- *Rotation* — Does the campus have a policy of rekeying locks or rotating locks on a regular basis? Has it proven effective?

- *Loss* — When a key is lost, is the lock rekeyed as soon as possible? Are master keys tightly controlled and limited?

- *Documentation* — Is the key control plan written down, adhered to, and evaluated? Is all rekeying and lock rotation recorded?

- *Technology* — Has the campus considered using technology to address key issues, such as electronic card access systems on exterior or interior doors?

Personnel

The campus must ensure that residence hall personnel are qualified to meet today's security standards. In addition to adequate staff training and supervision, it's important to ascertain the background of employees. Failure to properly screen staff assigned to the sensitive living areas of young people can result in litigation. These claims would allege institutional negligence.

CIGNA Education Insurance Services suggests that those hiring residence hall employees consider several pre-employment checks. For the ultimate protection of the students and school, references should be checked on character and credit, as should records on service in the armed forces and the possibility of a police record. This should be in addition to normal background checks. Security checks should also be conducted on non-residential staff with access to the student living areas. These include custodial services, maintenance and grounds crews, food service, and security personnel.

Background checks are an important part of the employment process, particularly when security is an issue. Make sure they are done and done right.

Reinforcement

Since crime never seems to rest, neither can campus officials charged with protecting people and property. In addition to reviewing campus residential policies, entry and access points, key controls, and personnel, campus officials should also make it a point to constantly re-assess program effectiveness. If change is needed, make a change. Keep students aware and involved. Help them protect themselves by conducting a well coordinated crime prevention program. Make everyone aware of the risks in residential settings and of what they can do to make campus living safer.

Common Sense

Most of the safety and security tips provided annually to students represent common sense. But no matter how obvious the warnings, take the time to make students aware again of the things they should know to live safer:

- Don't prop open exterior doors.
- Lock your door when sleeping or when leaving others sleeping.
- Keep items of value out of sight, and make sure they are marked with an identifying number.
- Ask strangers to identify themselves, and ask staff for credentials.
- Don't loan out your key or make a duplicate.
- Don't leave a note on your door or telephone answering machine announcing that no one is home.
- Report any thefts or suspicious events or people to proper staff.
- Let staff know about safety or security items that aren't working.

All campus staff involved in residence hall life should promote the idea of "living safer." They need to make clear to students that it's everyone's goal, and everyone has a role to play in the effort.

(For more information on CIGNA Education Insurance Services, contact CIGNA Communications, 1601 Chestnut Street, 6 TPL, Philadelphia, PA 19192.)

High Cost of Keeping Books

April 1990, July 1990

Question: What costs campuses millions of dollars a year, affects the quality of education and research, and is a growing problem? Answer: Theft of library materials.

This isn't just a student problem — it affects everyone on campus and in the community. And it's not just students taking away valuable resource materials. In recent years, campus libraries have also become a target for professional thieves interested primarily in rare book and art book collections. But other valuable resources, including manuscripts, full-color pictures from art books, and lithographs, are also subject to theft.

FBI to Throw the Book at Library Thief

Over 11,000 rare books, valued by the FBI at up to $20 million, have been seized in Iowa by law enforcement agents. The rare books and manuscripts were stolen from around the country in recent years, mostly from college and university libraries and private collections. The recovery of the books heightens growing campus concern about protection of rare book collections.

The suspect had been under investigation for over two years following a 1988 arrest in which he was caught outside the University of California-Riverside library carrying burglary tools. With evidence linking him to the theft of books worth $650,000 from the University of Oregon, police obtained a search warrant to enter the suspect's home. Finding a large quantity of rare books and manuscripts, they arrested the suspect on charges of interstate transportation of stolen property. That crime alone carries a maximum sentence of five years in prison and a $10,000 fine.

Various other charges related to the actual theft of the books may be filed by the many states involved. Books and documents found in the home indicate that stolen property came from a number of campus libraries, including Harvard, Notre Dame, Nebraska, Michigan,

Minnesota, and William and Mary. Rare book experts from the University of Iowa are helping police identify the many valuable items.

Security and Access

What can campuses do to protect their collections while keeping resources available for use? That's a central question today. Years ago, libraries were very reluctant to even mark rare books with any campus identifications; they didn't want to do anything to permanently affect the appearance or value of the items. New identification and marking systems have allowed libraries to more actively protect collections — but clever thieves can work very hard at breaching security systems. An example: the use of a hardware store stud finder to locate hidden magnetic devices!

One key to protecting library resources is a *good working relationship with campus security*. Cooperation and communication can help provide a more protective environment for valuable resources and facilitate recovery in the event of a loss. Security reviews and guidelines on reporting losses are two steps in the right direction. A periodic review of potential security problems in library facilities and systems can help reduce or limit losses. And when a resource is lost, campus services need to respond quickly to maximize the opportunity for recovery.

For libraries committed to reducing the opportunities for theft of valuable materials, experts suggest the following tips:

- Maintain a detailed record-keeping system and accountability procedures. Make the system work by providing the resources necessary to keep track of what belongs where and to whom items are assigned.

- Conduct regular inventories. If regular inventories of the full collections aren't possible, there should at least be special periodic inventories of valuable items.

- Keep important and valuable items in appropriate areas within library facilities. It's also wise to strictly maintain a log of personnel with access to key materials and a record of their use of those materials.

- Take the time to carefully screen personnel with access to important library resources.

- Provide training on the use and security of key resources to all staff with access, with follow-up training when appropriate.

- Conduct an environmental audit. Are there too many "hidden" corners in the library? Areas poorly lit? Unsecured or unalarmed exits?

- Educate staff and patrons on security systems and needs. Don't just lock things up: make people understand why some items need to be secured. Enlist the support, not the wrath, of the academic community in the security effort.

- Appoint a library staffer to serve as a liaison with law enforcement officials on campus.

- Establish a written protocol for incidents of loss, to ensure that everything that needs to get done is done properly and quickly.

In addition to the efforts of libraries to protect resources, security staff initiatives and advice are important. In reacting to a loss, cooperation and communication must be stressed. All parties must be prepared to work together swiftly for the best results. An initial step is proper planning for possible losses.

In the wake of a loss, calling in the right people as quickly as possible can facilitate the recovery process. Law enforcement officials offer the following recommendations:

- Don't offer rewards for recovery. This can lead to greater problems in the future.

- Preserve all evidence and the site of the loss for law enforcement investigation.

- Involve local and state law enforcement personnel in the recovery effort as appropriate.

- Notify the FBI if the lost item is valued at over $5,000, belonged to the federal government, or could be sent across state lines. Items valued under $5,000 might also be of interest to the local FBI. It pays to check.

- Begin an inventory to check for other losses that may be related to the security problem.

Campus security officials can also help prevent losses. For crime to occur, there must be an opportunity, and security staff can work closely with libraries to limit those opportunities. Among the measures security personnel stress:

- Adequate security during hours of operation. Material checkout systems need to be designed to protect materials. Limit access to the facilities.

- Book bags, briefcases, and backpacks represent special risks. They should be inspected on entry and exit in most circumstances.

- Door and window security is important. Windows must be modified to prevent the passage of materials. Emergency doors need to have alarm systems to eliminate casual use — or criminal use.

- Security personnel should be aware of library security procedures and knowledgeable about material use policies. Security audits and patrols should extend beyond high-traffic areas to include high-risk areas, such as document rooms, archives, and storage areas.

- Security doesn't end when the library doors close; recent thefts have served as reminders that crime can occur anytime. It's important to have adequate lockdown procedures for closing times, security patrols, staff screening and training, and monitoring equipment, including alarms.

Libraries represent a tremendous investment to colleges and universities. The costs of books and journals continue to skyrocket, placing increasing financial burdens on library systems. Important and valuable resource materials are vital to the educational and research efforts of an institution. The times, however, force an awareness of the potential for crime. The united efforts of libraries, security personnel, and patrons are needed to preserve important resources — for today and tomorrow.

Big Brother Comes to Computerized Campus

June 1991

Is Big Brother reading your electronic mail or storing ID photographs of you? Is Big Brother keeping track of the books you check out of the library or the movies you rent from the video shop? Is Big Brother a college or a university?

The privacy rights of students on some campuses have come into question in our age of technology. As more information is transferred and stored electronically, the danger of unauthorized or inappropriate use of personal information or materials grows.

The storage of library records became a concern at the State University of New York at Buffalo. At Dartmouth College (NH), the privacy of the campus electronic mail system has been questioned. And the storage and use of ID card photographs at Indiana University has raised concerns on that campus. While these privacy issues have not yet led to litigation in higher education, there already has been legal action on similar matters in the private sector. Are campus lawsuits next?

At Buffalo, the issue was the storage of electronic files that contained *library patron borrowing records*. Could that information become public? Does anyone else have any right to know what you're reading and when? Recording systems had been established as circulation control measures, but the possibility of misuse and abuse existed. As part of a probe of some international students, the FBI obtained these records.

Campus programs and procedures were modified to remove electronic links between specific books and specific borrowers. While some felt the information was "safe" inside the system, others recalled the confirmation hearings of a federal jurist, at which the electronic records from his video store were produced as evidence of his personal tastes in film. In maintaining records, it's vitally important to assess the need for keeping data and to address potential abuses.

At Dartmouth, concerns were raised over security of some popular campus *email services*. System procedures require that all information on the email server be backed up and stored. The campus has an internal policy, unpublished, against reading mail in the system. But officials concede that records of all "private" computer mail are saved, and that 12 to 20 staff people have regular access to the system.

What would happen if someone came to the computing center with a search warrant? One campus official says, "It hasn't happened but ... they are just like other documents. ... The courts can get access." The campus email guidebook offers student users some good advice: "Remember that some things are better said in person than via electronic mail." Some have suggested that fear of abuse is exaggerated, but others recall that during congressional hearings, email message files were brought forth that White House officials thought they'd deleted. In establishing backup systems, it's important to understand potential abuses and to take necessary precautions.

The storage of *ID card photographs* at Indiana University has also led to Orwellian concerns. Since well before 1984, the school has taken two ID photos of each student: one for the card and one for the Department of Public Safety. The department uses the photos for investigative purposes, to search for missing persons and to catch students using fake ID cards — arresting 120 students in this way last year.

Most students say they were unaware of the practice. Some are concerned about Public Safety keeping files on everyone on campus, and they have turned to the local American Civil Liberties Union for support. In this age of computer graphics and digitized photographs, photo storage has become more common — as is the potential for abuse. Campus officials should clearly think out and clearly communicate their policies on record-keeping and use.

Off campus, concerns over privacy in electronic systems have led to litigation. Employees at Epson Computers have filed a class-action suit, alleging invasion of privacy. They contend that the company routinely prints out private employee email. The employees argue that state wiretap laws should prevent company "snooping." While the company denies it "indiscriminately reads electronic mail," it argues that it owns the computer system and, therefore, the information on it. No trial date has been set.

With the storage of library records, email backups, and photo IDs, campuses may be able to better serve students. But with the obvious benefits come obvious risks. Officials need to consider record use, record-keeping, and potential abuse of records. They should:

- Maintain only those records necessary for campus operations
- Ensure that stored records are personally identifiable only as absolutely required
- Limit records access to only appropriate individuals

- Provide staff with adequate training on records security and privacy
- Conduct periodic systems audits to maintain security
- Establish personnel and student conduct regulations and discipline policies that deal effectively with record system abuse
- Advise students and system users of record storage policies and procedures, to prevent misunderstandings and avoid problems

Cover Your Assets

March 1994

Do you have a library or a museum on college or university property? Do you have archives with rare books and manuscripts? Do you have collections of historical significance or value? Are these items located in buildings of historical or architectural importance?

Campus museums and libraries are valuable and important — and often at great risk for losses. They must be protected.

Officials responsible for these facilities must work to ensure that collections are properly maintained and protected against loss. Failure to do so can lead to significant historical and financial losses, damage to academic scholarship, and litigation from donors. Administrators and staff need to understand the risks associated with museums and libraries, then take steps to control losses through prevention programs, plans for disaster response, and risk transfer.

Museum and library risk issues are considered in *The Delphian: The Journal of Risk Management for Higher Education* (3:2, October/November 1992). In an article entitled, "Managing Risks at College Museums and Libraries," insurance executives G. McGriffin and S. Spenser explore strategies for dealing with potential losses and litigation. They also outline a variety of suggestions to help protect campus collections.

Appropriate loss prevention efforts include a review of materials and reviews of facilities and building systems. All collections should be carefully documented. Campus staff should know the location of all materials as well as their condition and value. This information is needed, according to the authors, to develop an appropriate plan to protect them.

Facilities and systems require constant attention. McGriffin and Spenser suggest "frequent inspection and monitoring of the collections and facility." Inspecting for flammables and combustibles is critical, as is a review of climate control systems.

With fire a primary risk in older buildings, campuses are urged to consider the following questions when planning loss prevention programs:

- Does the facility contain old electrical wiring, poor insulation materials, or older plumbing?
- Is there a smoke detector and fire alarm system?
- Is there an adequate sprinkler system?
- Is there a fire department close by?

Developing a Disaster Response Plan

Loss prevention programs must anticipate problems. Good planning can minimize disaster losses.

When developing a response plan, McGriffin and Spenser suggest the following considerations:

- Set priorities. What's important? What should be saved first? How?
- Involve all staff in planning for disasters. What could happen and how? What are the most likely disasters to strike your facility, given its age, system, contents, and location?
- How would the staff need to respond? Who would do what? Assign responsibilities in advance.
- Make copies of the plan, review it with staff, and keep it up to date.
- Make sure the response plan will work. Test key telephone numbers. Have local emergency personnel tour the facilities to become aware of building design, collection locations, and special considerations.
- Be prepared to set up an alternative emergency work site and to move the collections if necessary. Where else can the work be done? Where can materials be taken for safekeeping in the event of a campus disaster?
- Make sure that emergency supplies are available and adequate. First-aid kits and communication systems are critical in early disaster response.

Given the value of many campus museum and library collections, as well as the value of the buildings, most campuses attempt to transfer some or all risks to insurance carriers. To do so, McGriffin and Spenser note that campus officials must consider several factors in advance, including the facility features, the collection itself, and disaster response costs.

Transferring Risks to Insurance

Insurance for the building should be based on a professional appraisal. Would the campus replace the structure with another if it was lost in a disaster? Or, would the structure be reproduced in great detail, due to its history and campus tradition?

An insurance policy for the facility must reflect the campus disaster plan to either replace or reproduce. Any campus insurance plan should also consider costs associated with student use of an alternative site during construction.

Insurance for the collection should replace lost items and restore any that are damaged. For full recovery, careful records on the collection are needed to document claims.

The insurance plan should also consider the various costs associated with disaster response. The campus might need to rent facilities, bring in staff on overtime, and make alternative communication plans in the aftermath of a major loss. An insurance plan can also provide coverage for these costs.

In "Managing Risks at College Museums and Libraries," McGriffin and Spenser point out how valuable campus resources can be to schools, students, and scholars. To protect these resources wisely, campus officials need to accept loss prevention plans, prepare for disasters, and consider risk transfer strategies.

Chapter 10:
STUDENT CONDUCT

Introduction

> Young people do not "shed their constitutional rights" at the school house door.
>
> *Goss v. Lopez*, 419 U.S. 565 (1975)

In the beginning, there was "in loco parentis." Today, the relationship between students and educational institutions is far more complex, but it still remains deeply rooted in the law.

At private and public institutions, students are expected to understand and comply with basic campus regulations and standards. When violations are alleged, they are reviewed and addressed through established disciplinary processes. Different standards may exist at public and private institutions due to constitutional considerations, but all students are entitled to fairness and compliance with established policies.

Students who have run afoul of campus regulations have often challenged campus practices in the courts. They often contend that campus systems have violated their constitutional or contractual rights, that they are unfair, or or that they failed to follow established policies.

Dealing with Dishonesty

November 1994

"I have cheated." In a 1993 survey of 2,000 of America's top high school students, almost 80% responded that, at some point in their high school careers, they had been academically dishonest. To the surprise of no one, this cheating carries over into the college years. Reports indicate that collegiate academic dishonesty is on the rise. Just what can campuses do?

Several sources have attempted to determine how much cheating goes on. In the second edition of *Issues and Perspectives on Academic Integrity*, Gary Pavela and Donald D. Gehring cite several campus-based studies indicating that 25% to 40% of undergraduates may have cheated during college.

A recently published federal government report suggests those statistics may be too low. A Department of Education Office of Educational Research and Improvement (OERI) report, *Academic Dishonesty Among College Students*, reviewed the types and causes of collegiate cheating and campus responses. The report also includes recommendations for higher education responses and considerations.

Academic Dishonesty reports survey data showing that collegiate cheating could occur among 9% to 95% of students. The wide range is explained in the report as caused by survey techniques, sample sizes, research methods, and differing institutions and cheating definitions. The survey also cites a comprehensive report, prepared in 1992, which reviewed academic integrity issues with over 6,000 students at 31 "highly selective" institutions. The report revealed that 67% of students admitted to some form of involvement in campus cheating.

Why?

The OERI report suggests several commonly accepted rationales for collegiate dishonesty. First, cheating among students is often related to pressures to succeed. Competition for scholarships, graduate and professional programs, and careers is intense, which encourages dishonesty.

The report also notes that many students are apparently indifferent toward cheating. This could be seen as a reflection of the dishonesty students observe in authority figures, such as parents, government officials, sports heroes, and teachers. A final suggested reason is confusion over what actually constitutes academic dishonesty. Some students may be unaware of their cheating, due to ignorance or the lack of clear guidelines.

The most commonly reported forms of campus cheating involve plagiarism and copying from someone elses' examination or paper. Other examples of academic dishonesty include purchasing term papers, submitting a paper for credit in several courses without permission, faking illness to avoid exams or paper deadlines, or adding false items to bibliographies. Student's efforts to help others cheat also constitute a common form of academic dishonesty.

What Can Be Done?

Surveys on campus cheating indicate that many campuses are not vigorous in identifying cheaters and enforcing academic dishonesty polices. What should be done to promote awareness and involvement? What can be done to improve academic integrity and limit opportunities for cheating?

Among the suggestions from experts to promote integrity, increase awareness, reduce opportunities, and deal effectively with those who cheat:

- Improved communication — Use campus publications and media to send messages on standards and the importance of academic integrity.

- Improved student involvement — Make sure that students are involved in the development and implementation of policies.

- Increased faculty involvement — Increase faculty participation in processes to promote awareness and help communicate campus values.

- Coordination of efforts — Ensure that consistent messages are sent to students; all academic integrity efforts should have some central purpose and direction. A single office should be designated or established to coordinate campus academic dishonesty policies, education, and enforcement.

- Development of academic integrity programs — Promote awareness campus-wide and support enforcement efforts, including training for faculty and teaching assistants, educational programs for students, assistance services for faculty members when faced with possible dishonesty, exam proctoring services, and positive recognition for faculty efforts to control cheating.

- Development of policies — Develop and adopt clear policies on academic dishonesty. Make sure that guidelines adequately consider definition and examples of permitted and unauthorized student collaboration. Use separate publications and printed materials in formats conducive to student comprehension to distribute policies to instructors and students, and make sure that the message gets out to the broadest populations.

- Enforcement process — Define and identify the process that will be followed to investigate and review allegations. Add strong sanctions to promote compliance.

- Class size — Recognize that dishonesty is more likely to take place in large, lecture-style classrooms.

- Evaluations — Develop a process of comprehensive student evaluation prior to testing to make course cheating less effective. This could include a major thesis or comprehensive examination at the end of a term or prior to graduation.

- Reporting — Establish a convenient and effective means of reporting suspected cheating.

- Education — Use orientation programs designed to promote integrity appreciation by new students.

- Sanctions — Publish sanctions throughout the academic community to serve as deterrents, and publish annual statistics on academic dishonesty and campus response.

Suggestions for Instructors

Instructors can battle cheating through the following means:

- Use the first class of each semester to articulate academic integrity standards for students.

- Use more frequent testing and written assignments during the semester, develop an understanding of student capabilities, and reduce the pressures associated with relying on a single exam or paper.

- Allow members of judicial or disciplinary boards to make class presentations or review standards with student leaders.

- Reprint campus academic standards on all syllabi.

- Require an outline and first draft of all papers and written assignments.

- Meet with students to discuss their paper topics to ensure student knowledge.

- Have students make oral reports on paper topics, or answer student questions in class.

- Scramble test questions and answer sheets to avoid in-class copying.

- Avoid using published standardized examinations, reusing examinations, and take-home tests.

- Require students to provide photo identification before entering the exam site.

- Collect exam books in an order that allows an instructor to ascertain seating location.

- Seat students randomly for exams, to break up potential dishonesty in pre-arranged groups.

- Provide adequate proctoring during exams.

- Require students to leave all personal items except writing instruments outside testing areas.

- Provide graders with answers to the course exams as needed, not all at once.

- Collect scrap paper after exams to prevent circulation of accurate questions and answers.

- Have each student sign each page of the exam to allow handwriting comparisons.

- Copy examinations and papers before returning them to students to discourage them from altering responses and requesting later reconsideration.

To preserve the value of collegiate learning and the degrees colleges and universities award, institutions must take effective steps to ensure academic integrity through policies and programs to promote awareness and limit cheating. Campuses must establish and maintain ethical academic standards for the benefit of all.

For more information: Academic Dishonesty Among College Students, U.S. Department of Education Office of Education Research and Improvement, 555 New Jersey Ave., NW, Room 615, Washington, DC 20208. *Issues and Perspectives on Academic Integrity*, 2nd ed., National Association of Student Personnel Administrators, 1875 Connecticut Ave., NW, Washington, DC 20009.

Everyone Has a Story for Sale

May 1994

The campus newspaper ad boldly stated, "Do you have a term paper assignment that's a little too much work? Are you cramped for time with a nightmarish deadline closing in? Let us help you." Many students did. They bought papers from "term paper mills" — companies that mass produce term papers for sale to college students.

Students who took advantage of this offer were assured of quality and safety. The company brochure said its products were "commensurate [sic] in quality with work sufficient to be submitted in a graduate program at an accredited university." The papers were said to be custom made and professionally typed and prepared by "writers who can handle any subject." Finally, to avoid "duplications," the company recorded the student's name, campus, instructor name, and course information to make sure that a similar paper was not provided to another student in the same program.

The state attorney general was not as impressed by the service as some students were. He sued in state court, attempting to halt the sale of mass produced term papers. In *State v. Saksniit*, 332 N.Y.S.2d 343 (1972), the court heard the state challenge.

Over the past two decades, term paper companies have put a new face on student cheating. Instead of copying off a classmate's test paper, college students can now peruse catalogs that list research papers available for sale. Term paper mills advertise in campus newspapers and national magazines and stress quality and confidentiality to would-be student buyers. But the submission of purchased papers for credit constitutes academic dishonesty, and a concerted effort has been made to prevent this form of cheating. A combination of federal and state laws and campus discipline reduced the use of purchased term papers but certainly did not eliminate it.

State Efforts at Control

As the term paper mill industry grew, so did the list of states that adopted legislation designed to control the industry. While enforcement of such laws has been limited, where enacted they are a means of controlling cheating of this type. State regulations usually prohibit ghostwriting or the marketing and sale of produced term papers.

Ghostwriting-for-profit laws, for example, can be found in Maryland and Pennsylvania, where "a person may not sell or offer for sale any academic paper" or "sell or offer for sale any assistance in the preparation of a dissertation, term paper, or thesis."

In New York, "No person shall prepare any written material intended for submission as a term paper by a student at an educational institution." At least a dozen other states have adopted similar language in the battle against purchased term papers.

Most state laws, however, require the seller to know or have reason to know that the product is going to be turned in for credit. To get around this, today's term paper mills offer "research" services, not finished products, according to their marketing materials. To enforce the laws, states must then find a link between the sale and the buyer's attempt to defraud. Sometimes marketing materials can be used to show seller's awareness of the purchasing student's intent.

New York has been the site of most reported litigation against term paper mills. In *People v. Magee*, 423 N.Y.S.2d 417 (1979), the attorney general tried to use company sales materials and product format to prove intent to sell papers for student submission. The company sought to protect itself from prosecution by including a disclaimer in its catalog. The materials indicated that the company's products were not "a substitute for the reader's own original research and writing." The company's small print noted that it did "not support or condone plagiarism or academic fraud."

But the state showed the court that the copy sent by the company to purchasers was typewritten in a format designed for immediate submission for credit. That, combined with the firm's marketing claims, led the court to ban the sale of the firm's products in the state. The court was convinced of the company's illegal efforts. It dismissed the company's other defensive effort, a student signature on a "condition of sale" statement. The court found the signed statement, by which the purchaser promised not to plagiarize, to be "patently tongue-in-cheek and executed with an obvious wink."

The court, in *Magee*, rejected the "for research only" argument as well. This defense was found to be "specious" because the papers were carefully designed to be used as term papers.

And in *Saksniit*, another New York court reviewed term paper mill company practices in an effort to determine legality. The court ruled against the firm, based on its advertising campaign and its product ordering process. Because the company emphasized the pressure students face and the high quality of the work, the court saw a clear intent to provide a product for submission as a student's own academic work. In addition, the ordering student filled out a form indicating topic desired, number of pages, and class information to avoid possible duplication. The court saw this as additional clear evidence of the firm's intended use of its products as student work.

The federal government may use postal regulations to control the "shopping for ideas" system. Federal law makes it unlawful to use the mail system in efforts to defraud. It allows the postal service to stop service to those involved in fraudulent activities. The denial of postal service has been used against term paper mills.

Under the law, use of the mail may be subject to an injunction when it is determined that an enterprise is fraudulent or is part of a fraudulent scheme. In 1973, the government halted mail service to a Massachusetts company found to be a term paper mill. That injunction was challenged by the company in *United States v. International Term Papers*, 351 F. Supp.76. The district court ruled in favor of the company, since a student — not the company — commits the fraud by submitting the paper. The court held that the company should not be penalized for the actions of the purchaser.

But on appeal, the Circuit Court ruled for the government, finding that the company was part of a scheme to commit fraud by supplying the product. Since the product and payment used the mail service, the court felt the injunction against the company was warranted. It was illegal, said the court, for the term paper mill to get payments through the mail for products that enabled students to commit academic fraud.

Campus Responses

Given the limited enforcement efforts at the state and federal levels, colleges and universities need to be prepared to deal directly and effectively with term-paper mills and those students using their products. In the *Journal of College and University Law* (18:2), an article by K.M. Capano focuses on "Stopping Students from Cheating: Halting the Activities of Term Paper Mills and Enforcing Disciplinary Sanctions Against Students Who Purchase Term Papers." In the article, the author suggests the following:

- *Regulate term paper advertising on campus.* This could be accomplished by eliminating ads (with the cooperation of campus newspapers) and removing notices from bulletin boards.

- *Use state and federal laws.* Under existing state legislation and postal service regulations, campuses can seek action to halt the sale of term papers to students.

- *Obtain the names of students using the products.* In an effort to investigate possible academic fraud, some schools have obtained or tried to get the names of students who have purchased products from term paper mills. In some cases, companies have been ordered to provide client lists for campus review. In other cases, purchaser privacy has been preserved.

- *Discipline students who purchase term papers.* To be effective, campus academic honesty statements should define plagiarism to prohibit the use of "outside sources" without acknowledgement. Sanctions for use of purchased materials can range from failure in a course to expulsion.

Taking Ideas Without Credit

March 1995

Plagiarism has been described as "a kind of theft; one writer steals the ideas or even the actual words of another writer without giving credit where credit is due." What constitutes plagiarism? How can campuses limit these violations of academic integrity?

Proper Academic Standards and Sanctions

She had been recruited to the university as a scholar and athlete. An injury ended her basketball career, but she stayed involved in athletics, providing support services to others. Her grade point average was 3.7, and she was under consideration for a prestigious international graduate study program. Then, her Spanish instructor accused her of plagiarism on a term paper.

The university had academic standards requiring acknowledgment of sources in written work, and students signed statements indicating that they had adhered to those standards. In this course, the plaintiff had selected a topic for a paper and her instructor had recommended a book as a good resource. In reading the term paper, the instructor felt material had been plagiarized directly from the resource book. She gave the student an "incomplete" and recommended a disciplinary inquiry.

A hearing board then found that the student had violated campus standards, and it recommended delaying her graduation by one year. After the president attempted to impose the sanction, the student took her case to court, in *Napolitano v. Trustees of Princeton University*, 453 A.2d 263 (1982).

There, a New Jersey appellate panel asked the campus to reconsider its decision, questioning whether the student really intended to "pass the submitted work off as her own." By a unanimous vote, the campus committee reaffirmed its earlier finding of responsibility and delayed her graduation.

The student returned to court, asking for her diploma. She maintained that the campus had failed to follow its rules, did not have sufficient evidence of wrongdoing, and had imposed a sanction that was too severe. The court disagreed.

It noted that Princeton's academic standards had been established in advance and that the committee's finding was reasonable and properly reached. The court found the term paper to "constitute a mosaic" of the works and ideas of another. Finally, in considering the one-year suspension of graduation, the court said:

> Plaintiff claims that the penalty is supposed to provide something educative in its imposition. She argues that the penalty here is improper because there is no educational value found in it. Perhaps plaintiff's self-concern blinds her to the fact that the penalty imposed on her, as a leader of the University community, has to have some educative effect on other students. ... To paraphrase the poet, "the child is mother to the women." We are sure it will strengthen her in her resolve to become a success in whatever endeavor she chooses.

Definitions and Advice

Students must be encouraged to read and understand campus academic dishonesty standards. These standards should include clear definitions and examples of plagiarism.

Each campus must establish its own definition of plagiarism. Most definitions focus on circumstances in which the words or ideas of others are represented as being one's own work. Many campuses also consider student intent in their definitions; their policies may require proof of intent: Did the student "knowingly or intentionally" attempt to deceive the instructor? For other campuses, intent is not an issue: they maintain that plagiarism may result from student negligence.

Whatever the standard selected, campus employees are urged to clearly word and widely distribute that standard to promote compliance and avoid challenges. In addition, experts suggest that students be reminded of how and when to document sources. Most resources suggest acknowledgments when using:

- A direct quotation
- A copied table, chart, or drawing
- A passage paraphrased
- Specific examples or facts, taken from specific sources, to explain or support

Strategies

Because plagiarism is widespread and often difficult to detect, instructors are encouraged to consider prevention strategies. Among the suggestions offered in *Academic Integrity and Student Development* (1988):

- Limit topics for class papers and presentations. This may restrict opportunities for prepared or previously used papers.
- Change topics regularly to avoid re-use of works previously submitted.
- Maintain precise format specifications for papers, making it more difficult to recycle or buy papers.
- Provide specific criteria for papers, and grade according to those criteria.
- Make students "show their work" by requiring that they get advance approval of their topics, submit tentative bibliographies and an outline draft prior to writing, and include a file with notes, drafts, and other work papers with the final paper.
- Make students stick to the topic. Students who change their minds late in the semester may be more apt to cheat, due to time pressures.
- Give a surprise quiz on the papers a week before they are due, to assess student knowledge.
- Retain submitted papers for several years, to allow for comparison.

These strategies should limit the opportunity for academic misconduct. Plagiarism is a serious problem that needs to be addressed through solid policies, education, and prevention strategies.

For more information, consult: Academic Misconduct: Cheating and Plagiarism, Ralph D. Mawdsley. Topeka KS: National Organization on Legal Problems of Education, 1994. *Academic Integrity and Student Development: Legal Issues and Policy Perspectives*, William L. Kibler *et al*. Asheville NC: College Administration Publications, 1988.

Courts Let Campus Arms Reach Out and Touch

May 1990

Can campuses pursue disciplinary sanctions against students for off-campus activities? This is a question of growing interest to campuess and communities nationwide, as increasing student problems compel campus officials to re-examine this issue. At stake are community relationships and the standards and safety of our institutions.

In response to demands for student freedoms, many campuses withdrew their interests and jurisdiction for off-campus occurrences in the early 1970s. As *in loco parentis* authority waned, institutional rules and regulations became more focused on campus occurrences. Students off campus, it was argued, were subject to community standards and enforcement mechanisms. If it happened off campus, let the community take care of it!

Less than two decades later, this approach is under severe scrutiny, as student vandalism, noise, parking, trash, and partying have municipalities looking back to campus for a strong response.

An obvious reaction is to make off-campus incidents subject to campus discipline. "Is it legal?" is always the first question asked. And the courts have consistently answered, "Yes."

An early case serves as a good example of the judicial support for campus discipline in off-campus incidents. In *Due v. Florida Agricultural and Mechanical Institute*, 233 F.Supp. 396 (1963), students sued after being suspended for off-campus contempt of court convictions. The student handbook stated that students could be disciplined if convicted of crimes. The federal district court upheld the suspension, finding adequate support for the discipline in the school's policies and ample evidence against the students.

But can students *automatically* be suspended from the school if convicted of off-campus violations? Automatic sanctions violate due process considerations, according to judicial decisions. In the early 1970s, the University of Texas System had a rule requiring a two-year suspension for any student convicted of drug-related offenses. In *Paine v. Board of Regents of the University of Texas System*, 355 F.Supp. 199 (1972), a federal district court overturned the rule, citing constitutional objections.

The automatic sanctions policy violated both due process and equal protection clauses, said the court — *due process* because a convicted student on probation had no opportunity to show that he posed no risk on campus, and *equal protection* because only students convicted of off-campus offenses were denied hearings on campus. Campus discipline could deal with off-campus occurrences, but it had to adequately protect constitutional rights.

Court Decisions Extend Campus Authority

Just what is the basis for campus authority over off-campus student conduct? Courts have long recognized the need for schools to establish and maintain standards of conduct. A series of key cases established justification for school discipline: to prohibit violations of the law and to promote the protection of the educational environment from disruption. Support for these principles can be found in U.S. Supreme Court cases, including *Goss v. Lopez*, 419 U.S. 565 (1975), and *Healy v. James*, 408 U.S. 169 (1972). Rulings of this type give colleges and universities the right to establish standards of conduct.

The validity of student conduct rules must also be examined. Rules and regulations have been upheld when they've been shown to be necessary to the educational environment and to campus discipline. But in drafting rules, officials should take care not to be vague or overly broad. Students must be able to understand rules and know what actions they permit or prohibit, and the rules must be reasonable in scope. Students should also have an opportunity to review the regulations.

Student conduct rules can also be seen as part of the campus-student contract. Courts are willing to enforce conduct rules that comply with legal requirements and that are incorporated into the contractual relationship, including rules that extend jurisdiction to off-campus events and incidents.

Two additional cases involving student discipline in Virginia and Maryland provide additional support for extension of campus sanctions to off-campus offenses. In both cases, the court upheld campus rights to discipline students for off-campus conduct.

In *Krasnow v. Virginia Polytechnic Institute*, 551 F.2d 591 (1977), the school disciplined a student who'd been placed on probation by a state court. Campus rules permitted discipline for both on- and off-campus drug use. The student sued to stop the disciplinary sanctions, but the federal appellate panel upheld the school's action. According to the court, the school "clearly has the prerogative to determine that any unlawful possession of drugs or criminal conduct of the students is detrimental to the university."

Off-campus drug use and student conduct discipline were also at issue more recently in *Sohmer v. Kinnard*, 535 F.Supp. 50 (1982). A University of Maryland pharmacy student participating in an off-campus clinical experience was found to be using drugs. He was later convicted of an unrelated criminal drug charge. His school conducted a disciplinary hearing and dismissed him for two violations: use of drugs on a clinical internship and off-campus possession of drugs. The student sued for readmission.

The court upheld the dismissal, in view of the school's interests, rules, and procedures, noting that "illegal use and possession of narcotic drugs would violate the law and the Code of Ethics of his profession and would therefore be detrimental to the interests of the University."

Policy Guidelines

Campus rules can be applied to off-campus incidents. But they must:

- Comply with established legal standards

- Be legally adopted and properly communicated to students

- Not be too vague or too broad

- Be written to clearly communicate to students what actions are permitted and prohibited

- Be fair and fairly enforced, with adequate due process and equal protection considerations

- Not limit student's exercise of constitutional rights

If they meet legal standards, student conduct regulations can be enforced to control behaviors detrimental to the campus, whether on campus or off. And intense community pressures are compelling more and more campus officials to do so.

Campus Hearing Option for Asult Victims

April 1993

In light of the negative realities of today's society, college campuses across the country are being forced to deal with sexual assault within the campus community. In attempting to respond, colleges and universities are re-evaluating campus sexual assault procedures and their relationship to off-campus proceedings.

Properly designed and supervised, campus conduct proceedings can be a viable option for student sexual assault victims who are uncertain about getting involved in more formal, off-campus criminal proceedings.

Because of lower standards of proof and other deviations from traditional courtroom procedures, campus hearings may provide an adequate and appropriate forum for sexual assault and harassment cases involving students.

Lower Standards Often Appealing

Many students pursue campus disciplinary procedures, rather than criminal procedures, because of a unique feature that many campus disciplinary systems have.

While traditional courts require prosecutors to prove guilt "beyond a reasonable doubt," campus proceedings often require only "clear and convincing evidence" or a "preponderance" of the evidence to find a party responsible. In addition, some forms of hearsay (testimony based on secondhand information) may be admissible in campus proceedings, and unanimous verdicts are generally not required.

These lower standards make it easier, in some cases, for victims to take campus action rather than criminal action against an accused student or students.

At the University of Pennsylvania, for example, a student was expelled for sexual assault charges that were never prosecuted in court. The campus, however, held its own two-day hearing and imposed the sanction. The decision was based on campus standards of justice.

The case involved charges of an assault in a fraternity house. The victim didn't report the incident for two months, so the local district attorney decided not to press criminal charges.

Harvard Wrestles with Definitions

Harvard University (MA) has struggled with changes in campus conduct language designed to attack the problem of acquaintance rape.

A task force suggested a policy that would have required "express consent" before any sexual contact between students. But an administrative board rejected that language, saying it was "impractical" and "inappropriate."

Campus discussion on alternatives continues. The university's Date Rape Task Force has offered a broad definition of acquaintance rape, which would include "any act of sexual intercourse that occurs without the expressed consent of the person, or is accompanied by physical force or threat of bodily harm."

The task force's proposal also says that "lack of consent may be indicated physically or verbally and need only be expressed once." The group has also suggested that "rape may also include intercourse when the person is incapable of expressing or withholding reasoned consent, or is prevented from consenting because of the intake of alcohol or drugs."

The task force's goal is to establish policies that clearly communicate acceptable and unacceptable practices and actions with regard to acquaintance rape.

More Modifications

At the University of North Carolina-Chapel Hill, the district attorney proposed modified guidelines for pursuing acquaintance rapists in off-campus courts.

The prosecutor insisted that a victim had to fight an assailant and make a clear statement against sexual contact for an act to be considered acquaintance rape. Under the new guidelines, however, a victim can communicate "her lack of consent by saying 'no,' or by other reasonable means which would indicate the victim is not a voluntary participant."

The guidelines are intended to help prosecutors in cases dealing with acquaintance rape issues. They come in response to several assaults in the area.

At Pasco-Hernando Community College (FL), a subcommittee of the governing board is developing new guidelines for the handling of sexual assault cases. Among the considerations are rape education programs and efforts to encourage more campus discussion of the issue and its impact.

Summary

Campuses should adopt and publicize written policies that condemn sexual assault. The policies should include appropriate definitions, guidelines, hearing procedures, and awareness programs.

Society is beginning to understand more about sexual assault and sexual assault issues. That means society will probably be focusing more attention on the way campuses implement acquaintance rape and sexual assault procedures.

Alcohol Sanctions: Suggestions for Change

July 1992

Alcohol consistently mixes into campus discipline cases. Found in assault cases, in accidents and injuries, in automobile incidents, and in unwanted sexual activity, alcohol also directly affects classroom performance, extracurricular behavior, and interpersonal relationships.

And research on campus alcohol use suggests that the problem will not be going away anytime soon. Consider the following statistics:

- Even though purchase and consumption is restricted to persons over 21, 90% of college students have used alcohol before college.
- College students drink far more heavily than do non-college students of the same age group and high school seniors.
- Male college students drink heavily twice as much as college women, but women began to catch up in the '80s.
- While daily alcohol use for high school students has declined this decade, a similar trend has not been found for college students.
- Getting "drunk" one to three times a month almost doubled in frequency for both sexes in college during the last decade.

While campus prevention and awareness programs have increased dramatically, college and university officials still need to be prepared to respond judicially to "problem" student drinkers. Campus discipline programs must be ready to intervene and act appropriately in order to protect students, the campus, and the community.

Discipline for alcohol-related incidents should be an important part of any campus alcohol policy. The Inter-Association Task Force Model Campus Alcohol Policy Guidelines, developed by a coalition of college and university professional organizations, recommend that campus alcohol guidelines clearly articulate procedures for adjudicating violations of alcohol policy; such procedures should include an explicit statement of sanctions.

Disciplinary Intervention

When necessary, the campus must intervene in alcohol situations. Essential to any intervention process are education and training. It is important to prepare personnel likely to come into contact with students in alcohol difficulty. They need to be able to identify students who may need intervention activity. This training is particularly important for residence hall staff, public safety officers, and judicial affairs personnel.

To assist in intervention, campus disciplinary personnel must be able to review incident reports to assess what actions may be appropriate. Among the options could be either referral to standard disciplinary hearings or referral to education or other support services.

Disciplinary processes, predicated upon an awareness of the impact of alcohol abuse on students and campuses, are helpful to develop appropriate sanction options. Administrators should make sure that some form of liaison between the disciplinary system and campus counseling or alcohol abuse support systems exists. The two working together may assist in the development of sanction alternatives.

Alternatives to Tradition

What if traditional forms of discipline are ineffective? Judicial systems should provide students involved in conduct violations an option between some form of an "encouraged recovery" sanction or a more traditional sanction. A recent review of college alcohol programs suggests the following possible alternative sanctions:

- Volunteer service hours in campus prevention activity
- Required individual substance abuse counseling
- Participation in a six- to eight-week alcohol education service
- Alcohol program contracts, agreements to work on modifying some behaviors
- Some form of group counseling sessions
- Outpatient treatment, with suspension a possible consequence of failure to participate
- Leaves of absence to seek extensive treatment, such as detoxification

If alternatives are to succeed in promoting the interests of the school and the student, they must build upon a well-defined referral system to support changed behaviors. An alternative system provides an opportunity for students to participate in an alcohol awareness education program as an alternative to other disciplinary sanctions. Such alternative systems promote learning and responsibility, not punishment *per se*. Granted, the student may choose to regard such alternatives as punishment anyway, even if they represent the lesser of two evils. But if campuses are truly concerned about altering behavior(s) and attitudes, they need to consider carefully whether a purely punitive approach will ever work effectively.

In alternative programs of this type, students are evaluated and then agree to a program of chemical-free activities and education. At the end of a specified period, the student is re-evaluated. At that time, the student can be returned to the program for further work, referred back to the discipline process for sanctions if he or she has not cooperated, or released from the program and sanctions if the process has been successfully completed. These programs are a positive alternative to other more traditional and punitive measures.

Summary

Alcohol use and abuse is a fact of life in the college population, and one that shows no signs of disappearing anytime soon. The realistic campus understands that it will probably never eliminate all illegal alcohol use or stop all student abusers. But an enlightened approach to the problem would take these as givens and try to tailor its response around them. As a result, in addition to appropriate awareness and education programs, the campus discipline process must be prepared to identify students with alcohol difficulties and provide appropriate intervention, processing, and referrals.

Due Process for Greeks

August 1990

Behind each newspaper headline concerning troubled Greek life on campus is some form of a disciplinary proceeding. A chapter, a national organization, a campus, or any combination thereof may need to take action. In a nation of laws and rights, what rights do the laws give to Greek-letter organizations and their members?

Background

Only in the last hundred years has the phrase "due process of law" taken on today's meanings. Prior to the Civil War and the 14th Amendment to the Constitution, "due process" was generally viewed as it was in 1215, when the Magna Carta called for government to act "by the law of the land." Government had to follow its rules.

Our more modern appreciation of due process may be best demonstrated by the language of *Hurtado v. California*, 110 U.S. 516 (1984): "Any legal proceeding enforced by public authority ..., in furtherance of the general good, which regards and preserves ... principles of liberty and justice, must be held to be due process of laws." Now, in addition to following rules, government needs to make sure that the rules promote liberty and justice.

Today, when we consider "due process," we are primarily concerned with two types:

- *Procedural* due process, which focuses on the fairness and validity of rules
- *Substantive* due process, which focuses on prohibiting arbitrary and capricious conduct that has no rational basis or is done in bad faith or with ill will

One key element in the matter of due process is *state action*. The federal and state constitutions restrict only the right of government to act. As written in the 14th Amendment (ratified in 1868), "Nor shall any State deprive any person of life, liberty, or property, without due process of law." Clearly, government and governmental units, including public institutions of higher education, are bound by the law to provide for due process, procedural and substantive, in disciplinary proceedings. Private schools and groups generally need only follow their own rules, as they're not normally seen as conducting "state action."

Due Process Considerations

When due process is required, what is it and how much of it is needed? These are basic questions that must be considered in any disciplinary process.

Generally, due process requires:

- Notice of time and place of hearing and the nature of any charges
- Names of witnesses and an opportunity to examine evidence
- An impartial hearing with an opportunity to present a case
- A finding of facts and reasons for sanctions

How much process is due depends on two factors: the extent of possible sanctions and existing campus or organizational policies. Impartial decision-makers are bound to follow policies, and the greater the possible sanction, the more due process that should be provided.

But in structuring campus or organizational Greek disciplinary processes, recall the words of a federal district court judge in *Bahr v. Jenkins*, 539 F.Supp. 483 (1982), who noted that if schools (or groups) have to "make a federal case out of every petty disciplinary incident, the whole purpose of having any discipline at all and any rules of conduct would be defeated."

When a campus must deal with discipline for a Greek organization or a member, normal campus procedures should apply. Many schools have separate Greek organization panels that hear Greek-related cases. Others depend on general student conduct boards. In either case, due process considerations must be consistent with previously established rules, the nature of the institution (private vs. public), and the extent of potential sanctions.

Chapter Discipline

Discipline of an organization by a campus or Greek governance body raises a basic question: Can an association or membership group be held liable for the acts of its members?

Yes, under certain circumstances, according to court rulings. For example, in *Federal Prescription Service v. American Pharmaceutical Association*, 663 F.2d 253 D.C. Cir. (1981), the court ruled, "It must be shown that the members were acting with apparent authority conferred upon them by the association."

The key words in this ruling are "apparent authority." *Actual* authority is an express grant of authorization to act. *Apparent* authority exists when it seems, to an informed outsider, that the act is being performed with group authority. The act doesn't have to be conducted with the express authority of the group; it need only *appear to a reasonable person* that the act is indeed authorized.

In judging whether or not group sanctions are appropriate, consider the following factors:

- The proportion of the membership involved in the incident or activity
- Any participation or prior knowledge of the activity by chapter officials
- The extent to which the group was aware in advance of the activity
- Any history of previous incidents
- Group cooperation in any subsequent investigation and group sanctions internally imposed

These factors can help determine whether group sanctions are appropriate. But in pursuing group sanctions, remember: groups can be entitled to due process as well as individuals!

Member Discipline

How much due process should members get from their chapters? Since the chapters are not, through campus recognition processes, considered to be part of the state, their acts are not generally viewed as "state action." Chapters are bound only to follow their rules.

But can there be limits on the rules? Can rights to due process be established under the group rules?

Yes. As first suggested by *Fraternal Law*, consider the case of baseball player Pete Rose a few years ago. In the midst of his legal troubles, he was able to get a county court to issue a restraining order temporarily preventing Major League Baseball from disciplining him. Why? Because baseball officials hadn't followed their own rules, which said sanction proceedings would be conducted "with due regard for all the principles of natural justice and fair play."

Case law has long supported the notion that private groups have to follow their own rules and play fair with members. In other examples, a professional organization and a youth group both were accused of expelling members unfairly. In both cases, judges provided strong language to guide other membership groups, such as fraternities and sororities.

In *Normali v. Cleveland Association of Life Underwriters*, 39 Ohio App.2d 25 (1975), the court extended due process rights to members of a private group. Said the court, in this case "due process ... is not derived from the Constitution, but is comprised of three basic elements: (1) absence of (individual) bad faith, (2) compliance with the constitution and bylaws of the association, and (3) neutral justice."

In a similar case involving expulsion from a membership organization, *Curan v. Mt. Diablo Council of Boy Scouts*, 195 Cal. Rpt. 325 (1983), a California court came to the same conclusion. Said the court, it "is deemed arbitrary and in violation of the common law right of fair procedure when the expulsion is substantively unreasonable, internally irregular, or procedurally unfair."

Private membership groups, such as fraternities and sororities, should provide members with due process even when the law doesn't explicitly require it, for two reasons: basic fairness and good risk management.

Summary

In disciplining students and groups, institutions are bound by the law and campus policies to provide appropriate due process. Public institutions engaged in "state action" must provide the basic elements of due process, with consideration to providing due process in proportion to potential sanctions. Private institutions should base their due process decisions on fairness and risk management. Group sanctions are justifiable when an incident occurs with the apparent authority of the group. Membership organizations must follow their own rules and play fair with members.

Due process means "with fairness." At all levels of the discipline process, it's important that all processes and decisions focus on fairness.

Be Sure It's the Real Thing

November 1990

An official transcript has often been called the single most important document or record issued by a college or university. Used to gain employment, financial aid, promotions, or admission to another school, the transcript represents a student's institutional history, including demographic and academic data. Given the wide use and importance of transcripts, transcript fraud comes as no surprise.

Background on Fraud

There are two types of transcript fraud: creation of academic records from fictitious schools and tampering with records issued by recognized institutions. Fake transcripts are generated the same way as the better-known "diploma mill" produces documents. They come from a "grades for hire" industry serving a population obsessed with success — at any price.

Alteration of official documents is, unfortunately, more common and harder to detect. Sometimes, the fraud takes place from within: employees and students can use official paper, seals, documents, computers, and other equipment. It's generally easier to identify external alteration of documents.

One major problem today is the number of transcripts in circulation. This has dramatically increased because of the Buckley Amendment. Under the Family Educational Rights and Privacy Act of 1974, all students and former students are entitled to receive copies of their transcripts. As a result, copies of campus records marked "issued to student" are now circulated in record quantities.

Most schools won't accept the student copy for official purposes; licensing and certification services require official transcripts as well. But due to cost and timing, some employers accept student copies — against the advice of school officials — which creates problems.

An additional problem is the high quality and greater availability of photocopy equipment. This has given unscrupulous students unprecedented opportunities to alter official or official-looking documents.

To maintain control over the accuracy of academic records, campuses need to encourage all transcript users to require official documentation. These records should be sealed, signed, and dated. In addition, the document should be delivered in some way other than by the student. The method generally preferred is mailing in a sealed envelope.

Transcript fraud enjoys an opportunity when campus controls over the process are weak or when transcript users accept unofficial copies. The campus has a responsibility to ensure the regulation of campus transcript processing and to educate users on the importance of accepting only official documents.

Guidelines

The American Association of Collegiate Registrars and Admissions Officers has established guidelines to discover and control the use of altered transcripts.

The quality of the transcript is the first defense against fraud. To make it harder to alter official records, campuses must insist on quality transcripts. They should be individually signed or certified, and they can be printed on special paper or with colored ink to make reproduction harder. The document should also indicate the quality elements necessary to make a document official, so that the person receiving it can verify its authenticity.

For mailing, transcripts can also be placed in institutional envelopes and posted with an institutional postage machine rather than a stamp. This can be an additional control factor, protecting the integrity of the transcripts.

AACRAO suggests that organizations and institutions examine the transcripts they receive for fraud, using these questions:

- Was the document mailed directly and stamped or marked by an institutional postage meter?
- Does it have a signature and seal?
- Is it recently dated?
- Does it appear to be altered in any way?
- Is it similar to the form used by other schools or to other documents received recently from the same school?

Guidelines have also been established to help transcript users respond when they sense a problem with a particular document.

Check with the issuing institution on the style and format of its documents and on student directory information for verification. If documents seem suspicious, return them to the issuing institution for review and reissue, or ask the student in question to request new official copies, to see what happens. Often, the issuing school will want to see the document in question to conduct its own investigation.

It may also be appropriate to talk with the involved student. During an interview, probe areas of concern on the transcript — and weigh the responses carefully.

When an employer or institution believes a document is fraudulent, several responses are suggested:

- Contact the issuing institution and send officials a copy for their own investigation.
- Report the incident to campus and local law enforcement personnel, as appropriate.
- Attempt to maintain any evidence, including the document itself, in its original condition.
- Respond positively to those who identified the false document.
- Fully review the incident with staff to promote greater attention to authenticity of documents.

Conclusion

Students who work hard for academic success deserve recognition for their achievements. If less conscientious students try to cut corners with fraudulent transcripts, campuses need to respond strongly. Campuses must remain vigilant in their efforts to control the integrity of the official academic record process — on and off campus.

Fake Diplomas a Big Business

January 1996

Just what is a medical degree worth to people these days? Somewhere between $5,000 and $27,000, according to law enforcement personnel who broke up a major fake college degree ring in New York City.

Officials there discovered at least four individuals trying to obtain medical degrees from an obscure Caribbean school. All four were indicted on charges of conspiracy to obtain fraudulent degrees. Their degrees, if awarded, would have provided the recipients with an opportunity to complete medical residencies in the United States. Indicted in the scheme were a college professor, a physician's assistant, a records clerk, and a laborer. The complete investigation into the Caribbean school resulted in over 20 arrests in the bogus diploma scheme.

How big is the business of false degrees? And what's being done about them to protect the integrity of legitimate college and university diplomas? A review of several notable cases may help answer these questions.

Sheepskins for Sale

The most recent information on false diplomas was developed by studies in the U.S. in the 1980s. They suggested that there were at least 100 schools in about 20 states offering bogus degrees at the time. The FBI estimated that the schools were selling between 10,000 and 15,000 fake degrees annually.

Experts categorize businesses selling degrees as either diploma "mills" or "factories." The factories simply sell degrees, whether from an unknown institution of their own or false copies of legitimate school degrees. The mills are more common. They generally offer degrees to "students" based on academic requirements that are far less rigorous than at other accredited schools. With the close correlation now between a college degree and personal earning power, business for diploma factories and mills appears to be booming.

Across the U.S., state and federal authorities have used prosecution and legislation to try to shut down these businesses. The latest effort involves the state of Wyoming.

Wyoming

Until last year, Wyoming had no direct standards on degree mills and factories. According to state officials, doctoral, master's, and bachelor's degrees were apparently available in the state through institutions that were not recognized by the state.

To get around state regulations, several diploma mills had filed incorporation papers, allowing them to do business in the state. Under Wyoming law, these corporations did not have to file anything with state education officials.

After the state education department got complaint calls from other states and other countries, officials decided to investigate possible diploma mill activity in the state. They found almost 60 companies operating as businesses with the words "school" or "college" or "university" in their titles. One report indicated that one company abroad was selling degrees for up to $700.

Acting on the complaints, Wyoming adopted legislation on diploma mills. Under the new laws, state corporations can no longer offer degrees solely for money or grant diplomas based only on "life experiences." State officials hope that the new rules will chase the companies out of business — or at least out of the state.

The case of one particular company from Wyoming shows how the mills worked under the old and new laws. The corporation, called George Washington University, Inc. (not related to George Washington University), filed to conduct business by stating that it worked in Germany and Nevada. When the new law went into effect, the corporation simply changed its name to George Washington International Students' Services, Inc. and tried to stay in business.

The Wyoming experience is similar to that of other states that have dealt with diploma mills in past decades. Because these business operations are relatively small and generally use the mail system for communication, they can move from place to place as necessary.

In the late 1970s, Missouri was a state favored by diploma mills, but increasingly tough laws forced most of the companies to move out. California was also once the home to hundreds of reported diploma mills. When the state strengthened its standards on them in 1991, those "schools" moved out.

Today, it is believed that Iowa has now become a home to at least a dozen diploma mills, because it doesn't yet have regulatory standards against them. Based on the growth of the mills in the state, education officials have now proposed new laws to control them.

Enforcement

While the New York City case of the Caribbean medical school degrees highlighted state enforcement efforts, federal authorities are also working on the problem. Consider the case of American Western University and the Northwestern College of Allied Science.

Despite their impressive names, the schools were simply diploma mills. They both sold degrees, at high costs, to individuals who wanted academic credentials without any academic experiences. In the mid-1980s, FBI agents conducted an undercover investigation into the schools, based on complaints.

With little police effort, FBI agents posing as "students" were able to buy any degrees they desired. One bought an M.B.A. for $510, while another purchased another management diploma for $830. For their money, the agents got more than just the fake diplomas: they also received complete academic transcripts, which indicated courses not taken and grades not received.

In *United States v. Geruntino* (1985), a federal district court in North Carolina heard evidence that the two schools had issued over 3,000 degrees and had related revenues of over $2.3 million before the government closed them down. The major operators of American

Western and Northwestern Allied Science pleaded guilty to federal mail fraud charges after the investigation was completed.

Use of False Degrees

While the business of degree mills may be moving from state to state, the risks of using unearned academic degrees remains constant, on and off campus.

In one case, a college instructor lost his job when officials discovered that he didn't have the degrees he had claimed. He was hired based on transcripts that included a B.A., an M.A., and even a Ph.D. from New York University. When it was determined that he had no degrees, he was fired and denied unemployment benefits. His case was also referred for possible criminal charges. By all accounts, he had done an adequate job teaching.

In another case, a medical student was successfully completing his education in medicine at West Virginia University and looking forward to getting his degree. Then, school officials discovered he had used false academic credentials to gain admission to medical school. When he was expelled, he sued.

In *North v. West Virginia Board of Regents*, 332 S.E.2d 141 (1985), the court upheld the student's expulsion, for breaching the WVU disciplinary code (although not yet a student at that time) and for fraud. The court found no reason to become involved in an academic dispute of this type, but the state's highest court did note that "a person who cheats to get into school and gets caught gets expelled."

Summary

Degree mills and factories continue to operate, and their diplomas continue to be used to fraudulently gain employment and collegiate admissions. State and federal authorities are using legislation and enforcement to ensure that degrees are earned, not bought.

For more information: Diploma Mills: Degrees of Fraud, by David W. Stewart and Henry A. Spille, 1988, published by the American Council on Education. Contact: Macmillan Publishing Co., Front and Brown St., Riverside, NJ 08075.

Campuses Try Mediation

February 1991

Are judicial processes the best method for a campus to solve problems and resolve conflicts? With the decline of *in loco parentis*, decades ago campuses began to lean heavily on legalistic methods of addressing conduct violations. Heavily dependent on due process, and with a strong emphasis on procedure, a variety of campus "courts" developed.

But some schools have challenged that approach and developed an alternative — mediation, a cooperative, problem-solving venture that gives conflicting parties an opportunity to work out their differences with the assistance of a neutral third party.

The benefits and process of mediation are featured in *Enhancing Campus Judicial Systems* (Jossey-Bass, 1987, New Directions for Student Services, 39). In their article, "Mediation: A Judicial Affairs Alternative," R. Serr and R. Taber consider the background and methods of mediation. More recently, the *NASPA Journal* (Spring 1990) contained an article by J. Hayes and C. Balogh, "Mediation: An Emerging Form of Dispute Resolution on College Campuses," which explores the features and extent of mediation efforts. Together, these two articles provide a comprehensive look at the elements and implications of campus mediation.

Conflict Resolution

Mediation is one of four generally accepted forms of conflict resolution:

- Negotiation — a bargaining process involving the parties in dispute
- Mediation — a form of negotiation assisted by an intervening, neutral third party but leaving the final decisions to the two parties in conflict
- Arbitration — a process in which a neutral third party makes the decisions in the conflict
- Judicial action — an adversarial process in which a binding decision is made favoring one part at the expense of the other

Mediation works best when dealing with situations in which conflict can be explored. It assumes the parties are interested in settling differences and allows the principals to develop an understanding of problems and to initiate solutions.

Mediation can become a formal method of resolving campus differences. While some higher education mediation systems differ to some degree, most programs follow these basic steps:

- Offer or referral — Once a problem is identified, a mediator can offer services to the parties. The benefits of the process and the methods to be used should be explained. In some schools, referral comes from student affairs, residence life, or public safety units.
- Discovery — After the parties agree on mediation, the mediator needs to assemble and review all relevant documents and meet separately with the parties. After this is accomplished, face-to-face mediation sessions can be scheduled.
- Sessions — At the start of any mediation meeting, it's important for the parties to understand the rules of procedure. Each party should be given an opportunity to present its case or issues, based on relevant facts. Once this is done, the

neutral mediator should begin to identify the areas of conflict in need of resolution. Attention then turns to brainstorming possible solutions and agreeing on steps to implement them.

Follow-up contacts by the mediator are appropriate after specified time intervals, to ensure that the parties are making progress.

Current Campus Programs

A collegiate survey from a few years ago indicated that fewer than three dozen NASPA member schools had mediation programs. Most of these programs were initiated during the past decade. A majority of the programs were found at public institutions. Schools of all sizes ran the programs. Other than staff time, the schools invested few campus resources: over half of the responding schools spent $1,500 or less in operating the programs each year.

Most of the campus mediation efforts currently concern disputes between students, many involving roommates. However, the process can be used to address a wide variety of other conflicts.

Campus Considerations

In establishing and maintaining a mediation program, a campus needs to consider and resolve several administrative issues. Among them are the size and scope of the program, resources, reporting relationships, training programs, confidentiality, program site, record-keeping, and resolution follow-up.

The variety of conflicts to be handled should dictate the *type of program* needed. Is it going to serve resident students? All members of the campus community? Local residents? What kind of disputes? Landlord-tenant? Roommates? Vandalism? Violence? Faculty vs. student complaints? In considering program size and scope, administrators should carefully review the range of cases to be handled and the potential populations to be served.

A quality mediation program can be developed with few *resources* beyond staff time. Some funding is necessary to support the program, including advertising, training, and office supplies.

A variety of *reporting relationships* are possible for a mediation program. Most reside somewhere in student affairs, but other options can be considered. Student committees can also be established to advise or supervise the program.

The survey of NASPA institutions showed that many of the current campus mediation programs are run by personnel without *formal training*. While some training programs have been used, most personnel receive "on the job" training. Appropriate staff training should make the program more effective.

What kind of protection should be given to mediation records? Are they *confidential?* Some states have taken action to protect records and to protect mediators from having to testify in court on matters in which they participated. Administrators should carefully review and understand the statutes of their state. Then they need to adopt strong campus policies on access to records, to prevent problems and confusion.

Where should the campus mediation program be located? How can the *site* affect program effectiveness? The program can be located independent of other units. It can also be physically within another unit, such as a dean's office, counseling center, or residence halls. Location can influence the type of case activity. An office will attract different conflicts depending on whether it's located in the housing office, the dean's office, or a counseling center. Officials should carefully consider the site to make sure it suits program goals.

Some program *record-keeping* is important to properly manage and evaluate the mediation effort. It's also helpful to have copies of agreements available to facilitate necessary *follow-up*.

Summary

Mediation is working on campuses today. With a relatively small investment of time and effort, officials can develop an alternative to the adversarial judicial approach to campus conflict. Only a handful of campuses have fully developed the model, but increased concern over conflicts may lead to a re-examination of mediation. It may find a more hospitable climate for growth in higher education in the years ahead.

Mediating Conflicts

October 1994

Within our academic communities, just as in our various off-campus contacts and relationships, conflict is inevitable. Litigation is costly, damaging to relationships, and lengthy, and it takes control of the solution out of the hands of the disputants and puts it into the hands of a judge or jury. How can we keep campus disputes out of the courts?

Individuals and groups on campus should have a variety of methods available to them for finding solutions to disagreements. An increasingly popular approach to settling disputes is mediation. Instead of having the parties involved confront and compete, mediation attempts to have them collaborate on a solution. An understanding of mediation principles and techniques may help promote and improve campus dispute resolution.

Definition

Mediation is based on voluntary participation in a structured process in which a neutral third party assists disputing parties to identify and satisfy their interests. Skills and techniques are combined to help the parties in conflict develop a fuller understanding of the conflict and facilitate their efforts to find ways to resolve it. Mediation on campus could give those in conflict an opportunity to be heard and to listen, hopefully to better understand each other's concerns, feelings, and thoughts. Hopefully, this can help identify creative ways to solve problems while developing stronger long-term relationships.

Principles

On and off campus, mediation processes are based on several key principles revolving around the role of an independent, third-party mediator. Generally, trained mediators:

- Only assist when the parties' participation is voluntary
- Protect the confidentiality of the parties and the process
- Assist in resolving identified conflicts
- Assist in drawing information and answers from involved parties, not telling the parties what to do or how it should be done
- Do not make determinations for the parties
- Facilitate the process by establishing ground rules, moving the process forward, and working toward a solution
- Attempt to create a "win-win" environment

Why Mediation?

Several theories underlying the dispute resolution process are identified in *Mediation: A Comprehensive Guide to Resolving Conflicts without Litigation* (Jossey Bass, 1984), by J. Folberg and A. Taylor. They suggest that participants in disputes can generally make better decisions about outcomes than can outside authorities. Participants may also be more willing to comply with resolution terms if they played an important role in the outcome, taking some responsibility for it. Additionally, an agreement is more likely to be sustained if it accurately reflects the needs, intentions, and abilities of the participants. Finally, since the mediation process is flexible, it allows for change to meet difficult or unique circumstances or issues.

Parties in conflict may have dispute resolution opportunities beyond mediation available to them. But other standard approaches have the potential for some negative consequences. Direct *negotiation* between the parties, without the aid of a third party, should be encouraged. But it is often unsuccessful, and direct confrontation can be harmful to long-term relationships. In *arbitration*, control of the solution is lost to the participants, as an independent party makes the final decision. And *litigation*, as reviewed earlier, has the drawbacks of time, expense, and complexity.

Mediation provides for the active involvement of an independent third party as a *facilitator*, in a confidential and relatively informal process that has a concern for the parties' continuing relationship.

Technique

Experts suggest a six-step mediation process that allows for opening statements, fact finding, an opportunity to frame the issues, review of options and negotiation, development of an agreement, and closure.

Beginning with *opening statements* allows a mediator to explain the process and the third party's role and establish other ground rules. At the opening, it's important for the parties to be convinced of the mediator's neutrality and competence.

The initial effort at *fact-finding* allows each party to describe the problem in detail. This is done for their benefit in an effort to clarify issues, agreement, and differences from their perspectives.

Once this has been accomplished, a mediator can *identify and frame* the real matters in dispute by trying to develop a "neutral" statement of the problem in conflict. This step also presents an opportunity to isolate issue components. A conflict may have many parts, and breaking it down into component parts may be important.

Next, the mediator will turn the parties toward *option-finding and negotiation*. The participants are urged to generate as many solutions as possible, reserving judgment on their acceptability until later. A mediator can keep the parties on the issues through questioning, clarifying comments, and pressing toward fairness and a common goal. During negotiations, the mediator tries to get the parties to consider how a problem should be addressed.

If an option proves to be agreeable, it needs to be clearly articulated on paper. An *agreement* should contain the exact intentions of the parties, to avoid continued or renewed conflict. A mediator can help the parties write how the issues have been resolved.

Ending mediation involves a confirmation of any agreement through the parties' signatures. An effort is made to summarize the process and settlement, to consider possible follow-up, and then close the process.

College campuses can be places of conflict, and those disputes can have an effect on any learning, living, and working environment. Non-judicial methods of dispute resolution, like mediation, are an efficient and effective approach to settling some conflicts.

For more information, contact: National Association for Mediation in Education, 205 Hampshire House, Box 33635, University of Massachusetts, Amherst, MA 01003; Ph: 413/545-2462 or *National Institute for Dispute Resolution,* 1726 M Street, NW, Suite 500, Washington, DC 20036; Ph: 202/466-4764. Or contact your local Better Business Bureau.

Chapter 11
STUDENT LIFE: ACTIVITIES, ORGANIZATIONS, AND ATHLETICS

Introduction

> While the freedom of association is not explicitly set out ..., it has long been held to be implicit in the freedoms of speech, assembly, and petition. There can be no doubt that denial of official recognition, without justification, to college organizations burdens or abridges that associational right. The primary impediment to free association flowing from non-recognition is the denial of use of campus facilities for meetings and other appropriate purposes.
>
> *Healy v. James*, 408 U.S. 169 (1972)

It is an old debate, but one that keeps coming back. What right do student organizations have to be on college campuses? What rules must they follow? What if they advocate ideas in opposition to school beliefs? In the 1960s, the debate focused on student activist groups. Most recently challenged have been the associational rights of groups based on sexual orientation interests.

While private institutions generally can be more restrictive toward student groups, public colleges and universities must offer them recognition unless the groups advocate violence, fail to abide by campus rules, or engage in disruptive activities.

Among the other legal issues of concern in today's student organizations: activity fees, advisor liability, cults, election requirements, liability for activities' use of logos and symbols, athletics, alcohol, and discipline.

Liability Risks for Greeks

July 1993

Risk and Greek letter organizations seem to go hand in hand in most campus liability discussions. Meanwhile, the media seem to report the latest transgressions of every fraternity and sorority, leaving national organizations and campus officials to worry about what will happen next and where.

Given the perceived risks associated with Greek life on college campuses, a Louisville (KY) insurance firm, Harris & Harris, studied claims filed against fraternities. The company found that, for many Greek groups, member fees for insurance are greater than general membership dues.

What kinds of claims, company officials wondered, could make insurance premiums so high for Greek organizations? And why, they asked, is coverage so difficult for them to obtain?

To answer their own questions, the firm analyzed the insurance claims filed over a four-year period against a sampling of national Greek organizations. To be as accurate as possible, the firm hired outside companies to research claims filed between 1987 and 1991.

The study looked only at claims filed, not at all incidents that could lead to liability. It's assumed that some cases are settled by the parties without filing an insurance claim, to avoid publicity or prevent insurance rate increases.

Therefore, the review is *not* an exhaustive look at all fraternity risks. But it does provide a fact-based listing of practices and incidents that result in liability claims against Greek organizations. These groups can use the data to plan educational programs that encourage change and promote safety.

The Top Three Risks

So what places fraternities and others at risk when it comes to fraternity activities?

The study found that slip and fall incidents, fights, and drinking and driving incidents were the top three reasons insurance claims were filed against Greek groups. Combined, these types of claims represent over 50% of those made against fraternities.

Slip and fall cases are generally caused by poor property management. Failure to keep stairwells clear, sidewalks shoveled, and floors well-maintained led to 30% of the liability filings against Greek organizations.

An active effort to correct common household hazards (e.g., wet floors, loose carpets) could prevent similar cases from occurring in the future.

About 15% of the claims filed against Greek organizations were related to *fighting*. Typically, the fights involved a member and a non-member and occurred during a house event involving alcohol.

By paying more attention to alcohol laws and preventative programming, Greek groups could decrease the number of these types of claims as well.

Member use of a vehicle after drinking made up the third-most-reported category of liability risk (8% of claims filed). These incidents generally occurred after house parties or other social events where alcohol was consumed. A fraternity member was found to be partly to blame for an accident or injury in most cases.

The survey found several other types of common claims against Greek organizations:

- Injuries from athletic events (7%)
- Damage to the property of others (7%)
- Charges of sexual abuse or harassment (5%)
- Falls from roofs (4%)
- Hazing incidents (3%)
- Fires (3%)

Not surprisingly, the study found a common link among most of the high-risk activities: alcohol. A few simple statistics tell the story:

- About 47% of *all* claims against fraternities involved underage drinking.
- About 86% of the claims involving a death also involved alcohol.
- Alcohol was a significant factor in many of the general liability claims.
- Alcohol was a factor in more than 96% of the fights, sexual abuse incidents, and falls from roofs that resulted in claims.
- About 87% of the automobile claims involved alcohol.
- About 65% of other "slips and falls" and 48% of the hazing-related claims involved alcohol.

The survey also illustrates the dangers associated with group activities. About 26% of the claims involved death, paralysis, or a serious injury.

The news wasn't all negative, however. About 54% of the claims against Greek organizations ultimately involved no monetary awards. Of those that did, 32% were less than $10,000, 9% were between $10,000 and $50,000, and only 5% were more than $50,000.

While newspaper headlines often print plaintiffs' demands for staggering damage sums, in the end, only 2% of all claims against Greek groups resulted in payments exceeding $100,000, the study found.

The study also found that the majority of claims were filed by members of the fraternities they were suing. Only 46% of the claims came from non-members.

Liability: A Continuing Risk

While campus and off-campus headlines may sometimes sensationalize the dollar claims associated with Greek liability incidents, they usually confirm that the risks for Greek groups and student groups in general remain significant. A quick review of recent campus newspaper articles demonstrates the point best.

At the University of Minnesota, for example, the latest liability claim against a fraternity involves *sexual harassment*. A female cook has filed a 10-charge civil suit against the Greek organization she worked for, claiming she was subjected to repeated incidents of sexual harassment and verbal abuse. She says she suffered emotional distress, mental anguish, and humiliation as a result.

She only worked at the fraternity for two-and-a-half months before filing her claim against 15 of its members. She has demanded an apology along with sexual harassment sensitivity training for the group. She also seeks damages of about $50,000.

At Southern University (LA), the claim against a Greek organization is *hazing*. A student says he was "physically beaten and abused" by a fraternity. He was hospitalized for various injuries and temporarily paralyzed, and he ended up blind. He wants the fraternity to pay damages for his injuries.

At the University of California-Santa Barbara, injuries suffered in an *alcohol-related accident* at a fraternity party were the subject of a recent court decision.

In 1989, a member of the group injured himself jumping into a shallow, artificial stream that served as a luau party decoration. He was paralyzed and accumulated over $600,000 in medical expenses. The parties recently reached an out-of-court settlement for $200,000 to avoid prolonged litigation.

Other fraternities on campus have since taken steps to prevent further incidents of this type. The amount of alcohol available at future events, for example, will be limited, and organizations will continue to explore ways to reduce liability risks.

Conclusion

These stories, combined with the findings of the insurance firm's study, serve as dual reminders of the many avoidable risks college students and their organizations face daily. The statistics highlight the extent of the problems, and the newspapers portray the damage that can result.

By knowing the risks and taking concrete steps to reduce liability (and accidents), Greek organizations and other student groups can do themselves a big favor — for the short term as well as the long term.

Greeks and Alcohol Don't Mix Well

May 1992

The presence of alcohol in campus Greek life has always created risks, but never more so than today. With the increased drinking age, numerous state hazing statutes, federal substance abuse legislation, the development of dram shop and social-host liability laws, increased awareness of the dangers of drinking and driving, sexual assaults, and continued reports of problems and litigation, it is clear to all that Greeks and alcohol should mix only very carefully, if at all. Colleges and campus Greek organizations need to understand the risks that alcohol represents to all students, organizations, alums, and institutions.

Criminal and Civil Liability Exists

Greek organizations and members risk *criminal* prosecution on alcohol-related matters, particularly when alcohol is distributed to persons who are minors or intoxicated. It's illegal to provide alcohol under these circumstances in most states. In addition, forced consumption of alcohol as part of initiation or affiliation rites may violate anti-hazing laws effective in at least 33 states.

Civil liability may be faced by Greeks over alcohol-related incidents due to dram shop and social-host laws. Some states have dram laws giving victims of alcohol-related incidents the right to sue persons or establishments that sell alcohol. Liability may be claimed for irresponsible distribution of alcohol that causes personal or property damage.

Social-host laws are also found in a majority of states. They extend liability to persons or groups that provide alcohol that causes damage or loss. Many establish liability when alcohol is provided to minors and those intoxicated, while others extend responsibility to all involved in the distribution process, regardless of the age or condition of the "drinker."

These laws, established by state legislatures and judicial decisions, create a variety of criminal and civil risks for Greek organization programming involving alcohol.

Cases of Concern

While fraternities will not be held liable in all instances of alcohol-related injuries or deaths, members do risk criminal responsibility and civil liability under social-host, dram shop, and tort laws every time they serve alcohol.

A 1987 court decision points out risks inherent in one typical Greek activity. A University of Illinois freshman passed out from excessive alcohol consumption during a pledge activity. He had been given a large pitcher of beer and eight ounces of liquor. Over 14 hours later, his blood alcohol content was still two-and-a-half times the level of legal intoxication. The student suffered permanent damage to arm and hand nerves and sued the fraternity. In *Quinn v. Sigma Rho Chapter of Beta Theta Pi Fraternity*, 515 N.E.2d 1125 (1987), the court ruled that the fraternity had a duty to its prospective members that was violated. The group provided alcohol to minors and then pressured them to drink.

Another case, involving a University of South Carolina student death, demonstrates how a civil court action can affect a student group. In a state with a .10 blood alcohol content (BAC) legal intoxication level, a pledge died after forced consumption led to a .46 BAC. Four pledges passed out during drinking games involving a mixture of beer, wine, and liquor. The fraternity left them alone to sleep it off. By morning, one pledge was dead. The state courts ruled that:

- Greek organizations have a *duty* not to injure members.
- The fraternity *breached* that duty by forcing alcohol consumption and not providing assistance when clearly needed.
- The group's actions and failure to respond were the *proximate cause* of the pledge's death.
- The death represented a damage or harm due to *injury* that was actionable.

Duty, breach, proximate cause, and injury are the four required elements in establishing legal liability. The court ruled that the group had acted in a negligent manner and it awarded the pledge's family $200,000 in compensatory and $50,000 in punitive damages.

The death of a first-year student participating in a Greek-run hayride at the University of Arkansas also resulted in a liability judgment against a fraternity. After drinking fraternity-provided alcohol on the hayride, the student was struck by a car while crossing a road. His family sued, and the group was held responsible for the death in *Alpha Zeta Chapter of Pi Kappa Alpha v. Sullivan*, 740 S.W.2d 127 (1987).

And in *Fassett v. Delta Kappa Epsilon Fraternity*, 807 F.2d 1150 (1986), a fraternity provided alcohol to a minor who subsequently crashed his car. He killed one passenger and injured another. The injured student sued, claiming the group was responsible for damages. A trial court, using traditional state law, found only the bartender from the Greek party liable. But an appellate court ruled that other members of the group could be held responsible as "accomplices," even though they did not directly provide the alcohol to the student.

Campus Groups Respond

Faced with increasing concerns over possible injury, death, or damages, Greek governing bodies on many campuses have responded with common sense regulations.

At the University of Arizona, groups have agreed not to sponsor events with alcohol service on weeknights and during exams. In addition, specific limits have been placed on the amount of alcohol that can be provided, based on expected attendance. Off-duty police officers patrol alcohol events that are registered in advance with the chapter advisor and local police. Other restrictions, including a limit on the number of events that can be scheduled on any given weekend, are also enforced.

Greeks at Purdue University (IN) adopted effective alcohol risk management programs that stress regulation, education, and enforcement. They prohibit the purchase of bulk quantity alcoholic beverages and the use of chapter funds for alcohol, and they require proof of age and non-alcoholic beverages. Among the time regulations are a four-hour service limit, no service after 2 a.m., and a continuation of music for at least 30 minutes after the service of alcohol has ceased. Designated drivers are also required. An alcohol policy committee was formed to implement the program and to conduct periodic educational programs for chapters. A judicial review board was also formed to counsel organizations on the policies and enforce the rules. They plan to make investigative visits to each chapter's function, some announced and some unanticipated.

Fraternities and sororities at the University of Akron (OH) have also adopted a progressive plan to reduce liability, promote health and safety, and enhance Greek-community relationships. Strict proof of age is required for service and campus ID cards are not acceptable proof. Alcohol cannot be purchased or distributed at an event, but may be consumed by those over 21 years of age who bring their own. Open parties are prohibited; all parties and all guests must be registered in advance. A team of chapter advisors, presidents, and governance officers are welcome to attend any event to ensure the regulations are followed. In addition to inspection visits, a sponsoring organization must provide one non-drinking monitor to promote safety and rule enforcement for each 25 guests.

Programs like those at Arizona, Purdue, and Akron are good examples of campus Greek efforts to minimize the possibility of injury, death, and civil and criminal sanctions.

Advice for Campuses and Groups

An American Council on Education (ACE) White Paper on fraternity and sorority liability issues recently summarized recommendations for all to consider that have a particular application to alcohol-related risks. Among the suggestions:

- *Promote education.* The dangers and need for personal responsibility need to be known.
- *Have clear conduct rules and enforce them.* Standards have to be established and maintained for the protection of all.
- *Preserve the separate identities of the campus and Greek groups.* Make sure that the proper relationships are maintained. Don't blur the responsibilities that each has.
- *Assume duties carefully.* Don't take on responsibilities for care and safety unless you mean to and are able to carry out these assumed duties.
- *Check for risks.* Make sure that past events and current practices are carefully reviewed to ensure appropriate application of the law and other legal duties.

Conclusion

Alcohol and Greek life together have had a troubled past. Help students understand the criminal and civil risks and cases of concerns *before* their next event. Help provide positive responses and advice and, working together, help change the future.

The Hazards of Hazing

January 1990

"*College people call it hazing rather than torture, but it amounts to the same thing.*"

That's the way a major newspaper article began its examination of pledge practices of national fraternities and sororities. But Greek organizations, campuses, and associations have begun to battle that reality and perception in a profound way.

A campaign of change is being waged on three fronts, with two major organizations adopting non-pledging programs through an all-out information campaign by the Inter-Fraternity Council, and with a new American Council on Education White Paper on campus relations with Greeks. The combination of the three efforts may have a significant impact on the future of Greek life on campus.

Student Life

Two Fraternities Eliminate Pledging

Two large national fraternities took the final first steps toward ending organizational hazing by eliminating pledging periods. The organizations — Tau Kappa Epsilon and Zeta Beta Tau — both moved to reduce the most abused membership time period.

Since the 1920s, Greek organizations have maintained a six- to eight-week period between the time a member is asked to join the group and his or her full initiation. This period is one in which pledges serve in a subordinate status while they prove themselves worthy of full-fledged participation.

Zeta Beta Tau has already eliminated the pledge period. It is now granting full membership to individuals at the time they're invited to join. After years of efforts to halt hazing, they've now eliminated the time period in which it would occur. Tau Kappa Epsilon is prepared to reduce the time period for invitation and initiation to no more than 14 days, for the same reason. In an effort to promote brotherhood and mutual respect, both groups have established programs to promote leadership skills, community service, and academic excellence.

Several other national organizations are preparing to follow this lead out of a desire to eliminate the problem — or out of fear of the responsibility for what could happen if they don't. Several schools have banned Greek organizations in recent years, and *self-regulation* seems to be a key to *self-preservation*.

National IFC Efforts

With the Greek population having doubled in the last 15 years to over 400,000 undergraduates, greater educational and awareness programming is necessary. The National Inter-Fraternity Council, an association representing 59 of the 62 national college fraternities, has publicly declared war on hazing. In ads in *The Chronicle of Higher Education* and fraternity magazines, the IFC declares that hazing "is a dangerous form of intimidation that makes a mockery of the whole concept of fraternal love. It does not strengthen bonds of friendship. It does not prove an individual's superior qualifications in any way."

Packets describing the anti-hazing policy were sent to 5,194 member chapters on 900 campuses across the country. Conference leaders have also begun a series of meetings with chapters and campus officials across the country to urge the development of new rules emphasizing positive behaviors. With at least 53 fraternity-related deaths reported in the past 10 years, this new awareness and educational program is needed *now*.

ACE White Paper

In an effort to redefine the proper relationship between campuses and Greek organizations, ACE has published a white paper for its members. The basic premise: that schools can best protect themselves from liability by offering programs that teach students to assume responsibility for their own conduct.

The White Paper contends that schools should treat students as adults and not subject them to special supervision or controls. This should be done in an attempt to avoid any appearance of *in loco parentis*, creating additional responsibilities to students or third parties.

On the question of hazing, the paper urges policies similar to those being promoted by the IFC. Schools should make sure that regulations clearly prohibit hazing — and that the rules are strictly enforced. In the event of hazing accusations, there should be an official investigation, with loss of campus reorganization a potential sanction for substantiated violations.

In establishing a proper relationship between a school and its Greek organizations, the ACE white paper makes several recommendations for campus consideration:

Emphasize education. If a campus wants to contend that it treats students as adults, it must make sure that students *understand* and *accept* that concept. Educational programs and materials must be developed to inform students of their duties and responsibilities. Campuses need to help "guide students in the exercise of their new adult freedoms." This education effort should begin with freshman orientation.

Establish clear conduct rules and enforcement. Rules should be clearly stated so that students understand fully their rights and responsibilities — and understand that they're "expected to assume personal responsibility as adults for their behavior, without supervision." Only those rules that can be enforced should be included in the regulations.

Ensure a separate legal identity for Greek organizations. A key to campus legal defense when faced with liability claims related to Greek activities is *separation*! Make sure that your school doesn't take "formal or informal actions that compromise the status of fraternities or sororities as independent corporations legally distinct" from the school. Avoid any actions or policies that could unintentionally establish a Greek organization as an entity of your school.

Don't assume duties. There's a general feeling that schools should be held responsible for ensuring Greek organization compliance with all conduct, health, and safety rules. Correct this misconception! Where the campus intends to regulate and supervise activities, it must do so "carefully and diligently."

Check danger areas. Risk management has become an increasingly important consideration. Campuses need to be aware of dangers and potential dangers associated with the practices and activities of Greek organizations — and they need to respond appropriately.

The ACE White Paper is designed to assist schools in establishing constructive and protective relationships with Greek organizations. A copy of the report, entitled *Colleges, Fraternities, and Sororities: A White Paper on Tort*

Liability Issues, is available for schools from ACE, Division of Governmental Relations, 1 Dupont Circle, Washington, DC 20036.

Summary

Greek organizations have grown dramatically in membership. And Greek members continue to die. In reaction, responsible organizations — chapters, student groups, and professional associations — have initiated efforts to provide for a safer and more legally responsible Greek experience. Through *education* and *awareness* comes *responsible action*.

Greeks: Initiation Rites New Wrong

April 1992

Only the tragic cases make the news. But you don't have to read many media accounts of fraternity hazing to get a sense of anger and frustration — anger that young people still are put, or put themselves, at great risk of injury and death, and frustration that the combined efforts of Greek organizations, campuses, and legislators have yet to end the threat. Has it been reduced? Yes. Is there much more to do? Unfortunately, yes.

From a quick read of campus and local newspapers from around the country, consider the following. They represent only a sampling of recorded incidents:

- A student at the University of Texas was chased by fraternity pledges over a cliff and died.
- Police are investigating the alleged fraternity kidnapping of a University of Oklahoma student. Three men attacked him while he slept, put a pillow case over his head, tied him up at knife point, and drove him miles from campus, leaving him in a ravine.
- Campus and national fraternity leaders imposed sanctions on a Rutgers University (NJ) chapter for branding pledges on their buttocks.
- Probation was the penalty for a University of Wisconsin chapter that spat soft drinks and dumped food on pledges in order to promote a more perfect union, a.k.a., "bonding." The group had earlier been sanctioned for "racist and discriminatory" activities.
- A Morehouse College (GA) freshman pledge died of cardiac dysrhythmia after a ritual "chest-pounding" by fraternity members.
- An Oklahoma State University chapter was suspended for tying a pledge to an attic ceiling beam and forcing him to drink large quantities of alcohol.

In spite of significant efforts to eliminate hazing and its threat to students, the concern remains and more work needs to be done by students, chapters, campuses, and national organizations.

Campus Responsibility Hazy at Best

In recent years, a series of cases have supported the principle that college students could be treated as adults and that they do not require special campus supervision or control. In *Beach v. University of Utah*, 726 P.2d 413 (1986), it was ruled that it would be unrealistic for the courts to impose a "custodian" role over adult students. Said the court, "Fulfilling this charge would require the institution to babysit each student, a task beyond the resources of any school."

Similar reasoning was used in a Pennsylvania case, *Bradshaw v. Rawlings*, 612 F.2d 135 (1979), in which a federal circuit appellate panel ruled that a campus was not responsible for drinking activities of a student group off campus property. To make the school responsible for the decisions made by adult students would be inconsistent with the goals of a college education and unenforceable, said the court.

But in the mid-1980s, a case involving a fraternity member, a trampoline, a can of beer, and the University of Denver strongly challenged the campus position of not providing special standards of care. In *Whitlock v. University of Denver*, 744 P.2d 54 (1987), an appeals court upheld a multimillion-dollar judgment against the school for its failure to supervise or control unsafe off-campus fraternity house conduct. It wasn't until the case reached the state's highest court that the *Bradshaw* and *Beach* principles were accepted. While the monetary award was ultimately rejected, there was obviously much judicial sympathy for the student, and there was a strong minority opinion that campuses do have a special obligation to provide care, control, and supervision to student group conduct. Can campus responsibility be extended to fraternity hazing?

Case Law Development Reverses Tradition

The campus legal community used to cite one case when arguing that schools had no special obligation to prevent harm to members of student groups. *Furek v. University of Delaware*, 594 A.2d 506 (1991), had its beginnings in a 1980 "Hell Night." A pledge was forced to eat food from a toilet, was severely paddled, and had food and liquids poured over his head. One member used oven cleaner on the pledge's head, resulting in severe burns and scarring.

The pledge sued, and a jury found the fraternity member and the campus responsible for injuries. But the judge rejected the liability claim against the school, using *Beach* and *Bradshaw* principles. In the years before the state's highest court heard an appeal, *Furek* was used as further support for the lack of campus responsibility for harms such as those resulting from hazing.

However, the Supreme Court of Delaware ruled that the school did have a duty to protect the student from hazing harm. Among the court's findings:

- Schools have an obligation to act with the knowledge of dangers inherent in the large concentration of young people, based on students' *need for a safe environment*. Campus security cases — notably, incidents of rape and murder — presented a better rationale for campus responsibility than alcohol cases.

- *In loco parentis* may not be "dead" in safety-related cases. While students have been given greater control over their lives by schools and society, making their private actions private, campuses may not say student safety is a student-only problem because they are adults.

- When the campus *participates in or has knowledge of dangerous acts*, it must act to protect. The campus had treated hazing cases in its health center, issued statements and letters on hazing concerns, and threatened to discipline chapters engaged in hazing. Some pledge activities had been observed by campus personnel. Using tort law, the court ruled that the school was involved in the issue, knew of the dangers and student practices, and, therefore, had a greater obligation to act to prevent harm.

- As a *property owner*, the campus had a duty to protect students from harms that were known or should have been known. Since the campus took some actions in response to hazing, it was aware of the danger, and had a duty to protect those on the property.

While *Furek* is only a state court decision, its implications for other colleges and universities must be considered. When a student is injured and student groups are involved, the campus rarely avoids litigation. And the damages can be significant, given campus "deep pockets." Plaintiffs will search very carefully for involvement, notice, or duties that would establish institutional liability. Consider how the *Furek* principles might be applied on other campuses.

Statutory Duties Becoming the Norm

In addition to case law, campuses may find a duty to act in state legislation. At last count, 33 states had adopted laws prohibiting hazing practices. While they differ in language and content, the laws generally make it a criminal offense to haze. In addition, some state legislation imposes a duty on colleges and universities to take proactive steps designed to reduce the incidence of hazing.

These laws may also require campuses to create anti-hazing student conduct regulations with enforcement and education programs. While not an intended outcome, these laws may open campuses to yet more litigation from students and parents.

Organizational Response Encouraging

Efforts to eliminate hazing have almost universal support and commitment. The American Council on Education (ACE) has recommended that pledging be eliminated. National Greek organizations have adopted new recruitment, orientation, and member education programs with a degree of enthusiasm. Group insurance programs have banned unsafe practices. Greek organization anti-hazing policies and education programs have been reinvigorated. And state legislators continue to create tighter guidelines and standards under the law, with Mississippi making jail time a hazing sanction and Florida extending its laws to private institutions.

Campuses have reviewed their rules and regulations and strengthened enforcement and education efforts. All of this has made a positive difference. But the problem remains.

In addition to understanding case law on liability and responsibilities, statutory obligations and sanctions, and organizational responses, campuses should consider strongly the policy guidelines developed by ACE for "Greek Organizations on the College Campus." Related to the elimination of hazing, ACE recommends institutional strategies include the following:

- Conduct standards and sanctions for failure to meet standards

- Regular self-studies and procedures for monitoring activities and behaviors

- Specific policies and penalties for hazing violations

- One institutional officer with oversight responsibilities

- Supervision standards for chapters and encouragement of faculty and staff advisement

- Educational programs on alcohol and other substance abuses

- Elimination of alcohol from rush processes as part of an overall assessment of rush activities

- Policies that eliminate pledge status as part of the membership process

Summary

Much progress has been made, but much more remains to be done. With the continued aggressive development, application, and enforcement of anti-hazing policies, newspaper headlines can be changed — and lives can be saved.

State Hazing Laws Force Accountability

June 1994

Despite the honest efforts and good intentions of many within national social fraternal organizations, colleges and universities continue to struggle with student hazing. During a past academic year, reports of student deaths, injuries, and abuse from all over the country drew attention and concern. In looking back at some cases from last year, campuses may be reminded of risks faced by students and institutions due to unlawful, unsafe, and outdated membership initiation practices. Consider these recent reports from Rutgers (NJ), Southeast Missouri State, Indiana, Nebraska, Dartmouth (NH), and Keene State (NH).

At Rutgers, the campus greek review board has suspended a chapter for 30 months due to hazing charges. The group forced pledges to endure calisthenics and slapping of their bodies. Campus police raided a fraternity meeting as part of a hazing investigation and discovered the practices. Seven fraternity members were charged with violating both state laws and university conduct regulations. The chapter has been suspended for the next five semesters.

The hazing death of a pledge left the campus of Southeast Missouri State University, and others, in shock. The chapter was expelled from the school, seven members were arrested on involuntary manslaughter charges, and six others face hazing law violations in criminal courts. The organization involved in the beating death had adopted a national "non-hazing" pledge process over four years ago.

According to local reports, the pledge was beaten repeatedly by members over the course of several weeks of initiation. The chapter had been suspended for a year in 1988 due to beating allegations and sanctioned by its national organization in 1991.

Two Greek letter organizations at Indiana University also found trouble, on and off campus, due to hazing. One organization faces civil suits and campus discipline as the result of pledge abductions. A pledge dislocated a kneecap when thrown into the trunk of a car while blindfolded. He spent a month in a wheelchair and the next six weeks in a full leg cast. The victim has filed a notice of suit with involved individuals, the chapter, and the national organization, seeking reimbursement for medical expenses. IU has filed charges against the organization for violating hazing and physical abuse sections of the school code of student ethics.

In a more serious IU case, another chapter has been suspended until fall 1997 due to hazing-related beatings. According to reports, a pledge required hospitalization after suffering two weeks of physical abuse. Police reports indicate that the pledge was beaten with a wooden paddle and slapped and had a folding chair broken over him during a two-week pledge period. The national organization outlawed pledging in 1985.

Five members of the group were arrested for criminal recklessness, including a law student who had been serving as chapter advisor. The chapter president also was charged. The organization agreed to a three-year suspension, preventing current members from participating in a new group, if formed later at IU.

A fall from a third-story window by a University of Nebraska fraternity pledge has led to the adoption of another state anti-hazing law. A pledge was forced by a fraternity to consume alcohol and fell from a house window. The injured student then spent more than three months at a rehabilitation center, and he needs continued therapy to overcome fall-related disabilities.

Under the law, adopted earlier this year, hazing became a crime punishable by up to six months in jail and a $1,000 fine. Organizations involved in hazing also face $10,000 fines under the law. The bill passed unanimously in the state legislature after university officials and fraternity members testified in its favor.

Campus officials felt the law was important because it prevents hazing students from avoiding responsibility. In the past, only student conduct regulations prohibited hazing. Accused students simply dropped out of school to avoid sanctions. Now, they would face criminal prosecution regardless of their student status.

In New Hampshire, college and university officials dealt with a new state law requiring campuses to report hazing to local police. The law covers acts by fraternities, sororities, and sports teams, and makes initiation and membership practices that could cause physical or psychological harm illegal. Violators could face fines of up to $1,200 and mandatory community service assignments. Fraternities at both Keene State College and Dartmouth College had a chance to learn about the law in its initial year.

At Keene State, a fraternity was disciplined during the first month of the fall semester for hazing. Fraternity members allegedly made pledges roll around naked in dog food. Administrators suspended the group for a semester, but after review, criminal charges were not filed by prosecutors.

However, criminal charges were filed under the statute at Dartmouth. There, two students were arrested for violating state hazing laws. According to police, the two forced an underage pledge to drink an unsafe amount of alcohol during an initiation rite. They then returned the intoxicated sophomore to a residence hall. Campus officials became involved when the student was found in the hall. Local police were informed of the incident, and made arrests after an investigation.

About 20 students have died in hazing-related cases during the past 10 years, and at least 39 states now have anti-hazing laws. Campuses and fraternities committed to keeping students safe and out of the courts need to be constantly aware of the risks of hazing and needed prevention strategies.

Student Organizations Fight to Survive

November 1990

At Colby College (ME), there are no recognized fraternities. However, when "outlawed" fraternities stole Christmas decorations from local houses or held initiation rites in a rented local hall, the school reacted: it punished members of unrecognized fraternities.

Now, years after Colby's trustees banned the organizations, the groups are fighting back. Members argue that the campus actions against them violate their constitutional rights to free association.

On Campus

"Right to associate" cases are generally first judged on the basis of *Healy v. James*, 408 U.S. 169 (1972). At issue then was the status of a Central Connecticut State College chapter of Students for a Democratic Society. Students wanting to form a chapter had received approval from the student affairs committee, but the college president denied their request for recognition.

The president argued that the group's aims were at odds with campus philosophy. He felt that the group could threaten academic freedom and be a disruptive and potentially violent influence on campus. He was also concerned about the chapter's relationship with the national organization. Based on this analysis, he refused to allow the group to form or meet on campus.

In reviewing the decision, the U.S. Supreme Court found only limited grounds for infringing students' constitutional rights to freedom of association. The court found nothing wrong with any national affiliation and noted that academic freedoms should protect, not deflect, dissenting points of view. As for potential campus disruption, the court saw the concern but ruled that more than an apprehension of violence was needed to support constitutional limitations.

In finding that denial of recognition could threaten the very existence of organizations, the court severely limited the campus decision-making process. However, the court upheld the need for group compliance with campus rules and regulations. If a group violates or "reserves the right to violate" campus rules, its status on campus can be revoked or denied.

Said the court:

> A college administrator may impose a requirement ... that a group seeking official recognition affirm in advance its willingness to adhere to reasonable campus law. ... This is a minimal requirement, in the interest of the entire academic community.

This ruling has withstood the test of time. A series of cases involving rights of association for *gay rights* advocacy groups on campus have been decided on the basis of *Healy*. These include *Gay Students Organization of the University of New Hampshire v. Bonner*, 509 F.2d 652 (1974), *Gay Activists Alliance v. Board of Regents*, 638 P.2d 1116 (1981), and *Gay Student Services v. Texas A&M University*, 737 F.2d 1317 (1984). The campuses sought to bar these groups, but the courts found no grounds to support such action. The groups agreed to follow campus rules and not turn to violence; they had a right to espouse a different or challenging point of view.

Adherence to campus rules isn't the only test for recognition. Other factors may be considered.

For instance, the campus rules that groups must obey cannot be unconstitutional or otherwise unlawful. In addition, groups can't be required to *waive other equally important rights*, such as free speech or expression, in exchange for recognition.

Campuses don't have to tolerate *"substantial disruption"* of the academic process. While the court didn't find this condition in *Healy*, it noted that "associational activities need not be tolerated where they ... interrupt classes ... or substantially interfere with the opportunity of other students to obtain an education." But again, the burden rests on schools to show that disruption has occurred or will occur, not merely that it is feared.

Healy also established another test for campus recognition. Campuses have the right to prevent group activities that are illegal or that direct others into illegal activities. This test was best defined by *Brandenburg v. Ohio*, 395 U.S. 444 (1969), preventing activities "directed to inciting or producing imminent lawless action and ... likely to incite or produce such action."

Off Campus

The *Healy* rules apply to recognized campus groups. Before 1984, Colby College recognized fraternities; today it doesn't. And the case going to trial now will determine what a school can or cannot do about unrecognized off-campus organizations.

After the incident of the stolen holiday decorations, Colby forced two unrecognized groups to disband in exchange for amnesty. The college also barred 16 seniors from graduation ceremonies and suspended 20 underclassmen for a semester for other Greek-related offenses — violating campus rules against exclusionary membership standards, hazing, and disruptive initiation practices. The students contend that they have a right to organize and assemble on or off campus.

The Maine Civil Liberties Union is providing legal support to the students and their organizations. Their case doesn't contest Colby's right to establish or enforce rules reasonable for the operation of the school. However, the students say the college has no right to interfere with their off-campus memberships.

Earlier in the year, a state superior court judge denied a motion to allow the sanctioned seniors to attend graduation ceremonies. On initial review, the court found the campus decision to be reasonable. The court said the evidence suggested that "this discipline was much more a traditional college discipline issue than sort of a civil rights ... matter." This ruling suggests that the trial will focus on *membership vs. activities*. Did the college discipline the students because they belonged to a group or because they participated in group activities that violated valid campus rules?

Six years ago, Colby banned Greek-letter organizations and barred practices such as rushing, pledging, and initiation. School trustees decided that the existence of the groups didn't support the school's mission and beliefs. However, Colby officials say their 1984 action barred *activities*, not *memberships*.

Attorneys for the students aren't so sure. They feel the college is punishing students for activities that should be beyond the reach of campus officials.

The courts have offered no relief to Colby College students concerned about Greek-letter organization membership. A recent legal attempt to block school efforts to sanction members of unauthorized organizations has failed.

Students accused of violating the campus ban against fraternities sued the school, citing a constitutional right to assemble as a legal basis for continuing Greek activities. The school had ousted the groups in 1984 and made it a violation of conduct rules to participate in fraternities and fraternity events. But last month, the Maine Superior Court ruled against the students. In *Phelps v. Colby College*, Case No. CV-90-287, the court rejected student requests to enjoin the school from enforcing its rules. In fact, the decision reversed the freedom of association argument presented by the Greek students. The court ruled that it had a duty to protect association rights, but protected the rights of the many students at Colby because it was free from Greek organizations. Recalling the movie *Animal House*, the court sided strongly with the school and non-Greek students.

Summary

Regulations regarding the recognition of campus organizations are fairly clear. *Healy* and subsequent cases have established tests for denying recognition requests:

- Does the group fail to agree to "adhere to reasonable campus law"?
- Does the group disrupt classes or "substantially interfere with the opportunity of other students to obtain an education"?
- Does the group engage in illegal activities or activity "directed to inciting or producing imminent lawless action"?

Off campus, no clear test has been established. What happens when a school imposes campus sanctions for membership in off-campus organizations?

Courts faced with this question must balance the interests of the school and the rights of the student. The school will have to show some relationship between its rules and the student activities. The students have a right to assemble — on and off campus. Courts will allow this right to be infringed only under limited circumstances when well-justified by campuses.

Who Controls the Right of Association?

April 1992

For years, student governments have fought with campus administrators to get student clubs and organizations recognized or registered. For a variety of reasons, colleges and universities found certain student organizations objectionable and placed roadblocks in their path, denying them use of campus facilities and services.

In a series of legal decisions, beginning with *Healy v. James*, 408 U.S. 169 (1972), student governments won the right to organize and operate clubs and organizations under limited campus controls. Campus administration saw its power to limit campus groups seriously eroded due to legal victories by student governments.

But today, the tables are turning at Auburn University (AL), where the campus administration has recognized a student organization over the objection of student government! After decades of litigation to obtain recognition, students are now considering court action to overturn recognition.

Issue Has Roots in '60s

In the national and campus turbulence of the late '60s came a request for campus recognition of a chapter of the radical Students for a Democratic Society (SDS) at Central Connecticut State College. After an initial favorable review, the college president rejected the request, citing the potential disruption of academic and campus life. The U.S. Supreme Court understood the president's concern, but could not accept his position. The court found the student organization had a legal right to exist if it agreed to comply with reasonable campus rules and regulations that applied to all similar groups.

Healy and related litigation involving the attempted denial by administrators of recognition for student groups have established a three-part constitutional test for colleges and universities faced with recognition conflicts:

- Does the group agree to abide by "reasonable standards respecting conduct" established by the school? (*Healy*)
- Will the organization interrupt classes, create a substantial disruption on campus, or "interfere with the opportunity of other students to obtain an education? (*Healy*)
- Does the student group act in violation of the law or act to "incite or produce such action"? (*Brandenburg v. Ohio*, 395 U.S. 444 (1969)

When a student group comes to campus or is formed on campus, the school must ask and answer these questions before denying recognition. Unless there is a substantial affirmative response to one or more of the test questions, recognition is constitutionally expected.

The Auburn Dilemma: Irony Abounds

Student government approval of club recognition is a fairly routine matter at Auburn University (AL) and other schools. A group comes to the government with a request for recognition and it's usually granted with little or no discussion. That was until the recognition petition of a gay and lesbian student group reached the Auburn University student senate. The group received probationary recognition from the senate in 1990. But citing a petition with over 400 signatures, health dangers, the fact that sodomy is against state law, and concerns that "public acceptance of homosexuality is the final stage in the destruction of a nation from within," the senate recently voted 23 to 7 to deny the group's charter. Without recognition, the group could not receive free meeting space on campus, student fee support, and discounted advertising rates in school publications.

The gay and lesbian student group, denied recognition by student government, turned to the university administration for help. And while the students took the issue to the top, the American Civil Liberties Union (ACLU) stood ready to assist if needed. Said one national ACLU official, "We would eagerly take on a case." But they may not have to. The Auburn vice president for student affairs and campus president overruled the student government decision and granted recognition.

Unhappy student leaders then gathered up more than 12,000 signatures of complaint and presented them to Auburn's Board of Trustees, hoping to again get the group barred from campus. Campus administration and trustees, however, held firm, based on their understanding of federal law.

Case Law Developments

Determining the rights of gay and lesbian student groups on campus has occupied considerable judicial time. Cases involving college and university groups include recognition, school image, funding, and access to campus services.

An early campus challenge came in *Gay Students Organization of the University of New Hampshire v. Bonner*, 509 F.2d 652 (1974), in which the state government barred the use of campus space for a gay student dance. A federal appellate court forced the school to open its facilities for future gay student functions, as the ban violated the "practicalities of human interaction."

Recognition was at issue in several notable cases. When Virginia Commonwealth University turned down a request for gay student recognition, its decision was swiftly overturned on constitutional grounds. The court, in *Gay Alliance of Students v. Matthews*, 544 F.2d 162 (1976), said the school action violated the group's freedom of speech, association, and equal protection rights.

Citing legal precedent for limiting constitutional rights where there is an imminent likelihood of unlawful activity, several campuses tried to deny gay student organizations recognition based on state sodomy statutes. Important to the courts was not the name of the student group, but its purpose. In *Gay Lib v. University of Missouri*, 558 F.2d 848 (1977), a student group received recognition because it was an advocacy group, promoting awareness, education, and changes in the law. A similar outcome was reached in *Gay Student Services v. Texas A&M University*, 737 F.2d 1317 (1984). The possibility that the group's activities might increase understanding and even encourage homosexual conduct did not support the rejection of recognition. "Fear or apprehension" of possible unlawful activities did not justify the violation of constitutional freedoms, said the court.

Concern that campus recognition might imply campus approval or encouragement of homosexual conduct is also no grounds for denial of recognition, as indicated in *Student Coalition v. Austin Peay State University*, 477 F.Supp. 1267 (1979).

And in more recent times, the battles over gay student club recognition at Georgetown University (DC) have led to a similar outcome. While the private institution has indicated that, due to its religious beliefs, it did not want to recognize the group, the school ultimately agreed to provide limited services — after extensive legal battles involving a District of Columbia human rights statute and threats of Congressional action.

Summary

Applying the judicially established test for student group recognition, Auburn University administrators determined that the proposed gay and lesbian student organization had agreed to comply with campus rules, did not disrupt classes, and did not incite lawless action. Recognition was therefore granted over some student objections. Campus leaders demonstrated an understanding of current case law. Student leaders are now advocating a challenge to the law, based in part on a dissent to the recognition standards written in 1978 by Justice W. Rehnquist. The students have asked the trustees to take the lead in overturning three decades of constitutional lawmaking.

Gay, Lesbian, and Bisexual Students Fight for Rights

October 1992

The debate over a gay-lesbian student group at Auburn University (AL) is only one of many current debates concerning homosexuality on campus. Across the country, gay, lesbian, and bisexual students are fighting for their rights and against the violence they fear.

A review of headlines from student newspapers reveals how widespread the debate, violence, and challenges are on today's college and university campuses.

"Auburn Fight Over Gay Group Shifts to U.S. Courts"

The governor, legislature, attorney general, influential alums, and the student government all agreed on something in this case — highly unusual in higher education! They all believed that a gay and lesbian student organization at Auburn should not be recognized by the school.

Last fall, the student government voted to deny the group organizational rights. But the AU administration overruled and allowed the group to begin meeting last spring.

Within weeks, everyone jumped into the fray. The school trustees ultimately agreed to send the issue to federal courts for guidance.

Auburn is now suing the organization seeking recognition as well as the student government that refused it, shifting the debate from campus to the courts. At issue is whether homosexual groups have the same rights as other groups do to organize on campus.

The issue has been to the courts before — and the right of such groups to meet on campus has been consistently upheld.

"Homosexual Group Funding Questioned"

Funding for a gay student group has been subject to debate and scrutiny at the University of Alabama-Tuscaloosa as well.

Motivated by the Auburn dispute, the UA student government voted to review whether it was "ethical and legal" for the government to provide $500 in annual funding to the Gay/Lesbian Alliance. The student government wants to get an opinion from the state attorney general on the issue.

Supporters of the request say the alliance sanctions illegal activities, since state law prohibits sodomy. But opponents say the review reinforces a "backward, redneck image of the state."

At the University of Alabama-Birmingham, a gay student organization has been recognized — but without funding.

"Gay Harassment Punished"

That was the headline last fall at Northern Illinois University, where gay students said they had been repeatedly harassed.

One group of NIU students, for example, gathered in front of a gay student's apartment, called the student names, and kicked in the apartment door. The accused were all members of a fraternity.

The campus judicial process recommended that two students in the group be suspended and a third be banned from campus. But the fraternity says it did not condone the actions, and that those doing the harassing "acted independent" of the organization and its members.

"Gay Rules on UW Housing Attacked" / "Students Say Policy Bars Gay Marriages"

The debates at the University of Wisconsin-Madison, Syracuse University (NY), and other campuses concern the rights of gay students in "family" housing programs.

A UW off-campus housing project, for instance, has been challenged over a tenant policy that allows only students who are married or are single parents. The units offer a low-rent option to UW students and families, and some have argued that gay and lesbian couples should be given equal access.

Speakers at a campus forum urged UW to provide "equal rights" to all. Only a few argued that non-traditional families should be limited to specified areas.

At Syracuse, a gay couple preparing for marriage has challenged a campus housing rule. Since they can't get a marriage license from the city, SU won't provide them with a room in married student housing.

One partner is a resident advisor. He petitioned the Residence Life Office to change its rules to recognize non-traditional couples.

The two contacted a lawyer to help them in their challenge.

"CGLA Files Suit to End Restraint on Publications"

The Carolina Gay and Lesbian Association at the University of North Carolina contested UNC student government's control of CGLA publications.

The CGLA filed a lawsuit against the student government, demanding the removal of budget restrictions that require CGLA to submit all publications for student government approval. The idea, according to student government, is to ensure that CGLA funds are not used for "political" purposes.

The CGLA says the rule prevents the group from commenting on HIV issues, legislation, or research funding proposals. Student affairs officials say the rule destroys diversity and promotes exclusiveness, not inclusiveness.

Even the student body president has spoken out against his own organization's rule. He says students shouldn't do anything to "impede activism on campus."

"Charges Pending"

That's how the challenge over gay rights has been headlined at the University of Nebraska-Lincoln, where a member of Queer Nation-Nebraska filed charges against a UNL student who allegedly pulled, kicked, and spat on him during an anti-ROTC rally on campus.

The gay student, from another school, says he was videotaping the rally when he was assaulted by the defendant. The victim says he hurt his shoulder and neck during the attack and lost his camera and eyeglasses.

"Fliers About Gays and Fraternities Taken from Kinko's"

The clerk at a local copy store near Kent State University (OH) didn't know what to do about the out-of-the-ordinary posters a man wanted to make — posters that linked three KSU fraternities to gay student activities.

So the clerk questioned the customer, who turned and left the shop with his original but no copies.

But some students saw the fliers around campus and complained to the fraternities, the student activities office, and the campus affirmative action office.

"Gay Alumni Group Promises to Sue OU"

The alumni organization at the University of Oklahoma has actively tried to support regional groups or individual campus associations. But when asked to form a gay and lesbian alumni association, it declined.

That negative response will now be tested in court. A gay rights legal defense fund has agreed to finance a challenge of OU policy.

According to the campus newspaper, the school turned down the group because it does "not wish to have specific-interest alumni associations." The school says that if too many sub-groups are formed, there is "no sense of identity." As an example, OU cited its previous refusal to form an ROTC alumni group.

The denied group, however, says the ROTC was given access to alumni publications that have turned the gay group away. In addition, the group says, African American and American Indian alumni associations have been formed in recent years by OU. The school, however, says those groups are protected by federal law, and that they help the school recruit new students.

The would-be gay alumni group is rewriting its bylaws so that they'll be similar to those of approved groups. That way, members say, the group will be able to argue that sexual orientation is the only difference between their group and groups that have been accepted.

As more gay students and student organizations come forward, campuses can expect more challenges, more changes, more litigation, and more headlines.

Tomorrow the headlines may be coming from your campus. Will you respond appropriately?

Activity Fees Are Not for Political Usage

October 1993

A campus collected a mandatory activity fee from students and turned a portion over to the student government to disburse under established guidelines. The student government used the money to support governance, a variety of student organizations, and students lobbying on behalf of student issues.

Will such fee systems exist in the future? That's the issue being debated in the courts, based on a student challenge to the constitutionality of typical mandatory fee systems. In *Smith v. Regents of the University of California*, 844 P.2d 500 (1993), the state's highest court considered claims that the use of student fees for lobbying and in support of "ideological" student organizations violated the free speech and association rights of dissenting students.

Do mandatory activity fees serve an educational purpose? Does the use of fees to support ideological student organizations represent speech by compulsion or coercion? Must a campus scrutinize each group for possible political or ideological actions before providing fees? Are students who disagree with the goals or positions of such groups entitled to refunds of mandatory fees? *Smith*, now under appeal to the U.S. Supreme Court, addresses all of these important student activity issues. The final resolution of the case could have a dramatic, national impact on how student fees are collected and expanded in the future.

The Background

Smith began in 1979, when four students requested fee reimbursement. They questioned the right of the University of California-Berkeley to force them to pay funds used to support causes and positions they did not support. Of particular concern was funding to advocacy groups, positions taken by the student government on national and social issues, and lobbying efforts funded by fee dollars.

The students demanded the right to deduct from their bills that portion of the mandatory fee used for "ideological" purposes. The university refused.

The Decisions

The California Supreme Court ruled that state university students can't be required to pay fees supporting campus political causes or lobbying activities. In a 5-2 decision, the court found constitutional objections to the state's mandatory fee system, noting "the constitutional guarantees of free speech and association do not permit the state to make speech a matter of compulsion and coercion."

Under the ruling, students objecting to particular uses of mandatory fees should be permitted to deduct that portion of the fee. The court said fee dollars could continue to support academic and cultural groups with purposes "germane to the university's mission." However, the court specifically limited funding to organizations whose educational functions are outweighed by other functions. Educational functions of a funded student organization cannot be "merely incidental to its political and ideological activities."

The student plaintiffs, in challenging the mandatory fee system, stressed a view expressed much earlier by Thomas Jefferson that "to compel a man to furnish contributions of money for the propagation of opinions which he disbelieves, is sinful and tyrannical." In related issues, this principle has led to recent court decisions prohibiting labor and membership groups from using compelled contributions for political purposes (*Abood v. Detroit Board of Education*, 431 U.S. 209, 1977; *Keller v. State Bar of California*, 496 U.S. 1, 1990).

The California Supreme Court used *Abood* and *Keller* to justify its limitation on student activity fee expenditures. In *Abood*, a labor union was forced to limit the expenditure of membership dues to only organization and collective bargaining issues. The money could not be diverted for political purposes. And in *Keller*, a state bar association's use of membership dues to support social and political issues was barred. The court held that the group may "constitutionally fund activities germane to (organizational) goals out of the mandatory dues of all members. It may not, however, in such manner fund activities of an ideological nature which fall outside of those areas of activities."

The court, in deciding *Smith* and its limitation on mandatory activity fees, also reviewed earlier student fee cases from other campuses. Two cases, both involving activity fee funding for a public interest research group (PIRG), dealt with political and ideological support. In *Galda v. Rutgers, The State University of New Jersey*, 772 F.2d 1060 (1985), students objected to fee support of organizations with a fixed political agenda. The court ruled that educational benefits offered by the PIRG did not justify the infringement of dissenting students' speech and associational rights.

And just last year, a similar challenge was raised in New York to student fee PIRG funding. In *Carroll v. Blinken*, 957 F.2d 991 (1992), students again challenged use of their fees to support a research and advocacy group. The group spent funding on and off campus on educational and lobbying efforts. While the court acknowledged infringement on dissenting students forced to fund political activities against their will, the ultimate decision found enough benefits to the campus to justify the policy. The group promoted extracurricular life, transmitted skills and civic duties, and stimulated campus debate, said the court. However, *Carroll* could not find similar support for the PIRG's off-campus activities and barred such funding.

Finding support in the PIRG cases (*Galda* and *Carroll*) and labor and professional organization cases (*Abood* and *Keller*), the California Supreme Court ordered an end to fee systems as currently exist in the state. The decision has left the state university system, and perhaps many others, with a series of difficult "what's next?" questions. What's next could be major changes in mandatory student fee programs.

Mandatory Student Activity Fees

November 1993

The University of California System has asked the U.S. Supreme Court to review a mandatory student activity fee case that could significantly alter campus student life funding. A lower court ruling, in *Smith v. Regents of the University of California*, 844 P.2d 500 (1993), placed what could be severe restrictions on the use of student funds. It limited the use of funds for lobbying, even lobbying associated with student or university issues. It also questioned funding of student organizations with political or social agendas. The educational value of some student groups was reviewed and the court ordered "check-off refund procedures" for lobbying, political, and ideological student groups.

Stating that the lower court finding was "a radical departure from educational reality and settled law," the University of California System has requested Supreme Court review.

Precedent

First, the system has asked that the ruling be overturned as being in direct conflict with an earlier federal decision. In *Carroll v. Blinken*, 957 F.2d 991 (1992), mandatory student activity fees were used to fund a public interest research group's on- and off-campus activity. At the State University of New York at Albany, the group sponsored debates, research, and projects on issues ranging from parking lot lighting to the arms race. Student fees were also used off campus to fund full-time lobbyists to work on issues. Some SUNY Albany students strongly objected to the use of fees for this form of "political activity" and sued. *Carroll* held that the use of fees for these purposes did "burden the dissenters' First Amendment Rights." But the court found three reasons to justify that burden, including:

- General promotion of extracurricular activities
- Provision of "participatory civics training"
- "Stimulation of robust campus debate" on public issues

The court found these to be reasonable justifications for expenditures of student fees and important enough to outweigh the interests of the dissenting students. In *Carroll*, the court upheld the on-campus use of mandatory student activity fees for ideological student organizations.

The educational justification was limited to on-campus activities only. The court ruled that the educational interests asserted by the university did not justify funding away from campus. It ordered the school to collect fees only to the level spent on campus.

The *Smith* appeal contends that *Carroll* represents decided federal law on the question. Therefore, the California system argues, it should not face more restrictive regulations than others. Under *Smith*, the colleges involved were required to "differentiate between (student) groups engaged in on-campus political speech, and to use the proceeds of the mandatory fee to fund only those groups which provide educational benefits that 'outweigh' the group's dedication to its political or ideological goals."

As a result of *Carroll* and *Smith*, the two largest public university systems in the U.S., New York and California, are governing student fees in opposite ways. In New York, lobbying and public interest research groups are OK; in California, they are not fundable. The appeal is designed to resolve this conflict.

One of the arguments favoring the appeal focuses on public debate and public forums. A series of earlier cases established strong judicial support for using fees for public speech. These involved student governments (*Lace v. Vermont*, 303 A.2d 478, 1973); student newspapers (*Hays County Guardian v. Supple*, 969 F.2d 111, 1992); and speakers bureaus, films, and conferences (*Veed v. Schwartzkopf*, 353 F.Supp. 149, 1973). These cases all supported the notion that mandatory fees can support public debate on state campuses. The reason is most clearly stated in *Kania v. Fordham*, 702 F.2d 475 (1983), a student newspaper funding case that supported public forums because they expose "the student body to various points of view on significant issues, and (allow) students to express themselves on those issues."

The *Smith* appeal argues that student fee organizations must be treated in a manner promoting free expression, the exchange of ideas, and the advocacy of divergent views.

Officials are concerned over the impact of *Smith* on today's college campuses. According to the request for review (petition for writ of *certiorari*), the lower court decision could bring political and ideological student-sponsored debate "to a screeching halt" on campuses.

Need to Assess Educational and Ideological?

Many administrators fear the potential establishment of a campus process to review the nature of student organizations. The *Smith* decision could necessitate some form of administrative procedure to evaluate the educational and ideological elements of each student organization. The appeal expresses concern over the burden that schools and organizations would bear if they had to weigh educational vs. ideological elements for every student organization.

Administratively, it suggests annual proceedings as student group goals change, even if the "amount in controversy for each individual student will be not more than pennies." Ethically, it brings up a quagmire of issues over who to choose to judge the student groups and whose criteria to use.

The *Smith* appeal also details concerns for the impact on student governments. Most take governmental positions on a variety of issues — campus related, as well as those of local, national, or even international interest. A court decision limiting ideological debates of student government can limit the educational value of the experience. *Smith*, it's argued, could cut student fee support for student governments if they become "ideological."

The loss of the right to lobby is also questioned in the appeal. Many student organizations actively pursue their interests, on and off campus. Student lobbies urge students to contact legislators, do research to support positions, encourage participation in local boards and civic organizations, and sponsor on-campus debates.

The *Smith* ruling found that the only educational value in lobbying was gained by the few student lobbyists themselves. But the Supreme Court appeal notes that effective lobbying involves group discussion, debate, and increased understanding. It argues that lobbying cannot be easily separated from on-campus political debate, and that it should be supportable with student fees.

Summary

Mandatory student fees support a wide variety of student-related programs. But the future of mandatory student fee systems, as currently operated, remains in doubt. The judicial preference for educational, not ideological, activities, as evidenced in the *Smith* case, appears to dismiss the educational value of political debate. If lobbying and some organizations are threatened today, some fear that student newspapers, speakers, government resolutions, films, and other forms of expression may not be far behind.

Note: The U.S. Supreme Court decided not to review a key mandatory student activity fee case, *Smith v. Regents*. A lower court ruling had earlier declared that the California University system campuses could not allow the use of student fees for "political, ideological, or religious" organizations.

Implementation of the ruling had been delayed by the schools as a result of the appeal. Student leaders in the California state system now expect campus officials to implement the limitations established by the court. They anticipate a review of all student organizations to determine their purpose in an effort to deny funding if necessary, based on *Smith*.

The impact of the actual decision is limited to the California system but it will certainly be considered by students in other states interested in challenging student fee systems or allocations for specific types of groups.

Student Control of Student Fees Questioned

May 1994

Are mandatory student activity fees being put to appropriate uses? Are there adequate fiscal controls? Are policies needed to promote responsible and ethical spending by student organizations and leaders?

These questions and others have been asked more and more often in the wake of news stories focused on questionable student stewardship over student fee dollars. Among the stories:

- There are allegations that a student government in the South used fee money to bribe political opponents and to reimburse themselves for conferences they did not attend.
- An audit of a Northeastern community college's student government exposed $30,000 in unexplained expenditures, which resulted in arrests when a meeting to deal with the problem got out of control.
- Charges that a student leader embezzled almost $10,000 in student fee funds led to an arrest on criminal charges.
- The president of a student organization was accused of stealing admission fees from a student event for personal use. Due to an earlier fraud conviction, the student had to serve jail time.
- Several student leaders from the Midwest are accused of spending over $2,000 at a conference on car rentals, taxi fares, and meals, even though they stayed in the conference hotel and their meals were included in a prepaid registration fee.

In perhaps the most publicized case of fee abuse, the annual budget of one organization at City University of New York — over $345,000 in activity fee money — was spent by a student leader in just six months. Expenditures included $24,000 on car rentals, beepers, and portable telephones and thousands of dollars in loans for students to attend a conference in Africa. Family members of student officers and campus senators were apparently given full-time employment at student fee expense as well.

The cumulative impact of stories like these has renewed college and university interest in the fiscal affairs of student government and organizations. Over two decades have passed since greater student responsibility for student fees was established in the wake of widespread national campus unrest. But now, in response to today's allegations of misuse and continuing student objections over some uses, campuses are considering different approaches to fee issues.

Structures

Student mandatory activity fee systems in today's higher education vary. At some institutions, students have complete control over activity funding, while differing degrees of administrative controls exist at other schools. And finally, where students have some or primary authority for student fees, there also exist institutional guidelines, generally established to assure some level of administrative input and oversight.

Student fees are collected by campuses through a variety of systems as well. The standard method of collection is mandatory assessment, a process found on many campuses. Every student in attendance is charged a fee that must be paid with other charges, such as tuition. While this practice has been found to be the least protective of individual student constitutional rights, courts have supported the process. The system, however, has created problems for students unhappy with the use of their fee dollars. Challenges to the system process by non-supportive students have included suits against health fees, athletic programs, college newspapers, and political and lobbying expenditures.

An alternative method of collection used by some schools is the *optional check-off* system. Under this system, a student decides whether or not to pay an activity fee, and he or she can indicate how it may be used. This is accomplished through tuition invoices on which students check off boxes to indicate fee levels and intended uses. A student supports only the organizations or causes he or she chooses to support. Voluntary check-off systems have not generated legal challenges, as they generally protect individual student constitutional rights.

A third system for student fee collection is based on a combination of the assessment and check-off processes. Fewer schools use this system, referred to as the "negative check-off." All students are charged a fee for student activities. The fee is mandatory and placed on student accounts automatically. However, students have an opportunity to request and receive a refund after payment. This system allows students to withdraw support for objectionable groups or efforts, but only after paying the fee and having it available for objectionable use for a limited time.

Most student fee litigation has focused on expenditures. But expenditure issues have also led to reviews of collection processes, as schools search for an appropriate balance between student control and administrative responsibility. The growing number of student challenges to fee systems and expenditures may motivate colleges and universities to consider alternatives.

Objections and Controls

Student fee systems use student dollars to support student activities and programs. That's the simple part. But when the fees are mandatory, they may require some students to support programs or activities that they disagree with due to political, religious, or ethical reasons. That's where it gets complicated.

The balancing test between the rights of individuals and the needs of student organizations was reviewed in *Good v. Associated Students of the University of Washington*, 542 P.2d 762 (1975). Students objecting to fee money used for anti-war protests sued their student government. The court recognized their individual constitutional concerns, but said:

> We must balance the plaintiff's First Amendment rights against the traditional need and desirability of the university to provide an atmosphere of learning, debate, dissent and controversy. Neither is absolute. If we allow mandatory financial support to be unchecked, the plaintiff's rights may be meaningless. On the other hand, if we allow dissenters to withhold the minimal financial contributions required we would permit a possible minority view to destroy or cripple a valuable learning adjunct of university life.

Good established a legal basis for mandatory student fees. But the extent of campus controls over expenditure has been regularly challenged over the years, as has been the judgment of those authorizing expenditures.

Campus control over expenditures has been tested in cases involving college and university attempts to halt student program funding. Once funding is established, the power of the administration to terminate the funding is heavily controlled by the courts.

Efforts to halt or alter student funding were blocked for X-rated movies (*Swope v. Lubbers*, 560 F.Supp. 1328, 1983), a campus newspaper with segregationist views (*Joyner v. Whiting*, 477 F.2d 456, 1973), and a magazine humor issue that administrators didn't find funny (*Stanley v. McGrath*, 719 F.2d 279, 1983). In each case, campus attempts to limit or eliminate funding were subject to a test for a compelling campus need, since constitutional First Amendment issues were involved.

Refund Systems

In recent years, some campuses have begun to look at student activity fee refund systems to better control expenditures and protect student rights. Fee systems that allow students to select programs for funding encourage fiscal responsibility. If programs are not well-run, students can withhold funding, ending the opportunity for abuse. And if some students find some programs objectionable, they can withhold their personal funding. In addition, the threat of funding loss may affect student decision-makers, leading them to moderate their actions.

Two collegiate cases in recent years have promoted consideration of fee refund systems. They dealt with campus publications (*Stanley v. McGrath*) and fees for public interest research groups on campus (*Galda v. Rutgers, The State University of New Jersey*, 772 F.2d 1060 (1985)).

In *Stanley*, a university attempted to establish a refund system in retaliation for a humor issue. That response was found to be unlawful. The court ruled that a refund system organized for that purpose was punitive and unconstitutional. The court did not find all refund systems illegal, only those designed to limit protected student press, speech, association, and expression freedoms.

In *Galda*, the issue of refunds was again subject to federal review. Students challenged activity fee funding for an off campus organization with a fixed political agenda. Under campus policies, certain organizations received student funding subject to refund-on-demand by dissenting students. The involved students sued, claiming that a system that took their money, even for a short period of time, was impermissible. And the court agreed, ruling that the process was a violation of their constitutional rights.

Campus Funding of Student Groups — Again

December 1995

The publication, *Wide Awake*, proclaimed its purpose:

> To challenge Christians to live in word and deed, according to the faith they proclaim, and to encourage students to consider what a personal relationship with Jesus Christ means.

The University of Virginia had a Board of Visitors policy that religious activities were ineligible for university funding. Under campus policies, funding was prohibited for any "activity which primarily promotes ... a particular belief in or about a deity or an ultimate reality."

In 1991, the student council appropriation committee denied Wide Awake Productions' request for $5,800 to pay its publication costs. The student government said the Wide Awake group was a religious organization, not eligible for funding.

But the student publication said its request was based on freedom of speech, not religious principles. WAP contended that it was denied funding only because of its editorial point of view. In making the funding request, the publication cited campus support for Muslim and Jewish student groups at Virginia. WAP wanted similar treatment for Wide Awake. The campus, however, said those groups were funded because of their cultural, not religious, nature.

Without campus support, the publication only lasted four issues. It later sued for university funding.

A lower court ruled in favor of the school, turning away Wide Awake's First Amendment argument. The court said it "cannot find any evidence to indicate that the decision to deny funding ... was based on discriminatory intent" in the record. A federal appellate panel agreed with that finding in 1994, noting that direct campus funding would violate the constitutionally required separation of church and state.

Arguments

Earlier this year, the case was argued before the U.S. Supreme Court. In previous proceedings, the State of Virginia had defended the university's decision to deny funding, but a change in government required a change in legal counsel. The state, instead of continuing to defend its flagship campus, actually filed a brief in opposition to the university's position. The UVa Board of Visitors was left to argue on behalf of the university's position without government support.

The arguments centered on First Amendment freedoms of free speech and religion. An attorney for WAP contended that the case was about discrimination based on religion. He argued that the publication was denied funding solely because of its religious beliefs, while the campus would have recognized and supported "vegetarians, black separatists, and members of Students for a Democratic Society" rather than Christians.

Wide Awake also argued for the freedom of the campus press. Since the university had already decided to support other student press activities with fee funding, attorneys maintained that "the state should be completely indifferent to whether students use those benefits to participate in religious activity." The Constitution, attorneys contended, required "neutrality between religion and its various ideological competitors in the marketplace of ideas." As an example, an attorney noted:

> If a group of students qualify to form a newspaper ... or media group, they could not be excluded ... because they espouse ... a controversial opinion of a secular sort.

Several justices questioned the Wide Awake arguments. They asked whether student organizations were really the same as religious publications, noting a distinction between recruiting members and working to "recruit adherents to God." They also wondered about how readers would or could separate the opinions of the university-funded publications from the opinions of the university. The Court also considered that there was no precedent for direct government funding to support a religious activity.

In these Supreme Court arguments, counsel for UVa defended the school's policy in the face of strong questioning about alleged inconsistencies. Wasn't allowing the groups space a form of support? How was giving them funding so different? Counsel also argued that students had a right to publish a magazine on political or religious issues, just not with campus support or funding. UVa, said its lawyers, attempted to avoid any constitutional problems of religious establishment or entanglement by denying funding to all religious activities. It asked the court to support that principle.

Decision

Earlier this summer, in a 5-4 vote, the U.S. Supreme Court ruled that the University of Virginia decision to deny funding to Wide Awake was unconstitutional. The justices said that the denial violated protected student free speech rights. The Court provided a majority opinion, a concurring opinion, and a dissent, all of importance to today's collegiate environment. The court said:

> It is axiomatic that the government may not regulate speech based on its substantive content or the message it conveys. ... Discrimination against speech because of its message is presumed to be unconstitutional.

Justice Anthony M. Kennedy used these principles to provide a framework "forbidding the State from exercising viewpoint discrimination, even when the limited public forum is one of its own creation." This gave Wide Awake access to campus funds. Of the limits on government restrictions on speech, Kennedy wrote:

> The viewpoint discrimination inherent in the university's regulation required public officials to scan and intercept student publications to discern their underlying philosophic assumption respecting religious theory and belief ... . That course of action was a denial of the right of free speech and would risk fostering a pervasive bias or hostility to religion.

In a dissent, written by Justice David H. Souter, four justices strongly disagreed with the direct funding of a core religious activity by an arm of the state. They contended that this level of support violated the establishment of religion principle. After an extensive review of the four Wide Awake issues, the dissent noted:

> This writing is no merely descriptive examination of religious doctrine or even of ideal Christian practice in confronting life's social and personal problems. ... It is straightforward

exhortation to enter into a relationship with God as revealed in Jesus Christ.

The *Rosenberger v. Rector and Visitors of the University of Virginia*, 115 S.Ct. 2510 (1995), decision has forced colleges and universities to re-evaluate student mandatory activity fee policies. Many had regulations, based on the establishment clause, that denied groups and program funding for religious purposes. Based on the new decision, however, religious groups that are recognized, distinguish their activities from those of the college or university, and have student funding pay bills directly may be entitled to campus funding.

The first policy change came at the University of Virginia. Just before the start of the school year, the Board of Visitors changed campus fee guidelines to reflect *Rosenberger*. Under the new policy:

> No student group ... shall be deemed ineligible for funding on the grounds that the ideas or viewpoints expressed or advocated by such group are religious in nature.

In early November, UVA adjusted its policy to allow funding for political organizations as well. The policy also includes an "opt out" clause, so that students can choose to withhold funding if they disagree with a publication or group.

Next Case

How long will any student organization be eligible for student or campus funding? That was the issue raised in *Rosenberger* by Justice Sandra Day O'Connor in her concurring decision. While agreeing that *Wide Awake* was entitled to funding, she noted that the constitutionality of the entire collegiate student activity fee system is subject to challenge, writing:

> I note the possibility that the student fee is susceptible to a Free Speech Clause challenge by an objecting student that she should not be compelled to pay for speech with which she disagrees.

Justice O'Connor further noted, "There currently exists a split in the lower courts as to whether such a challenge would be successful." Her comments are based, in part, on a recent California Supreme Court decision on the use of mandatory fees for political purposes.

In *Smith v. Board of Regents of University of California*, 844 P.2d 500 (1993), the state disallowed fees to groups with political purposes and agendas, not just political groups. The state court held that mandatory fee support of groups with political agendas violated student free speech and association rights.

Rosenberger was the first collegiate separation of church and state to reach the Supreme Court in almost 15 years. The decision overturned a generally accepted collegiate policy. It also left campuses wondering if the next case could overturn fee systems themselves.

Sports in the Courts

November 1993

Intercollegiate sports, from the earliest days of student rowing competitions, focused on strength and endurance. Sports were intended to concentrate on individual and team development. And sports issues were resolved on the playing fields, not in courtrooms.

Yet, in local papers all around the country, intercollegiate sports headlines can be found in the news sections, not the sports pages. Instead of concentrating on the action on the playing fields, coaches, players, and administrators today find themselves spending increasing time inside courtrooms.

The wide variety of cases demonstrates the potential for litigation. Sports programming has legal risks, as demonstrated by these recent cases, and colleges and universities must understand those risks. Among the potential risk areas: stadium alcohol, scholarships, discrimination, and coaching complaints. What is not a concern on campus today may become a complex legal and sporting question by tomorrow!

Alcohol, Scholarships, and Defamation

While it's against the law to serve beer and other alcoholic drinks on Mississippi campuses, they can be served on other state properties. So beer sales were proposed to cover an operating deficit at the Jackson State University football stadium. A facility commission approved the beer sales at the 60,000-seat stadium — over the objections of some students, alums, public officials, community leaders, and even the university president.

When public pressure failed to sway the stadium commissioners to change their plans, a local judge banned the sales until a full hearing could take place on the issue.

In East Lansing (MI), an issue concerning intercollegiate sports scholarships is in the courts. A former basketball player recently sued Michigan State University, claiming breach of contract. The player argued that his sports-related scholarship was taken away without a school hearing. He sought $10,000 in damages from MSU.

But school officials said it should not have been a surprise that the athlete lost his scholarship, since they acted after he was arrested on cocaine charges. MSU also contends that the player broke the terms of the scholarship by taking cash payments from team boosters, a direct NCAA violation.

A judge heard the arguments and ruled that the player had lost his right to the scholarship through his actions. An appeal has been discussed but not yet filed.

Title IX suits remain fairly common in today's collegiate sports world. For example, at Colgate University (NY), the women's ice hockey program remains in court over equity issues. And at the University of Minnesota, a women's gymnastics coach has filed suit against the school, claiming unequal pay for the same work as the men's coach and wrongful discharge. The civil suit will be heard in a state court, and Minnesota will argue that NCAA violations, not discrimination, led to the problems.

A newer area of claims against schools involves the methods and decisions of team coaches. Courts are hearing cases involving the University of Wisconsin-Madison, Purdue University (IN), and the University of Miami. All involve player claims against coaches.

At UW-Madison, a state court last year reviewed claims by a female basketball player that her coach defamed her at a team meeting by calling her "a disgrace" in front of the team. The comment reportedly came during a meeting to discuss an assistant coach who was fired after allegedly having a personal relationship with the player.

The player sued, claiming that the head coach had violated her privacy by revealing the personal relationship. While the jury did not support all of the coach's methods, it did vote 10-2 against the player's claim. It found no intention by the coach to harm the player, a necessary element in a defamation claim.

Abuse and Disappointment

At Purdue, a football player and his parents have sued the school over the conduct of the football coach. They claim the coach abused the player, driving him to alcohol use and suicide fears. The former all-state high school player claims that the coach's abusive methods forced him to give up his scholarship and leave the school.

Some of the accusations are that the coach regularly "hit, punched, kicked, and shoved" players. As a result of this alleged treatment, the plaintiff claims he experienced suicidal thoughts, abused alcohol, and suffered from deterioration of social relationships and poor academic performance. His parents say the coach perpetrated a fraud in recruiting their son to attend Purdue without disclosing the extreme coaching methods.

In addition to the claim against the coach, the family also named the athletic department and school officials as defendants. They contend that the department and officials knew, or should have known, of the coach's abusive conduct and should have stopped it. The suit seeks damages for pain and suffering and punitive damages. The family also wants a payment equal to the value of a full Big Ten scholarship.

"Unfounded" is the coach's reaction to the suit. He says he knows he's tough on his players but that he doesn't plan on changing his methods. He contends that his approach is fair and his expectations reasonable.

Coaching decisions are also under fire at the University of Miami, where athletic officials face an interesting $20 million question. A former player has filed a 25-count lawsuit against Miami, claiming that the school's failure to keep commitments and its negligence may have cost him a professional football career. The case was recently filed in federal court in New Jersey. The university and eight officials were named as defendants.

The plaintiff, currently the starting quarterback at Rutgers University (NJ), began his collegiate career at Miami after being heavily recruited. Shortly after he signed a letter of intent to attend Miami on a scholarship, the school's head football coach left for a professional football job. The school refused to release the scholarship students who had just signed commitments. They had to play for Miami, even though the coach who had recruited them was gone before they arrived on campus.

The new head coach at Miami allegedly reassured the quarterback that he would be groomed for the top job on the top-ranked team. After a year of waiting, another player was selected as the starting quarterback. According to the suit, this "traumatized" the plaintiff and, "in order to save his collegiate football career, he was forced to transfer to Rutgers University, where he hoped he would still be able to achieve his destined, successful, and lucrative pro-football career." The transfer to Rutgers cost the plaintiff one year of eligibility, forcing him to sit out the year.

In addition to claiming injury because the coach did not select him as the starting quarterback, the former Miami player is also suing over financial matters. He says he was one of 91 students an athletic department academic advisor fraudulently signed up for federal financial aid. As a result, he illegally received financial aid and was questioned repeatedly by federal investigators. He claims he was "intimidated" by that investigation process and that the threat of criminal prosecution "distracted" him from football. Again, this had a negative impact on his career, according to the suit.

These cases are just a sampling of the concerns facing college and university officials. Be prepared. No matter what the sport, the name of the game is litigation.

Court Ruling Gives Title IX Renewed Strength

October 1992

The case didn't involve a college or university. It didn't involve a sports team either. But the U.S. Supreme Court's decision in the case has sent campuses a strong message about gender equity in college athletic programs.

In *Franklin v. Gwinnett County Public Schools*, 112 S.Ct. 1028 (1992), the Court ruled that victims of sex discrimination could sue for monetary damages.

For years, Title IX of the Education Amendments of 1972 has prohibited sex discrimination at schools receiving federal dollars. Most school officials understand that law. Many, however, believe the risk of losing federal funding for non-compliance is very low.

But Title IX has grown teeth as a result of the Court's recent decision — and people are going to find out how sharp those teeth really are!

The Franklin Case

In *Franklin*, the high court heard the case of a high school student who had been sexually harassed by an instructor. The school listened to her complaints, but failed to take action — so the student took her case to court.

But why? What was she entitled to? What remedies exist for her and for other victims of sex discrimination?

Before Title IX, people claiming sex discrimination tried to use the Constitution's "Equal Protection" clause as a remedy vehicle. Courts looked at sex-based decisions (like allowing separate sports teams in high schools and colleges) and adopted a "separate but equal" approach.

But in 1972, Title IX, 20 U.S.C. sec 1681, directly addressed the issue of sex discrimination. It said:

> No person in the United States shall, on the basis of sex, be excluded from participation in, be denied the benefits of, or be subjected to discrimination under any education program or activity receiving federal financial assistance.

So aside from a few stated exceptions (social fraternities, sororities, and other traditionally single-sex youth service organizations), educational institutions cannot discriminate on the basis of sex.

But Title IX didn't specify what sanctions could or should be imposed on violators. So legal experts argued that courts finding unlawful sex discrimination at educational institutions could not award monetary damages.

In previous sex discrimination cases — almost all of them involving employment — courts had ordered illegal activity halted and awarded back pay. But what could these remedies offer to the student in *Franklin*? She had long since graduated from high school, and the accused teacher had left the school district.

The Court decided that it could use any available remedy — unless Congress had excluded a particular remedy when writing the law. Said the Court:

> If a right of action exists to enforce a federal right, and Congress is silent on the question of remedies, a federal court may order any appropriate relief.

So now, *Franklin* will have to go to a new trial in the lower courts to determine the level of damages the victim will receive. She originally requested $6 million from the school district.

Title IX's New Impact

Title IX, now revived, directly affects college athletics. Section 106 specifically requires equal opportunity in "interscholastic, intercollegiate, club, or intramural athletics." The law also prohibits discrimination in athletic scholarships, cheerleading, and physical education classes.

But does Title IX mean the end of separate men's and women's teams or competition?

Some have argued that the "Equal Protection" clause should open up all competition to all competitors, regardless of sex. But Title IX doesn't go that far. Instead, it establishes a test for equity, based on the "contact" nature of the sport.

If a sport is based on "contact," a school can have separate teams for each sex — or one team for only one sex. But if a school offers a contact sport to only one sex, it must offer another opportunity in its athletic program to make up for the inequity.

On the government's current list of contact sports: boxing, wrestling, rugby, ice hockey, football, and basketball.

For non-contact sports, if a school has only one team, it must be open to both sexes.

But if a college or university has separate teams in some sports and only one team in others, how can the school's gender equity be judged?

That's been an important question on many campuses, and it may receive even more attention in light of *Franklin*. Title IX doesn't require total budget equity between men's and women's sports teams on campus. However, a school must provide "equal athletic opportunity for members of both sexes."

To judge equity in athletic programs, the Court suggested that campuses (and other courts) look at several factors, including:

- Sports selected and level of competition
- Equipment and supplies used
- Game and practice time schedules
- Allowances for travel and per diems
- Coaching and tutoring offered
- Number of coaches and tutors (and their compensation)
- Locker rooms, practice, and office sites
- Medical and training facilities and services
- Housing and dining facilities
- Publicity provided

Status Quo Won't Do

The re-emergence of Title IX has led to a variety of challenges to the "business as usual" attitude in intercollegiate sports programs. Across the country, women's sports teams are searching for equity through the schools and the courts.

At the University of Texas-Austin, for example, seven female athletes filed a class-action suit, saying they've been denied the opportunity to participate in intercollegiate sports. Using Title IX, they say they've been victims of discrimination because their sports are offered only at the club or intramural level.

The lawsuit seeks to force the school to offer women's softball, soccer, crew, and gymnastics as intercollegiate sports.

Currently, UT has nine men's and eight women's teams. But only 23% of the school's athletes are female, though women account for 47% of the student population.

Funding reductions at Brown University (RI) have also led to a Title IX athletics case. Facing a huge deficit, the school cut four athletic programs — two men's teams and two women's teams.

But the women affected, members of the gymnastics and volleyball teams, have gone to court claiming inequity. Even though more men than women were affected by the cuts, the women say they "were not on an even playing field to begin with."

At Bowdoin College (ME), the women's hockey team has filed a complaint with the U.S. Department of Education, claiming it was poorly treated compared to the men's team.

The women's volleyball team at California State University-Fullerton recently agreed to settle its Title IX complaint against the school.

After the players got a preliminary injunction against the school's decision to drop the program, officials agreed to reinstate the team, start a women's soccer program next year, and improve the proportion of female athletes over the next decade to within five percentage points of the campus male-female ratio.

Currently, only 29% of the school's athletes are women, though women make up 55% of the student population.

At the City University of New York Brooklyn College, coaches recently challenged campus sports programs on Title IX grounds.

Two female instructors filed a complaint with the Department of Education, alleging inequities in the school's sports program. The school provided equal scholarship opportunities to men and women, but the DOE found disparities in coaching salaries, scheduling, equipment, locker room facilities, and recruitment policies.

In settling the case, the campus agreed to work toward full compliance with Title IX. The school is also evaluating coaching assignments and student interests, and it is adding sports teams as well.

At the University of Massachusetts at Amherst, a faculty senate committee is investigating the treatment of women's sport teams. The women's tennis team is contemplating legal action in response to a decision to cut the team's funding and reduce the team to the club level.

At Northeastern University (MA), members of the women's hockey team have reviewed their rights with an attorney after their scholarships were withdrawn and their coach resigned in protest.

Two other Title IX cases have also received DOE scrutiny recently. Inequities in athletic recruiting policies led to violation findings at Western Carolina University (NC) and the University of Wisconsin-Madison.

WCU, the DOE found, paid visiting expenses for 90% of its male recruits but for only 17% of its prospective female athletes. At UW, the DOE found that the school spent only 12% of its total recruiting budget on women's athletics.

The DOE reviewers are part of an enforcement effort that has been revitalized by the Office of Civil Rights. The DOE has made equity in athletics a priority, according to officials, and has urged schools to voluntarily comply with Title IX.

One notable effort came recently from the Big Ten athletic conference. The presidents at Big Ten schools have adopted a plan to increase female athletic participation to 40% of available intercollegiate athletic opportunities in the next five years — a 10% improvement over the current rate.

Summary

Title IX, after its initial adoption, sparked renewed interest in women's sports on college campuses. But after initial improvements, progress slowed considerably. There was even a four-year period of non-enforcement by the federal government in the 1980s.

But today, Title IX is back, stronger than ever, giving higher education notice of sweeping changes ahead. Considering the commitment of coaches and athletes, the impact of *Franklin*, the threat of monetary damages, and the renewed pressure from the DOE, presidents, and some athletic conferences, gender equity in collegiate sports may be on the horizon.

Look for more Title IX complaints and cases, all arguing for change — which will come either voluntarily or through the courts.

Note: In 1995, a federal district court ruled that Brown University does not provide female athletes with sufficient opportunities to compete in sports. Brown has filed an appeal, claiming that the court misapplied the law and that the test for Title IX compliance is flawed.

Absent Supervisor Liable for Cheerleader Injuries

September 1993

The school's cheerleading squad received funding from both the school and student organizations. The team performed at various events for the campus, some athletic and others promotional. Its first faculty advisor actively supervised the team and stressed safety. But a new advisor, assigned by the campus, didn't even attend practices.

When the campus mat room was not available, the team practiced on an astroturf surface that was much harder. After the team changed a routine to make it faster, a first year cheerleader fell, breaking her elbow and ankle on the surface. After her injury, the campus hired an experienced program supervisor to lead the team. However, this was too late for the injured student.

Were the school and absent advisor responsible for the student's injuries? She thought so, and she sued for damages. Her negligence claims included failure to provide adequate supervision, training, and coaching; failure to provide proper equipment, such as padded mats; and failure to provide proper instructional and safety materials. Her claim was one of many suits in recent years filed against colleges and universities based on potential liability for activities and advisors.

Campus Duty

Every year, claims are made against campuses and campus personnel related to student organizations. Students injured in student activities often blame the school or advisor, and seek damages from the campus. Sporting events, recreation, and the use of alcohol by student groups all represent liability risks.

Generally, courts have not found a duty for campus advisors to supervise student organizations, and their activities, in a manner designed to protect students from harm. In many cases, courts have recognized that a campus today has a limited ability to control student behavior. But when the campus provides inadequate supervision, or fails to stop obviously dangerous activities, the campus and staff can be found liable.

When a student is injured in a student organization or campus-sponsored activity and files a legal claim, the court considers several elements before making a decision. To hold the campus or an advisor responsible, the court usually must find that:

- The school or the advisor had a duty (responsibility) to supervise the students or activity
- The school or advisor intentionally or negligently breached that duty.
- The breach by the campus or advisor caused student injury.

Does the campus have a duty to supervise? When deciding this, courts consider the extent of control the institution exercises over a student group. If institutional control suggests that the group is part of the institution or is an agent of the school, the school may be liable for harms caused by the group. However, the more independence shown by the student group, the more likely it is that the group, not the campus, will be held liable.

Non-Campus Control Standard Set

The non-campus control standard was perhaps most significantly established in *Bradshaw v. Rawlings*, 612 F.3d 135 (1979). A campus and an advisor were not held responsible for injuries caused in an alcohol-related student accident following an off-campus class picnic. The event was advertised on campus, and an advisor had authorized expenditures for the picnic, but no one from the campus attended or exercised supervision. The injured student claimed that the school knew or should have known that minors would be drinking, and had a duty to control the class.

The federal court disagreed. Noting that "the modern American campus is not insured of the safety of its students," it found the school and advisor not responsible. The court considered:

- The notion that campus students are seen today as adults rather than children
- The lessening role of campuses as protectors of students
- The obvious difficulties campuses have in attempting to control the behaviors of today's students.

The court found students capable of making adult decisions and obligated to live with the consequences.

Other cases support the general limited institutional or advisor liability principle for student events. In *Baldwin v. Zoradi*, 123 Cal. App 809 (1981), a resident advisor did not have a special duty to protect a student from drinking and driving injuries. The accident was judged not to be so foreseeable that the advisor had a duty to act. And in *Hartman v. Bethany*, 778 F.Supp. 291 (1991), a campus was judged not responsible for an assault at a bar adjacent to the school. The court found the campus had no duty to advise students about possible off-campus risk, although there are other legitimate motivations to do so.

In addition to alcohol cases, there are other risk areas as well. Sports and recreation often cause injuries for which students claim campuses are responsible. In *Gehling v. St. George's University School of Medicine*, 705 F.Supp. 761 (NY 1989), a medical student died after running a race conducted by the school. His estate sued, but the court found no institutional liability. The campus provided reasonable facilities and services and was held to have no further duties. And in *Nganga v. Wooster*, 557 N.E. 2d 152 (1989), a campus was found not responsible for injuries from an intramural tackle-football incident. The court did not find negligent supervision. The student assumed the risk of such injuries in a heavy-contact sport, said the court.

Similar decisions were reached in cases involving pushball, trampolines, recreation areas, and ski equipment. No supervision of a student pushball game was required in *Rubtinchsky v. State University of New York at Albany*, 260 N.Y.S.2d 256 (1965), unless the sport was held to be "inherently" dangerous. In *Whitlock v. University of Denver*, 744 P.3d 54 (1987), lower courts held the university liable for an off-campus fraternity house injury on a trampoline. But while the trial court said it was unreasonable for the school to allow the activity to continue, the higher court said the campus was responsible for conduct only when:

- It has undertaken to supervise conduct to prevent specific harms
- It fails to exercise that supervision
- Either the student relied on that supervision or the lack of expected supervision increased the risks.

In *Whitlock*, those conditions were not found, freeing the school from liability. But in some cases, institutional liability can be established where inadequate supervision or inherently dangerous activities take place uncontrolled.

Liability for Dangerous Activities

Consider the case of the university employee who failed to properly inspect the snow ski bindings before renting skis to a student. In *Meese v. Brigham Young University*, 639 P.2d 720 (1981), the court found the campus negligent. And in *Brown v. Florida State Board of Regents*, 513 So.2d 184 (Fla. Dist. Ct. App. Dist. 1987), the court supported an action against a school for operating a canoe rental service in a dangerous manner, including a lack of supervision and safety instructions.

Finally, the case of the injured campus cheerleader is another example of liability. In *Kirk v. Washington State University*, 746 P.2d 285 (1987), the state's highest court reviewed a lower court liability decision for over $350,000 in damages due to the student's permanent injuries. The Supreme Court of Washington upheld the award. The lower court found the student partially responsible for her injuries under an "assumption of risk" principle, and the higher court agreed. But the campus and advisor remained substantially liable due to their negligence. The activity was school funded and the school provided an advisor, who unlike predecessors, did not participate and stress safety. The activity was school approved and the potential risks were known. The organization was under the "control" of the campus, not independent. The school was held liable.

Clarify the Risks

At the root of all of these cases is the relationship between the campus and the student organization. A clear understanding of the involvement can help avoid unwanted confusion, frustration, and litigation.

Does the campus sponsor, supervise, sanction, permit the reserved use of space, or allow only the use of public spaces? The greater the level of involvement, the greater the liability risks. Campus officials need to take the time to understand these relationships and make sure that the potential for liability is considered carefully by all.

Three Cheers for Safety

April 1991

Cheerleading has become a standard part of college athletics. At intercollegiate athletic events across the country, squads lead cheering crowds and perform stunts. For the spectators, they add excitement to the event. But some administrators and parents are fearful of the potential safety risks faced by young people performing intricate routines using trampolines, tumbling, and human pyramids.

A Washington state case points out some of the dangers and legal issues related to cheerleading, while a recent *NASPA Journal* article looked at campus cheerleading safety practices. Reviewing both will help colleges and universities stay out of the courts.

High Cost of Negligence

In *Kirk v. Washington State University*, 746 P.2d 285 (1987), the state Supreme Court heard an appeal of a case involving injury to a college cheerleader. She had suffered permanent injury to her arm and elbow after falling during a practice session. The team had practiced on mats in the past but recently had been forced to move to an area with synthetic turf flooring, a much harder surface. The team advisor was new and didn't participate in any training activities.

The cheerleader sued WSU, claiming that negligence led to her injuries, which included permanent arm disability and severe mental depression that caused prolonged hospitalization. A jury found the plaintiff in part responsible for her injuries but awarded her damages totaling $350,000. The jury concluded that the school had failed to take reasonable steps to protect cheerleaders from harm. Negligence was found in the school's failure to:

- To properly train, coach, and supervise
- To provide proper materials on safety
- To provide appropriate practice facilities
- To warn about the hard floor surface

The jury didn't award the amount of damages sought by the plaintiff because it found an *assumption of risks* on her part. This principle, a defense against some claims of negligence, states that a person who exposes himself or herself to a known or obvious danger may not recover for related injuries. The jury felt that, to some extent, the cheerleader should have been aware of cheerleading dangers, and that she had assumed a personal risk in participating. The plaintiff appealed the jury decision in hopes of greater compensation.

In a final review of *Kirk*, the Supreme Court of Washington looked at cheerleading, assumption of risks, and the level of damages. WSU claimed that, since the plaintiff had participated in cheerleading voluntarily, she couldn't make any claims for monetary damages. Not so, said the court. It found that assumption of risks is only a factor to consider in assessing negligence, and that it doesn't preclude recovery of damages. The jury had been correct in making voluntary participation in a dangerous activity a limiting factor in determining damages.

The ultimate award in *Kirk* points out clearly the need for appropriate campus supervision of cheerleading activities.

Give Me an S, an A, an F, an E, a T, a Y

That's the focus of a *NASPA Journal* article, "College Cheerleading: A National Survey of Current Safety Standards and Practices," by S. Johnson, A. Aagaard, J. Rhatigan, and J. Addison (Spring 1990). The authors cover the key issues of campus cheerleading concern — supervision, insurance activities, injuries, and safety guidelines — and make recommendations. The article is based on a survey of all NASPA institutions, with 63% of member institutions responding.

Respondents reported various levels of campus *supervision*. More than 80% of schools provided some level of supervision. Half of all supervisors have been campus cheerleaders, and a quarter participated in summer training programs. But almost 10% of supervisors have no previous experience. Only a third of responding institutions reported that supervisors attend practices.

About 80% of schools with cheerleading squads reported carrying some form of *insurance*. Generally, coverage is limited: a third have no medical coverage, half have no accidental death coverage, and two-thirds have no paraplegic or quadriplegic coverage.

Almost 75% of the squads perform human pyramid activities. Most pyramids reach a height of two-and-a-half persons. About 18% responded that their squads have suffered some pyramid injuries, including head injuries, paralysis, and fatalities.

And 75% of the schools allow pairs routines that sometimes appear to be complex and riskier. Pairs routines, also known as partner stunts, were the cause of most cheerleading *injuries* over the past five years. A quarter of schools reported partner stunt injuries, which included knee injuries, dental injuries, sprains, and broken bones. Jumps were the third leading cause of college cheerleader injuries.

While safety is an obvious concern, almost 30% of responding schools indicated that they have no *safety standards* for cheerleaders. Those schools with guidelines generally depend on established national or athletic conference standards.

Recommendations

In summary, the authors point out that, although cheerleading injuries aren't excessive, they remain a concern. Their recommendations to campuses:

- Develop a cheerleader injury data base.
- Further research and analyze cheerleading-related issues.
- Provide more complete insurance coverage.
- Establish safety guidelines.
- Continuously update supervision skills.

Campuses with cheerleading programs need to understand the risks inherent in the activity and respond appropriately. While a participant can be said to assume some associated risks, as in *Kirk*, colleges and universities still have a duty to their cheerleaders — and legal liabilities.

One key to meeting this duty is good supervision. Squad supervisors and advisors should pay close attention to the essentials:

- Carefully evaluate participant skill levels.
- Provide proper instruction.
- Ensure suitable facilities and equipment, including appropriate inspections.
- Closely plan and evaluate activities.
- Establish technical and safety guidelines — and adhere to them.
- Provide first aid and emergency care.
- Furnish suitable transportation and establish travel procedures.
- Maintain adequate insurance, inform participants of potential dangers, and use specific waivers of liability.
- Ensure that supervisors are present at practices and events.
- Properly train, evaluate, and supervise squad advisors and supervisors.

Cheerleading adds a colorful and exciting element to college sporting events. To reduce the potential for related injuries and litigation, good cheerleading needs good supervision.

Use the lessons of *Kirk* and the survey reported in the *NASPA Journal* to promote a review of current campus practices. Then, make improvements — improvements in cheerleading and improvements in risk management. Give everyone, including administrators and parents, something to cheer about!

Guide to Advising Groups

August 1995

So you've been asked to serve as an advisor to a student group. Some would extend congratulations — while others would offer condolences!

In recent years, concern over liability has made some faculty and staff reconsider involvement with student organizations. Just what are some of the legal risks associated with being an advisor? What can be done to limit potential liability? Key considerations should include torts, contracts, and statutory and constitutional issues.

Torts

Can an advisor be found responsible for the negligence of the student organization? Yes, if the involved faculty or staff member does not act as another "reasonably competent person" would.

Common negligence law says that liability can be established when the following conditions are found:

- There is some duty of care to the person or situation
- That duty is breached.
- The breach results in injury, harm, or loss.
- The breach is the proximate cause of the damage.

Under these circumstances, legal responsibility can be established. As a student group advisor, you may have a duty and special relationship. If so, you could be liable for directing or supervising activities that breach duties and cause harm.

What can be done to minimize the advisor's risk? Most legal experts agree that promoting two legal principles within the organization can reduce potential liability. Understanding and applying the principles of "reasonable standards of care" and "due warning" can help advisors avoid loss and related liability. Advisors should be aware of the principles and work to incorporate them into organization activities.

"Reasonable Standards of Care"

"Reasonable standards of care" require those responsible for a program or activity to know and adhere to guidelines and standards of safe conduct. They are expected to ensure that they and others behave in such a manner as to reduce risk. These standards are based on what others would do in the same or similar circumstances with appropriate education and experience.

This is the "reasonably prudent person" standard. Advisors will be expected to know what other advisors elsewhere are expected to know and to act accordingly.

Other protective standards that should be considered come from professional organizations. They generally establish recommended levels of training, equipment, and procedures necessary to conduct activities and services in a safe manner.

Who, for example, would operate a swimming area without first considering Red Cross guidelines? Many organizations, like those for fraternity and sorority advisors and faculty working with the student press, have created specific guidelines for advisors. Persons serving as advisors in these areas would generally be expected to obtain, review, and understand the guidelines and procedures established by related organizations. Campus or individual membership in appropriate organizations should be encouraged as well.

Developing an understanding of existing guidelines and attempting to conduct activities in a prudent and safe manner are the keys to providing reasonable standards of care within a student organization, protecting both the group and the advisor!

"Due Warning"

An advisor can also help the organization avoid loss and injury by promoting the provision of "due warning" when appropriate. Those responsible for programs should provide notice of foreseeable risks to those likely to come in contact with hazards.

Warnings should be provided about risks that sponsors know about, or should know about, through reasonable review. The warning could be through a sign promoting caution or through use of a formal waiver of liability detailing possible risks. The type and level of warning should reflect the nature of the risk and the likelihood of loss or harm.

An advisor can help an organization provide due warning that meets reasonable standards of care by conducting a thorough risk assessment before each activity:

- What are the possible risks involved?
- How can they be avoided?
- What are the established guidelines?
- How will they be implemented?
- What risks should participants be aware of before participating?

Working to provide organizational reasonable standards of care and due warning can significantly reduce the potential for advisor tort liability.

Contracts

The invoice arrives on your desk after the party. The student organization had a great time at the event and loved the music. But the money ran out before all of the bills came in, and the band never got paid.

Is the advisor responsible for the bill? No, not if the advisor understands his or her role and has taken appropriate steps *in advance* of receiving the bill.

All organizations need to understand basic financial structures and responsibilities. Guidelines and budgets need to be established and followed. Everyone involved needs to know who is authorized to make transactions in the name of the organization and to understand the personal consequences of exceeding their organizational authority.

To avoid individual financial liability, advisors generally should not enter into agreements on behalf of their groups, unless absolutely necessary. If signing something in your role as group advisor, make sure that your relationship is noted clearly on the document. Don't just sign your name or your name and school name. That could lead to unwanted individual and even institutional liability.

Statutory/Constitutional/Institutional Issues

Student organizations and their events, activities, and programs must operate within the boundaries established by government and the college or university. Advisors should be particularly aware of how some constitutional issues can affect student organizations. Depending on the public or private nature of an institution, consideration must be given to freedoms of speech, association, and assembly. Elements of due process may also be required of the organization.

Particular attention should also be paid to non-discrimination and sexual harassment laws and policies. Within the campus environment, student organizations must adhere to the law. Membership practices or activities that could be perceived as discriminatory or harassing must be ended.

Advisors should work with groups to ensure that their members understand the law and the principles the law promotes. Advisors must also remember that the student groups have some rights, and that their rights to be recognized and to use facilities must be understood and respected.

What Can Be Done?

Perhaps issues related to tort liability, contract law, constitutional and statutory limitations, and related concerns may explain why some colleagues might offer their condolences when you are appointed to advise a student group. The concerns are significant. But steps can be taken to reduce potential liability:

- Secure well-written position descriptions from the college or university, indicating duties, authority, and institutional protections.

- Review professional organization standards to ensure a full understanding of the organization and operating principles.

- Review insurance policies. Would you be covered under a campus policy? An organization or association policy? A plan of your own?

- Establish a good risk management program within the organization to provide for reasonable standards of care and appropriate due warning.

- Understand the law as it relates to student organizations and their rights and responsibilities.

- Make sure there are good financial policies in place. Sign documents to clearly indicate group obligations, not individual or institutional ones.

- Understand that alcohol is a significant risk factor; develop plans with students to prevent underage drinking and service to those intoxicated.

Above all, to be an effective and legally smart advisor, act as would a "reasonably prudent person." That's the standard by which you'll be judged.

'Tis Better to Have Won and Lost (Not!)

June 1992

"Winner must be present to claim the prize." Did all of the printed materials for the Kent State University (OH) football halftime contest include that phrase? One angry New Jersey family is trying to find out after "winning" and then "losing" a trip to France!

The family's name was pulled from a barrel of tickets during the last home game of the season. Although not at the game, friends from KSU called them at home to congratulate them on their prize. But when they called the KSU athletic department, they stopped packing their bags.

Representatives from KSU and a travel agency that sponsored the contest said the rules required the winner be present to claim the prize. But a check of campus newspaper ads and contest posters only turned up a few references to that limitation.

The original winning family says they're confused because an usher at an earlier game told them they could win even if not present. Since they were from out of town and would not be at the final game, they filled out the ticket only after speaking with the usher. They also want to know why another name wasn't called at the game when they failed to claim the prize.

While one school spokesperson said a winner was called and "details are being worked out," the family has been told the prize was unclaimed and will be given away at a future KU sporting event.

In this contest, it's clear there were no "winners;" not the family and certainly not KSU!

Unworthy Student Fund-Raisers: Evaluating Charitable Causes

April 1993

Many groups on college and university campuses participate in a wide variety of charitable programs and events throughout the year, most for good causes. But sometimes, that's not the case.

Unfortunately, in recent years charitable fraud has become more prevalent, placing campus efforts at risk. What can campus groups do to prevent becoming involved in fund-raisers for unworthy organizations? Since over $130 billion nationally was given to charities last year, it's important to know who campus groups are fund-raising for — and where the dollars go when they leave campus!

Experts suggest seven steps to consider before getting your campus, group, or organization involved in a charitable cause. These steps consist of:

- Find a cause that "moves" the group, that gets people really involved.
- Find an agency doing service work in your area.
- Make a donation through the United Way or a local foundation.
- Obtain a charitable organization's latest audited financial report or tax filing.
- Review the charitable organization's most recent annual report.
- Visit the charitable organization you might work with.
- Check with "watchdog" organizations on the group's status.

Given the time, effort, and energy that campus clubs and organizations put into charitable fund-raising, it's important to make sure that the cause is worthy.

Finding a cause that *moves the group* is an important first step in avoiding charity fraud. If the campus group is involved in a cause (such as AIDS prevention, hunger, education, or homelessness), the members will take a more active role in the charitable group beyond fund-raising. Simply sending checks with donations to charitable groups can lead to misuse. Active involvement in the charity by a fraternity or sorority, or a faculty club, can help ensure that the charity is worthy of campus group support.

The campus organization's level of awareness and involvement can be greatly increased if the chosen charitable group is *doing service work in your local area*. If it's a nationally known organization, does it have an active presence in your community? If it does not, the group is reduced to a "by mail" relationship, providing opportunity for abuse. If a campus group is unsure about what groups to support in the community, consider checking with local foundations. They provide their support to agencies only after a comprehensive evaluation. The support of an agency by a local foundation can be a very good indication of worthiness.

An alternative to screening national and local community service and charitable organizations yourself is to have your campus group *donate directly to a United Way chapter or a local foundation*. They traditionally scrutinize community needs and use their resources to provide needed support. They will provide a donating student or campus organization with periodic information on how their money is being used to aid the community.

If your campus group chooses to work directly with a charitable organization, make sure, in advance, that you are comfortable with how the agency works. How does it collect and expend its funds, and what are all the elements of its program? When the local news media produces their "exposés," on a group you support, it's not enough to respond by saying, "We didn't know." Before getting involved, you should know!

As a start, ask for a copy of the charity's *latest audited financial report or tax filing*. Read the materials carefully, and consider how much of the group's resources go into service. What does the group spend on overhead? Does this include executive salaries, fund-raising, and other administrative expenses? The Better Business Bureau requires member charities to spend no more than 50% of their resources on administration, while other "watchdog" groups only approve agencies that put at least 60% of contributions back into service.

If the available financial information is adequate, then get your campus group to review the agency's *annual program report* carefully before getting involved. Consider these questions when reviewing the program:

- What are all the services and programs?
- How are they managed and evaluated?
- How involved are other known service agencies?
- Who sits on the board of directors?
- Is the board broadly based?
- Are members of the group being served on the board?
- What is the level of corporate involvement? Are corporations involved for marketing and public relations purposes or are they truly participating?

Another key element to consider before getting campus groups financially involved with a charitable agency is a *site visit*. What does the agency site look like? Talk to some volunteers. Talk to some people being served by the group. Volunteer yourself and your members to see if this is really what you want to be supporting. How effective is the agency? How efficient is the service? What more does it need?

Finally, check on your chosen group with established charity *"watchdog" organizations*. These include the Better Business Bureau, the National Charities Information Bureau, and the American Institute of Philanthropy. Also consider checking with the state attorney general's office in your area.

Service to communities is an important lesson for students and their organization and an important purpose for institutions of higher education. Fund-raisers may be an element of that service commitment. But make sure that the causes supported within the community are worthy causes!

Concert Crush Teaches Lessons

May 1992

The legal capacity of the school gym was listed at 2,700 people. The videotape reviewed by police suggests that as many as 2,000 more had packed the hall for the celebrity-charity basketball game. The planning may have seemed like just one of thousands of similar events held each year on college and university campuses, but the reality turned out to be a veritable nightmare. Before the game began, nine people were dead, and a community, a college, and its staff had all become victims.

The tragedy at the City University of New York's (CUNY) Harlem Campus sent shock waves through campus networks of special events coordinators, student programmers, and athletic departments. The seemingly annual deaths of English soccer fanatics overseas had long been reported in the American press, but the Cincinnati concert of mega-stars "The Who" had previously served as the only stateside warning to those responsible for spectator events. By understanding what happened at CUNY, and by knowing the law involving spectators and facilities, campuses can protect themselves and others from damages, injuries, and even deaths in the future.

Several years ago, the death of spectators trying to push into a Cincinnati arena for a rock concert provided programmers with an ugly lesson about open seating and general admissions. Young music fans, desperate to get the best seats, simply pushed their way toward the entrance doors, unintentionally trampling and crushing those in their path. History painfully repeated itself last year at CUNY.

A student organization arranged with the CUNY student government to hold an event in the school's underground gym. The organization filled out some forms in a campus student affairs office. According to the college, a small crowd was anticipated for a celebrity basketball game being played on behalf of AIDS education. While not directly managing the event, the college did provide the facility and security. Required liability insurance was never purchased by organizers.

The celebrities, it turned out, were local and national rap artists, and ticket sales soared as word spread through the community. Police estimate that room capacity had been exceeded by almost 70% before the incident; tellingly, tickets were still being sold even as nine people were being crushed to death by the overwhelming crowds.

According to published reports, the game was scheduled to begin at 6 p.m., but hadn't started by 7. And eager fans began to crowd the facility hours before the scheduled tip-off. The crowd was admitted into the gym very slowly, due to a lack of organized ticket lines and a security frisk of all spectators.

People trying desperately to push into the gym broke glass doors and rushed down a staircase to find another set of locked gym doors. But the crowd continued to surge down the steps, and medical reports indicate that nine victims were asphyxiated, being "squeezed from front to back." One of the victims was pregnant.

When the game was called off due to the deaths, the crowd was further panicked and more injuries occurred. In the end, at least 28 people were injured, including five emergency medical technicians who responded to police calls. Campus police called twice for local law enforcement officers, and they were present but not in control of the situation at the time of the incident. In an investigation into the lack of a strong security presence in the facility, police indicated that the school was responsible for security. They also felt a highly visible police presence could have been "provocative" and led to additional crowd violence.

Investigators had many other concerns as they probed causes of the CUNY tragedy. They questioned the school's relationship with students and their organizations, the club advisement system, the facility reservation process, the lack of required facility supervision or management, and the role of campus security personnel and local police. The lack of an identified charitable organization to receive generated contributions, the ticket sales process, and other promoter activities were also reviewed.

In addition to possible criminal charges and civil litigation, which could name all involved parties, early post-incident victims were the campus student affairs personnel most closely involved. They lost their jobs; they either were fired, quit, or found themselves reassigned.

Spectator, Facility, and Emergency Medical Case Law

Campus event programming carries inherent liability risks. In response, campuses need to protect themselves, students, and visitors by developing good risk management programs involving spectators, facilities, and emergency services protection measures.

Campuses have a duty to *spectators*. Courts have ruled that schools can be held responsible. A general principle states that "the operator of a place of public entertainment owes a duty to keep the premises safe for its invitees." An example of this principle could be *Bearman v. University of Notre Dame*, 453 N.E.2d 1196 (1983). There, the school was held responsible for injuries that occurred in a parking lot. A spectator was injured by drunken students while walking to her car after a sporting event. The court found that the school had a duty to protect visitors at the school's events.

United Educators Insurance Risk Retention Group, Inc., an education insurance company, suggests the following risk management considerations when dealing with spectators:

- Alcohol policies that cover the time before, during, and after campus events, including tailgate party regulations
- Appropriate crowd control measures, including ticket and security plans
- Necessary spectator warnings prominently posted on facilities

Campuses also have a duty to provide adequate and safe *facilities* for crowds. The premises must be maintained in a reasonably safe condition. While many legal cases have focused on athletic playing fields, others have concerned design and equipment in facilities. As an example, glass near sports playing areas has resulted in negligence judgments against Syracuse University (NY) and local school boards. At Syracuse, the school was held responsible for having a dangerous glass door near a gym floor in *Eddy v. Syracuse University*, 433 N.Y.S.2d 923 (1980).

Failure to maintain *equipment* for spectators can also create campus liability. Seating has led to substantial litigation, including collapsing bleachers, seats not properly attached to floors, needed repairs, failure to inspect, or seats improperly constructed out of poor materials.

With regard to facilities, legal experts and insurers suggest the following:

- Install safety glass in doors and entrance areas.
- Conduct routine maintenance and safety reviews of facilities and equipment.
- Develop and implement appropriate safety and operational rules.
- Warn spectators and participants of hidden defects and dangers.
- Obtain adequate liability insurance.
- Have an adequate staffing plan for events.
- Have crowd control policies to protect spectators.
- Consider safety in building design and renovations.
- Watch for "dangerous" activities in halls, lobbies, and stairwells.
- Check outside lighting for spectators, surrounding buildings, walks, and in parking areas.

When an accident occurs that injures a spectator, a college or university should have a plan and resources to provide *emergency medical services*. Transportation to obtain assistance may also be needed. The duty to provide medical services may be established by state statute or case law. Many states have laws requiring the presence of medical personnel at large-crowd events. In other states, courts have recognized the duty in legal decisions involving negligence claims.

In *Clark v. State of New York*, 99 N.E.2d 300 (1951), a facility owner was sued for failing to provide adequate medical care to an injured party. But the case was dismissed when the court found that the facility had provided a doctor, blankets, a stretcher, and prompt transportation to a hospital. This met court standards for adequate care.

Many of the emergency service cases come from high school sporting events, including football games. Failure to provide prompt medical attention resulted in school liability in *Mogabad v. Orleans Parish School Board*, 239 S.2d 465 (1970).

Earlier cases have supported another principle for emergency medical service: it's sometimes better to transport a victim than to wait for medical aid to arrive on site. A parent challenged a school's policy to transport, not treat, injuries in *Sayers v. Ranger*, 83 A.2d 775 (1951). But the New Jersey court rejected the negligence claim, supporting the school's decision to transport injured students.

When there is a duty to respond with medical assistance, a campus events staff must also provide a reasonable facility for care and skilled first-aid personnel where appropriate.

As a result of state statutes and related case law, for campus events, colleges and universities should:

- Have and follow emergency medical procedures, including access to emergency telephone numbers, equipment, and facilities.
- Have emergency training drills and manuals for facility and program staff.
- Have emergency transportation available.

Summary

Big crowds on campus can mean big liability risks. Colleges and universities need to control their facilities, understand potential risks, and work to limit the opportunity for loss, damage, injury, or death. Campuses need to care for spectators, design and maintain safe facilities, and plan and respond appropriately to emergencies. Let the CUNY tragedy be a lesson to all and not be a sign of more tragedies to come.

Student Stampede Raises Issues of Safety

April 1994

As is often the case, at a moment of triumph, tragedy strikes. That was certainly the case in the closing seconds of a key football victory. University of Wisconsin fans stampeded from the stadium stands. According to reports, over 70 persons were injured — three left the field as "pulseless non-breathers" — when thousands rushed onto the field from the student section as the game ended. In the hours and days following the incident, even while some of the injured began to file their legal claims, the university moved swiftly to respond to the crisis.

What did UW-Madison do to limit losses? How did the campus and community respond? And what can be learned by others in an effort to provide for safe environments and reduce liability risks?

As the tragedy unfolded, campus and community officials moved swiftly in a combination of efforts that addressed assistance, investigation, information, acknowledgment, and prevention planning concerns.

Assistance came to those in need in a variety of forms from various sources. Right away, rescue and medical support was provided by staff from 23 campus Health Sciences departments. Some personnel were in the stadium and came down on the field when needed. Others were at home, watching the game on television, and drove to campus to provide aid. Within the community, emergency crews from five municipalities rushed to the scene. The injured were transported to two local hospitals, in addition to the UW Hospital. Members of the campus counseling staff met the injured in local emergency rooms and with their families and friends to offer support. The staff set aside time to spend with involved and concerned students, provided aid to parents, and established "walk-in" hours at their campus facility.

In addition to the important medical and counseling assistance, victim support was also offered through the Dean of Students office. The family of each injured student was contacted directly by UW. Every student's instructors were contacted as well, in an effort to deal with individual academic issues and problems.

Letters were sent to teaching faculty, asking them to monitor students for signs of stress or other emotional difficulties. If personal problems were suspected, they were asked to remind students about the counseling support services that were available. As the week went on, at least four debriefing sessions were held to give students and others a chance to speak out about the event and their related feelings.

In an effort to respond to the need for a full *investigation* into the incident, the UW Police immediately set up a command center to field inquiries and plan the review process. With other campus officials, law enforcement personnel participated in a press conference to assure the community that a proper probe would be conducted. It was to be an effort to find out what had actually happened and how it might be prevented in the future. The command site remained active throughout the week, as the previous week's event was reviewed and the following week's game was planned.

In responding to any crisis, *information* becomes a critical factor in addressing immediate needs and limiting damage. Public affairs staff from Health Sciences responded to hundreds of medically related calls from family members and media representatives. They were interested in obtaining accurate information on individual patients for reassurance or broadcast purposes.

The campus assistance center quickly set up a telephone information hotline that remained open overnight after the game and most of the following day. It handled calls from students, family members, alums, and the media which began as the game ended.

The need to deal with media requests required an extraordinary response from the campus public affairs staff as well. It handled hundreds of requests for materials and information and set up press conferences. In addition, it arranged for interviews with students, counselors, campus and athletic administrators, and security staff as requested. A special letter was prepared and sent to parents of undergraduates through a family publication. And a videotape of the incident was prepared and distributed to media representatives.

When so much happens so swiftly and so many work to limit the damage, it becomes important to ensure there is proper *acknowledgment*. In response to the football game stampede, words of acknowledgment came appropriately from the Board of Regents and campus officials. Within a week of the tragedy, system regents passed a resolution honoring the emergency personnel and medical facilities that responded. They were praised for their "skillful, coordinated work" that saved lives. The campus chancellor, in a published message to the entire campus community, offered a "heartfelt personal thank you to the students, staff, and faculty members who worked so hard to limit damage" and worked to avoid a recurrence. And in a final acknowledgment, prior to the next football game, those in attendance were asked to "join ... a quiet moment of reflection" on the event, the response, and the "ongoing process of healing."

With another game only a week away, *prevention planning* began immediately. The prevention effort was based on a quickly developed understanding of what had gone wrong. New fencing with break-away gates was installed to respond to crowd pressure. Extra loudspeakers were placed in the student seating section to ensure that crowd control and safety messages in the stadium could be heard. Public service announcements were broadcast and printed urging students to "celebrate responsibility." Student passes, usually used to get into games, were exchanged for one-time-only paper tickets to better maintain appropriate crowd levels. Hand stamps were also used to prevent unauthorized spectator traffic in and out of the stadium during the game. Special field-level seating was established for the marching band to ease pressure in the student seating section, where the band was traditionally placed. A cover was also installed over the field entrance for the visiting team, for the protection of players and coaches. Finally, a pep rally was planned for the stadium on a weeknight before the next game, with an emphasis on responsible celebrations.

A crisis can occur anytime on any campus. And when it does, the college or university will be faced with the same response needs as UW-Madison was — a need for assistance, investigation, information, acknowledgment, and prevention planning. How well-prepared are you to respond?

Preventing Violence at Student Social Events

October 1993

As violence in society increases, fear of violence at student social events on campus grows. Campuses concerned with the safety of student and institutional liability need to understand the causes of student event violence and employ risk-prevention strategies to prevent or limit violence and related liability.

In an effort to better prepare colleges and universities to deal with a growing trend of violence, a private organization, Campus Crime Prevention Programs, has developed a guidebook for administrators. *Preventing Acts of Violence at Student Social Events* provides information on related issues and concerns as well as sample campus policies and event regulation and planning forms. Events the guide pertains to include concerts, dances, speakers, activity fairs, fraternity parties, and football games. Two important sections of the guidebook deal with the causes of campus violence and liability issues.

Causes

To prevent or limit event violence, the campus needs to understand its root causes. Among the contributing factors:

- *Alcohol and abuse of other substances* — Increased aggressive behavior is often a consequence of substance use and abuse.
- *Attendance by non-college youths* — Non-students are not as likely to have institutional ties that might lead them to better know and observe campus rules and respond to campus authority.
- *Overcrowding* — This has been a critical factor in several significant violent situations on campuses in recent years. A lack of space for people to circulate or interact can lead to violence. Overcrowding makes it more difficult to control crowds and respond swiftly and appropriately when problems develop. Large crowds can make it difficult to find the people creating problems.
- *Poor lighting* — Inadequate lighting can create an environment in which some feel they can act without being seen. Low lighting also makes it more difficult for staff to properly observe and manage situations to prevent violence.
- *Poor supervision* — "Who's in charge here?" is a fair but sometimes difficult question to answer at some student campus events. Campus activities professionals must be properly trained, and they must be present at events to maintain a safe atmosphere. Supervision concerns extend to faculty or staff organization advisors. Their "adult" presence can help an organization make good decisions and good plans, and these lead to good events. The advisors also need training, and they need to be present to be effective.
- *Student organization controls* — Any organization sponsoring an event has to be responsible for its outcomes. When the group is not adequately prepared, trained, and held accountable, the risk of violence increases. Organizations may need to be reminded that, in the event of a problem, they may face loss of recognition, loss of funding, and disciplinary actions.
- *Inadequate security* — The presence of trained, supervised, and uniformed safety or security officers can deter student event violence. Officers need to have an adequate presence to allow effective action, if required.
- *Rivalries* — Conflicts exist on campus, and common student conflicts, if unchecked, can be the source of student event violence. Possible rivalries include conflicts between fraternities or between Greeks and athletes. The presence of gangs in the community also may be a source of potential violence on campus.
- *Interpersonal relationships* — Domestic disputes between or among two or more persons can escalate from verbal threats to physical abuse in social settings.

All of these causes of campus event violence today may not be present on any one college campus at any given time. But it only takes one factor to create a situation that ends in violence.

Cures

How can campuses, aware of the threats and causes of violence at student events, be prepared and respond? The Campus Crime Prevention Programs guidebook suggests several policies and procedures designed to assist activity officials in reducing the risk of violence:

- *Adequate event scheduling* — It takes time to do things right. An event should be planned, scheduled, and approved well in advance to allow adequate time for review and implementation. Staff must be given enough time to make necessary preparations, including scheduling of personnel and services for the program. It is also important to give appropriate consideration to event beginning and end times. The timing of events must allow for adequate staffing and safe exiting from the activity. Officials need to consider the parking situation, bus schedules, and other possible conditions that might cause difficulties, such as an end time that coincides with bar closing time.

- *Alcohol policies* — Prohibitions against alcohol at student events can effectively curb some of the potential for student event violence. Campus policies should be clearly posted, and they must be adequately enforced. It is also important to deny access to intoxicated people or remove them safely from the event.

- *Admissions controls* — Of key importance at an event is who is let in, how many are let in, what are they carrying in, and whether they leave and then freely return. Many campuses recommend a "no re-admittance" policy. This prevents students and others from leaving a controlled environment and then returning after drinking outside. An accurate system of counting the number of persons entering events is critical to avoid dangerous overcrowding.

- *Metal detection* — In an effort to control crime and violence, many large events now use metal detectors to scan for weapons. These units, walk-through or hand-held, can be effective as they visibly show campus concerns for security, deter persons from attempting to enter with weapons, identify weapons if they are concealed, and represent a significant institutional commitment to controlling liability.

- *Adequate lighting* — In order to effectively prevent violence or adequately respond to factors that could lead to violence, there must be a minimum level of lighting at events.

- *Active staff and advisor role* — Campus activities personnel need to have an active role in pre-event planning and an on-site role throughout an event. They must work with students to ensure compliance with school regulations and respond, as necessary, to circumstances to protect students, sponsoring organizations, and the institution. Advisors need to be adequately trained, in advance, to assist the organization in proper and safe event management. In addition, the advisor needs to be present at major events to help the organization comply with event regulations. In the event of a problem and possible lawsuit, courts judge liability case by case. However, supervisors are generally responsible for ensuring that participants are aware of known risks and that the activity is held in a manner that promotes safety.

- *Prepared and responsible student organizations* — The student group needs to be trained on event management techniques and requirements. It also must have an adequate number of members present and identifiable to effectively coordinate the program.

- *Public safety presence* — If dictated by the type or size of an event, campus police presence may be necessary. Officers on site need to be well-informed about plans for the event. They need to be visible, patrol interior and exterior areas, respond to trouble, assist in dismissal of the crowd, and help in post-event evaluations.

- *Campus sensitivity* — Staff and students must become aware of growing conflicts and seek to resolve them before violence occurs. A general knowledge of the campus climate is a necessity.

Conclusion

Many causes of student violence at campus events are predictable or controllable. To be able to adopt policies and procedures designed to limit or eliminate the risk of violence at events, campus officials need to assess possible causes, review event planning, and implement programs with students, advisors, and staff today to control violence at student events before it's too late.

FINAL THOUGHTS

Maintaining Perspective is clearly not a definitive text on all of the issues presented in these pages. Instead, it reflects the stories of today's colleges and universities as they struggle to meet the legal challenges that are so common in today's higher education environment.

The stories, and the schools involved, change over time, but the basic principles remain constant. It is hoped that the principles emerging from *Maintaining Perspective* will assist all in meeting challenges today and tomorrow.

Index

A

Abood v. Detroit Board of Education 264
abortion 130-132
Abrams v. Illinois College of Podiatric Medicine 2
academic freedom 5-6, 21, 26-27, 40, 71, 124
academic standards 5
access 119-120, 122-123
ACE 255-256
acquaintance rape 241-242
activity fees 263-264, 266-267
ADA
    See Americans with Disabilities Act
Adelphi University
    See also *Harte v. Adelphi University*
advertising 98
advising 1, 4
    risks 3
    training 3
advisors 283
affirmative action 13-15, 263
Age Discrimination in Employment Act 24
agency law 2, 4
Ahmed v. University of Toledo 128
AIDS/HIV 119, 127, 133-137, 193-194
Alabama State University 179
Alana Shoars v. Epson America Inc. 81
Albright College 94
alcohol 119, 140-143, 242, 251-254, 256-258, 269-270, 277, 280, 283
    and fraternities 252
    use and abuse 243
alcohol and other substance abuse 282
Alexander v. Trustees of Boston University 105
Alford v. Emory University 96-97
Aliens and Nationality regulations (1990) 16
Allen v. County of Westchester 150
Allen v. Rutgers State University 149
Alpha Zeta Chapter of Pi Kappa Alpha v. Sullivan 254
alcohol 143
American Association of Collegiate Registrars and Admissions Officers (AACRAO) 245
American Association of Law Schools 102
American Association of State Colleges and Universities 57
American Civil Liberties Union (ACLU) 261
American College Health Association 191-192
American Council on Education (ACE) 254, 257
American Institute of Philanthropy 279
American Western University 246
American Youth Hostels 169
Americans with Disabilities Act 119-123, 125
    Section 504 120-122
Amherst College 89, 93

Amherst College v. Assessors 93
Anti-Drug Abuse Act, 1988 106
Antioch University 219
Appeal of the University of Pittsburgh 93, 95-96
arbitration 247, 249
Argen v. State Board of Bar Examiners 125
Arizona State University 68
asbestos 119, 147
Asher v. Harrington 10-11
Associated Press v. Walker 34
Association for the Study of Higher Education 26
association rights 269
assumption of risk 167
athletes 194
athletic programs 98
Atkinson v. Board of Trustees of the University of Arkansas 29
Attention Deficit Disorder 124
Auburn University 260-262
Austin Peay State University 261

B

Bahr v. Jenkins 243
Baker v. Lafayette College 35
Bakke v. Regents of University of California 13, 117
Baldwin v. Zoradi 273
bankruptcy 114
Bankruptcy Reform Act 115
Barlow's, Inc. 228
Barnes v. Glen Theater, Inc. 63
Bartlett v. Pantzer 3
Bauer v. Board of Regents of University of Nebraska 86
Bauer v. Murphy 36
Beach v. University of Utah 149, 256
Beaman v. Des Moines Area Community College 12
Bearman v. University of Notre Dame 280
Beesinger 157
Belmont University 79
Ben-Shalom v. Marsh 103
Berg v. Hunter 37
Bethany College 223
Better Business Bureau 279
Big Ten athletic conference 272
bills of attainer 105
Bishop v. Aronov 71
Blackman, Justice Harry 26-28
Blair Academy v. Blairstown 94
Blair v. Wayne State University 86
Blank v. Board of Higher Education of the City New York 2
    Brooklyn College 2
Blide v. Rainier Mountaineering Inc. 169

bloodborne pathogens 147
Boettner 225
Boston College (MA) 222
Boston University 50
Boucher v. Riner 169
Bowdoin College 169, 272
Bowling Green University 102
Bradford v. Regents of the University California 85-86
Bradshaw v. Rawlings 149, 256, 273
Brandenburg v. Ohio 52, 56, 259, 261
Brigham Young University 158-159, 274
Bristol County Stadium, Inc. 169
Brooklyn College 2
Brooklyn College Department of Education 272
Brooks v. Auburn University 80
Brown University 111, 113, 272
Brown v. Board of Regents of University of Nebraska 70
Brown v. Florida State Board of Regents 274
Brown v. Trustees of Boston University 50
Brush v. Pennsylvania State University 67-68
Buckley Amendment 136, 181, 183-185, 187-190, 245
Burke v. Raschle 86

C

California State University-Chico 104
California State University-Fullerton 272
California University System 266
California Western School of Law 224
campus advisors 273
Campus Crime Prevention Programs 282
    guidebook 282
Campus Security Act 190
Campus Sexual Assault Victim's Bill of Rights 182-183
Cantwell v. Connecticut 52
Capano, K.M. 238
Carley v. Arizona Board of Regents 5, 19
Carolina Gay and Lesbian Association 262
Carolinian Creed 64-65
Carroll v. Blinken 264
Central Connecticut State College 259-260
Central Michigan University 221
certiorari, writ of 265
CFC's 146
Chaplinsky v. New Hampshire 52, 56, 60
Chapman v. Thomas 74-75
charitable causes 278
charitable organization 278-279
charitable remainder trusts 90
charity fraud 278
cheating 235-237, 239
cheerleaders 273-275
    insurance and 275
    safety and 274
Chess v. Widmar 73-74
Chrisman 226, 228
Christian 268
Christian student groups 267
Chrysler Outboard Corporation v. DILHR 134
City of Boulder v. Regents of the University of Colorado 96
City University of New York's (CUNY) Harlem Campus 279
City University of New York (CUNY) 41, 266, 279
City University of New York Brooklyn College 272
City University of New York Queens College
civil liability 253
civil rights 260
Civil Rights Act of 1964 24, 42-43, 108, 110
Civil Rights Act of 1991 174

Civil Rights Restoration Act of 1987 44
Civil Rights, Office of 272
Clark v. State of New York 280
Close v. Lederle 69-70
cocaine 269
Cohen 226
Cohen v. California 52
Colby College 259
Colgate University 269
Colin v. Smith 53
Columbia University 113
Committee for Public Education v. Regan 73
Commonwealth v. McCloskey 228
confidentiality 26, 180, 186-187, 190, 192-193, 195-196, 248
conflict resolution 247
Connelly v. University of Vermont 8
Connick v. Meyers 37-38
Constitution 268
constitutional immunity 95
contract 1, 3, 92, 277
    contract law 1, 3, 92
    contract theory 1
Cook County Collector v. National College 94
copyright 197-207
Cornell University 65, 96-97, 104, 113
Cornell University v. Board of Assessors 96-97
Corstvet v. Boger 108
County of Westchester 150
crank 36
credentials 22
    employment 21
Creighton University 11
Crime Awareness and Security Act 182
Cripe v. Board of Regents 35
Cubby, Inc. v. CompuServe, Inc. 83
Cuddihy v. Wayne State University 2
Curan v. Mt. Diablo Council of Boy Scouts 244
Curtis Publishing Company v. Butts 34
cy pres doctrine 89

D

D'Amico v. New York State Board of Law Examiners 122
D'Andrea v. Adams 38
Dartmouth College (NH) 113, 258, 232
defamation 34, 36, 51, 53, 193, 270
degrees, false 246-247
DelSanto, Jr. v. Bristol Cty. Stadium, Inc. 169
Delta Kappa Epsilon 150
Denver 149
Department of Defense Authorization Act 104
Department of Education 272
Deptartment of Education Office of Education Research
    and Improvement 235
DePauw University 35
Derdeyn v. University of Colorado 194
Detroit Board of Education 264
DeVito v. McMurray 11
Dickinson v. Bell 105
Dickson v. Oakland University 36
Dickson v. Sitterson 80
Dilworth v. Dudley 35
*Dinsmore v. Pugh and Regents of University of California
    at Berkeley* 124
diploma mills 246-247
diplomas, fake 245
disability 119, 121-122, 126
discrimination 87, 268

AIDS 133-134
   handicapping conditions 119
   health insurance 128
   race 13, 15, 18, 115
   sex 18-19, 26- 270, 49, 109-110
   sexual orientation 101, 103, 106-107
discrimination, religious 268
dishonesty 235-237
   standards for 239
Disney World 167
Doe v. Selective Service System 104
Doe v. University of Michigan 56
Doelker v. Ohio State University 157
Donnell v. California Western School of Law 224
Doyle v. Bowdoin College 169
draft registration 104
Drake University 102
Dronenburg v. Zeck 103
drug testing 119, 194
Drug-Free Schools and Communities Act 119, 140
drugs 119, 140-141
due process 85-87, 240, 243-244, 247
   fairness and 244
Due v. Florida Agricultural and Mechanical Institute 240
due warning 276
Duke University 142
Duke v. North Texas State University 38
Dunismur Joint Union High School District 153, 155
Dunlop v. University of Kentucky Student Health Clinic 157
Dunn v. Blumstein 133
Duquesne University 189
Dyson v. Lavery 5, 18-19

E

Eastern Michigan University 195
Eastern Montana College 35
ECPA
   See Electronic Communications Privacy Act
Eddy v. Syracuse University 280
educational use 93-94
EEOC
   See Equal Emplyment Opportunity Commission
EEOC v. Franklin and Marshall College 28
EEOC v. University of Notre Dame du Lac 27-28
Eiseman v. State of New York 224
Electronic Communications Privacy Act 82
email 81-83
Emory University 55, 96-97, 167, 169
Emory University v. Porubiansky 167, 169
Employee Polygraph Protection Act 44
Employee Retirement Income Security Act 24
Equal Emplyment Opportunity Commission 108
Equal Opportunity Employment Commission 26
Equal Pay Act 49
equal protection 42, 86-87, 103, 240, 271
equal rights 262
Erzinger v. Regnets of the University of California 131
Essignmann v. Western New England College 6, 8
Estate of Buchanan 91
Ethics Reform Act 29
evaluation, facultly4, 18
   proper usage 5
   validity 5, 20
evaluation, student 19

F

failure to warn 12
Fain v. State Residency Committee of University of North Carolina 88
Family Education Rights and Privacy Act 177, 181, 183-185, 187-191, 245
Family Policy Compliance Office 181
Fassett v. Delta Kappa Epsilon 150
Federal Prescription Service v. American Pharmaceutical Association 243
FERPA
   See Family Educational Rights and Privacy Act
free speech 269
Fifth Amendment 105, 117
fighting words 51-54, 56, 58-61
financial aid 270
   race-based 115, 117-118
First Amendment 6, 21, 36, 41-42, 51-56, 58, 60-64, 66, 105, 131, 265-268
flags 65
Flanagan v. President and Directors of Georgetown College 117
Fleming v. New York University 123
Florida Board of Regents of the Department Education 86
Florida State University 180
Fontbonne College 153-155
Forklift Systems, Inc. 174
Fourteenth Amendment 15, 44, 133-134, 243
Fourth Amendment 194
Fox v. Board of Trustees of the State University of New York 66
Frame v. Residency Appeals Committee 87-88
Franklin and Marshall College 28
Franklin v. Gwinnett County Public Schools 110, 270
fraternities 253, 255, 258-260, 271, 282
fraternity 251-256, 256, 258, 262
fraud 244-245
   resume 21
   tort law 2
free speech 26, 36, 51, 53-54, 56-57, 60, 62, 76, 103, 107, 269
freedom of assembly 251
freedom of association 251, 259, 261
Freedom of Information Act 177-180, 182
freedom of petition 251
freedom of speech 251, 261, 268
fund raising 89-90, 92, 278
Furek v. University of Delaware 256
FUTA 46

G

Galda v. Rutgers State University of New Jersey 264, 267
Gay Activists Alliance v. Board of Regents 259
Gay Alliance of Students v. Matthews 261
Gay and Lesbian Student Association v. Gohn 107
gay and lesbian student groups 261
gay and lesbian students 259, 262
Gay Lib v. University of Missouri 261
Gay Student Services v. Texas A&M University 259, 261
gay students 263
Gay Students Organization of the University of New Hampshire v. Bonner 259-261
Gay/Lesbian Alliance 262
Gehling v. St. George's University School of Medicine 273
gender equity 272
George Mason University 58, 63, 221

George Washington International Students' Services, I 246
George Washington University 130, 246
Georgetown College 117
Georgetown University 107, 117, 261
Gettysburg College 154
Gillespie v. Southern Utah State College 153
Girardier v. Webster College 114, 189
Gleeson v. Beesinger 157
Glusman v. Trustees of University of North Carolina 86
Gonzaga University 12
Good v. Associated Students of the University 267
Gooding v. Wilson 52
Goodman v. University of Illinois Foundation 94
Gore v. TriCounty Raceway, Inc. 169
Goss v. Lopez 235, 240
Goyings v. Jack and Ruth Echerd Foundation 169
grades 6-7, 9
Graham v. Richardson 133
Gray v. Board of Higher Education of City of New York 28
Greek organizations
    fighting and 252
    See also Fraternities
    liability and 252
Gross v. University of Tennessee 29
Gustafson v. California State University-Fresno 114

H

Hafer v. Melo 33
Handsome v. Rutgers University et al. 115
Hannibal-La Grange College 91
harassment 51, 54-55, 241
Harbin 154-155
Harrell v. Southern Illinois University 67
Harris and Harris Study 251
Harris v. Board of Trustees of State Colleges 36
Harris v. Forklift Systems, Inc. 174
Harte v. Adelphi University 11
Hartman v. Bethany College 223, 273
Harvard University 19, 25, 65, 107, 113, 181, 241
hate speech 53, 58-60
Haug v. Franklin 114
Hayes v. Board of Regents of Kent State University 87
Hays County Guardian v. Supple 265
hazing 252-259
Healy v. James 240, 251, 259-260
Healy v. Larsson 2, 4
Hebrew University in Jerusalem 111
Heisler v. New York Medical College 8
Helms, L.B. 26
Hewitt v. Miller 170
Hickingbottom v. Easley 38
Higher Education Amendments of 1992 190
Highland Community College 78-79
Hill v. National Collegiate Athletic Association 194
Hines v. Rinker 6
Hively, Robert 57
Hoch v. Prokop 35
Hofstra University
    See Sheilds v. School of Law
Holloway v. University of Montana 4
Hopwood v. Texas 13-14
Howard Savings Institution v. Peep 89
Hurtado v. California 243
Hustler Magazine v. Falwell 53

I

Ianiello v. University of Bridgeport 12
IFC 255
Illinois Benedictine College v. Wilson 4
Immigration and Nationality Act (1952) 16
Immigration and Naturalization Service 17
in loco parentis 239, 247, 255, 257
In re Albright College 94
In re Dinnan 27-28
In re Estate of Bacheller 91
incitement to lawlessness 51-52
independent contractor 47
Indiana University 111, 232, 258
Indiana University Foundation 180
INS
    See Immigration and Naturalization Service
insurance 277
    health 127-130
Inter-Fraternity Council 254
international student 16
    employment 16
Iota Xi Chapter of Signa Chi Fraternity v. George Mason University 62
irrevocable pledge 92
IRS Revenue Ruling 87-41 47
Irvine Valley College 7

J

Jack and Ruth Echerd Foundation 169
Jackson State University 269
    beer sales and 269
Jacksonville State University 185
James v. Jane 32-33, 156
James v. Nelson 67-68
Jawa v. Fayetteville State University 5, 18-19
job references 193
Johnson v. Edinboro State College 115
Johnson v. Honeywell Information Systems, Inc 22
Johnson v. Southern Greek Housing Corporation 96
Johnson v. Sullivan 8
Johnson v. University of Pittsburgh 18-19
Jones v. Wittenburg University 215
Joyner v. Whiting 267
judicial action 247
judicial deference 1
Juras v. Aman Collection Service, Inc. 114

K

Kania v. Fordham 265
Kansas State University 211
Kanton v. Schmidt 4
Katz v. United States 227
Kaufman v. American Youth Hostels 169
Keane v. Rodgers 226
Keegan v. University of Delaware 73-74
Keene State College 258
Keller v. State Bar of California 264
Kelm v. Carlson 87
Kennedy, Justice Anthony M. 268
Kent State University 33, 66, 102, 263, 277
Kersey v. Harbin 154-155
Kestenbaum v. Michigan State University 189
Kibler, William L. 239
Kirk v. Washington State University 274

Kleinknecht v. Gettysburg College 154
Korematsu v. United States 133
Krasnow v. Virginia Polytechnic Institute 240
Krause v. Rhodes 33
Krauss v. Nassau Community College 189
Krebs v. Rutgers 185

L

Lace v. Vermont 265
LaGuardia Community College 68
lead 146
learning disabilities 123-126
Lehigh University 49, 183
Lemon v. Kurtzman 71, 73
Levin v. Harleston 40
Levitou, P.S. 16
Lexington Theological Seminary v. Vance 108
liability insurance 279-280
Lieberman v. Gant 5, 18-19
Lindsey v. Board of Regents 38
Lindsey Wilson College 90
linkage
    aid and substance abuse 106
    draft 104, 106
Louisiana State University 30, 142, 191
Louisiana State University School of Music 107
Lovelace v. Southeastern Massachusetts University 5, 19
Lowenthal v. Vanderbilt University 11
Lowry v. Adams 144
LTV Recreational Development, Inc. 169

M

Maas v. Corporation of Gonzaga University 12
MacMurray College v. Wright 95, 97
malpractice, educational 10-11
Mapplethorpe, Robert 69
Marquette University 167
Marquez v. University of Washington 7
Marshall v. Barlow's, Inc. 228
Massachusetts Institute of Technology 112
Matthews v. Marsh 103
Mawdsley, Ralph D. 239
Mazart v. State of New York 107
McGill v. University of South Carolina 48
McIntosh v. Borough of Manhattan Community College 6-7
mediation records 248
mediation, ending 249
medical files 178, 191
Meese v. Brigham Young University 274
Meritor Savings Bank v. Vinson 108, 174
Michigan State University 179, 189, 269
Midland Lutheran College 69
Miller v. California 52, 56
Miller v. State of New York 224
Mitchell v. Wisconsin 63
Minnesota Public Interest Reseach Group (MPIRG) v. Selective Service System 105
Mogabad v. Orleans Parish School Board 153, 155, 280
Mohawk Valley Community College 68
Monnacept 170
Morale v. Grigel 227
Morehouse College 256
Mucklow v. John Marshall Law School 17, 19
Mullins v. Pine Manor College 223

murder 257
mutual consent 92

N

Napolitano v. Trustees of Princeton University 238
Naragon v. Wharton 107
NASPA 248, 274
    See National Association of Student Personnel Administrators
Nassau Community College 189
National Association of College and University Business Offices 47
National Association for Foreign Student Affairs 112
National Association of Student Personnel Administrators 16, 25
National Charities Information Bureau 279
National Inter-Fraternity Conference 255
NCAA 98-100, 270
Nebraska University 258
negligence 2-3, 280
    advisors and 276
    safety and 274
negotiation 247
Nero v. Kansas State University 211
New Mexico State University 68
New York Law School
    See also *Susan M. v. New York Law School*
New York University 96
    See also *Paynter v. New York University*
New York University v. Taylor 96
Nganga v. Wooster 273
Nieswand v. Cornell University 1
Nomi v. Regents for the University of Minnesota 103
Normali v. Cleveland Association of Life Underwriters 244
North Carolina State University 73
North Lake College 69
North v. West Virginia Board of Regents 247
Northeastern University (MA) 222
Northern Illinois University 67, 71, 262
Northwestern College of Allied Science 246
Northwestern University 95, 193

O

O'Connell v. Walt Disney World Company 167
O'Conner v. Peru State College 18-19
O'Connor v. Ortega 83
O'Connor, Justice Sandra Day 42, 174, 269
Oakland University 180
obscenity 51-53, 56, 63, 76
OERI 235
Ohio State University 79, 97-99, 102, 132, 157, 184
Oklahoma State University 68, 108, 195, 256
Older Workers Benefit Protection Act 24
Open Records Law 19
Orleans Parish School Board 153, 155
Overlap Group 112-113
Oyama v. Calilfornia 133

P

Paine v. Board of Regents of the University of Texas System 240
Palm Beach Community College 180
Pandazides v. Virginia Board of Education 124
Papish v. Board of Curator of the University of Missouri 75

Parate v. Isibor 6
Pasco-Hernando Community College 241
Paynter v. New York University 10-11
Pell grant 106
Pennsylvania State University 33, 35, 79
People v. Boettner 225
People v. Cohen 226
People v. Lanthier 228
People v. Magee 237
People v. Volpe 228
Perez v. Rodriguez Bou 32
permanent irrebuttable presumption 87
Peterson v. San Francisco Community College District 224
Pfaff v. Columbia-Greene Community College 6-7
Phelps v. Colby College 260
Pi Kappa Alpha Fraternity 150
Piazzola v. Watkins 228
Pine Manor College 223
Pine Manor College (MA) 223
plagiarism 235, 237-239
    defining 239
Podberesky v. Kirwan 117-118
Podberesky v. Kirwin 118
prayer 72
prevention planning 281-282
Princeton University 65, 113, 239
privileged communications 27
exemption, taxes 93, 95-96
protected communications 27
Public Interest Research Group (PIRG) 264-267
Purdue University 254, 270

Q

Queens College 11
Queer Nation-Nebraska 263
Quinn v. Sigma Rho Chapter of Beta Theta Pi Fraternity 253

R

R.A.V. v. City of St. Paul 51, 60, 62
radon 146
Rainier Mountaineering Inc. 169
rape 257
    See acquaintance rape
reasonable accommodations 126
reasonable means 85
reasonable standards of care 276
Red and Black Publishing Company, Inc. v. Board of Regents 190
Regents of the University of California v. Bakke 116
Regents of the University of Michigan v. Ewing 1
Rehabilitation Act of 1973 120
    Section 504 123
Rehabilitation Act of 1974 119, 123, 133-134
    Section 504 133, 144
Rehnquist, Chief Justice 261
Rekas v. Illinois 228
Relyea v. State of Florida 224
right of association 259-260
right to privacy 103
Riner 169
risk management 280
risk management programs
    and reasonable standards of care 277
risk-prevention 282
Rochester Institute of Technology (NY) 225

Roemer v. Maryland Public Works Board 73
Rosen v. LTV Recreational Development, Inc. 169
Rosenberger v. Rector and Visitors of University of Virginia 71, 269
Ross v. Creighton University 12
ROTC 101-103, 263
Rubtinchsky v. State University of New York at Albany 274
Rutgers
Rutgers State University
Rutgers University 149, 185-186, 256, 258, 264, 267, 270

S

Saksniit 237
Samuel v. University of Pittsburg 86-87
San Francisco Community College District 224
San Francisco State University 69
Saturday Evening Post 34
Sayers v. Ranger 155, 280
Schact v. United States 63
Scheiber v. St. John's University 71
Scheuer v. Rhodes 33
scholarships, athletic 269-271
School Board of Nassau County v. Arline 133
Seal, J. 26
Selective Service System v. Minnesota Public Interest Group 105
self-incrimination 105
Selkirk v. University of Oklahoma 191
separation of church and state 268
sex discrimination 270-271
sexual assault 241, 253
sexual harassment 108, 252, 271
sexual orientation 251
Shamloo v. Mississippi State Board of Trustees 144
Shapiro v. Columbia Union National Bank/Trust 89
Shields v. School of Law 3, 8
Simonsen v. Swenson 135
slander 35-36
Small v. McRae 35
Smith v. Board of Regents of University of California 269
Smith v. Duquesne University 189
Smith v. Goguen 66
Smith v. Regents of the University of California 263-264
Smith v. University of Tennessee 80
smoking 119, 137, 139
Social Security Number 185-186
Society of Professional Journalists and Millhollen v. Louisiana State University 191
Sohmer v. Kinnard 240
sororities 251, 254, 258, 271
Souter, Justice David H. 268
Southeast Missouri State University 258
Southeastern Louisiana University 78
Southeastern Massachusetts University
    See also *Lovelace v. Southeastern Massachusetts University*
Southern Illinois University v. Booker 95-96
Southern Oregon State University 99
Southern Technical College 1
    See also *Will v Delta School of Commerce*
Southern University 252
Southern Utah State College 153
Southwest Missouri State University 68, 183
Southwest Texas State University 75
sovereign immunity 93, 95
Spark v. Catholic University of America 37
Spas v. Wharton 114
speech codes 57, 62-63

Index

Spelmen College 26
Spence v. Washington 66
St. George's University 273
Stanford University 54
Stanley v. McGrath 267
Star Publishing Co. v. Pima County Attorney 83
Starns v. Malkerson 87
State of New York University at Buffalo Law School 101
State University of New York College at Buffalo 224
State University of New York at Albany 264
State University of New York at Binghamton 107
State University of New York at Buffalo 104, 232
State University of New York at Stony Brook 4
State University of New York at Stony Brook 224
State v. Johnson 226, 228
State v. King 228
State v. Pi Kappa Alpha Fraternity 150
State v. Saksniit 237
State v. Wingerd 226
Steshenko v. Texas 81
Stevenson v. Board of Regents of the University of Texas 8
Stineman v. Fontbonne College 153-155
Street v. New York 56, 66
Student Coalition v. Austin Peay State University 261
student conduct 235
Student Cooperative of Stony Brook 150
Student Press Law Center 76, 183, 185
studying abroad 111-112
substance abuse 242
suicide 270
Supple v. Hays Guardian 76
supremacy laws 96
Susan M. v. New York Law School 9
Swope v. Lubbers 267
Symantec Corp. v. Borland International Inc. 81
Syracuse University 93-94, 222, 262, 280

T

Tarka v. Franklin 188, 190
Tau Kappa Epsilon 255
Temple University 102, 138
Temple University Law School 106
Tennessee State University
    See also *Parate v. Isibor*
term paper mill 237238
termination
    faculty 18
Terminiello v. Chicago 52
testamentary capacity 91
testing 124
Texas A&M University 157, 259, 261
Texas Review Society v. Cunningham 75
Texas v. Johnson 66
Till v. Delta School of Commerce 2
Title IX 109-110, 269-272
Title VI 115, 117
Title VII 42, 108, 110, 174
Toll v. Moreno 86
tort law 2, 4, 34, 257
tort liability 277
torts 276
transcript fraud 245
    types of 244
transcripts 114
Trenton State University 165

TriCounty Raceway, Inc. 169
Troy State University 38
Trustees of Columbia University v. Jacobson 12
Trustees of University Delaware v. Gebelein 89
Tufts University 123
tuition tax 96
Tunkl v. Regents of University of California 167, 169

U

UBIT
    See Unrelated Business Income Tax
undergraduates
    cheating and 235
undue influence 91
United Educators Insurance Risk Retention Group 280
United States v. Associated Press 21
*United States v. Board of Trustees for the University of
    Alabama* 123
United States v. City of Philadelphia 103, 106
United States v. International Term Papers 238
United States v. Payner 227
United Way 278
University of Akron 254
University of Alabama 26, 68, 71, 104, 180, 184
University of Alabama at Birmingham 69, 123
University of Alabama-Birmingham 262
University of Alabama-Tuscaloosa 262
University of Arizona 38, 142, 254
University of Arkansas 107, 111, 130, 253
University of Buffalo 79
University of California 54, 60, 85, 167, 169, 212, 263-264
    Davis 13
University of California-Berkeley 49, 263
University of California-Irvine 92
University of California-Riverside 230
University of California-Santa Barbara 25, 61, 158, 252
University of Cincinnati 102, 104
University of Colorado 96
University of Colorado-Boulder 194
University of Connecticut 20, 54, 60, 85
University of Delaware 73, 111, 256
University of Denver 224, 256, 274
University of Florida 35, 79
University of Georgia 27, 34, 107, 190-191
University of Hawaii 71
University of Houston 221
University of Illinois 253
University of Illinois at Urbana-Champaign 81
University of Iowa 26, 231
University of Kansas 19-20, 36, 102, 184
University of Kentucky Student Health Service Clinic 157
University of Louisville 138
University of Marylan-College Park 117
University of Maryland 78, 86, 118, 240
University of Maryland-Baltimore 77
University of Maryland-College Park 77-78, 194
University of Massachusetts 55, 69, 222
University of Massachusetts at Amherst 272
University of Massachusetts-Dartmouth
    See also Southeastern Massachusetts University
University of Miami 270
University of Michigan 47, 53, 56, 58, 60-62, 81, 86-88, 179
University of Minnesota 30-31, 76, 79, 102-103, 107, 193-195
    and sexual harassment claim 252
University of Minnesota-Duluth 49
University of Missouri 261
University of Missouri at Kansas City 89

University of Missouri-Columbia 75
University of Missouri-Kansas City 73
University of Montana
    See also *Johnson v. Sullivan*
University of Montana Law School 3
University of Nebraska 33, 43, 70, 72, 81, 86, 193, 258
University of Nebraska-Lincoln 180, 263
University of Nebraska-Omaha 81
University of Nevada-Reno 195
University of New Hampshire 40, 259, 261
University of New Mexico 26, 58, 65, 119, 228
University of New York at Albany 274
University of North Carolina 31, 49, 68, 86, 262
University of North Carolina- Charlotte 30-31
University of North Carolina-Chapel Hill 61, 66, 68, 88-89, 98, 142, 241
University of Notre Dame 280

University of Oklahoma 72, 191, 256, 263
University of Pennsylvania v. Equal Employment Opportunities Commission 26-27
University of Pennsylvania 26, 28, 113, 241
University of Pittsburgh 87, 93, 95-96
University of Puerto Rico 32
University of Rochester 97
University of Rochester v. Wagner 97
University of South Alabama 195
University of South Carolina 64-65, 195, 253
University of South Dakota
    See also *Hines v. Rinker*
University of South Florida 222
University of Southern California 219, 224
University of Southern Maine 221
University of Texas 54, 81, 98, 240, 256
University of Texas Law School 13-14, 114
University of Texas-Arlington 130
University of Texas-Austin 272
University of Toledo 127, 180
University of Utah 149, 159
University of Vermont 89
University of Virginia 49, 71, 132, 267-269
University of Washington 37, 120, 160, 193, 267
University of Wisconsin 55, 57, 59-60, 186, 256, 262, 281-282
University of Wisconsin-Madison 30, 36, 61-62, 68, 102, 107, 132, 138, 187, 262, 270, 272
University of Wisconsin-Platteville 187
University of Wisconsin-River Falls 65
University of Wisconsin System 187
Unrelated Business Income Tax 97-100

USC 159-160
exemption, tax 95
Utah State University 87, 225
UW-Madison 164-165
UWM Post, Inc. v. Board of Regents UWI System 58

V

Valencia Community College 68
Veed v. Schwartzkopf 265
Villanova University 100-101
Vinson 174
Virginia 268
Virginia Commonwealth University 261
Virginia Polytechnic Institute 10-19, 240
    See also *Dyson v. Lavery*
visa, student 16
Vlandis v. Kline 85, 87

W

Wai-Chung Ng v. West Virginia Board of Regent 12
waiver of liability 276
Walter v. United States 227
Walters v. Churchill 42
Washington State University 274
Washington University 120
Washington v. Chrisman 226, 228
Washington v. Smith 36
Wayne State University 86
Webster College 189
Welch v. Dunismur Joint Union High School District 153-155
Wellcome v. Student Cooperative of Stony Brook 150
West Virginia University 78-79, 168, 170, 184, 221, 247
Western Carolina University 272
Western Kentucky University 90
whistleblowers 38
Whitlock v. University of Denver 224, 256, 274
Wide Awake Productions 267
Widmar v. Vincent 74
Wilbur v. University of Vermont 89
Wilson v. Illinois Benedictine College 1
Wisconsin v. Mitchell 62
Wittenburg University 215
Wood v. Davison 107
Wood v. Strickland 32
Woodruff v. Georgia State University 8
Woodward v. United States 103
Writ of Mandamus 3
Wynne v. Tufts University School of Medicine 123-124

Y

Yale School of Medicine 138
Yale University 92, 111, 113, 221

Z

Zeta Beta Tau 255
zoning 100
Zumbrun v. University of Southern California 2